RAGNAR AXELSSON

LAST DAYS
OF THE ARCTIC

RAGNAR AXELSSON

LAST DAYS

OF THE ARCTIC

Text by MARK NUTTALL

CRYMOGEA

CONTENTS

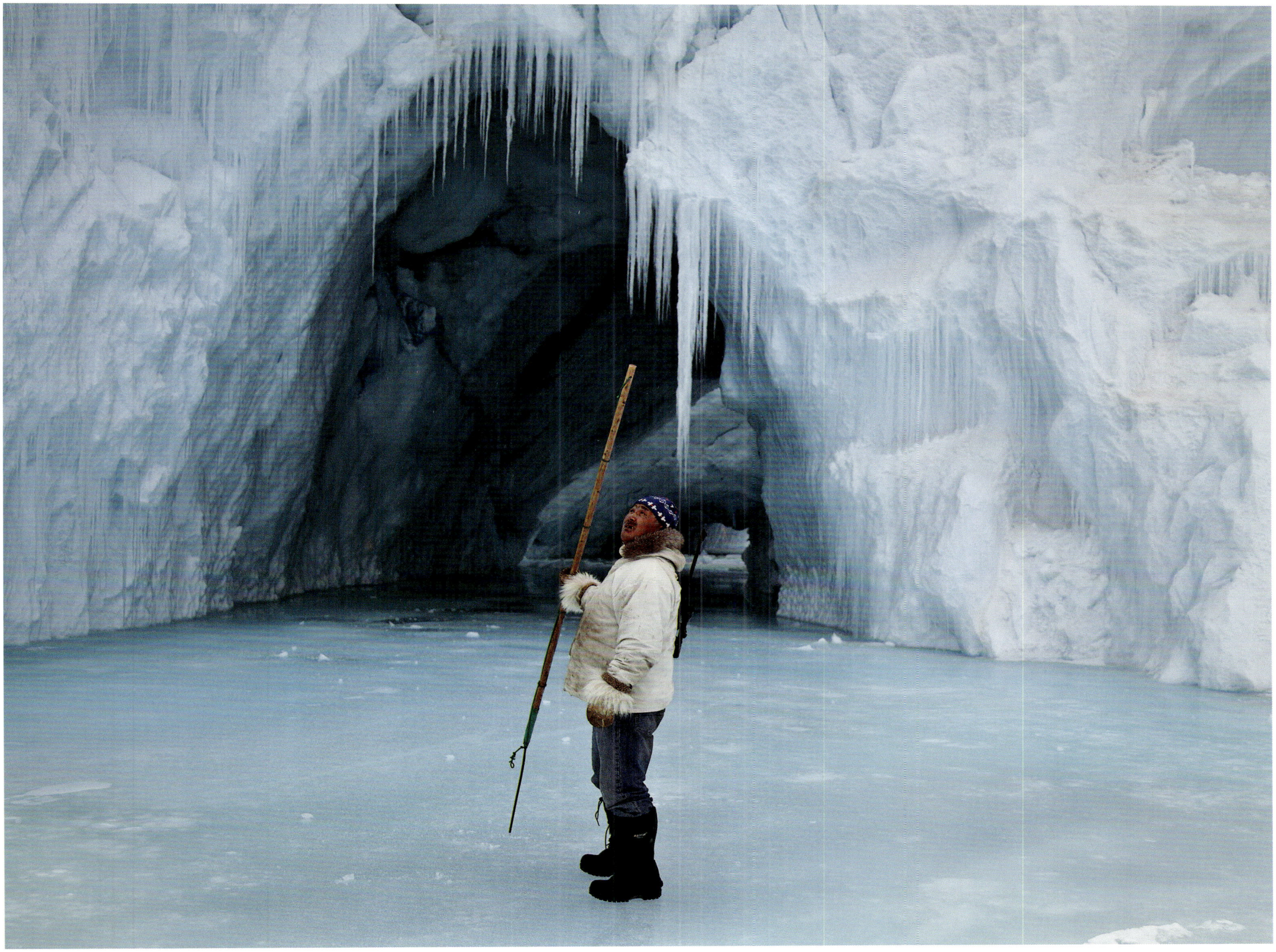

A hunter tests the safety of the ice underneath this icicled natural arch near Qaanaaq in North Greenland.

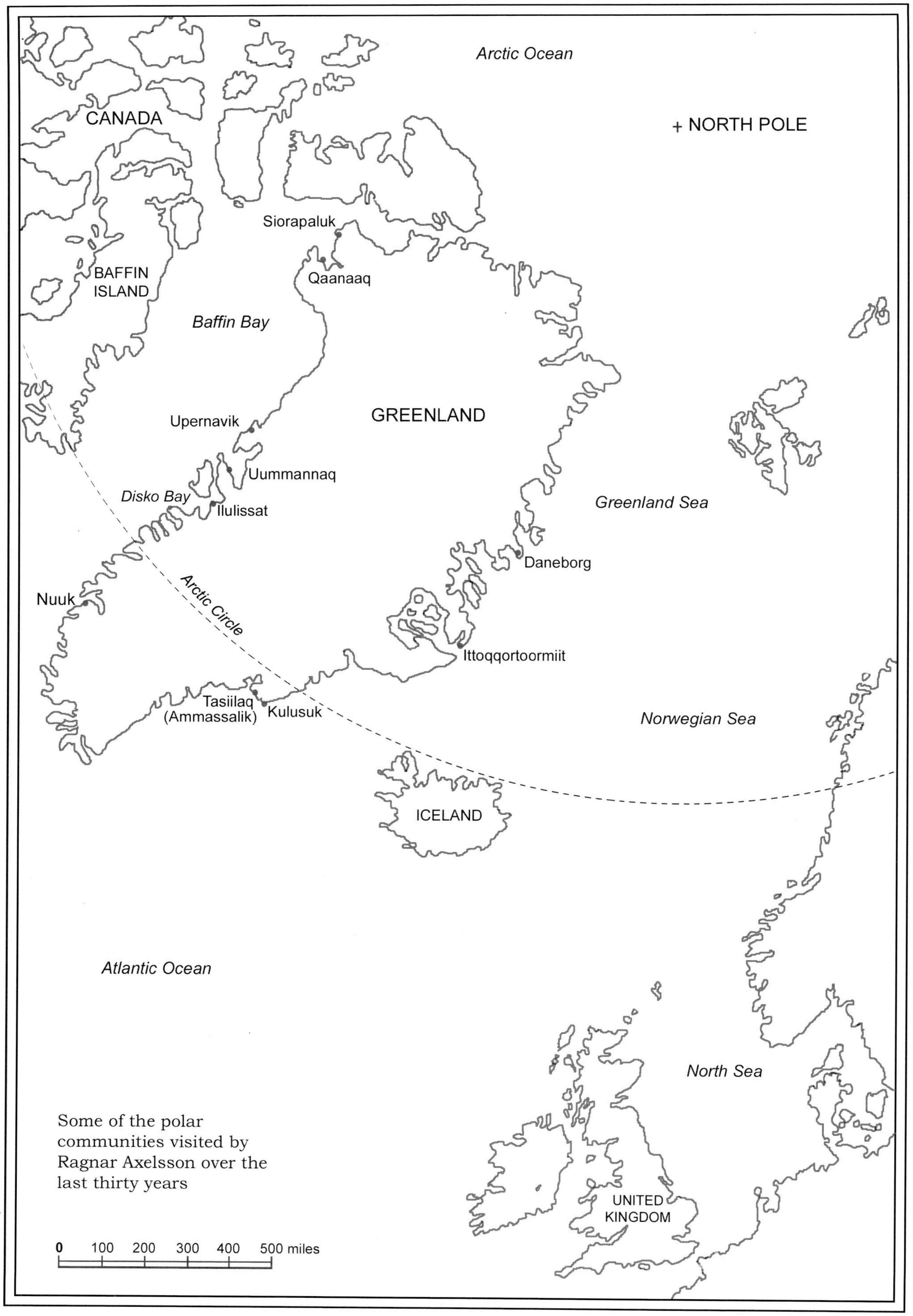

Some of the polar communities visited by Ragnar Axelsson over the last thirty years

A JOURNEY NORTH

Imagine taking a journey by land to the waters of the High Arctic from the northern reaches of the boreal forest, perhaps in Canada or in Siberia. Having left this evergreen subarctic region, you would find yourself travelling in the forest-tundra ecotone, a boggy transition zone of mosses and lichens, sparse dwarf willows, birches, and alders. You would come across sedge meadows — depending on which part of the circumpolar North you are in, this is prime grazing habitat for caribou, reindeer and muskoxen. As you travel farther north, the landscape becomes more open, with fewer trees and sparser vegetation. Eventually you would enter a treeless region called the tundra. The tundra has low species diversity and mosses and lichens are the most common forms of plant life found here. Lakes and ponds may abound, and groundwater seeps up to the surface from melting permafrost during summer helping the growth of tundra plants, but it is a land with little free water and little precipitation. Yet despite this, the tundra attracts huge numbers of shorebirds, waterfowl and other birds which arrive to nest during the summer, and many species of land animal roam this apparently barren landscape. Heading farther north, you would enter a cold, dry realm of true High Arctic polar desert, a landscape of exposed bedrock, gravel plains and frost-shattered rocks. It receives no solar radiation for six months of the year and the summer growing season is frighteningly brief, restricting opportunities for animal life to flourish there in abundance. Eventually, you would reach the Arctic Ocean, an immense body of water almost closed off from the world's other oceanic systems save for a few narrow and shallow passages, and with an interior covered by perennial (albeit diminishing), or multi-year, pack ice. If you were to make such an Arctic journey, through its various habitats and ecosystems, and in all seasons, encountering its wildlife, its people and their cultures, you could hardly help but feel astonishment and wonder.

The Arctic has been inhabited by indigenous peoples for millennia. In Arctic cultures, all human and animal life is interdependent. Around the circumpolar world animals, and their relationships with people, have formed the basis of social and economic life, and of a rich cultural history. In Greenlandic, the word for traditional Inuit foods is *kalaalimerniit,* which literally means "a little piece of a Greenlander". In this sense, the distinction between human and animal disappears — both humans and animals share the same spiritual essence. Hunting and the eating of the meat of animals is an act of regeneration, both of human society and of the animal. If animals are not respected, either when alive or dead, they will not allow themselves to be hunted and "give" themselves up to their hunter.

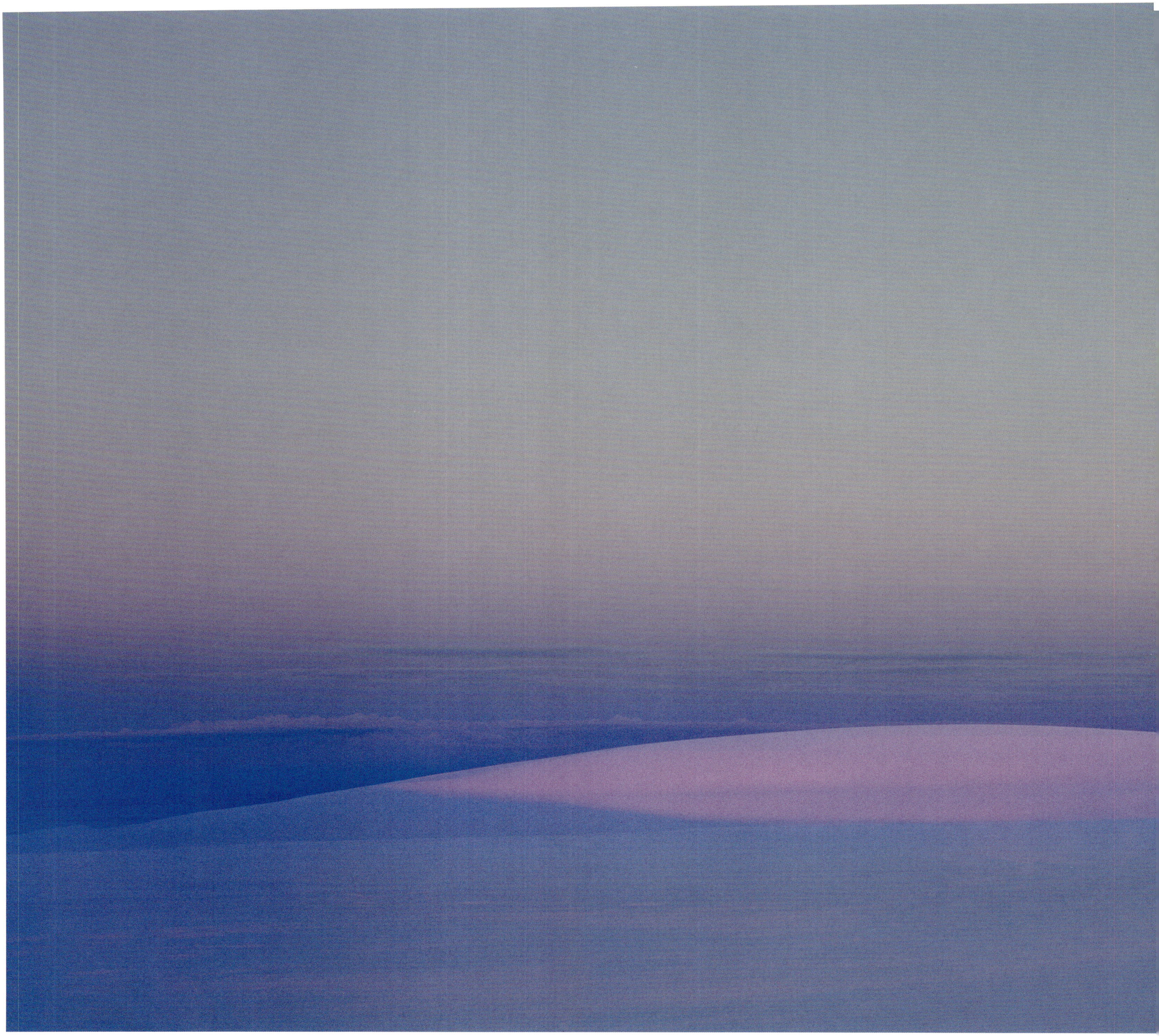

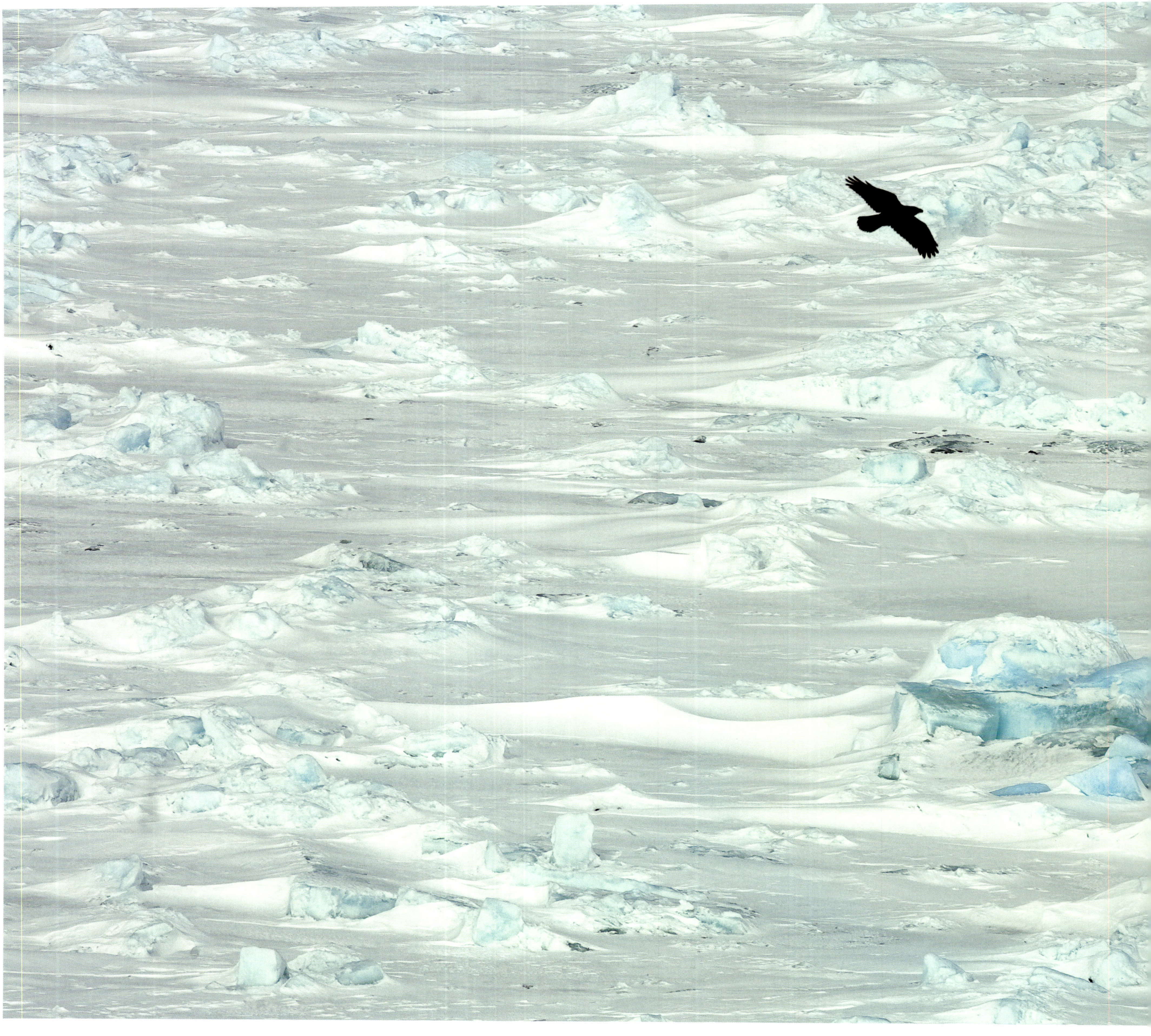

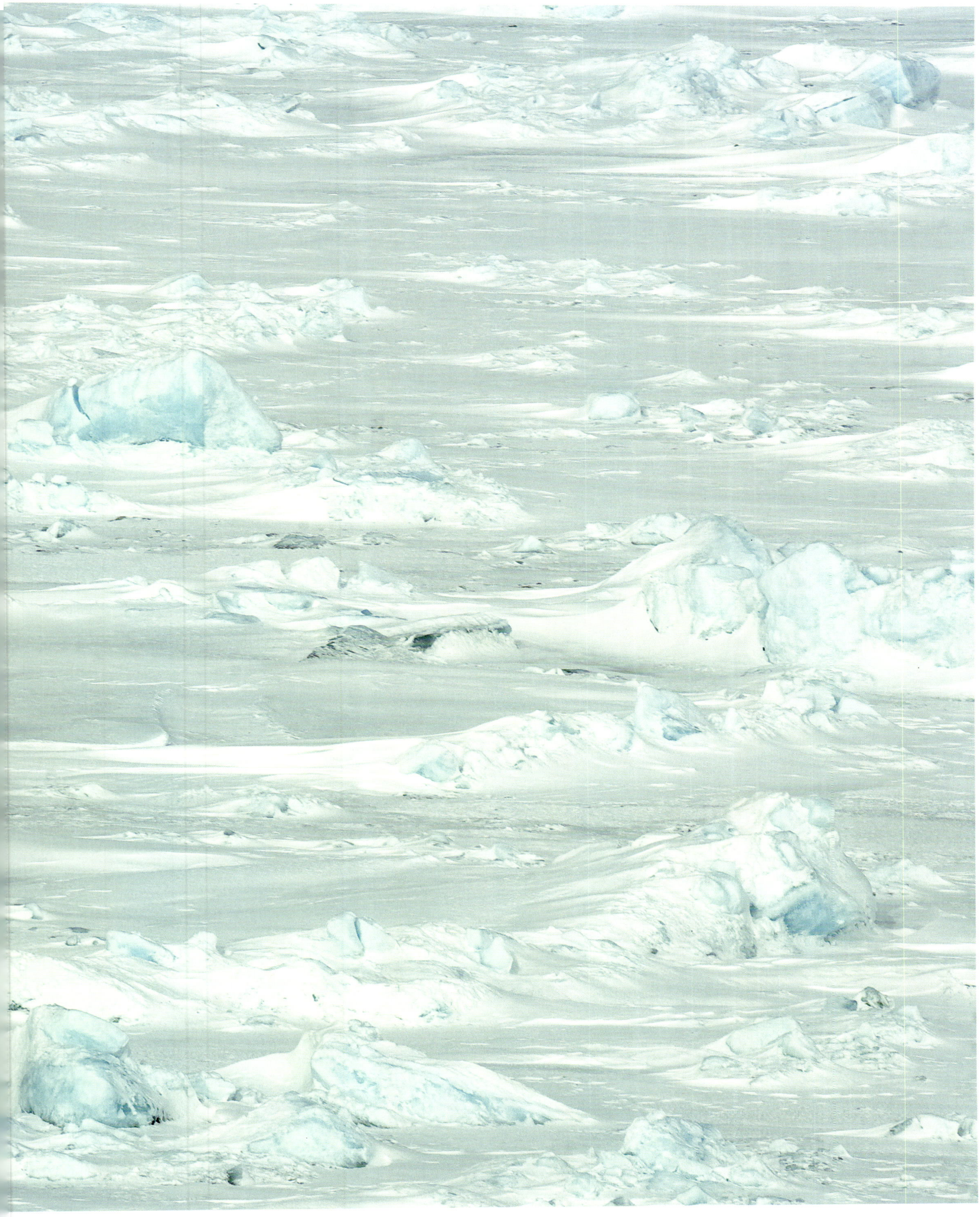

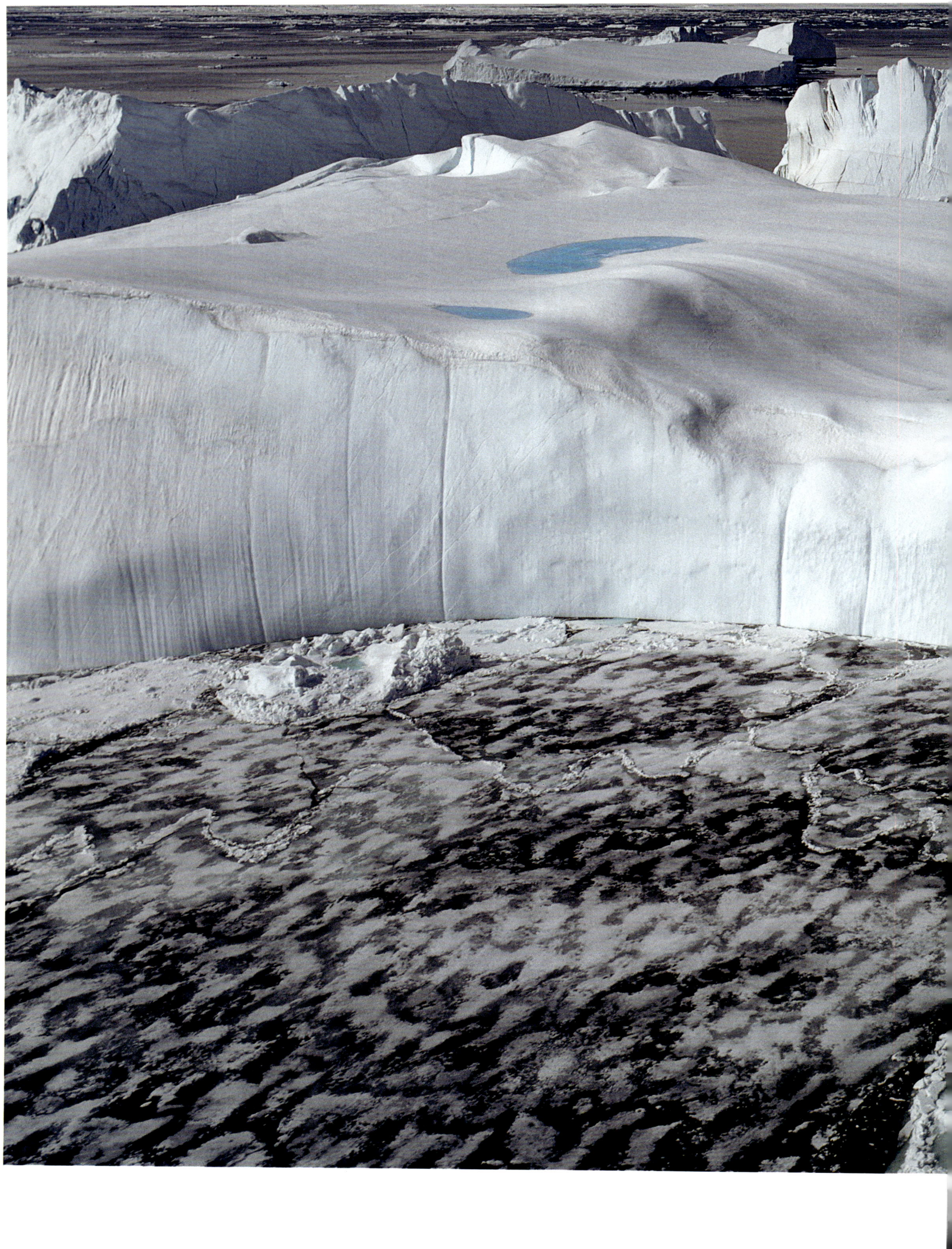

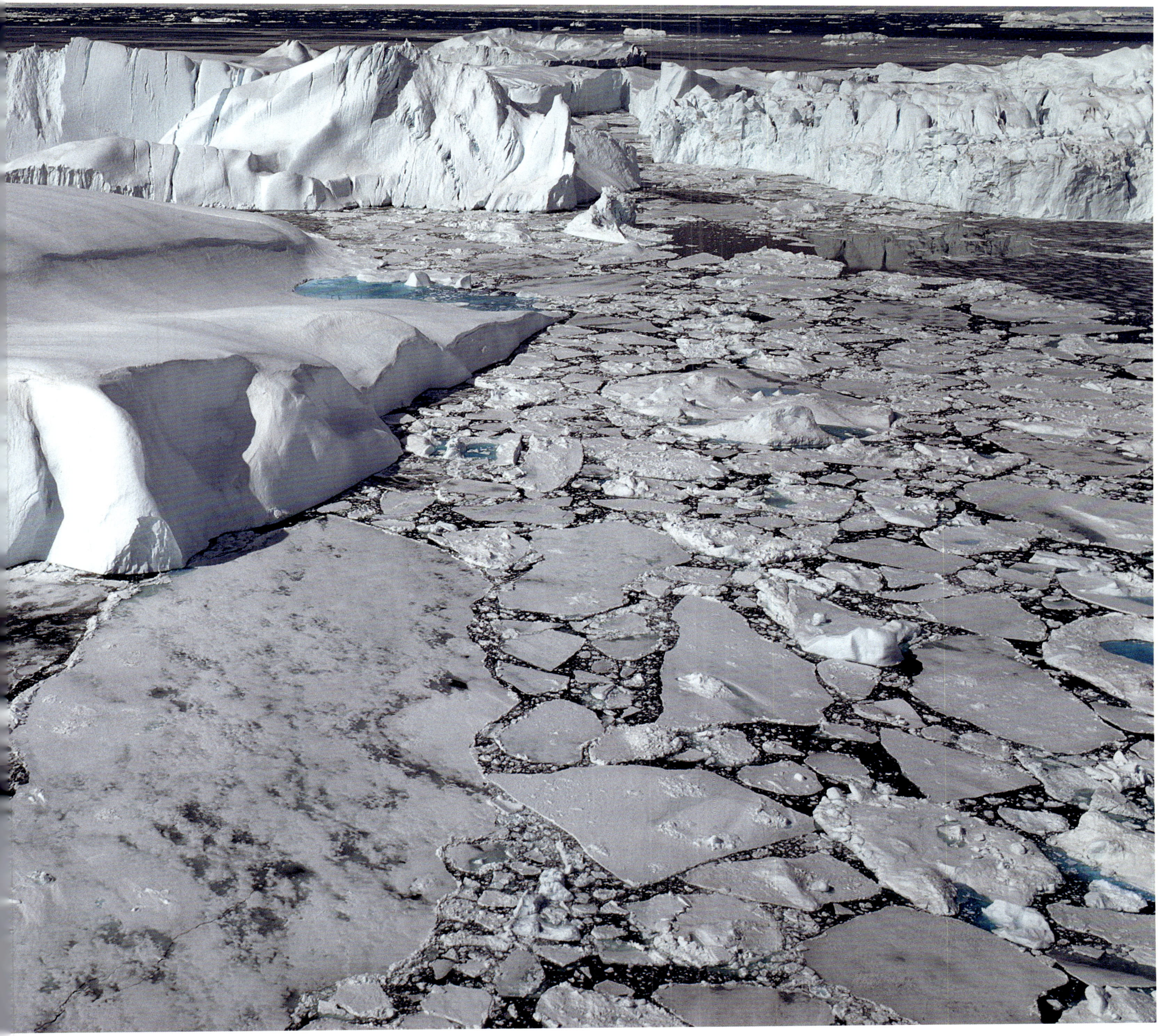

FOOTPRINTS ON THE LAND

pp. 8–9
Greenland's inland ice is the second largest ice mass on the planet after Antarctica's vast, 13 million square km ice sheet. In Greenlandic it is known as *sermersuaq*, "the great ice". View over Qeqertarsuaq glacier on Disko Island or Qeqertarsuaq (Large Island).

pp. 10–11
The raven can be spotted throughout the Arctic. Among Alaskan Inuit groups the raven is a trickster who emerged from the darkness at the beginning of time and created the world.

pp. 12–13
Every year, 20 billion tons of ice calves from the Sermeq Kujalleg glacier into the Ilulissat Fjord on the west coast of Greenland, making it the most productive glacier in the world. This is the same amount of water as the residents of New York City use each year.

This book is about the changing Arctic and specifically about Inuit experiences of this change. Through Ragnar Axelsson's photographs, we journey into the lives and lands of the Inuit in Greenland, and glimpse not only the resilience of those lives, but also the vulnerability of Inuit communities facing the challenges of social change as well as climate change.

When I first went to Greenland in the late 1980s, I lived with a family of Inuit hunters and fishers in a small community on the northwest coast of Greenland. Johannsi K. was the head of the family and respected as a great hunter (*piniartorssuaq*). Johannsi had first accompanied his father on caribou hunts in the mid-1930s, and he had made hunting expeditions to find caribou every autumn since until the early 1960s, when the animals could no longer be found. His last visit was in 1966 and, by that time, wildlife biologists were telling the local hunters that the caribou had disappeared, possibly because of overhunting or environmental change, or a combination of both. While respectful of this view, Johannsi, like his fellow hunters, did not believe the scientists. "The caribou have not disappeared, these places no longer contain the essence of caribou, that's all — they have moved on," he once told me. "One day, they will return and let us know."

Twenty-two years after his last trip, Johannsi woke one morning and told us of a dream he had about caribou living beyond the mountains to the east of the village. He set off with two of his sons on a reconnaissance trip, to see if he could locate any caribou, or at the very least, he said, to find the essence of caribou in the landscape. Five days later, having sailed deep into the inner fjords and walked a considerable distance over hills and along valleys, they returned. "Well?" asked his eldest son, who had remained behind, "Did you find any caribou?" "No," replied Johannsi, beaming from cheek to cheek, "but I found my footprints at the site of my last camp." To someone outside the family and the village, it may be hard to understand the significance of this. It had personal and family meaning, but also wider meaning for an Inuit community and its relationship with the landscape. One person's imprint on the landscape is interwoven with the imprints of others to express and sustain a rich diversity of human-environment relations.

Johannsi's lasting footprints in the landscape tell us three things: Firstly, far from being the empty wilderness many believe it to be, the North is a human world of cherished landscapes and ancestral memoryscapes. Although finding one's footprints in the landscape decades after you have left them may be astonishing and worthy of continual storytelling, I was surprised at how unsurprising it really was when people spoke about it. I came to understand that, from a local Inuit perspective, it was an ordinary thing — after all, people walk around and leave their footprints in many places. What was significant was its celebration of the ordinary, everyday world.

Secondly, wherever you stand in the circumpolar world, and gaze from the ground around you to the vistas stretching out and beyond, no matter how remote a place you may imagine yourself to be in, it will be a place infused with the history of human movement, imagination, ambition, dreams and desire. This is a place where indigenous peoples like the Inuit have survived, thrived and adapted for millennia, and have left their cultural imprint on the land; a place marked by the history of global interconnections; a place across which people, ideas, knowledge and innovation have moved and continue to move; and a place where more recent settlers have made homes and lives for themselves.

And thirdly, when you leave your mark on the Arctic landscape, it remains there for a long time. These lasting impressions speak of the resilience of indigenous cultures. Footprints on the landscape — whether real or metaphorical — become important for establishing land use and informing land claims; other kinds of marks on the environment provide evidence of intrusion and remind us of the brittleness and vulnerability of the Arctic. They challenge us to remember the importance of the Arctic, and find the most appropriate ways to ensure its protection.

Today, the Arctic regions of the circumpolar North have moved from the periphery of mainstream political, economic and scientific interest to the centre of global debate about the planet's future. Climate change is not only most striking in the Arctic — recent scientific research suggests that climate change has now brought the region to the point of no return. Glacial melt is accelerating and within the next decade the Arctic Ocean may become completely ice-free during the summer. The changes are unprecedented and possibly irreversible. They test the resilience of Inuit and other Arctic peoples. We may truly be witnessing the last days of the Arctic.

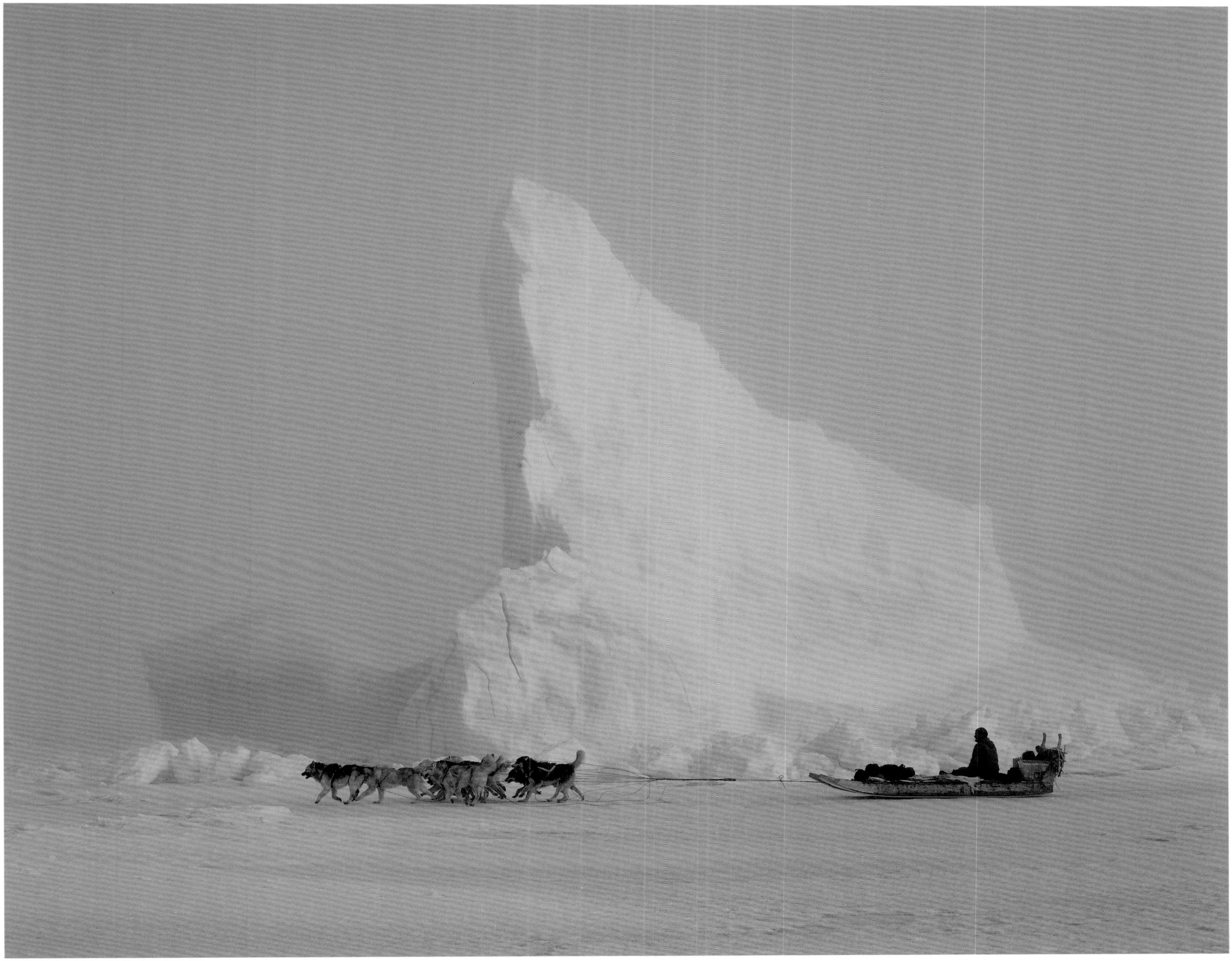

A hunter with his dog sledge on the ice near Qaanaaq in North Greenland.

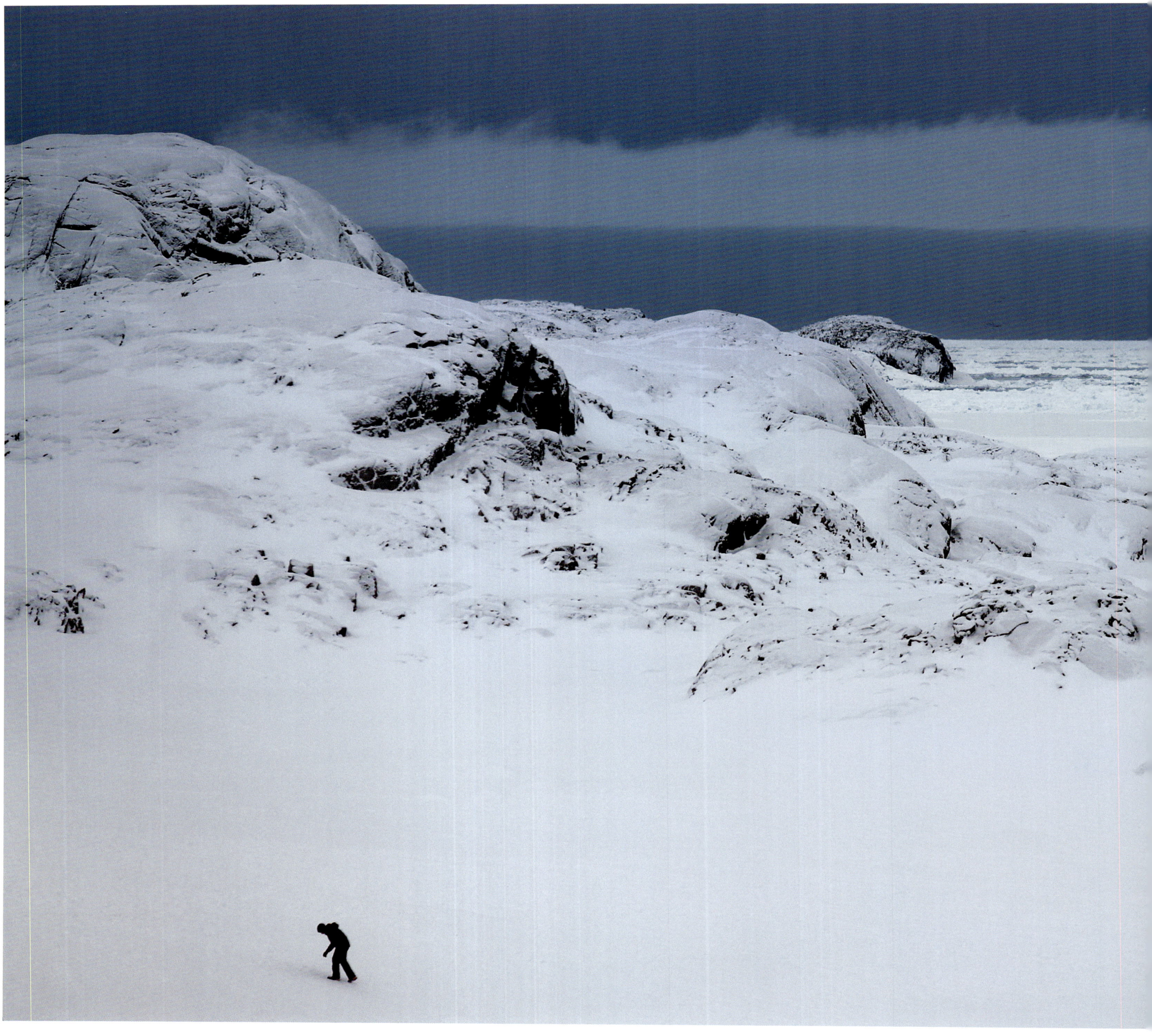

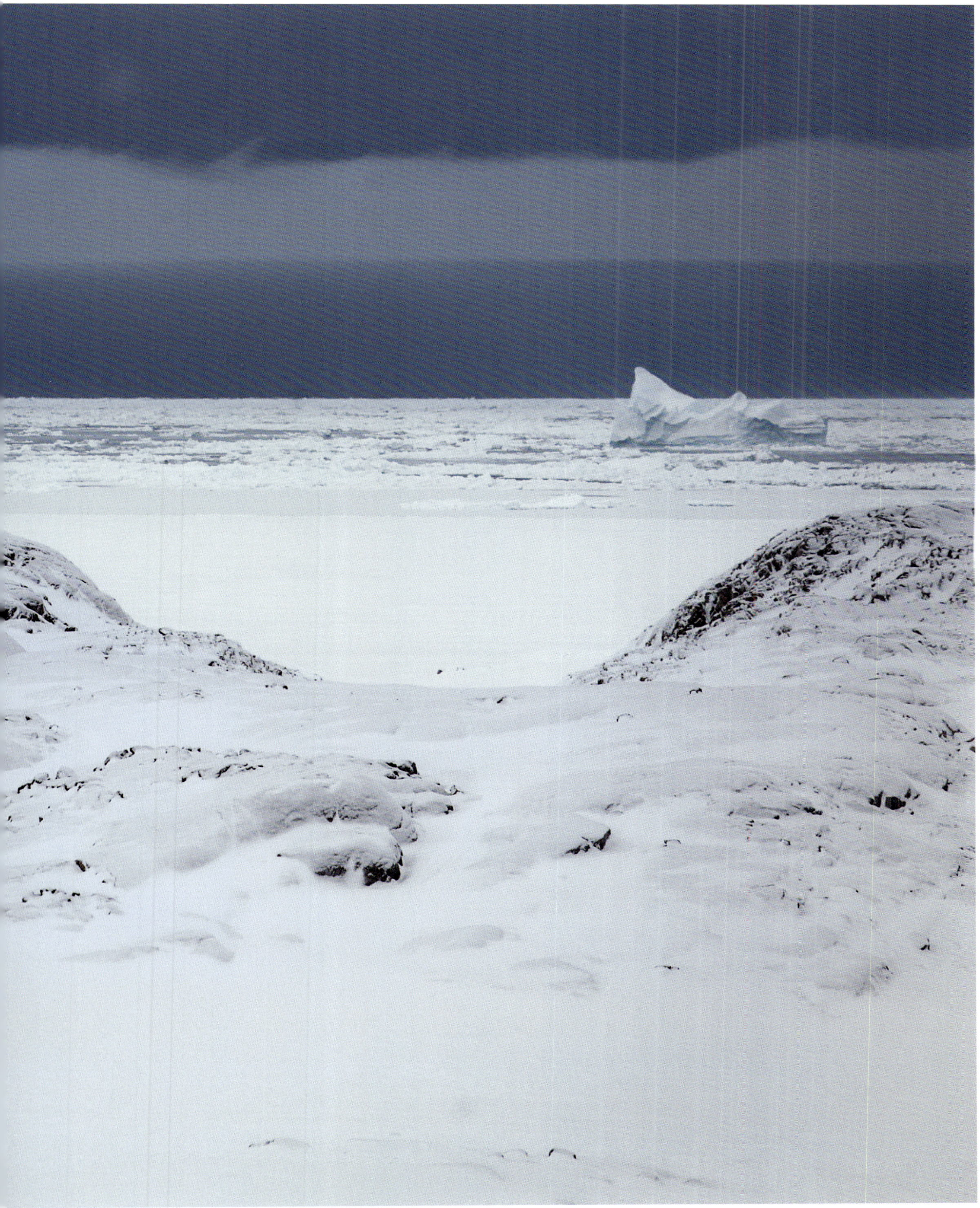

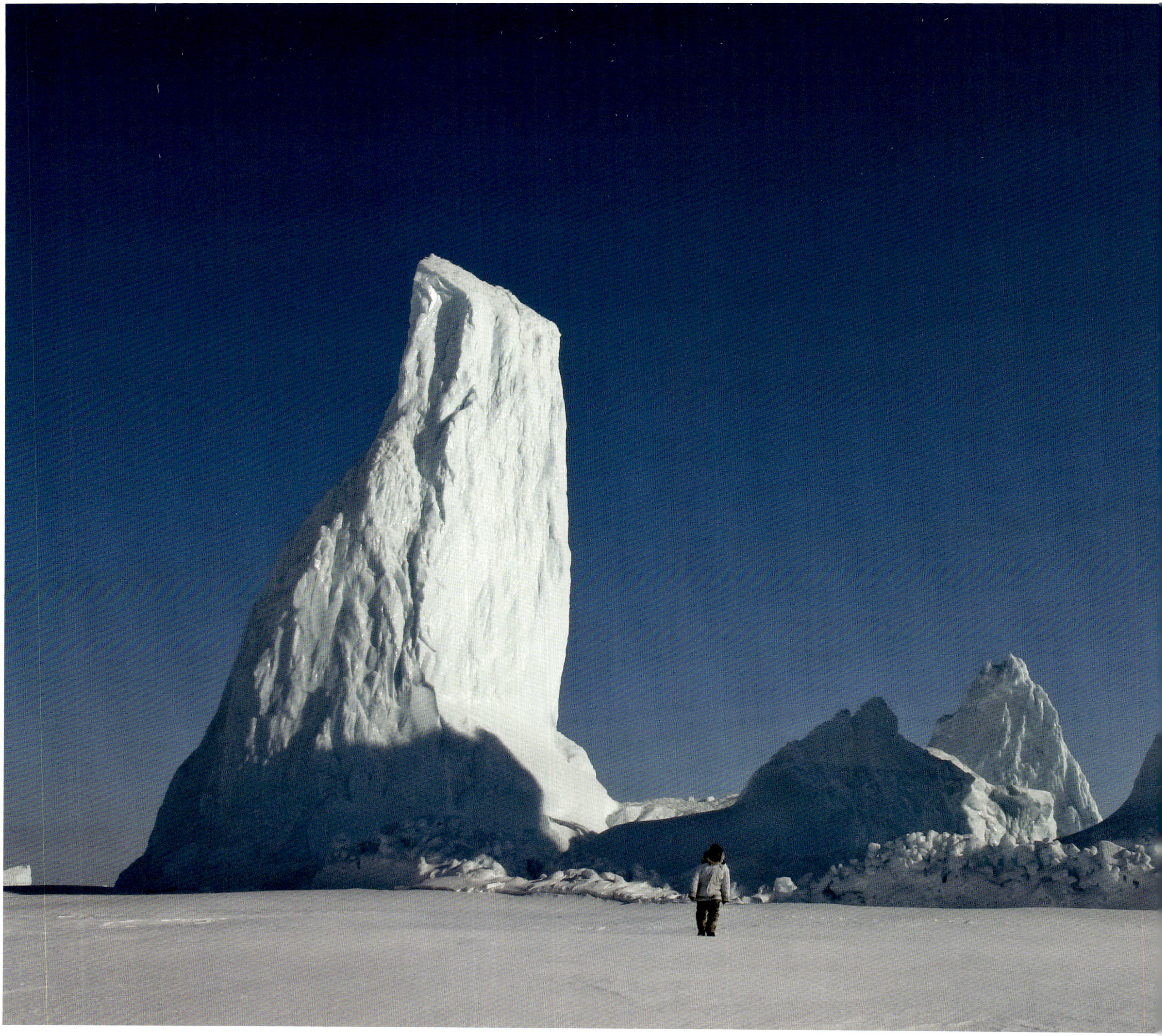

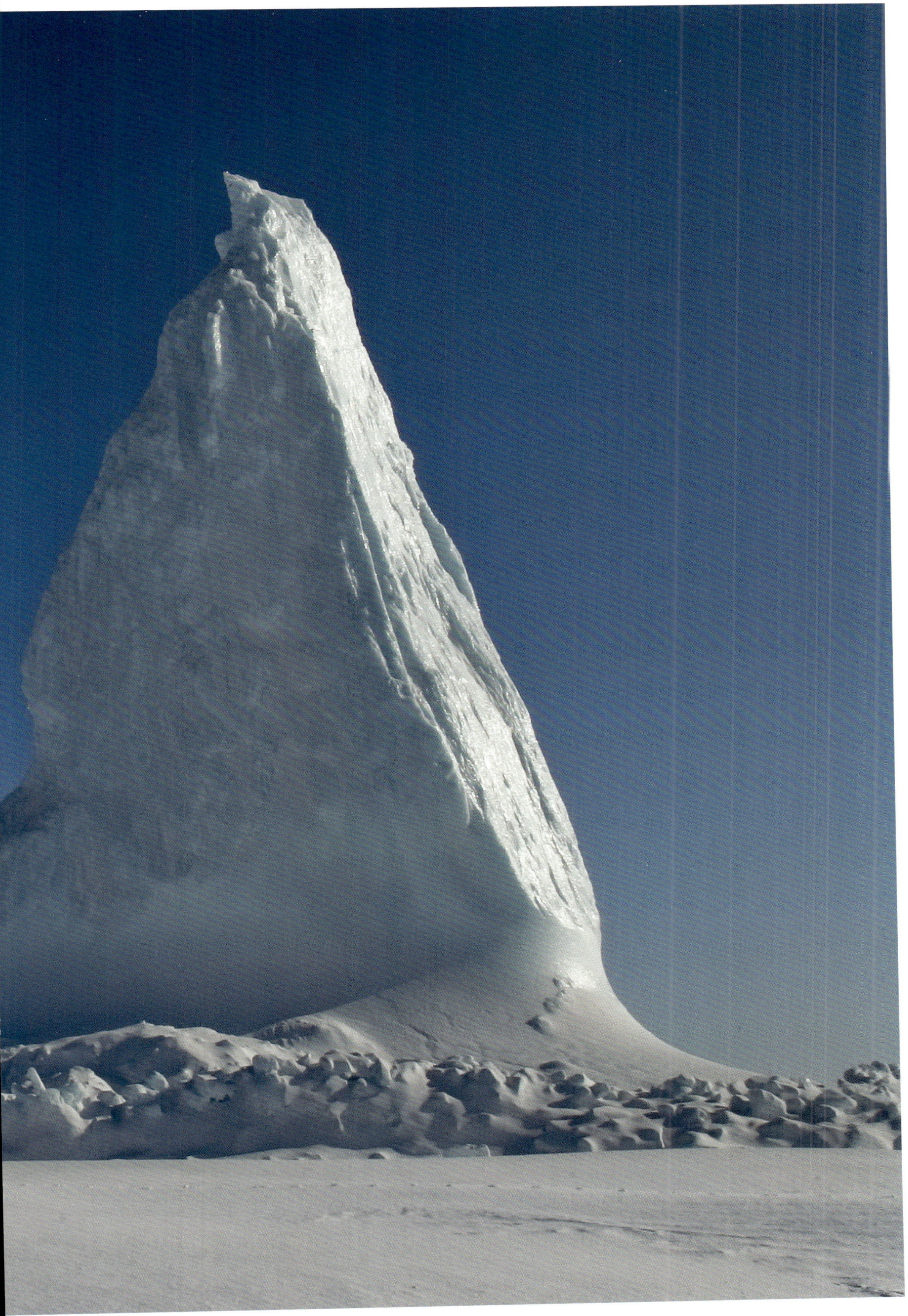

INUIT

pp. 16-17
One of Kulusuk's hunters searches for prey along the shore. In recent years, the ice sheet has become increasingly thin, making traditional hunting more difficult than before.

pp. 18-19
From a distance, the countless icebergs trapped in the seasonal ice between Baffin Island and Greenland look like castles.

The word *Inuit* (the singular form is *inuk*) means "the people" or "humans" and is applied generally to refer to the northern peoples whom outsiders have called "Eskimos." However, while there are compelling similarities from Siberia to Greenland, the general use of the term, implying that Inuit are a single people with a single culture, is deceptive. In Greenland they call themselves Kalaallit and Inughuit; Inuit and Inuvialuit in Canada; Iñupiaq, Yup'ik and Alutiiq in Alaska; and Yup'ik in Siberia. In their own languages, each of these names is a variant of "the people".

However, Inuit as a more general and political term of reference was adopted in 1977 in preference to Eskimo by the Inuit Circumpolar Conference (the ICC, now called the Inuit Circumpolar Council), an NGO established to represent the rights and interests of all Inuit peoples. Many scholars have argued that "Eskimo" originated from a French derivation of a term from an Algonquian language in eastern Canada, assumed to mean "eaters of raw flesh". Whatever its origin, the word Eskimo is generally seen as a derogatory term in Greenland and Canada while this is not the case in Alaska, where Iñupiaq and Yup'ik (the singular forms of Iñupiat and Yupiit) are suffixed with "Eskimo". Archaeologists, anthropologists, historians and linguists also often refer to Eskimo cultures, Eskimo peoples and Eskimo-Aleut languages. "Inuit" is linked etymologically to "existence" and "the state of being alive". In Greenlandic, for example, a newborn baby is spoken about as being brought to a "state of life" (*inunneq;* life, or literally "the state of being a person"). While *inunngorpoq* is often translated to mean "to be born", its literal meaning is "becomes a person/human" (*inuk:* person/human + *nngorpoq:* "becomes").

Around 155,000 Inuit inhabit the Arctic today, occupying a vast geographical area stretching westward from east Greenland across the Arctic islands and mainland of northern Canada to the coast of Alaska and across to Chukotka on the Russian side of the Bering Strait. The most northerly Inuit community (indeed the world's most northerly indigenous community) is the tiny village of Siorapaluk at 77°47'N in northwest Greenland, while Rigolet, located at 54°N at the entrance of Hamilton Inlet on Labrador's east coast, is the farthest south. Inuit political leaders call this immense territory Inuit Nunaat, the land of the Inuit. It is not an expression of hopes for an independent homeland, however, but a term used to signify that these northern lands are inhabited by Inuit who share a similar culture and who face similar social, political and environmental challenges.

Despite living in what are assumed to be the coldest, most barren, outermost and least habitable fringes of the world, the Inuit have survived, thrived and adapted in the Arctic for millennia. They have hunted marine and terrestrial mammals and fished cold inshore waters, freshwater lakes and rivers. They have seen opportunity and possibility in a landscape which outsiders have been predisposed to think of as an empty, harsh, cold, wilderness with only meagre resources. Their lifestyles are finely-tuned to the vagaries of weather and climate and they have developed rich cultural forms, beliefs and systems of kinship and social organisation that say much about the unique relationships they have nurtured with the animals and environment with which they have co-existed and which continue to sustain them.

Many archaeologists and anthropologists trace the origin of present-day Inuit to Siberia and possibly Central Asia. The Paleo-Arctic and Paleo-Eskimo ancestors of modern Inuit entered North America by crossing Beringia, an intercontinental land bridge connecting Siberia to Alaska during the Pleistocene, although water crossings were also probably made in boats covered in walrus skins, similar to the ones still used for hunting and travel by Yup'ik Eskimos living in coastal villages along the Bering Strait today. Arctic North America was not peopled by a rapid, large-scale migration from Asia, but by a gradual process of movement across the land, taking place over several thousand years and beginning as a search for new hunting grounds, rather than new land to settle.

Inuit cultures, both in the past and present, are diverse, but share specific common features. The Inuit depended first and foremost for their existence on seals, whales and other sea mammals, caribou and fish. Social organisation was built around the immediate family and broader kin group — social obligations to help one's kin and to share meat and fish were key cultural principles. On the whole, Inuit hunting groups were small in number, were based around nuclear families and were largely nomadic.

During the brief summers, families traversed wide-reaching hunting and fishing grounds looking for game. During the lengthy northern winter, families tended to group together in semi-permanent settlements. During long winter journeys, some Canadian Inuit groups built shelters from blocks of snow (the common misconception

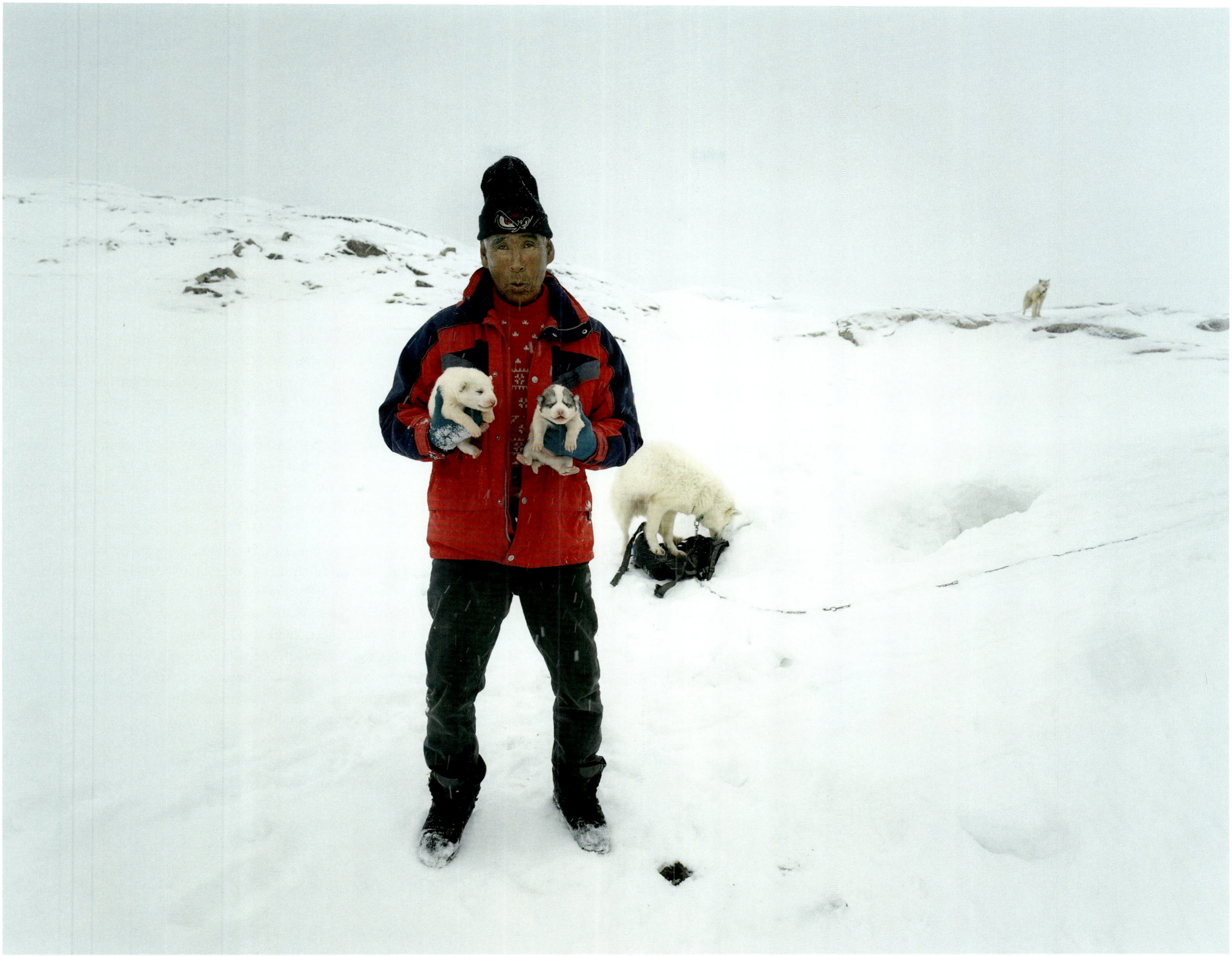

These husky puppies seem a little helpless in the hands of this old hunter in Kulusuk. The sledge dog is the working animal of the Inuit, and is perfectly adapted to the Arctic.

PINIARTOQ: Hunter

Translates literally as "one who wants". To hunt is to strive for something one wants and needs. Animals are wanted and needed for human survival. A second meaning of *piniartoq* is "provider." Animals not only sustain Inuit in an economic and nutritional sense, they provide a fundamental basis for social identity, cultural survival and spiritual life, making them no less important as cultural resources than economic ones.

IMARIPPOQ / MALLIALLERPOQ: Calm / Strong Sea

The sight and sound of water, its many and constantly changing moods and colours, are everyday topics of conversation. The sea is perceived and experienced as constantly changing, an environment of opportunity, of constantly unfolding possibilities. Hunters and fishers not only watch the changing appearance of the sea or the ice, they listen to it and learn to be attentive to sounds telling them about the behaviour of water, ice and icebergs.

NUNA: The Land

The land is a place in which people dwell and engage in elaborate and rich social relations, but also enjoy close relationships and partnerships with animals and the living environment. It is not completely accurate to translate *nuna* simply as "land" - it is the place which is underneath, above and all around. For Inuit in Canada's eastern Arctic, the Inuktitut word for environment, *avativut,* does not just describe the natural world, but also the surroundings in which a person lives and which are the vital components for balance and well-being. They include everything from one's personal name and identity, family and household, to plants, animals, the air one breathes and the water one drinks.

is that these shelters were called igloos, when in fact iglu is the Inuit word for "house").

Traditional Inuit religious beliefs were animistic — everything in the universe had a spirit which could affect the lives and fortunes of humans. Much of daily life was spent not only trying to procure food, but ensuring that taboos and rituals were observed to avoid harming the spirits of animals. Despite the conversion of the Inuit to Christianity, traditional beliefs concerning human-environment and human-animal relations and the reincarnation of the human soul have not disappeared entirely to this day.

Today, the Inuit fall within one of the following geographical and cultural groupings: the Greenland Inuit (living on the west, northwest and east coasts of the country); the Canadian Inuit (living in Labrador, Quebec, Nunavut, and the Northwest Territories); the Alaskan Eskimos, who are divided into Iñupiaq, Yup'ik, and Alutiiq/Sugpiaq peoples (living in the northern, western and south-western parts of the state); and the Siberian Yup'ik of Chukotka in north-eastern Siberia.

GREENLAND INUIT

The coastal areas of Greenland have been inhabited by Inuit groups for about 4,500 years. Since 1979, the country has been known officially as *Kalaallit Nunaat* ("the Greenlanders' Land"), although both "Inuit" and "Greenlanders" are used as more generic and interchangeable terms to refer to the indigenous population. The Inuit population is comprised of three distinct cultural and linguistic groups: the majority Kalaallit, living along the west coast; Inughuit (popularly known as the Polar Eskimos and famous as the world's most northerly indigenous inhabitants) in the north; and Iit on the east coast.

European settlement in Greenland can be traced to around 985 AD, when the Icelander Eirik the Red, outlawed from his homeland, sailed west to Greenland to establish two colonies in the south and southwest. The Norse existed in Greenland for almost 500 years. Exactly what happened to them has not been resolved definitively.

Danish colonisation dates from 1721. For over 200 years the Danes followed an isolationist policy towards Greenland and the indigenous Inuit, effectively keeping it a closed country. After World War II, however, Denmark ended its isolationist policy and emphasis was placed on social welfare and on infrastructural change as part of a process of modernisation of both the country and Inuit society. Commercial fishing was made the basis of economic development and people were moved from small hunting settlements and resettled in larger towns on the west coast.

By the late 1960s and early 1970s, the majority of the Inuit population now lived in these fast-growing west coast towns, a demographic transition which brought its own problems. While life in small settlements had been characterised by and organised around kinship, the move to towns disrupted kin-based groups leading to alienation, social and economic marginality and discrimination. This was aggravated by ethnic tensions and increasing numbers of Danes living in Greenland because of the need for construction workers, teachers, doctors and administrators.

One direct result of these social changes and upheavals was the emergence of Inuit political parties and a heightened sense of Inuit identity. Greenlanders became the first population of Inuit origin to achieve a degree of self-government in 1979. While Greenland remains a part of the Kingdom of Denmark, the Home Rule authorities have embarked on an ambitious policy of nation-building. Fishing for cod and shrimp is vital to the country's economy and many small communities still depend on marine mammal hunting, but in the future Greenland is likely to develop its rich mineral and hydrocarbon resources. On 21 June 2009, a new form of self-government called Self-Rule, with even greater autonomy, was instituted.

CANADIAN INUIT

Canadian Inuit live across the entire length of the Canadian North, from the Mackenzie Delta region near the Alaskan border, to Baffin Island and farther south in Quebec and Labrador. Until the middle of the twentieth century many Inuit groups in Canada still pursued a semi-nomadic lifestyle based on seal and caribou hunting.

The Hudson's Bay Company dominated Canada's fur trade from the time it received its charter in 1670 right up to the early twentieth century. During this period, the Canadian Inuit became dependent on Hudson's Bay Company trading posts, cultural values were changed and the spiritual relationship between the Inuit and the animals they hunted was altered. Following World War II, mining activity grew and, together with hydroelectric projects, created a southern Canadian vision of the Far North as a vast storehouse of natural resources, the development and exploitation of which was necessary for the future Canadian nation. In recent years, however, major industrial projects have been opposed by environmentalists and Native peoples, fearful of the social and environmental impacts they could have on the Canadian North.

Canada decided on active intervention in the 1950s and began to move the Inuit off the land and settle them into permanent communities. Inuit children were sent to school and had to learn English. These government resettlement policies only exacerbated the erosion of the Inuit subsistence hunting culture and increased Inuit dependency on the Canadian government and institutions, as well as resulting in tremendous social problems. The presence in small Inuit settlements of large numbers of southern Canadians as administrators, trade managers, teachers and construction workers caused considerable resentment among the Inuit and ethnic conflict between the two groups was common. Since the 1950s, the Canadian government has aimed at

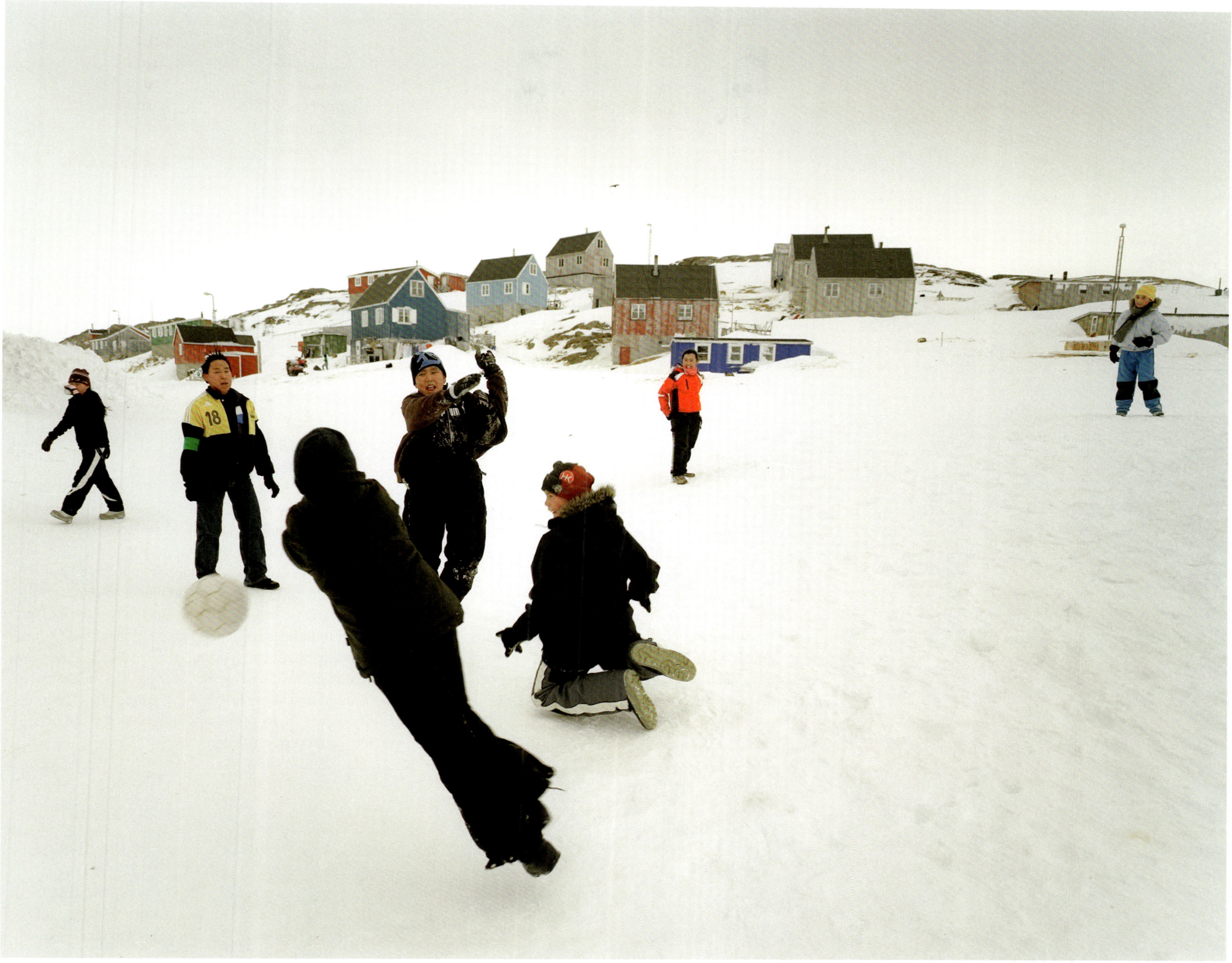

In the main town square in Kulusuk, youngsters gather after school for some ice football. In a place like this, nobody worries about the traffic.

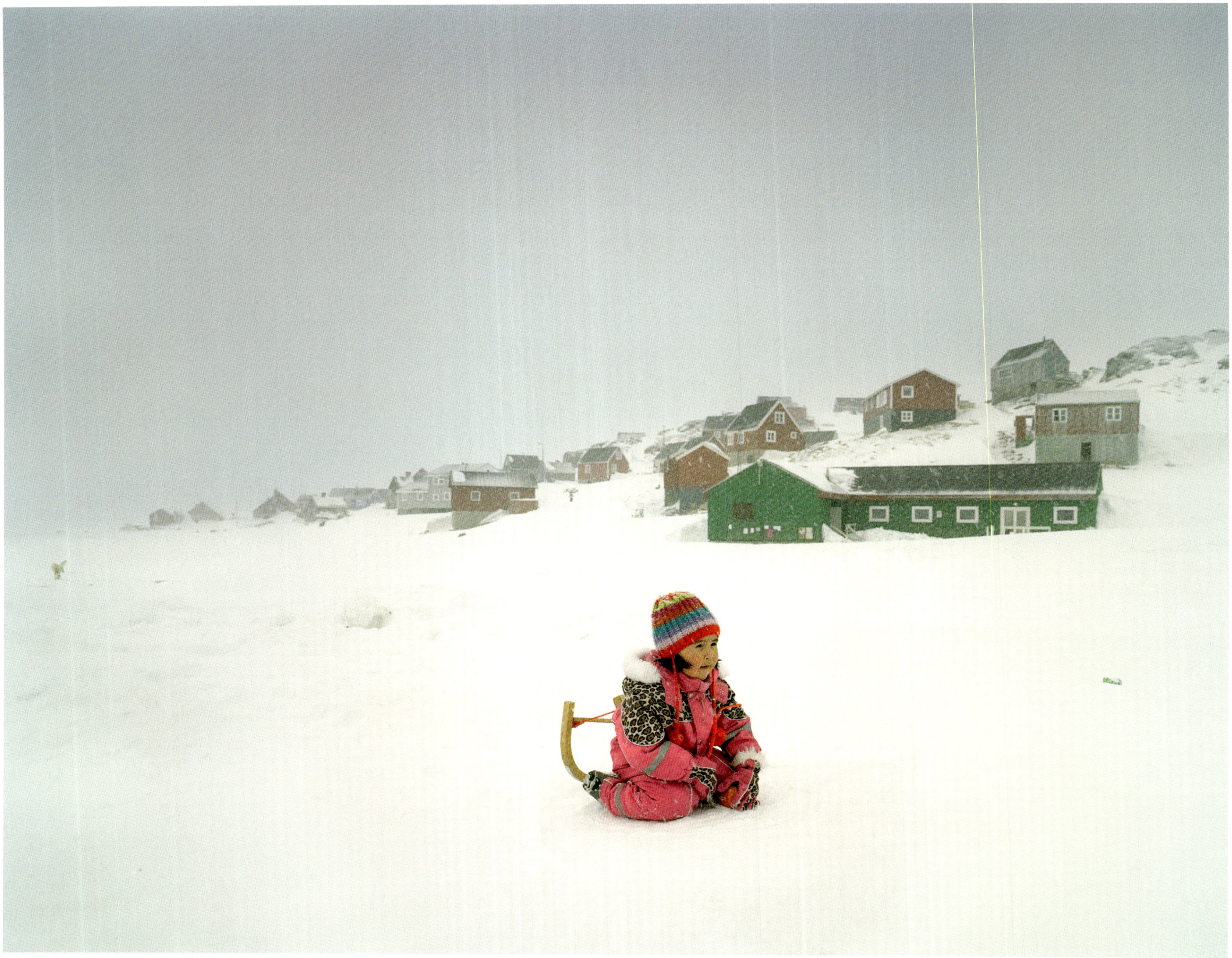

The vastness of Greenland's ice cap separates the East Greenlanders from the majority of the country's population on the southwest coast.

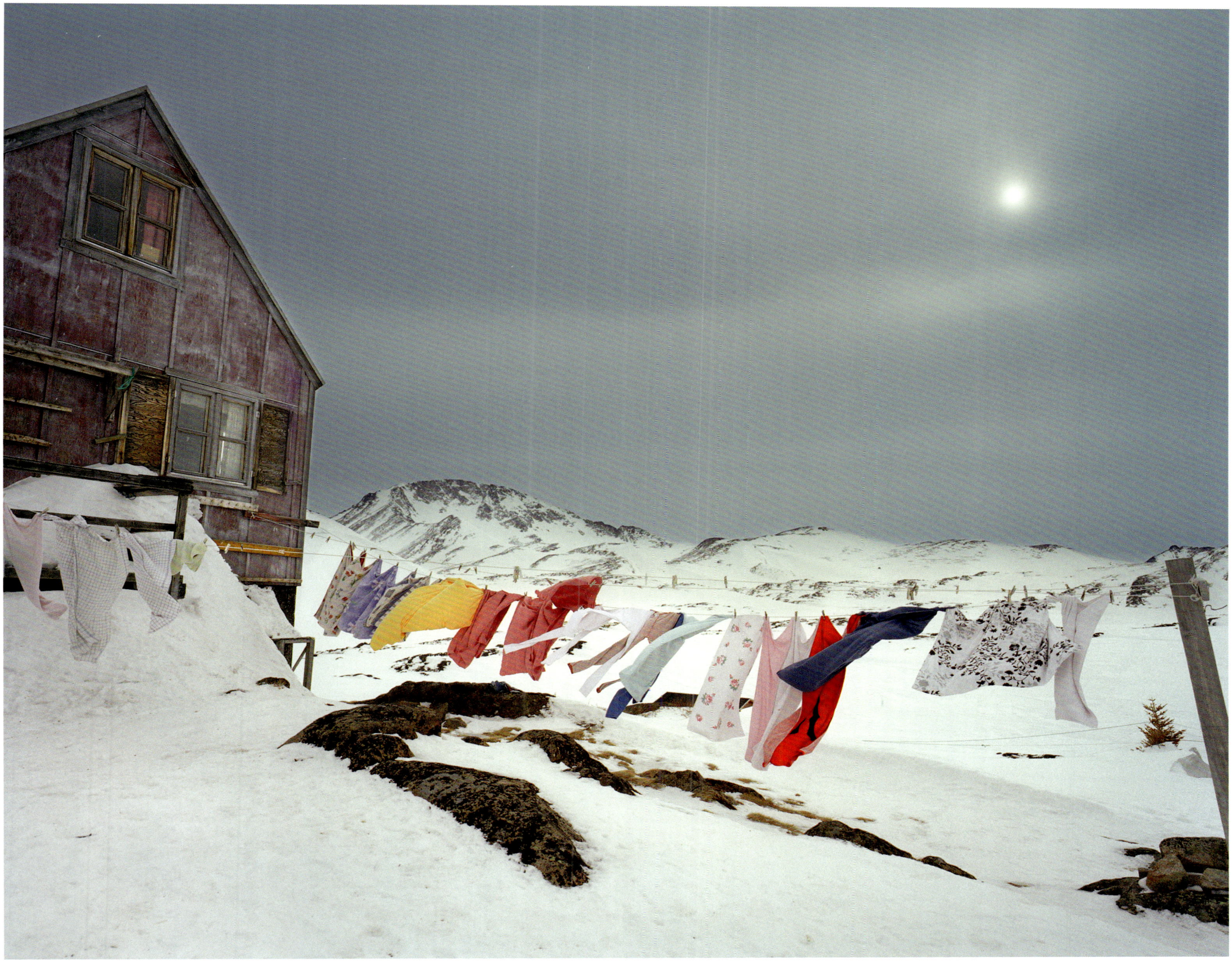

It's early spring and the sun rises rapidly again after the dark winter months. Kulusuk is far enough south, however, that the villagers never experience total darkness.

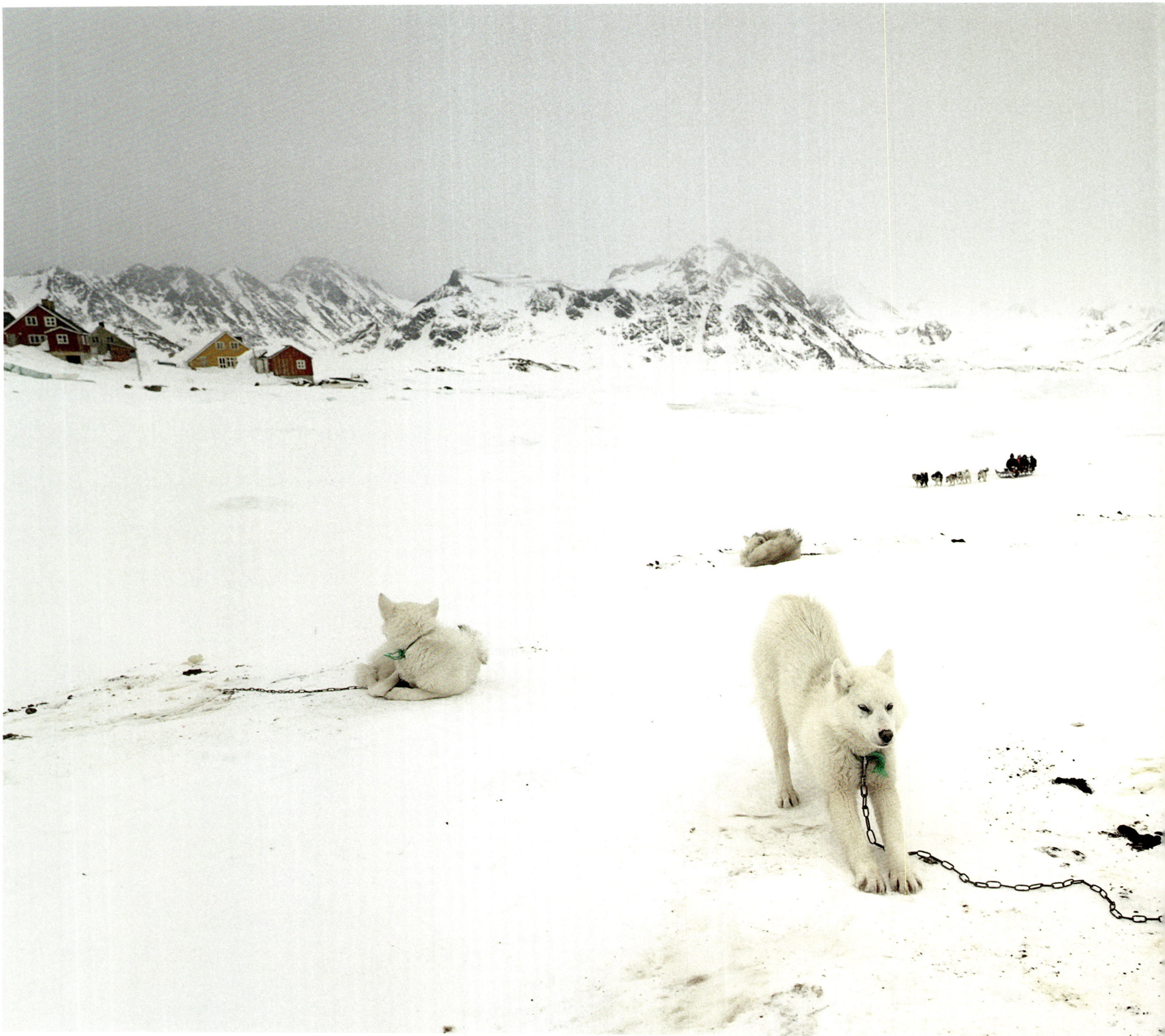

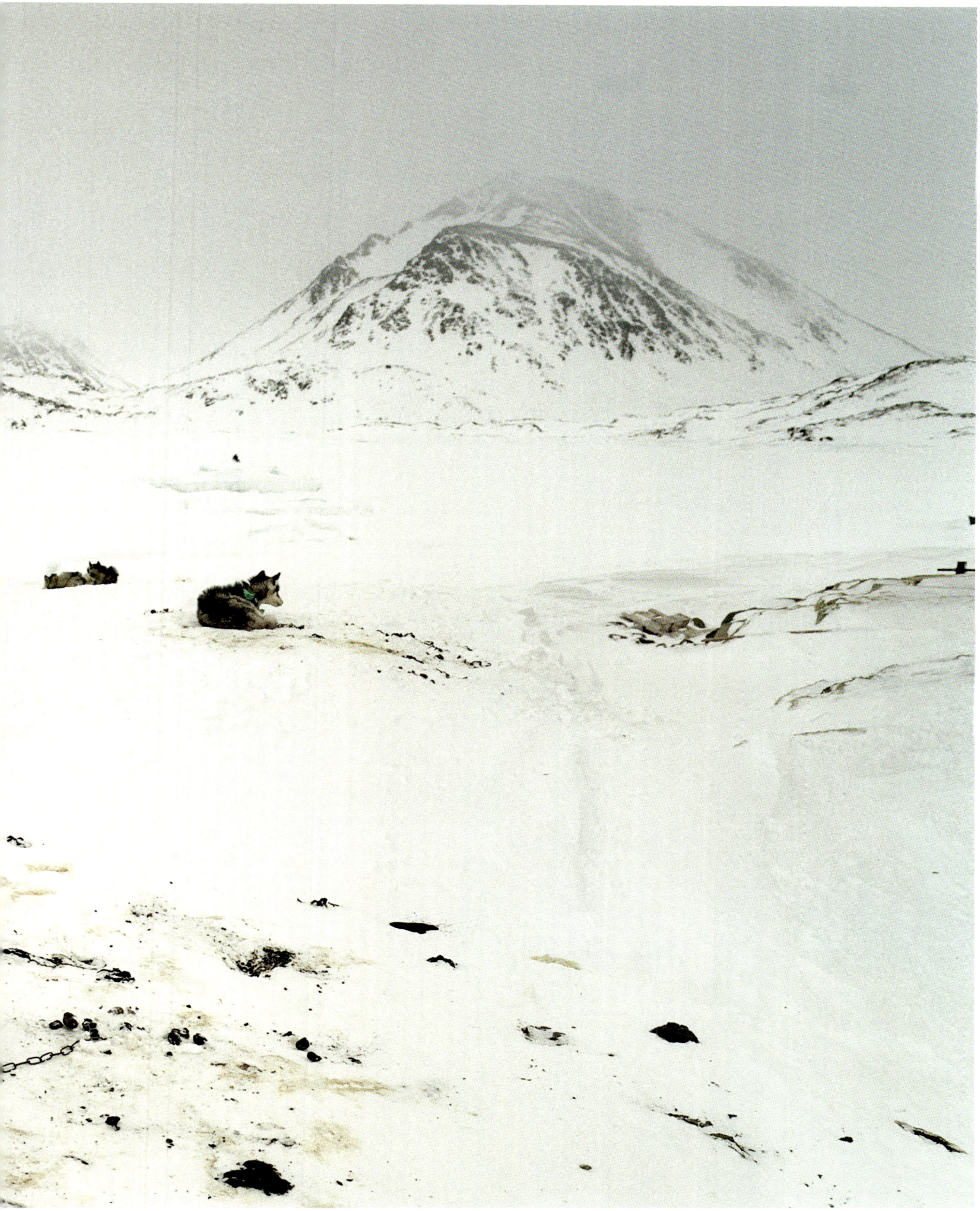

QANIK / APUT:
Falling snow / snow on the ground

A common misunderstanding is that the Inuit have dozens of words for snow. Essentially, there are two: *qanik* and *aput*. In addition, however, there are words and terms that describe, for example, the consistency of snow, such as *masak aput* (wet snow), or snow that is good for making water (*aniutaq*). Recent, deep snow that is difficult to walk on without sinking is *apijuq*, while hard snow that is good for making snow houses and can be cut into blocks relatively easily is *sitilluqaq*. Sometimes snow falls merely as light flurries, *qanniliqtaqtuq*, but a wind can also blow around snow that has already fallen, making it *natiruviktuq* – to seem as if it is snowing. Bad weather can bring strong winds, heavy falling snow, and make it natiruviktuq all at once. In Inuktitut, this is called tammajarnaqtuq, something that in English would be described as a blizzard.

SILA: Weather or climate

Considered the fundamental principle underlying the natural world, a life-giving spirit, a universal consciousness or breathing soul that is found in each person. A person who lacks *sila* is said to lack the essential relationship with the environment necessary for human well-being. *Silaqaraluarneq* is the state of being out of one's mind, but it can also mean "the weather is out of its mind", used in discussing changes in weather and climate that are unusual or difficult to account for.

pp. 26-27
Throughout Greenland's hunting villages, chained sledge dogs can be seen yawning and stretching when they are not on duty. They stay on bare cliffs in all weather, even during snowstorms and in the freezing cold, and bark angrily at each passerby, obeying no one but their master.

pp. 30-31
The biggest town in southeastern Greenland is Tasiilaq. The towns here are without doubt some of the most isolated human settlements on the planet, although flights from West Greenland and Iceland to Kulusuk bring some tourism to the region.

incorporating the Inuit into mainstream Canadian economic, social and cultural life. While it is easy to judge this as misguided from today's perspective, it is important to recognise that successive Canadian governments believed this paternalistic approach was a good thing for the Inuit. After all, in the popular imagination as well as in official legislation, the Inuit were believed to be living on the edge of starvation in a barren, inhospitable wilderness. Through education and training, the indigenous inhabitants of the Arctic were to become modern Canadians, improving their lifestyle options in a new period of economic development on the Canadian Arctic frontier.

In response to social change and large-scale economic development, a Canadian Inuit political elite have worked tirelessly to achieve specific degrees of self-determination and self-government in recent decades. Faced with oil and gas development in the Mackenzie Delta, the Inuvialuit formed the Committee of Original People's Entitlement (COPE) in 1969, and in 1971 the Inuit Tapirisat of Canada (ITC, and now called Inuit Tapiriit Kanatami, or ITK) was founded in Ottawa as a national voice for Inuit throughout Canada's North. In 1984 the Inuvialuit Final Agreement accorded title to 35,000 square miles of the Northwest Territories to the Inuvialuit, together with financial compensation and other rights (including gas, petroleum and mineral rights for 5000 square miles) as a final settlement of territorial claims. In 1975 the Inuit of northern Quebec signed a land claims agreement against the backdrop of controversy surrounding hydroelectric development in James Bay. In 1992 the Tungavik Federation of Nunavut and the Government of Canada signed an agreement on Inuit land claims and harvest rights committing the federal government to establishing Nunavut ("our land") in the Canadian Eastern Arctic. The territory of Nunavut, comprising 818,962 square miles of northern Canada, was inaugurated on 1 April 1999.

The population of Nunavut is around 80% Inuit and the government is effectively Inuit-led. While the settlement did not create a new ethnic Inuit state, Canadian territories and provinces have extensive public self-government within the limits defined by the Canadian constitution. Nunavut has given the Inuit of the eastern Arctic a greater degree of autonomy and self-government than is enjoyed by any other aboriginal group in Canada. The Inuit homeland of Nunavik in northern Quebec is currently subject to negotiations for status as a self-governing region within the province, while following ratification of the Labrador Inuit Land Claims Agreement, the government of Nunatsiavut was established in 2005 to represent the rights of Labrador Inuit.

ALASKAN ESKIMOS

The Alaskan Eskimos are the most culturally diverse of all the Inuit populations and encompass the *Iñupiat,* the *Yup'ik, Alutiiq* and *Sugpiaq* (the latter two traditionally referred to as Pacific Eskimos).

Prior to European contact, the coastal Iñupiat Eskimos specialised in hunting the bowhead whale, walrus, seals and polar bears, while the social and cultural life of inland groups revolved around caribou hunting. Today, whaling and the hunting of other marine mammals remain a strong part of Iñupiat culture and economic life. Due to the central importance of whaling, a distinctive and more socially-stratified society emerged on the North Slope. Inuit social status has traditionally been determined by the skill and knowledge of the hunter, his ability to catch an abundance of game and share the meat with others in the community. The captain of a whaling crew is known as an *umialik* and the *umialik* and his wife have traditionally held a high social position in Iñupiat Eskimo society. In complete contrast to the Inupiat of the North Slope, the Yup'ik peoples of southwest Alaska inhabit a subarctic landscape rich in natural resources. The Yup'ik are seal hunters, although they also catch beluga whales and walrus, and take advantage of the abundance of different types of fish found at sea and in the thousands of miles of rivers that cross the Yup'ik homeland. The Yup'ik are renowned for their complex ceremonial life. For example, elaborate masks carved from wood, or made from sealskin, and depicting animal spirits and mythical figures, are worn at community feasts and dances in memory of the ancestors. The Pacific Eskimos of the southern part of Alaska include groups who prefer to see themselves as either Aleut, Koniag, Alutiiq or Sugpiaq-speaking. They inhabit largely mountainous coastal areas and traditionally combine whaling, sealing and fishing. Traditionally, Pacific Eskimo societies had higher population densities and were more hierarchically-complex in terms of social organisation than other Inuit.

The European discovery of Alaska is accredited to Vitus Bering, a Danish explorer on a Russian expedition, in 1741. When Bering's expedition returned home with sea otter pelts, the subsequent course of Alaska's economic development based on exploitation of its natural resources began. Alaska was a focus of both Russian and British fur trade and, over a period of 140 years, fur seals, sea otters and some species of fur-bearing land mammals were exploited to near extinction. Beginning in 1847, American whalers from New England hunted the bowhead whale in the waters of Bering Strait, seriously affecting the viability of the indigenous Iñupiaq hunt. From the 1880s onward, gold mining formed the basis for the expansion of the Alaskan economy and its subsequent settlement by non-indigenous peoples. The discovery of vast reserves of oil and gas at Prudhoe Bay on the North Slope in 1968 has dominated Alaska's late-twentieth/early twenty-first century economic development. While hunting and trapping remains an important and integral part of the Iñupiat and Yup'ik village economies, many people now find permanent and seasonal employment in commercial fishing, in the petroleum industry or in urban centres such as Anchorage and Fairbanks.

Integration of the indigenous Iñupiat and Yup'ik Eskimo peoples into mainstream American social, cultural and economic life has followed a pattern similar to the experiences of Inuit groups elsewhere in the Arctic. Until the mid-1970s, the education system in rural Alaska's native communities-had assimilationist objectives. Native children were to be educated as US citizens and many had to leave their villages for a high school education. In 1975 a revision of the educational administration established regional school districts and village high schools. While this did help empower communities with regard to education, the curriculum was unchanged. Native schoolchildren studied the same subjects as US children elsewhere. Although schools in rural Alaska are effectively under local control today, they remain institutions that are not really part of the social and cultural fabric of Native communities.

SIBERIAN *YUP'IK*

The Siberian Yup'ik (pl. Yupiit) speak one of four Yup'ik dialects (the others are spoken in Alaska), although theirs is perhaps linguistically more closely related to the language of the Chukchi of Siberia. The Siberian Yup'ik communities are thinly scattered along the isolated coasts of Chukotka in north-western Siberia and number around 2,000. Their economy has revolved traditionally around the hunting of bowhead and grey whales, seals, walrus, caribou and polar bears. Like other Inuit groups, their social organization, culture, spiritual beliefs, religious practices and mythology have been inextricably linked to the animals they depend on for survival.

Contact between Siberian Yup'ik and Europeans first occurred in the tenth century, but extensive and prolonged contact with Russians only began in the eighteenth century. Once this contact was established, a familiar pattern followed: Siberian Yup'ik communities experienced wave after wave of epidemics, which seriously affected the demographic composition of north-eastern Siberia. Yup'ik communities were also extremely hard hit by Soviet economic policies in the twentieth century. With the establishment of the Soviet Committee of the North in 1928 Yup'ik economic life was collectivised and boat crews organised into seasonal hunting co-operatives. Following the end of World War II, many Yup'ik villages were closed down by the Soviet authorities and their inhabitants resettled in Chukchi villages. This set in motion a process of social and cultural integration with the Chukchi population which continues today.

In the 1950s and 1960s what was left of traditional Yup'ik culture and livelihoods was marginalised even further by resettlement, reducing the number of Siberian Yup'ik villages from 50 to 12. Major social, economic and infrastructural changes swept across the region — the construction of roads, pipelines, nuclear power plants and military installations had a massive impact on the human and physical environment.

Despite the tremendous changes that have transformed much of their traditional life, the Siberian Yup'ik have maintained a distinctive ethnic identity within Russia. Since the collapse of the Soviet Union in 1991, this identity has gained new strength.

THE INUIT AND SELF-DETERMINATION

In the Arctic today, indigenous peoples' organizations are challenging the authority of the state and questioning the processes and meanings of modernity, globalization, and development. They have taken a lead in pressing regional and national governments to offset the impact of social and economic change and have taken action in persuading governments to work on implementing measures for environmental protection and sustainable development. Notable success stories include the United Nations, where the Permanent Forum on Indigenous Peoples is a body of 16 representatives that meets annually to examine indigenous issues. Arctic indigenous representatives — particularly Inuit — have played a significant role in the Permanent Forum and have often led the way in how global indigenous movements can find a way of negotiating at international levels.

The Inuit, like other Arctic peoples, face threats to their culture, livelihood and homelands from environmental problems, such as trans-boundary pollution and climate change, large-scale industrial activity, rapid social transformation and other exogenous forces. Animal-rights groups and environmental movements campaign against traditional Inuit hunting activities, such as sealing and whaling. In Inuit society, no individual can claim to own the animals. Access to resources is based on communal rights and hunting is guided by community regulations, which are often unwritten. Sharing of the catch remains at the very heart of the hunting culture. From an Inuit perspective, threats to wildlife and the environment do not come from hunting, but from airborne and seaborne pollutants entering the Arctic from industrial areas far to the south. Extraction of non-renewable resources, such as oil and gas and minerals, pose other challenges.

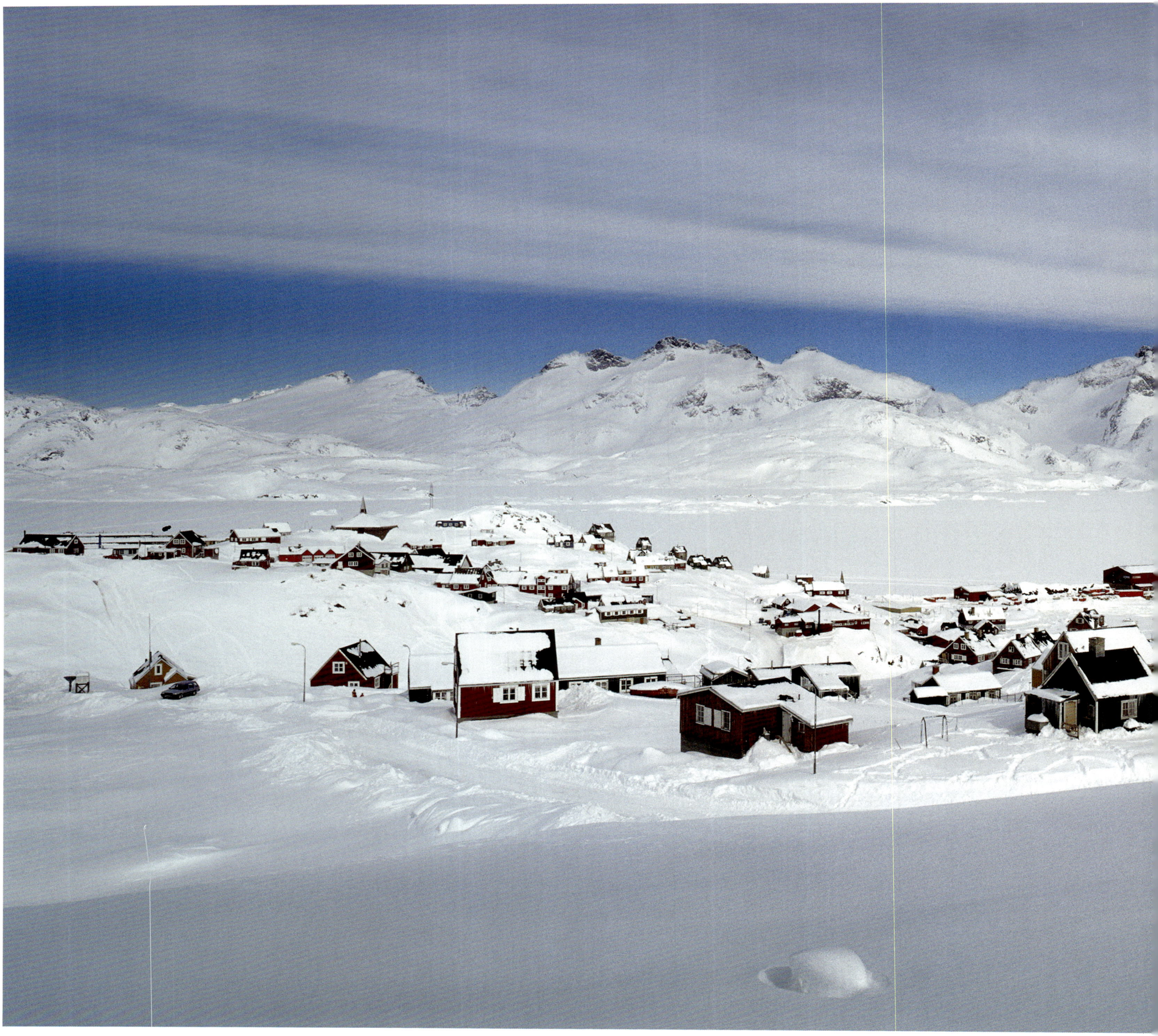

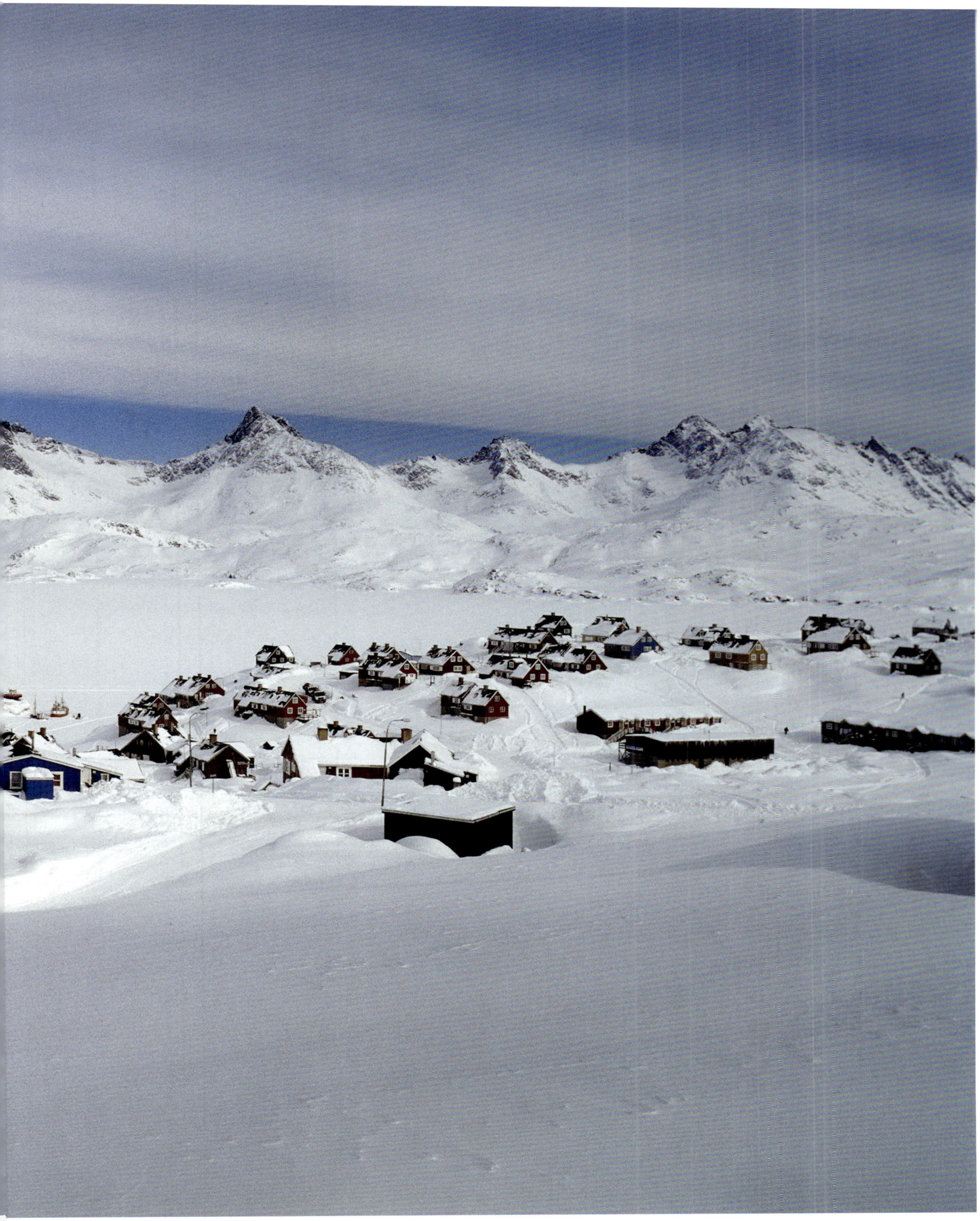

THE LAST DAYS OF THE GREAT ICE?

Covering an area of 1.7 million square km, Greenland's inland ice is the second largest ice mass on the planet after Antarctica's vast 13 million sq. km ice sheet. In Greenlandic it is known as *sermersuaq*, "the great ice". Elsewhere in the circumpolar North, smaller glaciers and ice caps cover significant areas, especially in the Canadian Arctic islands, Iceland, Svalbard and the Russian archipelagos of Franz Josef Land, Severnaya Zemlya and Novaya Zemlya. Together, Arctic ice masses form almost 15% of the world's glaciers and ice caps. Glaciers and ice sheets exist in the Arctic today because of both past and present climatic conditions, but the enhanced warming of the global atmosphere is threatening them and scientists now report worrying rates of accelerated melting and glacial retreat.

The melting of the Greenland inland ice has captured scientific and public attention as one of the starkest examples of global climate change. Scientific climate models suggest that Greenland's climate will warm by more than 3° C during this century, which would mean long-term melting of the inland ice. The entire Greenland ice sheet contains enough water to raise global sea levels by seven metres. Today's alarm about the melting of the Greenland inland ice arises from scientific scenarios that suggest the scale and nature of climate change in the coming decades may be greater than previous changes ever experienced in the Earth's history.

As the inland ice melts, a new Greenland is emerging. Geographically, mountains, headlands and islands are appearing and cartographers are beginning to revise maps and charts. Glaciologists may not yet have all the answers to why glaciers surge and retreat, but Inuit stories of glacial movement often speak to the sentience of these vast bodies of ice. Like everything else in the environment, they are aware, living beings. And perhaps one reason they move is that they are attentive and sensitive to human behaviour.

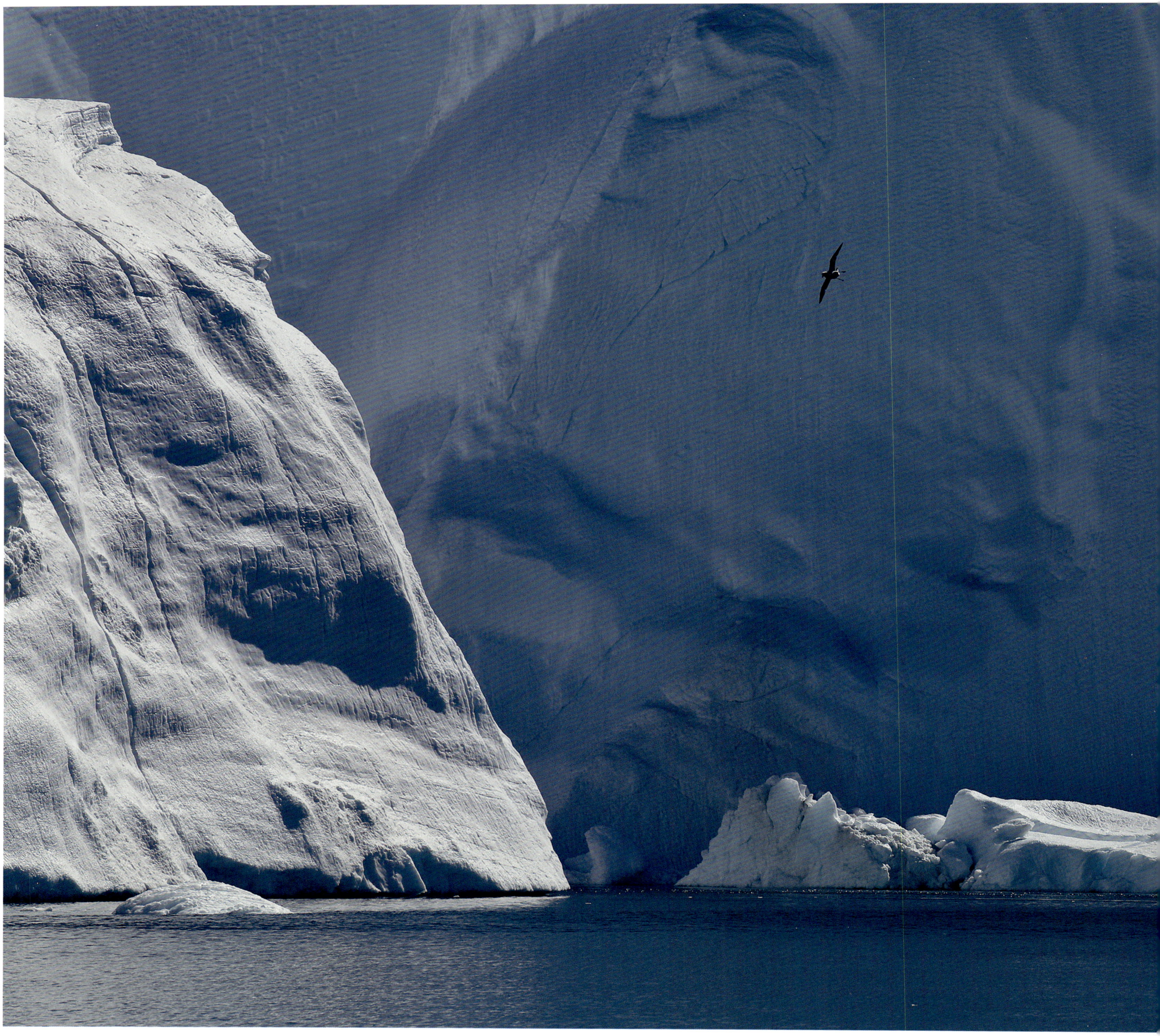

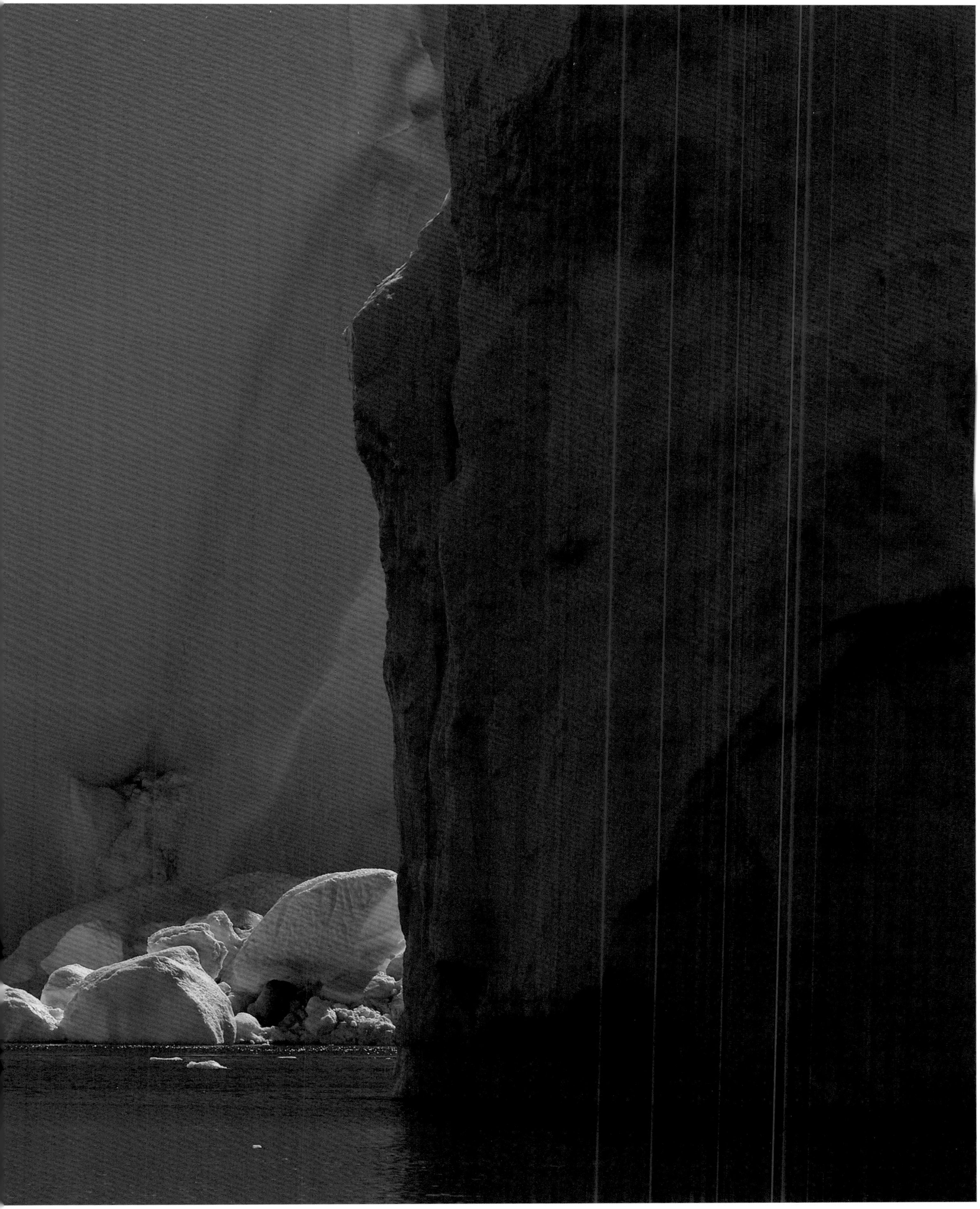

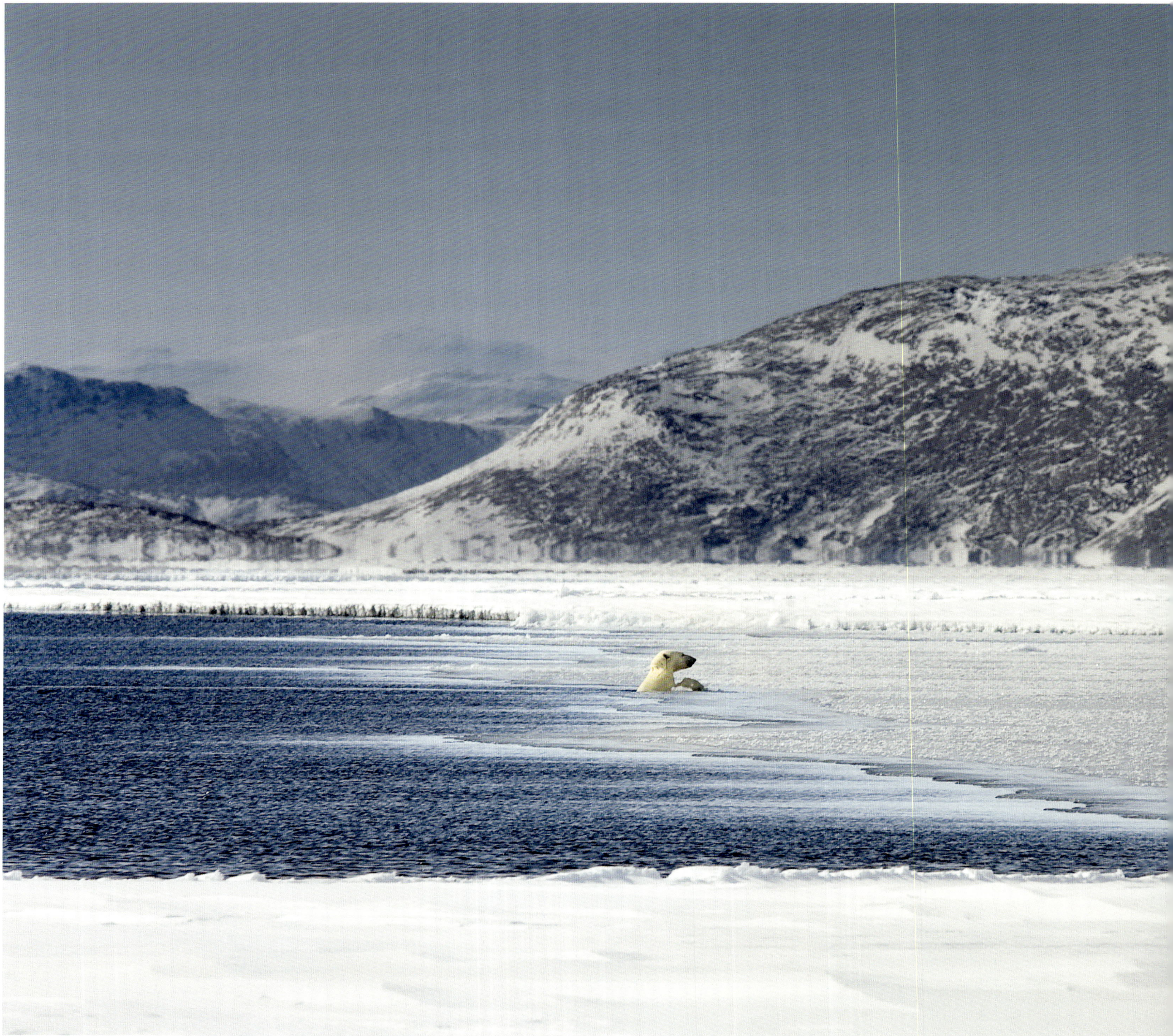

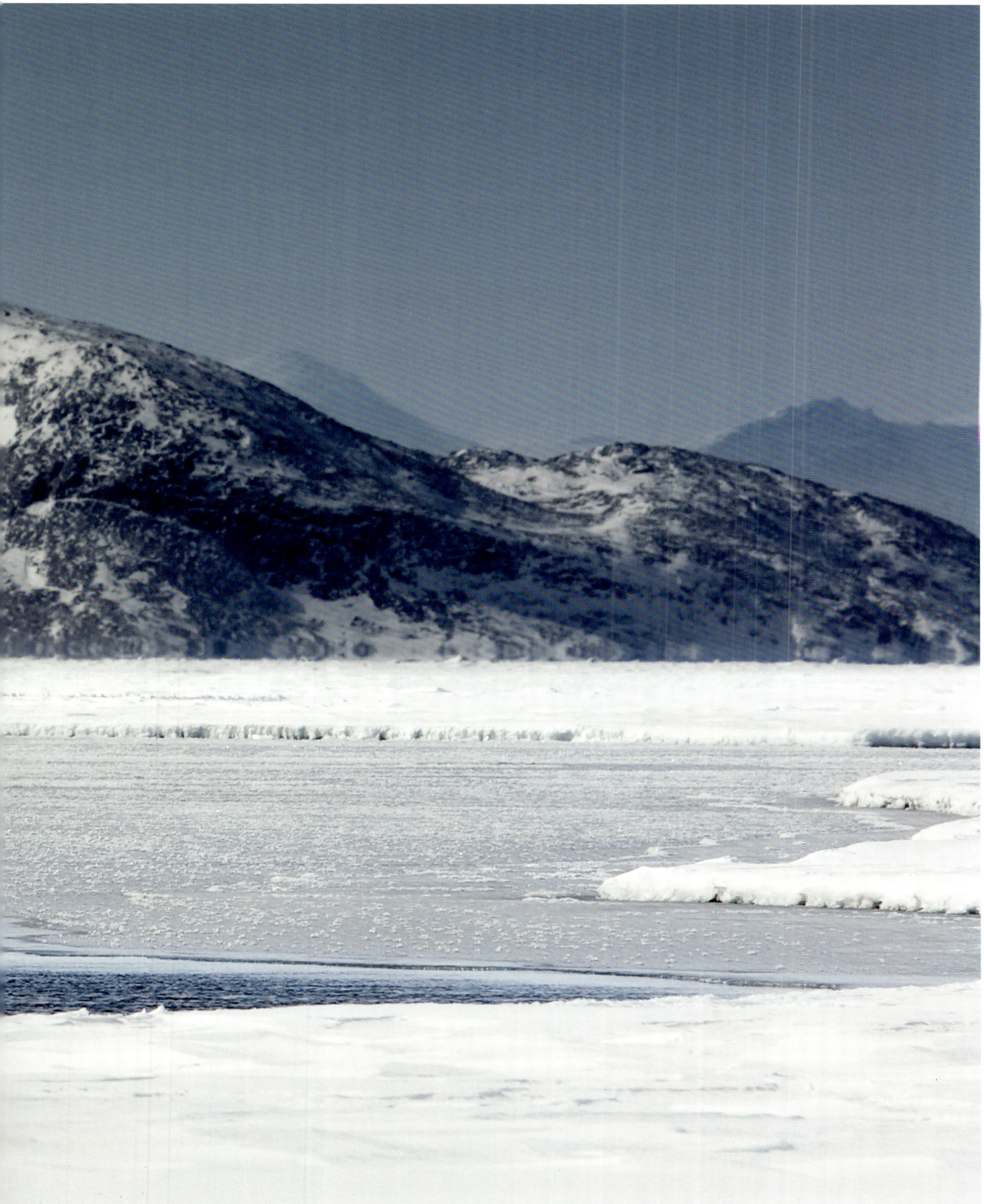

THE WARMING ARCTIC

pp. 34-35
Many icebergs that calve out of the glaciers in Ilulissat fjord and then drift into Disko Bay are hundreds of metres high. Some are so big that they become stuck on their way out to the ocean and can remain in place for years.

pp. 36-37
On the shores of Baffin Island a polar bear returns from a swimming tour and tries to balance itself on the ice floes. Despite being one of the largest land mammals on the planet, the polar bear possesses an incredible grace when it comes to walking on thin ice.

The Arctic as a place without snow and ice is seemingly unimaginable. Indeed, the imagery of snow and ice defines the region and tourists who visit the Arctic in summer are often surprised (and sometimes disappointed) when they see the land free of white and carpeted with tundra plants, grasses, sedges and flowers such as saxifrages (in fact around 900 varieties of flowers are found in the Arctic). It confounds the stereotype they have of the Arctic as a land of perpetual cold.

The popular perception of the Arctic is a place at the top of the world which is vast, timeless and unchanging, a place characterized by extreme cold and seasonal variations of light and darkness and one of the few locations on Earth to be virtually untouched by humans. Yet the Arctic continues to undergo changes in its climate and environment; today these changes are occurring with dramatic speed. The scientific consensus is that the region is now being affected by a human-induced warming trend unknown in its history. Sea ice is thinning, permafrost is melting, there are significant reductions in seasonal snow, and glaciers are beginning to recede at a rapid rate. Recent research has demonstrated that there has been a distinct warming trend in lowland permafrost of 2–4°C over the last hundred years.

Climate change will have a potentially devastating impact on the Arctic environment and on the peoples who live there, particularly the indigenous peoples of the region, whose livelihoods, societies and cultures are inextricably bound up with the Arctic environment and its wildlife. The migration routes of caribou, seals, whales, fish and geese will be disrupted and are likely to shift, with consequences for the hunting, trapping and fishing economies of many small, remote Arctic settlements. Permafrost will thaw more quickly in spring, but take longer to refreeze in autumn, and permafrost boundaries will gradually move poleward, with most of the ice-rich discontinuous permafrost disappearing by the end of the twenty-first century. At the same time, the tree line will move farther north. The dark evergreen forests characteristic of the boreal regions south of the tree line will advance northwards into areas where cedars, firs, pines, spruces, birches have not been known to grow.

Further warming will also increase the likelihood of natural hazards for people (increasing the risks involved in travelling on the land and sea, for example, or increased exposure to ultraviolet radiation), and posing challenges to buildings, communication and transportation links, industrial infrastructure, and oil and gas pipelines and production facilities.

TOWARDS AN ICE-FREE ARCTIC OCEAN

As much as 90% of the surface of the entire Arctic Ocean is covered by ice in winter and 70% year round. The ice is constantly battered by winds and shunted around by currents. Broken into floes which collide and grind together, forming walls of ice known as pressure ridges often several metres in height, it drifts slowly about the Arctic Ocean in two large gyres, or circles. It is an ocean in constant movement.

As the Arctic warms, the most noticeable changes are already being observed in the shrinking extent of sea ice and permafrost, the decrease of ice in lakes and rivers, pronounced reductions in seasonal snow, and the disappearance of the region's existing glacier mass. This is shifting terrestrial and marine ecosystem processes, and changing the very appearance of the Arctic. Over the last 100 years there has been a significant reduction in the extent and thickness of the Arctic ice cover. In the last thirty years alone, the area of multi-year sea ice cover of the Arctic Ocean has decreased by around 14% and scientists say that record reductions of sea ice coverage were already observed in the Beaufort and Chukchi seas in 1998. The extent of the sea ice in the Arctic Ocean in 2007 appears to have been the lowest on record. Because sea ice is highly dependent on the temperature difference between ocean and atmosphere and on near-surface oceanic heat flow, it reacts quickly to changes in atmospheric conditions. Atmosphere-ocean climate models predict a reduction in sea ice of around 60% in the next 50–100 years.

So what will the elimination of multi-year ice in the Arctic Ocean and other northern seas mean? For one thing, it will have tremendous consequences for Arctic wildlife. As the amount of sea ice decreases, seals, walrus, polar bears and other species that rely on it would suffer drastically. Most Arctic marine species depend upon the presence of sea ice and many Inuit coastal communities depend on harvesting marine species. The Arctic's ice-edge is unique among the world's ecosystems in that it moves thousands of kilometres each year, north in spring and south in autumn. Walrus, numerous species of seals, and cetaceans such as belugas and narwhals all follow the ice-edge as it moves, taking advantage of the ready access to food and (for the walrus and seals) the availability of ice to haul-out on for sunning, mating and raising pups in late winter and spring. Climate variability appears to have already caused relatively rapid shifts in the organization of Arctic marine ecosystems, especially in the Bering and Barents seas.

INUIT AND CLIMATE CHANGE

Many scientists seem certain that the climate of the Arctic is now at a "tipping point" beyond which irreversible changes will transform the ecology, economy and society of the region. And what happens to the climate of the Arctic, it is argued, will be an indication of the changes to happen elsewhere. For many Inuit, climate change is considered a human rights issue and they strive to have their voices heard in international policy-making, arguing that Inuit cultural survival is dependent on the continued presence of ice and snow.

The Inuit have long adapted to changes in the environment. Their ability to survive in an extreme environment and hunt and fish in the far northern reaches of the planet has often been influenced or affected by climatic variation, the changing ecology of the Arctic, and the availability of animals in specific habitats. Inuit societies have developed the capacity and flexibility, as well as the skills and technology, to harvest a diversity of animal and plant species and to do so in all seasons and in all weathers. Climate change, however, now appears to be testing the Inuit in ways they have not encountered in living memory and in many parts of the Arctic indigenous peoples are reporting that they are already experiencing the effects of climate change. Inuit accounts say that changes in climate and local ecosystems can be noticed not only in animals such as seals or caribou shifting their migration routes and altering their behaviour, but in the very taste of animals. I recall an elderly Inuk from western Nunavut at a community workshop on climate change in Iqaluit once describing the difficulty she found in sewing caribou skins to make clothing. There was something not quite right with the fur of the caribou now, she told us. She had also noticed that caribou were leaner and the meat was not easy to cook. Nor did it quite taste the same. Hunters and fishers in northern Greenland tell me that travelling to the edge of the ice (*sinaaq*) makes them anxious in a way it has never done — they say it is "more slippery" (*quasarpoq*) than they have known it, and that they feel more secure travelling by dogsledge on the solid ice that is attached to the shore. Changes in snow cover are also causing difficulty in accessing hunting and fishing areas by dogsled or snowmobile, making local adjustments in winter travel, hunting practices and harvesting strategies necessary. In Canada's Nunavut Territory, Inuit hunters have noticed the thinning of sea ice and the appearance of birds not usually found in their region; Iñupiat hunters in Alaska, as well as Inuvialuit in the Mackenzie Delta, report that ice cellars dug deep into the permafrost are too warm to keep meat and fish frozen. In Tuktoyaktuk, the community's ice cellar was excavated more than 50 years ago to keep seal meat, fish, and whale meat, as well as caribou and other traditional foods frozen. The permafrost is glacially-deformed and inside the cellar it is possible to catch a fascinating glimpse of the ground-ice stratigraphy that was formed during the last glacial-interglacial period. Yet, local residents now remark on how much warmer it is in the cellar than usual and prod at meat that is partially defrosted — "It shouldn't be like this," they say, "we worry that our food supplies are beginning to rot away."

In western Alaska several Inuit communities in low-lying coastal and island areas, including Shishmaref, Kivalina and Little Diomede have been affected by recent climate changes. The Iñupiaq Eskimo village of Shishmaref, located on Alaska's Sarichef Island in the Chukchi Sea is home to some 560 people who rely on a subsistence lifestyle of hunting and fishing. Coastal erosion and the frequency of storms have forced the residents to vote in favour of relocating the village to the Alaskan mainland.

Climate change cannot be understood in isolation from other environmental changes, rapid social and cultural change and global processes. No matter how remote, isolated or small they may be, Arctic communities are tightly tied politically, economically and socially to the national mainstream, as well as being linked to and affected by the global economy. Climate change is but one of several, often interrelating problems affecting their livelihoods. Combined with the Arctic's natural vulnerability, this magnifies the potential effects of global climate change on Inuit communities.

pp. 40-41
A part of Greenland's inland ice melts during the summer months, especially at lower elevations. For the last decade the melting of the ice sheet has gradually extended beyond the coastal areas and in summer 2012 satellites recorded for the first time that the surface of nearly all the ice sheet was melting. This development was also clearly visible when flying over Greenland. The usual whiteness of the ice was replaced with grayish slush and blue rivers.

pp. 42-43
When the hunters have reached their destination the dogs rest for several hours while their masters wait patiently for a seal to come up for breath or a whale to swim by, as here near Uummannaq, West Central Greenland.

pp. 46-47
The melting water on the surface of Greenland's ice cap in June and July 2012 flowed into vast lakes that dotted the entire glacier, even at latitudes over 70° north.

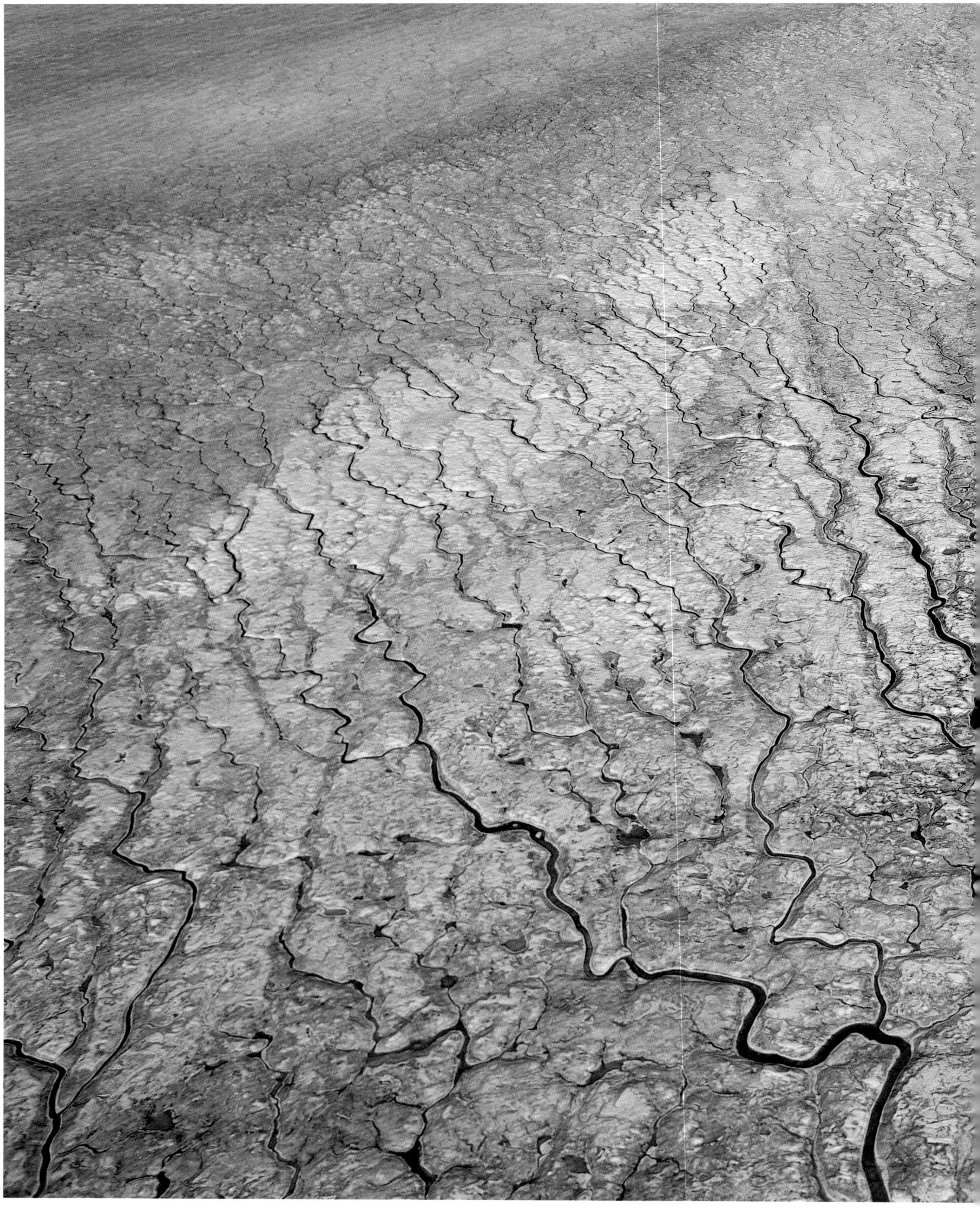

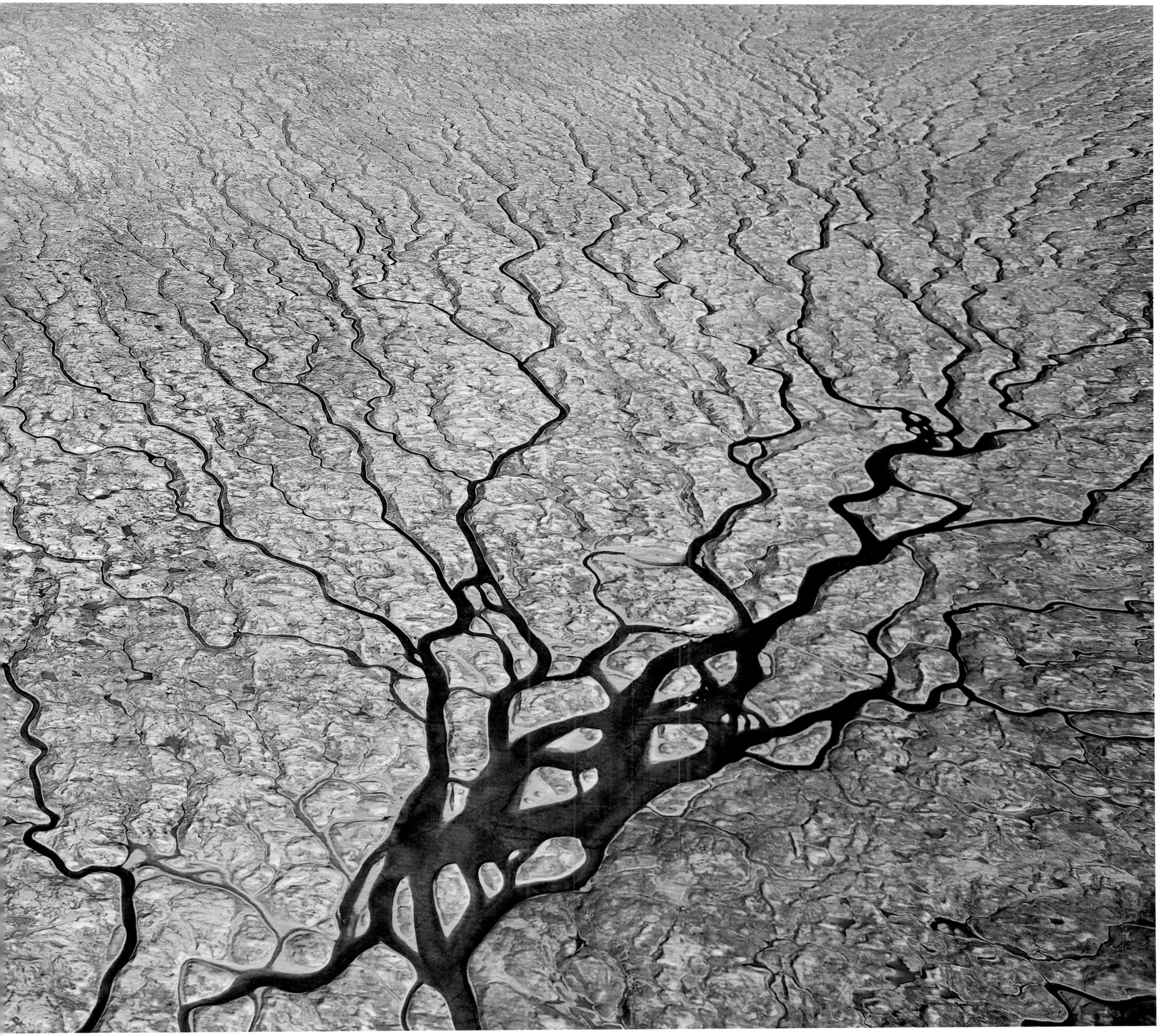

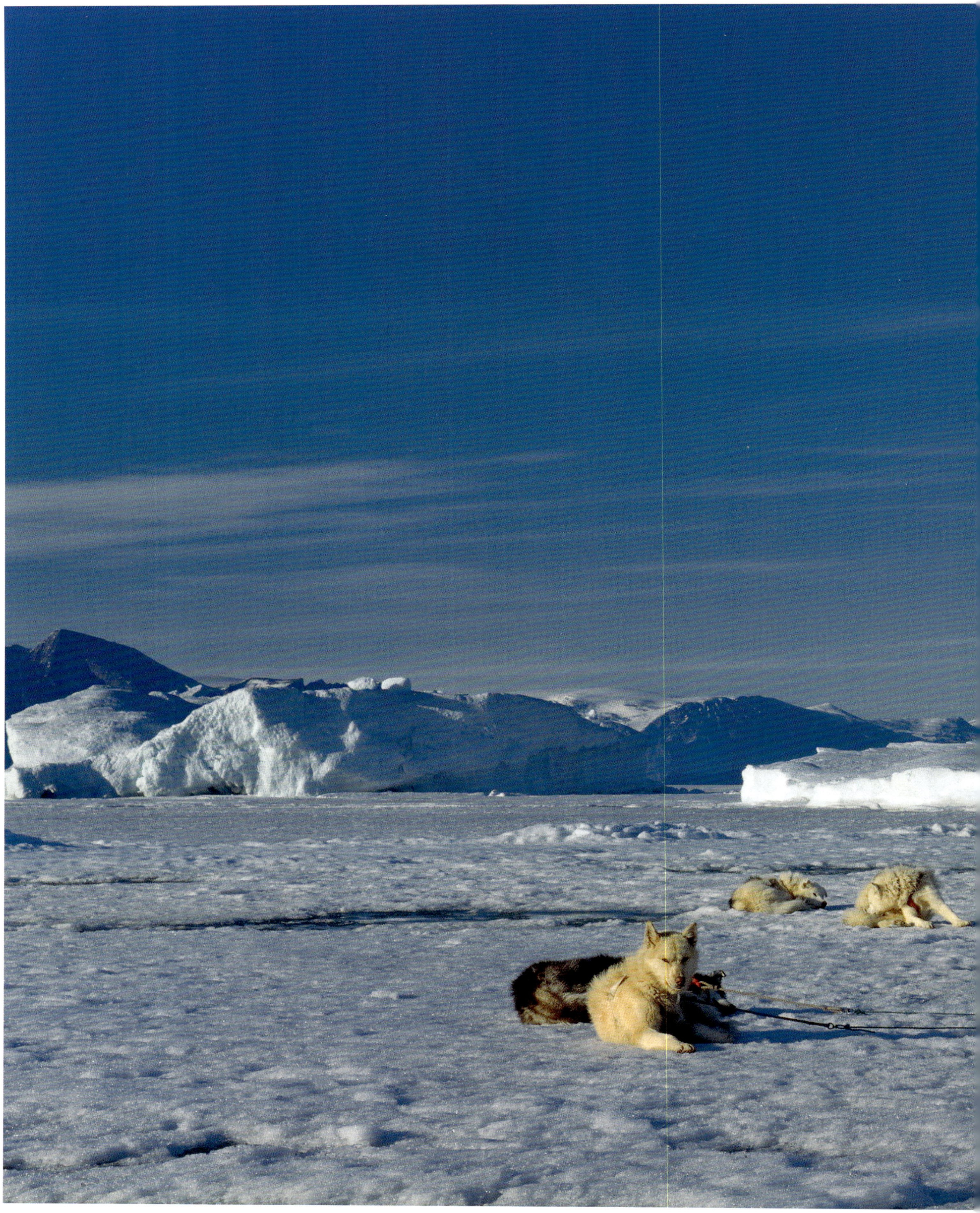

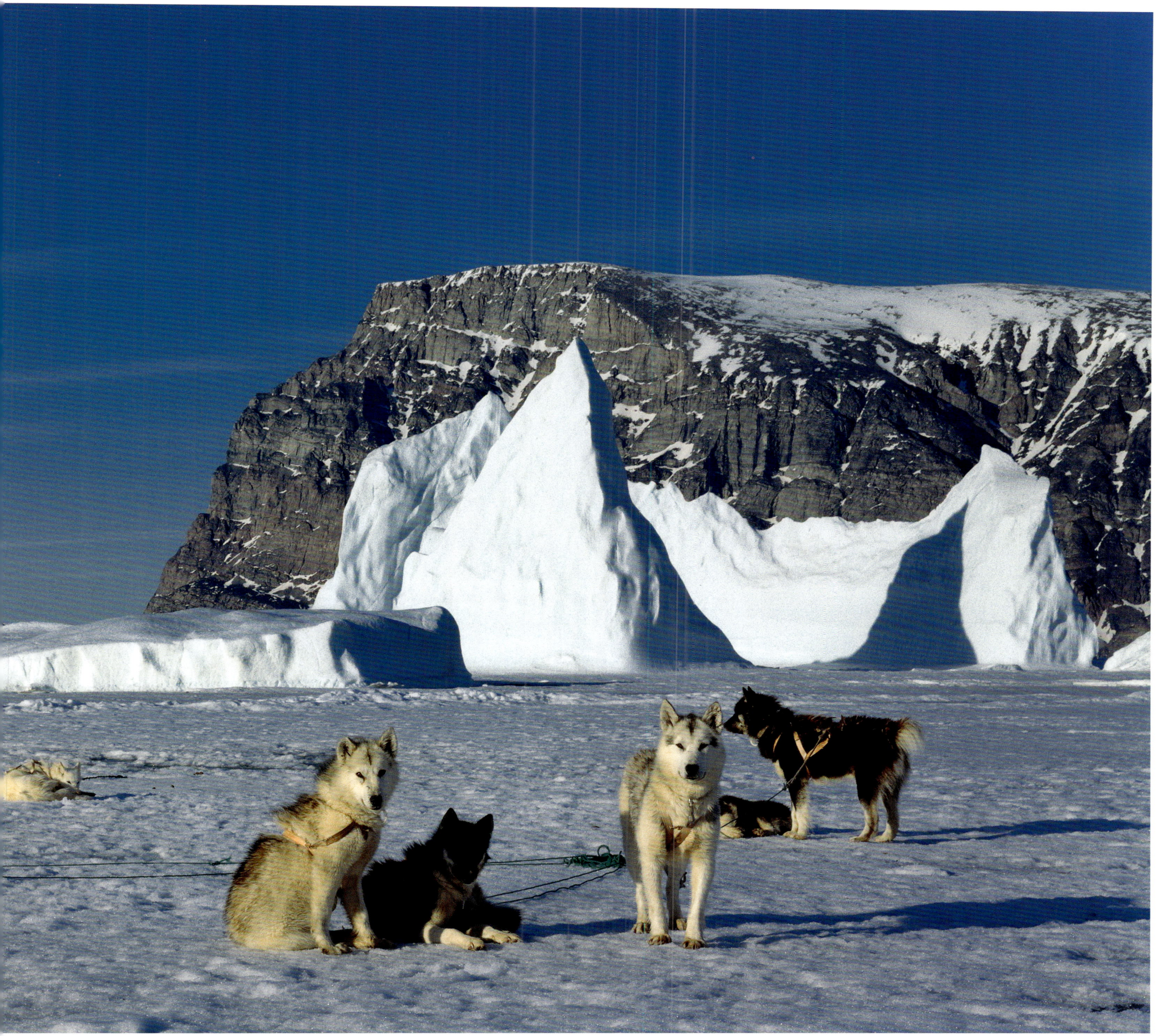

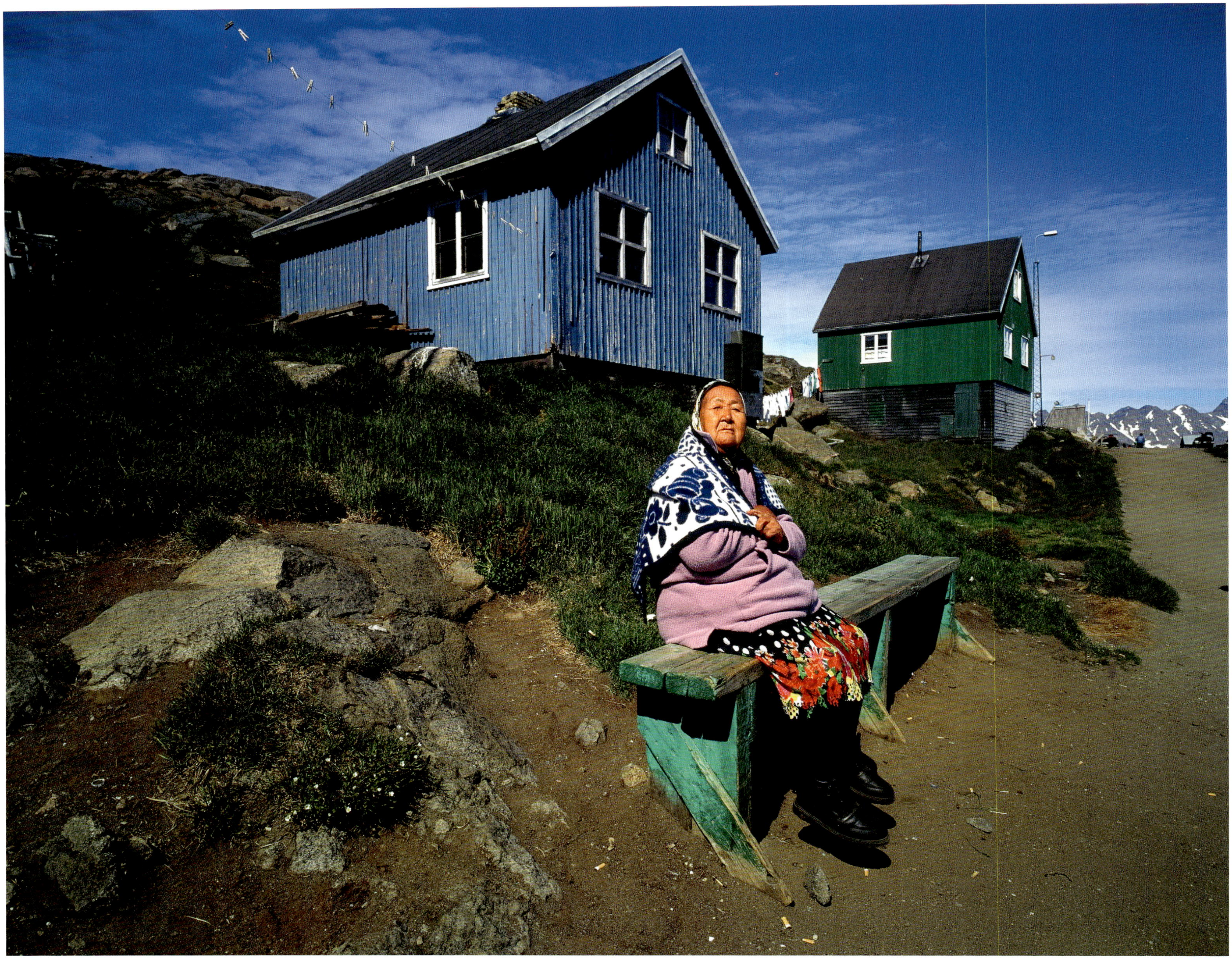

Many villages in Greenland are strikingly Scandinavian, with homes built of imported wood and often painted in vivid colours.

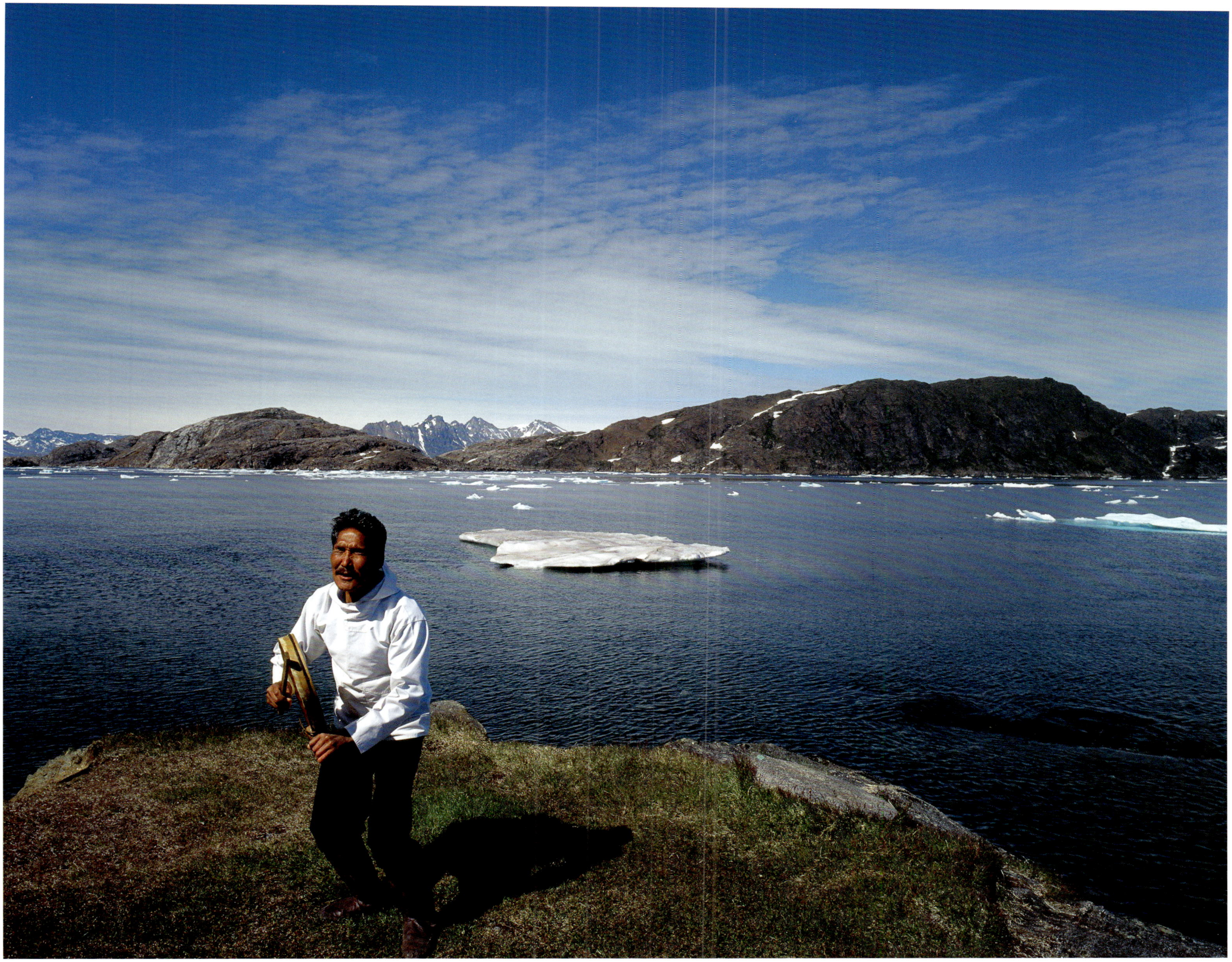

The drum dancer Anda Kuitse from Kulusuk performs his traditional drum act on his favourite stage with the waters of the Ammassalik fjord in the background.

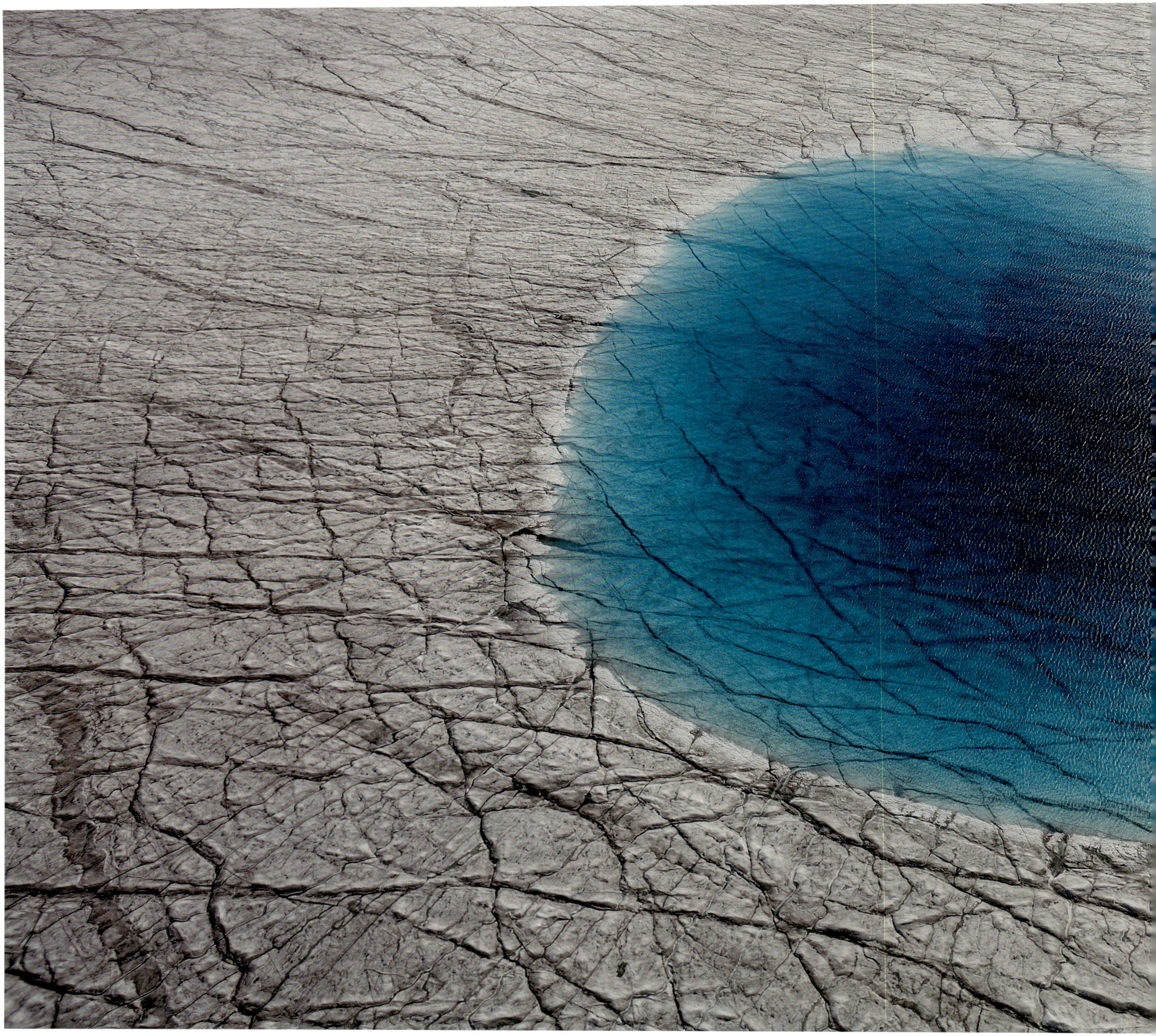

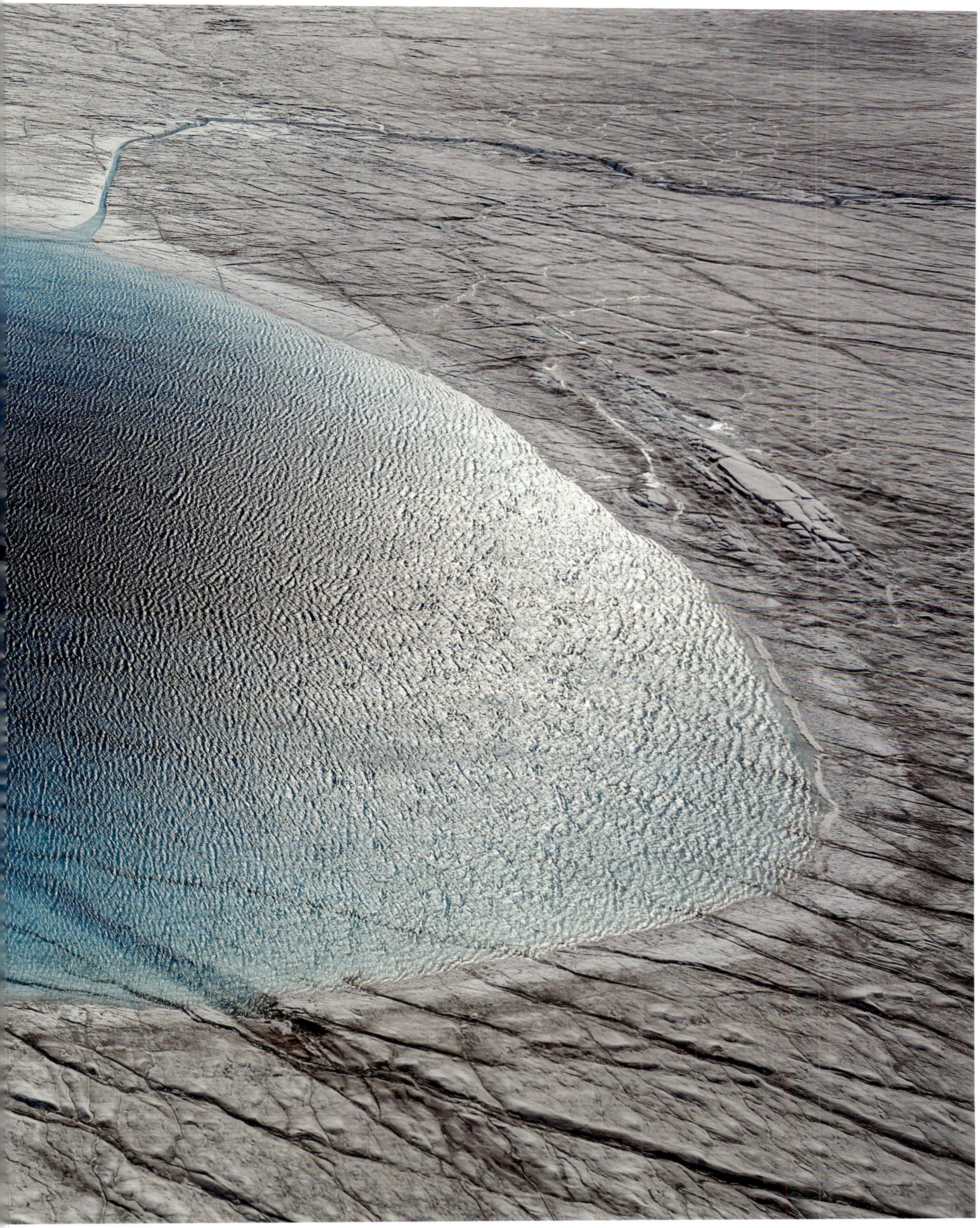

NANOQ: THE POLAR BEAR

The Inuit know the polar bear as *nanoq* (in Greenlandic) or *nanuq* (in Inuktitut and other dialects). *Nanoq* is a great wanderer. Its name probably derives from the Inuktitut root *nani-*, meaning "where." In Greenlandic *nanivaa* means "finds" in the sense of finding something one has been looking for with purpose and intent rather than having discovered something inadvertently. A lantern is *naneruarfik,* a torch *naneruaq* and a candle is *naneruut,* meaning things which are used for finding things or looking for something. *Nanoq*, therefore, could mean "one who is good at finding something," or "one who is good at finding the things it is searching for." Perhaps another meaning is "one who is good at looking."

The polar bear is a migratory animal and an iconic species, symbolic of the Arctic and the health of its ecology. Contaminants, pollution and climate change have made polar bears emblematic of Arctic ecosystems at risk. Toxic chemicals, such as PCBs and pesticides affect their hormonal development and immune systems, and they are frequent casualties of oil contamination. Some 500-900 polar bears are hunted each year, mainly by Inuit subsistence hunters. For conservation groups and the media they have also become a supreme image that represents the plight of all the world's animal species endangered by human activity.

Polar bears are dependent on sea ice — they hunt seals and use ice to travel from one area to another. Seal hunting success, and hence the survival of polar bears and their families, depends on good spring ice conditions. Global warming is now seen to be the biggest threat to their survival and polar bears have become an indicator species of the rapid nature and extent of climate change in the Arctic. Polar bears have been transformed in the public imagination from symbols of cold, unbounded polar wastes, to symbols of an ecosystem in crisis and a planet in peril.

The predictions for the future of polar bear populations — and the health of the Arctic generally — are stark. Scientists and environmentalists worry that polar bears are unlikely to survive as a species if there is an almost complete loss of summer sea-ice cover, which is what most climate models indicate will happen by the end of this century.

Polar bears continue to have considerable social, cultural and economic importance in many Inuit communities. They are hunted for their meat and their skins, and are a central feature in Inuit cosmology. To go polar bear hunting (*nannunniarpoq*) is a tremendous adventure and a polar bear hunter is a special kind of hunter — a *nannunniaq*. Inuit leaders claim that Inuit hunters have conserved polar bear populations at healthy levels through proper and responsible wildlife management and sustainable hunting practices. For many of the Arctic's indigenous peoples, consuming food from animals is a fundamental part of social identity and personal and cultural well-being. To be cut off from hunting, to be denied access to animals that nourish one in a nutritional, cultural and spiritual sense is to be denied cultural and spiritual rights.

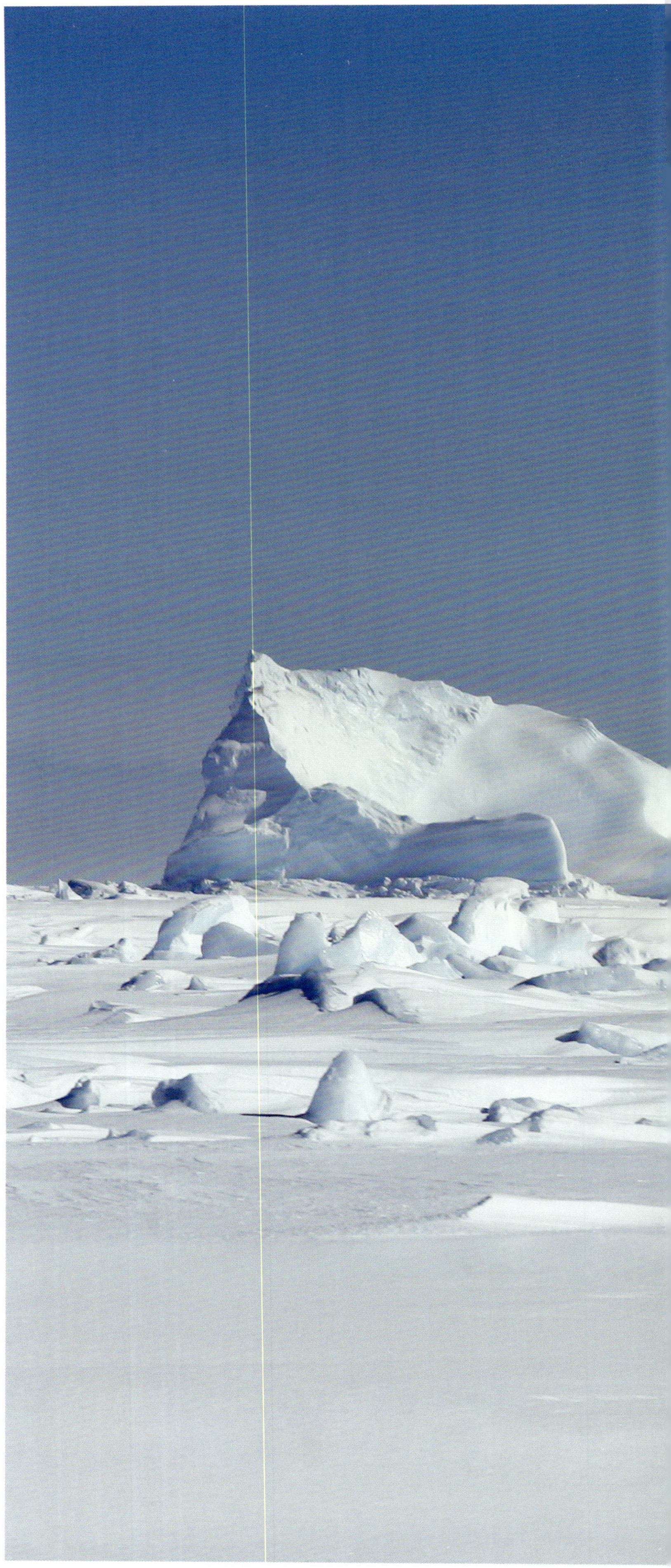

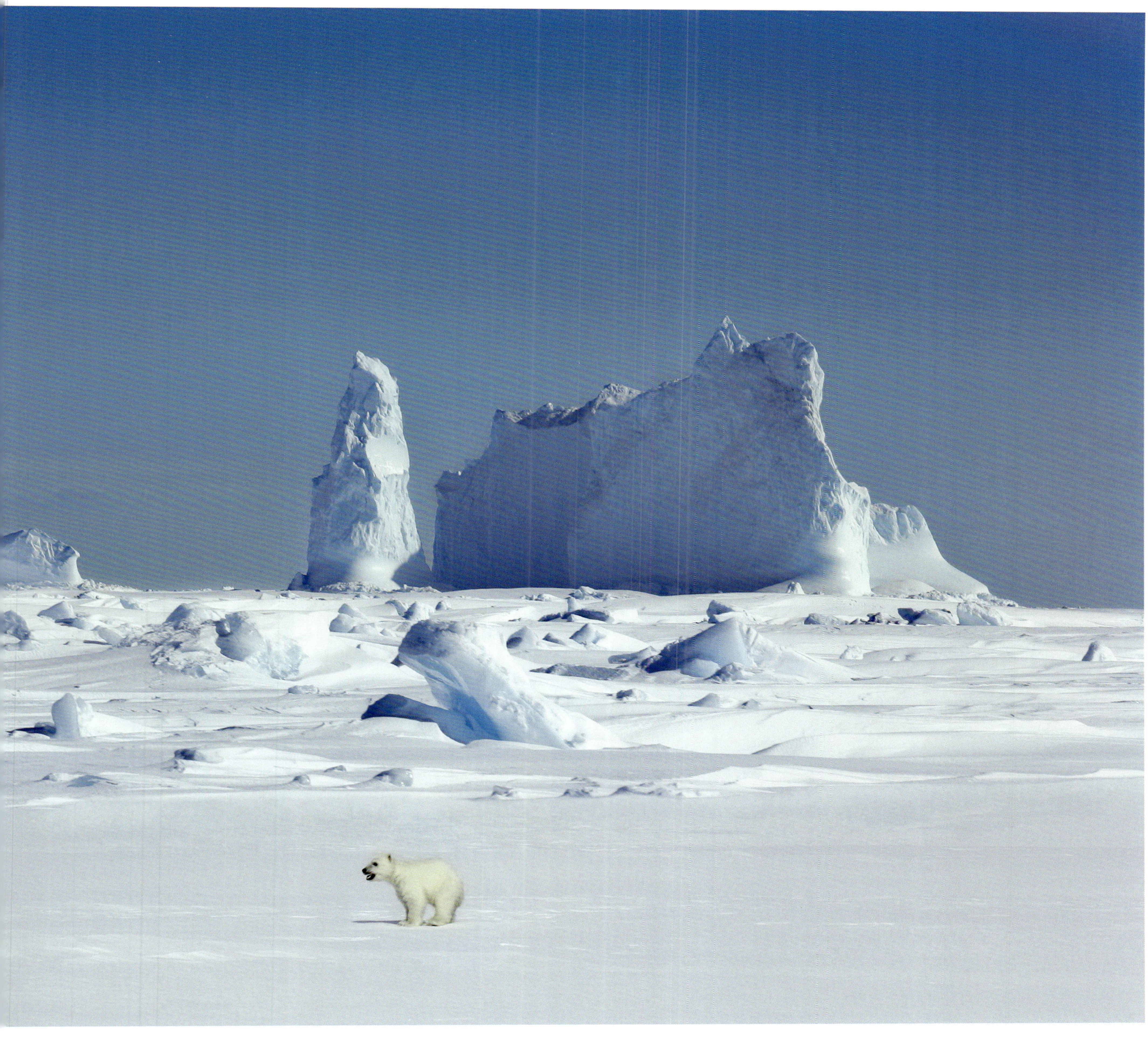

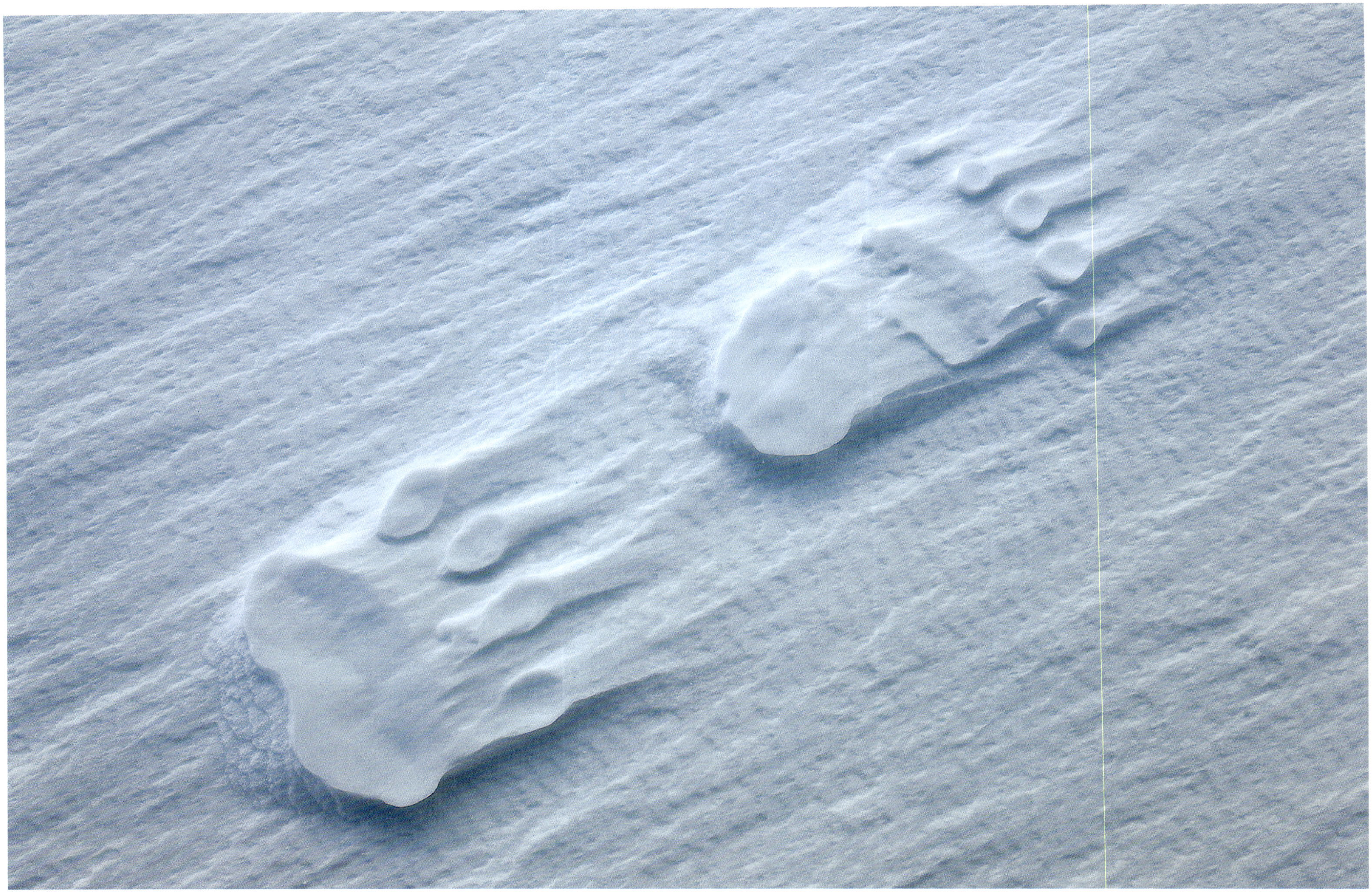

Footprints on the ice near Ittoqqortoormiit in East Greenland.

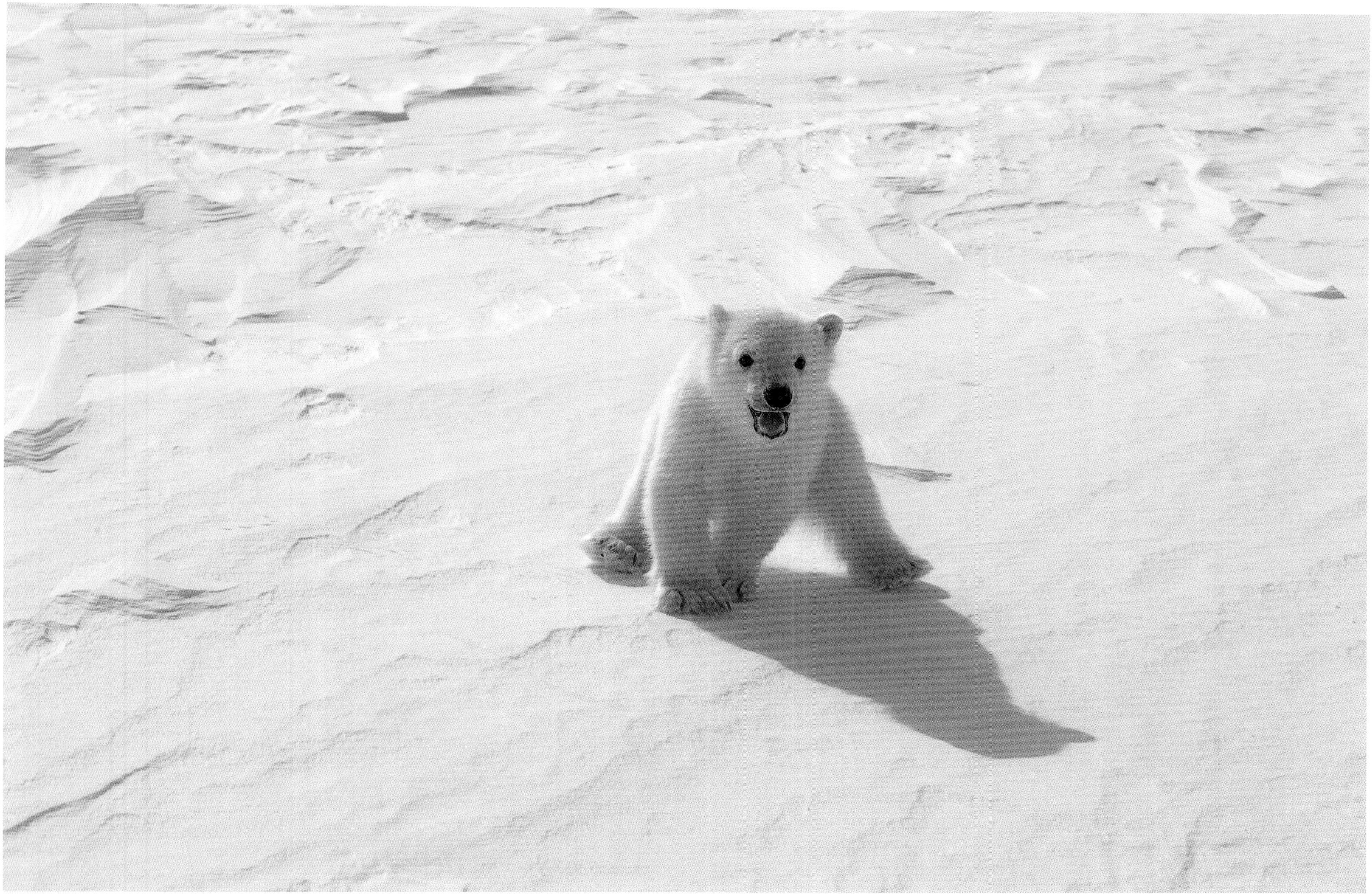

Out of fear of his mother the hunters try to avoid the friendly polar bear cub.

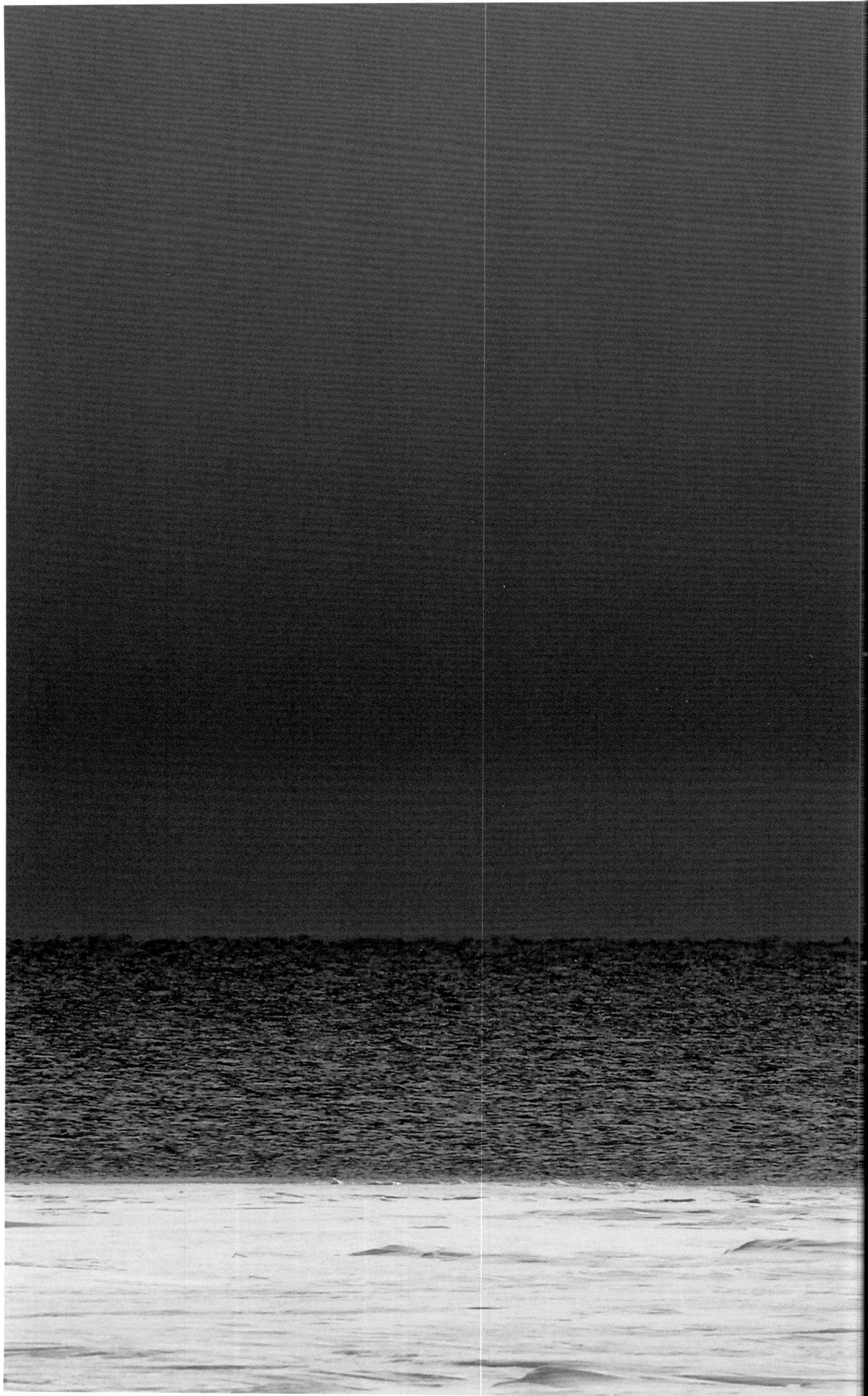

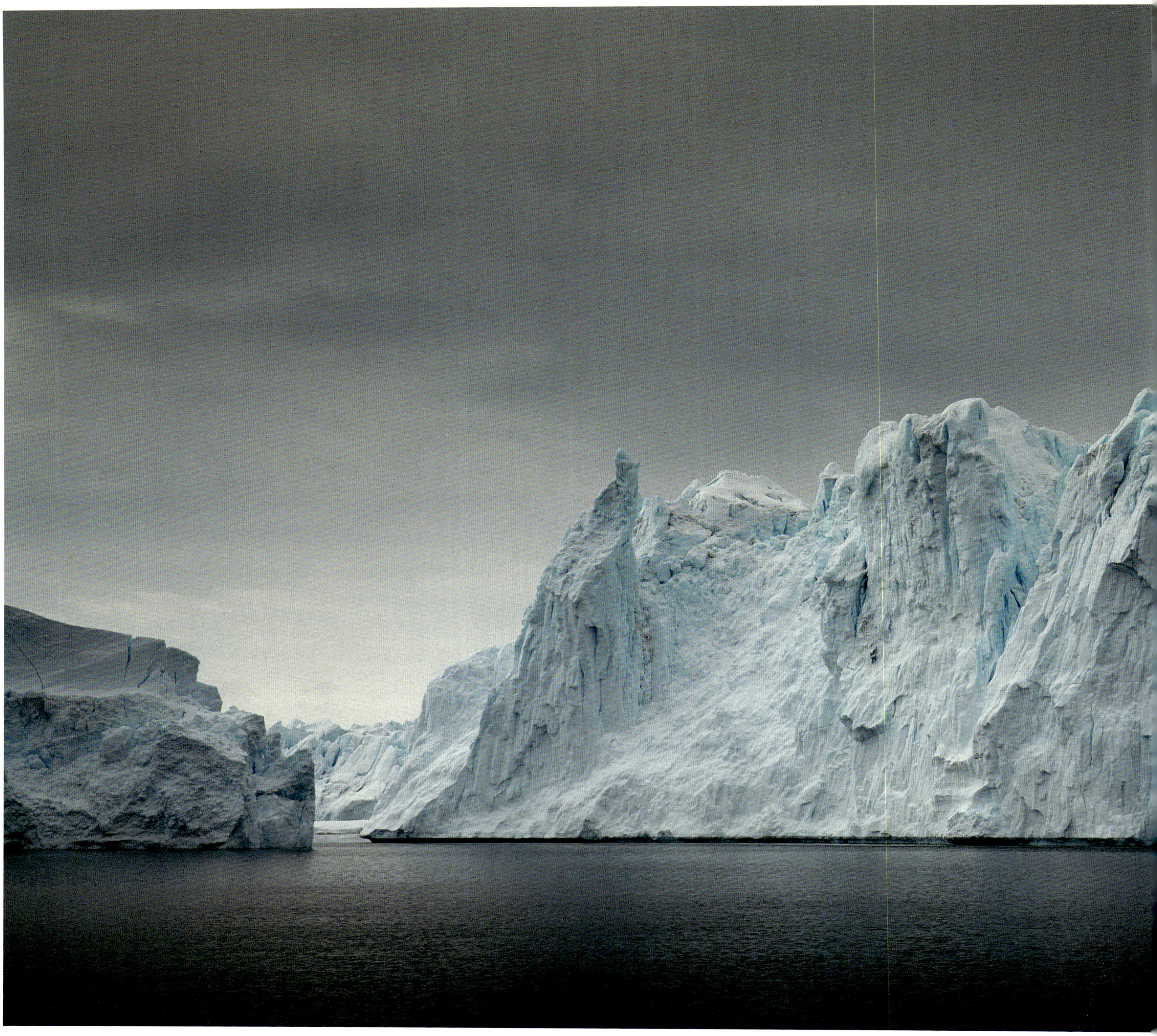

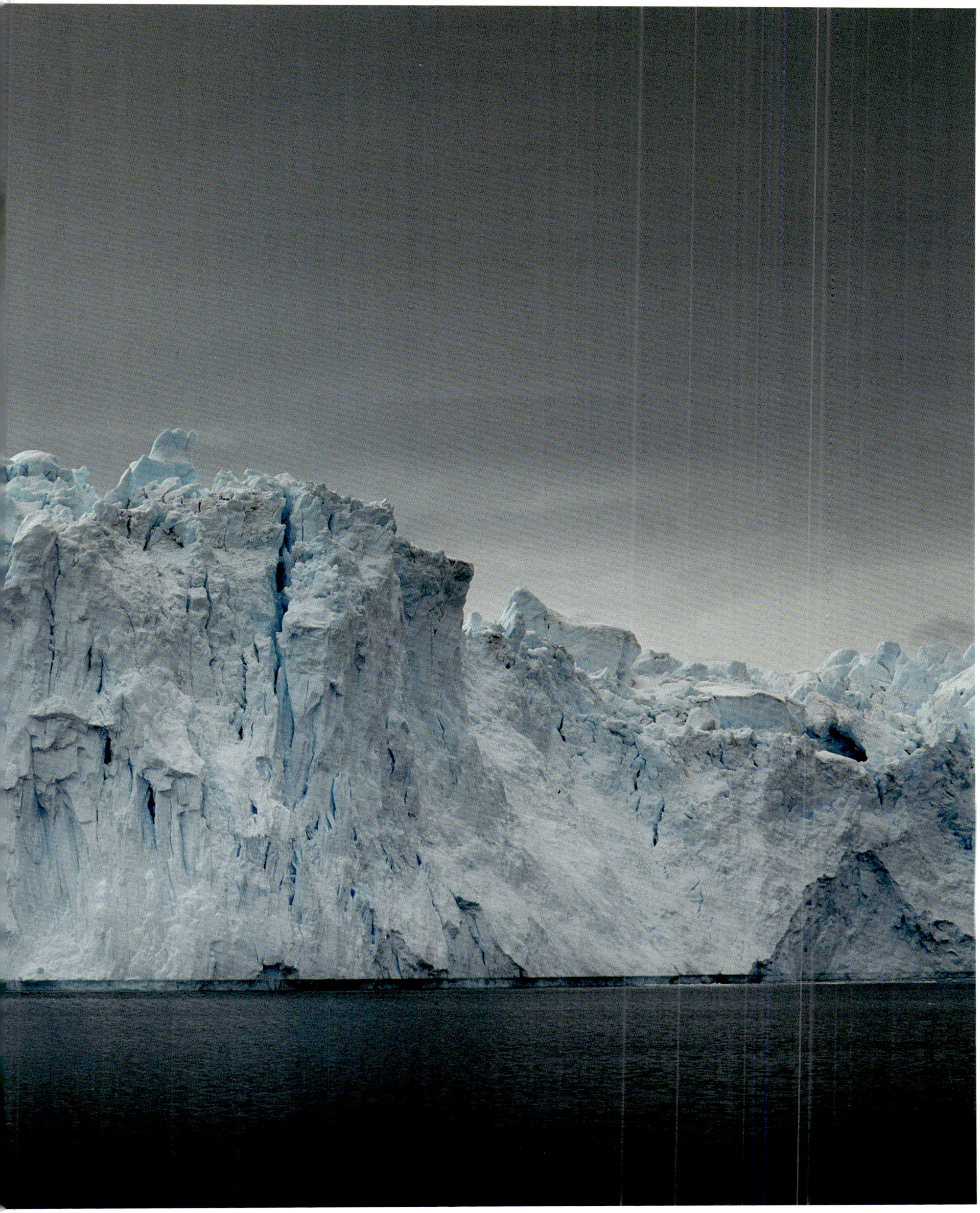

THE GLOBAL ARCTIC

pp. 50-51
A polar bear cub calls for its mother near the shore of Baffin Island. The mother is not far away and has already warned her offspring of the danger. The hunters watch from a distance and try to avoid confrontation with the mother as local laws expressly forbid killing polar bears with cubs.

pp. 54-55
The polar bear has become the emblem of the uncertain future awaiting animals and humans in the Arctic, following the global increase of air temperatures and depletion of the Arctic ice sheet. But the polar bear population is threatened by many other factors, such as sea pollution, mainly caused by industrial nations far away.

pp. 56-57
The Ilulissat fjord where one can witness the alarming speed of climate change has been declared a UNESCO World Heritage Site. Massive icebergs float on the fjord and drift farther into Disko Bay.

Stories of vast mineral wealth, of mountains of silver and gold in Greenland, Baffin Island and other Arctic islands abounded in Europe for centuries until organized mineral exploration hinted at the realities and possibilities of real discoveries. In North America, the gold rush opened up Alaska and Canada's Yukon in the 1890s bringing thousands of prospectors from all over the world hopeful of making their fortunes, while a massive industrial transformation of the Russian North and Siberia began in the 1920s. Today, coal, nickel and copper are mined near Norilsk, and gold, diamonds, uranium, and other minerals have been found in great quantity in other northern parts of Russia. High grade iron ore is mined at Kiruna in northern Sweden and gold is mined in south Greenland, while in Subarctic Canada and Alaska there is a wealth of mineral resources — for example uranium and diamonds in the Northwest Territories, zinc and lead in northwest Alaska. While mining is set to increase in importance in the Arctic, the world's ever-growing demands for resources and energy are focusing global attention on the planet's high latitudes and it is being seen as one of the last great frontiers for discoveries of oil and gas.

THE ARCTIC ENERGY FRONTIER

Like other parts of the Canadian western Arctic, the Mackenzie Delta in the Northwest Territories is a land relatively rich in resources. As is true for many other Arctic regions, the popular image of the Mackenzie Delta is of an untouched, pristine wilderness. Yet its history tells us a compellingly general story about indigenous peoples, the changes they have endured in recent times, how outsiders have viewed the Arctic, and how both indigenous and non-indigenous peoples imagine its future.

The essence of the story can be told almost universally across the high latitudes of the circumpolar North. Seals and, importantly, whales formed the backbone of the local Mackenzie Eskimo community. The Inuvialuit engaged in extensive interregional trade. Russian trading goods entered the local economy via trading partners in Alaska in the 18 th century and, when the first fur trade posts were opened on the Mackenzie River, the Mackenzie Eskimos found opportunities to create new relationships with Dene and Europeans further south.

As in practically every other part of northern Canada, fur trading soon became the primary economic activity in the Mackenzie Delta and Mackenzie Valley, shaping the livelihoods of indigenous peoples as well as the fortunes of outsiders from the early nineteenth century until the 1930s. But fur trading was never sustainable — a combination of overexploitation of fur-bearing animals and changing global fashion tastes saw to that. It is an example of the boom and bust nature of non-renewable resource development often experienced by Northern indigenous peoples and circumpolar environments since their incorporation into the global economy.

Dramatic changes came to the Mackenzie Delta and other Inuvialuit communities in the Beaufort Sea region when American commercial whalers arrived in the second half of the 19th century. Disease, epidemics and famine followed in the wake of the whalers with devastating results. When the whalers first went north, around 2,500 Mackenzie Eskimos lived in the region. By 1905 there were 250 left. The remnants of the Mackenzie Eskimo population soon became part of a larger group of mixed local and Alaskan descent. By the 1970s, prompted by growing political consciousness and local reaction to oil drilling activities, the people of the region asserted a new identity, calling themselves Inuvialuit, "the real people". In 1984, the Inuvialuit became the first aboriginal people from Canada's Northwest Territories to negotiate and sign a comprehensive land claims agreement with the federal government.

The history of contact in the Mackenzie Delta and its consequences for indigenous peoples is one which is familiar in so many other parts of the circumpolar world. In addition to its earlier potential for supplying furs, the Arctic has long been seen as a mineral and hydrocarbon-rich resource frontier vital for Canada's development as a nation. And just as whalers sought resources to fuel the gaslights and industry of North America and Europe, this part of Canada's North is today on the verge of a major boom in oil and gas exploration and associated activities. Oil and gas companies are positioning themselves to exploit northwest Canada's energy resources.

For some time, it has been assumed by petrogeologists, oil and gas companies and politicians that much of Canada's undeveloped oil and gas potential lies in its northern Arctic and Subarctic areas. One recent assessment by the United States Geological Survey suggests that 25% of the world's untapped reserves in areas known to contain oil could be found in the Arctic. This not only makes it attractive to the oil and gas industry as (perhaps Antarctica

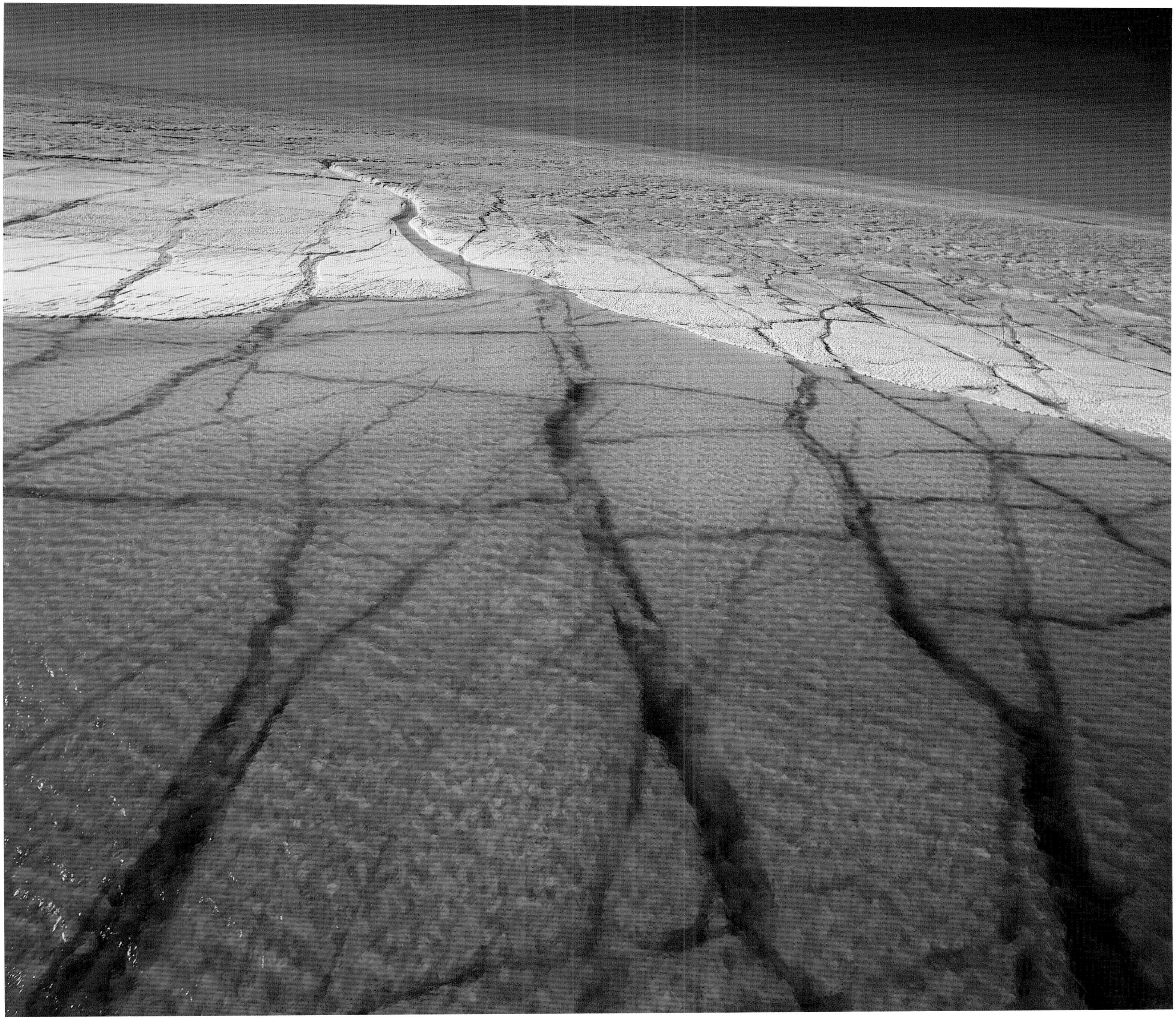

Melting water on Greenland's inland ice forms large seasonal rivers and lakes on the surface.

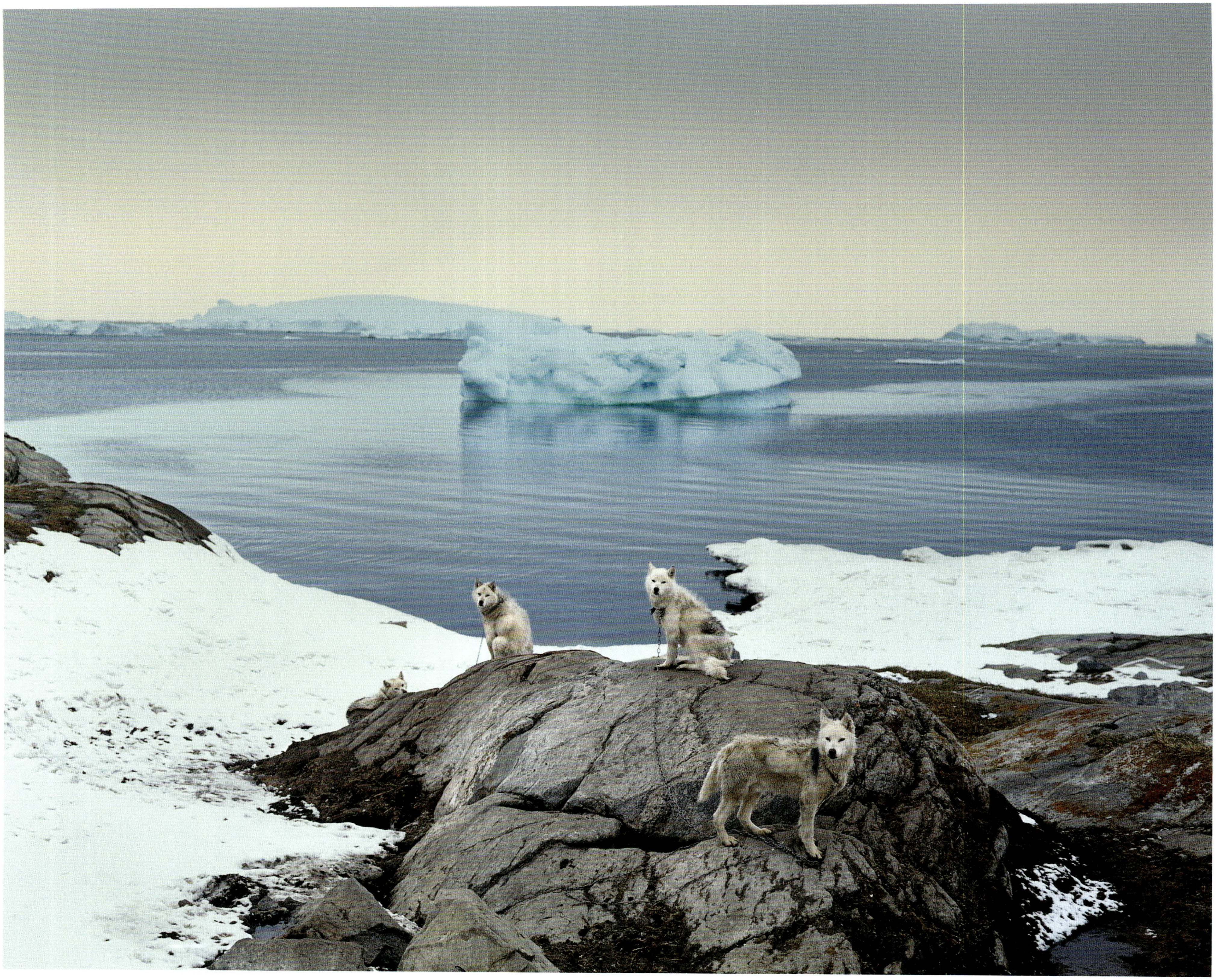

Stoic huskies stare into the Arctic ice fog near Uummannaq.

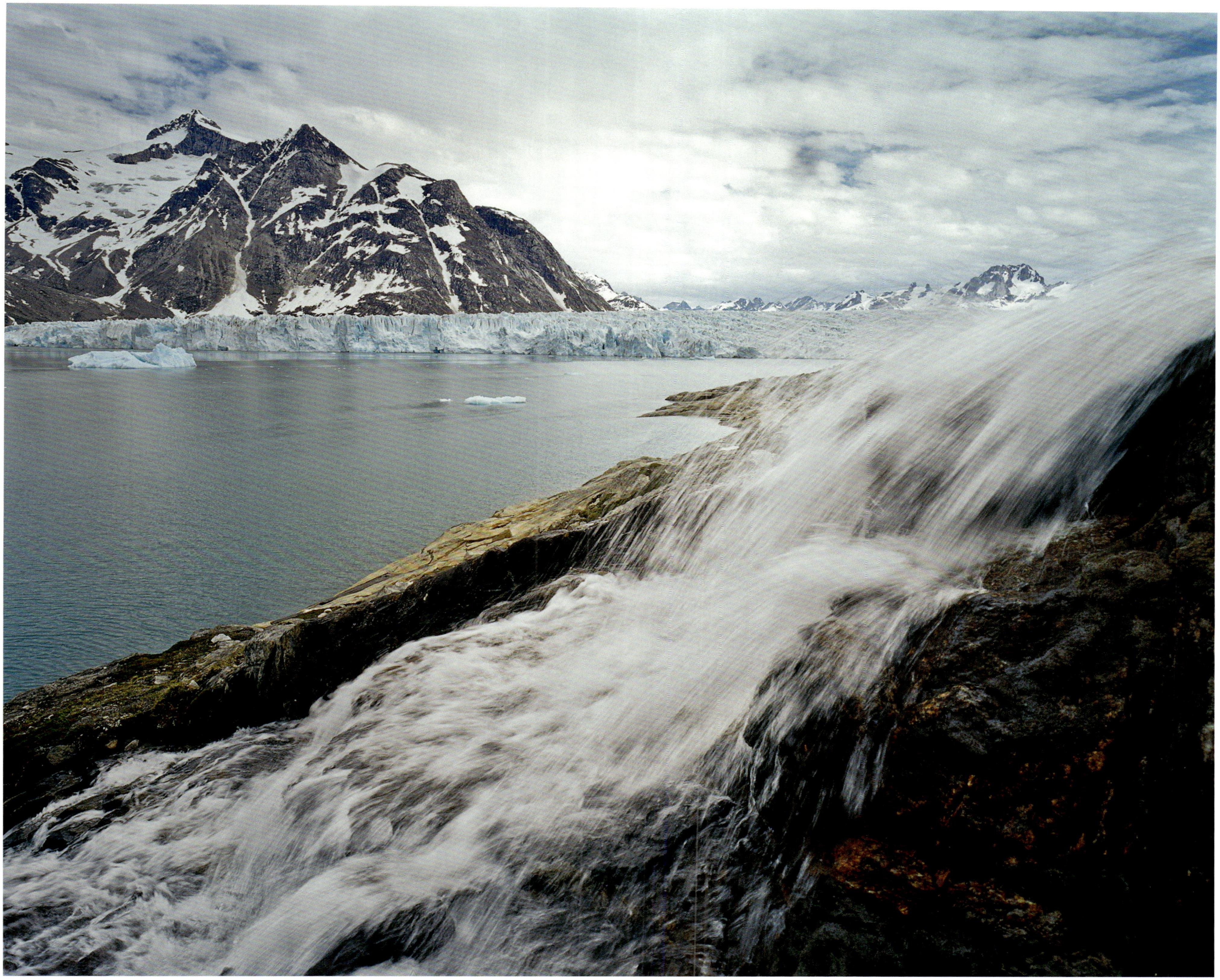

At the bottom of Sermilik fjord in East Greenland water flows from melting glaciers.

INUA

Every feature of the environment has its own essence, which Inuit refer to as *inua* (pl. *inuat*), which also means "owner" or "dweller." For example, *qaqqap inua,* means "the essence of mountains," or *sermersuap inua,* "the essence of the great ice."

UUMASUT: Animals

The correct treatment and propitiation of animals and their souls are central concerns of daily human life. Animals are considered non-human persons, endowed with intelligence, consciousness, will and purpose. Among all Inuit groups, animals' souls are particularly significant, and rituals and ceremonies are often devoted entirely to ensuring that the souls of whales, polar bears, walrus, seals and caribou receive proper treatment and respect. Mistreating an animal or failing to observe a taboo may result in poor hunting, illness, misfortune, famine or bad weather. Care must therefore be taken to ensure that animals and animal spirits are not offended or harmed by hunters.

ANGAKKOQ: Shaman

The angakkoq played a central role in traditional Inuit society as a mediator of relations between humans and animals, especially as an intermediary in transactions between humans, animal souls and animal guardians.

PUISI: The seal

In many north Greenlandic settlements, ringed seals (*natseq*) are the main food source for much of the year, but other seals are hunted in various seasons. There are many names for seals, not only to describe the particular species, but which categorise their age and also their position both in the water and while basking on the ice. In Greenlandic, a bearded seal is *ussuk* (but *taqammuaq* in the northern parts of the country), while a young bearded seal is called *teqilluk* or *ussuaraq*. A bearded seal that has hauled itself up out of the water to bask on the ice in spring is *ussuk qassimasoq*.A rutting male seal is called a *tiggak,* whereas any old male seal which gives off a horrible smell is called *tigganitsoq*. The generic word for seal, *puisi,* is derived from *puivoq,* meaning "to raise its head out of the water."

excepted) the final frontier for hydrocarbon development, but also alarms indigenous peoples, conservationists and environmental groups already concerned with lobbying states to protect the Arctic from contaminants and the impacts of climate change.

CLAIMING THE ARCTIC: A RUSH FOR RESOURCES?

As an energy-hungry world looks northwards for its oil and gas, territorial challenges are provoking nations like Russia and Canada to reassert their claims over their northern hinterlands. Both countries have emphasized that their futures lie in the Arctic. The Northwest Passage, however, is not recognized as Canadian waters by the United States which, instead, argues it is an international strait. Russia faces similar issues over the future use of the Northern Sea Route.

There is no doubt that current developments and further exploration will likely continue throughout the Arctic as climate change contributes to reducing sea ice, opening new sea and river routes and reducing exploration, development and transportation costs. The Arctic may be increasingly accessible in the future, but diminishing sea ice and climate change are not the drivers for this flurry of activity over territorial claims. Russia, Norway, Denmark/Greenland, and Canada have been mapping the sea bed to gather an enormous body of scientific evidence to assert ownership of as yet undiscovered resources.

ENERGY DEVELOPMENT

Oil and gas development activities in the Arctic are of critical importance to the present and future social, cultural, economic and ecological circumstances of Arctic indigenous peoples, and they have both negative and positive impacts and consequences. Some scenarios suggest that by 2050, 50-80% of the Arctic will be disturbed by development. In the Russian North, the oil and gas industries are the biggest sources of pollution, affecting reindeer pasture and marine and freshwater environments. Onshore oil and gas activities, such as construction of pipelines and the actual production of oil and gas, also impede access to traditional hunting and herding areas, which disrupt community activities and traditional practices.

Not all indigenous people see energy development in their traditional territories as negative, however, although there are certainly strong and emotional concerns expressed by people who are faced with oil and gas development projects. Whaling captains and fishermen worry over the presence of seismic survey vessels near whale migration routes, while hunters and trappers are anxious about seismic cuts and pipelines disrupting traplines and traditional hunting lands, as well as the desecration of sacred sites. However, in Alaska, Canada and Greenland, the settlement of land claims and the introduction of self-government have meant that many indigenous communities have entered into resource development projects through joint ventures with industry and government, impact benefit agreements, and environmental monitoring projects. Although traditional practices remain important to the daily lives of indigenous peoples, oil, gas and mining activities increasingly provide employment in some areas. Far from being mere victims of the impacts of industrial development, indigenous peoples are participants in, and increasingly beneficiaries of, the development of the Arctic resource frontier.

THE FUTURE OF SMALL COMMUNITY LIFE

The Arctic is an increasingly urban world, with a cultural and ethnic mix of populations. In Greenland, some 47,000 people out of a total population of around 57,000 live in towns; over 80% of the population live in the towns of 1,000 people or more, with 60% concentrated in six towns on the west coast. Modern Nuuk, with almost 16,000 people, is creating a new identity for itself not just as Greenland's dynamic capital but as an Arctic metropolis, a vibrant city in which a younger, cosmopolitan-minded generation, many of them well-travelled and often fluent in several languages, wants to live — and to which many more people from other parts of Greenland aspire to move. Rather than being seen as a place which sits uneasily in the Arctic, many people who like living there argue that this is where Greenlandic culture is produced and reproduced, through its politics, its debates about language and identity, its educational institutions and its creative arts scene. Indeed, as Greenland's political culture and sense of itself as a modern nation in the making has developed, it is the villages which are now regarded to be a problem and many Greenlandic politicians ask where the old hunting way of life fits in with Greenland's desire to become a modern nation.

Over the next two or three decades we are likely to see the abandonment of many settlements in Greenland and the continued decline of Inuit life based on small-scale hunting and fishing. This is the reality of a continuing trend of social and economic change but it is also going to be an effect of government attitude and policy towards non-urban centres with small populations. Many settlements are experiencing a population drain, mainly of young women, but Greenlanders are not only moving from smaller settlements to larger towns in Greenland. In many cases they are also moving to Denmark. While some of these migrants to Denmark return home after a few years, many choose to settle there permanently. One argument put forward is that climate change will lead to people migrating from small Arctic communities. I see it differently: people are already leaving for reasons that have little to do with climate change and a lot to do with lifestyle choices, ambition, education and the desire for an urban, cosmopolitan future. Migration away from Inuit communities has been ongoing for decades and it may well be that climate change just becomes another

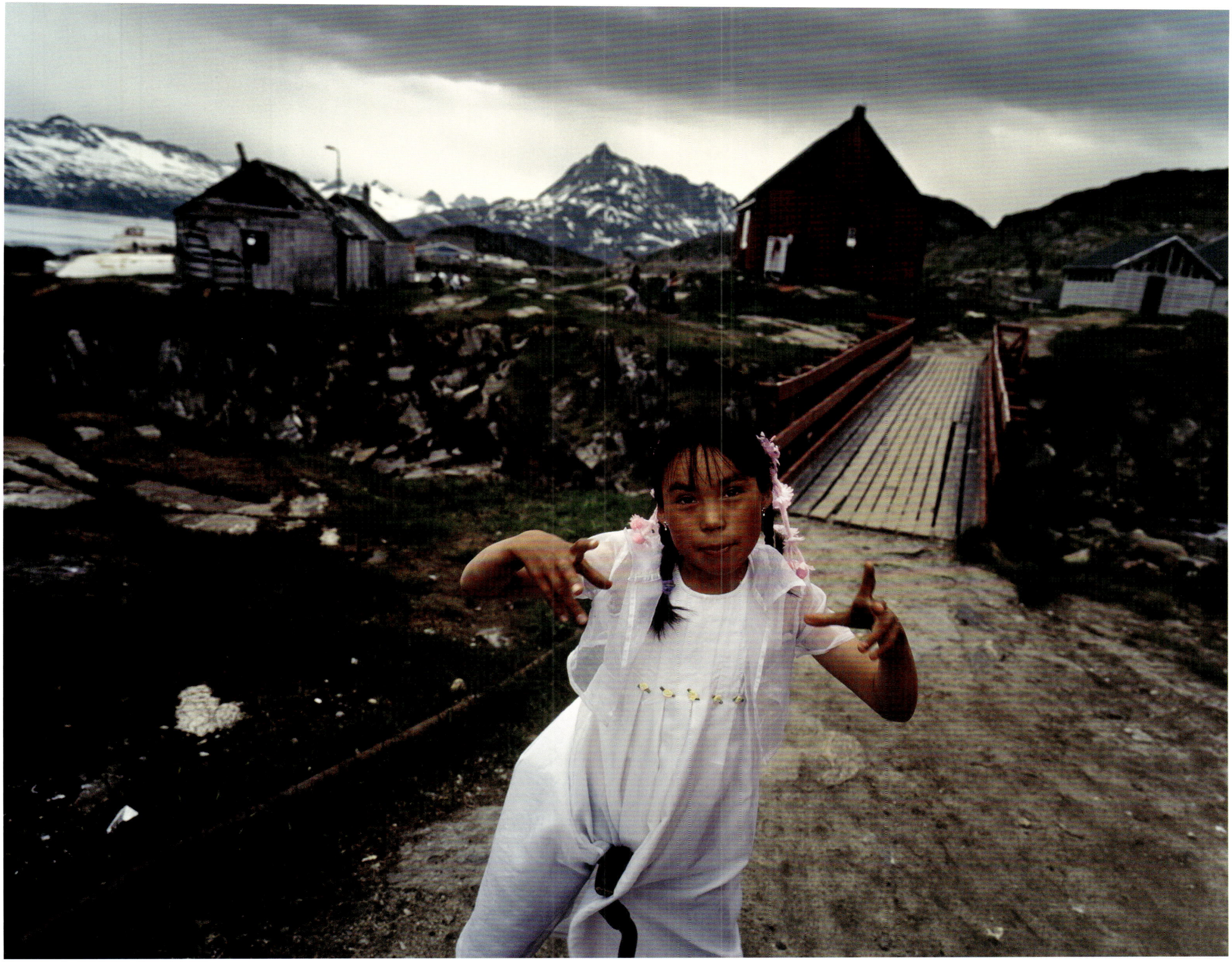

In Kuummiut in East Greenland a girl is on her way to church on Sunday. The temperature hovers arourd freezing but that does not stcp her wearing her best summer dress.

Seasons

Visitors to the Arctic from temperate regions, accustomed to dividing the calendar year into four seasons, must adjust their orientation to this high latitude world to include six seasons – perhaps even seven or eight, depending on which Inuit community they visit. A visitor to Baffin Island would have to learn at least six Inuktitut words to describe the seasonal changes. From November to March, it would be *ukiuq*, winter; from March to April *ukiuq* gives way to early spring, *upirngatsaaq*, before changing to *upirngaaq*, spring, between April and June; *aujaq* is the short season of summer, lasting from the end of June to early September; then, from mid-September to October *ukiatsaaq* describes the period of early autumn, followed by *ukiaq*, when darkening days and falling snow hint at the winter to come.

PINNGORTITAQ

The Greenlandic word *pinngortitaq* is often simply translated as "nature" or "creation", but its literal meaning is "to come into being". It derives from *pinngorpoq*, a process of "becoming," and "coming into existence," referring to the unfolding of possibilities and opportunities. The world is thus a work in progress.

pp. 68-69
The town of Uummannaq stands on rocks above the Uummannaq fjord for a good reason. The shore is often hit by enormous, almost tsunami-like waves, caused by immense icebergs calving from glaciers nearby.

pp. 70-71
The calmness of the water in Ammassalik fjord causes a disorienting effect with the reflection. What is up and what is down?

push factor rather than a primary reason. This is true of many other parts of the Arctic, not just Greenland. Young Inuit in Nunavut see Iqaluit as a place to move to because it is believed to offer opportunities (although overcrowded housing conditions and even homelessness are major problems in the territory's capital), while many more move to large cities further south. Montreal, Ottawa, Toronto, Winnipeg and Edmonton all have significant Inuit populations. In fact, over 8,000 Inuit live in urban Canadian settings outside the Inuit homelands of Nunavut, the NWT, Nunavik and Nunatsiavut and this figure, according to the Canadian census of 2006, represents around 17% of Canada's total Inuit population.

Although the economic significance of the traditional way of life is steadily decreasing, hunting is still a crucial part of Inuit identity and this is reflected in the fact that more people hunt for leisure than those for whom it is their sole occupation. Yet, the divide between town and village life has come to stand for and perhaps define the whole idea of political and economic development in Greenland. Although few Inuit politicians would publicly admit that it would be better to close some hunting communities and relocate their inhabitants to larger villages or towns, the reality is that hunting, while informing Inuit cultural identity, contributes little to the economy of this nation in formation.

THE GREENING LAND

The Icelandic Saga of Eirik the Red famously relates how, in the late 10th century, Eirik named the land to the west of Iceland "Greenland" because people would be attracted to go there if it had a favourable name. Thus enticed by the promise of verdant pastures and boundless opportunities in a new world, a group of colonists followed Eirik from Iceland in 985 to settle and farm in south Greenland. What they actually encountered in this subarctic environment was undoubtedly different from what they had heard about the country from the pioneering Eirik. Yet Norse farming communities eventually prospered in two settlements along the fjords of the southwest coast for around five hundred years.

The story of the success and ultimate disappearance of the Norse settlements in Greenland continues to fascinate archaeologists and historians of the North Atlantic. The generally accepted view as to why the Norse Greenlandic settlements disappeared sometime in the fifteenth century is because they failed or did not know how to adapt to climate change. In short, as the climate changed and cooled in Greenland during the Middle Ages, the Norse Greenlanders simply failed to adapt to new environmental conditions, while the Inuit moved along the coasts and thrived as they took advantage of the opportunities climate change brought.

Today, like Eirik the Red's efforts, Greenland's politicians and business leaders of the new millennium are eager to attract energy multinationals, mining companies and aluminium-producers, and are extolling the virtues of their country as a green land, or at least a land that is getting greener. It is distinctive in the way it differs from many other indigenous responses to the scientific rhetoric about Arctic meltdown as a social and environmental crisis.

Elsewhere in the circumpolar North, particularly in Canada and Alaska, indigenous politicians, community leaders and activists portray indigenous peoples as victims of climate change. Canadian Inuit leaders, for instance, have stressed the human rights dimensions to climate change, arguing that what is at stake with the melting sea ice and thawing permafrost is the cultural survival of the Inuit as a distinct people who are dependent on the continued presence of snow and ice.

By stark contrast, the Greenlandic official response to climate change diverges from this prevalent view. Climate change is happening and Greenland is getting warmer and greener, but rather than portraying themselves as victims of climate change and its impacts, Greenlanders are being encouraged to think positively about the opportunities that climate change is bringing. As Greenland melts, the country is preparing for frontier fever and an influx of foreign workers attracted by jobs in the extractive industries. The "greening of Greenland" is a metaphor for a warming politics of autonomy, self-governance and possible independence.

Inuit society has always responded to new encounters and new challenges and today the Inuit, along with other circumpolar peoples, are preparing to meet the challenges of a new Arctic. Self-determination is also about the right to development and, based on the ancestral and human rights of people to govern themselves, Greenland's industrial ambitions remind us that self-determination is also about the right to make decisions and choices that determine the path development should take.

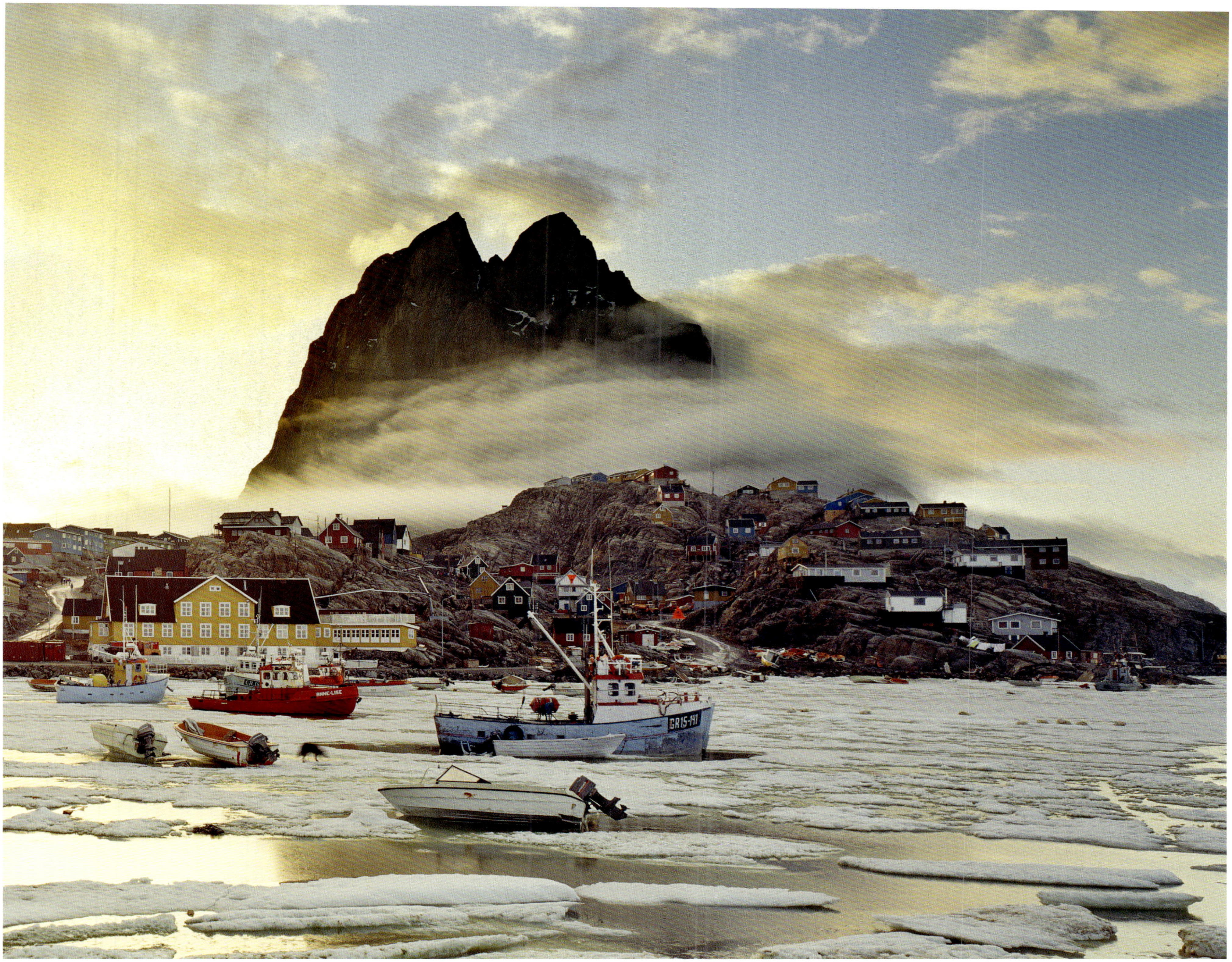

The horns of the Uummannaq mountain rise out of the fog, bathed in the otherworldly Arctic light.

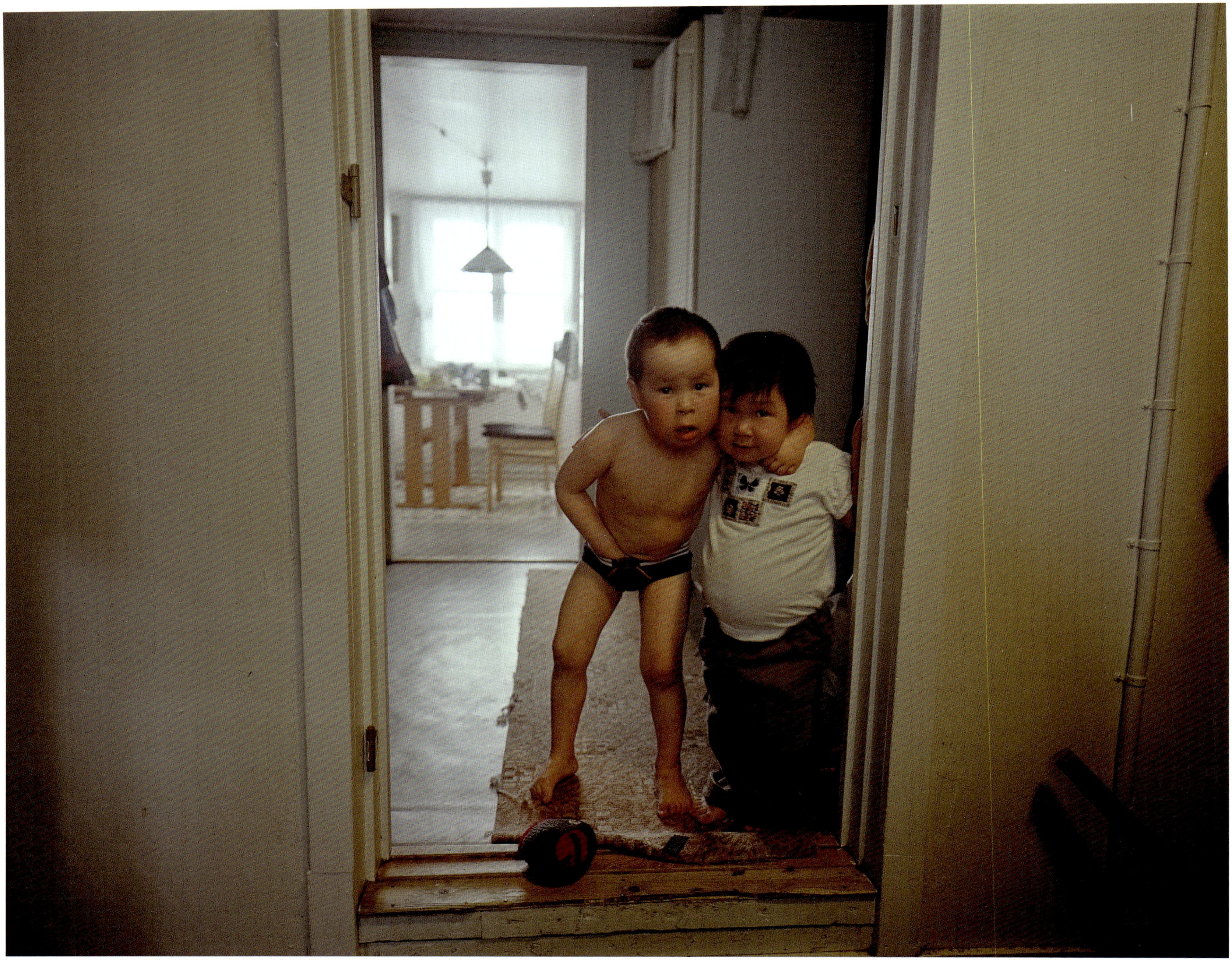

The houses in Greenland are well heated, but the Inuit also claim that their traditional diet of seal and whale products gives them the necessary warmth to endure the cold climate.

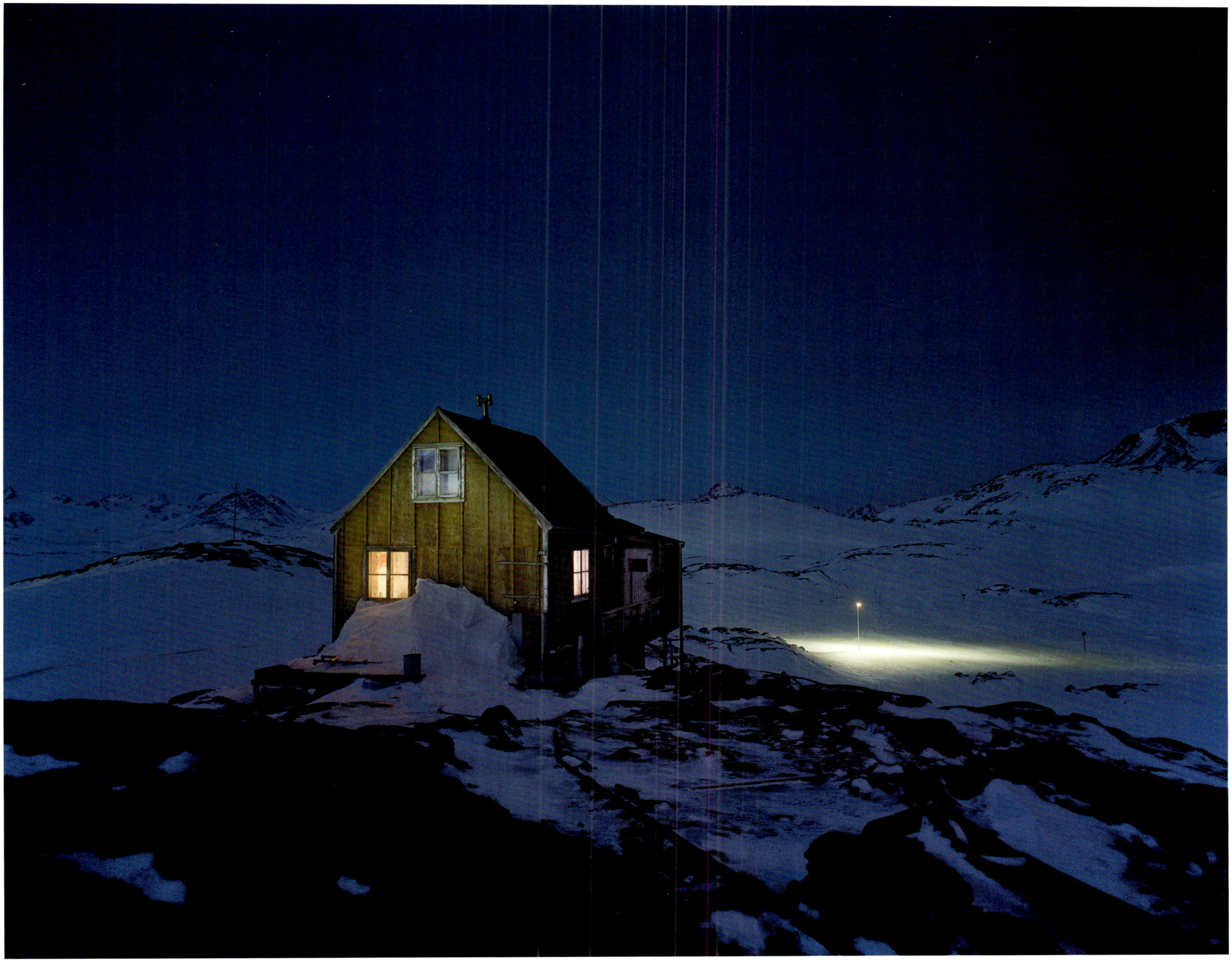

The lonely house of the drum dancer Anda Kuitse in Kulusuk. Drum dancing is one of the pillars of traditional Inuit culture, where the dancer recites stories, legends and myths.

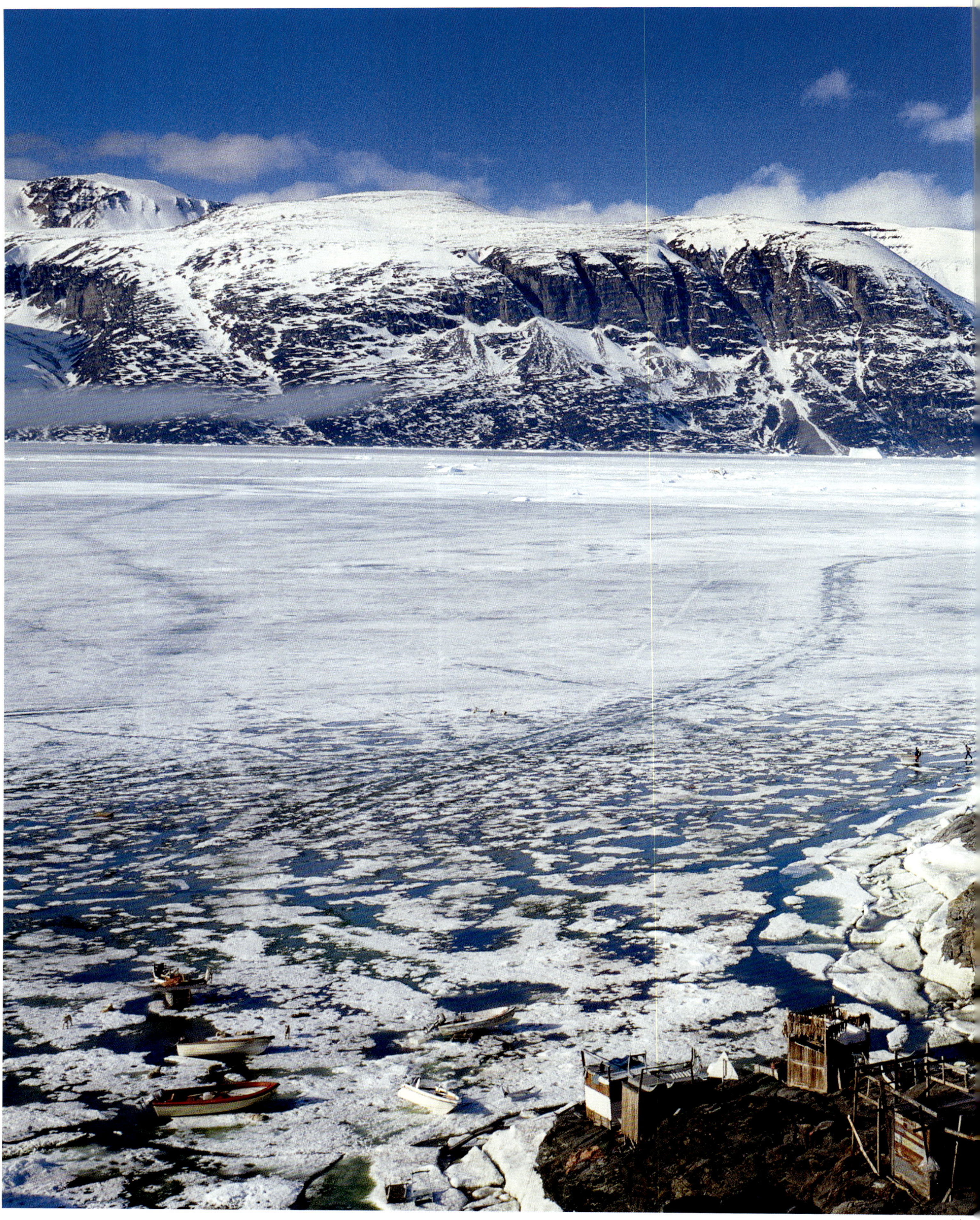

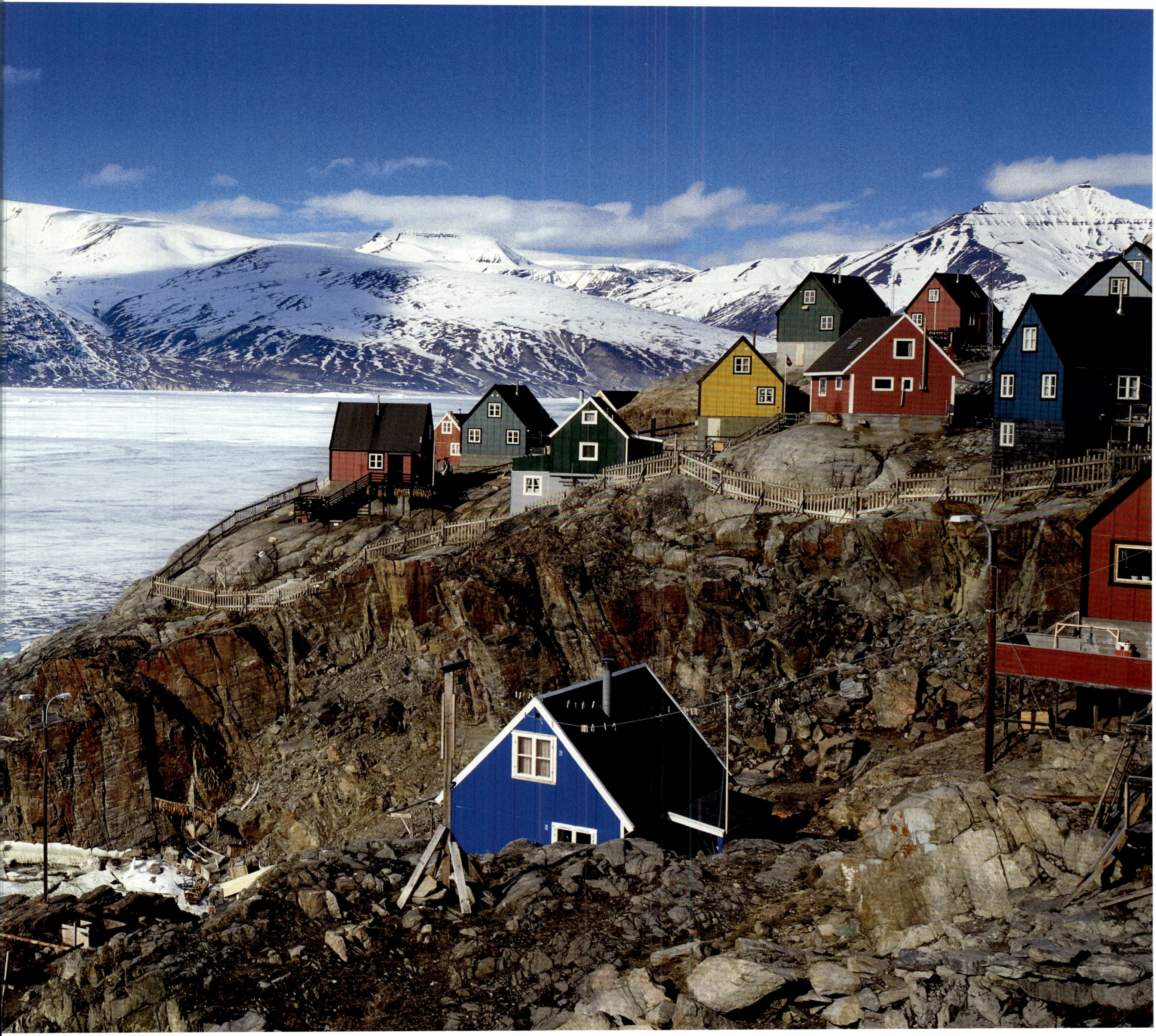

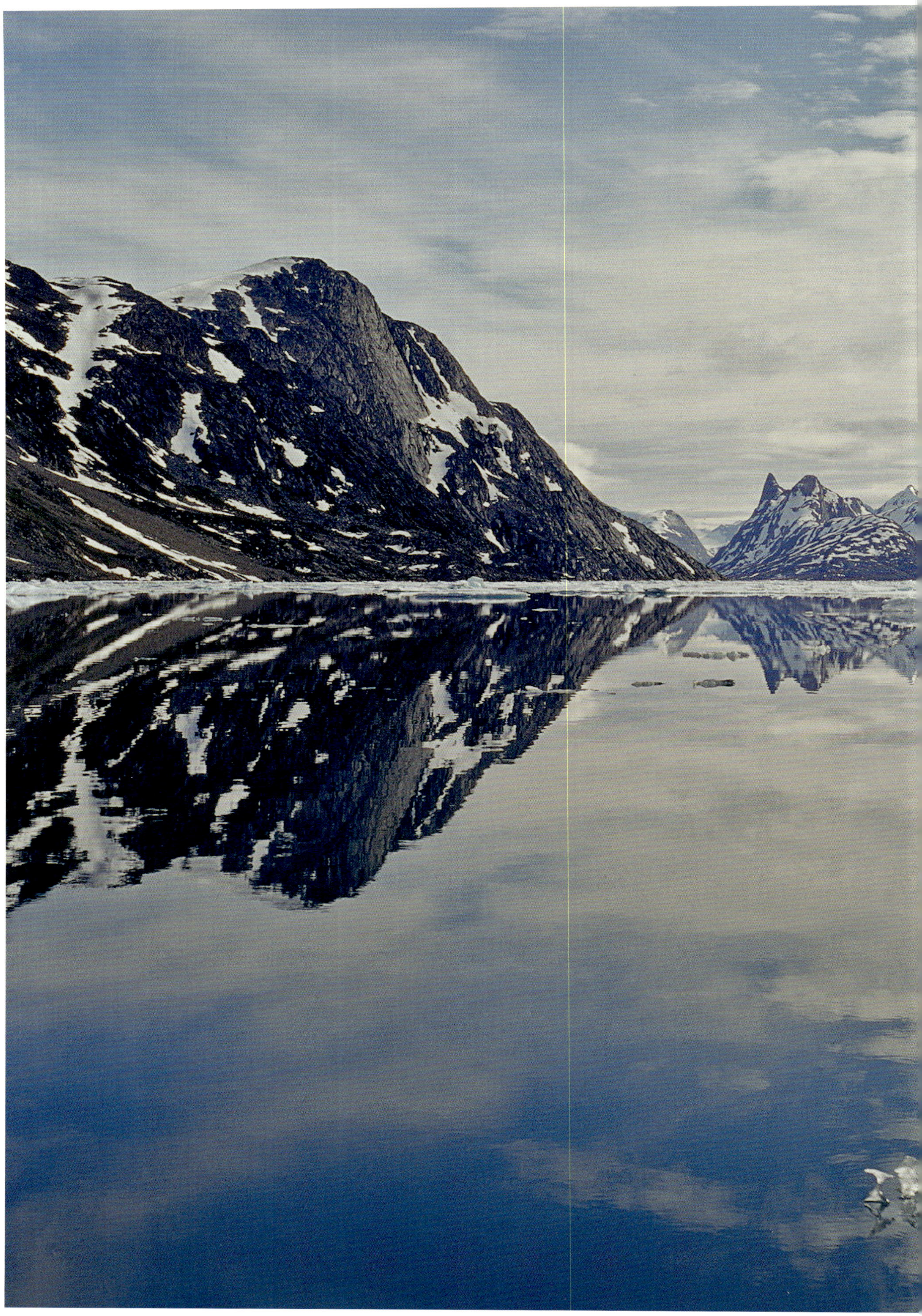

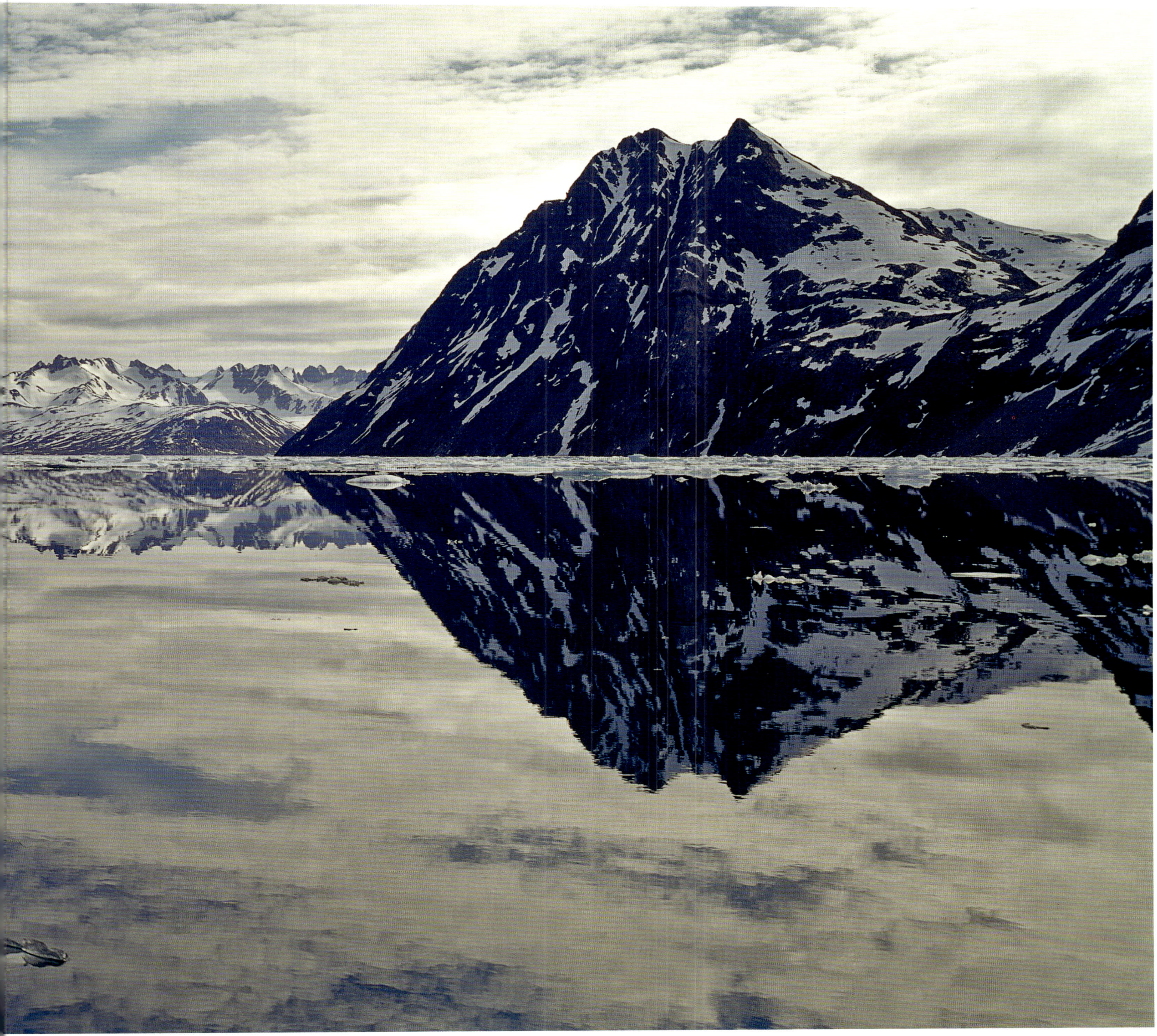

OUTSIDE A GLACIAL STORM ROARS AND THROWS LOOSE ITEMS OUT TO SEA. INSIDE THE WARM INUIT HOMES, SEALS ARE SKINNED, SKINS ARE CLEANED, AND BIRDS ARE FLAYED. LAUGHTER SOUNDS AS STORIES OF HEROES, STORMS AND HUNTING TRIPS ARE TOLD UNDER THE BEATING OF THE DRUM. EVERYTHING BECOMES A PICTURE.

RAGNAR AXELSSON

Waiting for the Prey

The air is filled with a sense of threat. The howling wind hurls up the snow so one can barely see between houses. A glacial storm, piteraq, is looming. It forms when strong winds blow down from mountain summits 3,000 metres high. The cold and heavy air speeds down the glacier, accelerating like a huge invisible river rushing out to sea and sparing nothing in its way. In its worst form, the storm is so powerful it shreds houses to pieces. It has been disastrous to the inhabitants of Greenland's East Coast.

People are running around the village, fastening down anything that could blow away, tying up the dogs and feeding them. The dogs curl up in the snow and preserve their body heat until the snow covers them. The windows are covered with ice so little can be seen through them. Walking around the village, everything becomes a picture. Time passes and it gets colder. Snow is blowing from all directions so there is no shelter to be found. The lens is saturated with snow and there is not a dry patch anywhere to wipe it off. Every now and then someone dashes past on their way for a visit or to the store. Life can be hard in the villages when fighting the forces of nature day after day, for weeks on end.

It is warm and cosy inside the Inuit homes. There, seals are skinned, skins are cleaned, and birds are flayed. People laugh heartily at stories of heroes, storms, and hunting trips, some which ended in tears, others in joy. The beating of the drum enhances the storytelling. The party lasts long into the night.

An old woman sitting on the side of a bed speaks Greenlandic to a guest who cannot understand a word. But it doesn't really matter; a lucid and innocent gleam in her eyes says it all. The walls are adorned with pictures of family members and Jesus Christ.

The next night the house burns to the ground. It is consumed by flames in less than half an hour. The old woman is rescued in the nick of time. The following day she sits devastated by the ruins of the house. She can no longer gaze at her village through the window.

In another house, another grandmother tells her grandchildren the story of when, at the age of five, she once sat on her father's sledge out on the ice. He was hunting food for the family and the dogs. (The dogs are the working animals that pull the hunters' sledges across the ice fields, bringing sustenance to the people; to accomplish this the dogs must also be well fed.)

The children listen in awe as their grandmother tells them how her father waited by a hole in the ice for a seal to surface. The moment the seal stuck its head through the hole its time was up. Suddenly, the hunter looked up and saw a polar bear running at full speed towards the sledge where the child was sitting. The polar bear is an unpredictable creature and capable of anything when hungry. In a split second the hunter grabbed his gun and shot, saving his daughter from the clutches of the bear.

"I was lucky," the daughter says now. "The polar bear fell dead at my feet, only a metre away." The children's eyes are big and fearful as they watch their grandmother imitate the polar bear by making noises with a pair of pot lids.

"You can't go out into this weather without eating some seal," says the old woman to me. When I have thanked her for the meal she brings out a polar bear skull and says: "This is the polar bear from the story. I've had it for eighty years, but now it is yours to keep. It comes with good luck, remember that." It would be an insult to say no to the old woman. The gift warms the heart as I look back towards the house through the storm.

After the storm the landscape of the village is transformed. There are huge piles of snow everywhere. Houses are buried and people have to be dug out of them. The children of the villages are all alike, cheerful and playing outside all day long, often dressed poorly. The tolerance for cold is much greater here than with most people. The seal meat and fat that is eaten in large quantities in Greenland's villages plays a big role in keeping them warm.

On a starry night in the Arctic, it is magnificent to see the northern lights dance throughout the heavens. The escalating cold of the night fades in the presence of this beauty. One can stare at the sky for hours on end; nowhere else can one spot so many stars as in Greenland.

It can be a bit dangerous to take photos in the middle of the night when beer is being heavily consumed. Without any warning, a window of a small house opens, an armed man sticks his head out, yells into the air, and fires his gun a few times. The bullets bouncing off the rocks make a disturbing sound. The man yells again and closes the window; he probably thinks he saw a ghost and that he's taken care of it with his gunfire. After this episode, it is not entirely comfortable to go back to taking photos of the northern lights, but they are just so beautiful this particular night.

The following morning the same man is in the sweetest mood, gearing up his dogs for a hunting trip out onto the ocean ice field. He is happy to let me come along for the trip. We are not going very far out and will be back before evening.

The dogs become restless when they sense what is about to happen. Three untied puppies are playing around. The dogs are fed. They are bound with chains. The puppies look on as the large dogs tear a piece of meat to shreds. The fierce growling does not bother them. All of a sudden, the puppies jump simultaneously towards the meat. They are able to grab some of it and drag it far enough away, so that the large dogs cannot reach them because of the chains that pull tightly at their necks. The three puppies eat the meat calmly in front of the furious dogs, which are fighting their chains just a few centimeters away. There is tangible excitement in the air. The dogs are ready for the trip onto the ice where adventures await. The little thieves are sleepy after their big meal and watch as the sledge glides onto the ice.

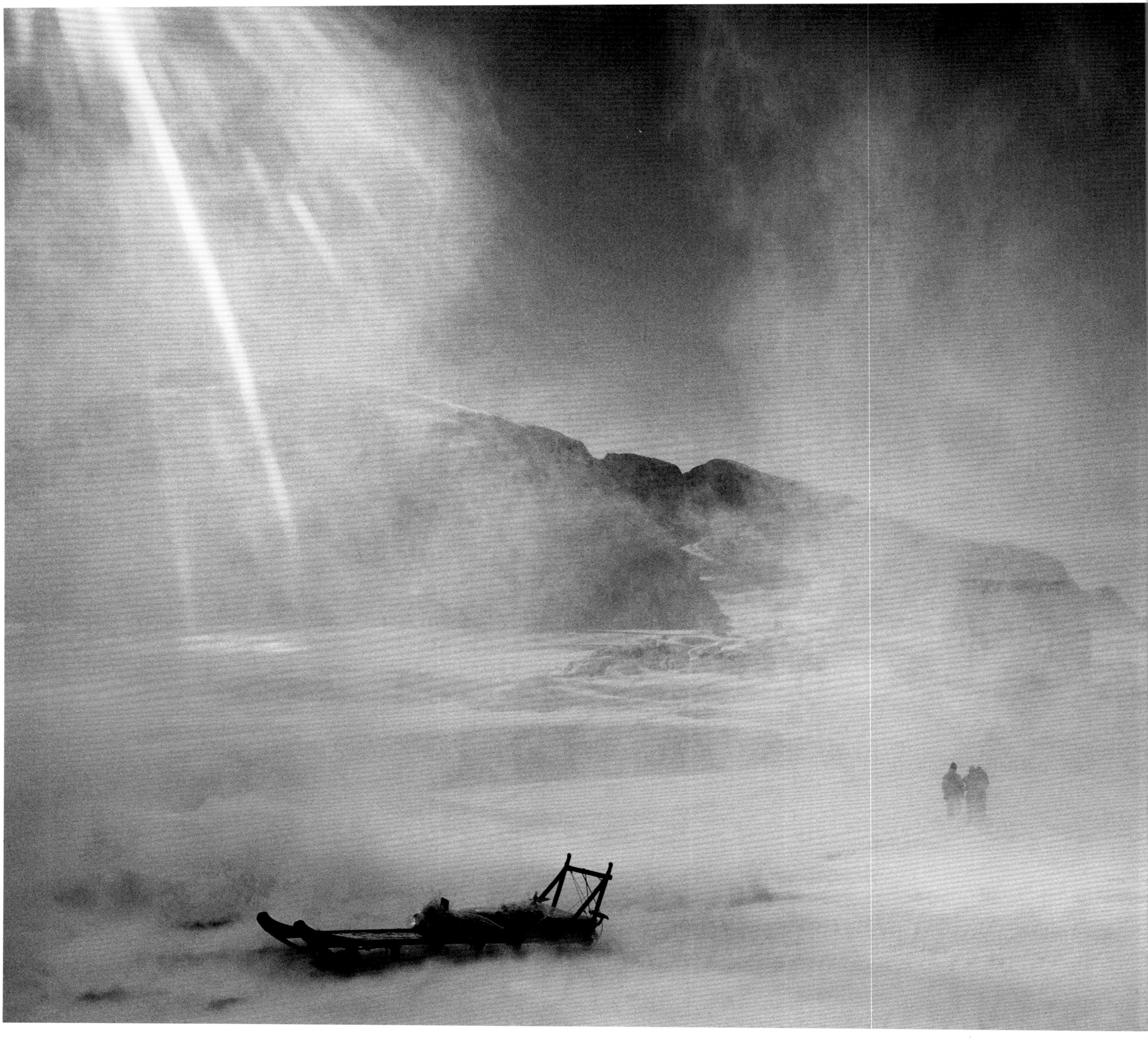

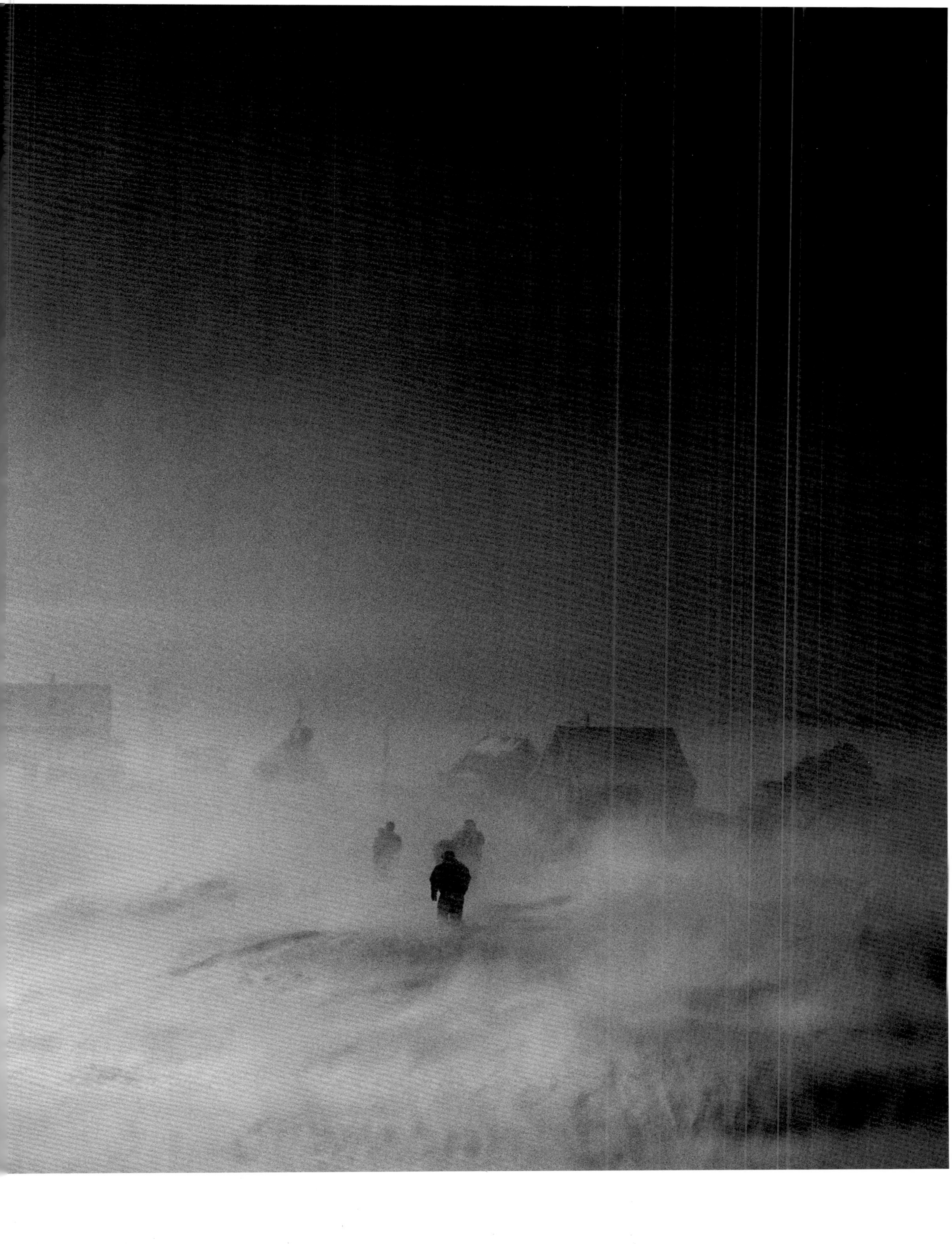

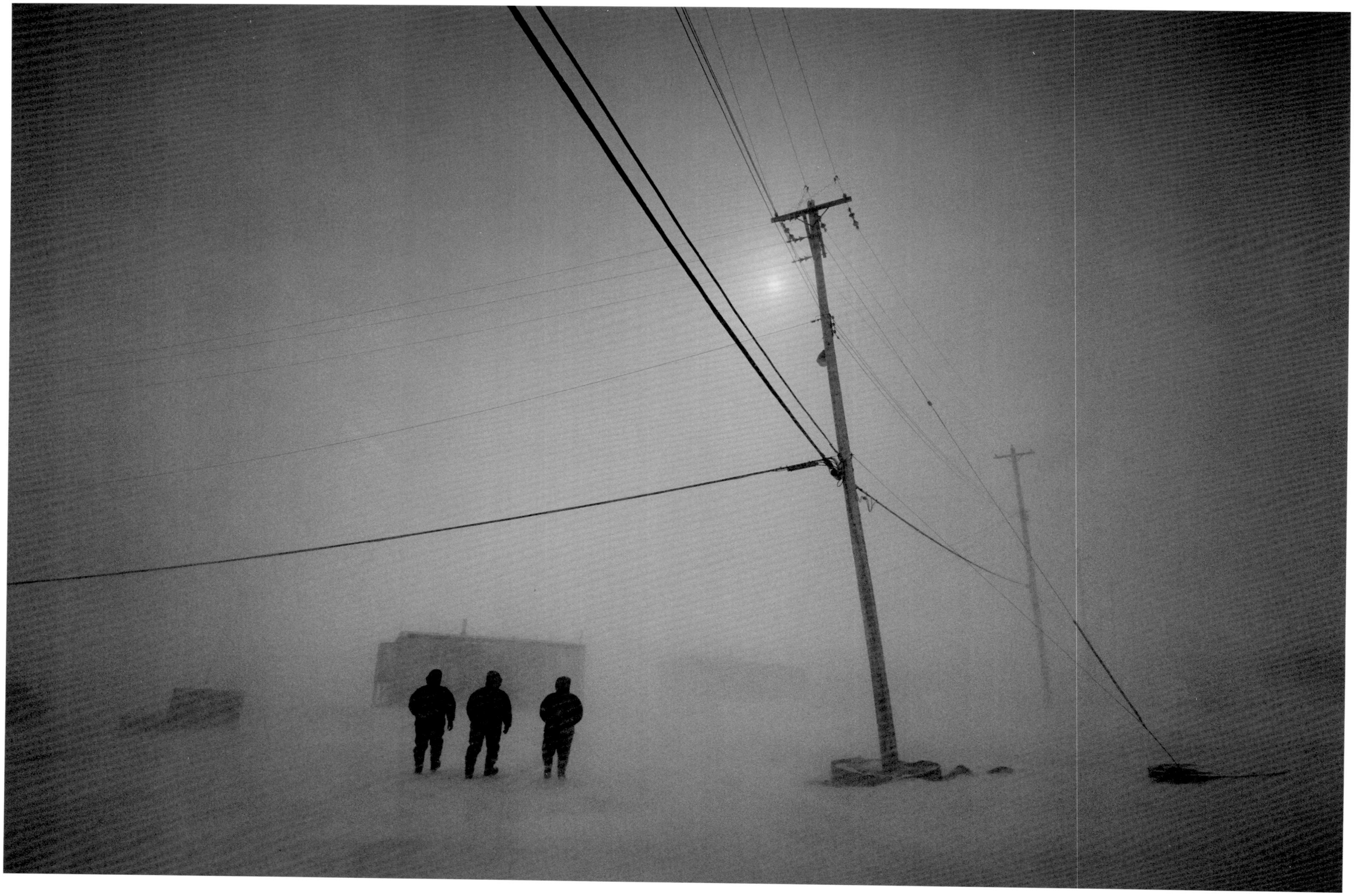

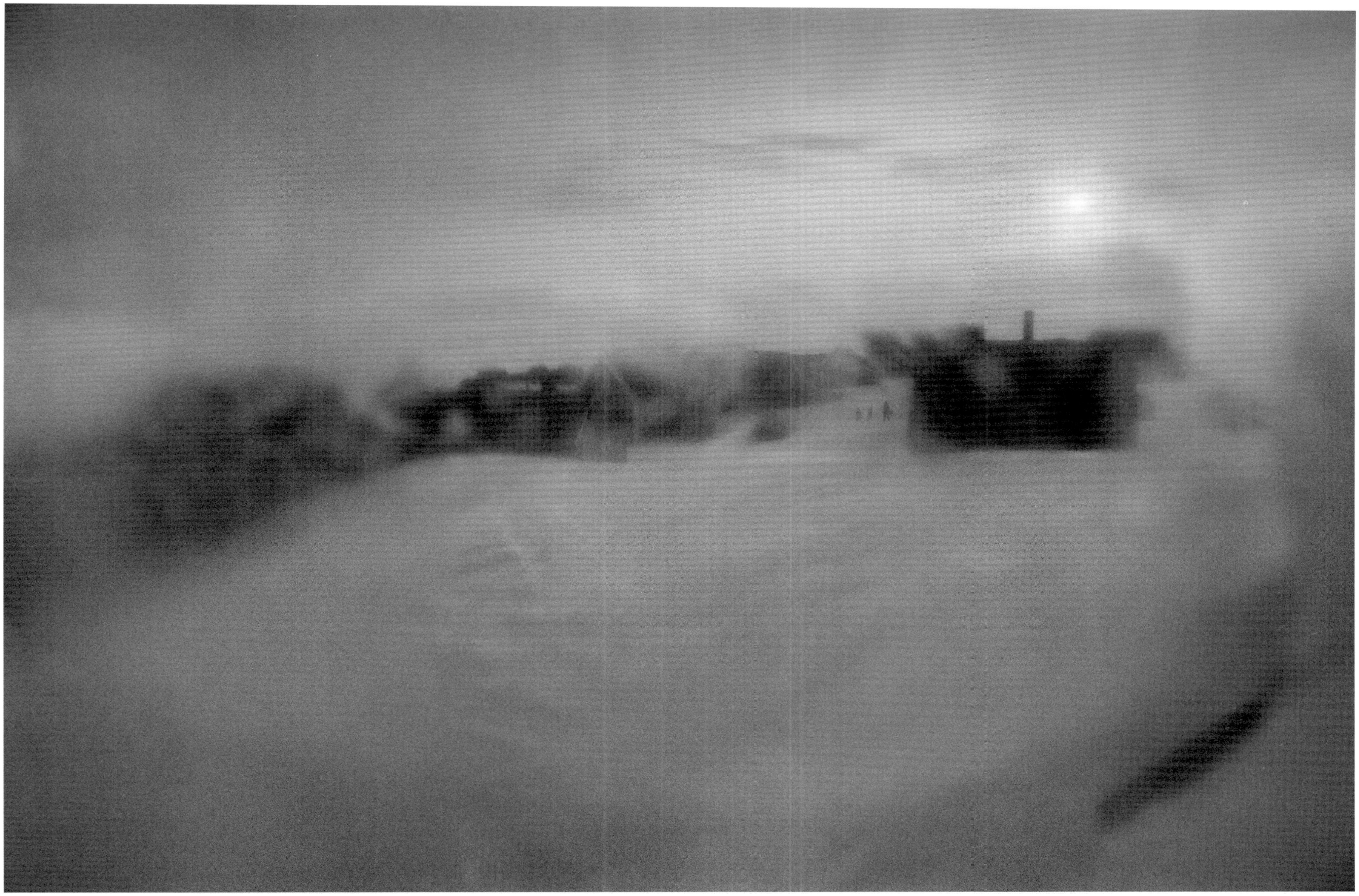

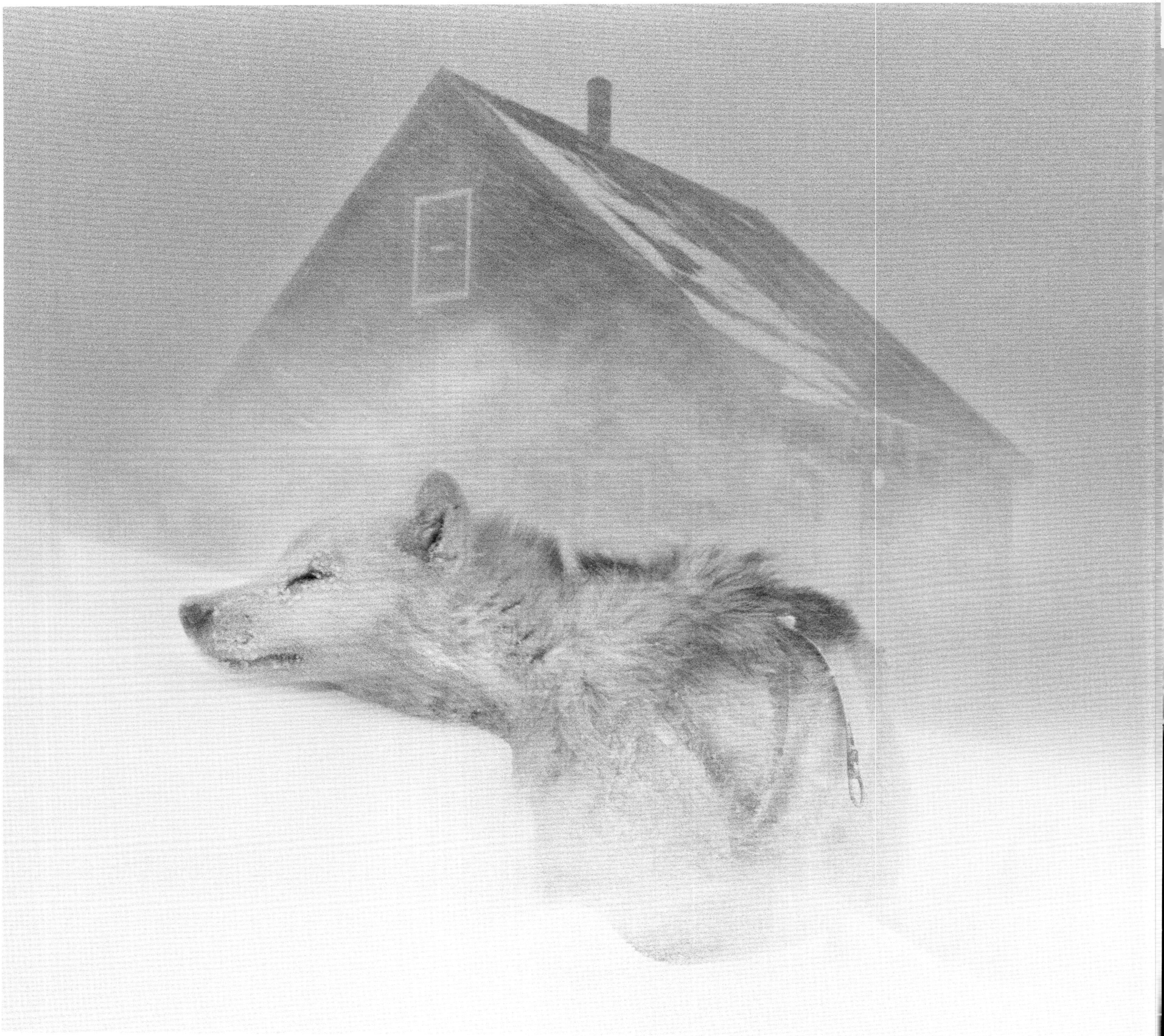

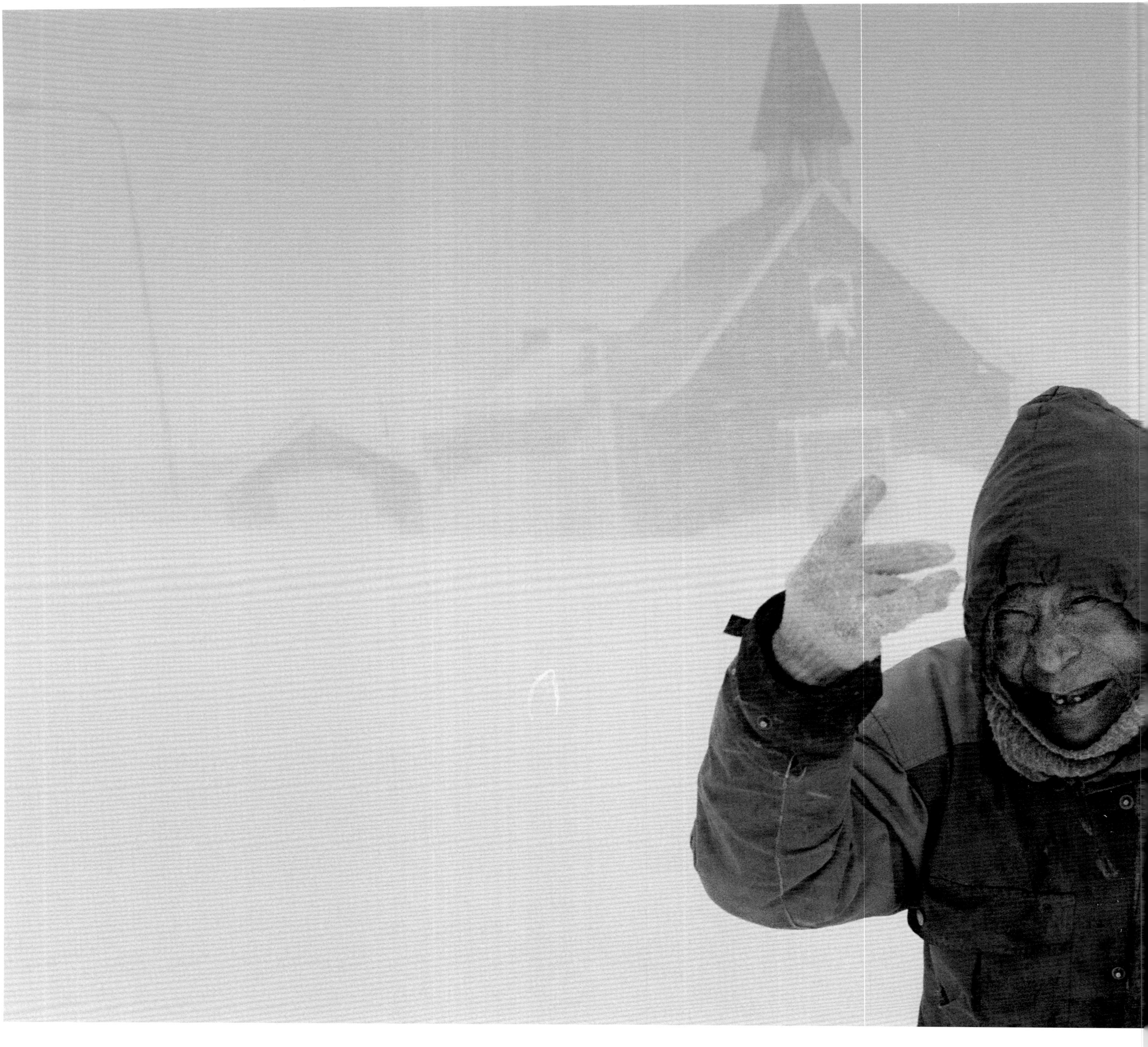

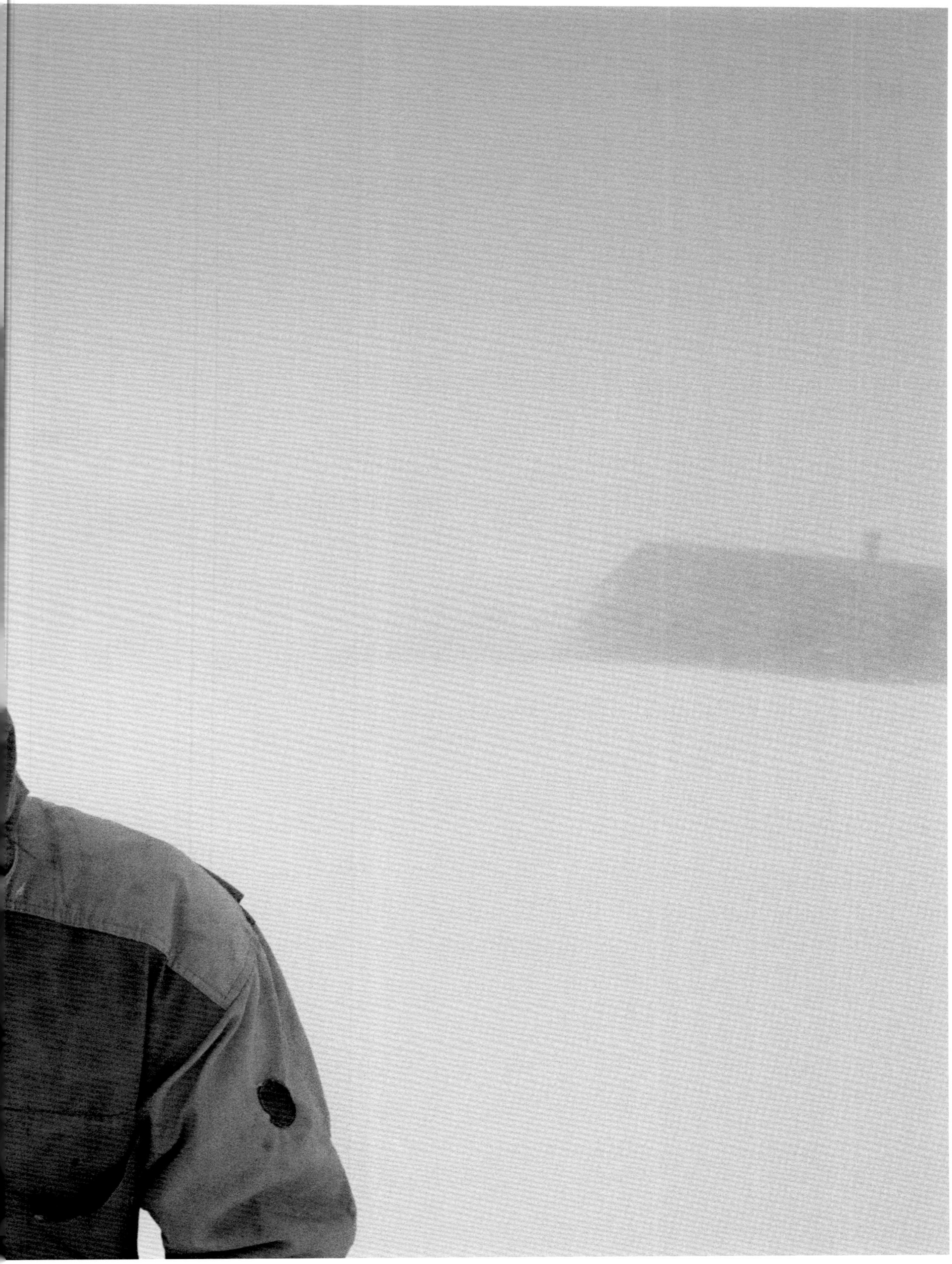

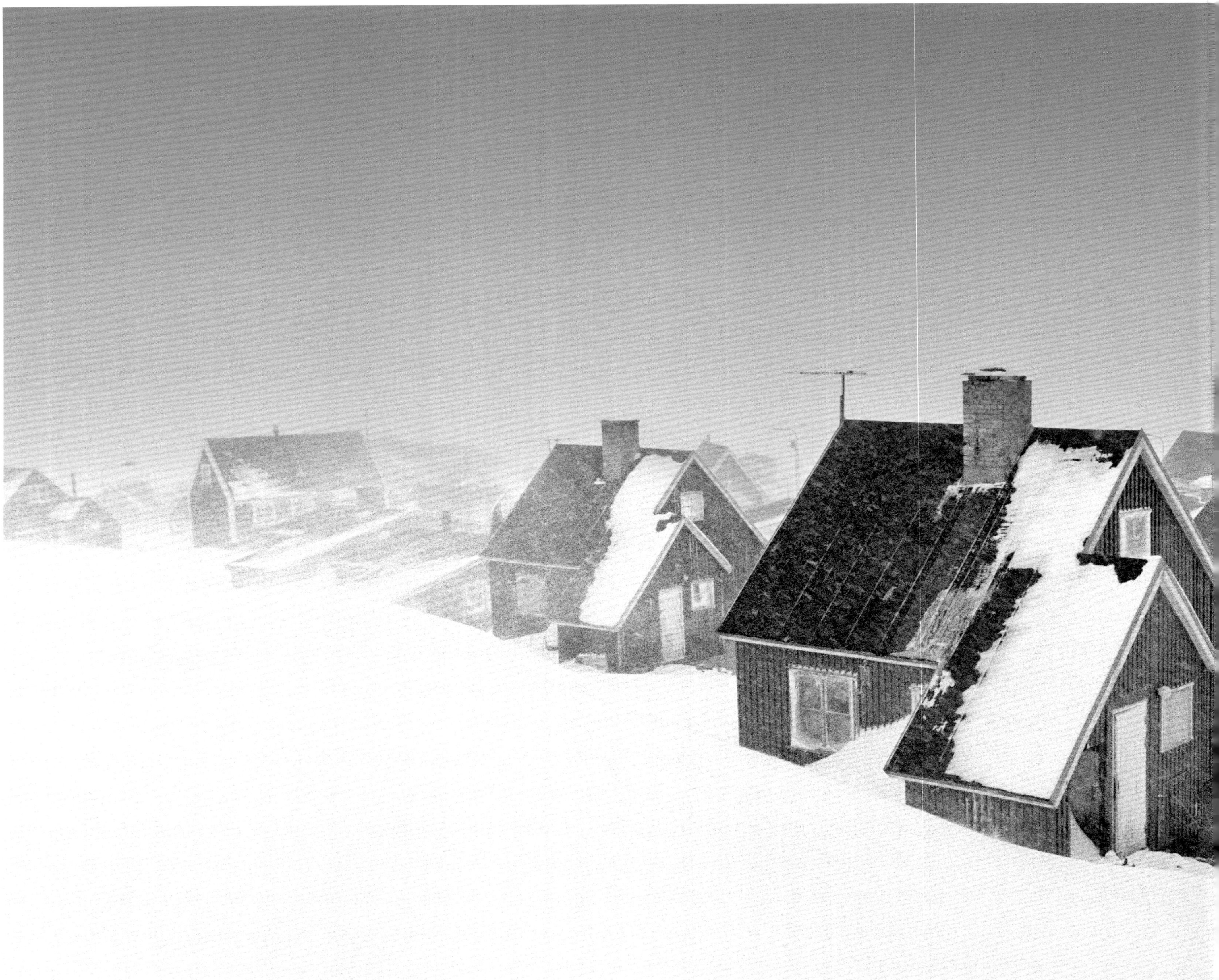

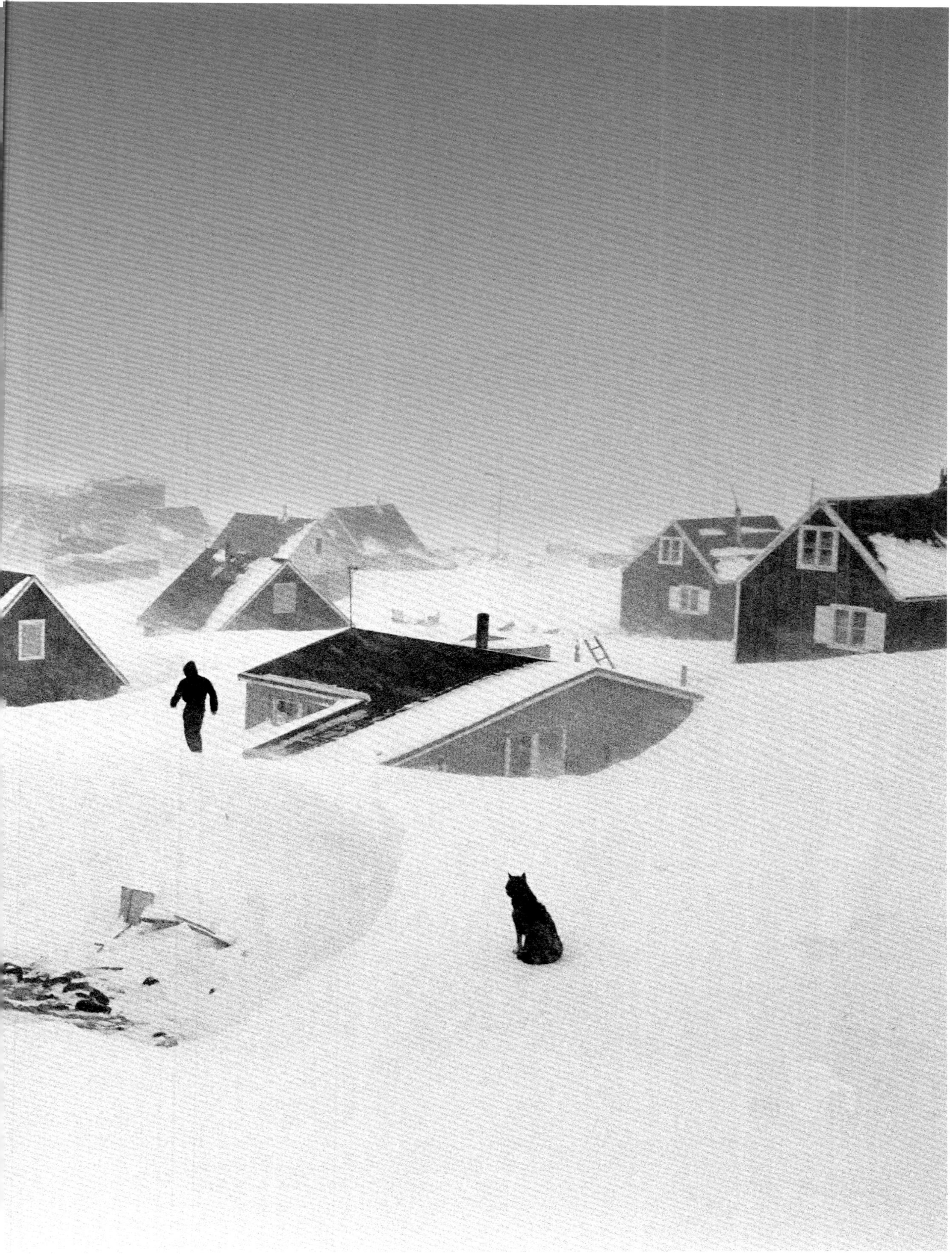

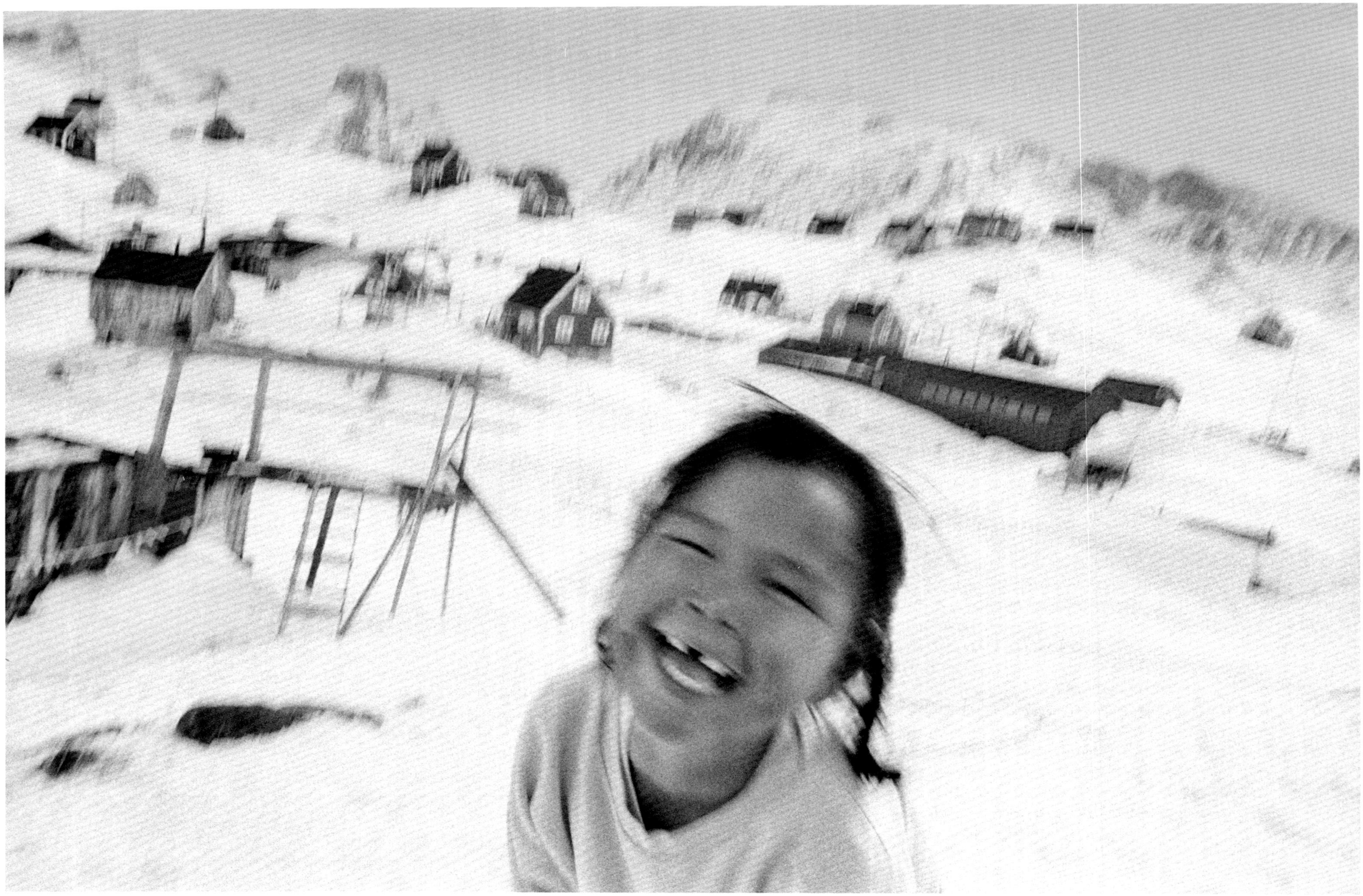

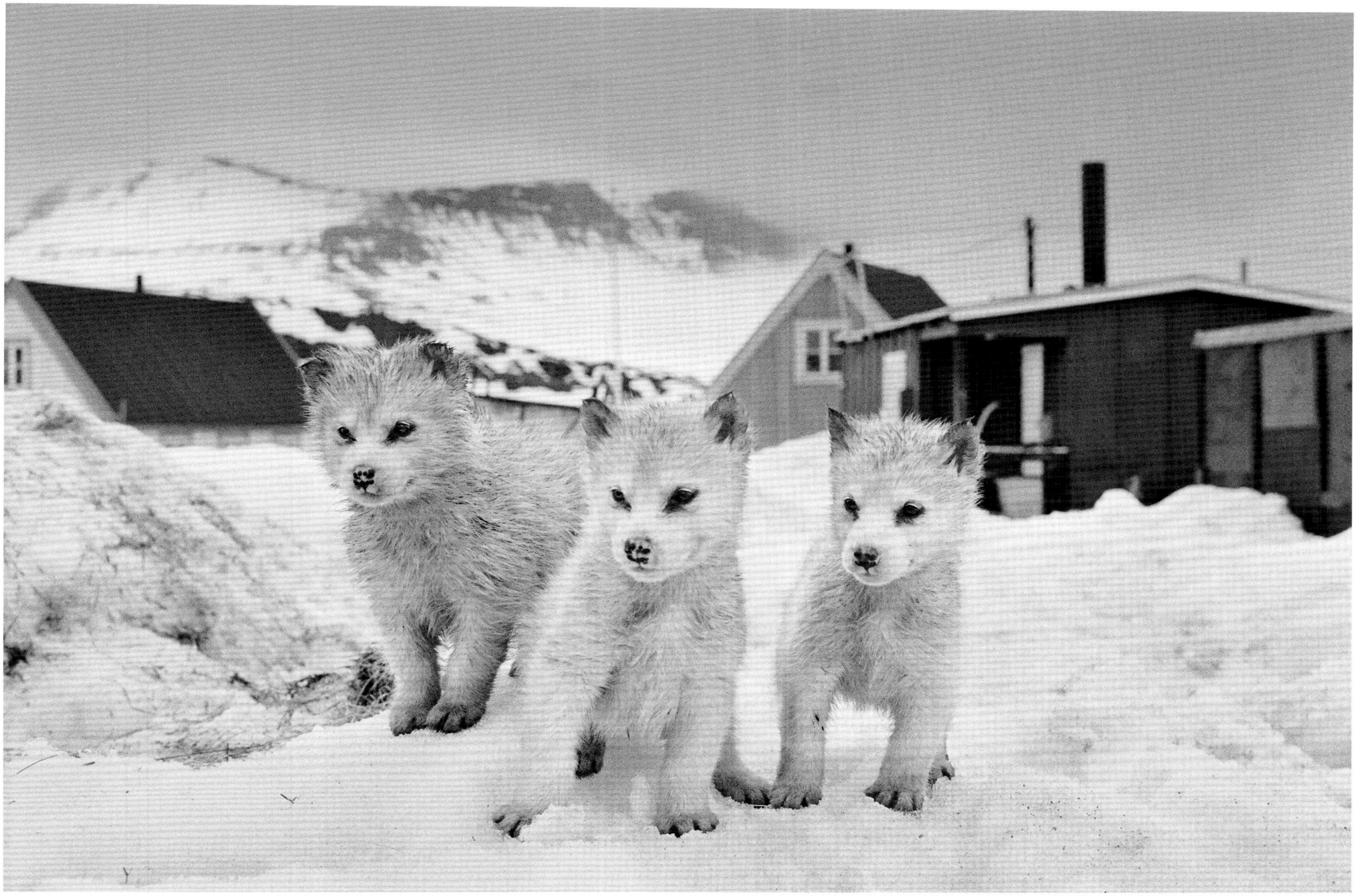

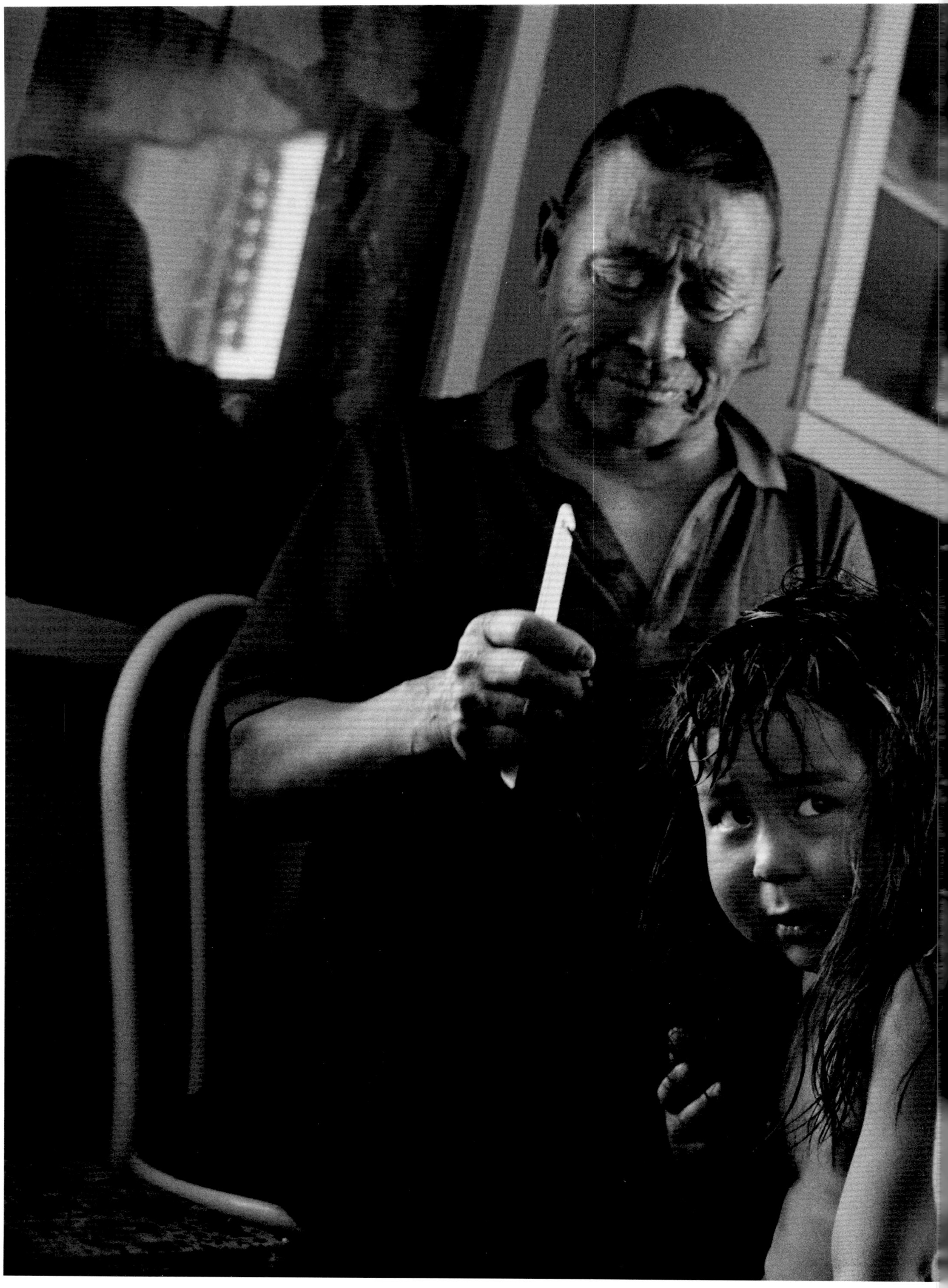

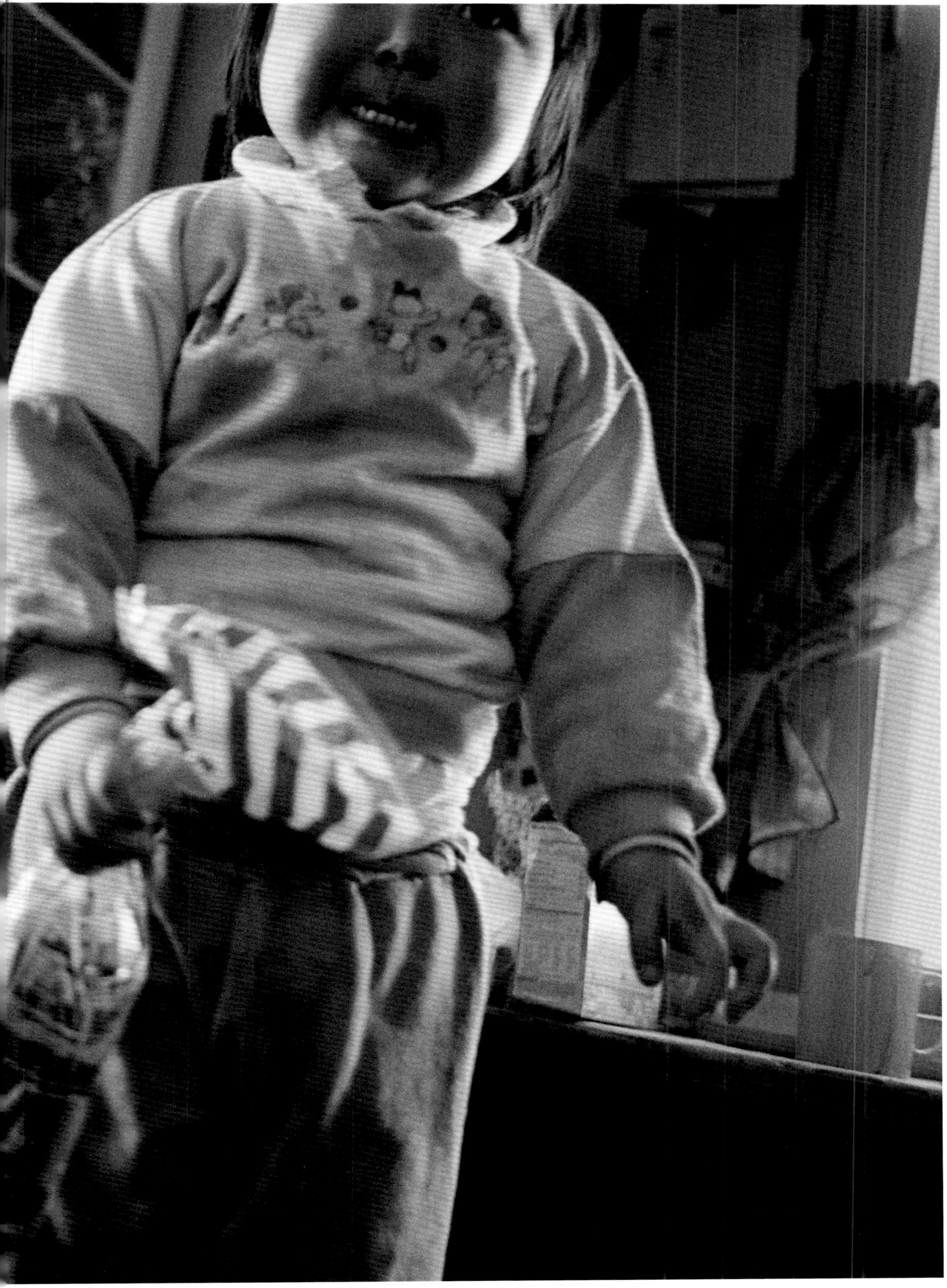

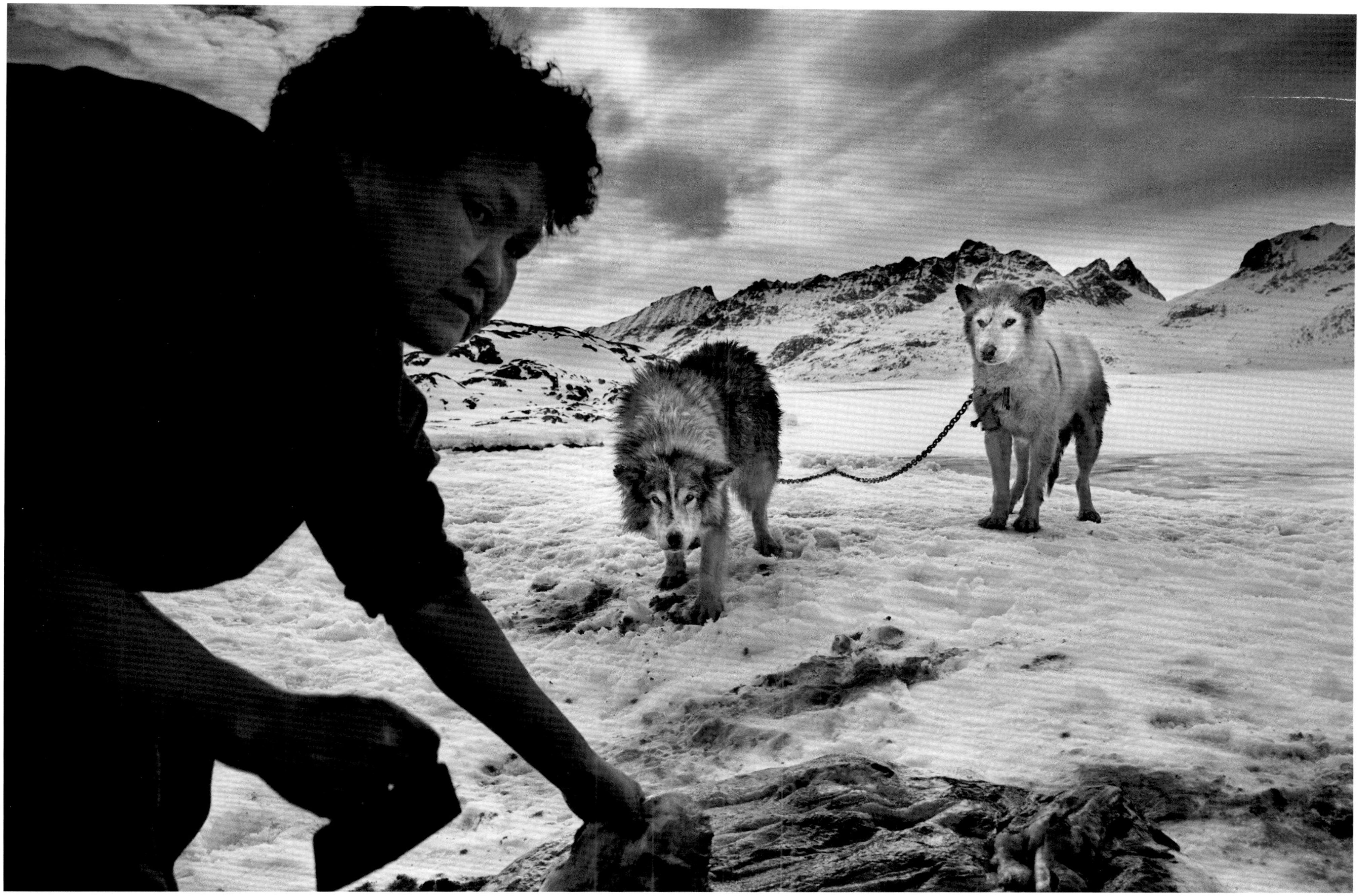

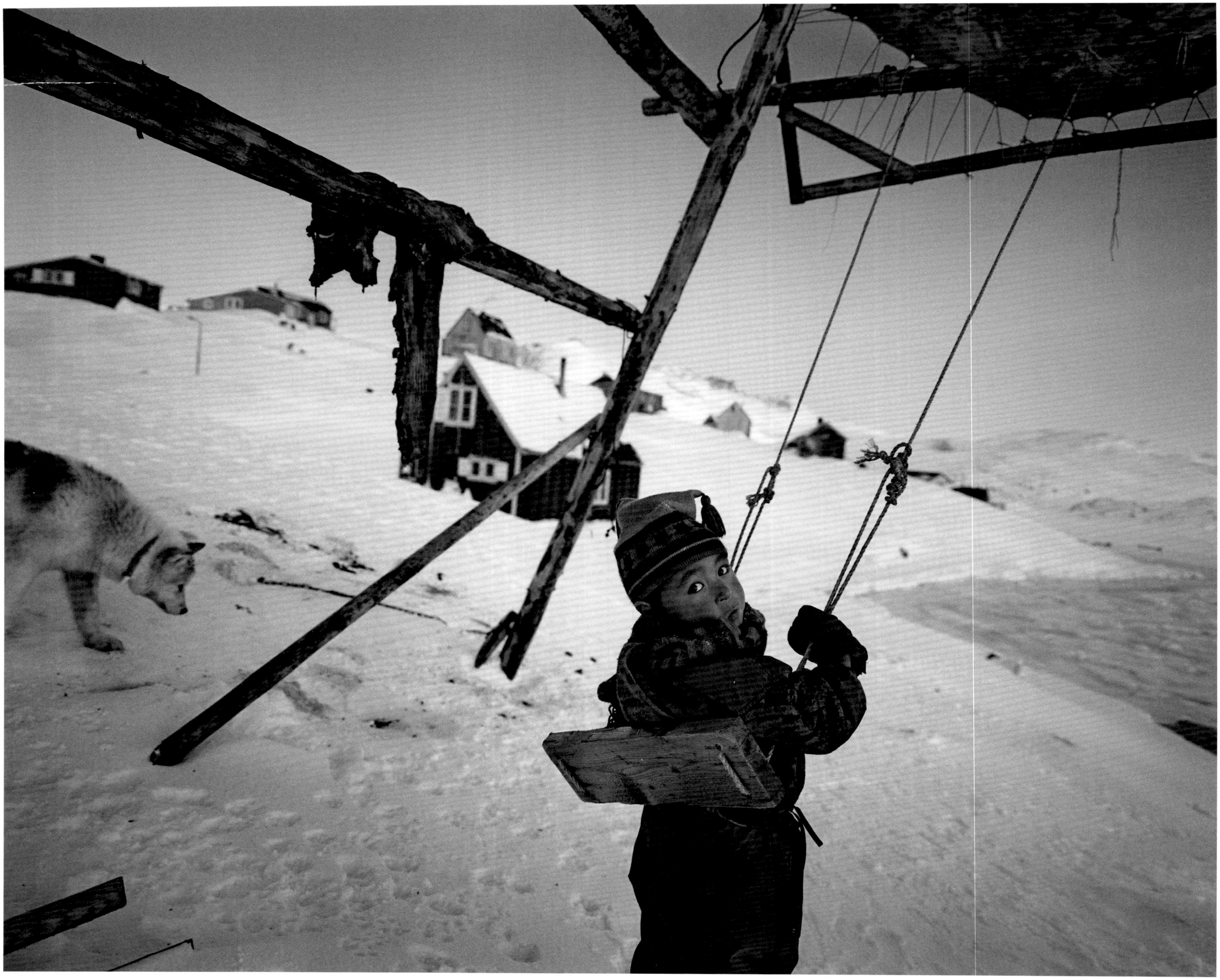

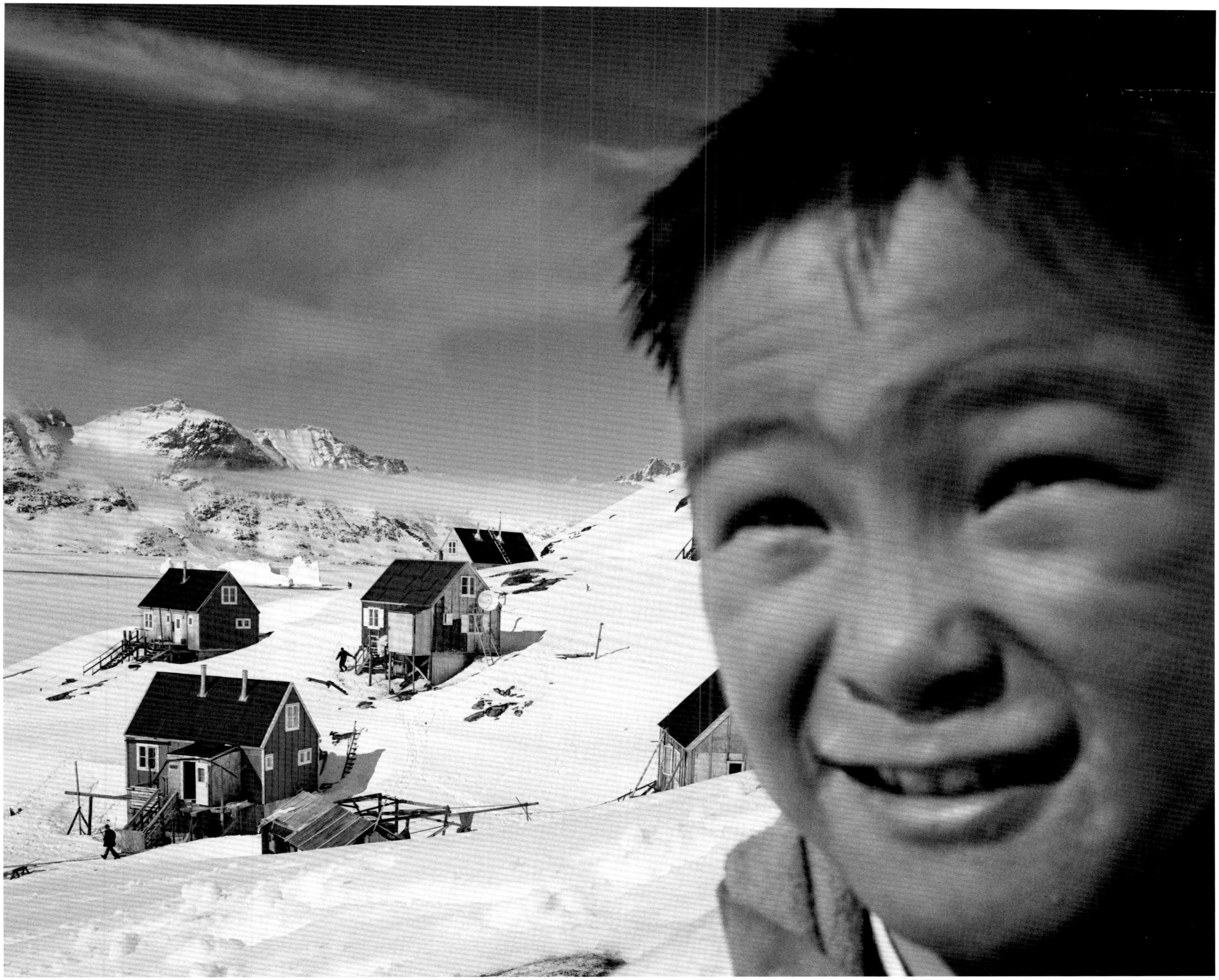

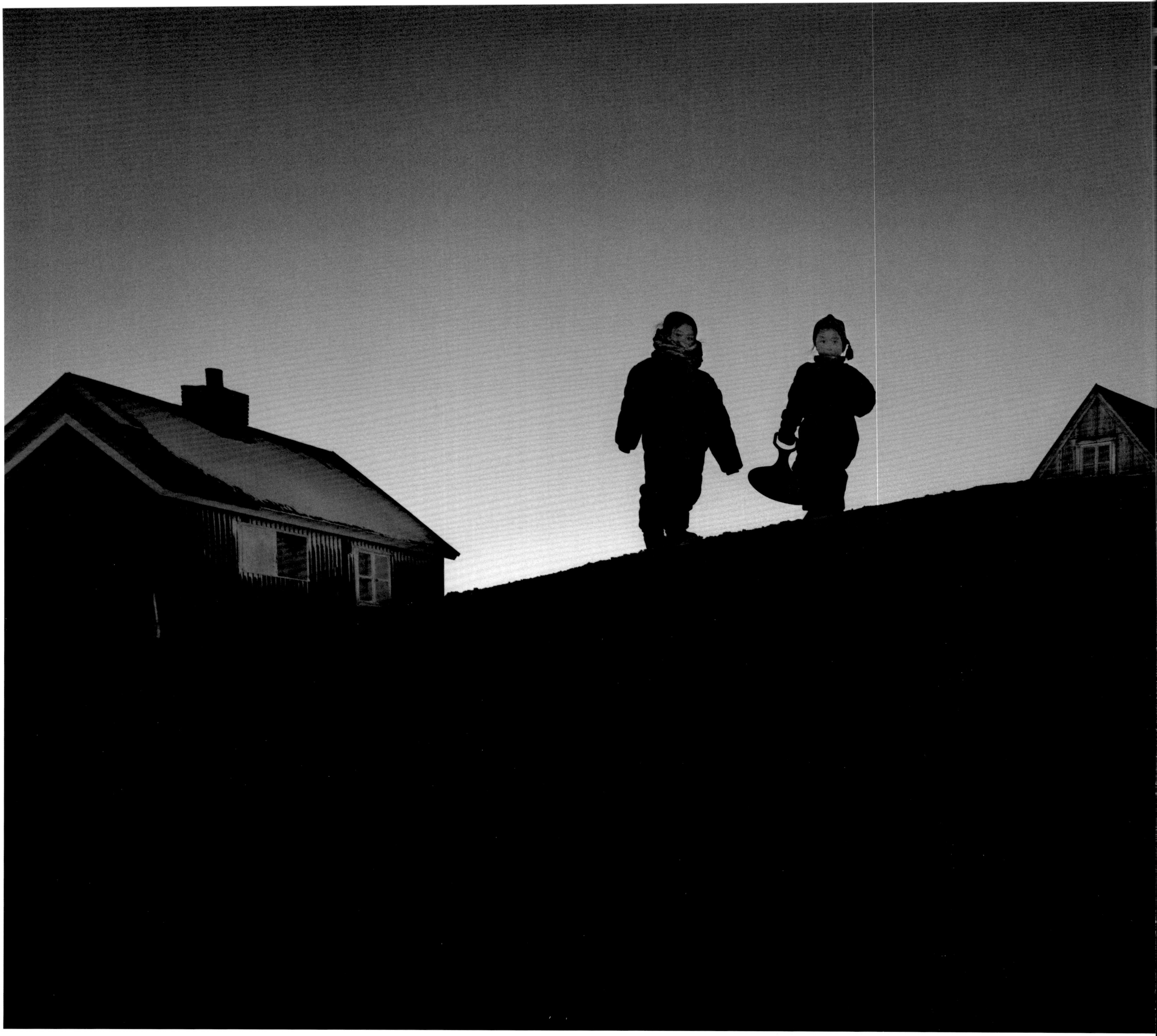

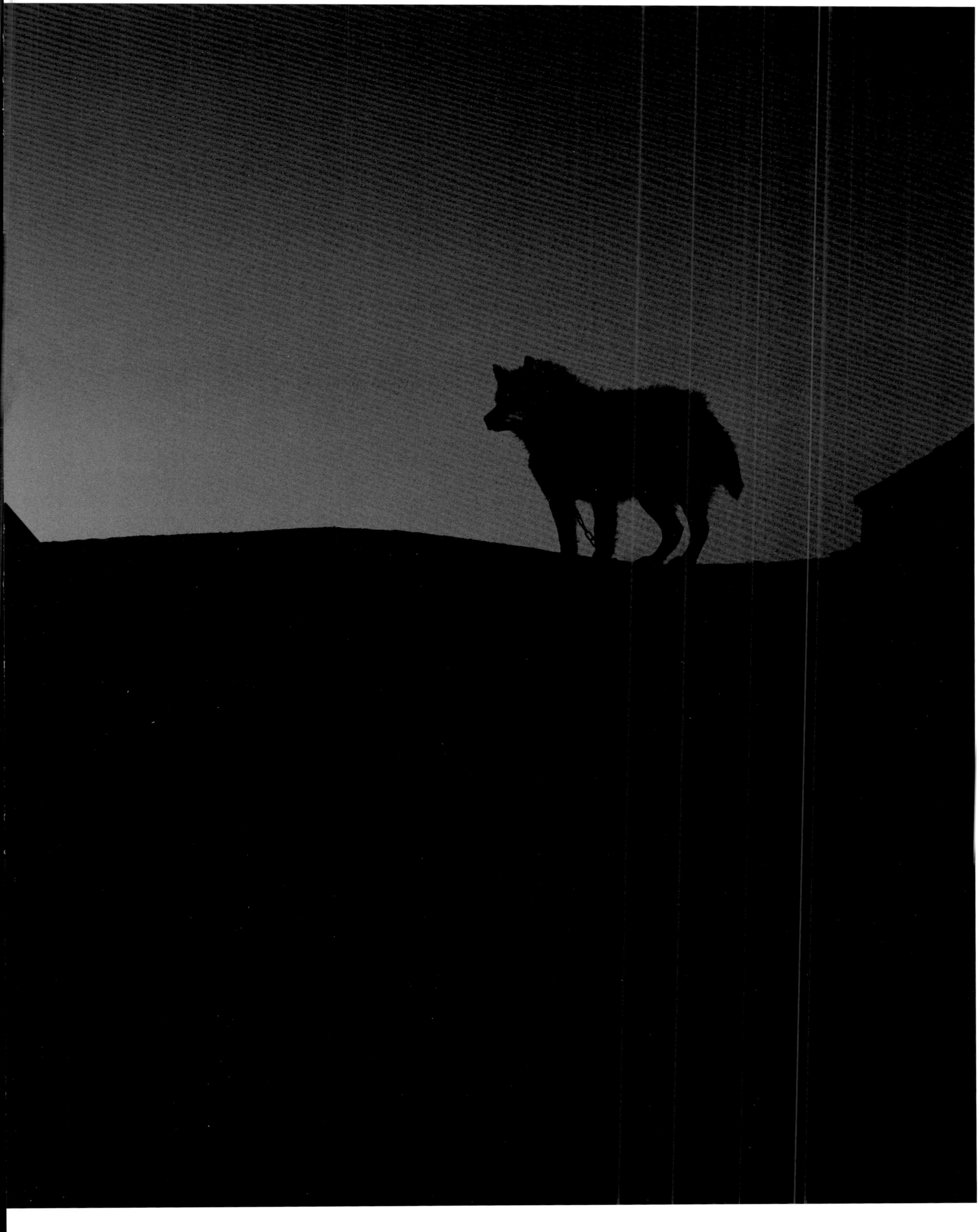

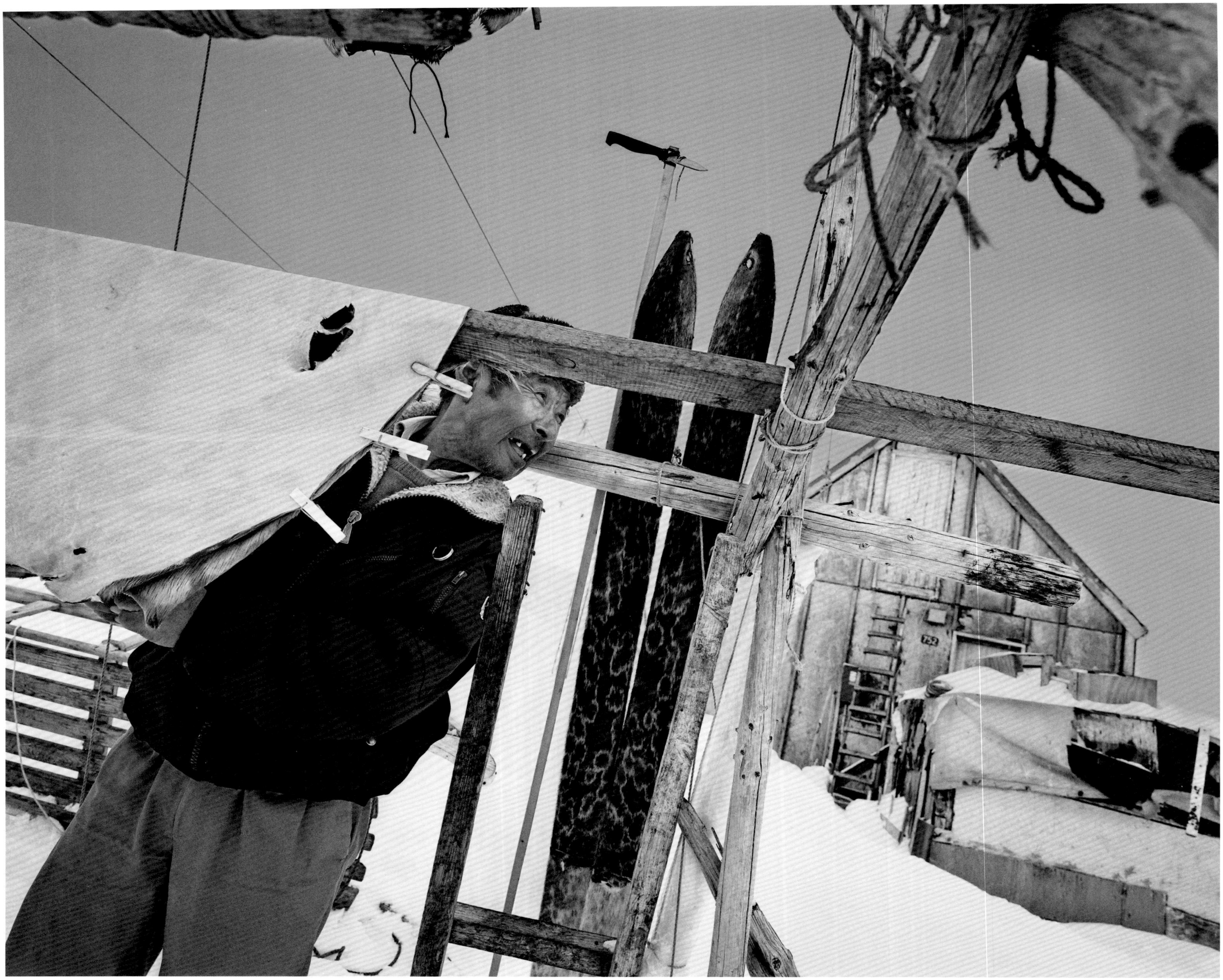

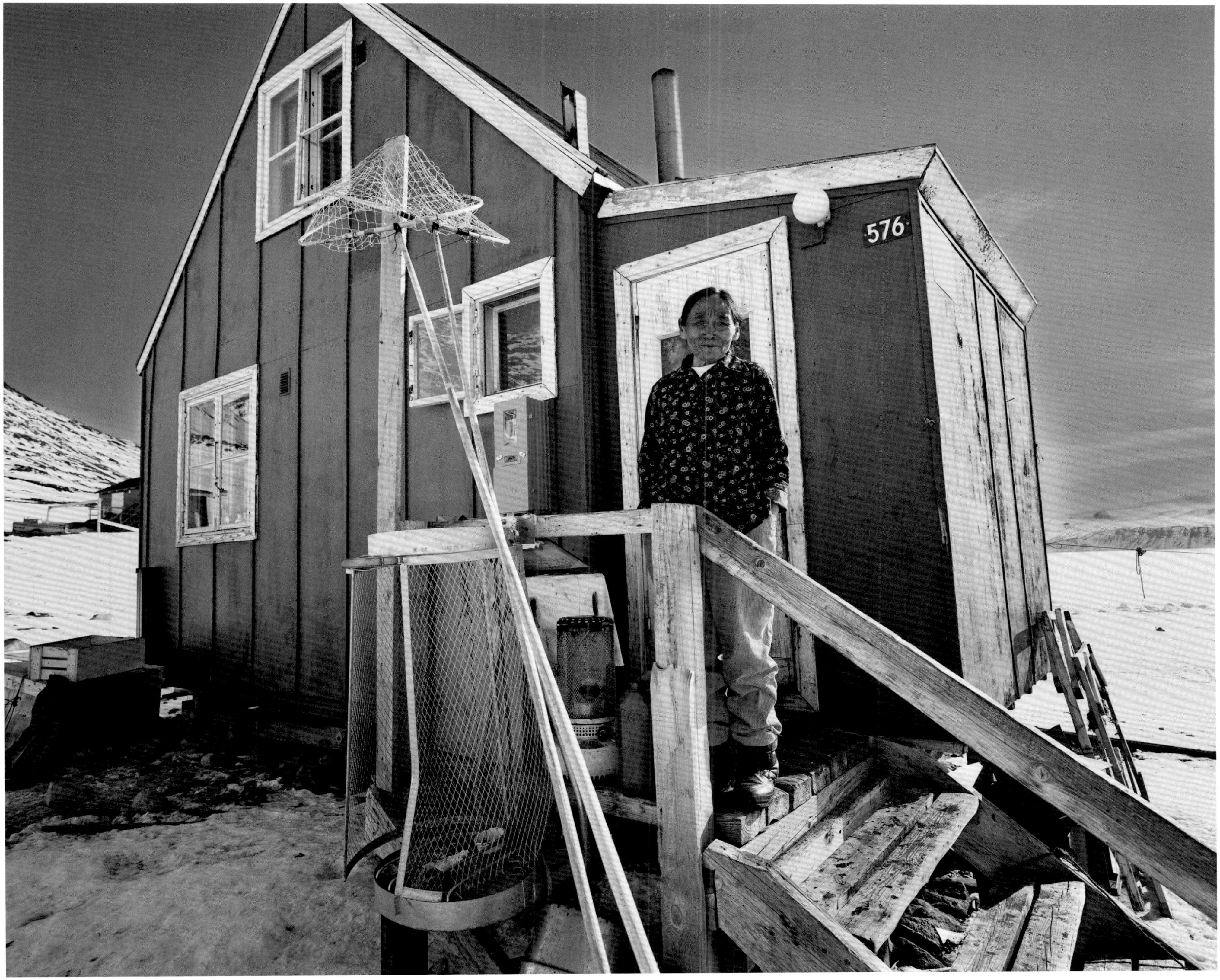
576

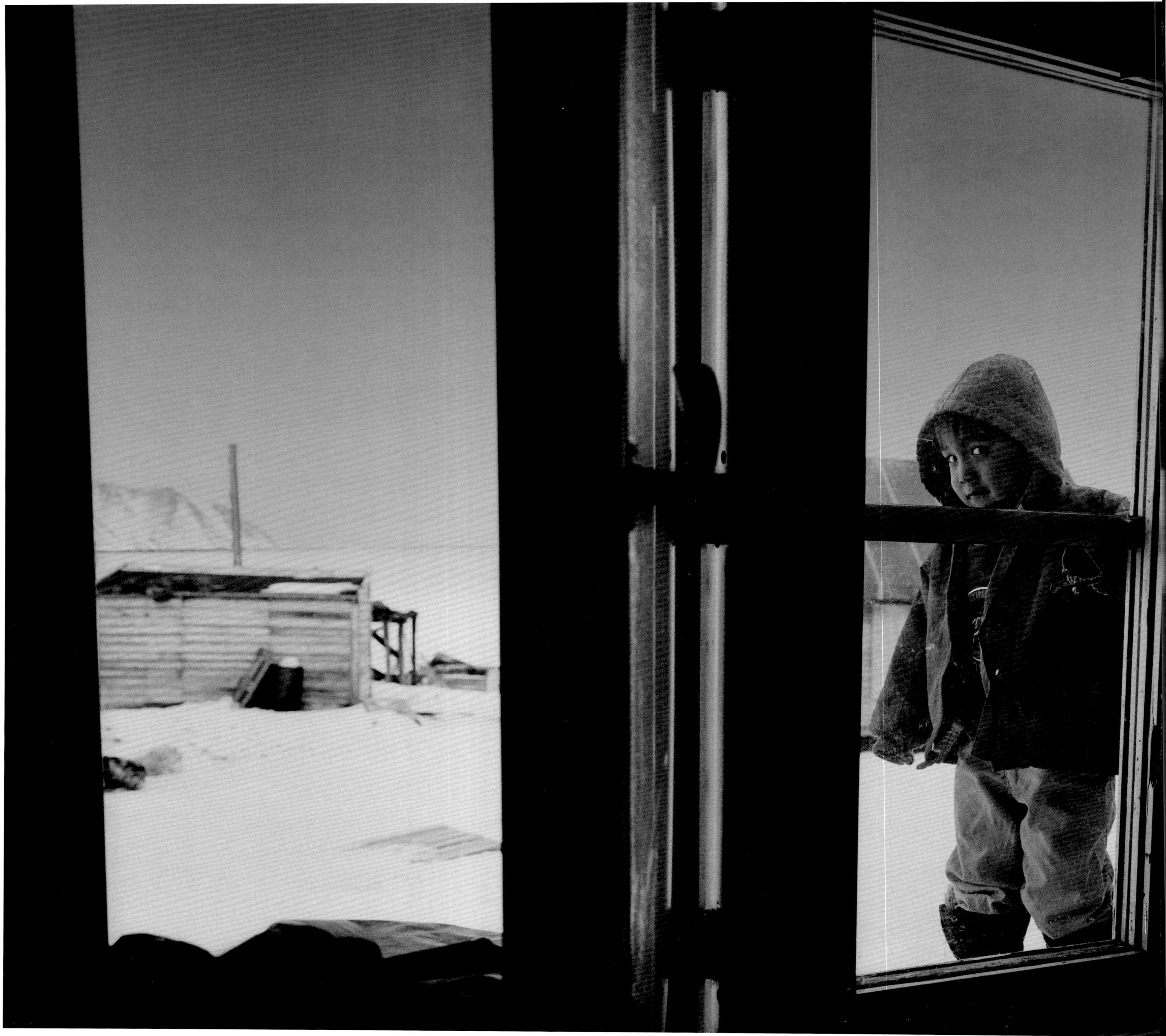

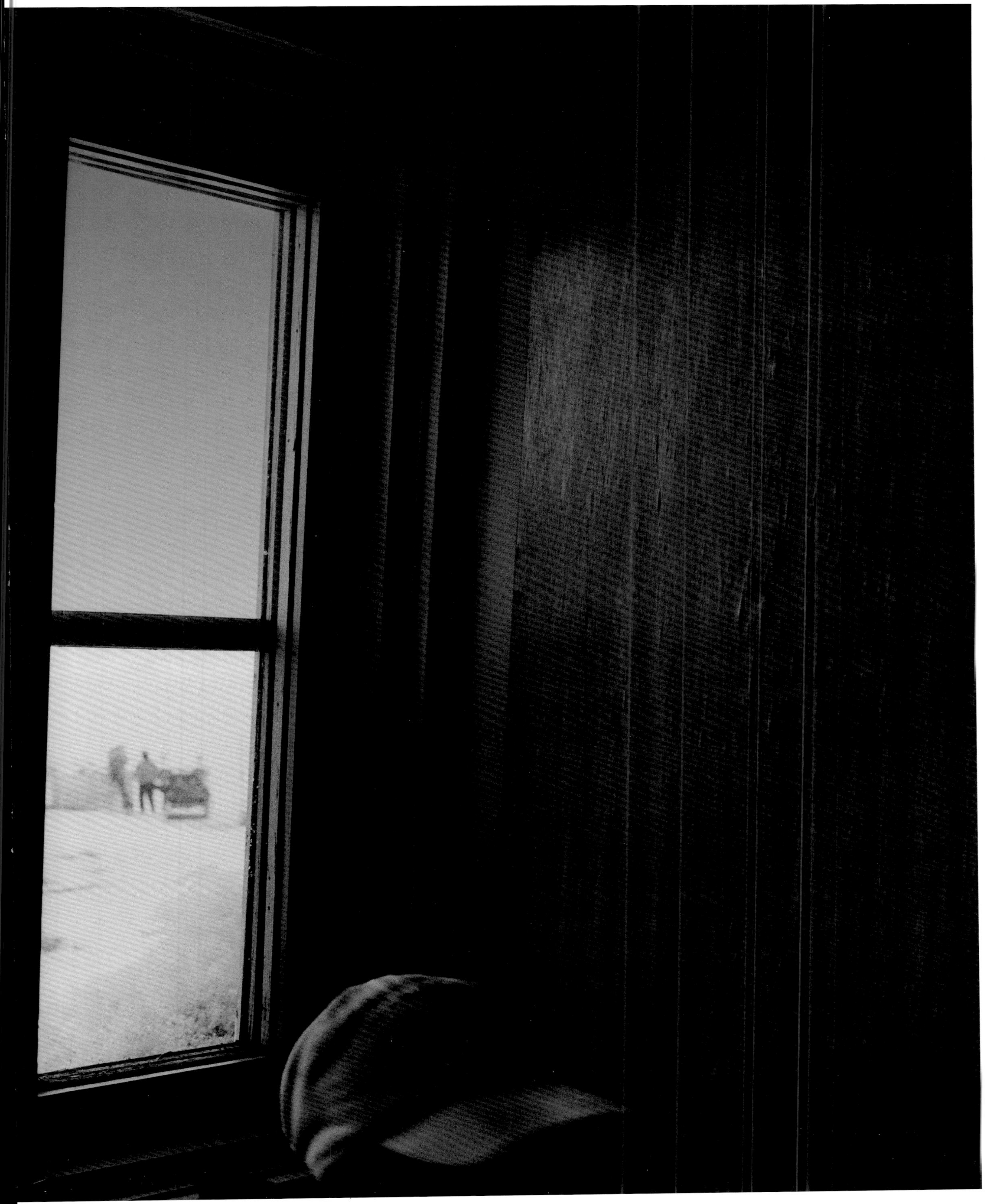

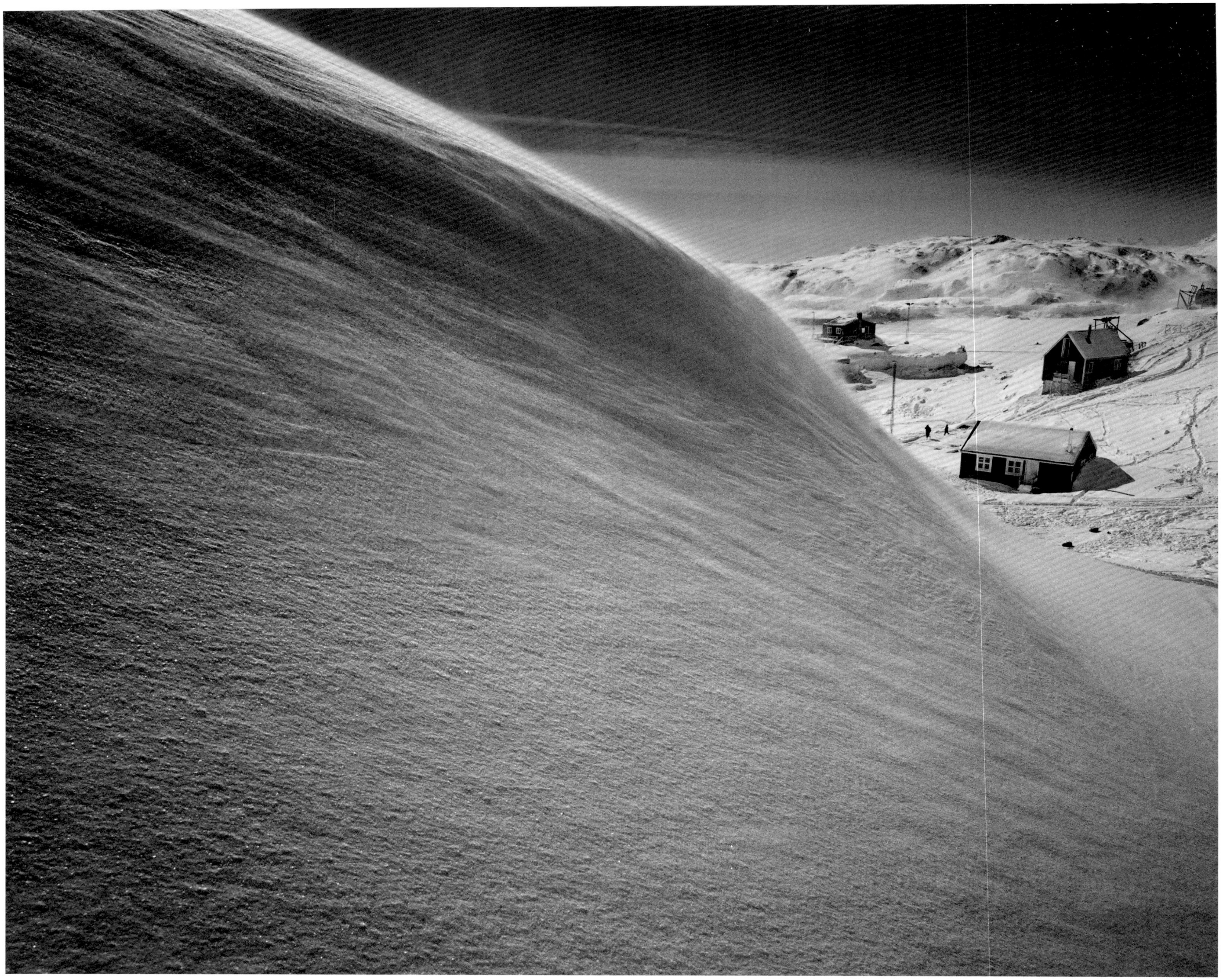

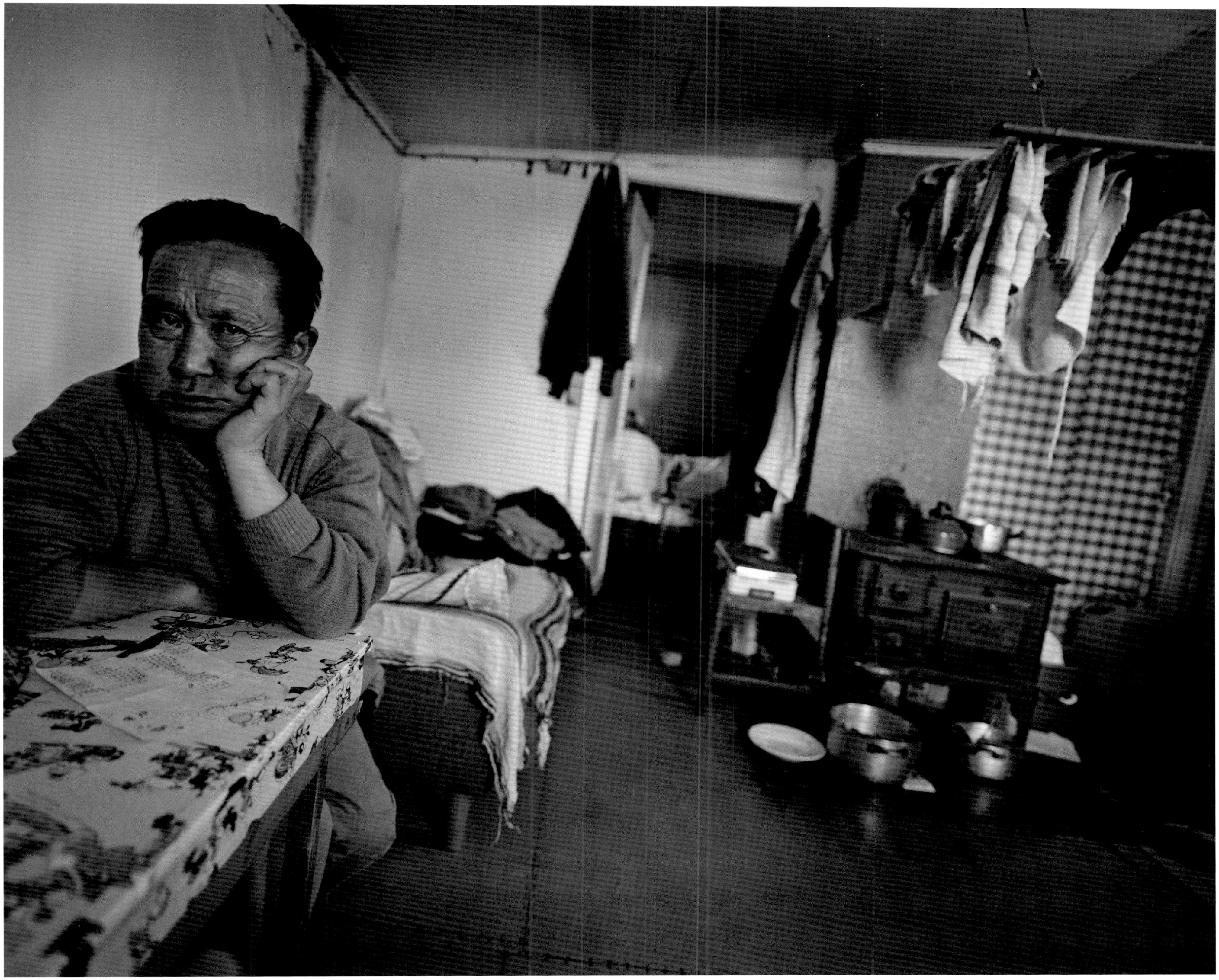

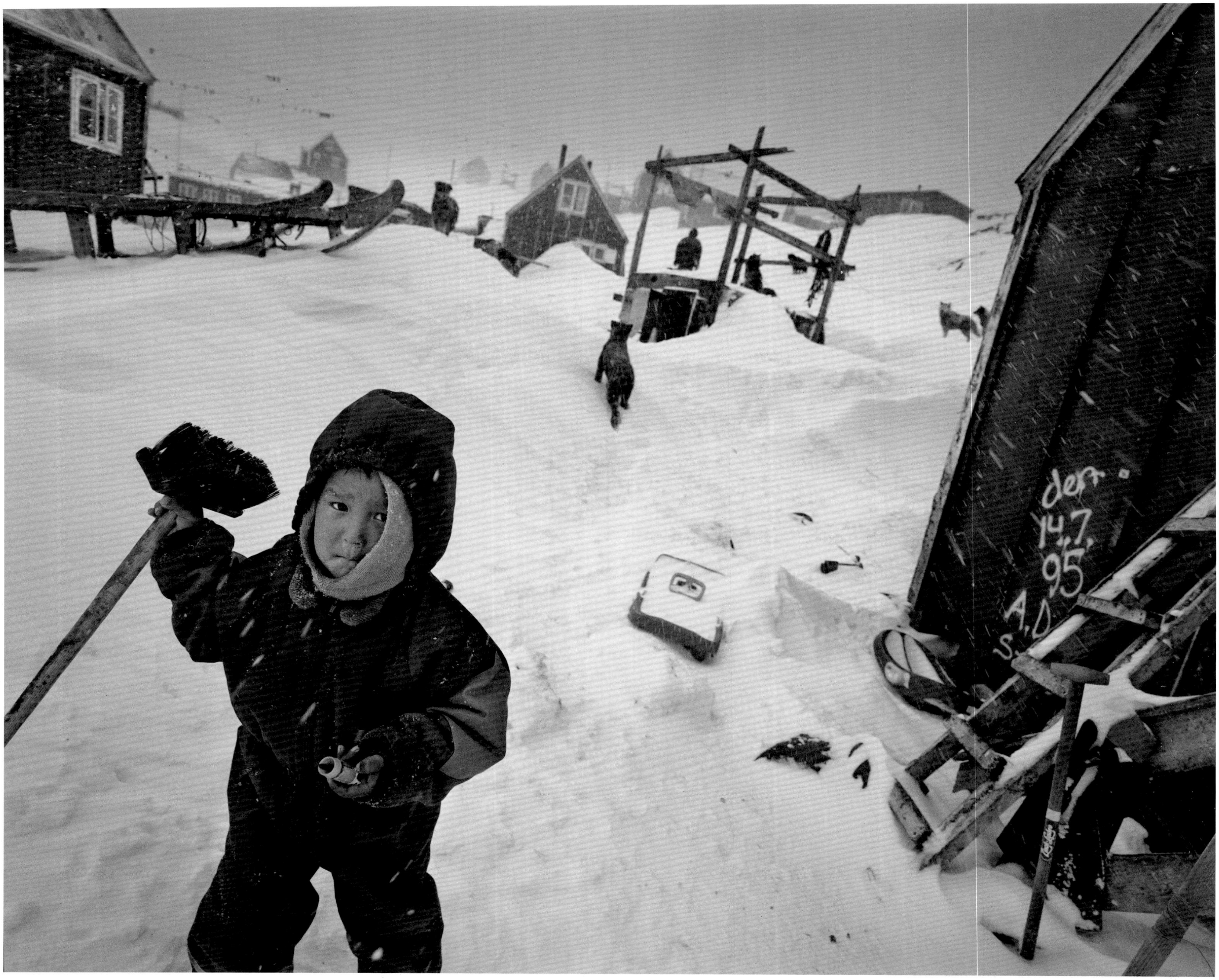
14.7.
95

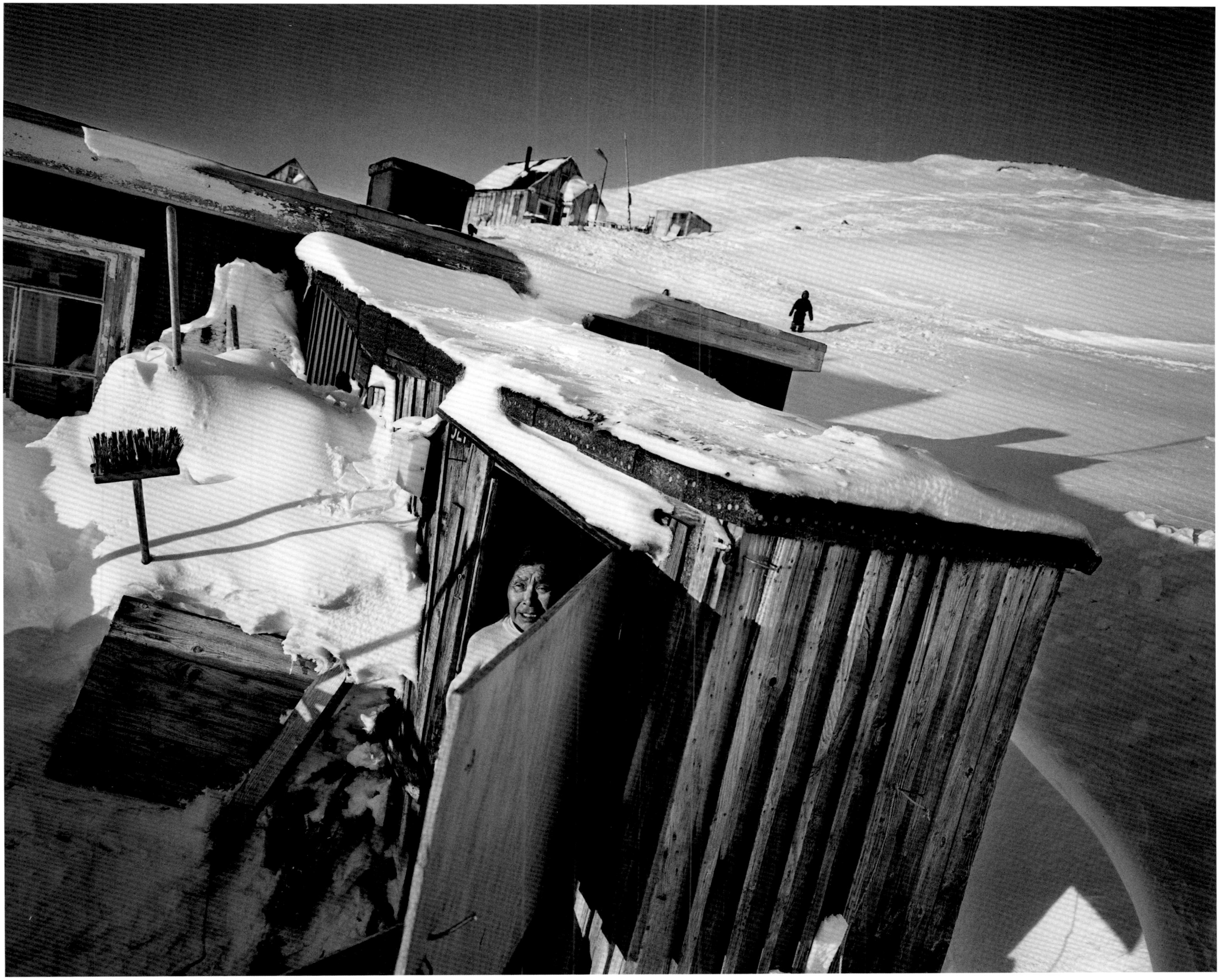

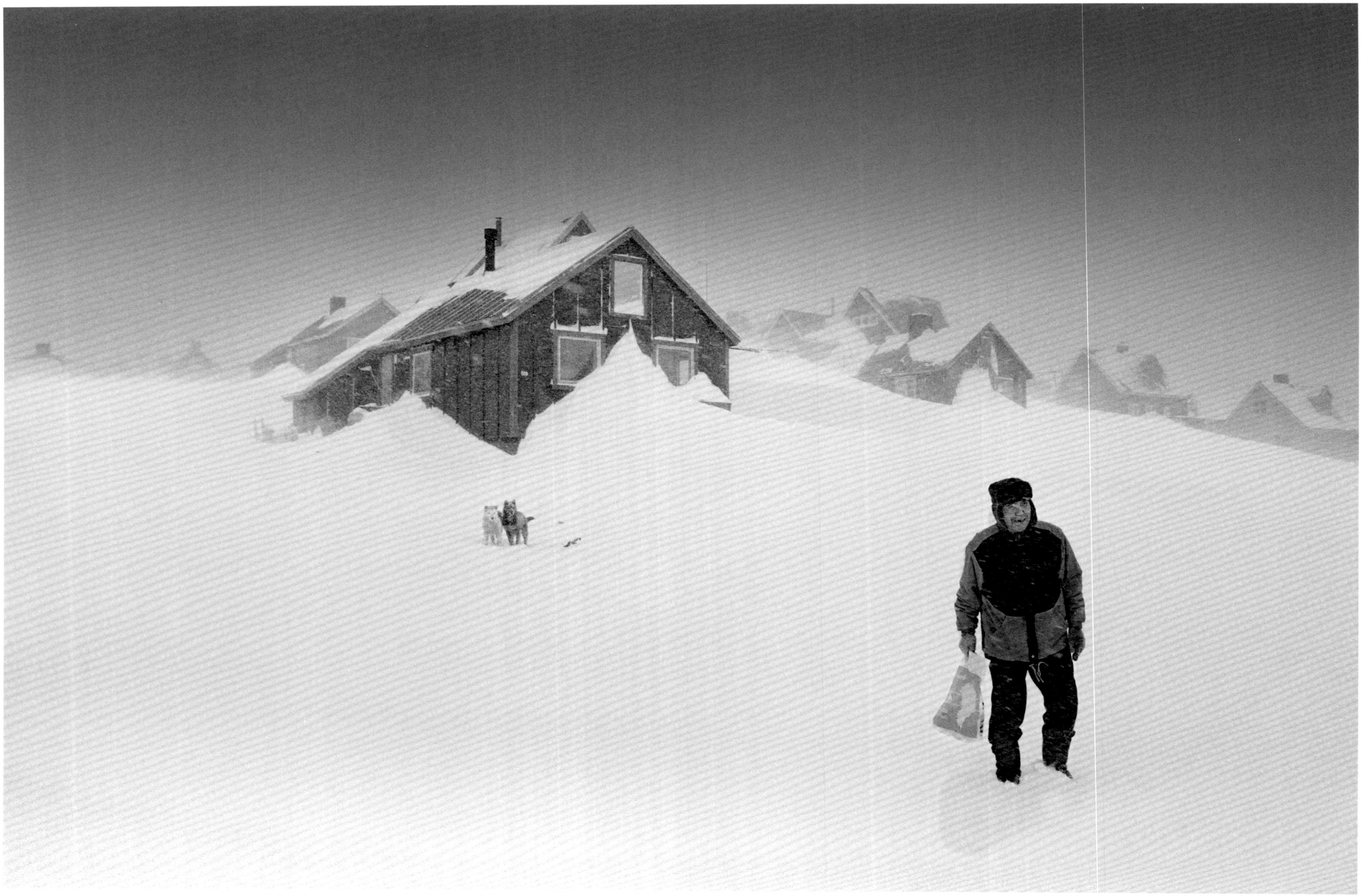

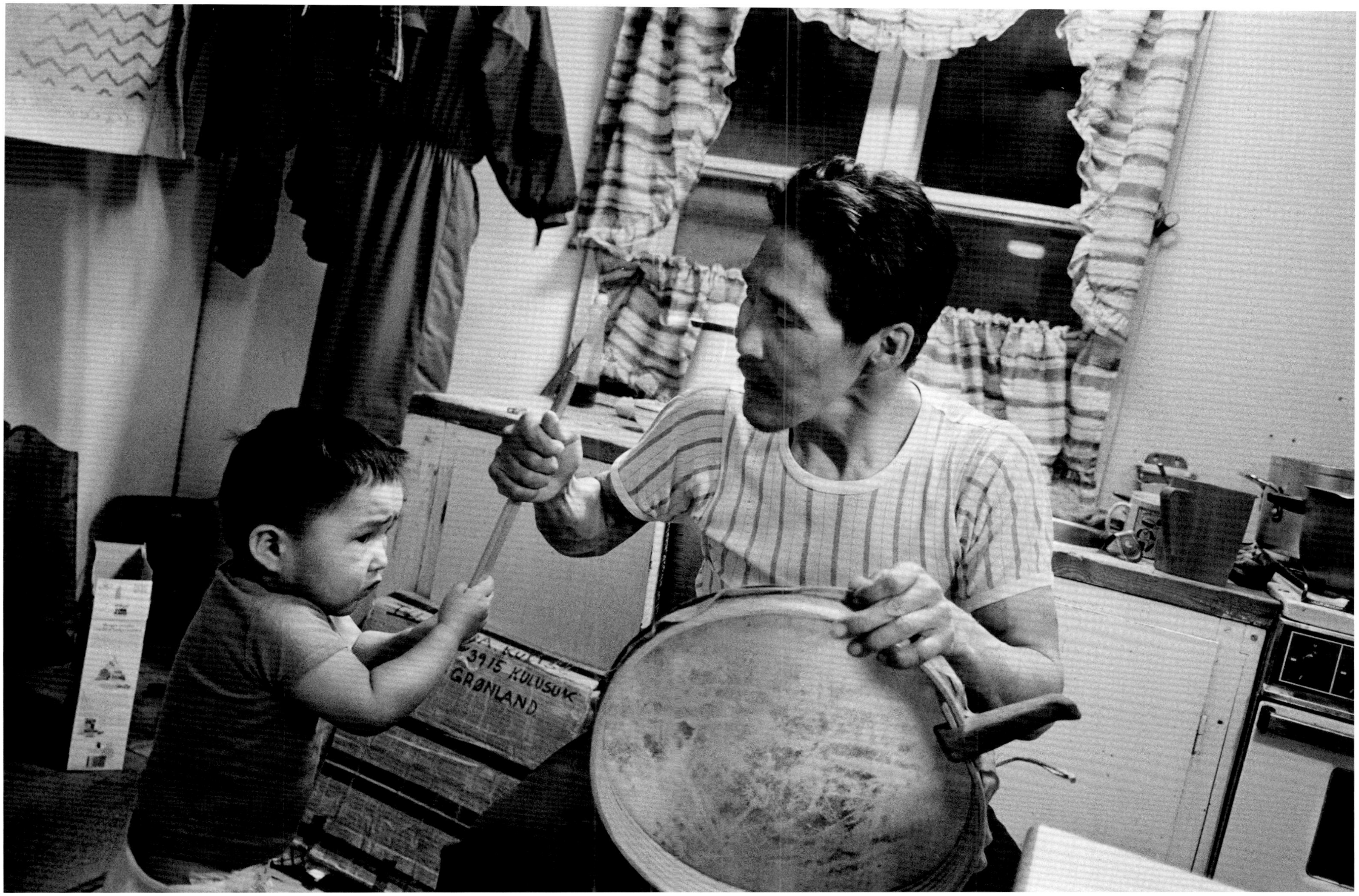
3915 KULUSUK
GRØNLAND

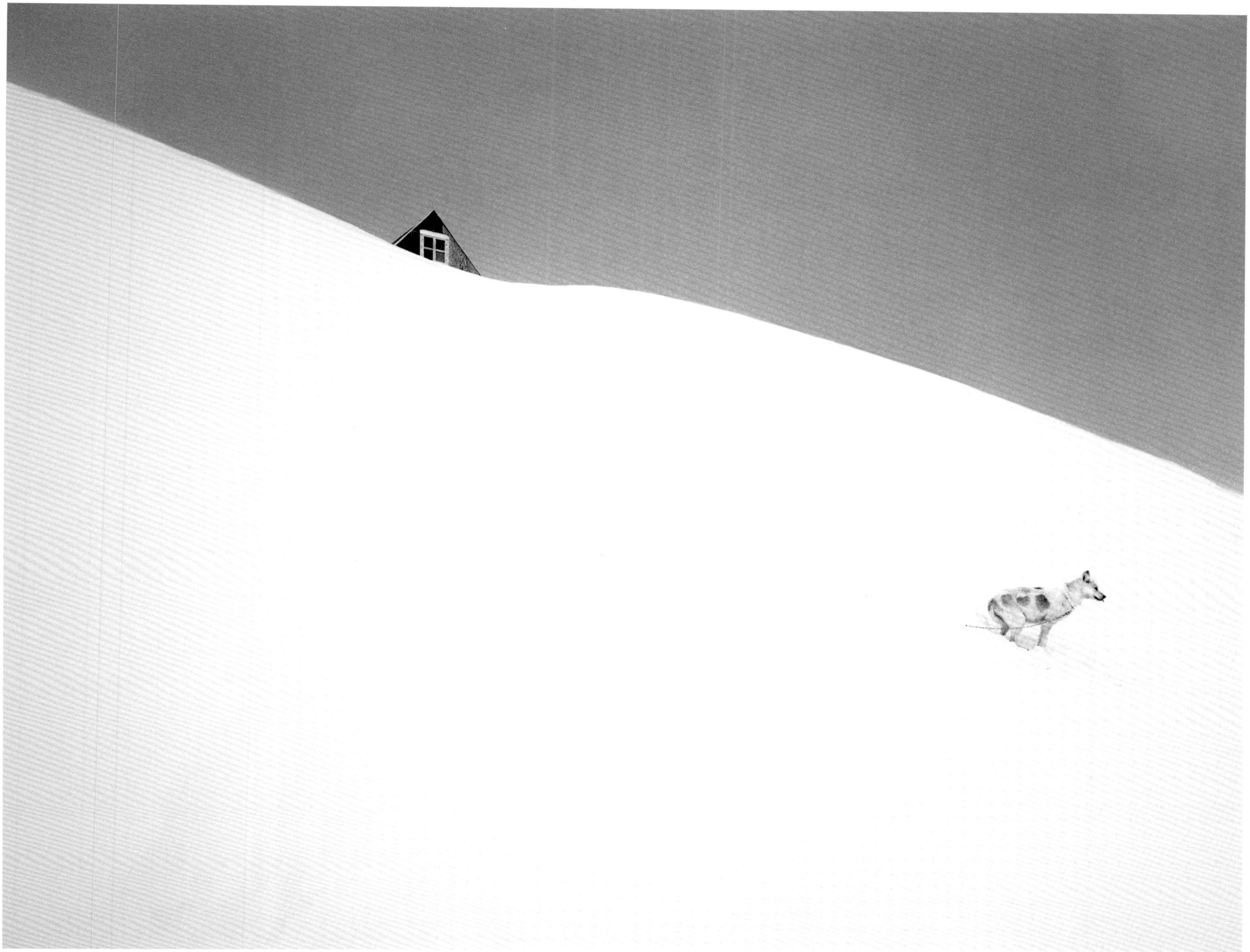

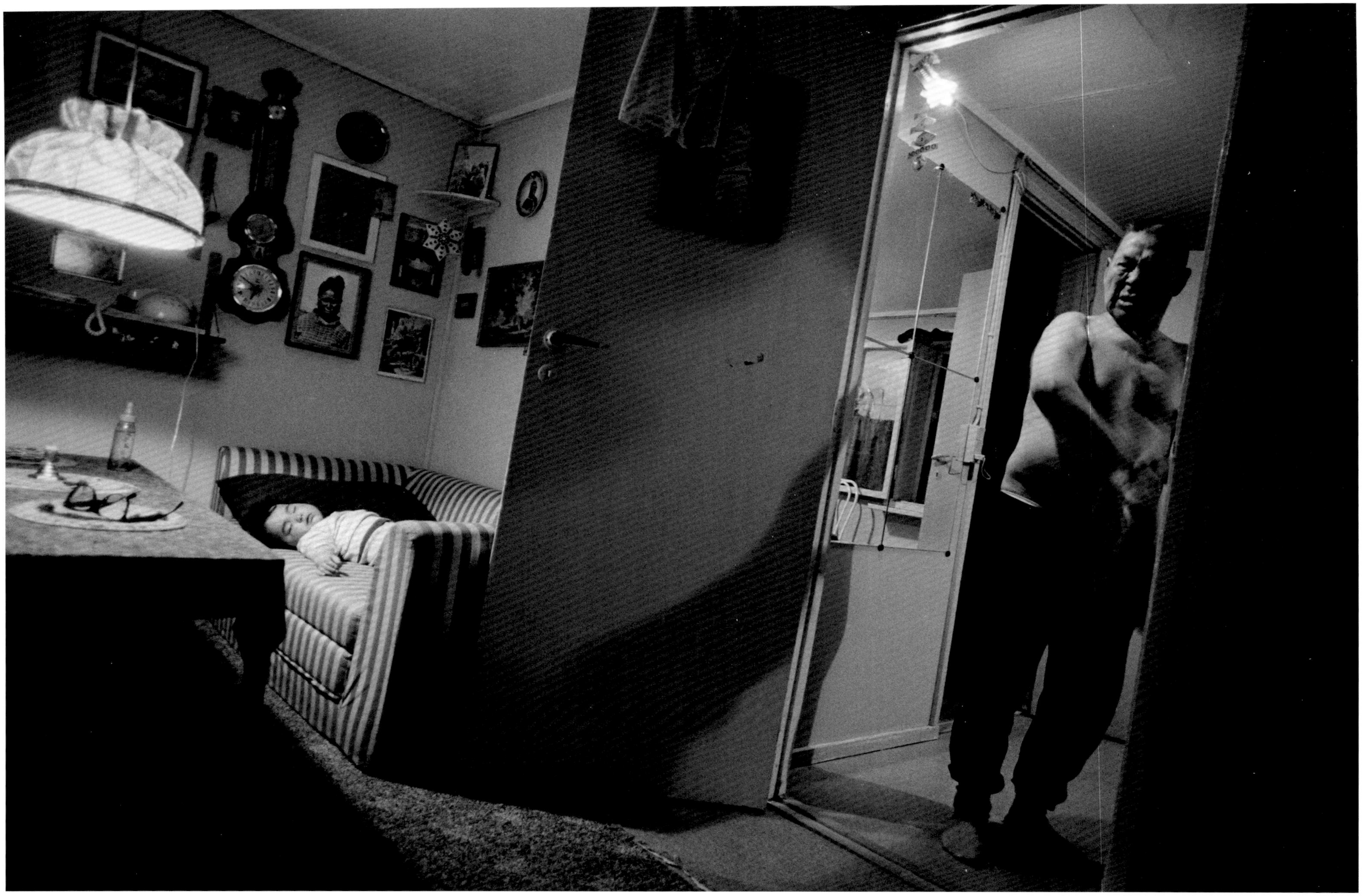

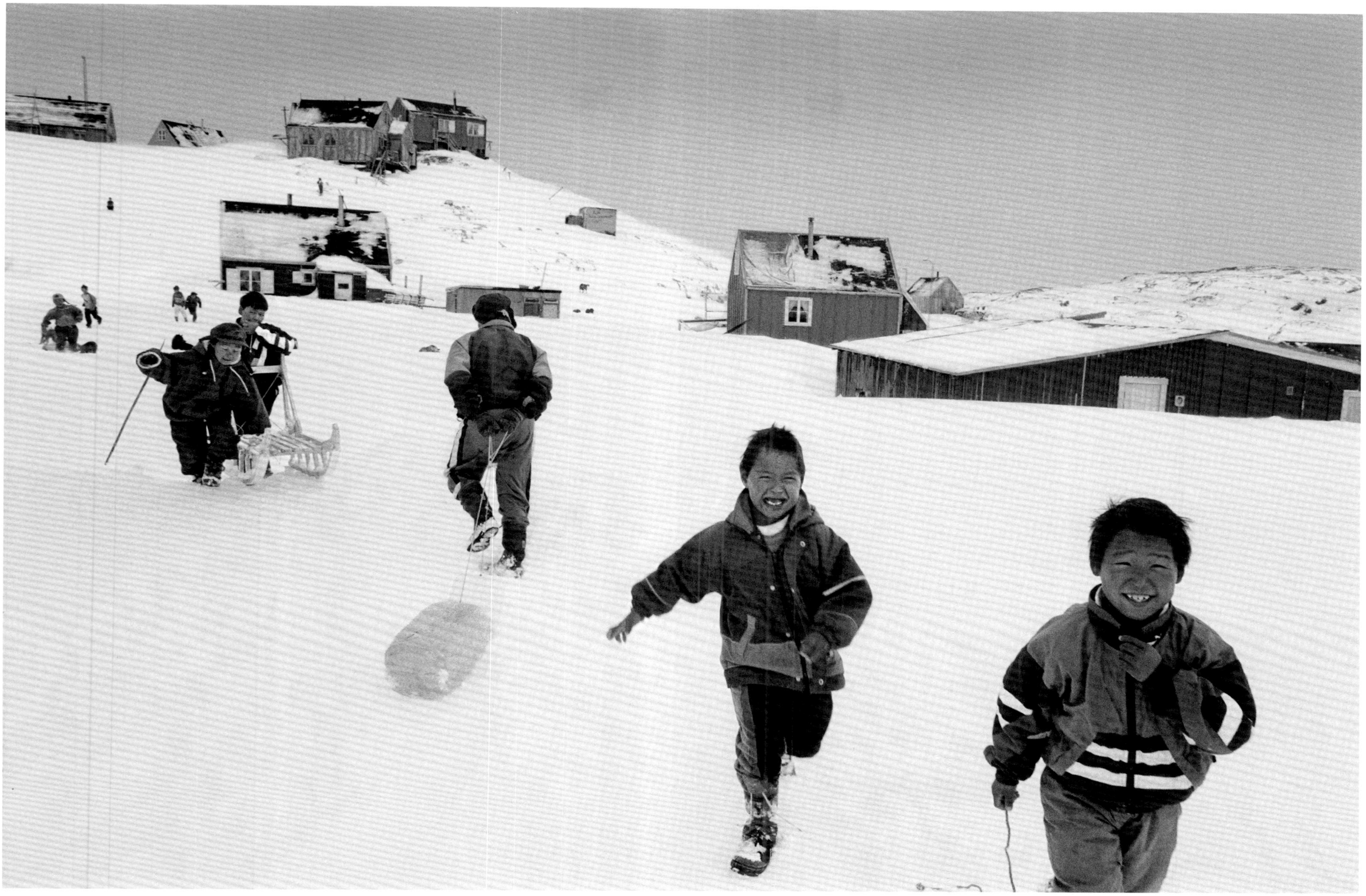

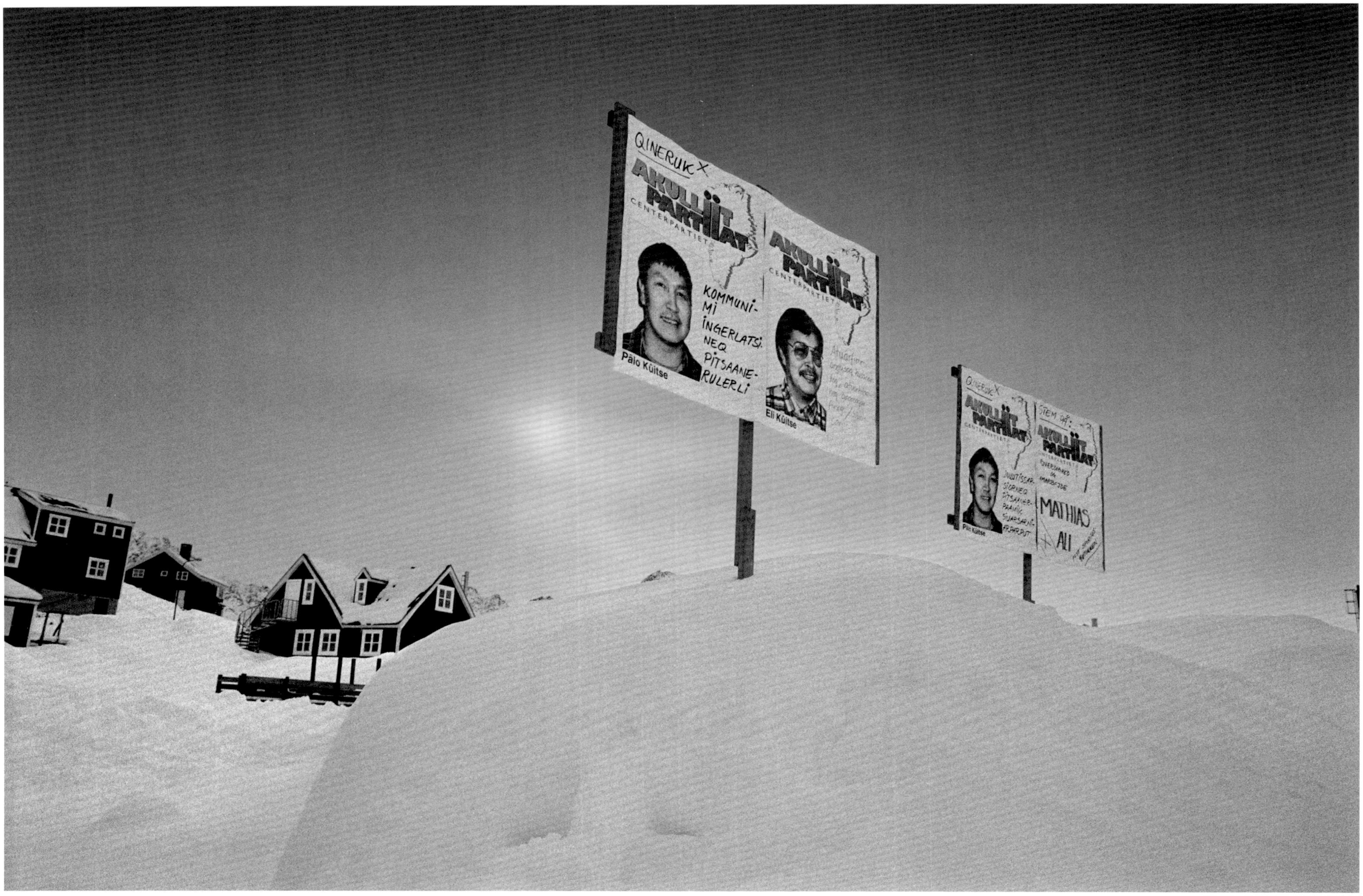
QINERUK X
AKULLIIT PARTIIAT
CENTERPARTIET
KOMMUNI-MI INGERLATSI-NEQ PITSAANE-RULERLI
Pâlo Kûitse
AKULLIIT PARTIIAT
CENTERPARTIET
Eli Kûitse
MATHIAS
ALI

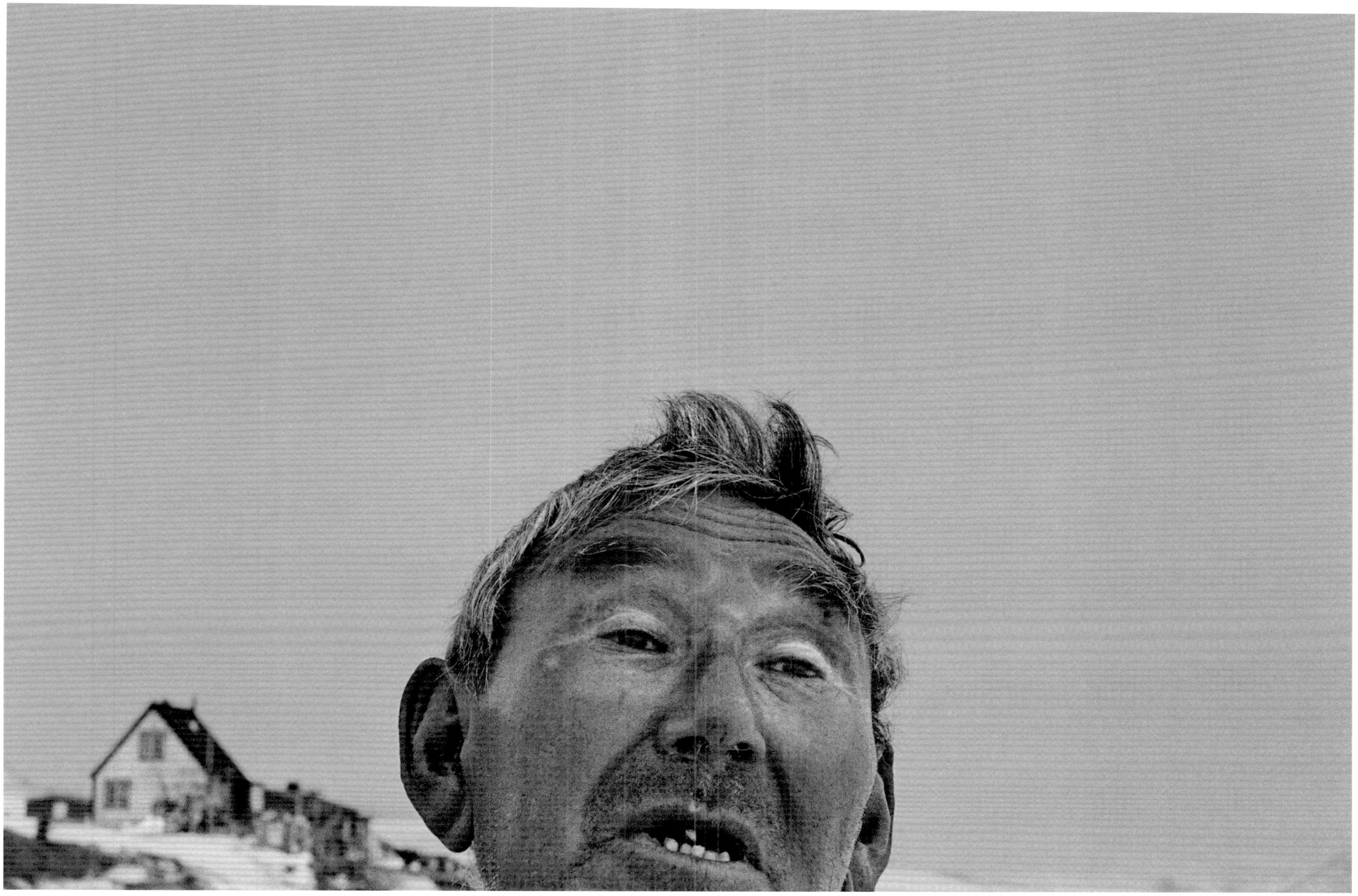

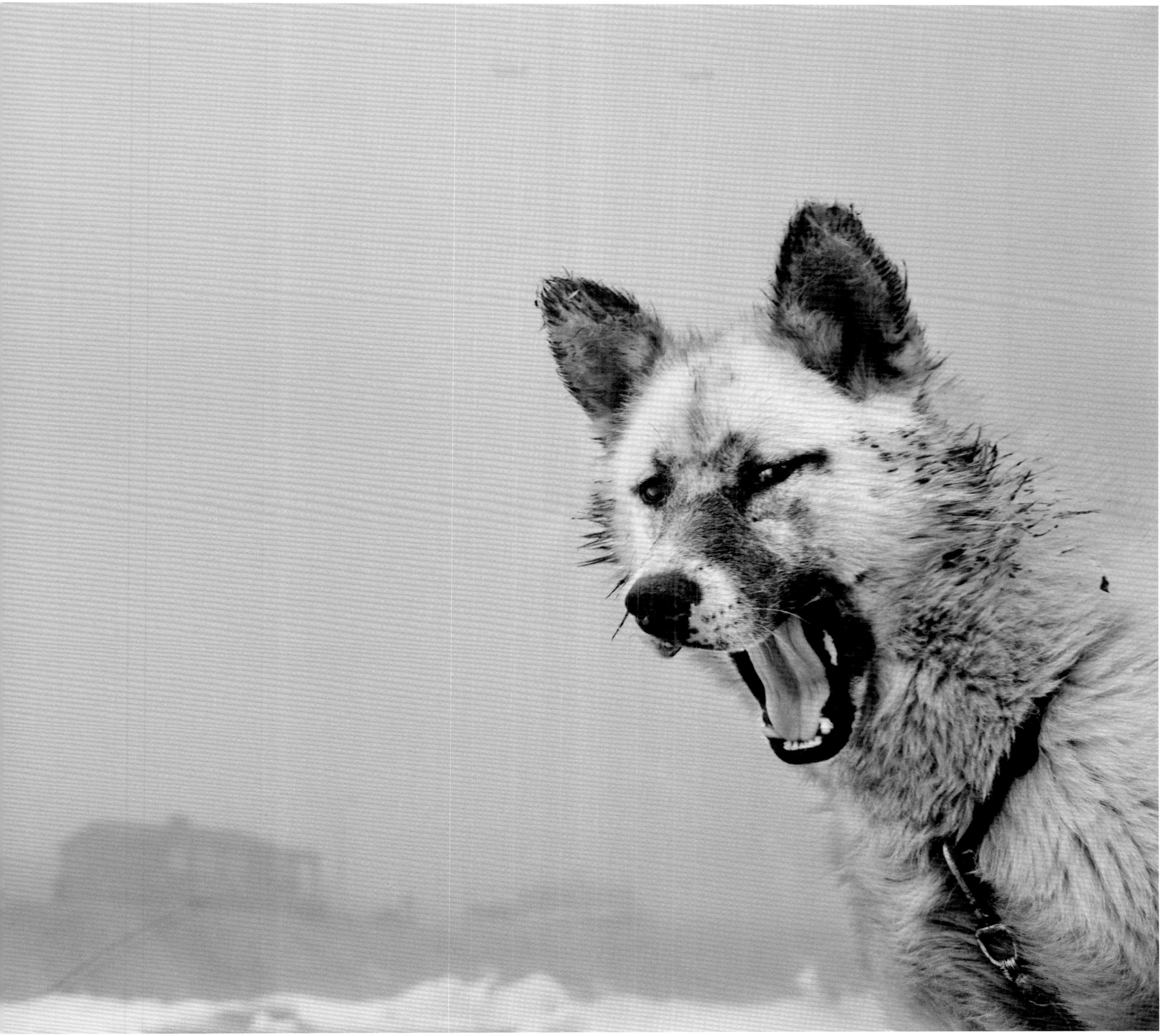

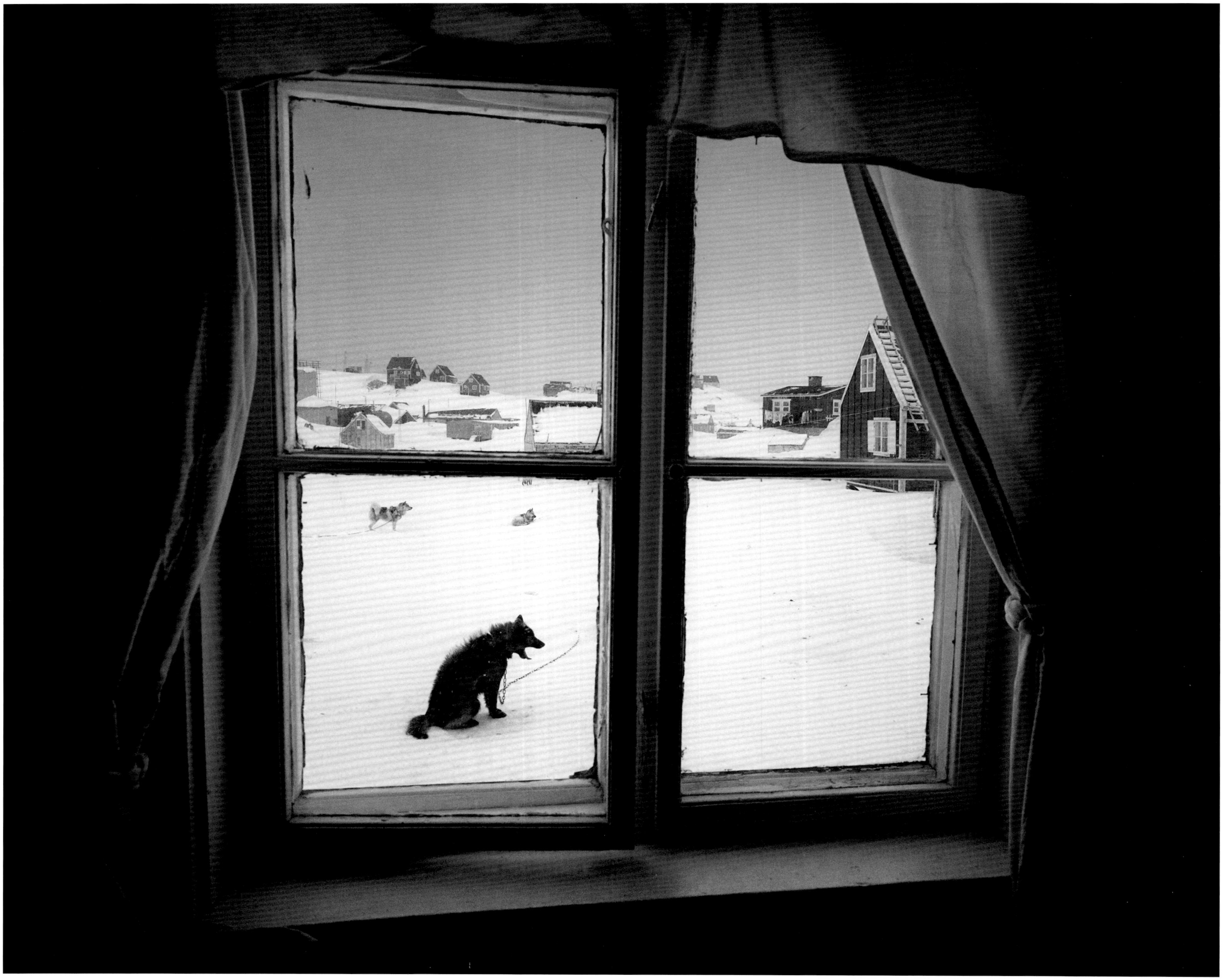

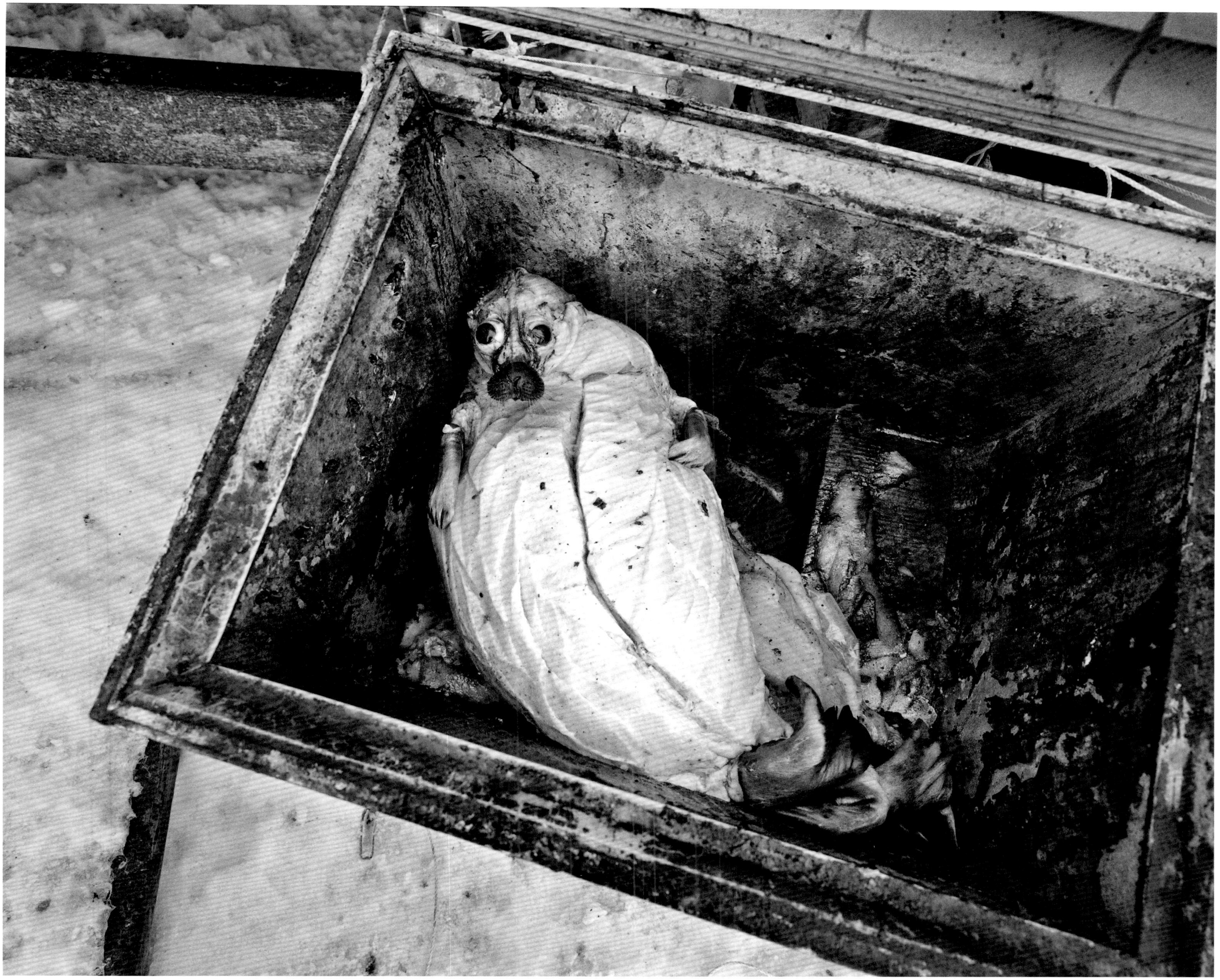

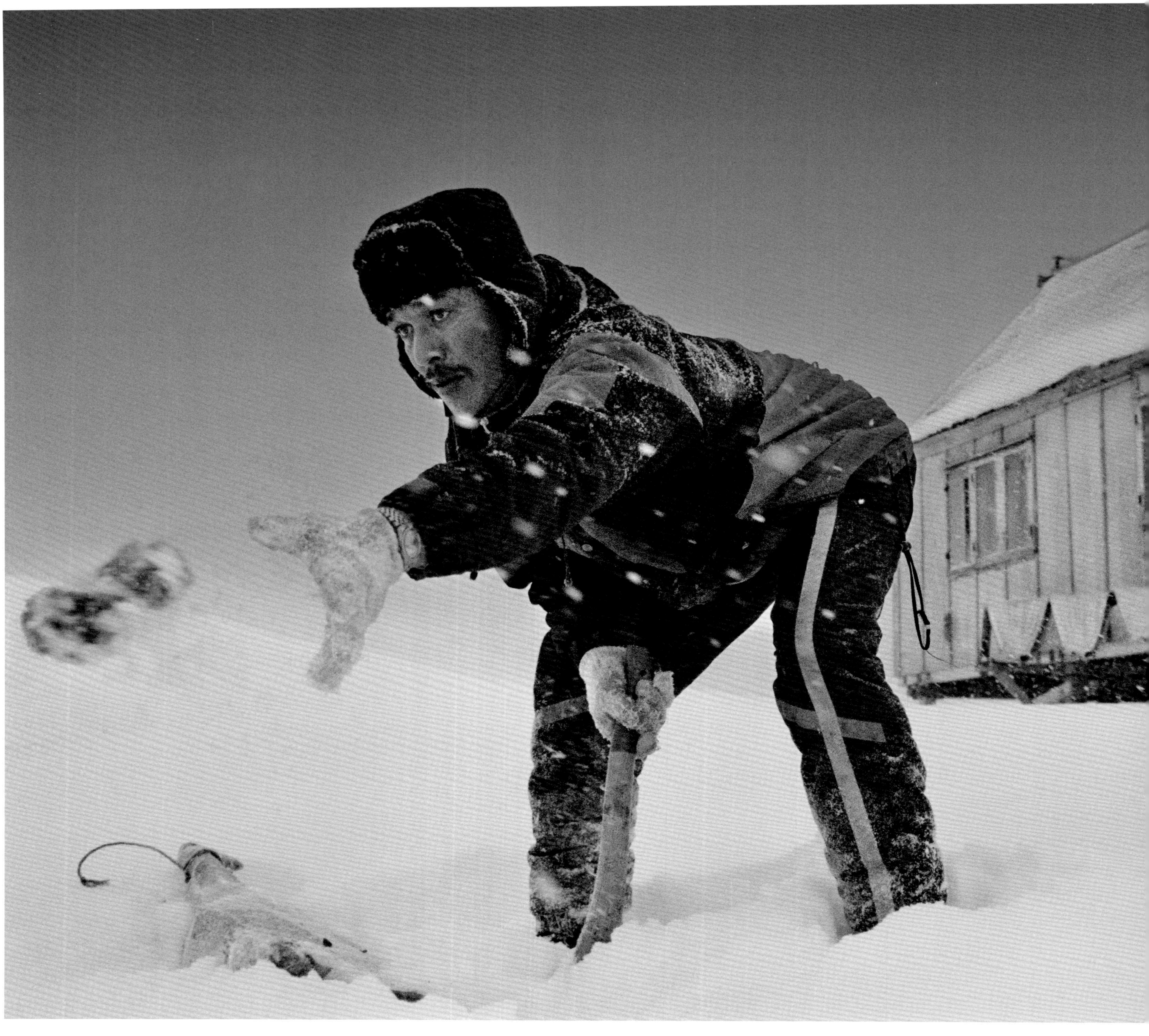

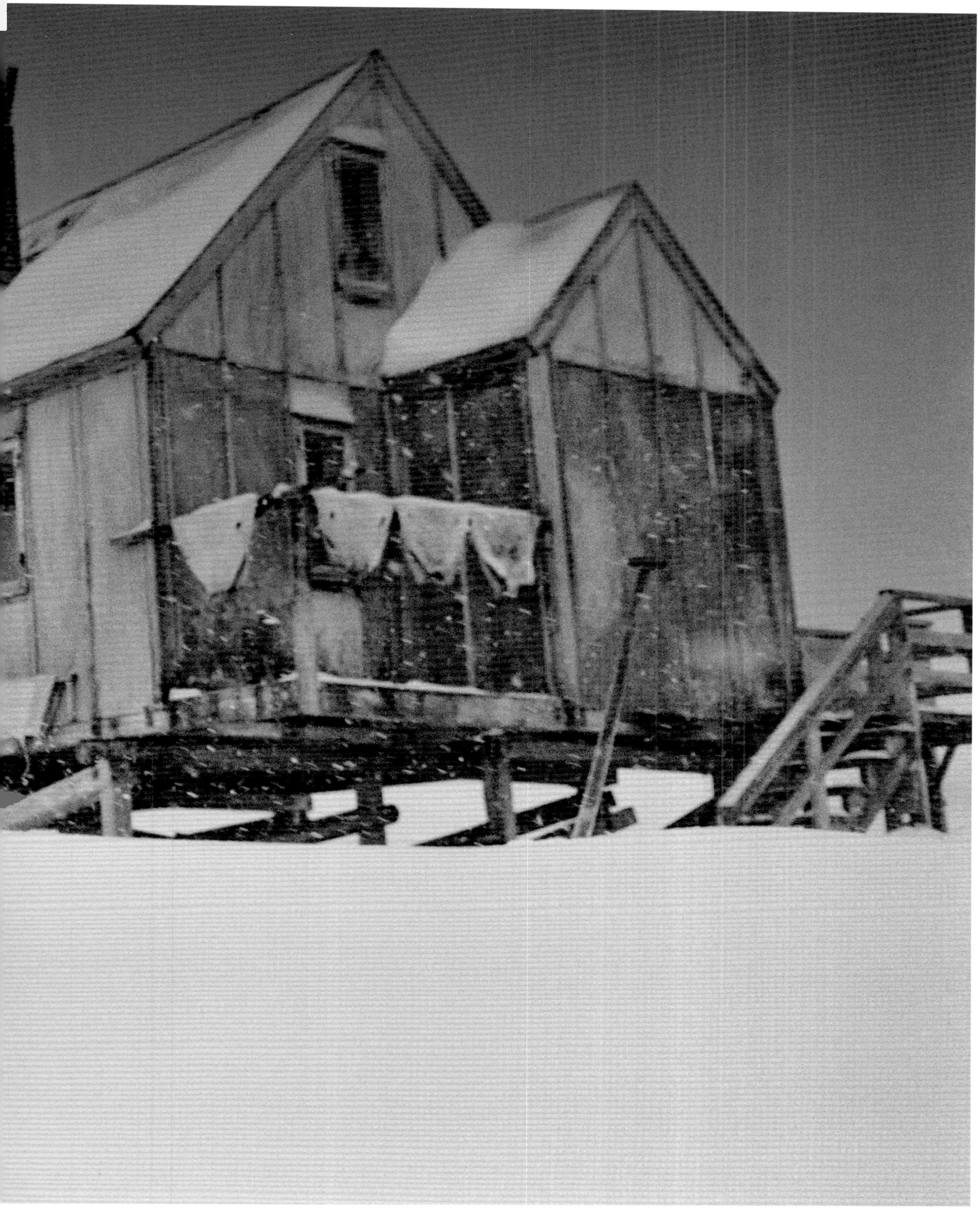

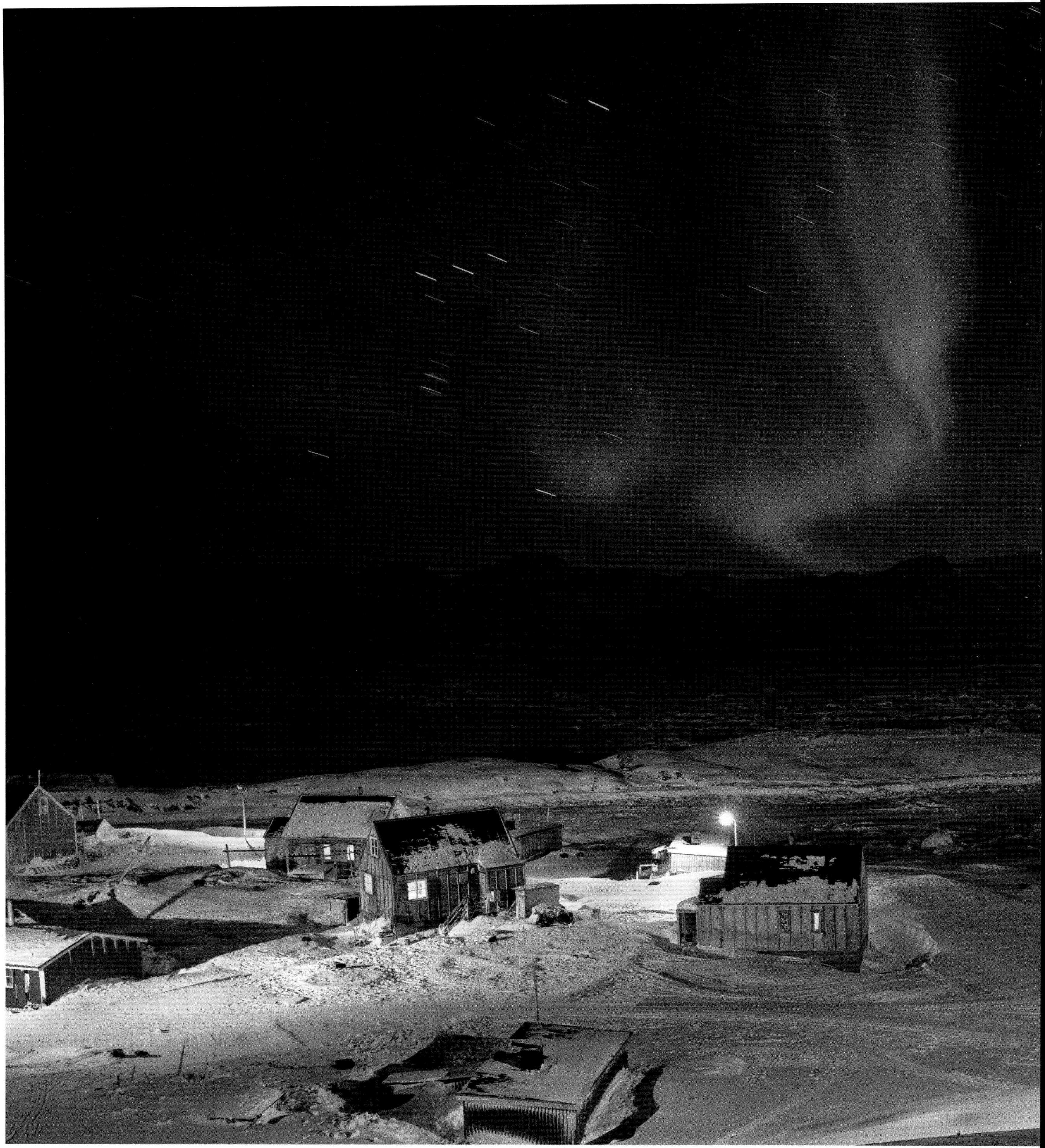

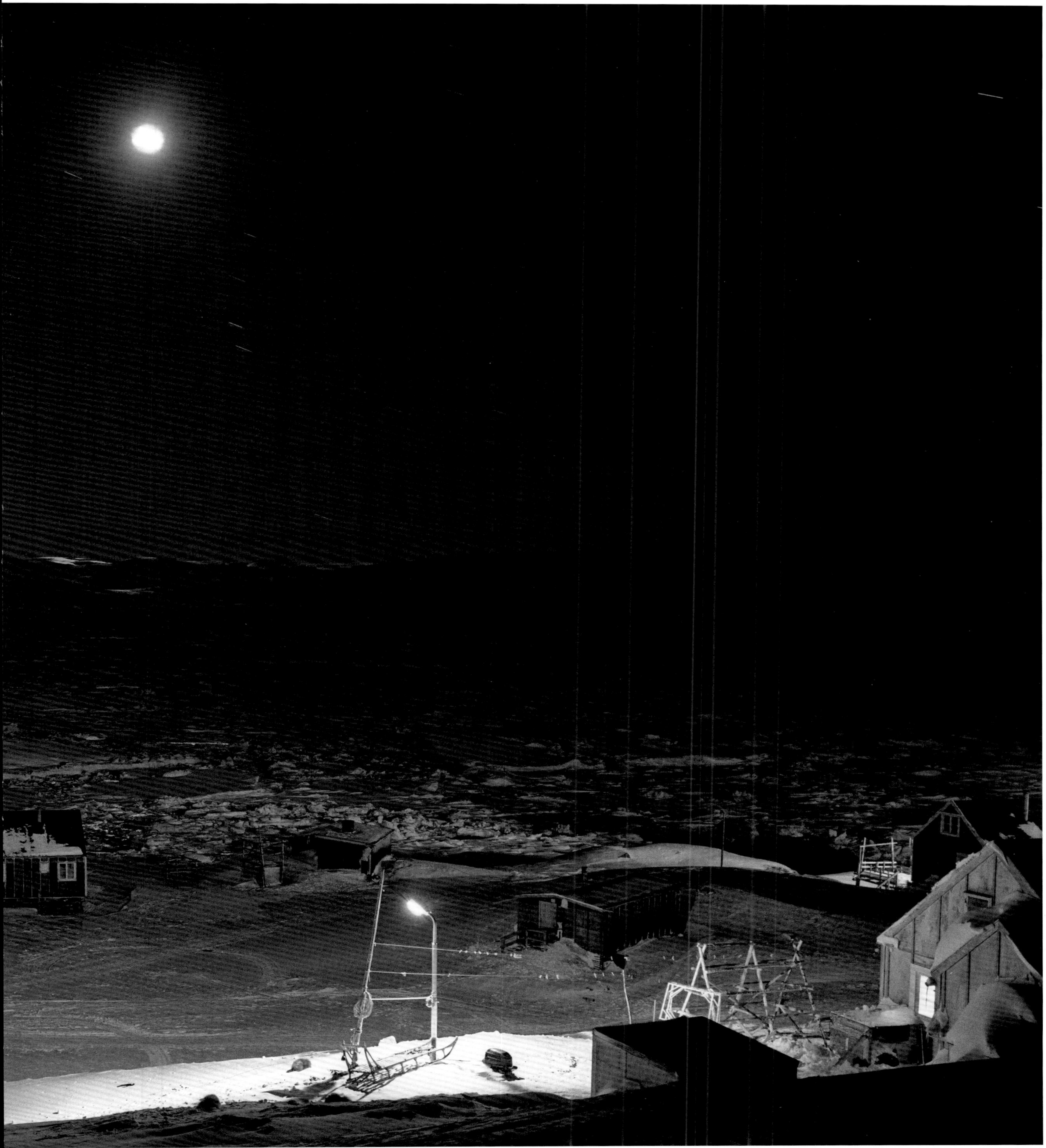

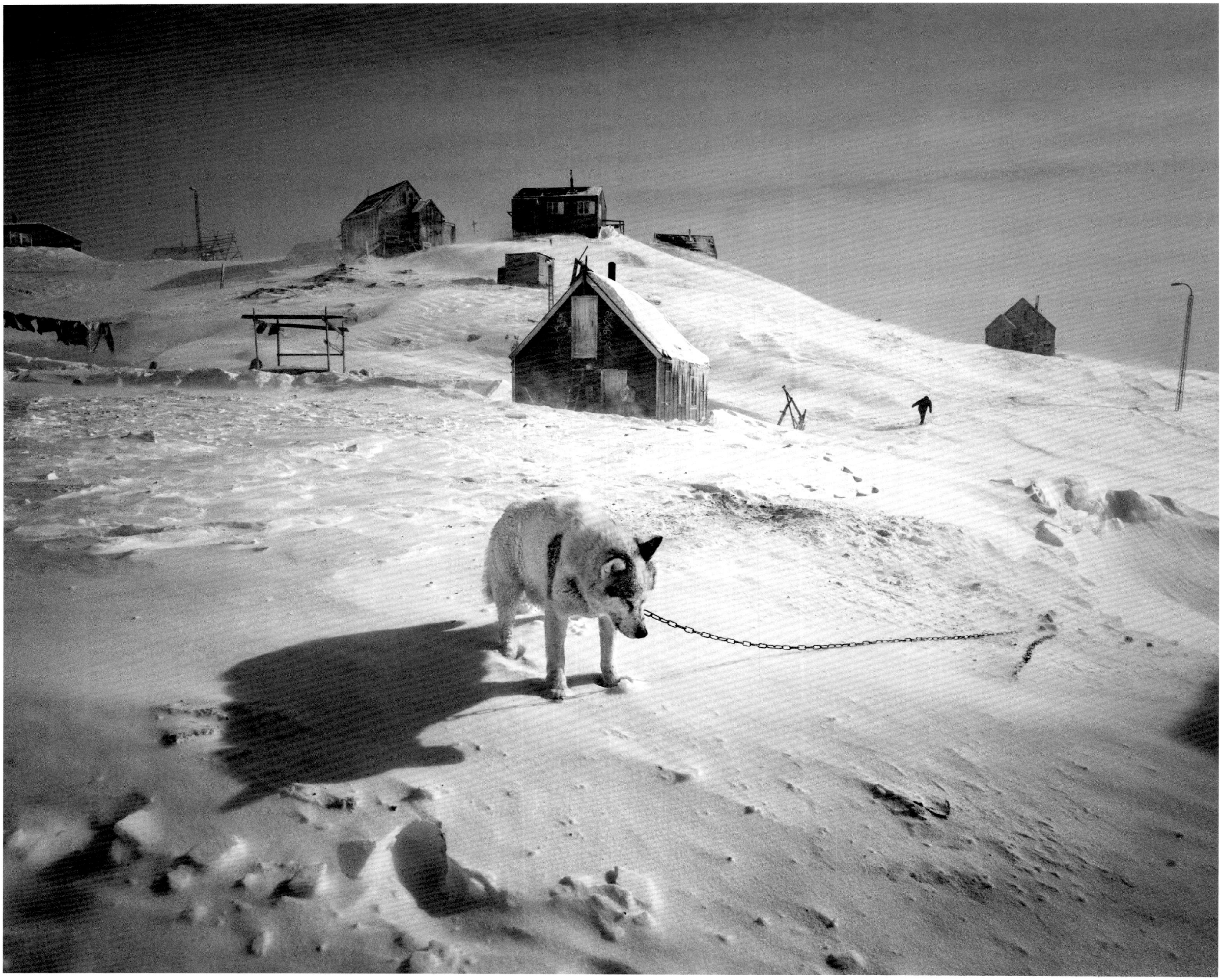

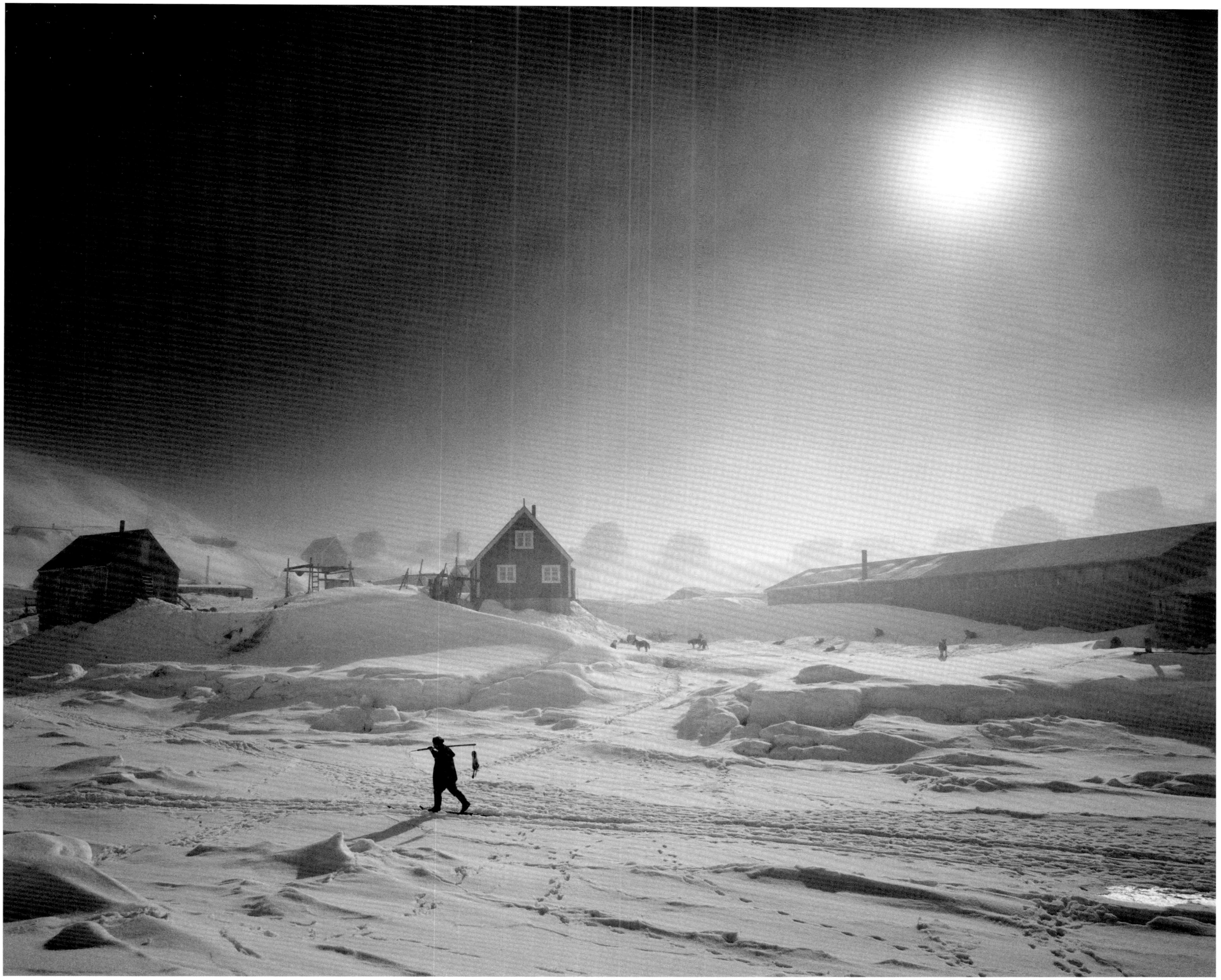

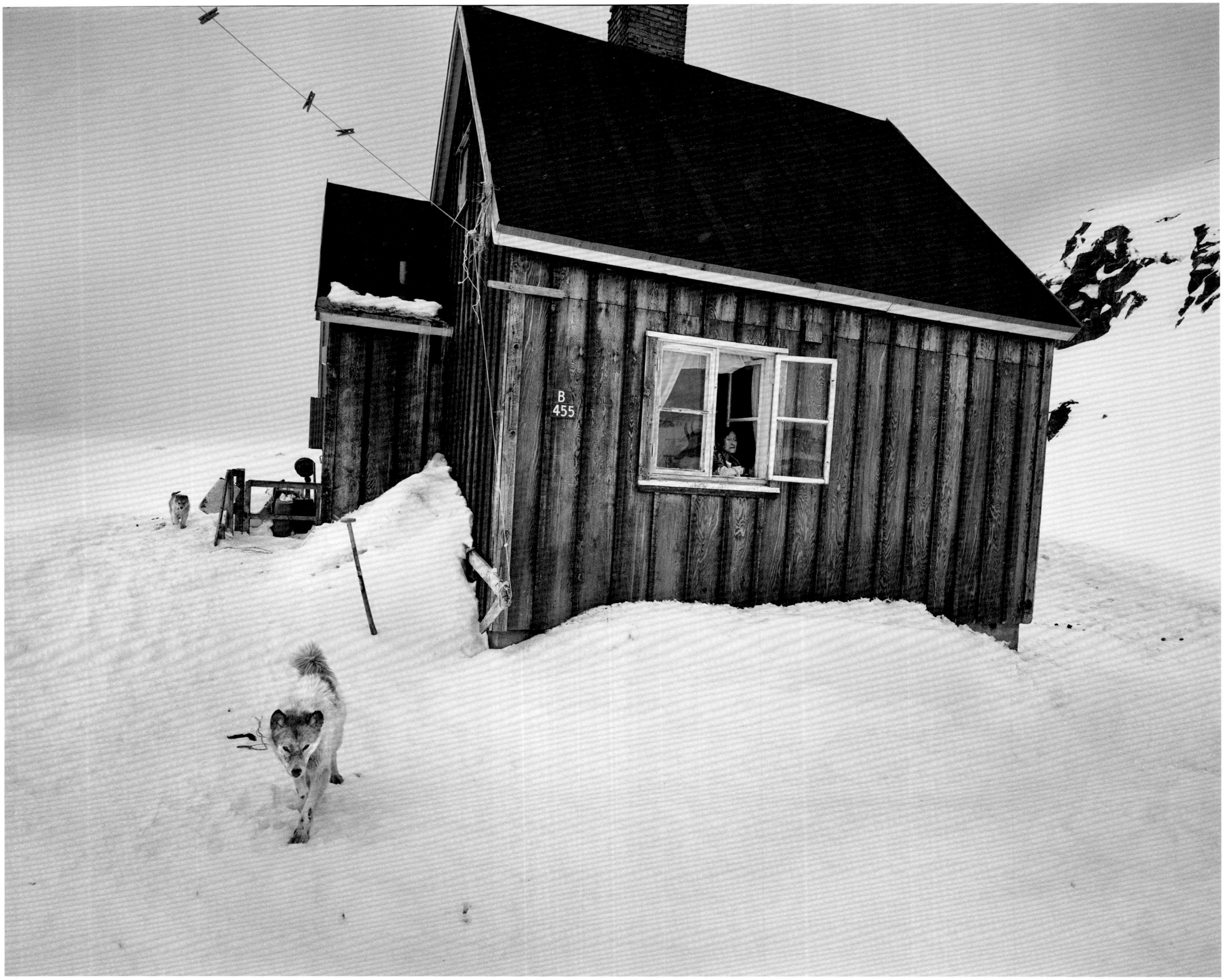
B
455

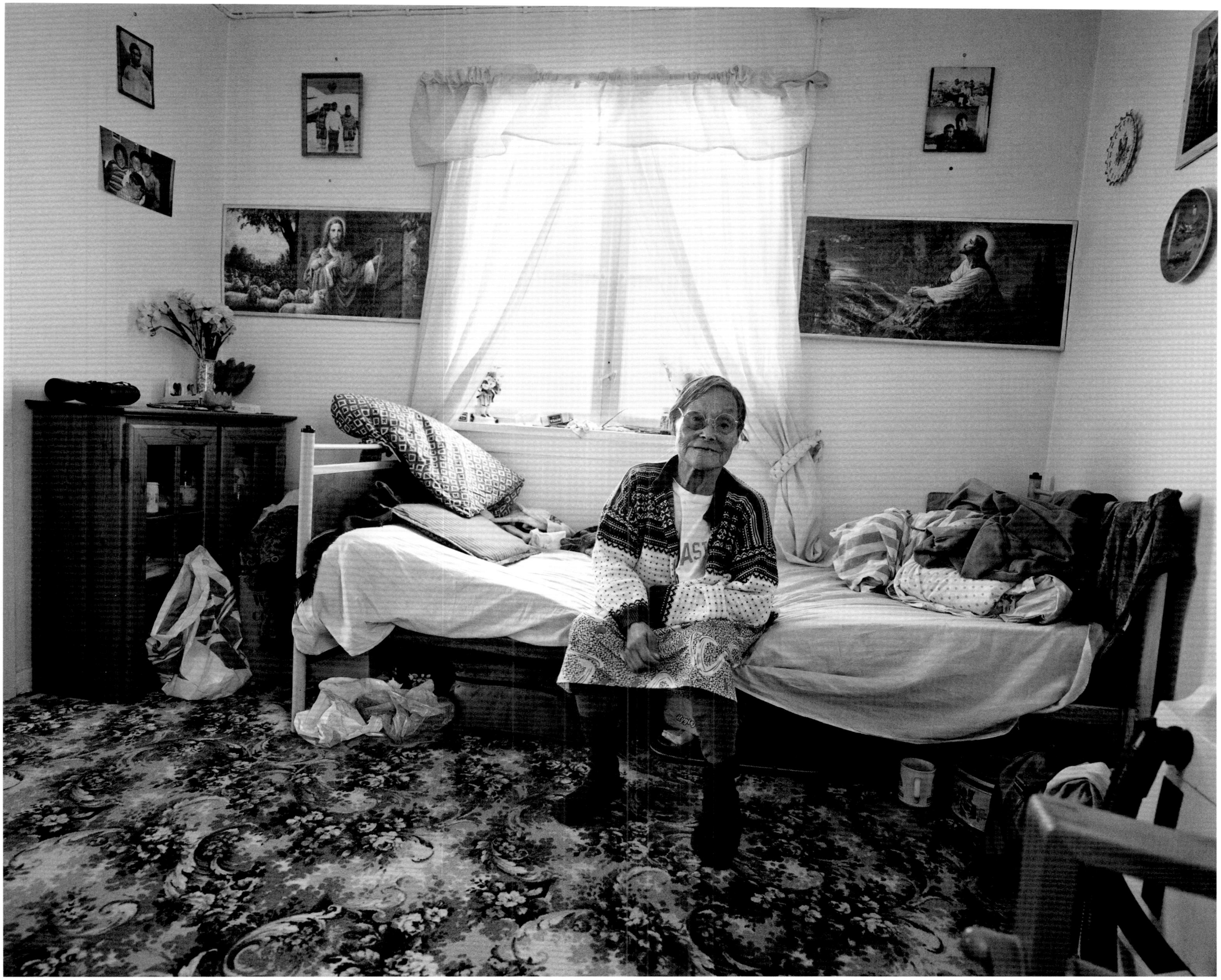

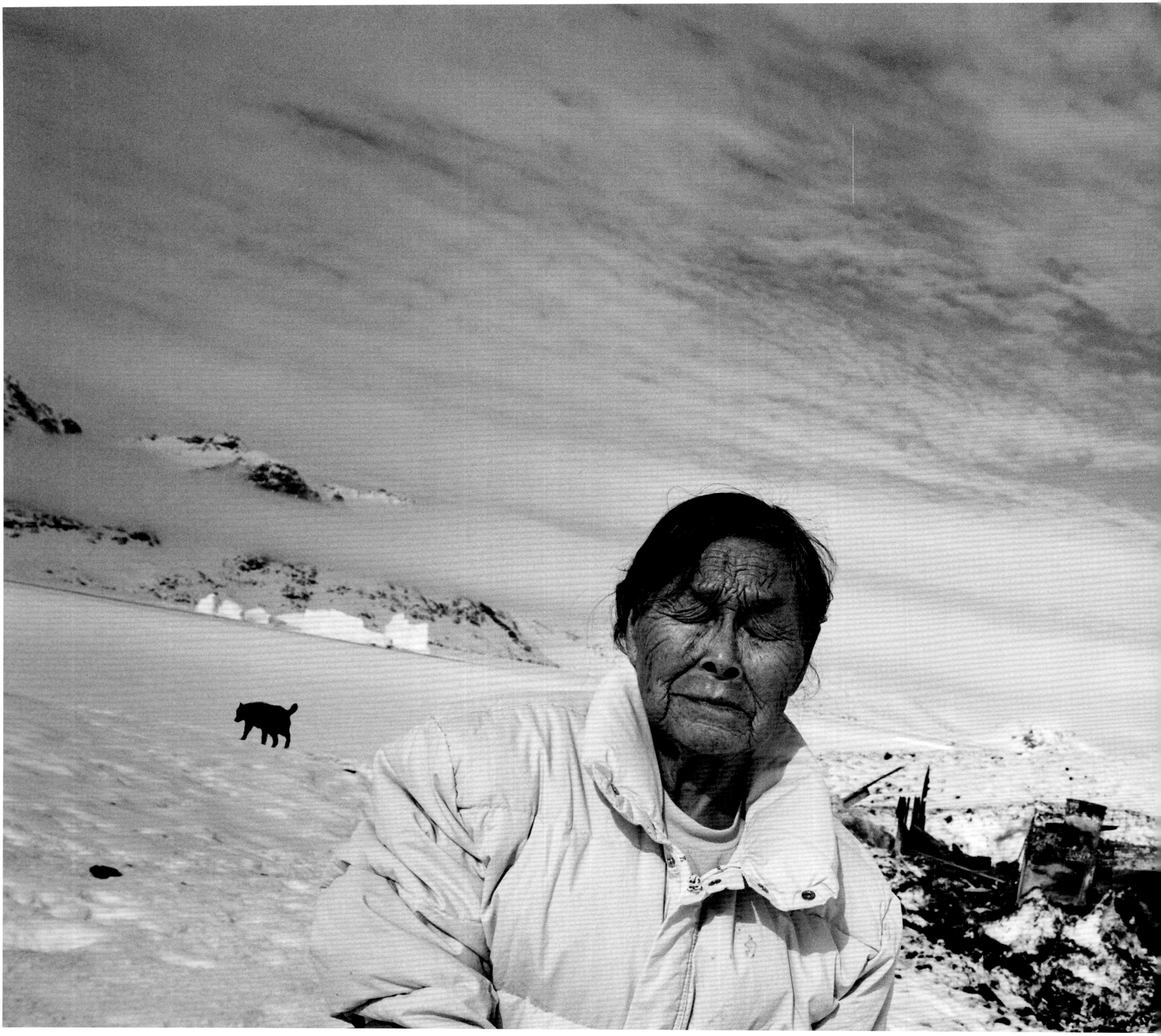

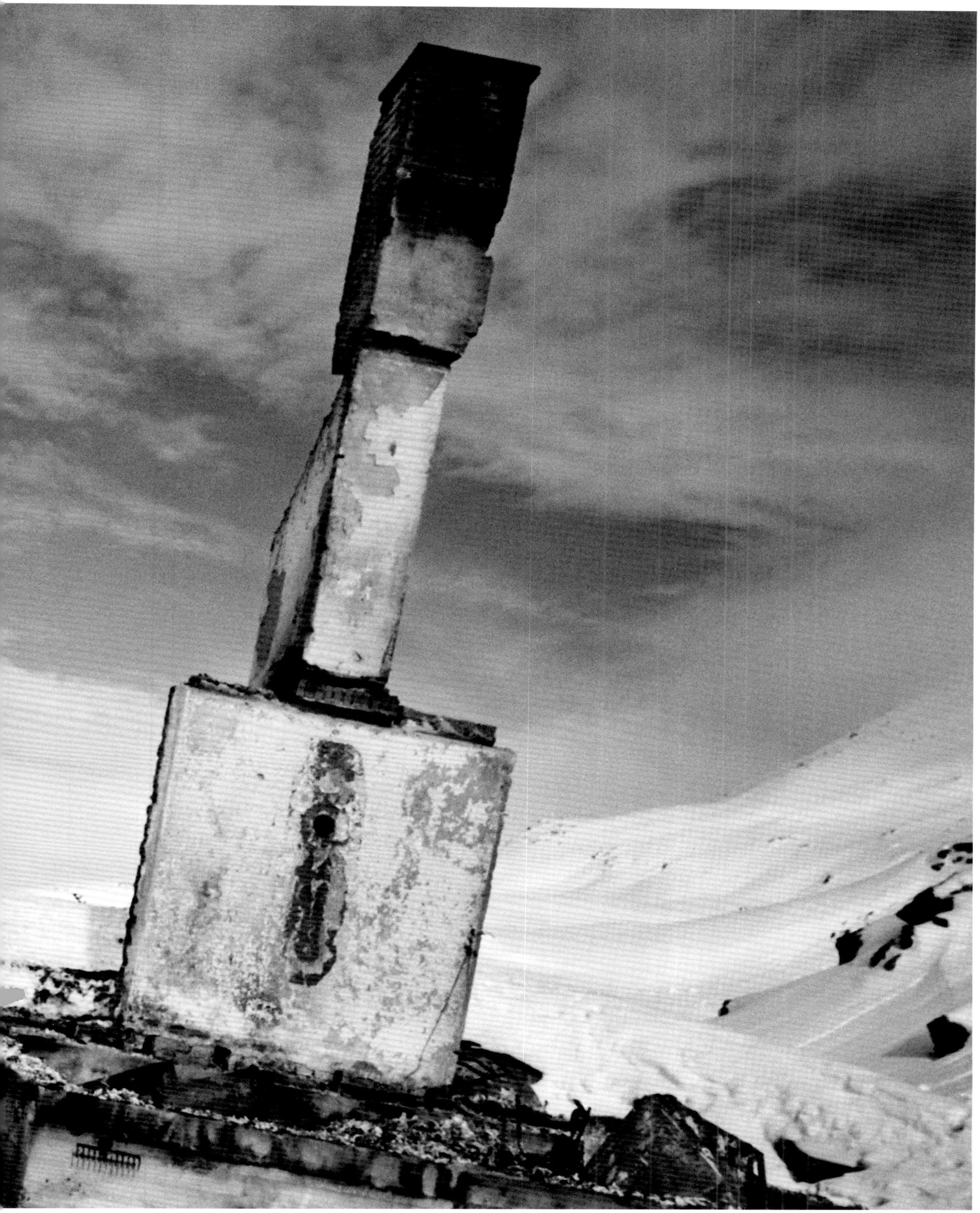

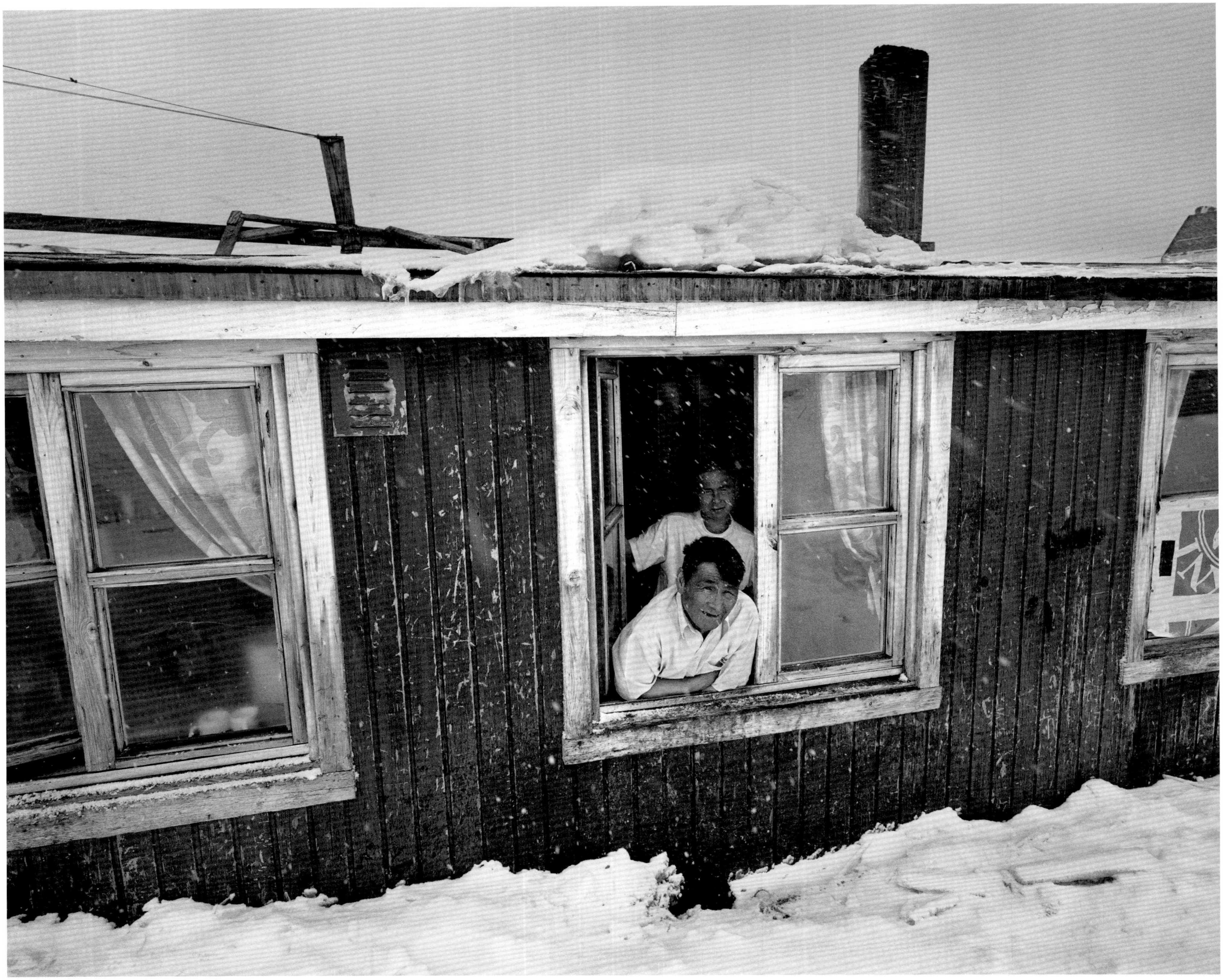

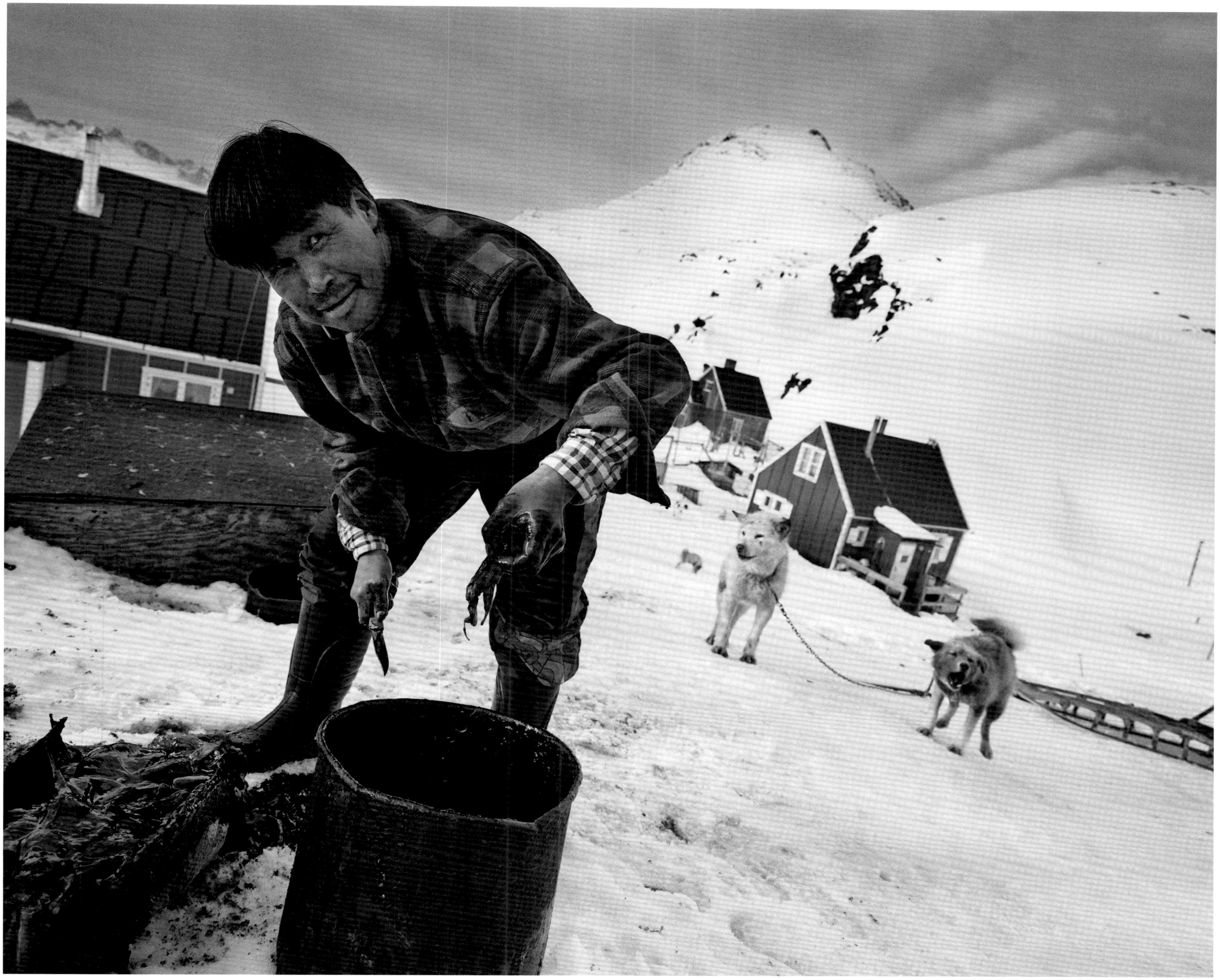

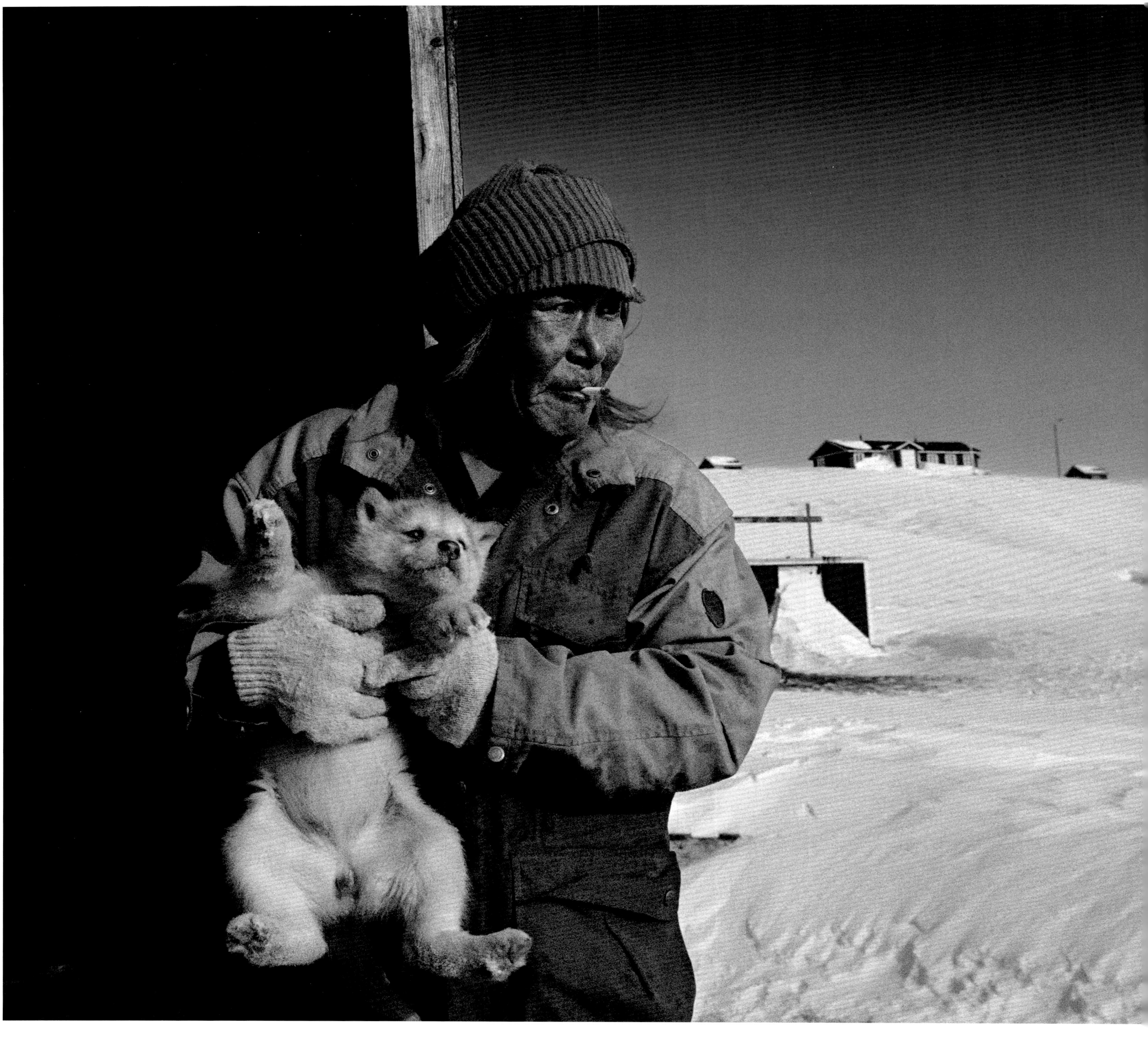

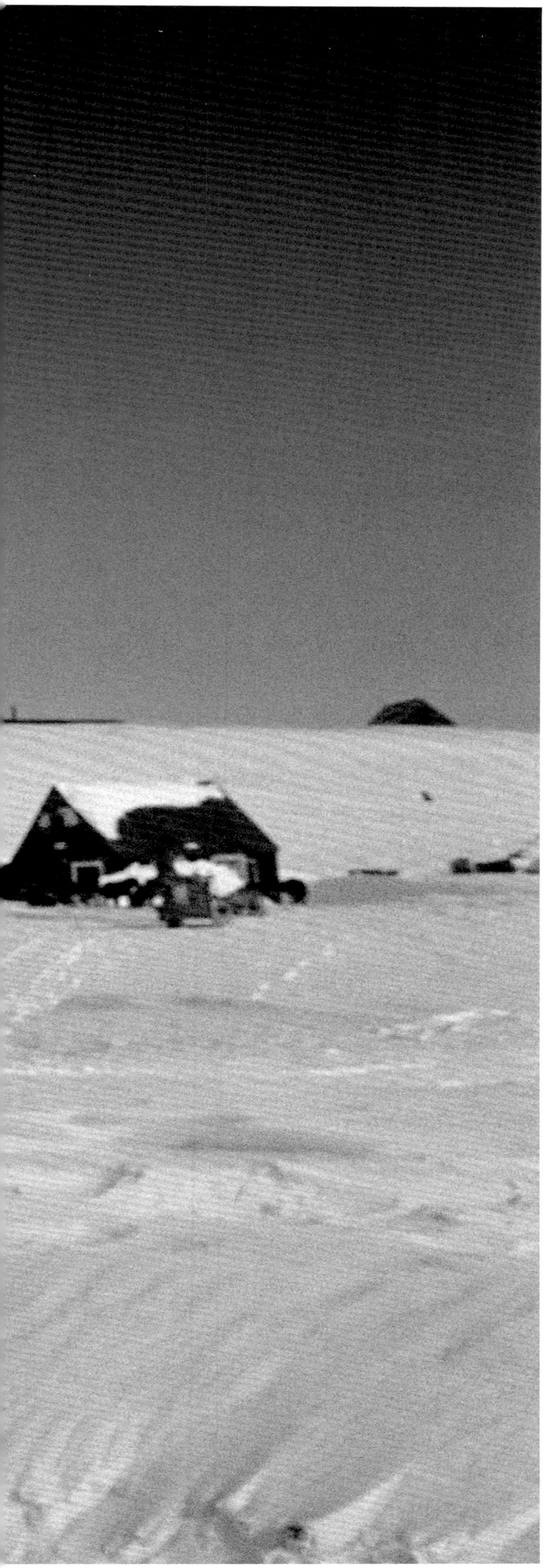

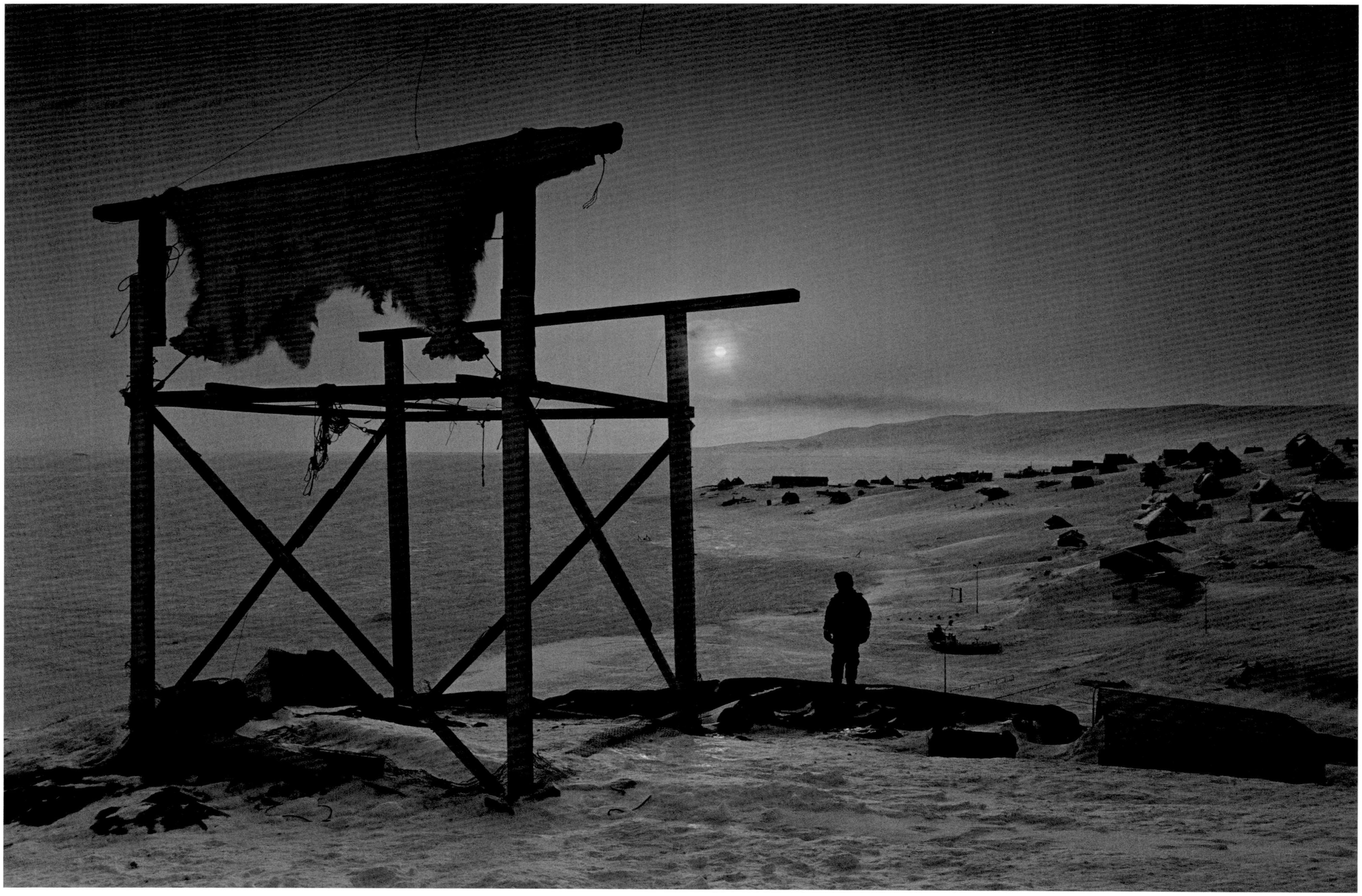

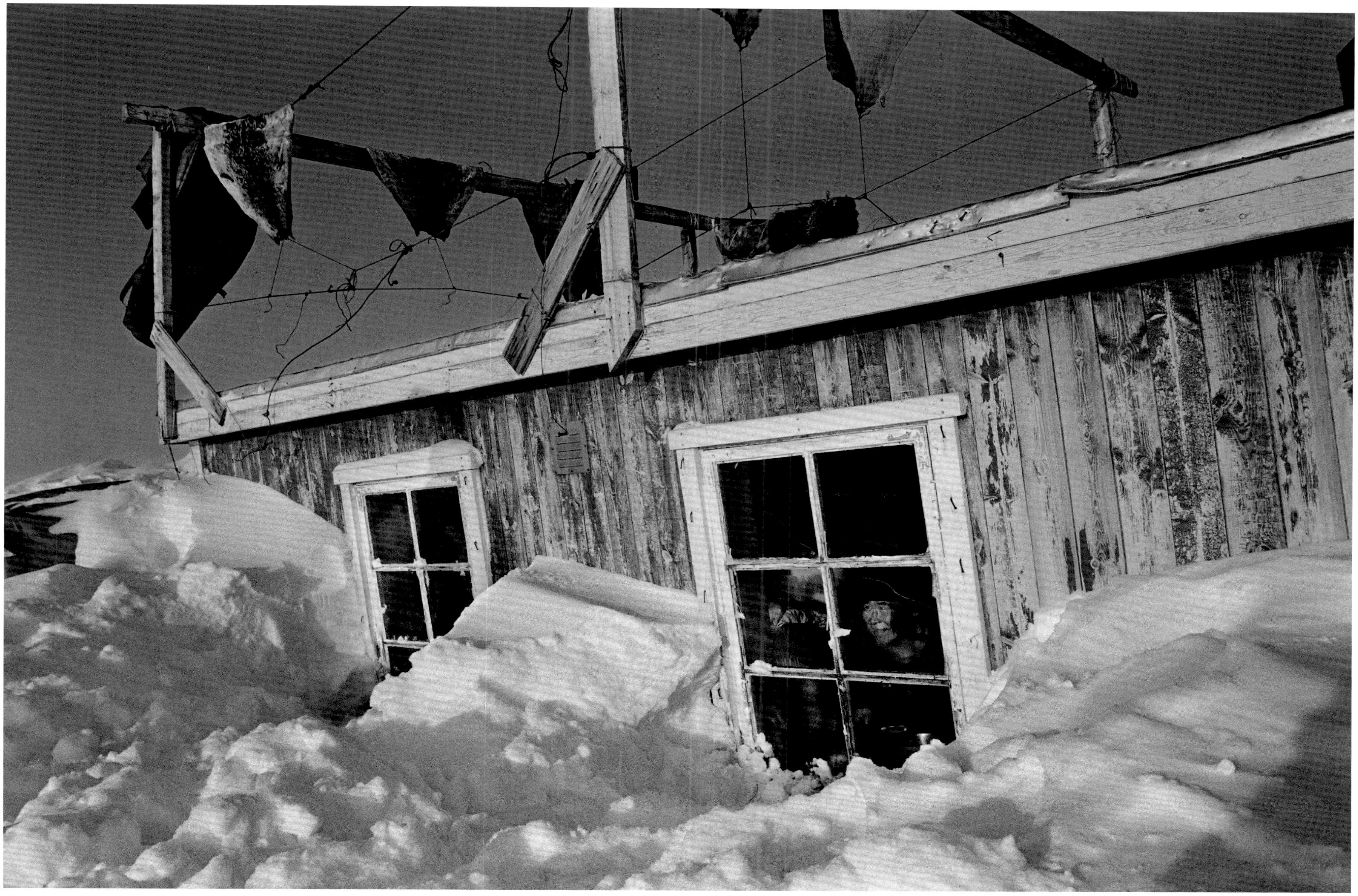

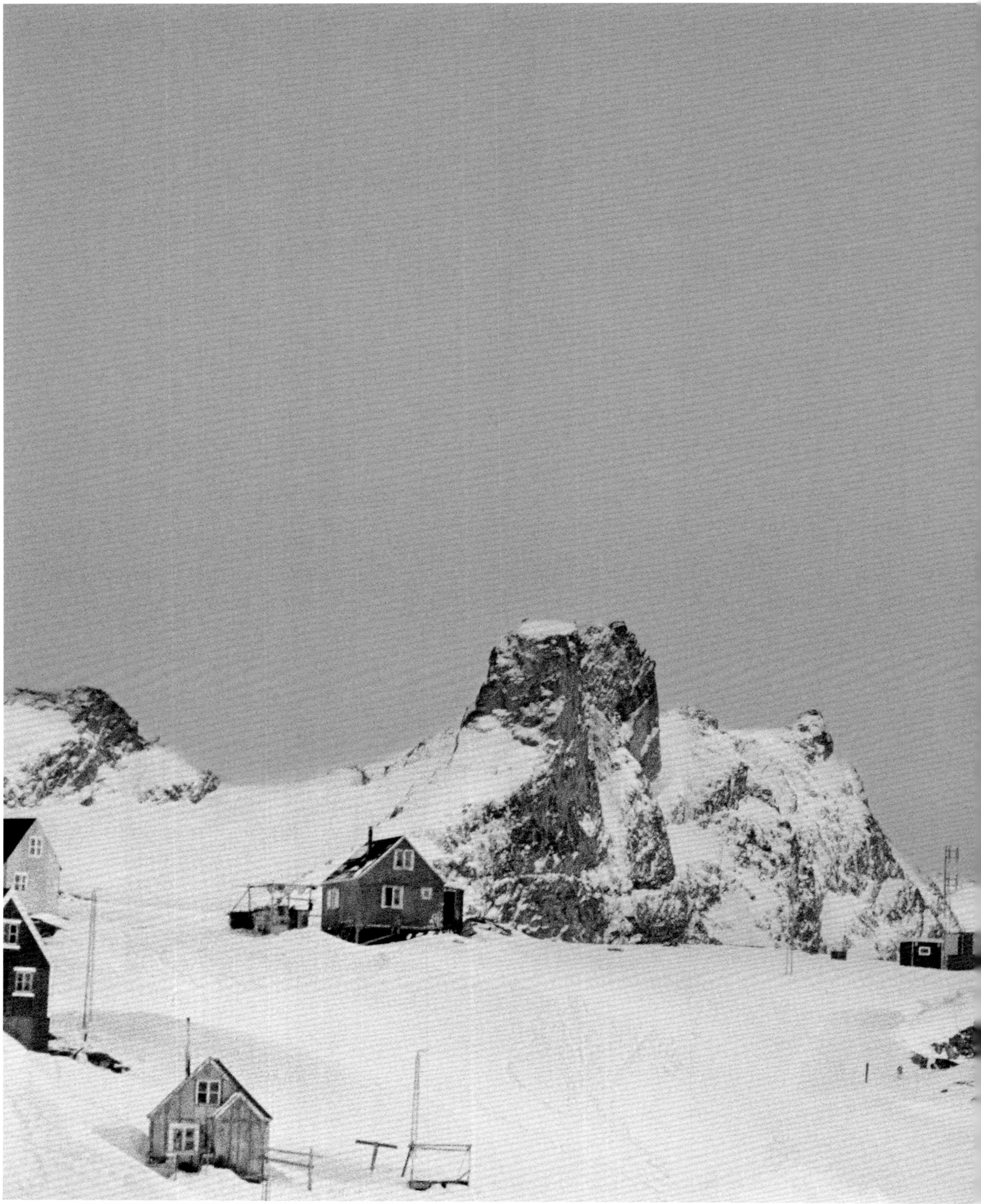

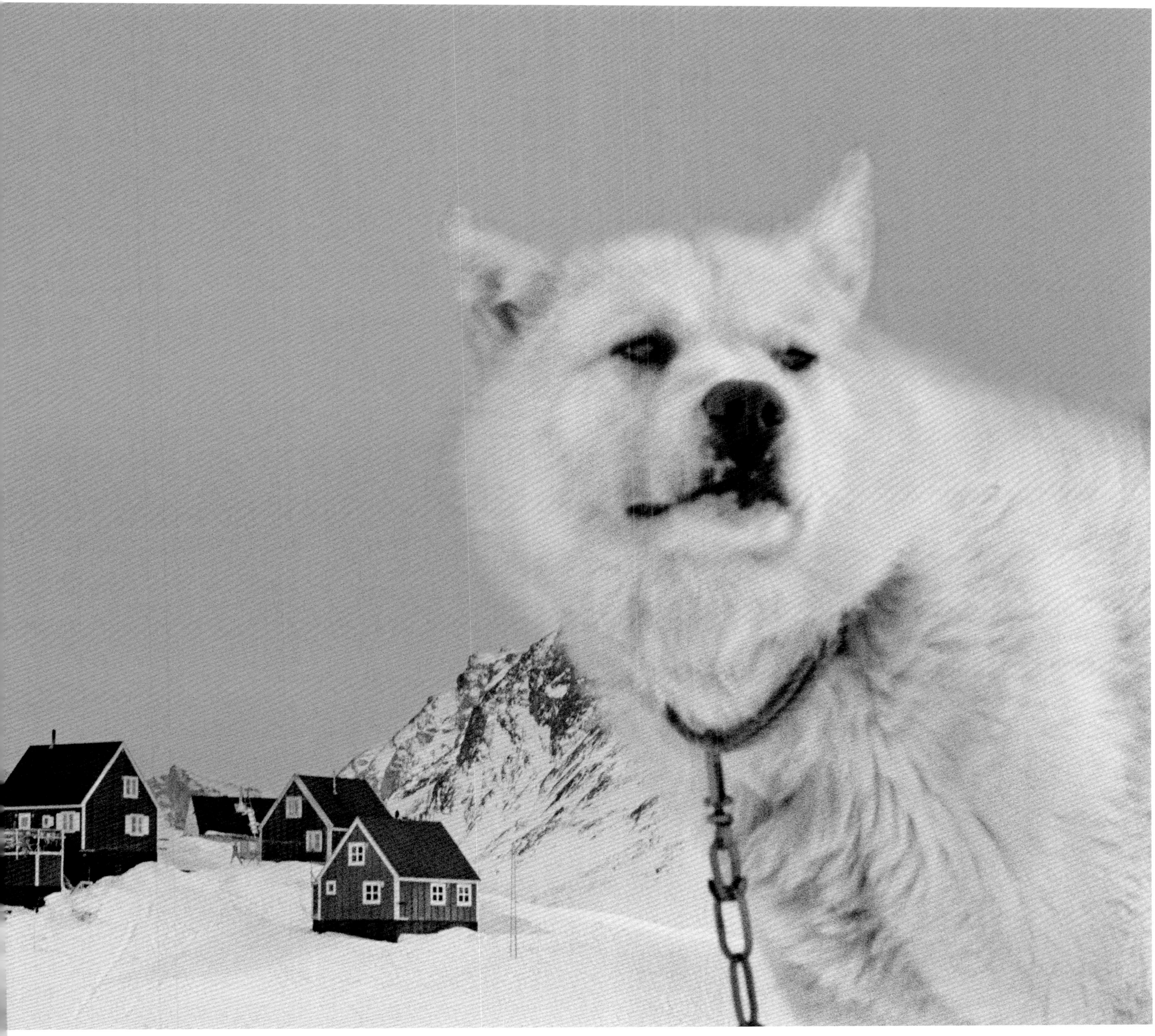

Out on the ice

The freedom of being out on the ice seems boundless. The sound of silence feels strange to the ears. The cracking ice and howling wind seem to tell a story one can hear but not understand. It is no small feat to have lived for thousands of years, as the Inuit have, under the oppressively cold claw of the ice, fighting for their lives every single day.

It can be challenging to wait around in the villages for a chance to go with the hunters out onto the ice shelf. Hunting relies on the weather, and even though the trip may start out under fine conditions, it is almost inevitable for bad weather to descend once the trip is underway. All hunters know the weather can change without warning.

The hunters sometimes stay for weeks, or even months, out on the ice. Travelling without means of communication, if the hunter gets into trouble, no one will know where to find him. The hunters have to rely on themselves. It is a remarkable experience for someone who is used to being able to follow news from every corner of the world all the time, to suddenly spend weeks without having any idea of what is going on in the world. Out on the ice, men are in the world's largest art gallery. Everywhere you look there are ice-sculptures the size of multi-storied buildings decorated with unimaginable patterns and figures.

The snow crunches as we step off the sledge by a large iceberg. We drink tea to get some warmth into our bodies. Little has been eaten for the past two days and the hunters are becoming weak from hunger after a long stretch out on the ice. They will have to hunt a seal today. Willpower and determination is visible in their eyes as they sense the presence of prey; seals, walruses, whales, and polar bears are close by. They have to be careful around the iceberg; a polar bear could be lurking there. While drinking their tea, the hunters tell stories. They recollect the time they followed a large polar bear for two days, trailing his fresh steps. As one of the hunters carefully approached an ice cave by an iceberg the polar bear came out from hiding and lunged at him, but he was able to shoot the creature mid-air. The other hunters saw this from afar and had the dogs run as fast as possible, in order to rescue their hunting-mate, who lay motionless. It took them a while to pass over cracks in the ice to reach him, only to find the bear was dead and the hunter was suffocating under its weight. The hunters laughed hysterically at the misfortune of the man who lay there trapped under the animal.

Seals and narwhals are swimming by the ridge of the ice. The group is silent. Men walk slowly around the ice and put their kayaks afloat. A pod of whales is oblivious to any sort of danger when a harpoon shoots through the air and plunges into the body of one of them. The whale immediately goes under water and the hunters move fast. An inflated seal skin floats in the water by a line that is attached to the harpoon head, showing the hunters where the whale is located. Now we have a game of life and death. There is jumping and running between icebergs, and the excitement of catching the whale eliminates all fear of falling into the ocean. The whale receives a fatal wound. It takes a long time to heave it up onto the solid ice. Mistakes are not acceptable here. Falling into the water can easily be deadly. Later that evening, the men are in good spirits. They play cards under the light from the gas lamp that heats up the tent.

It is pitch black and very windy. The ice is cracking and its eeriness makes it impossible to sleep. Sounds from ice plates grating against one another can be heard from afar. All of a sudden the ice begins to break form the weight of the sledges. The dogs howl in warning. The men immediately pack up the equipment, fasten the dogs to the sledges, and drive as fast as possible towards a safe piece of ice. They wind is getting stronger and it pushes the sledges in the direction of the ocean. Day is breaking. The ice is too slippery for the dogs. They whimper as they scratch their claws into the surface of the ice, barely able to get a grip. Finally, the ridge of the solid ice is close by. The hunters yells at the dogs that if they don't fight the storm they will end up in the ocean.

A lining of snow on top of the ice saves the day. The dogs manage to latch on to the ice again and press forward. For ten hours they struggle to reach solid ground. That evening, the small hunting hut feels like a palace. The hunters fetch some polar bear meat stored in the snow by the hut, and prepare a feast, even though they are completely exhausted.

The dogs get a long needed rest after their efforts and lounge around on the ice. The hunters remain vigilant, listening to every movement outside, ready to move when the opportunity arises. Suddenly, one of the hunters wrinkles his brow, silences the others and whispers, "nanoq". A polar bear has been spotted out on the ice. It is not aware of us. Even those who had been sleeping jump to their feet, dizzy and sleepy, to chase the polar bear.

They run and jump between icebergs that have broken off from the main ice. The bear knows it's being chased and is on the run. The five hunters follow him closely. The chase goes on for about an hour, but the bear manages to escape. The hunters begin to realise that the ice is too sparse and dangerous. It takes them a long time to get back.

Ravens fly over the ice. They are among the few creatures of the north that Inuit do not eat. We are on our way home and getting closer to the village. We are returning from a fantastic world that is difficult to describe with words, a world which is simultaneously terrifying and sublime.

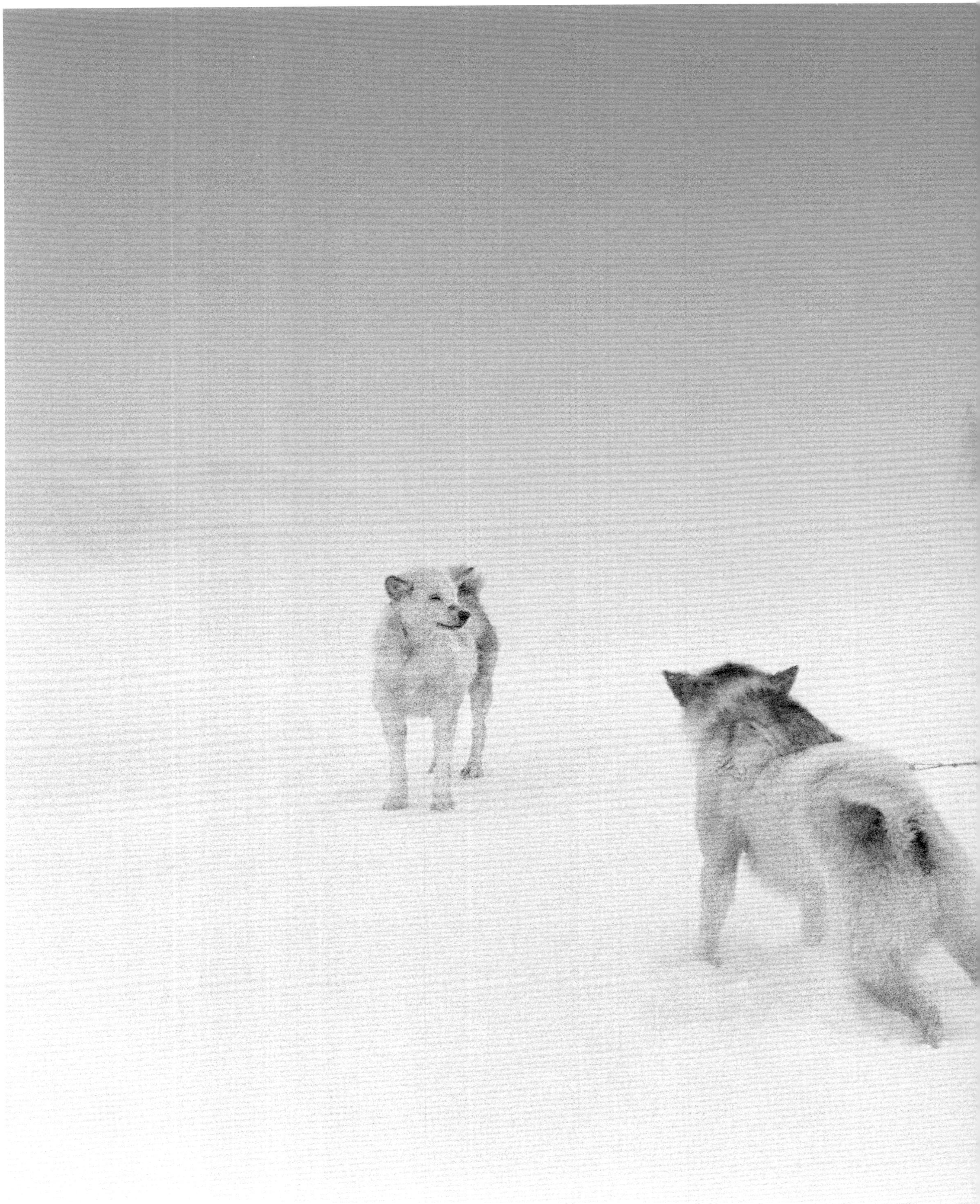

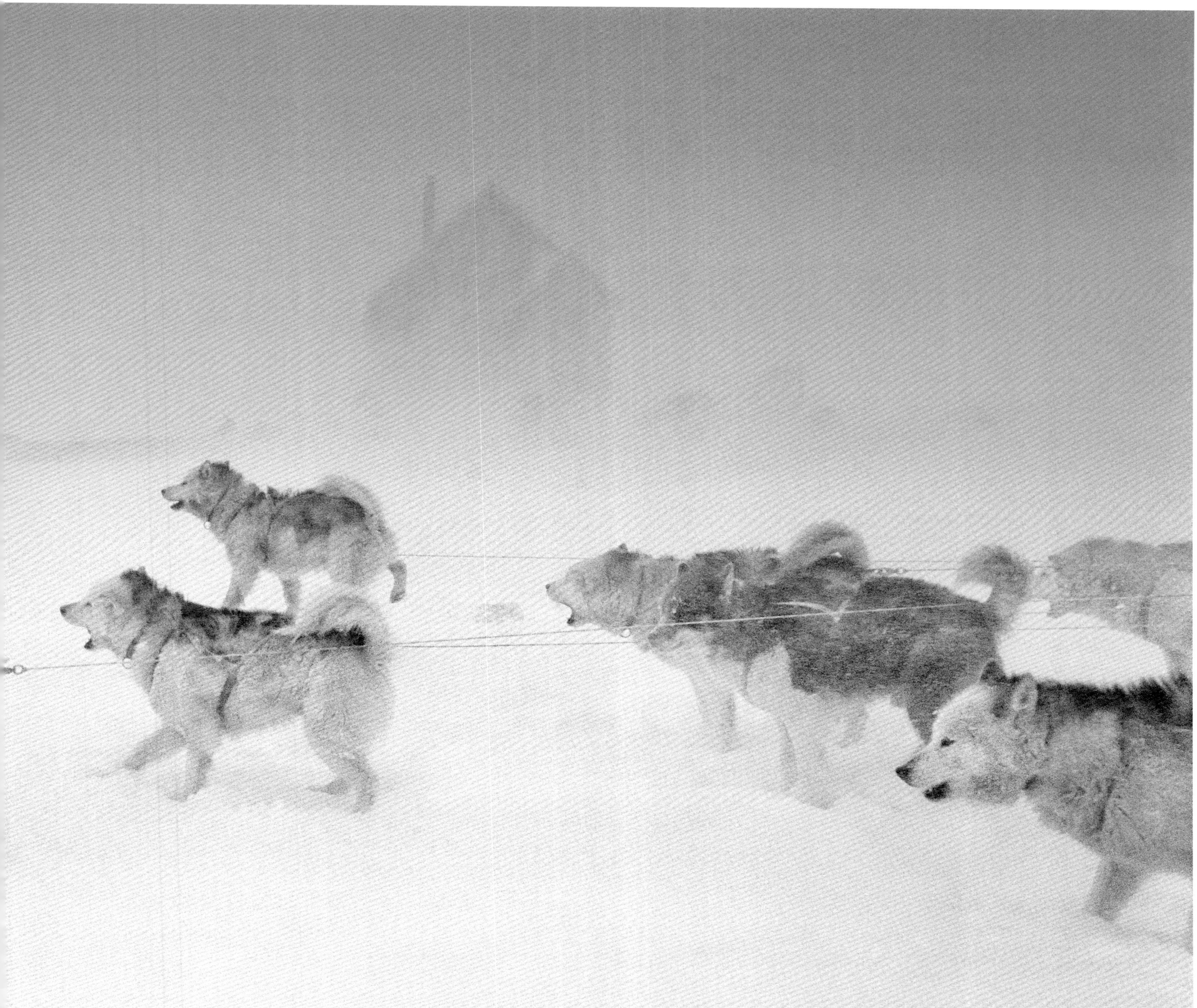

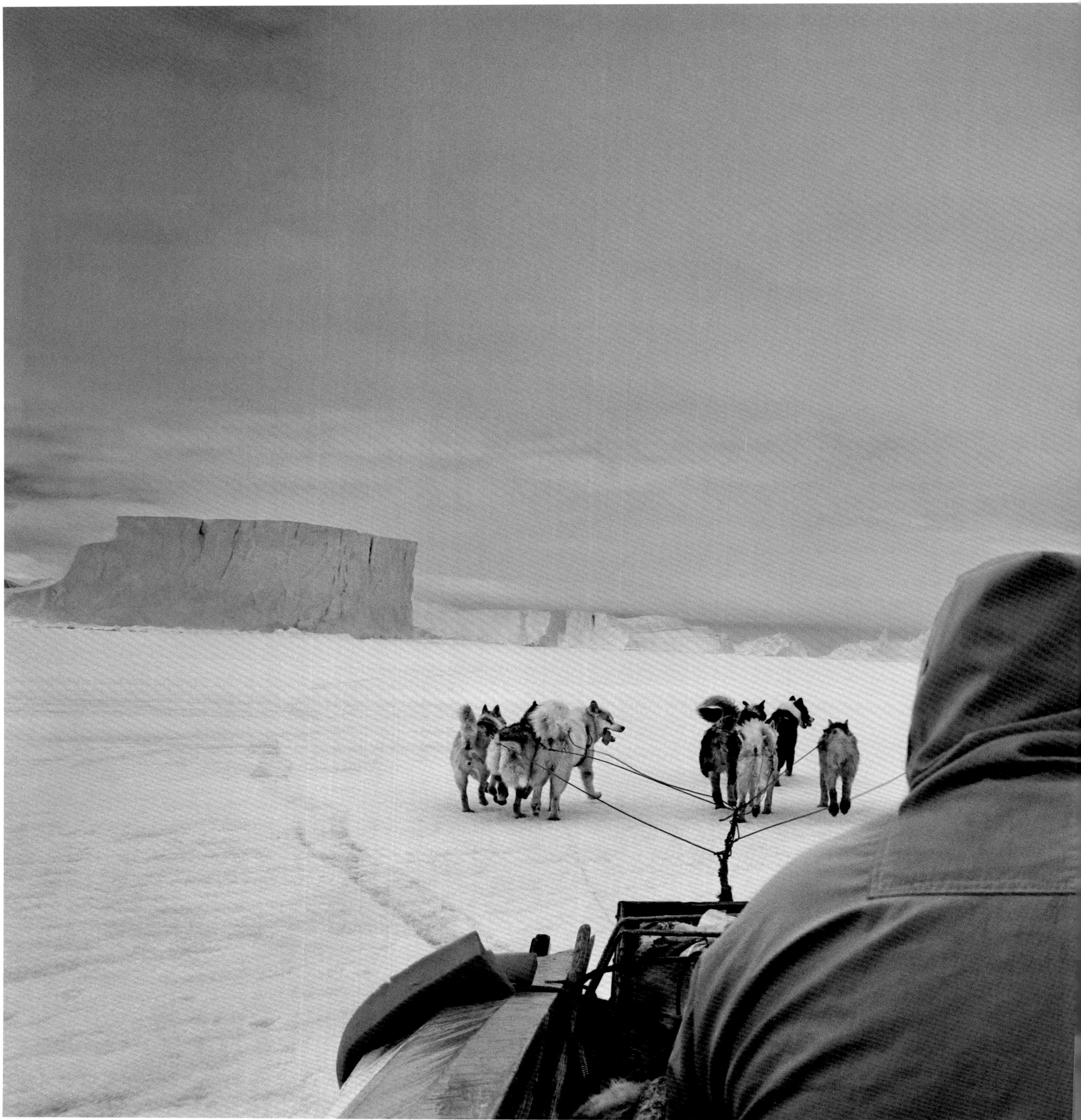

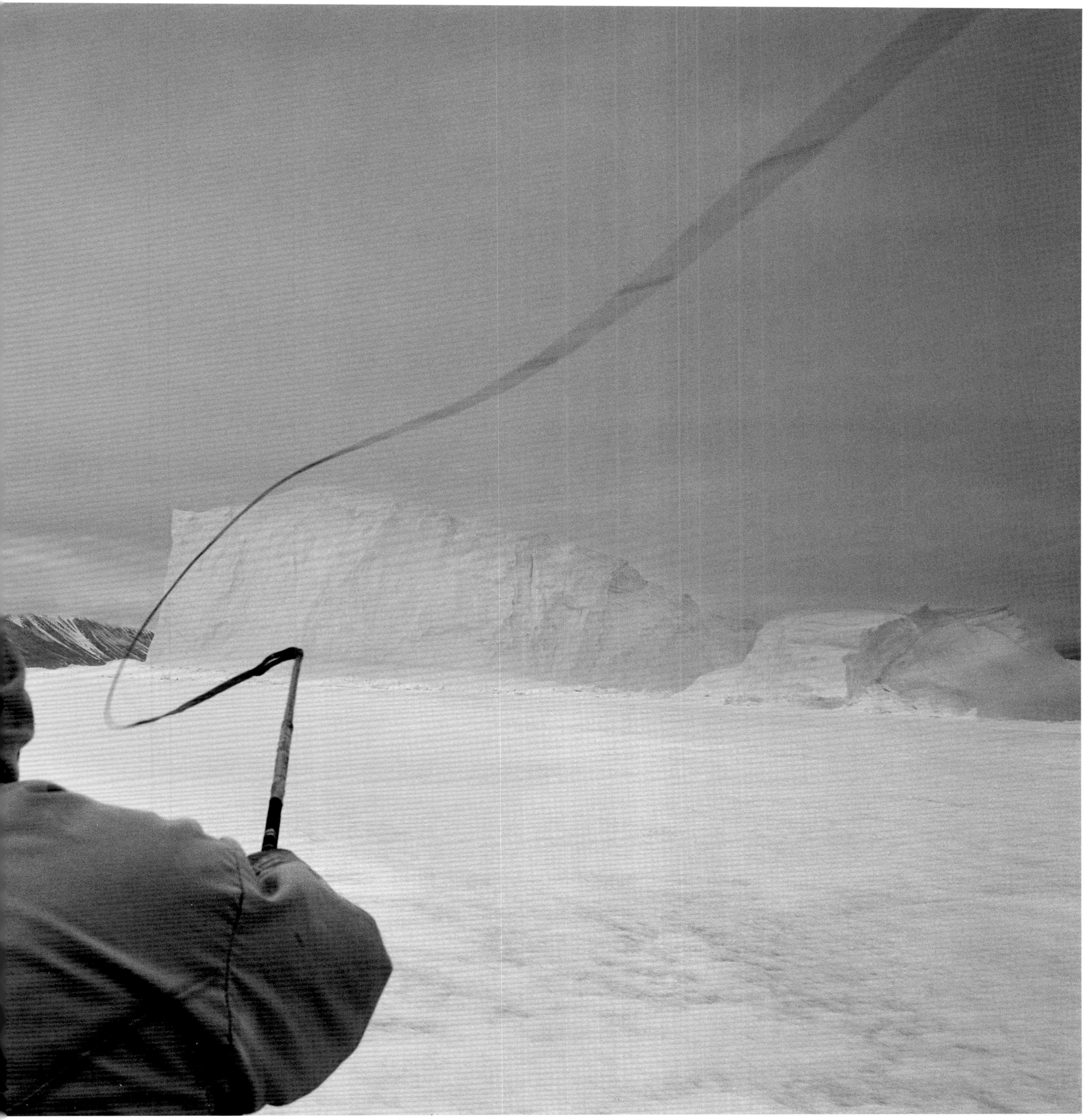

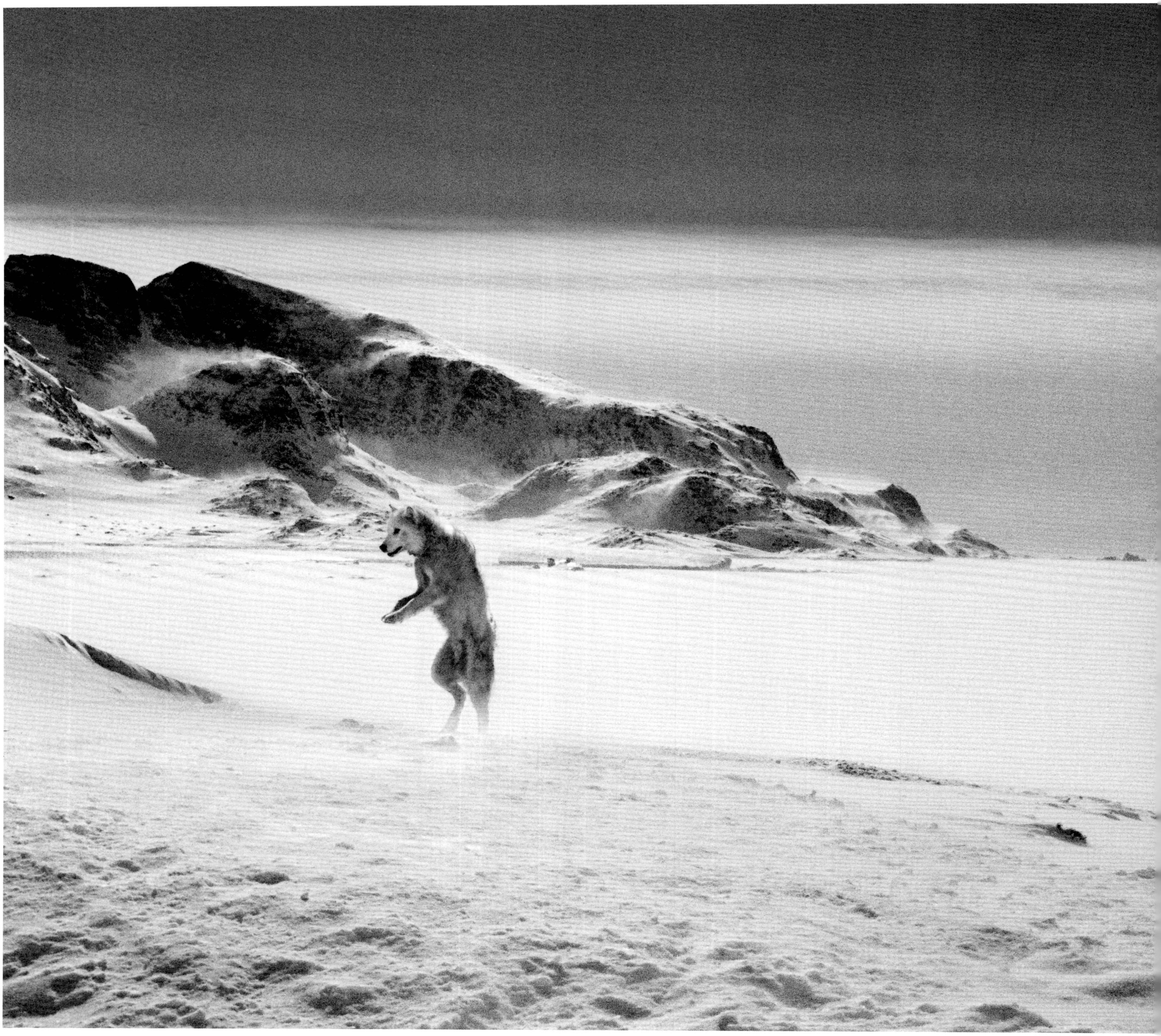

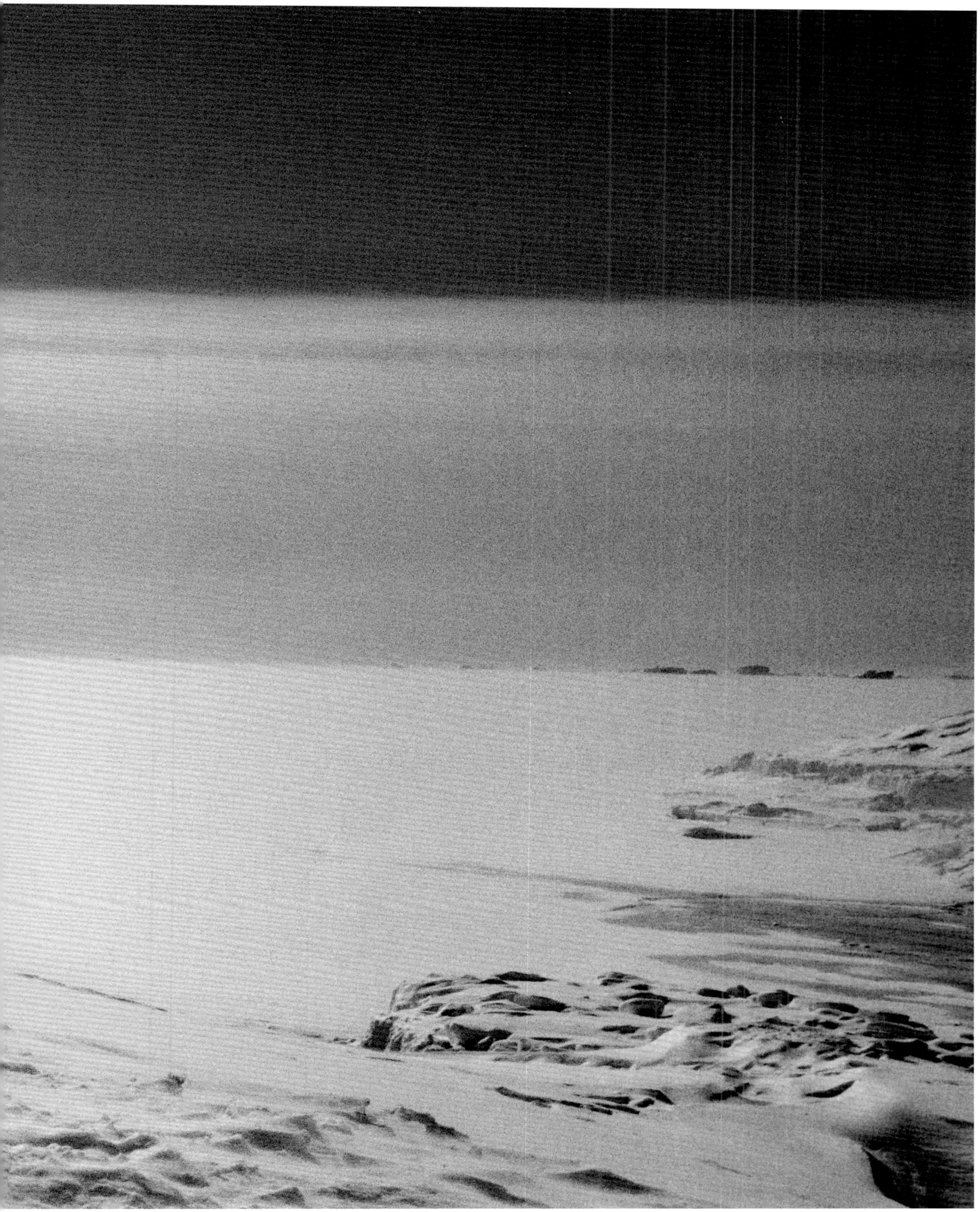

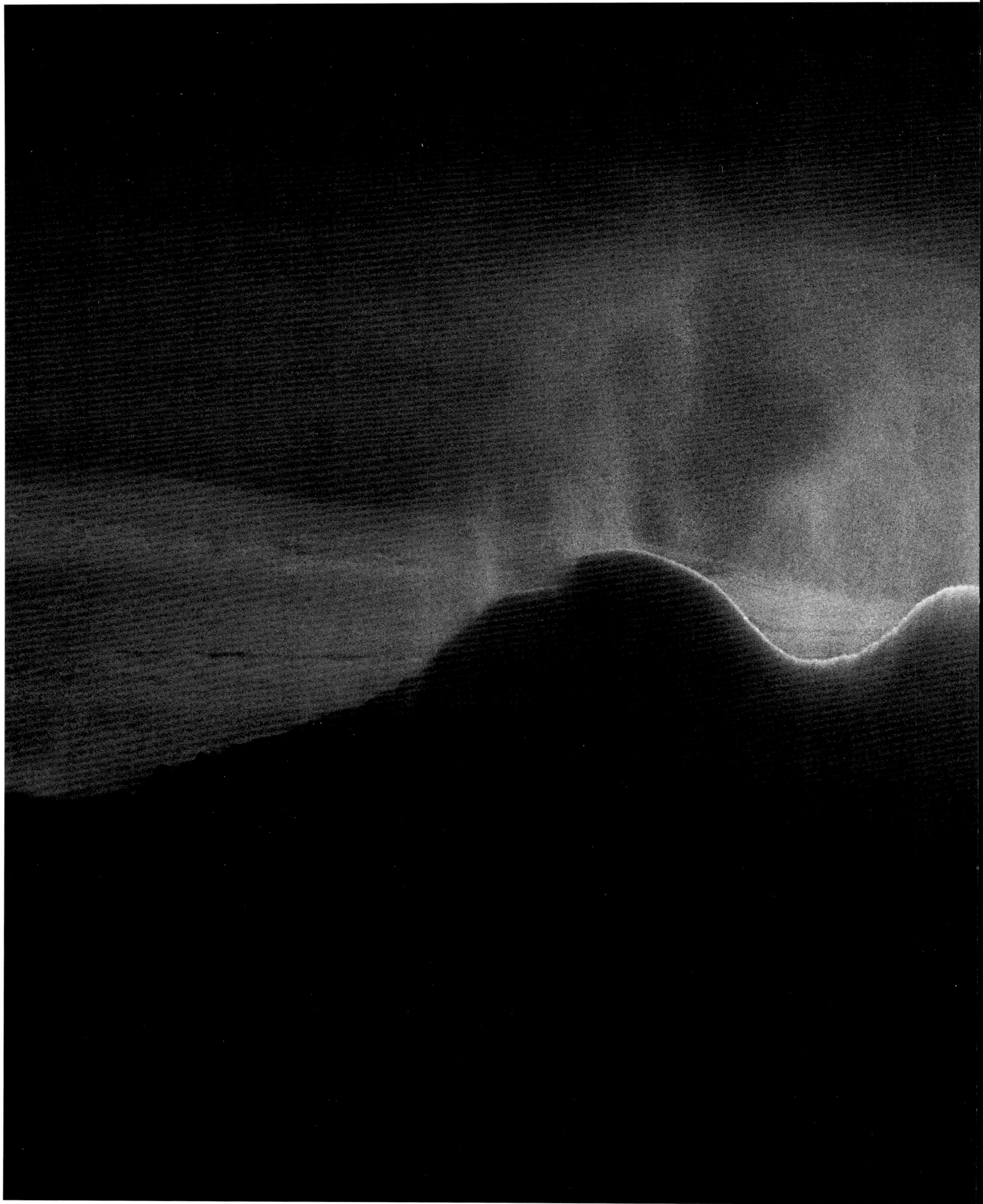

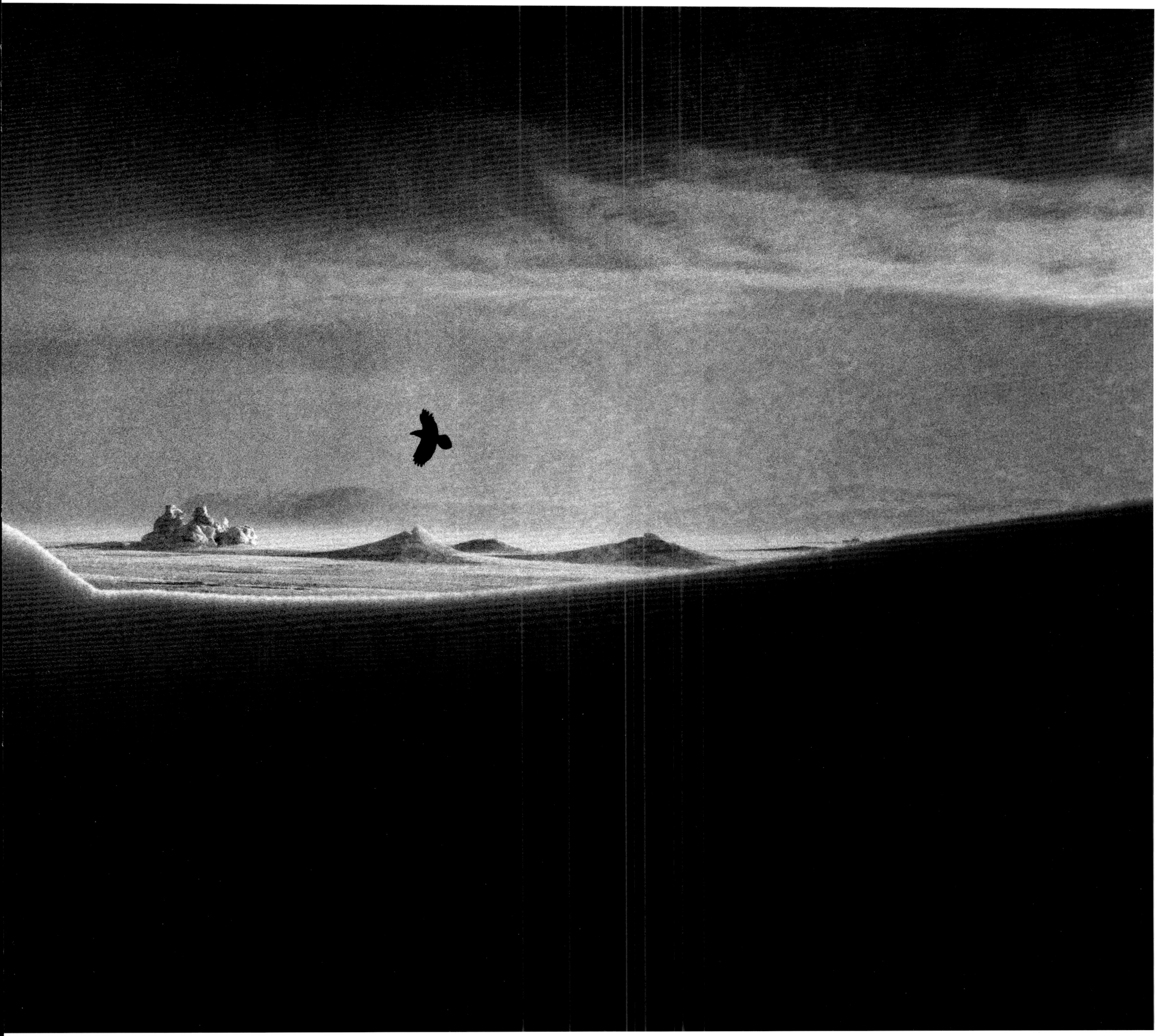

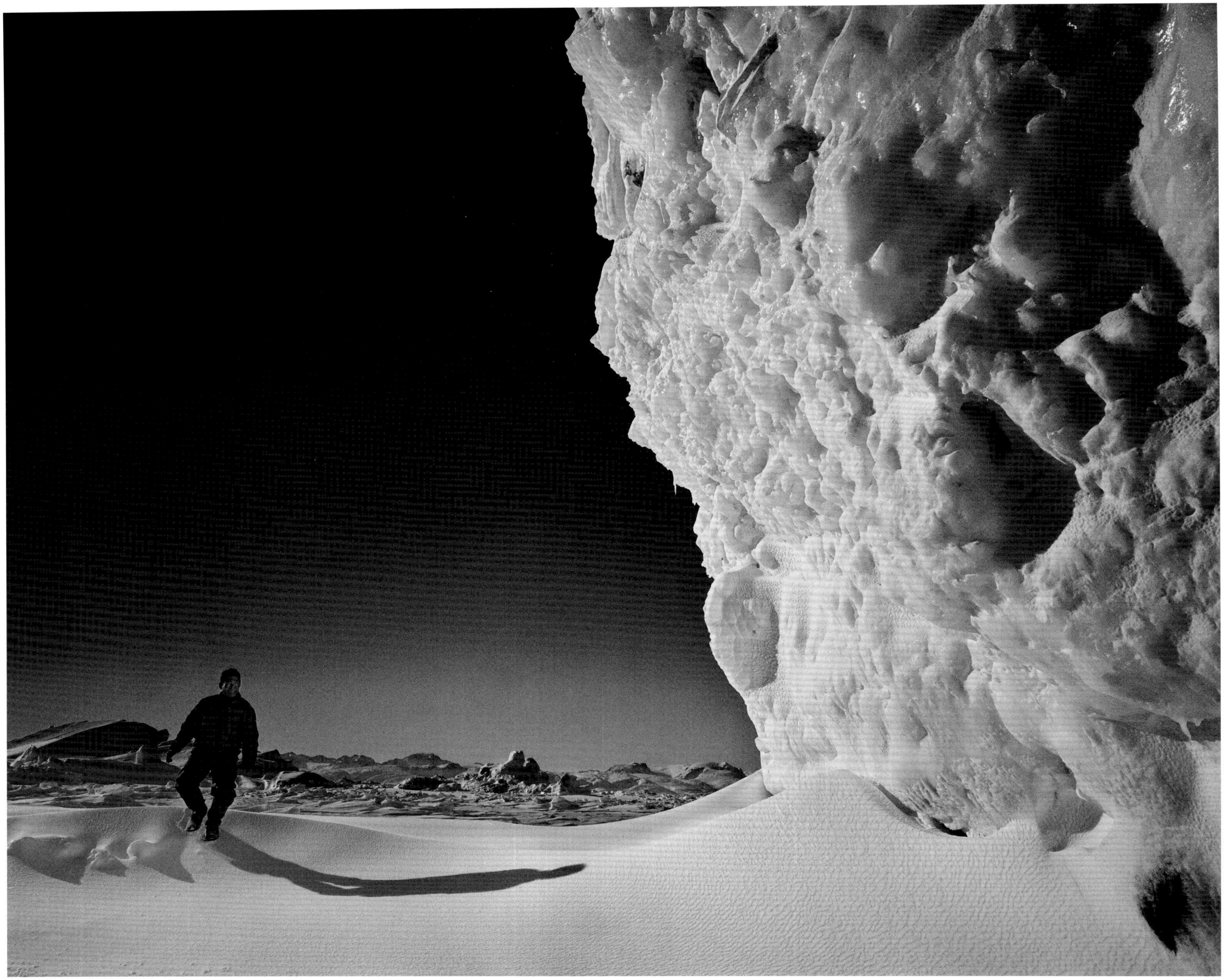

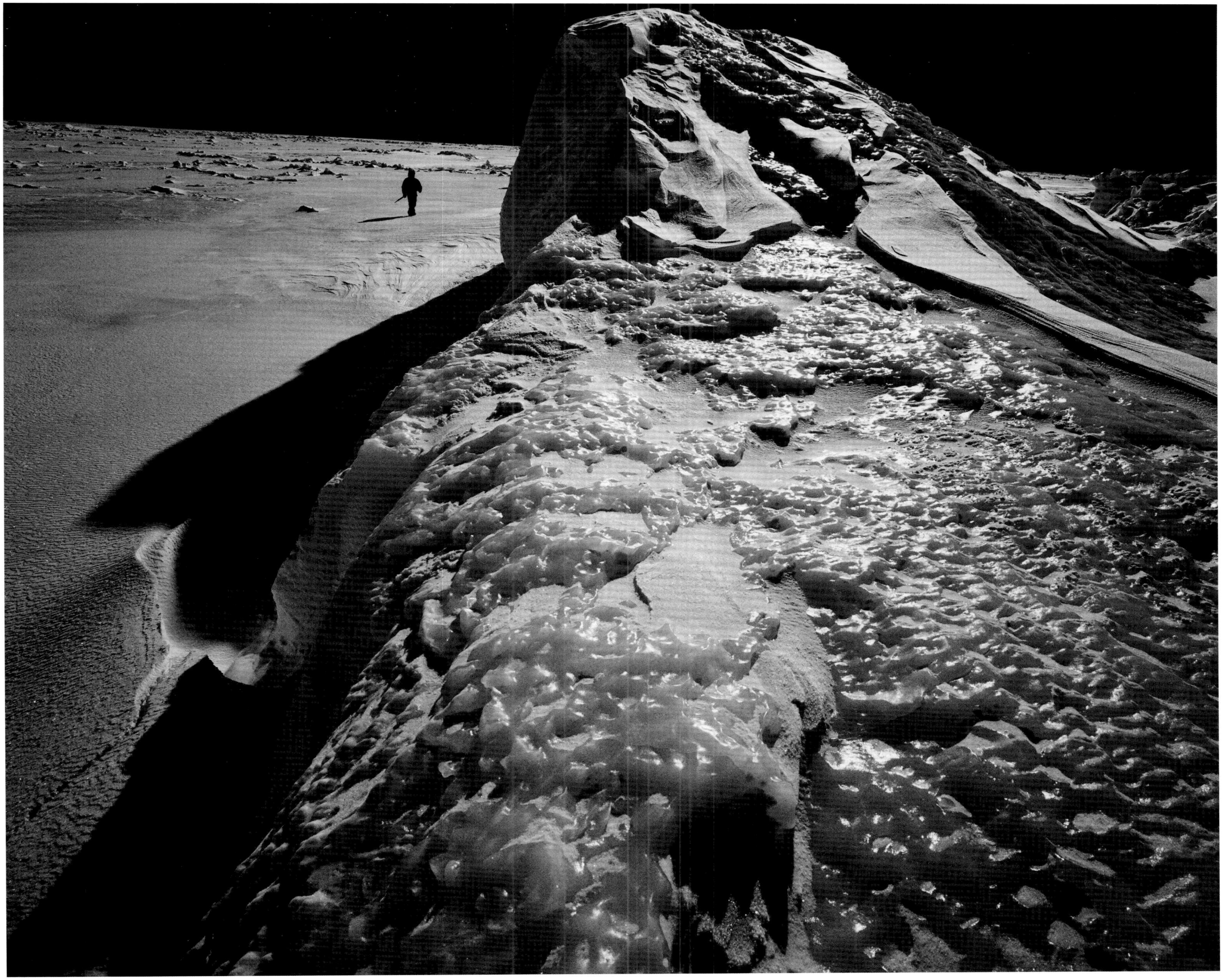

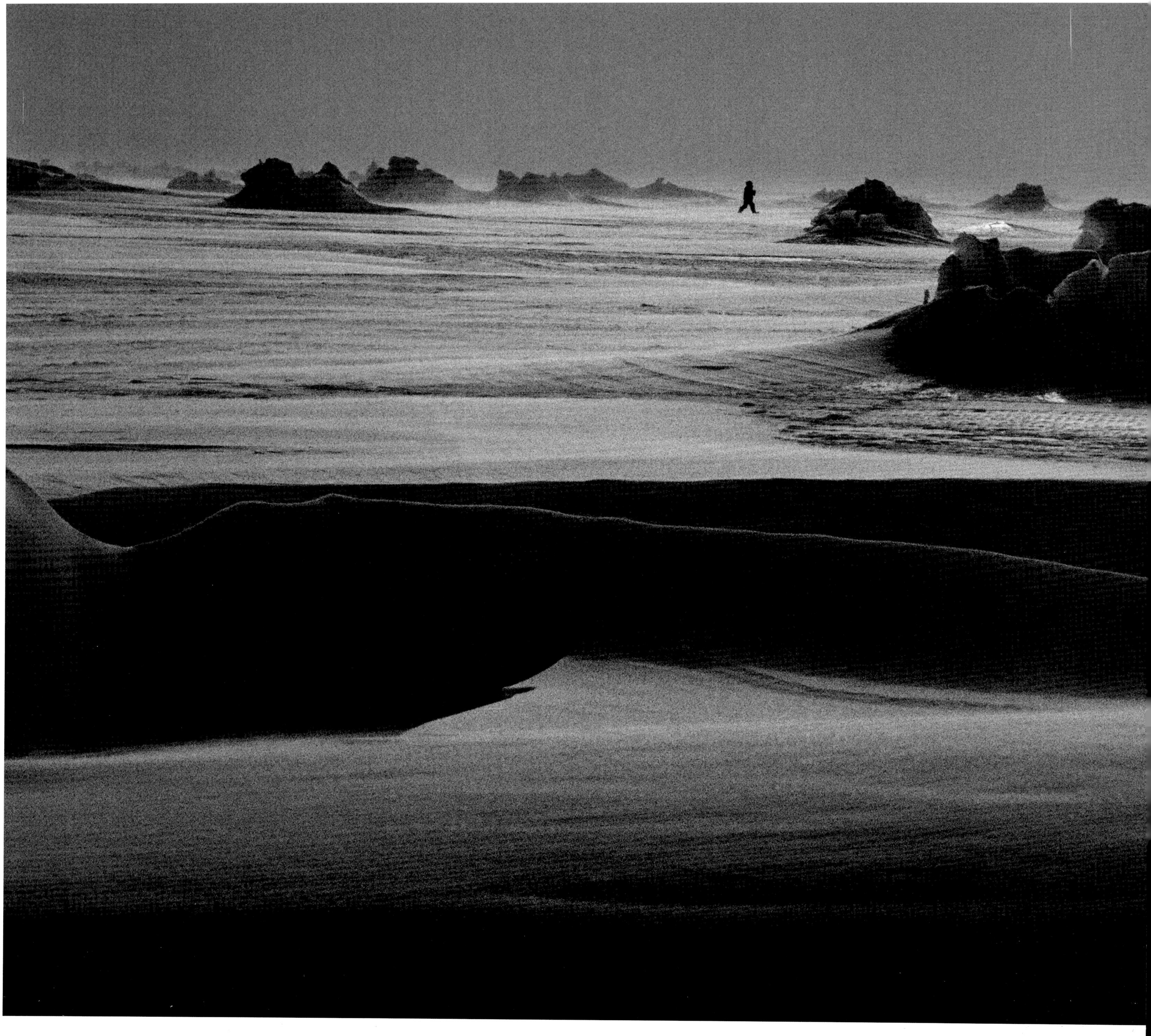

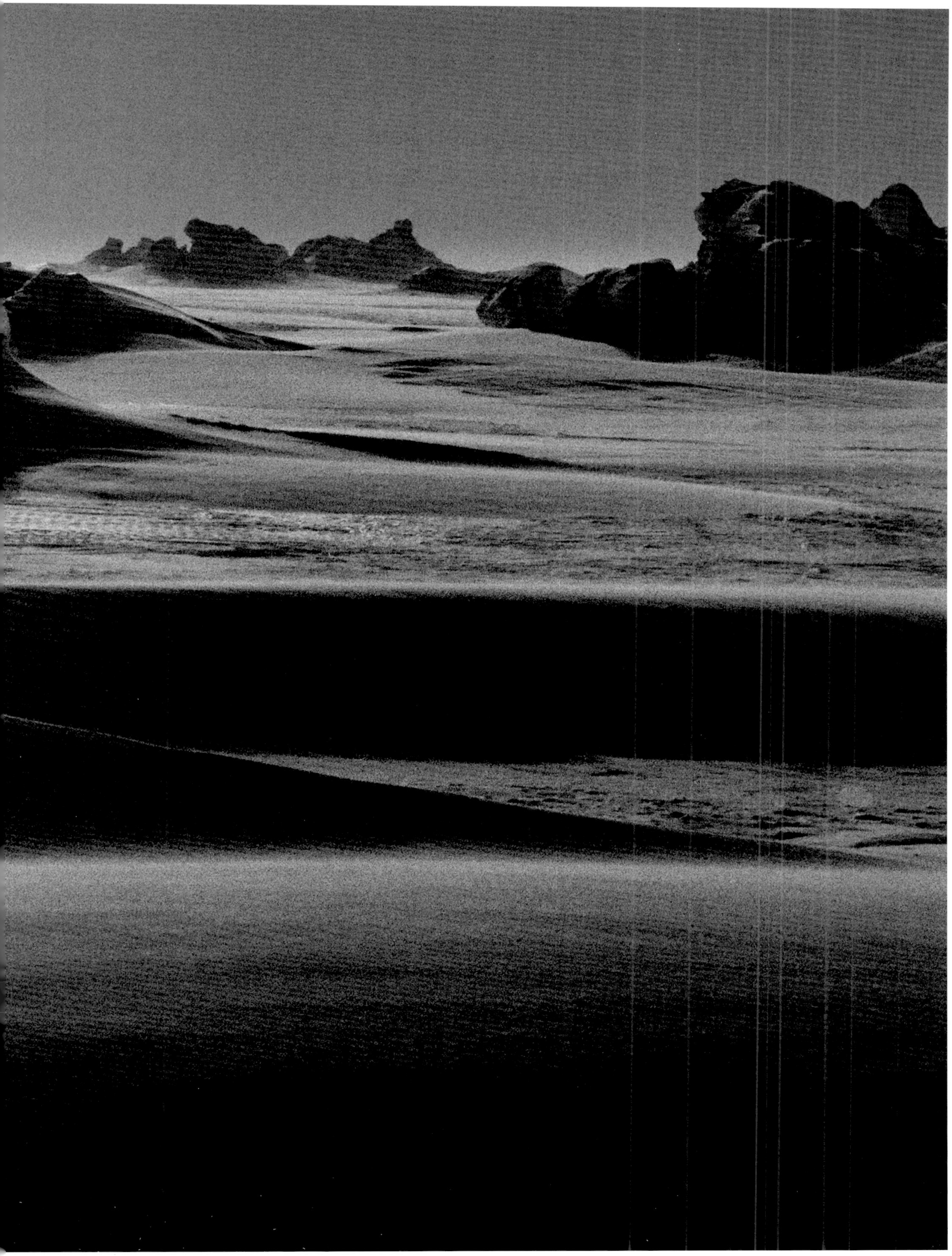

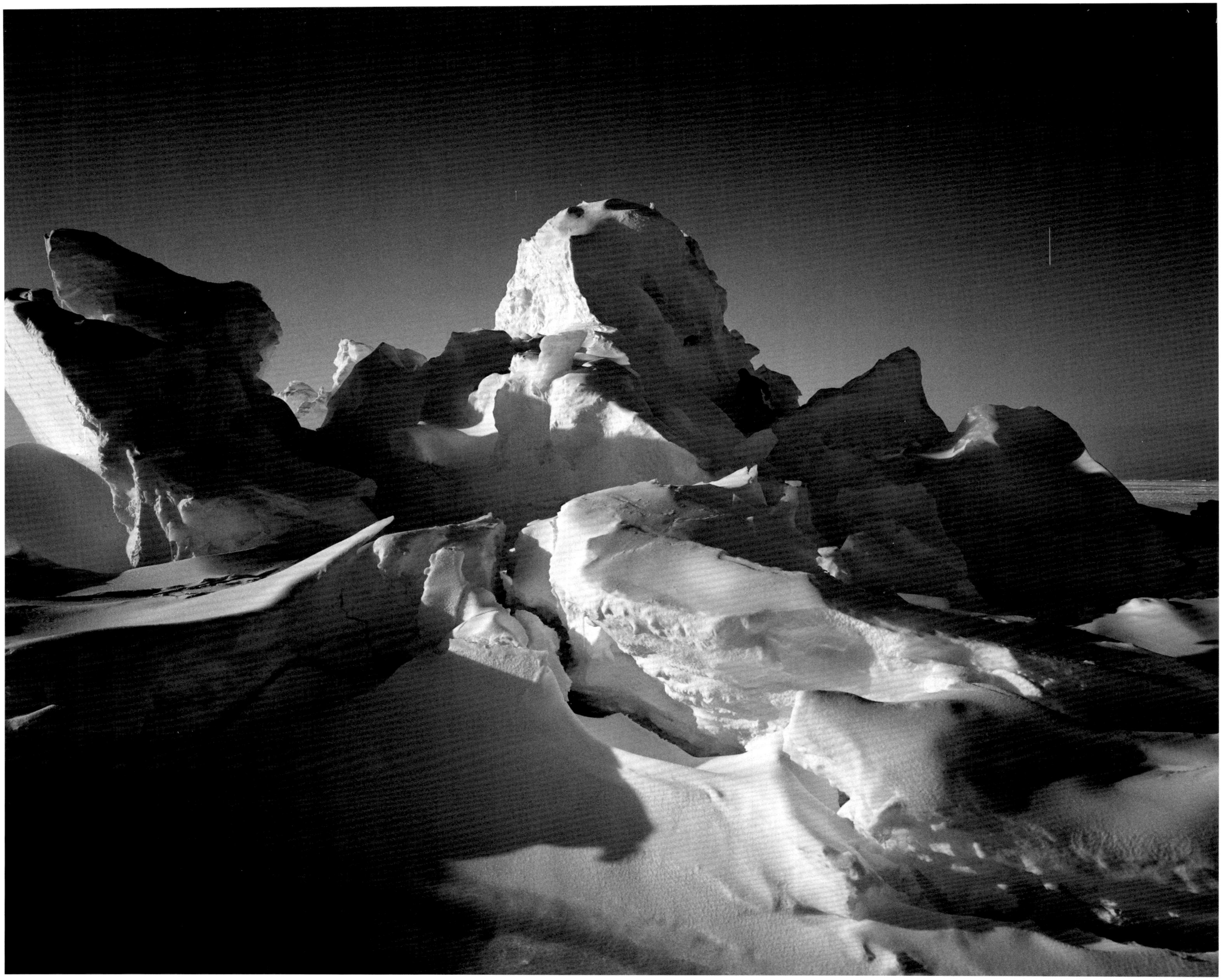

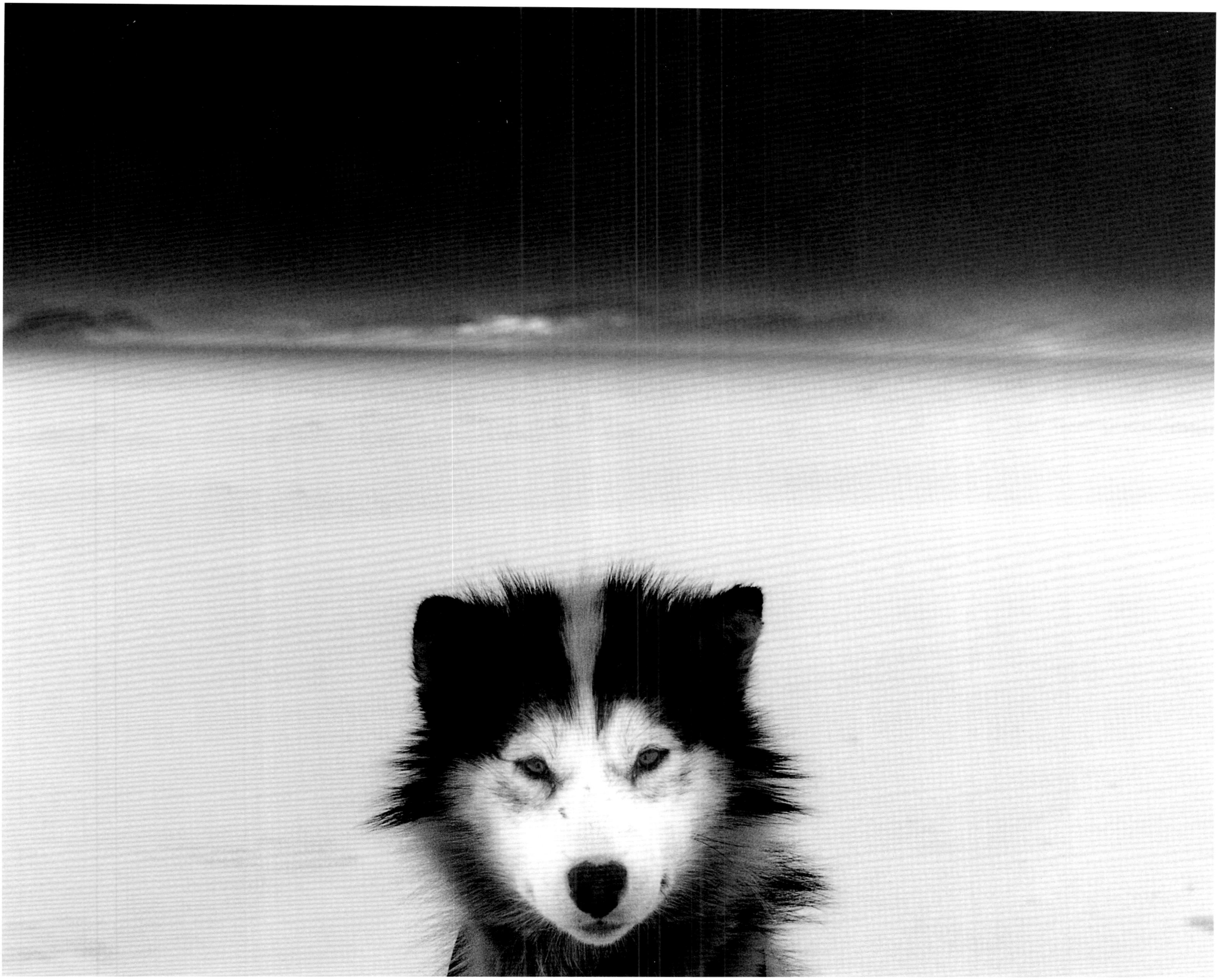

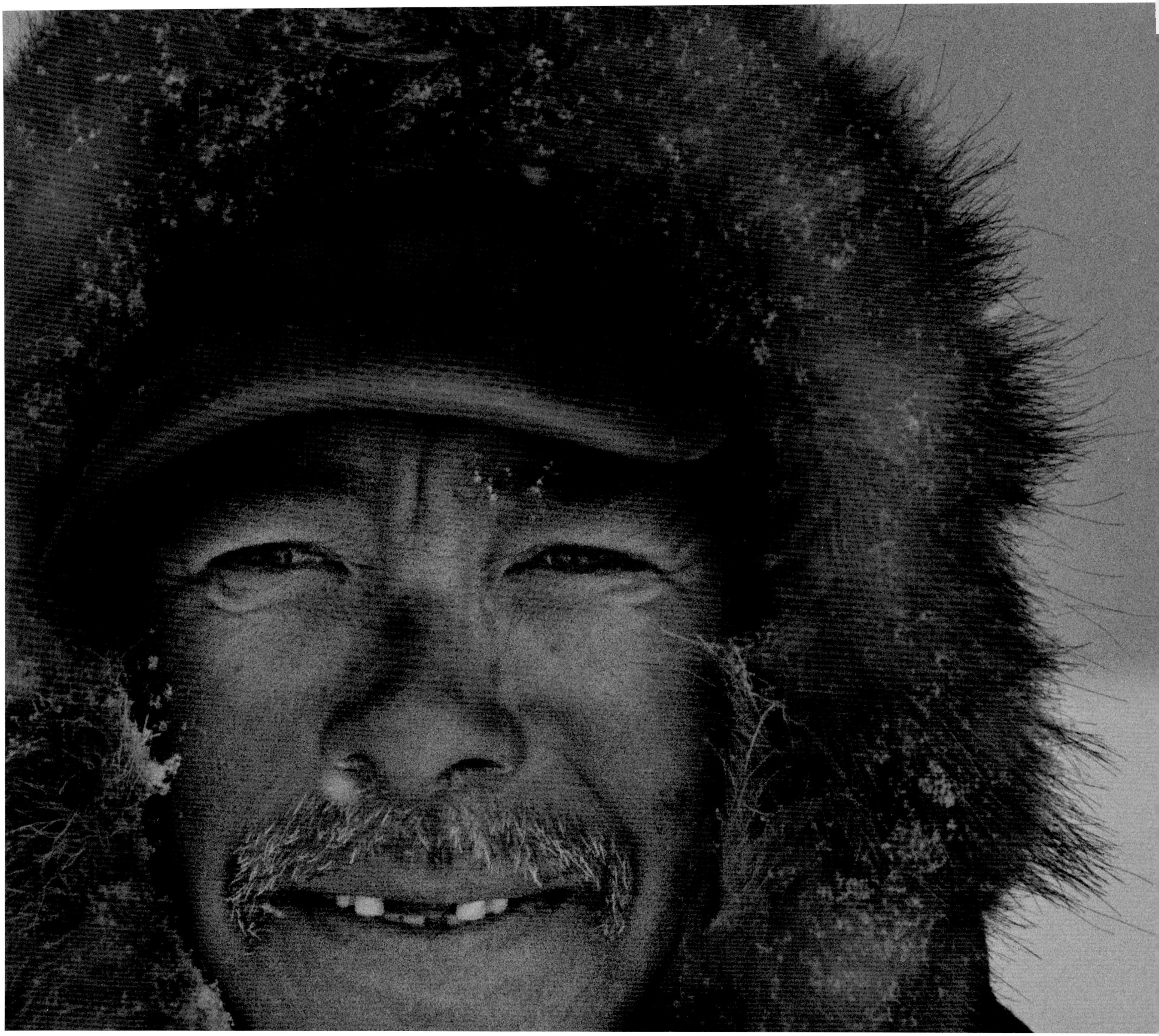

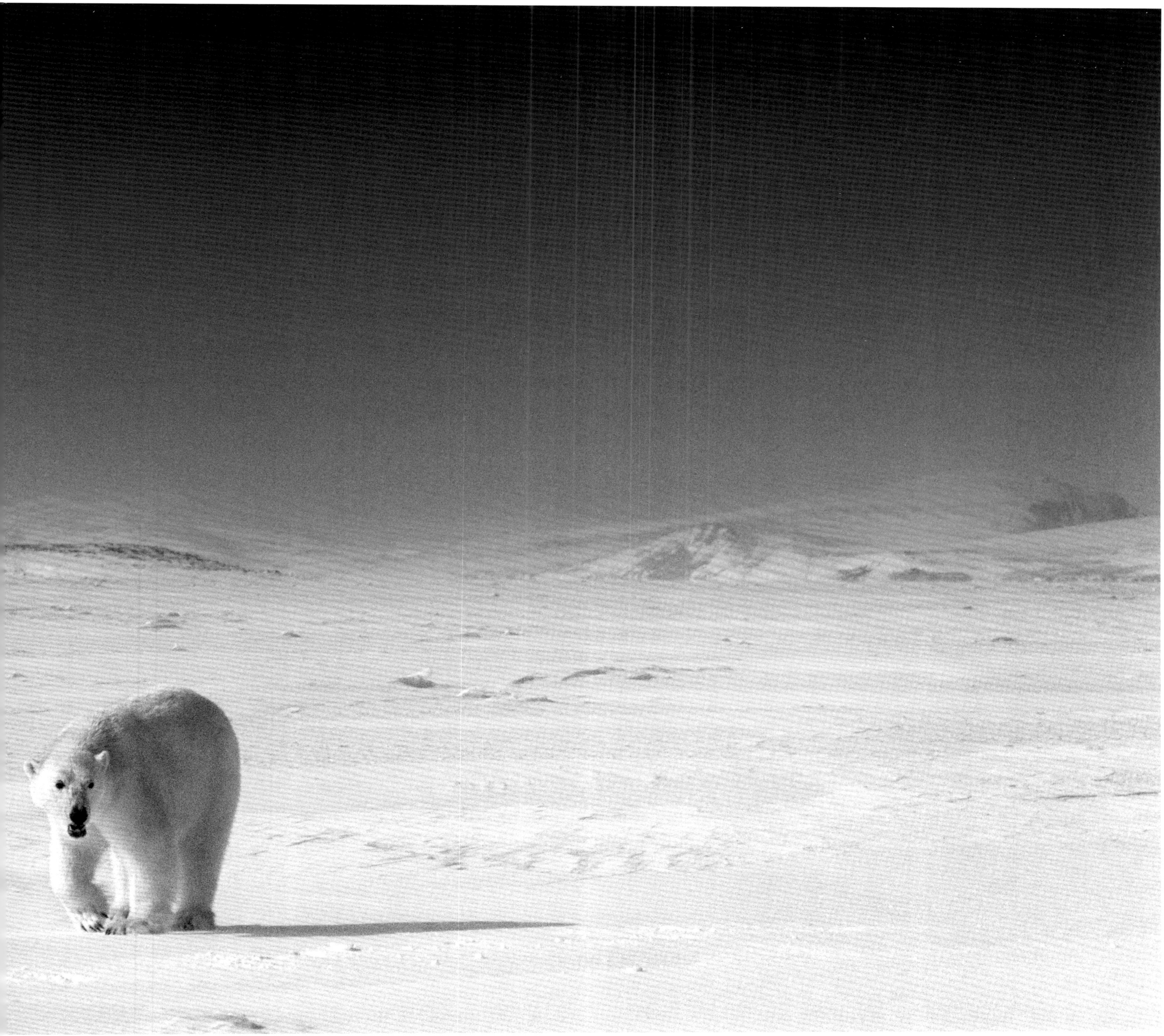

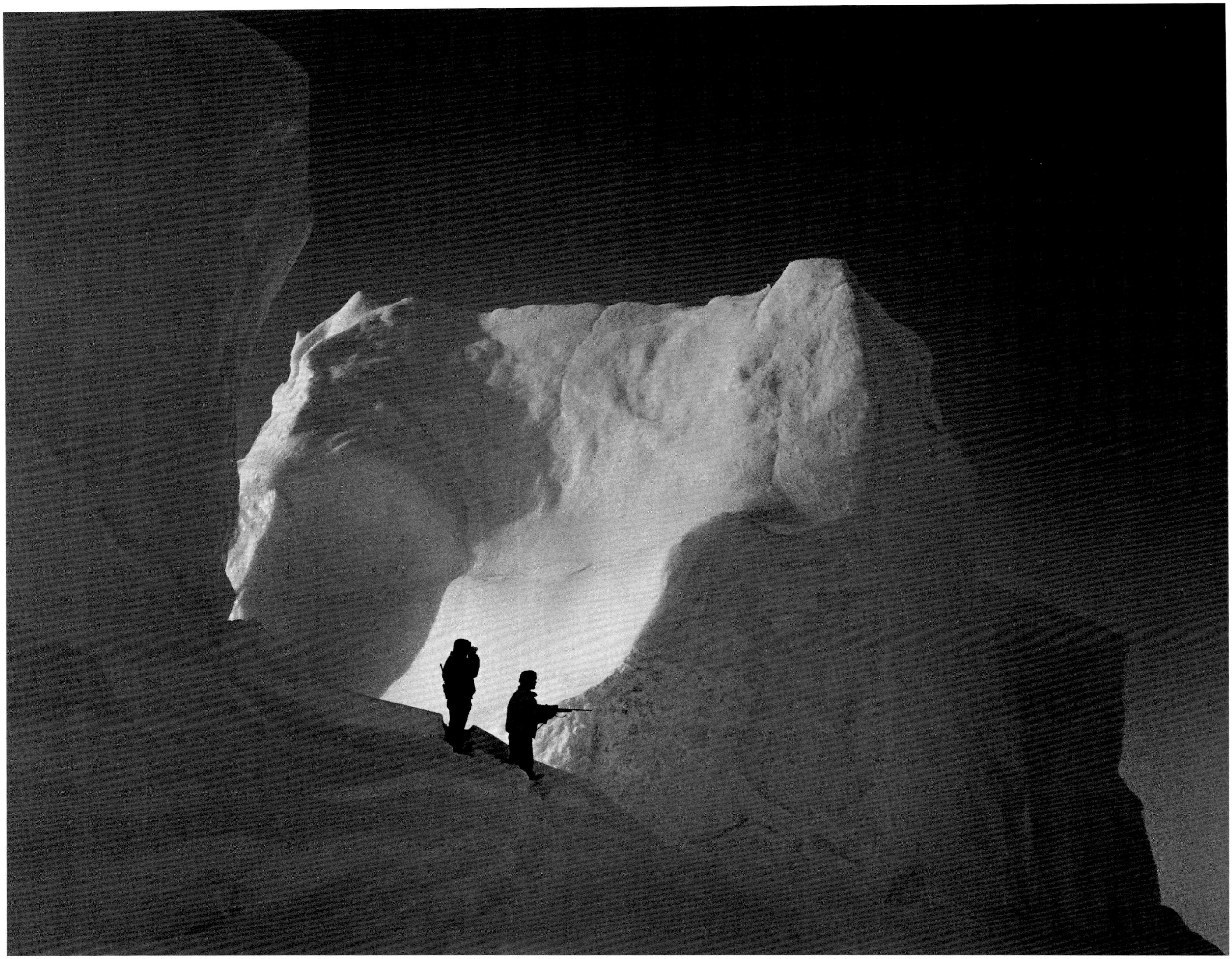

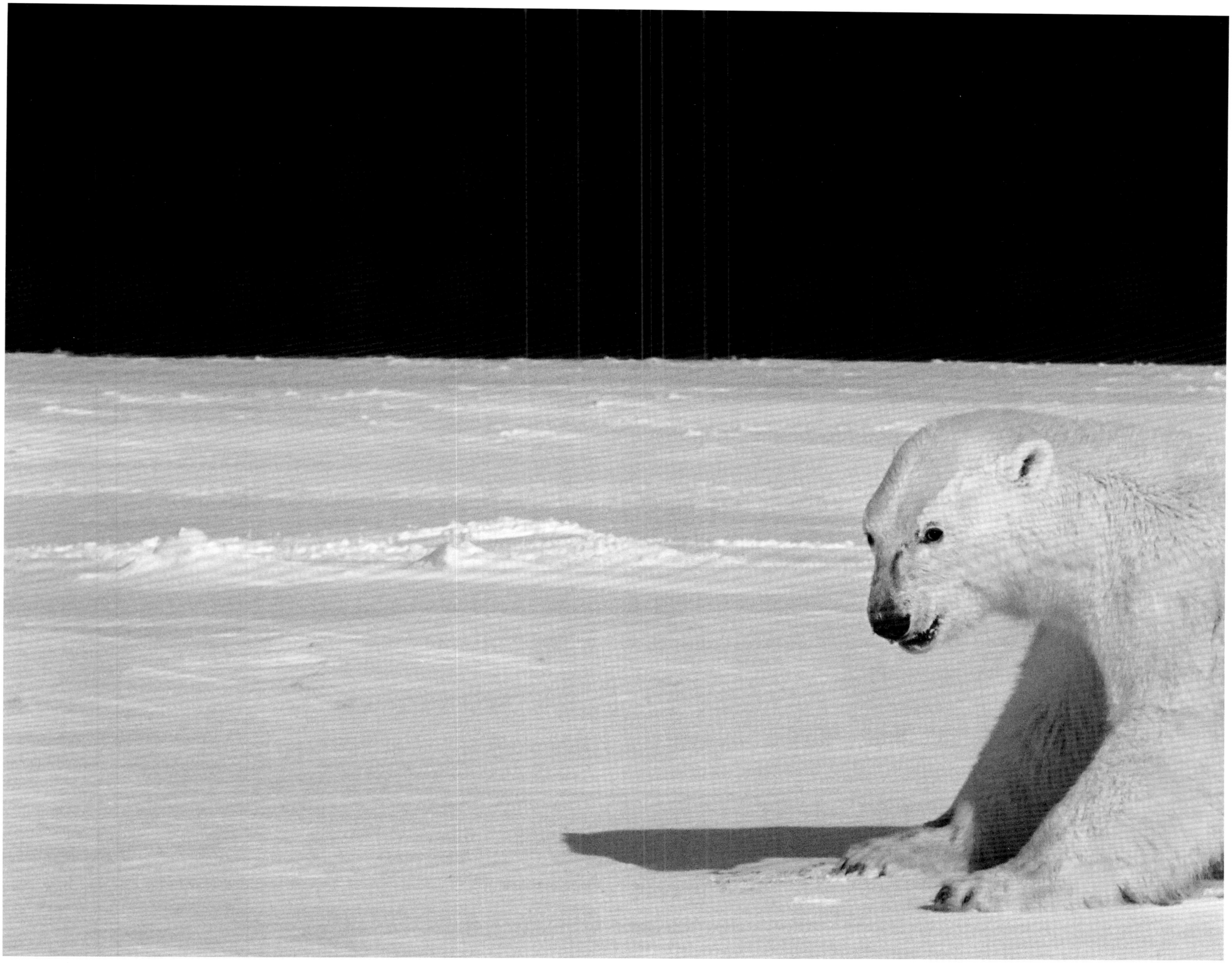

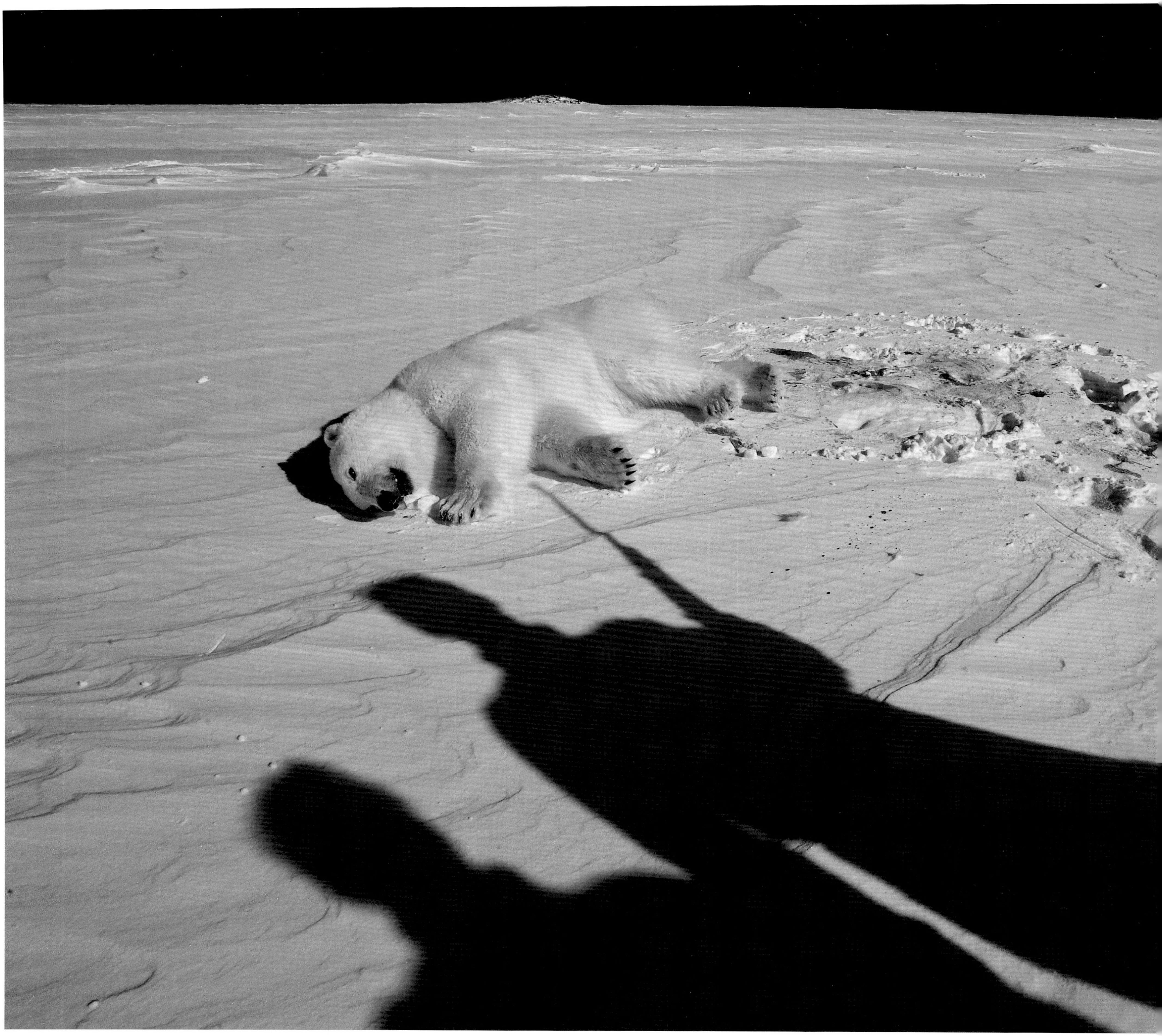

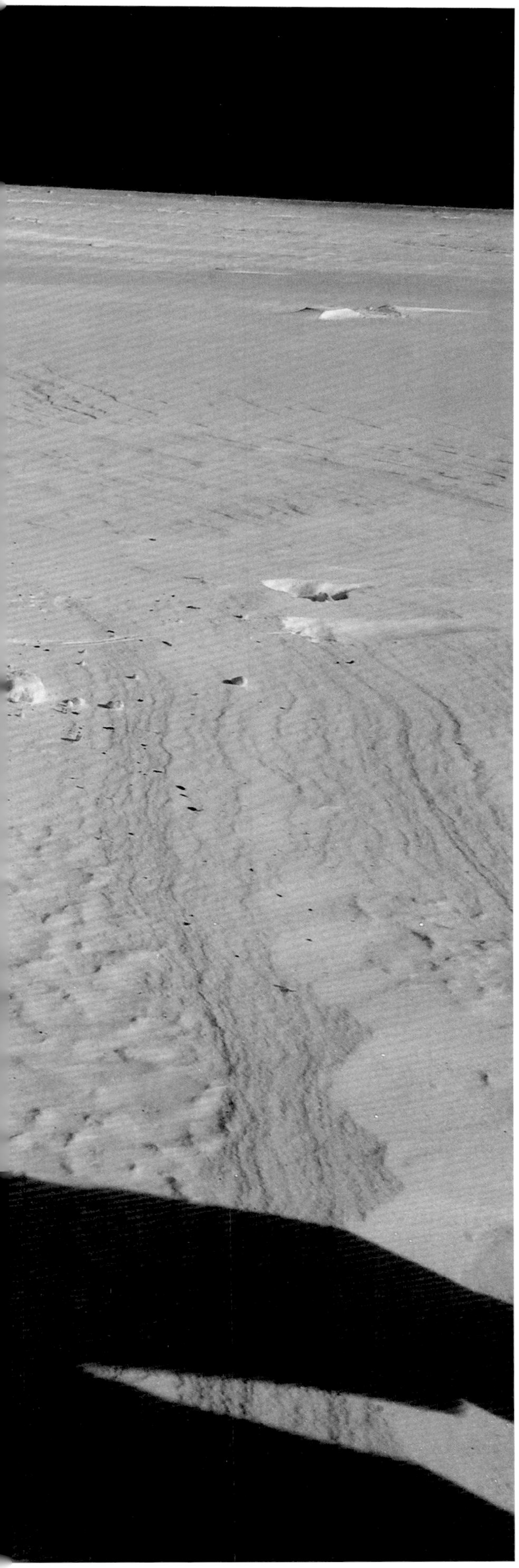

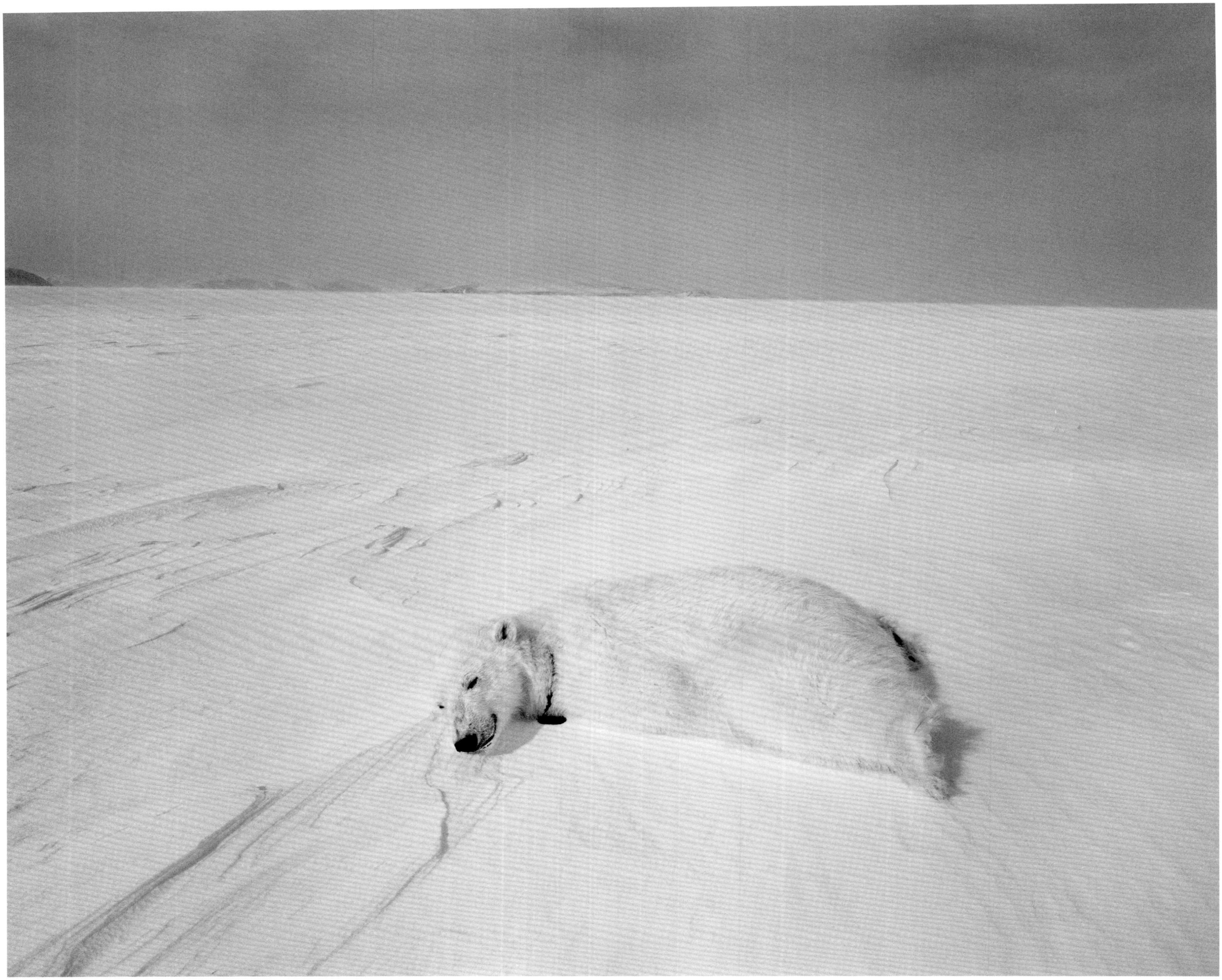

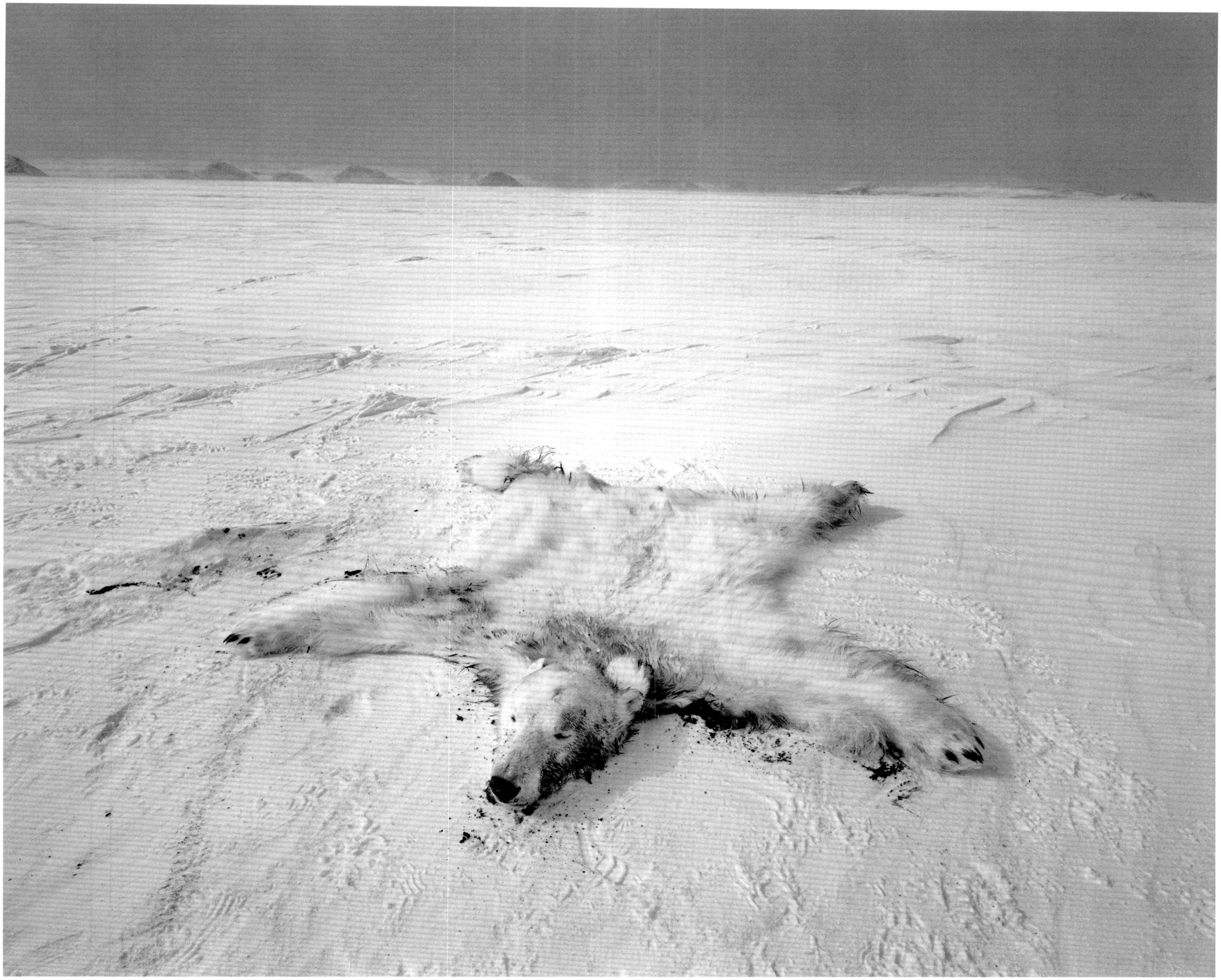

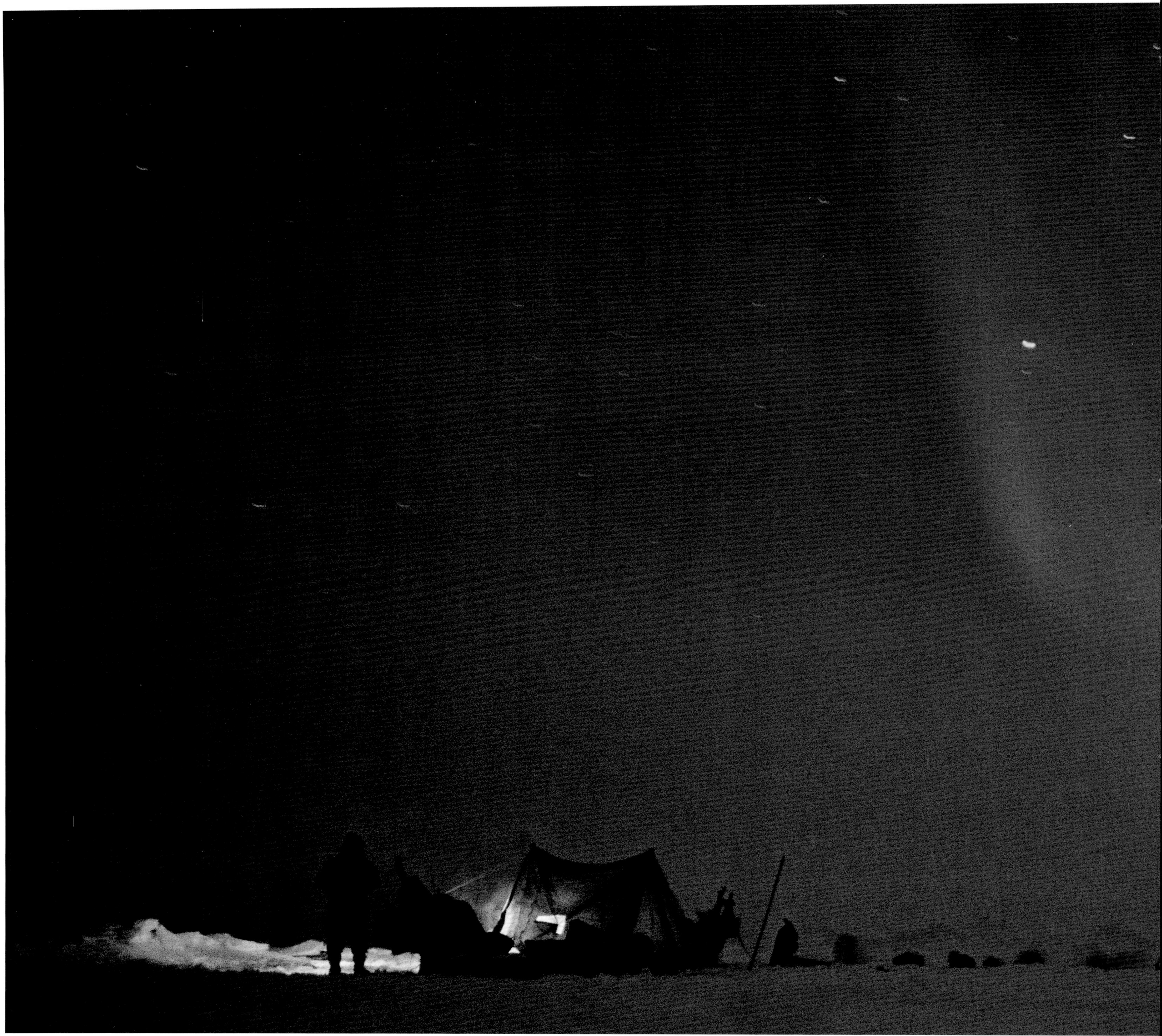

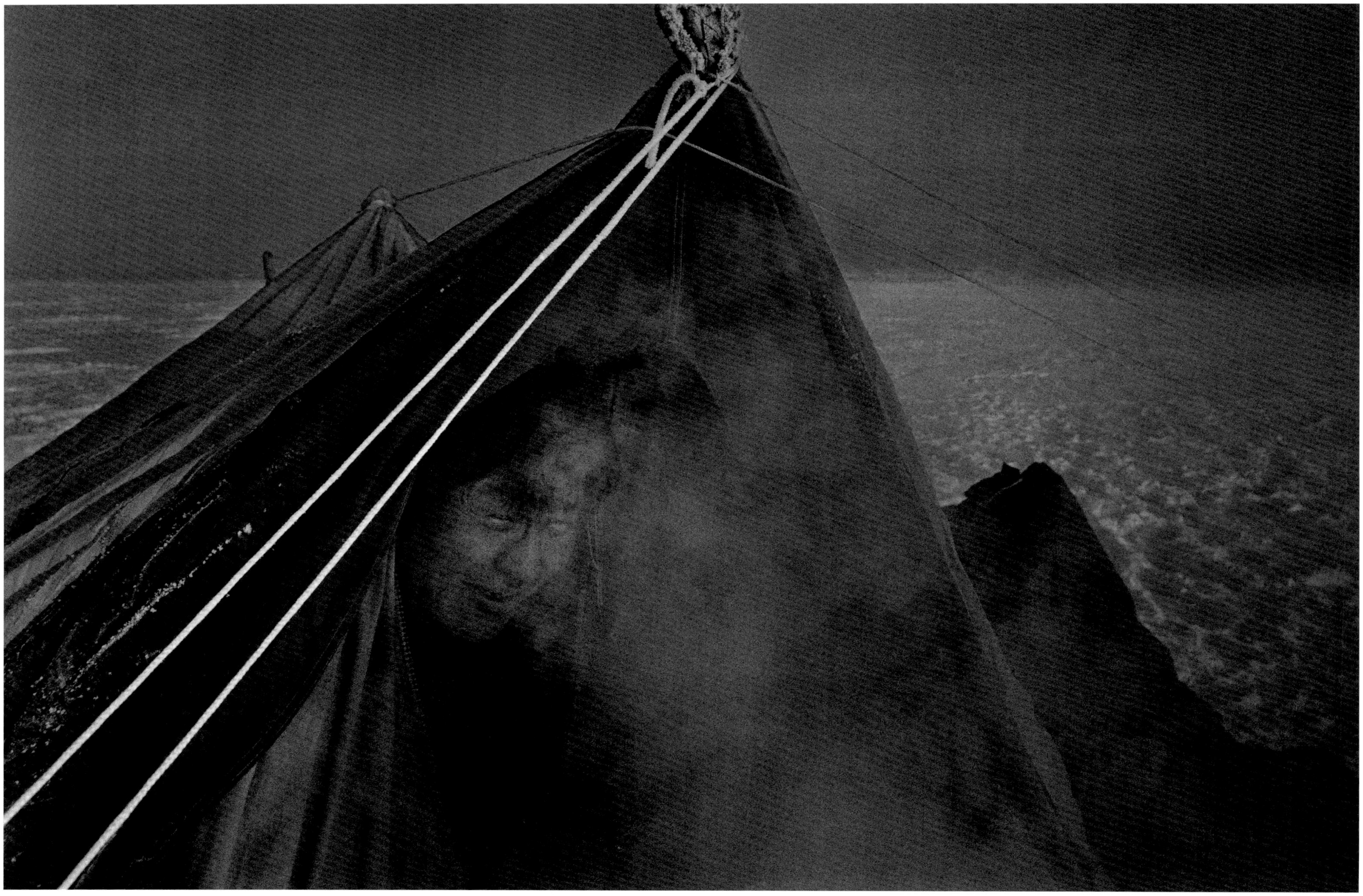

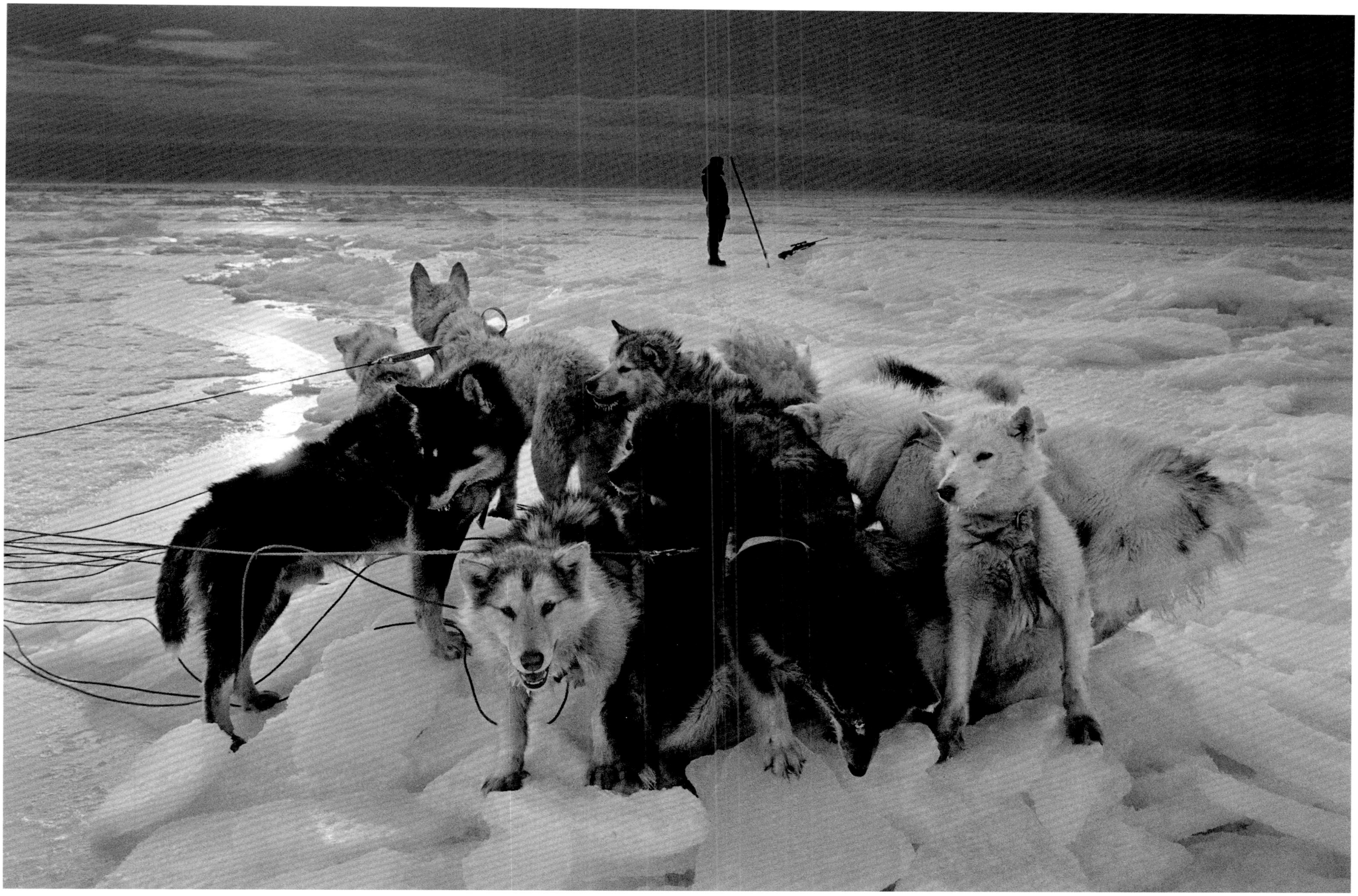

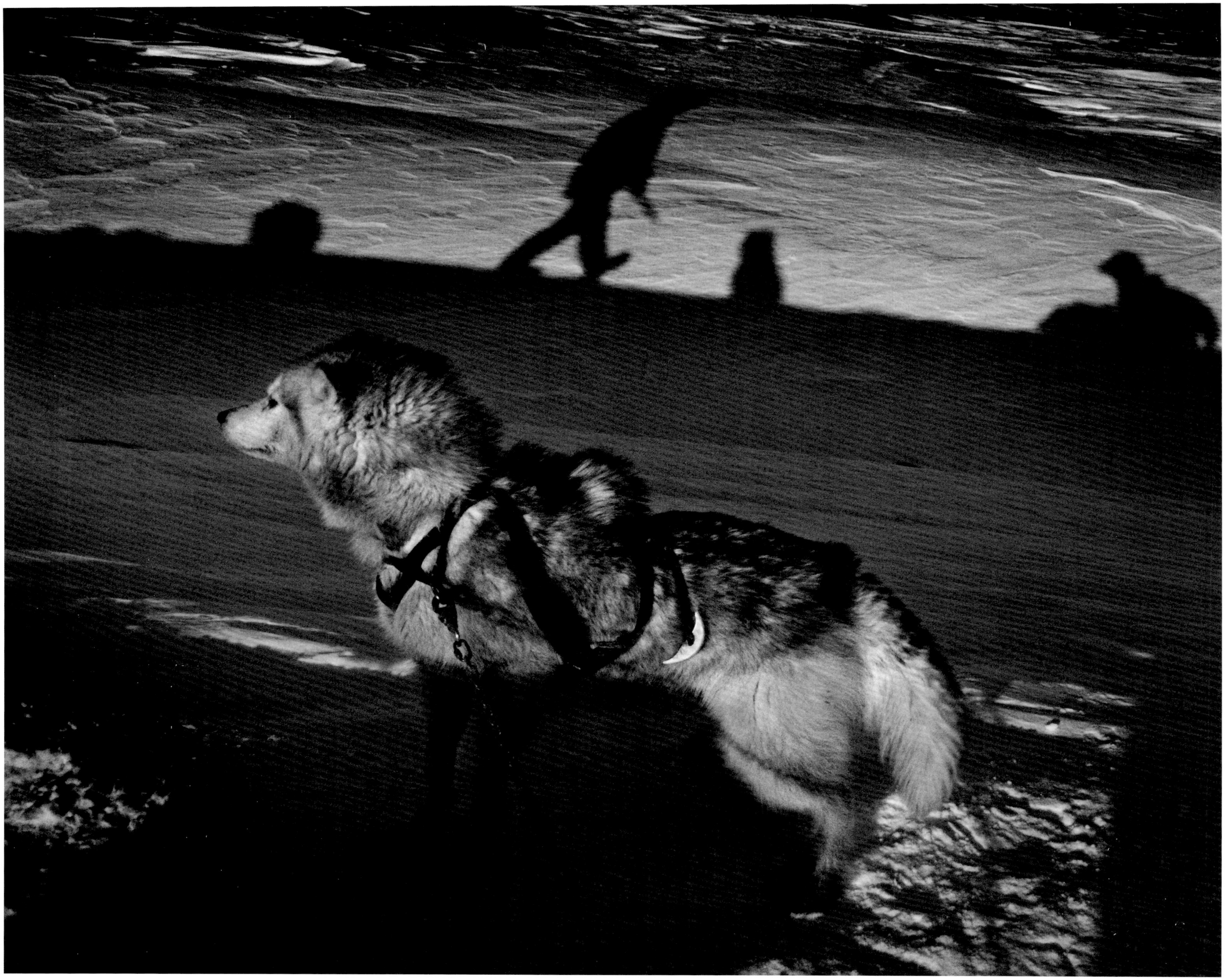

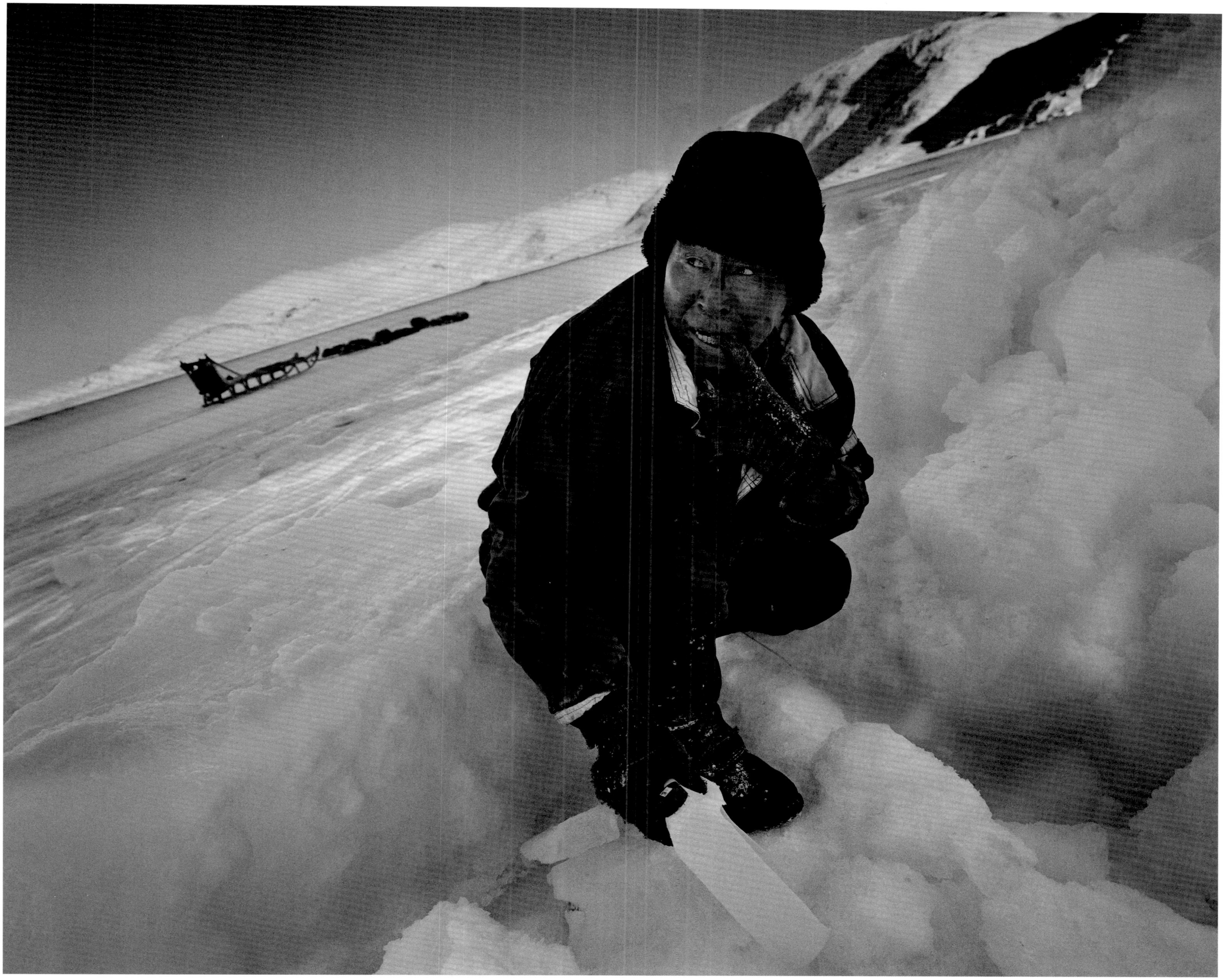

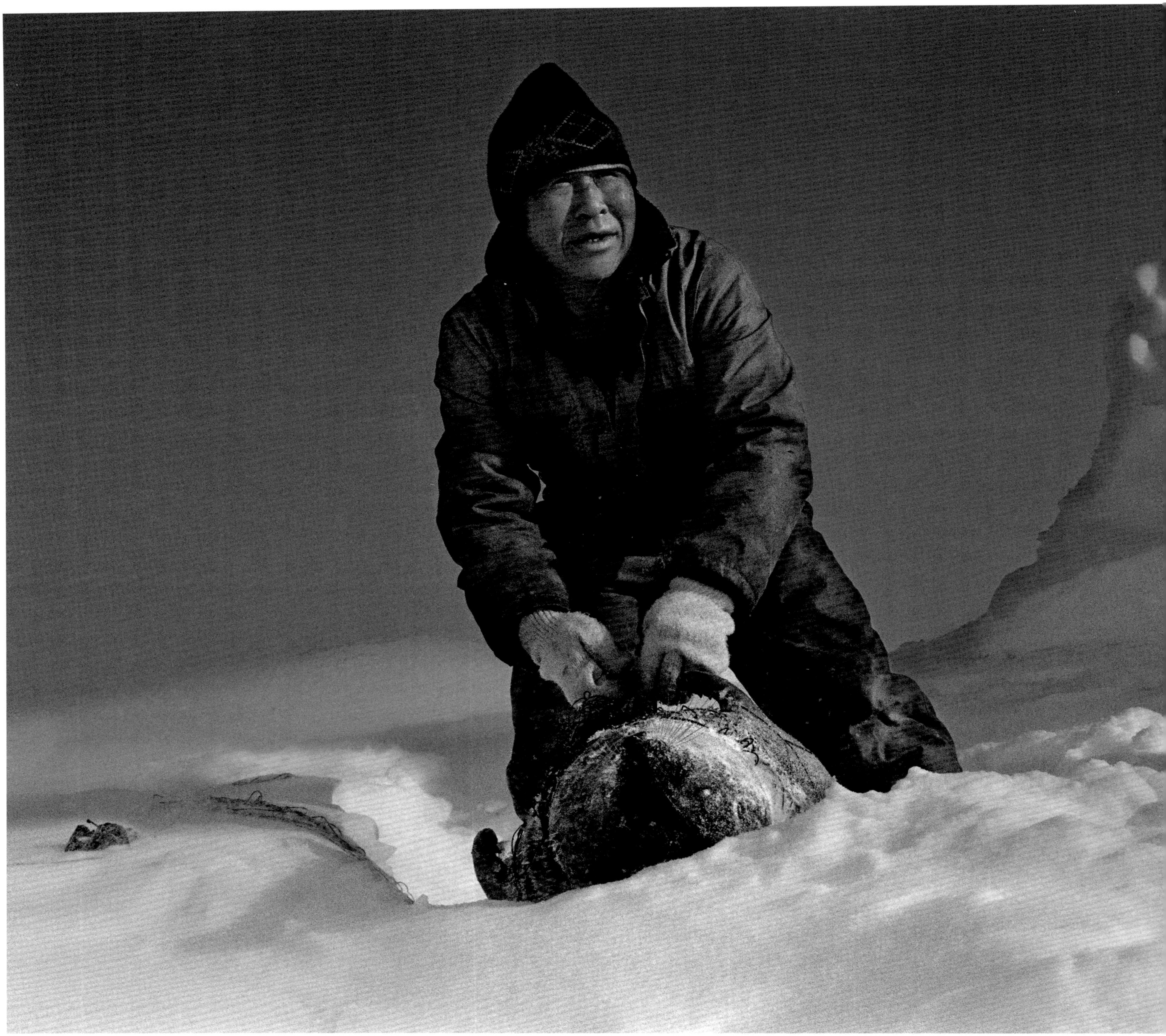

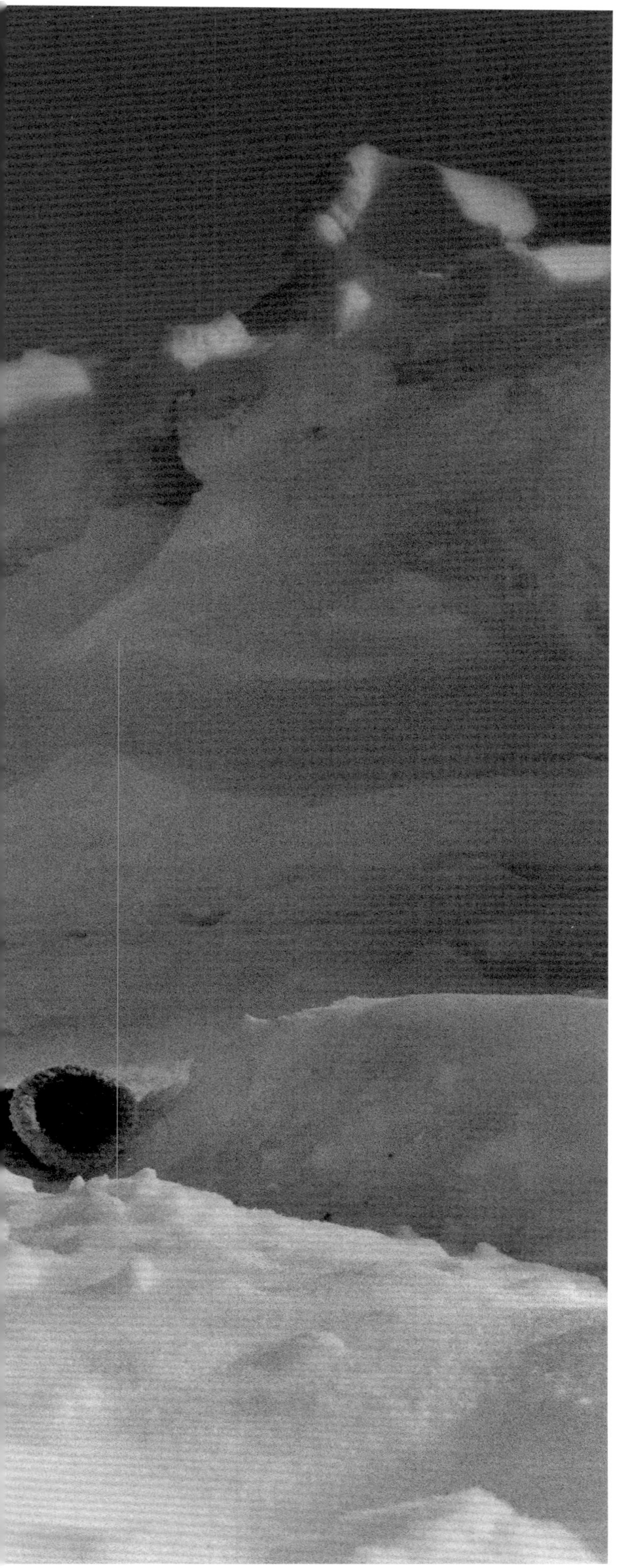

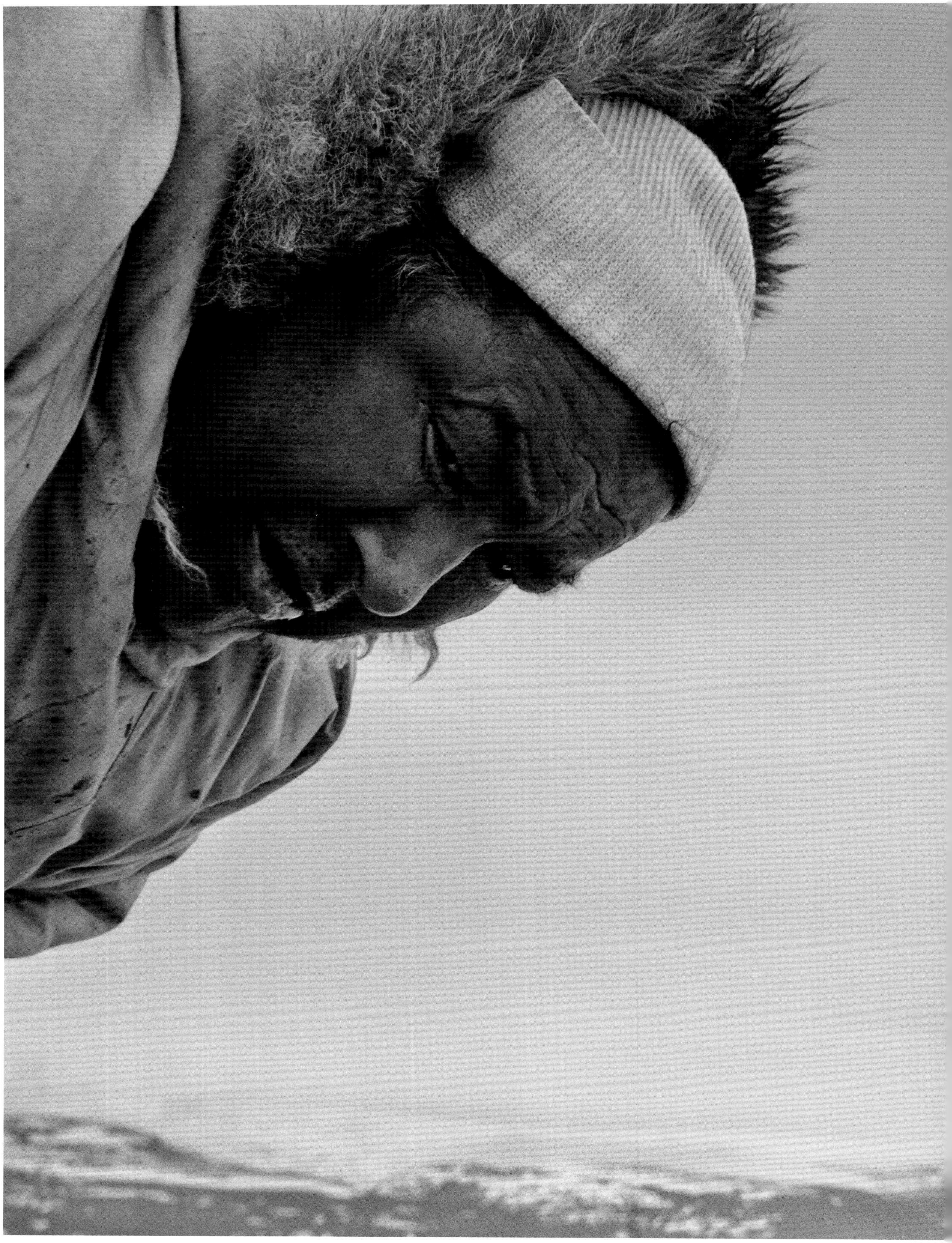

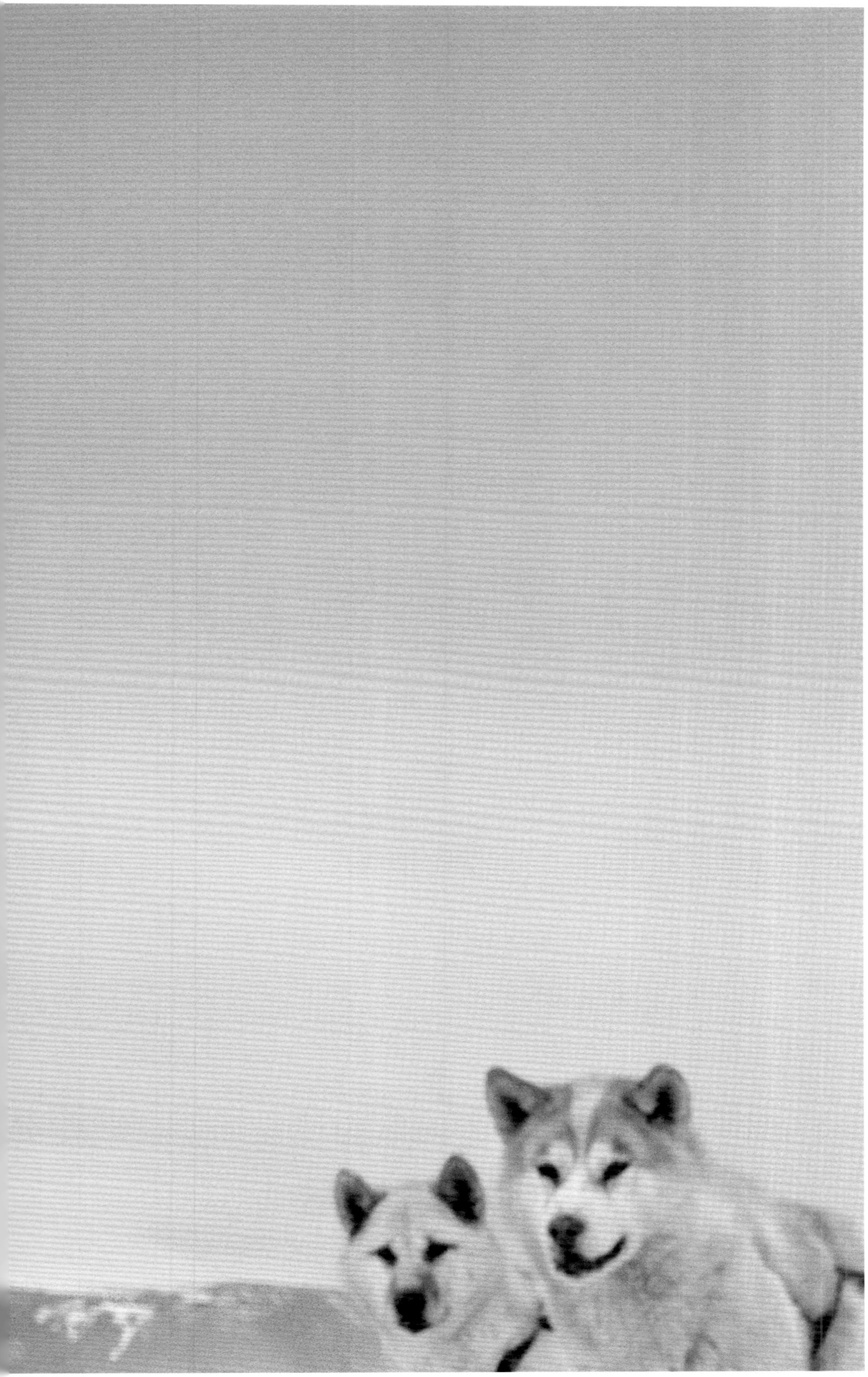

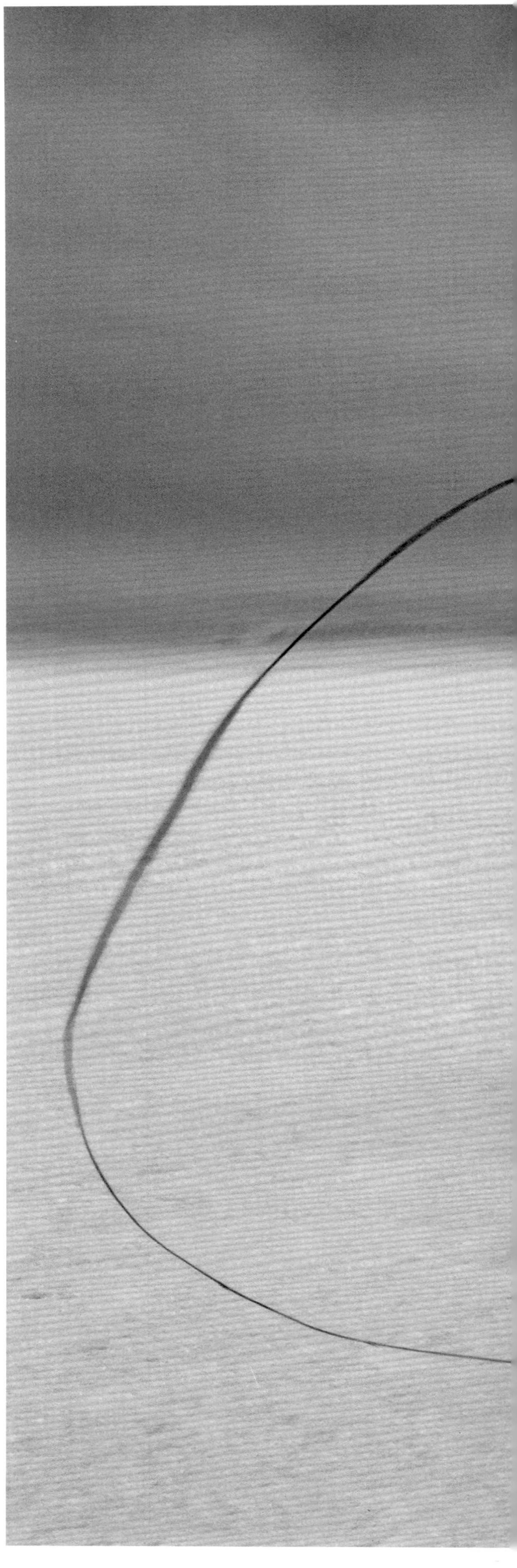

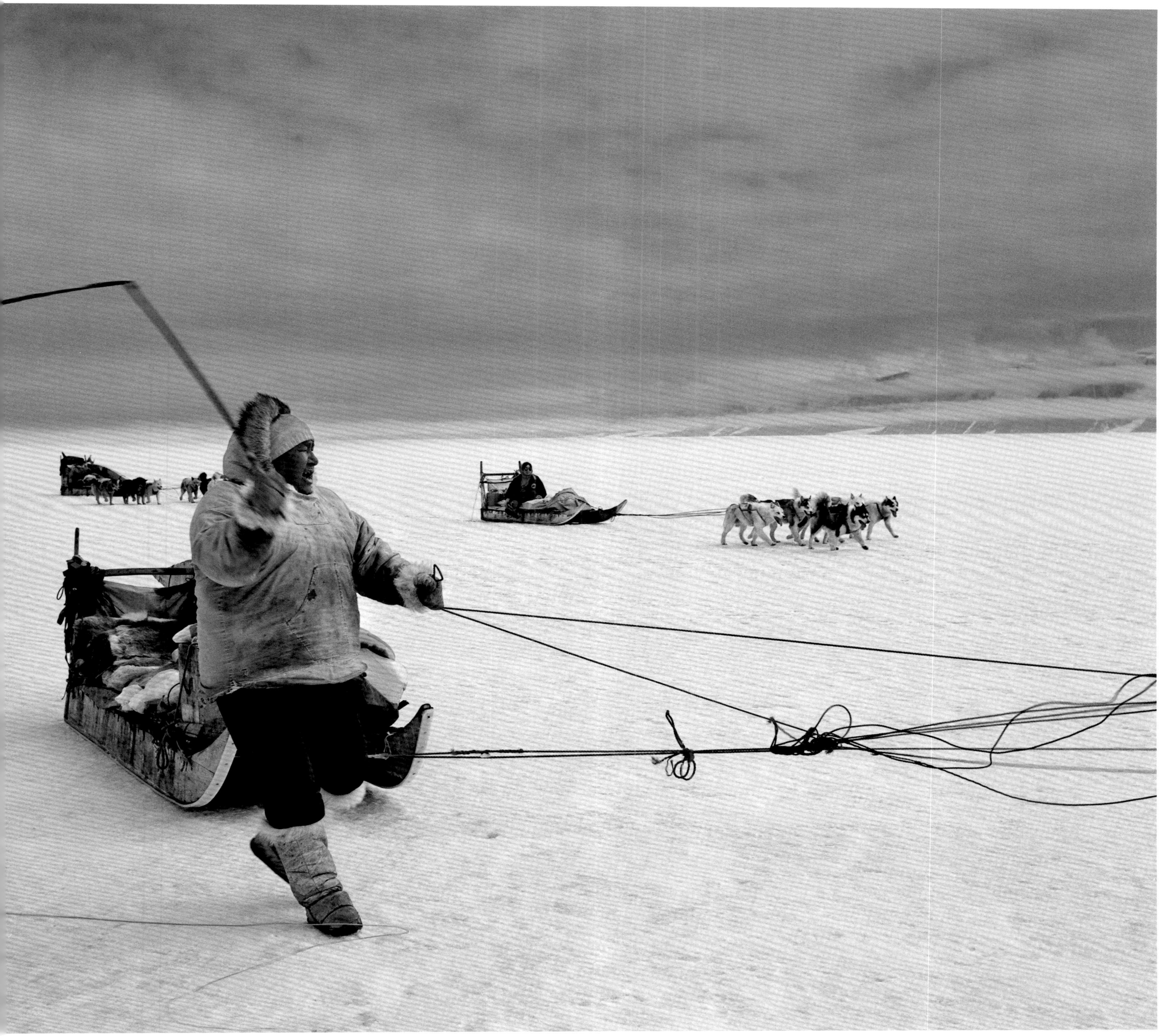

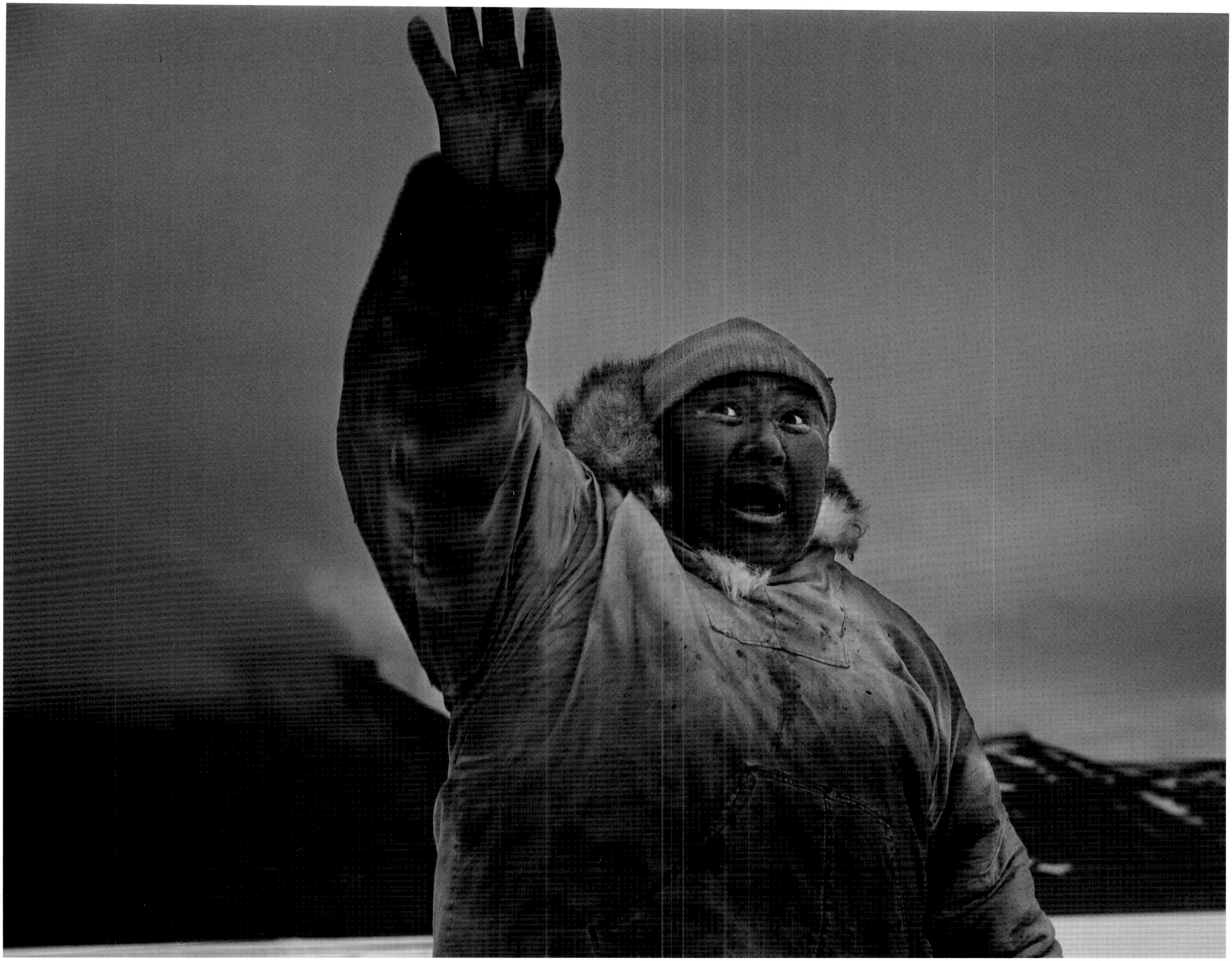

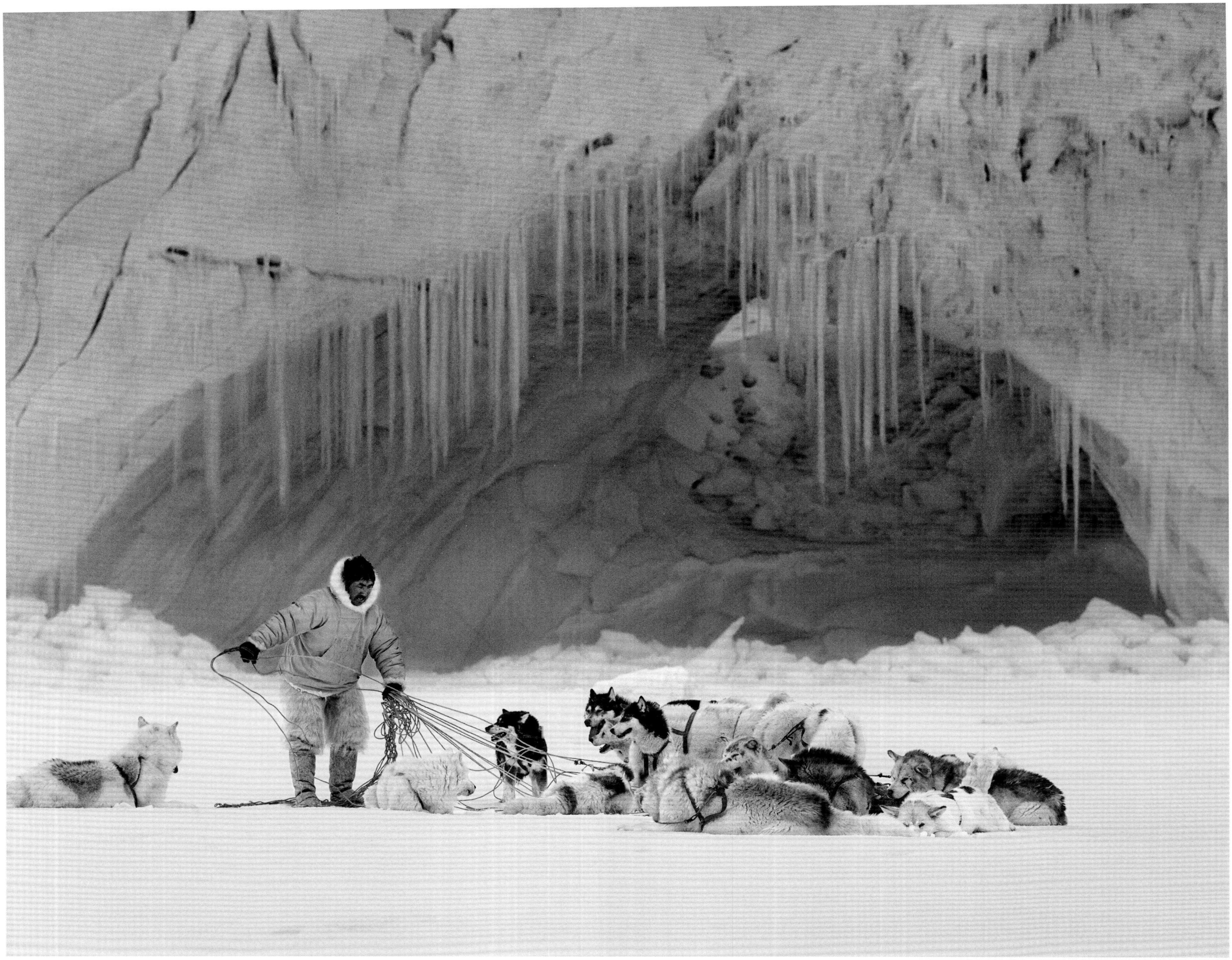

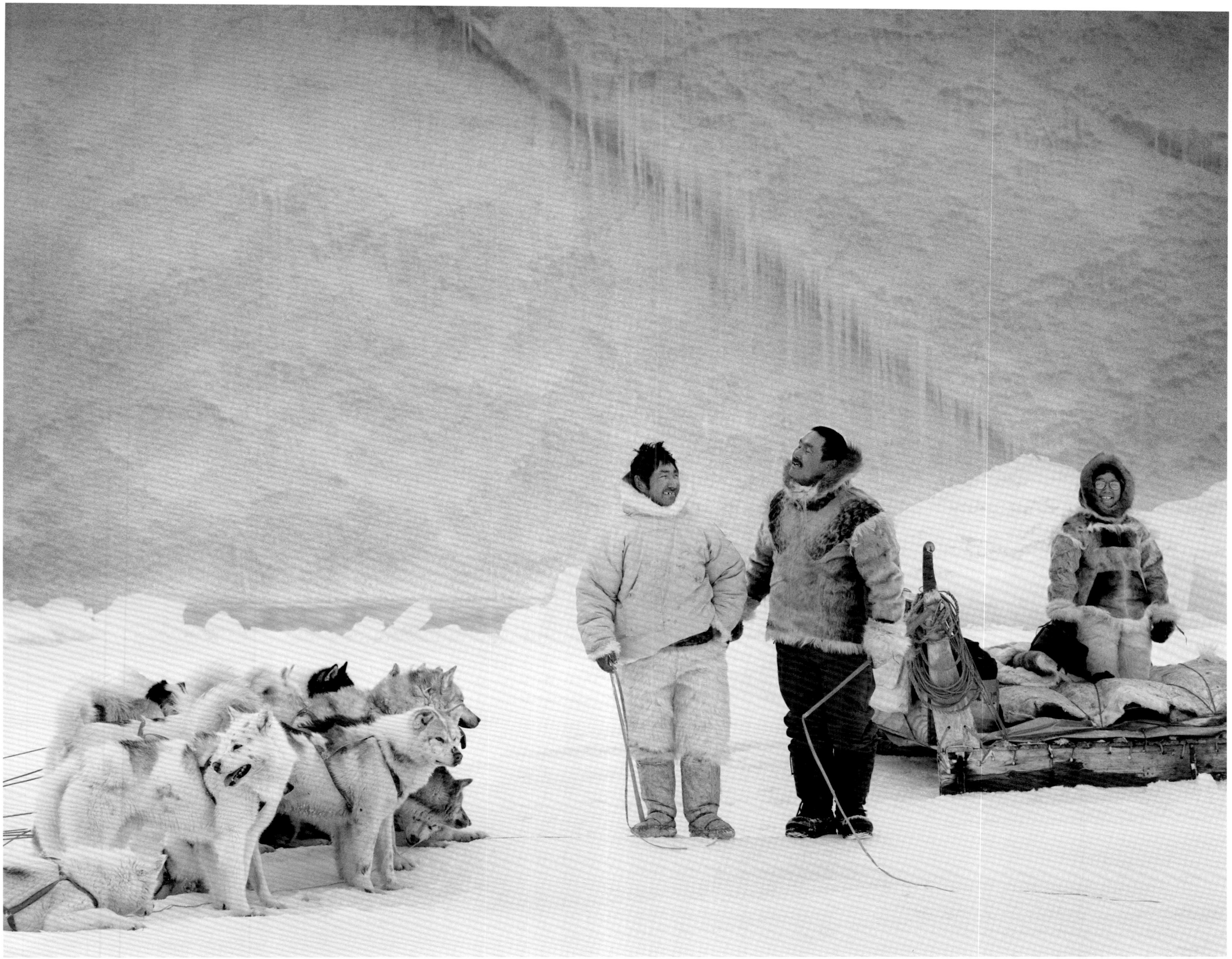

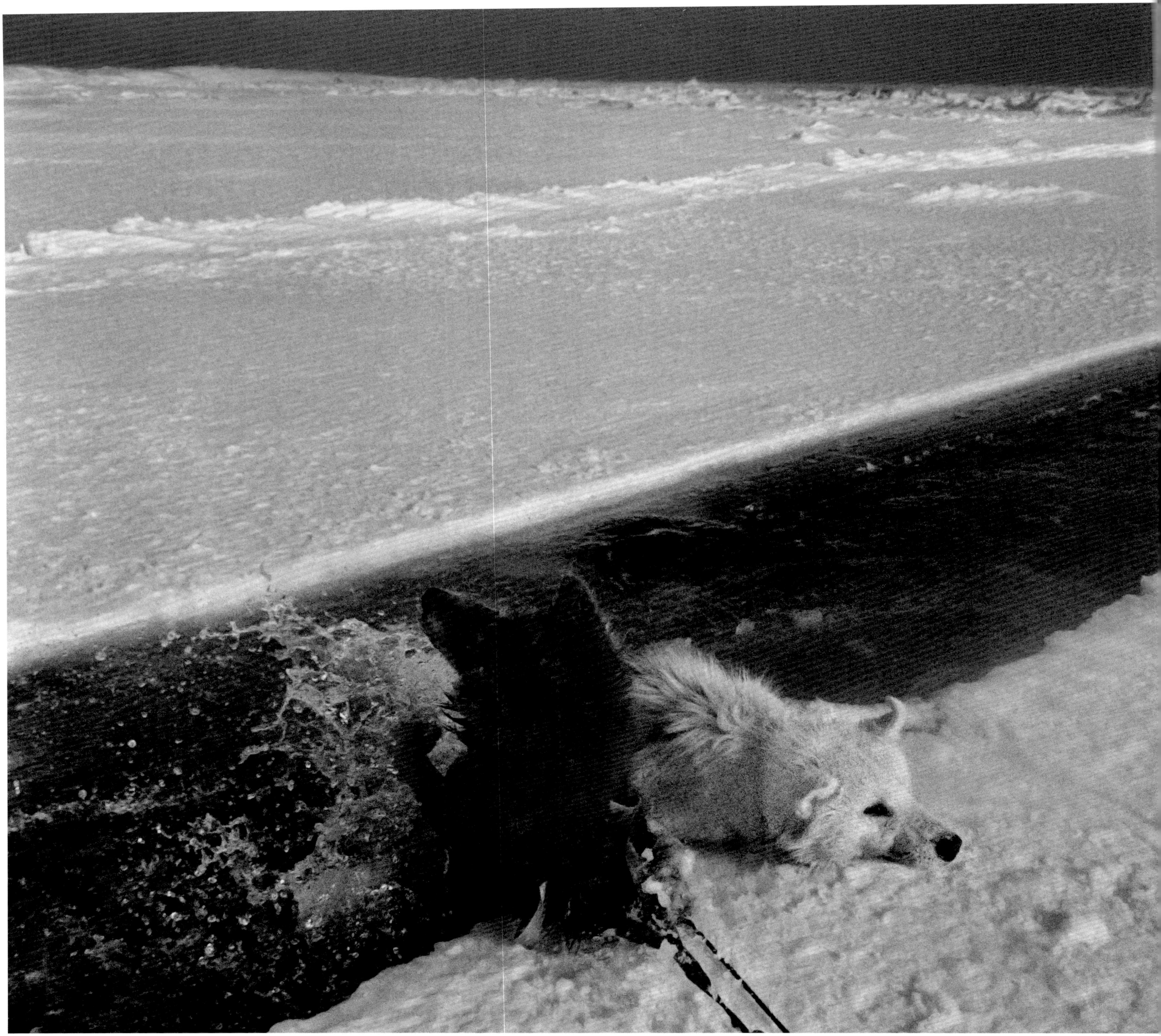

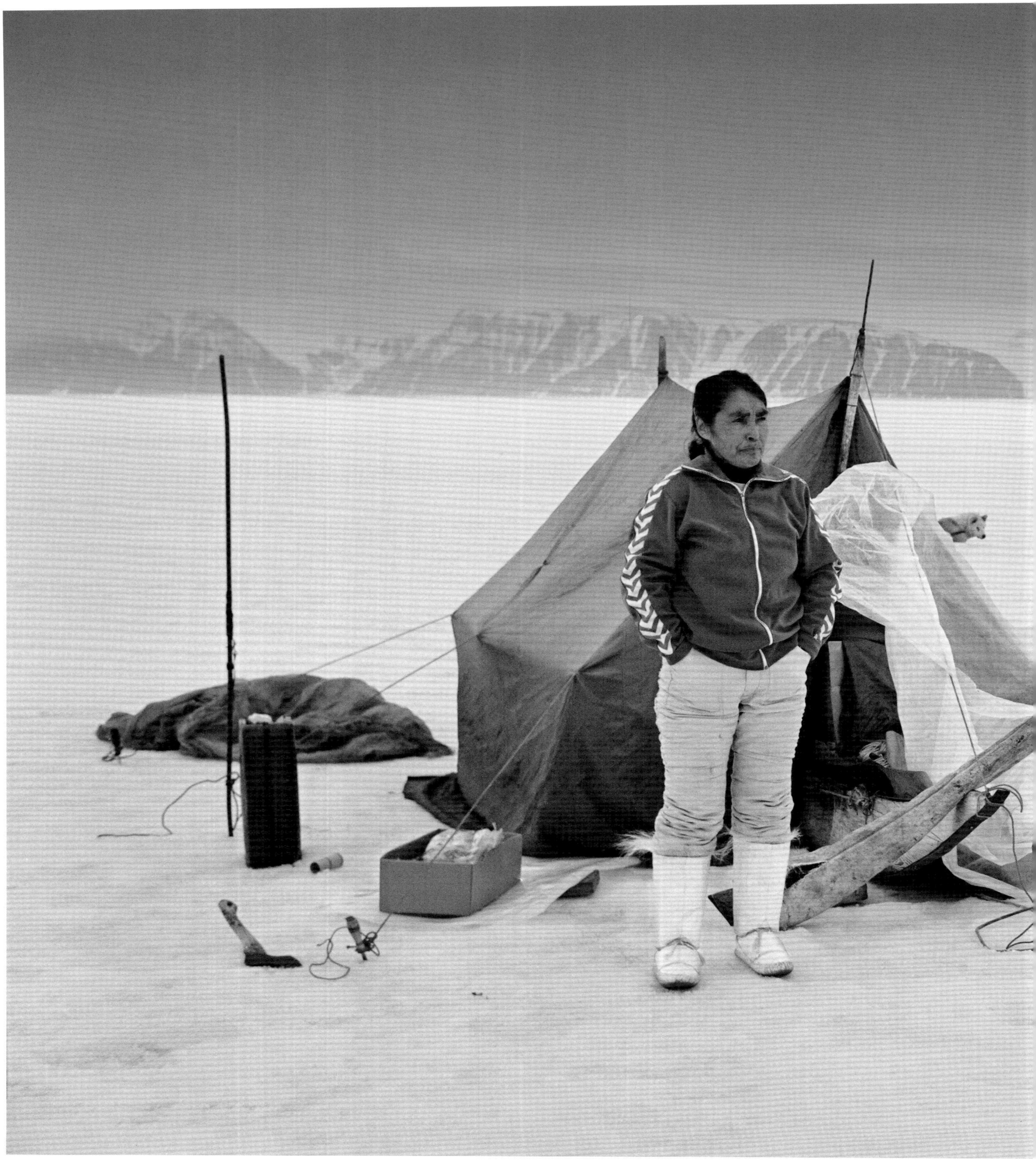

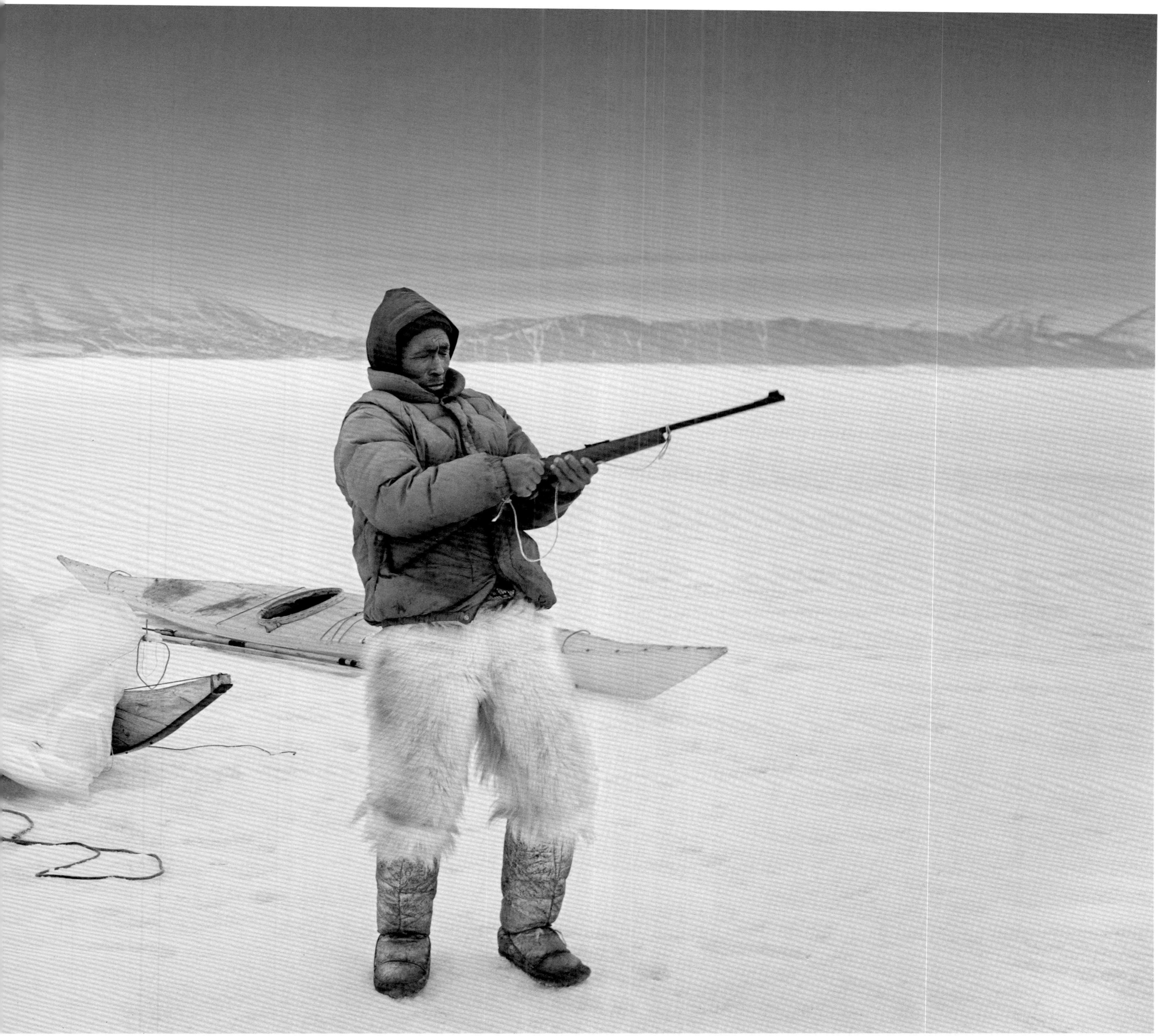

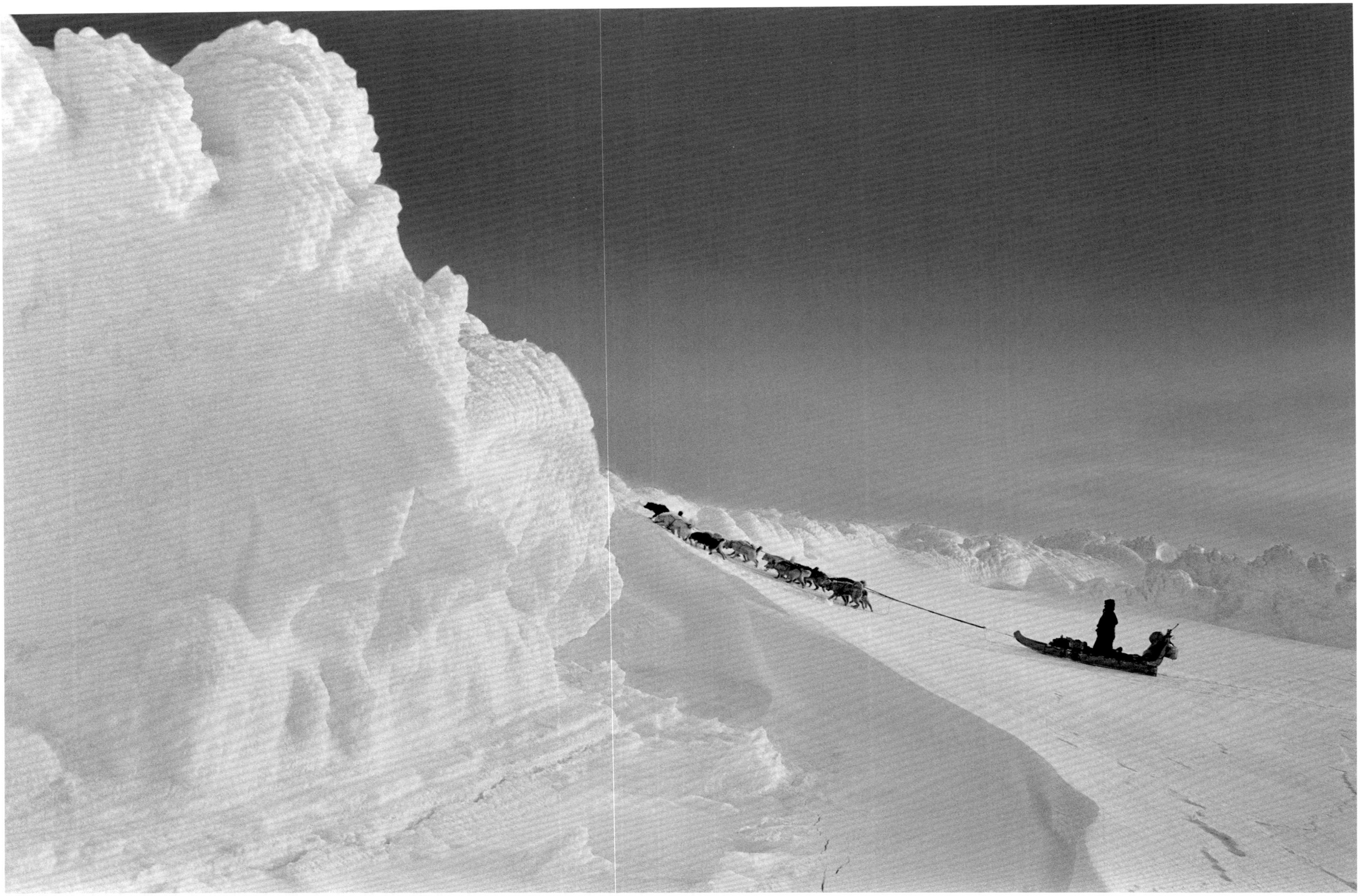

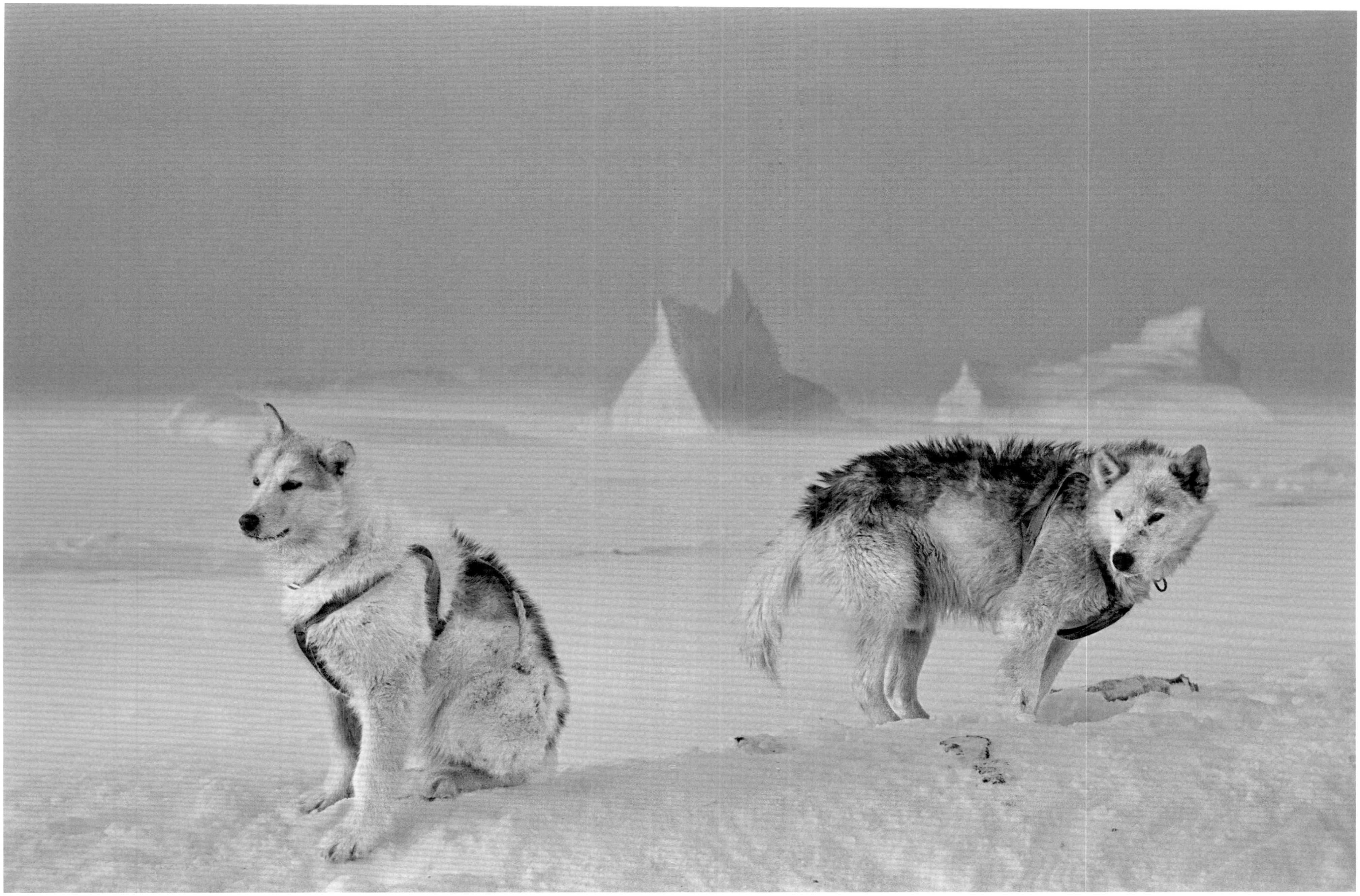

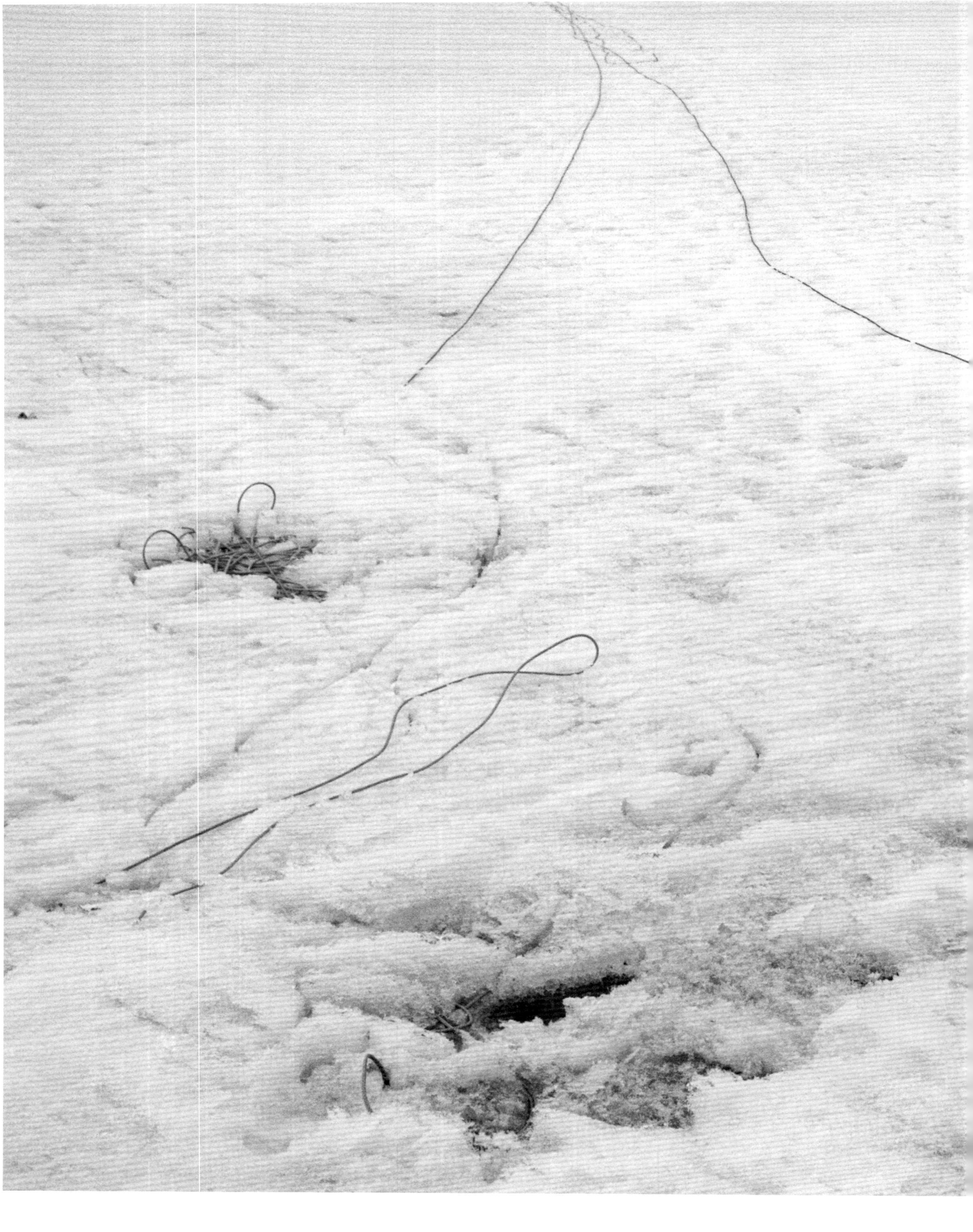

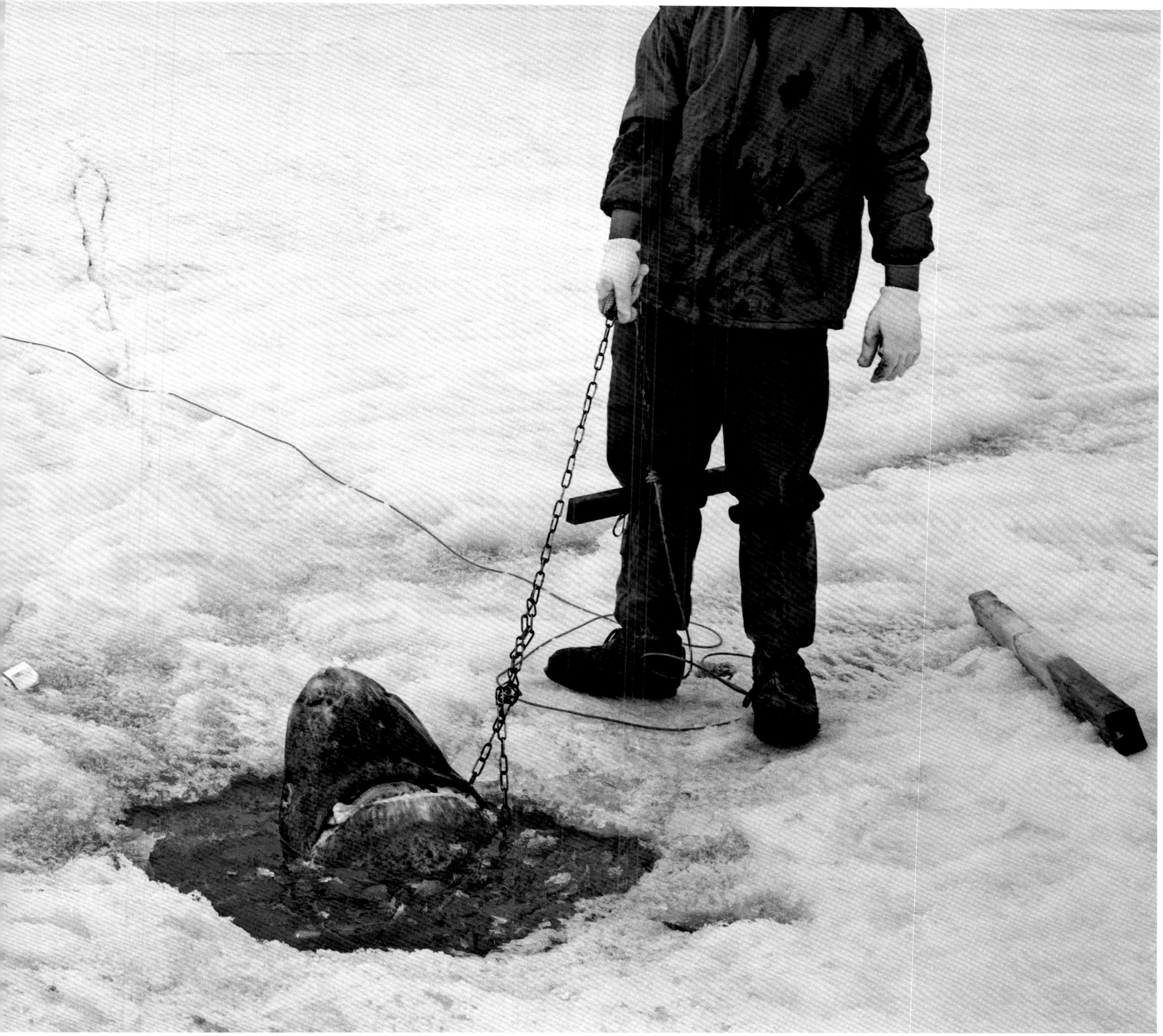

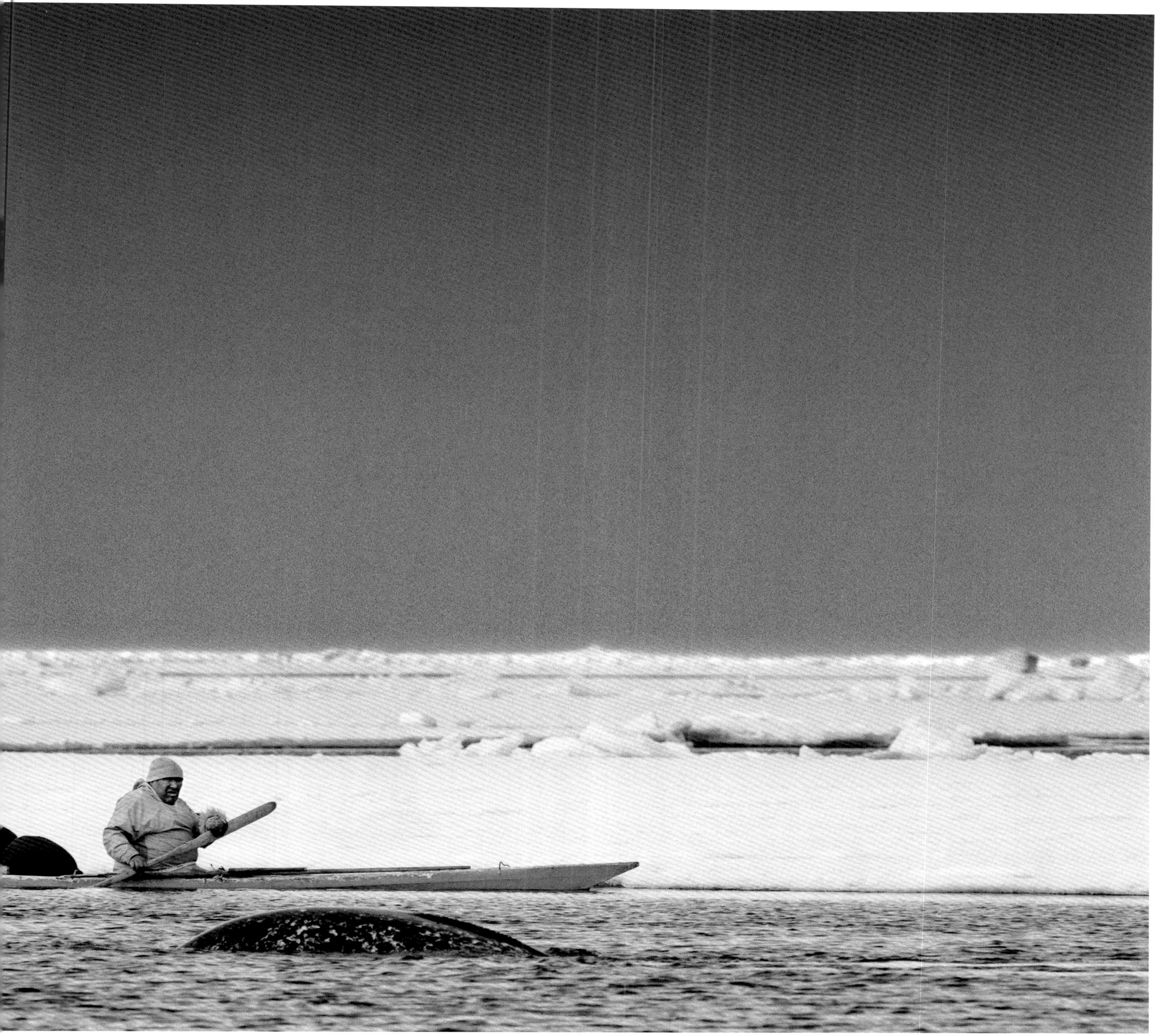

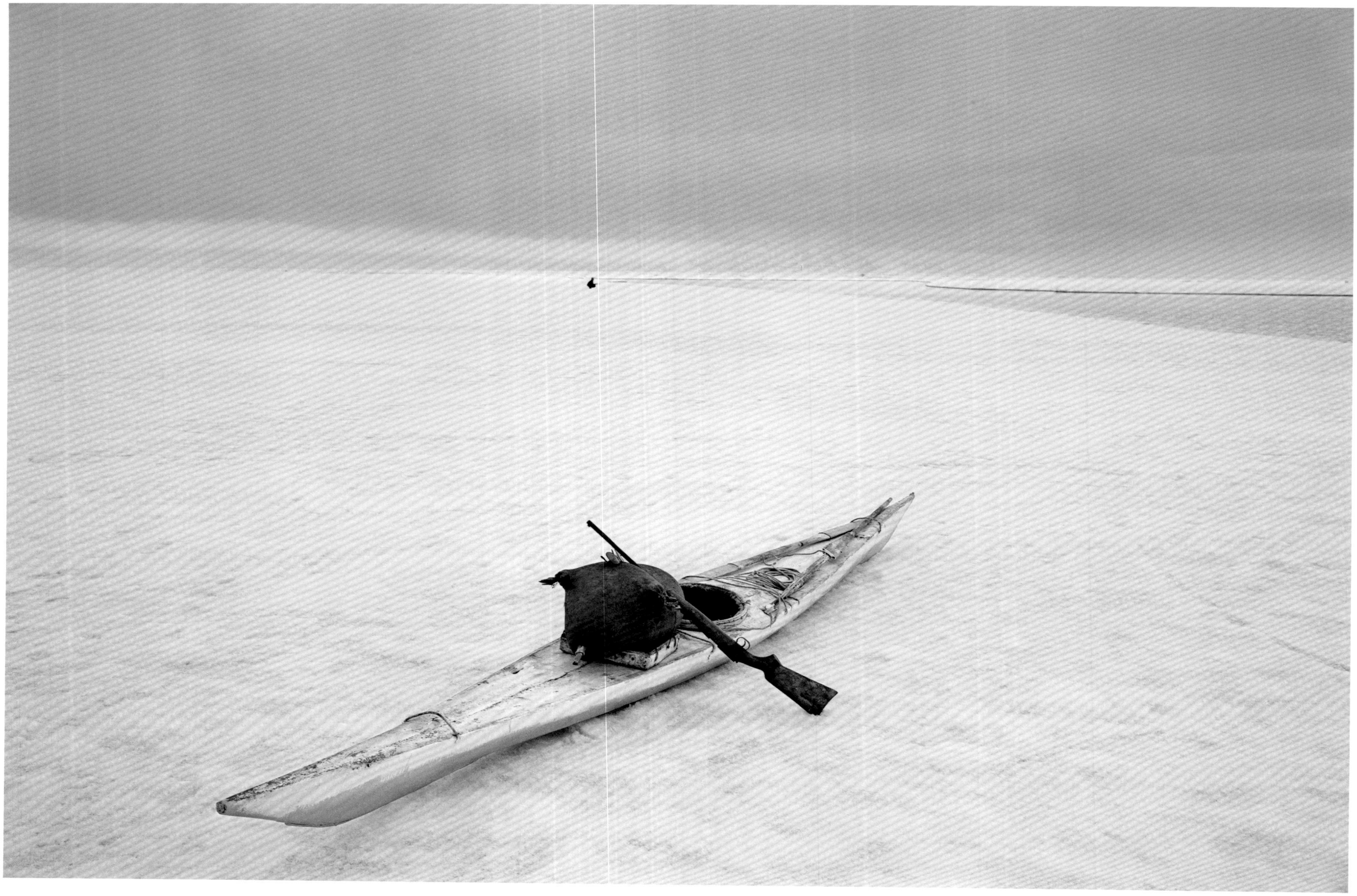

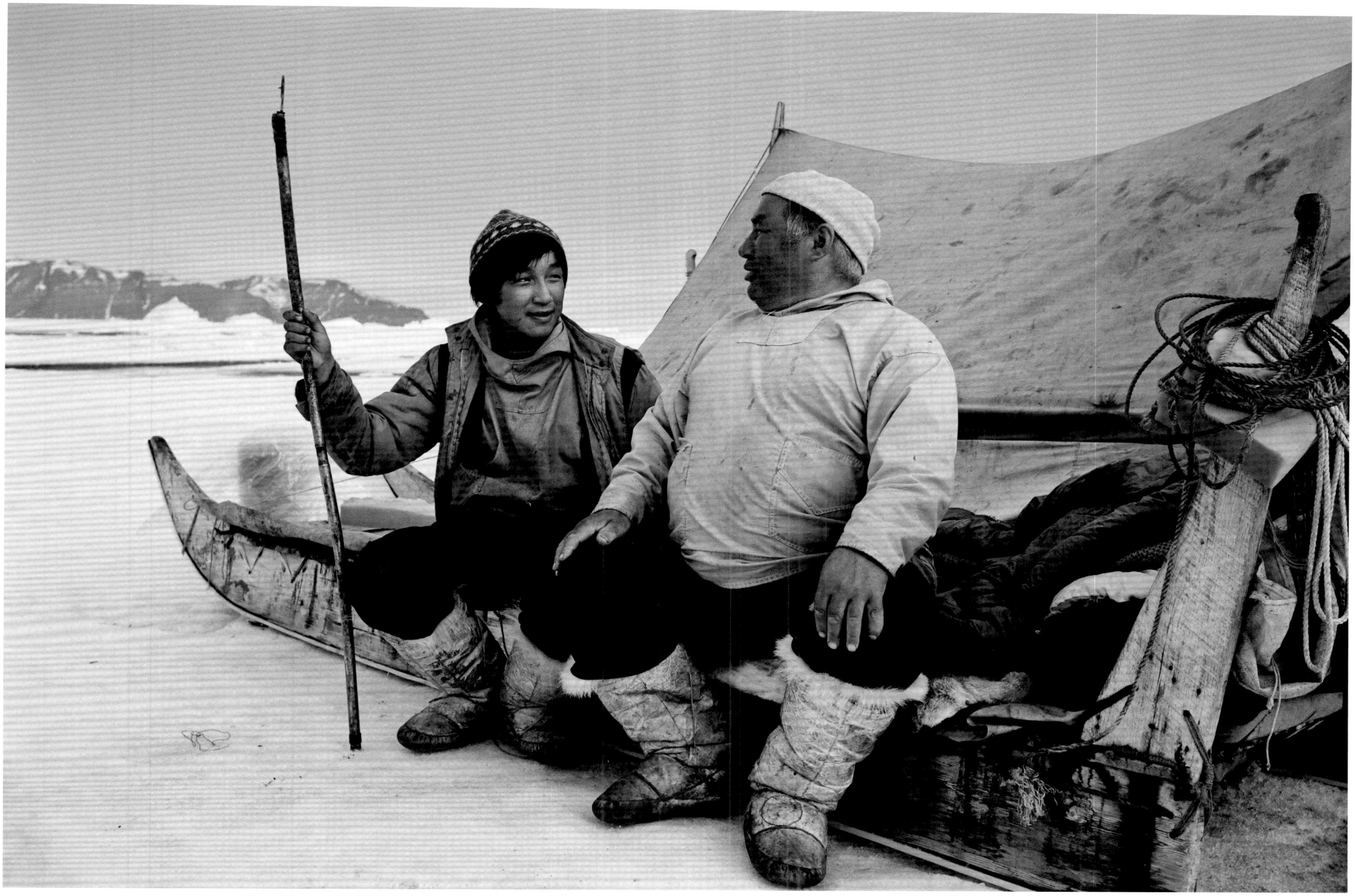

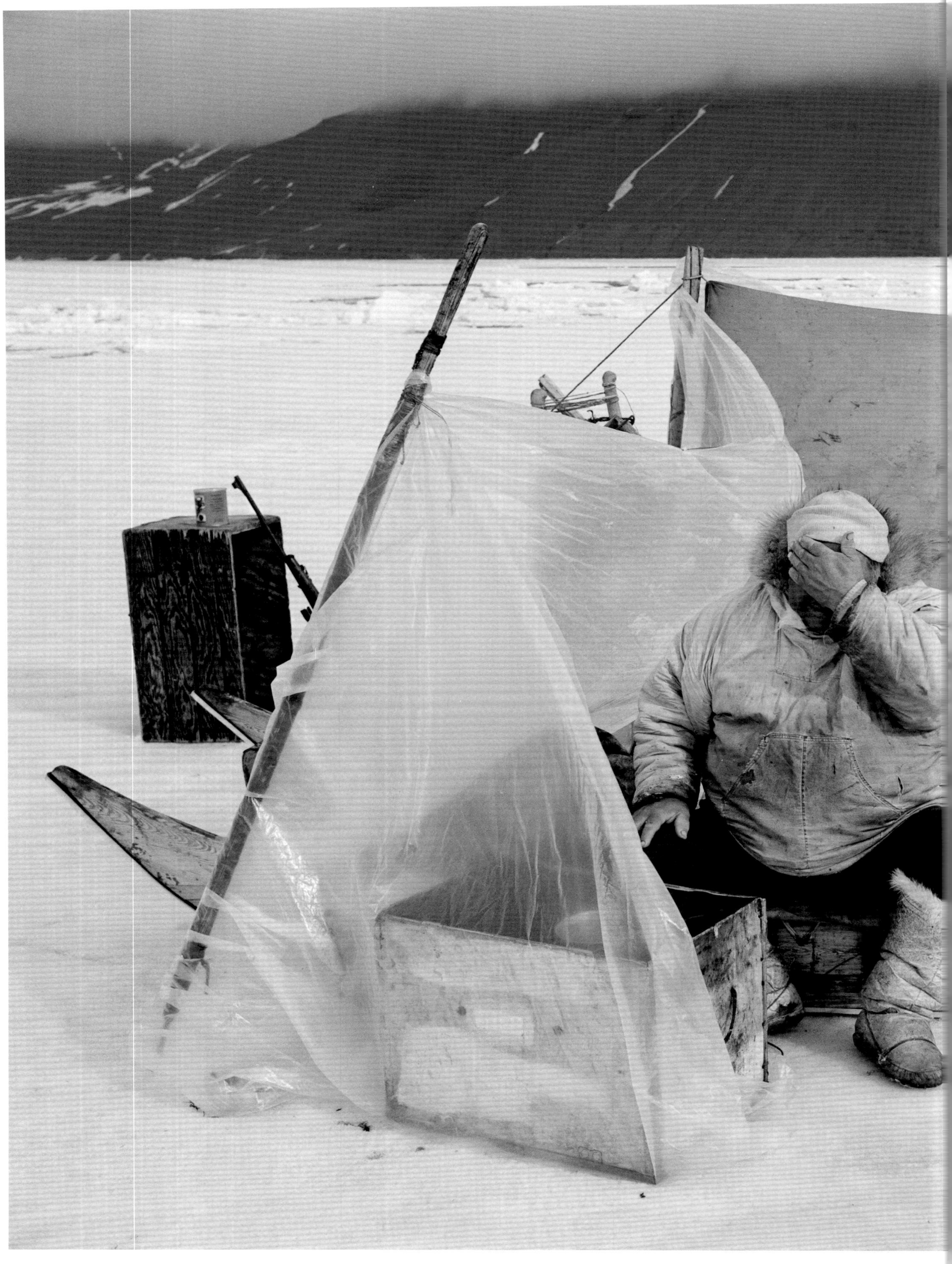

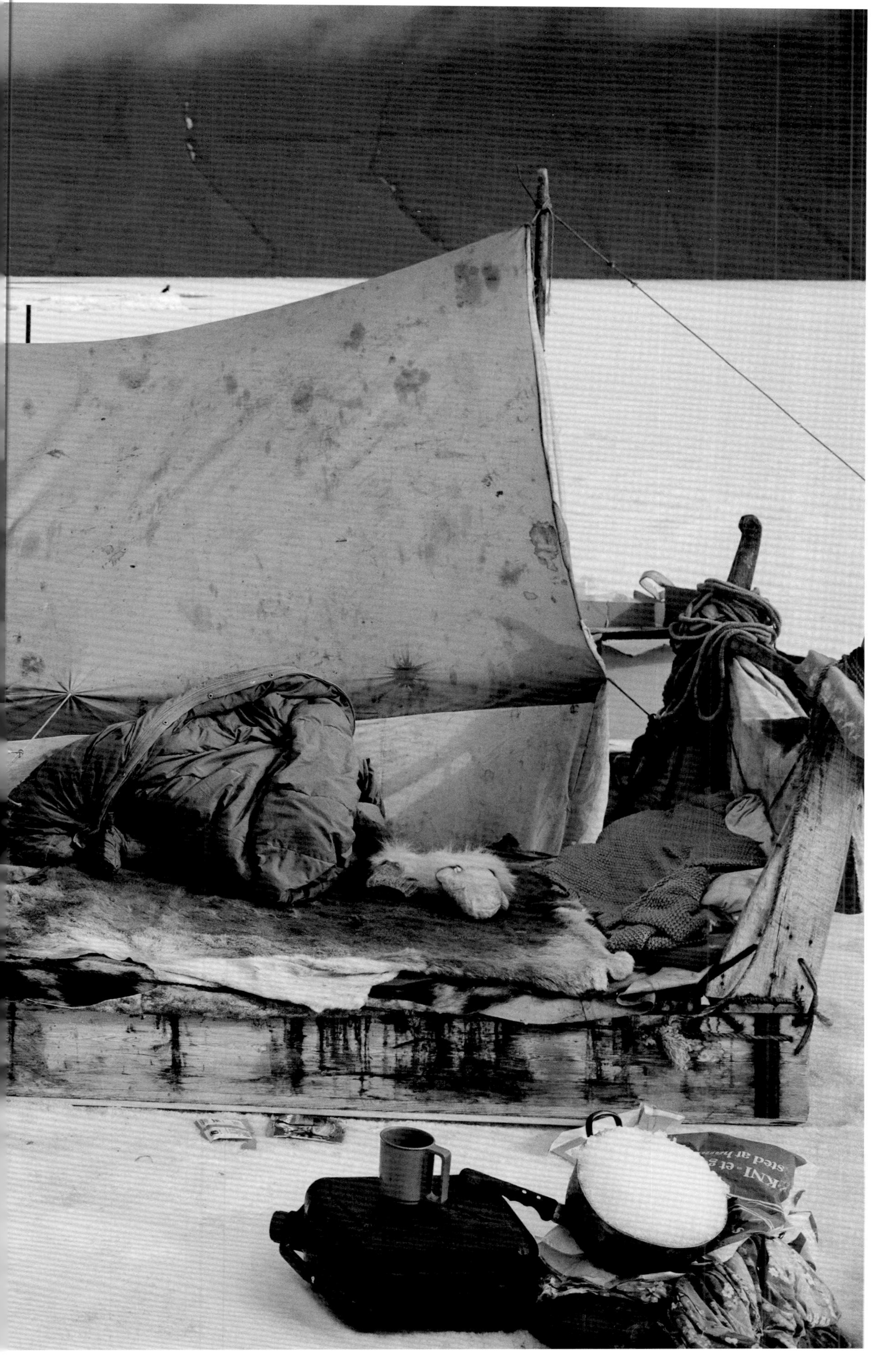

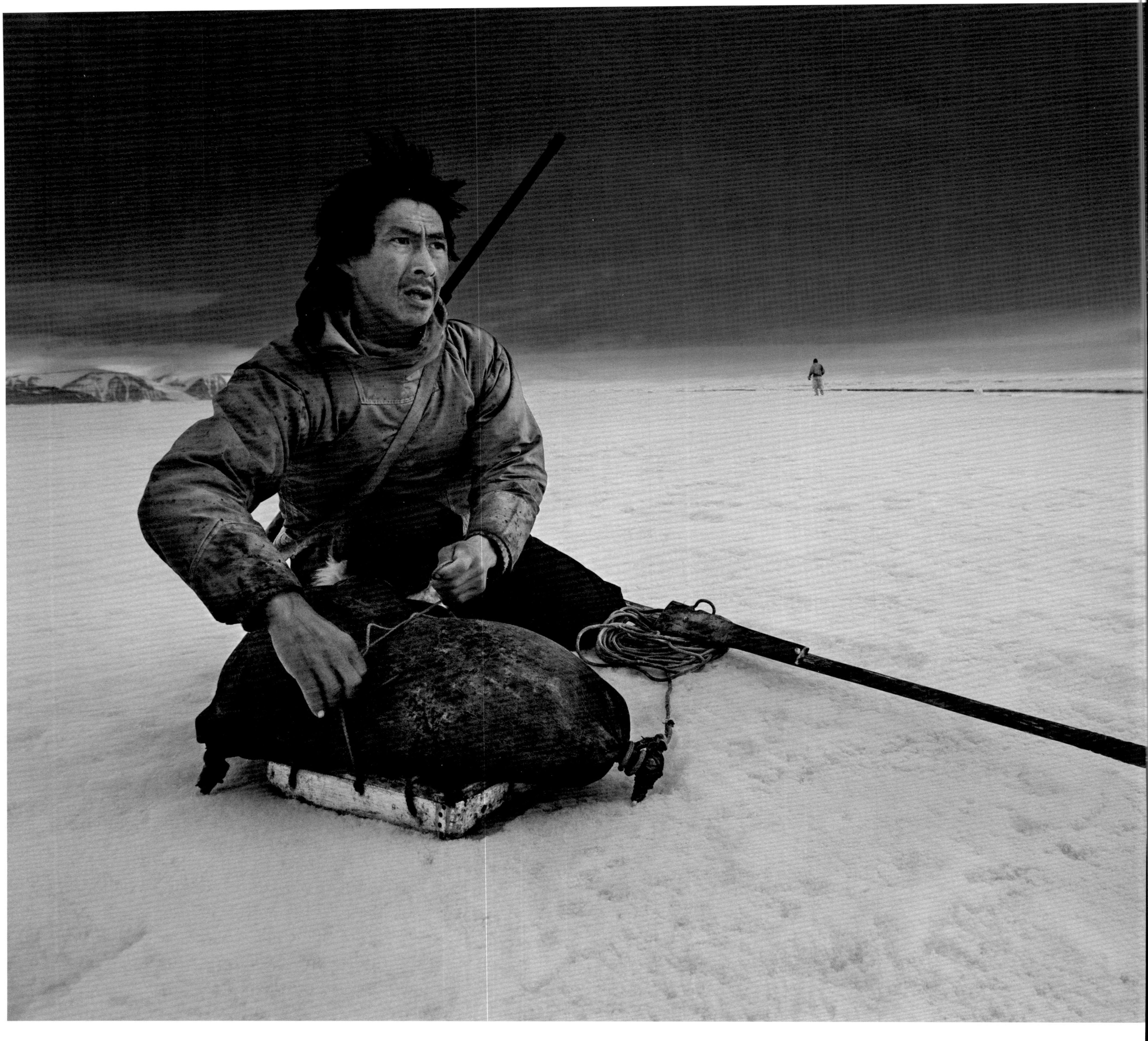

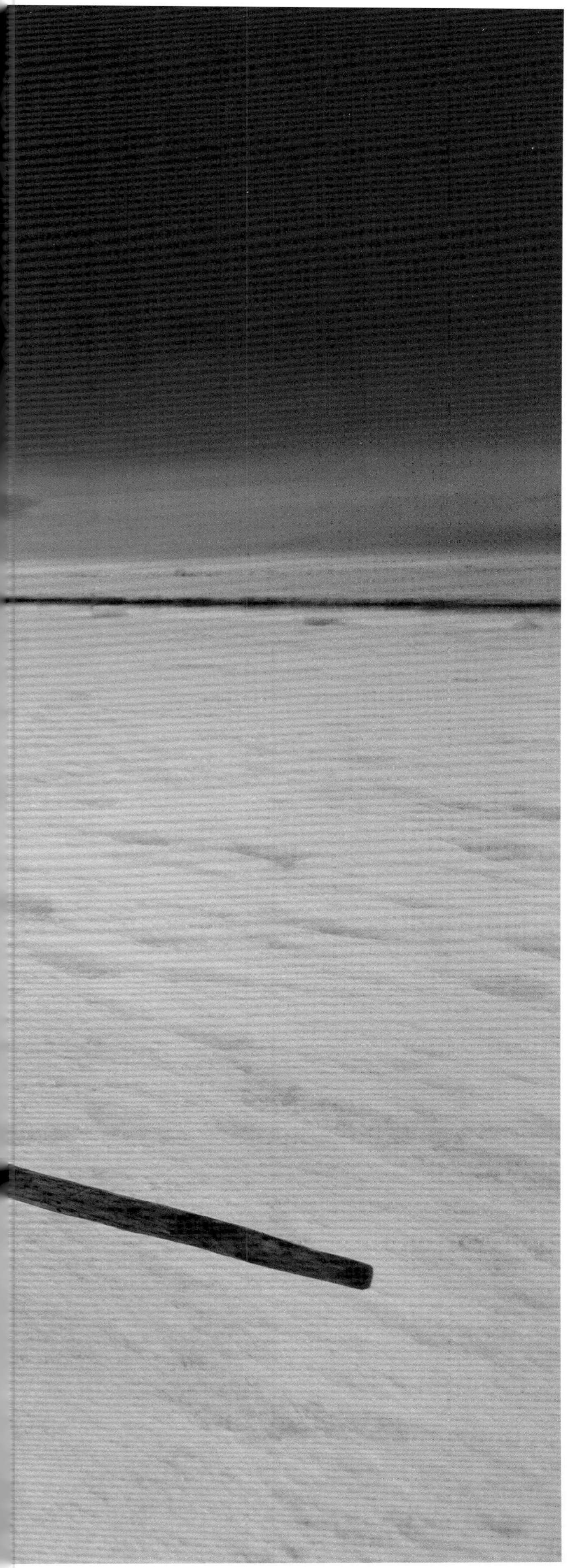

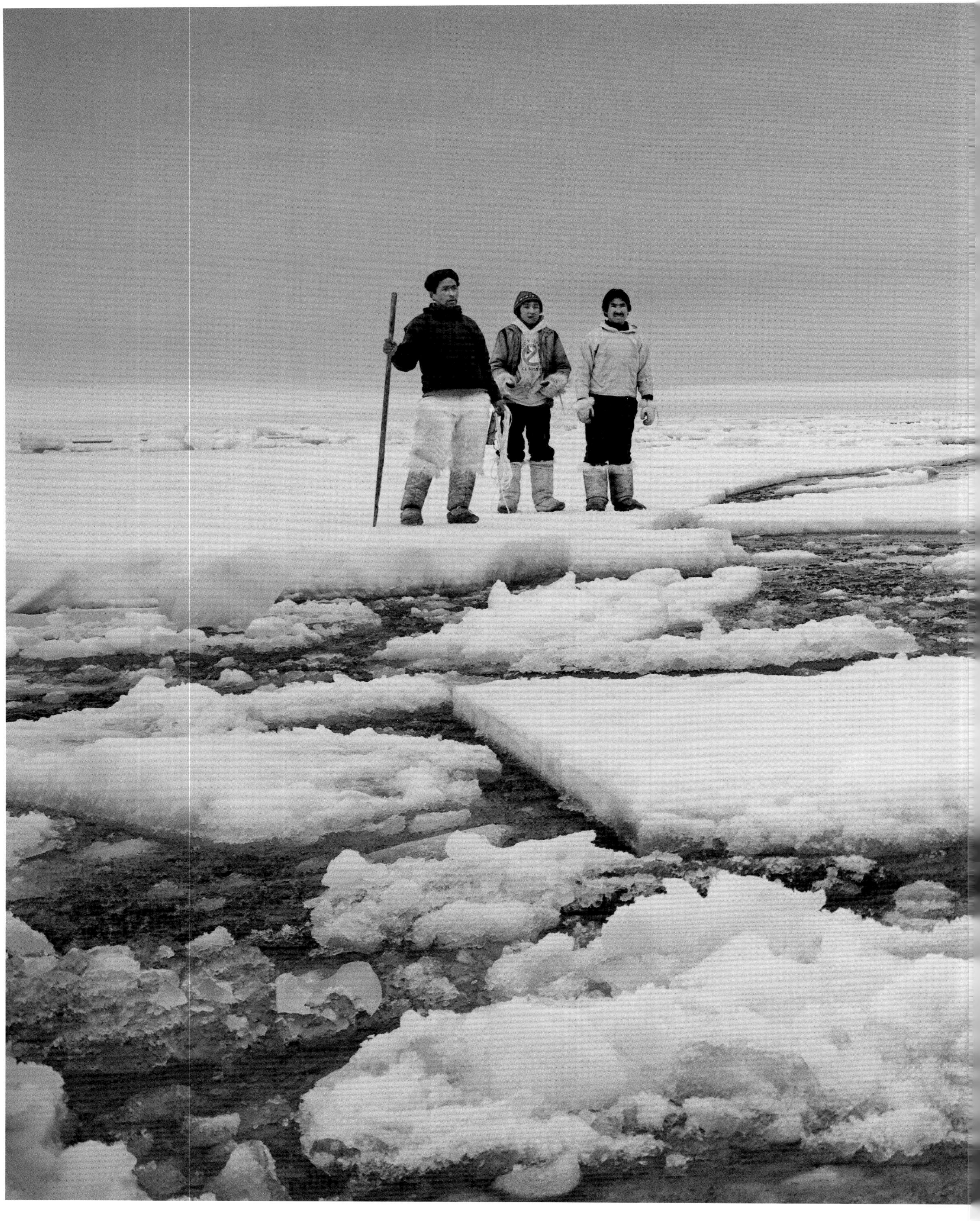

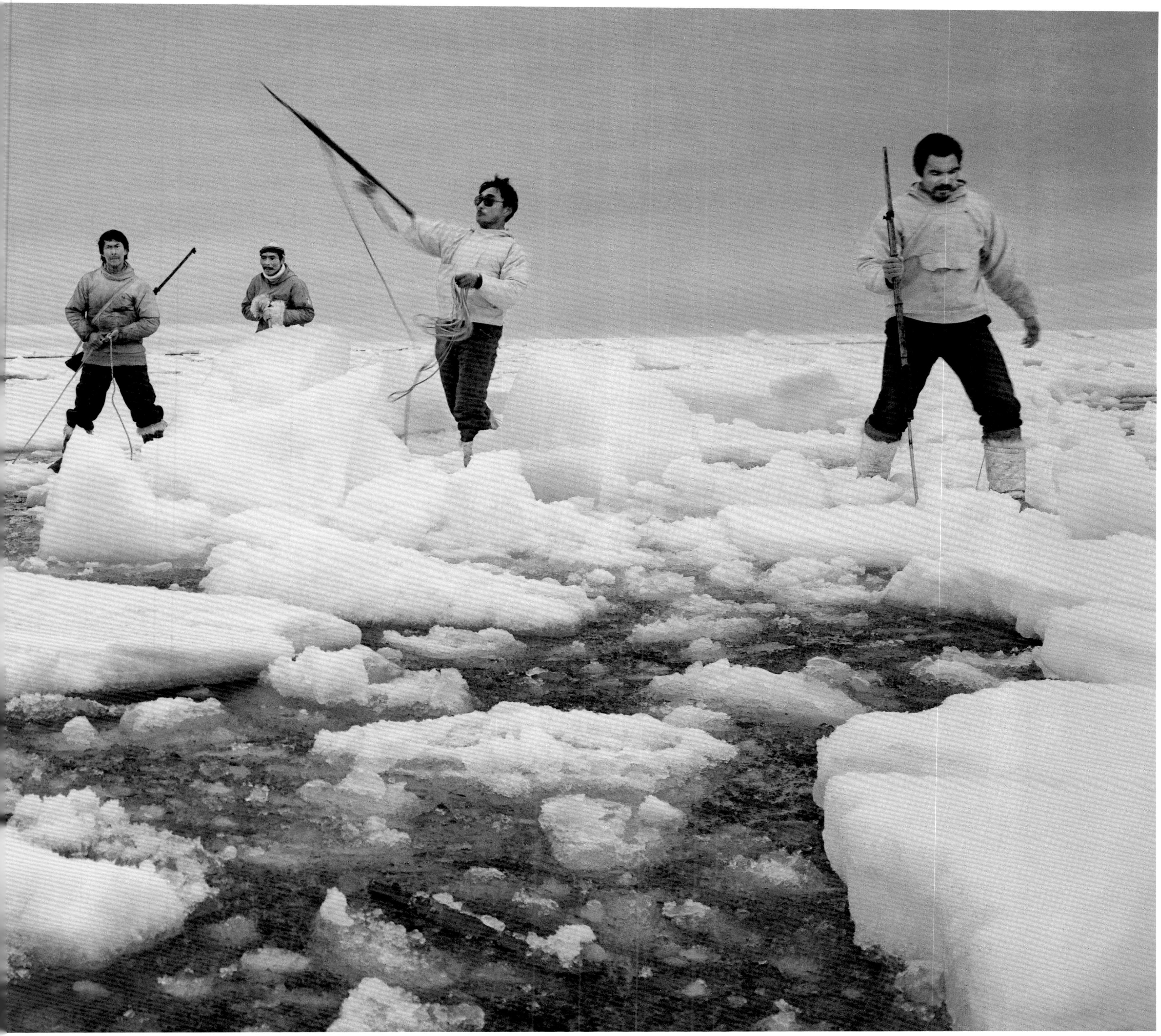

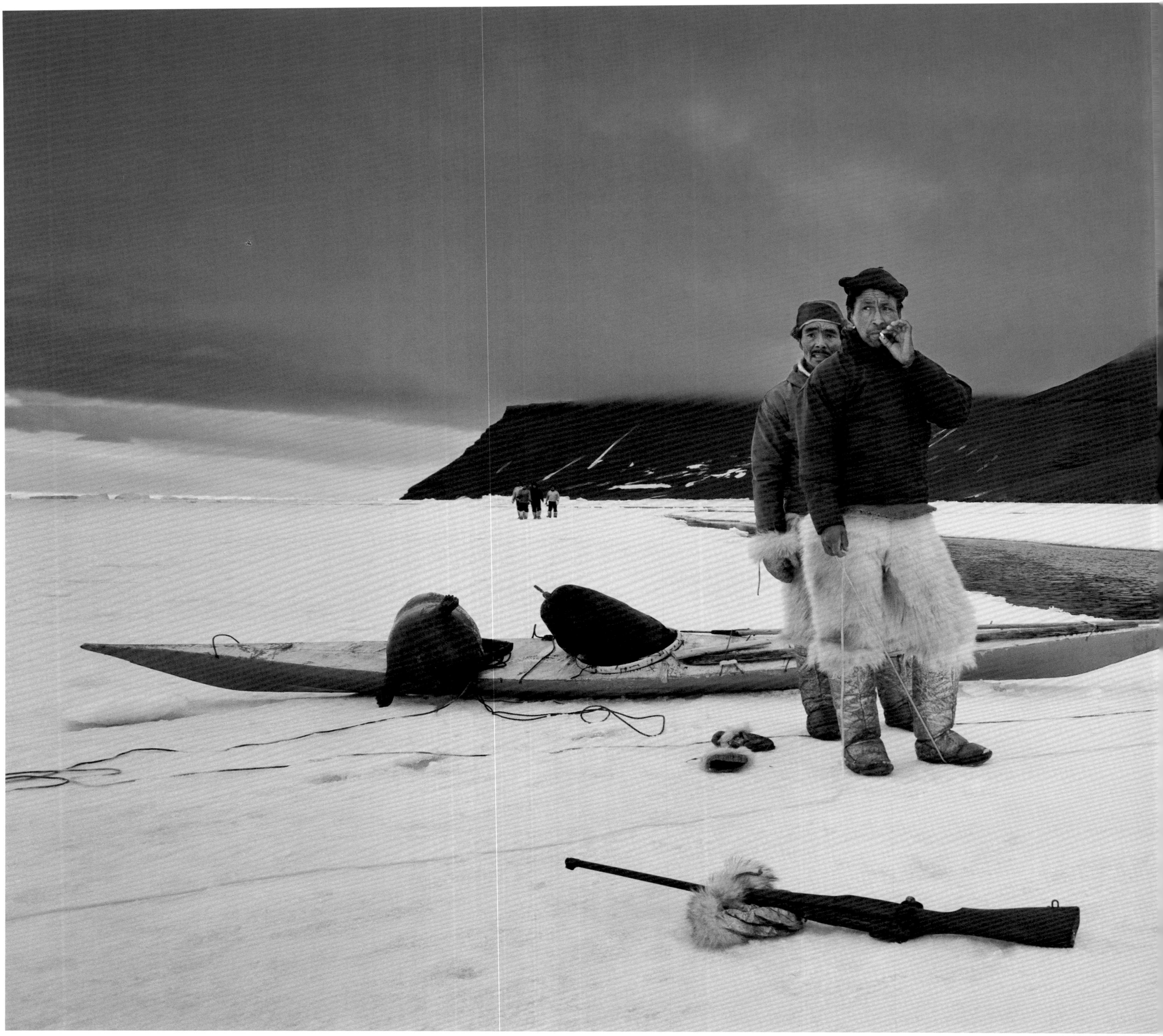

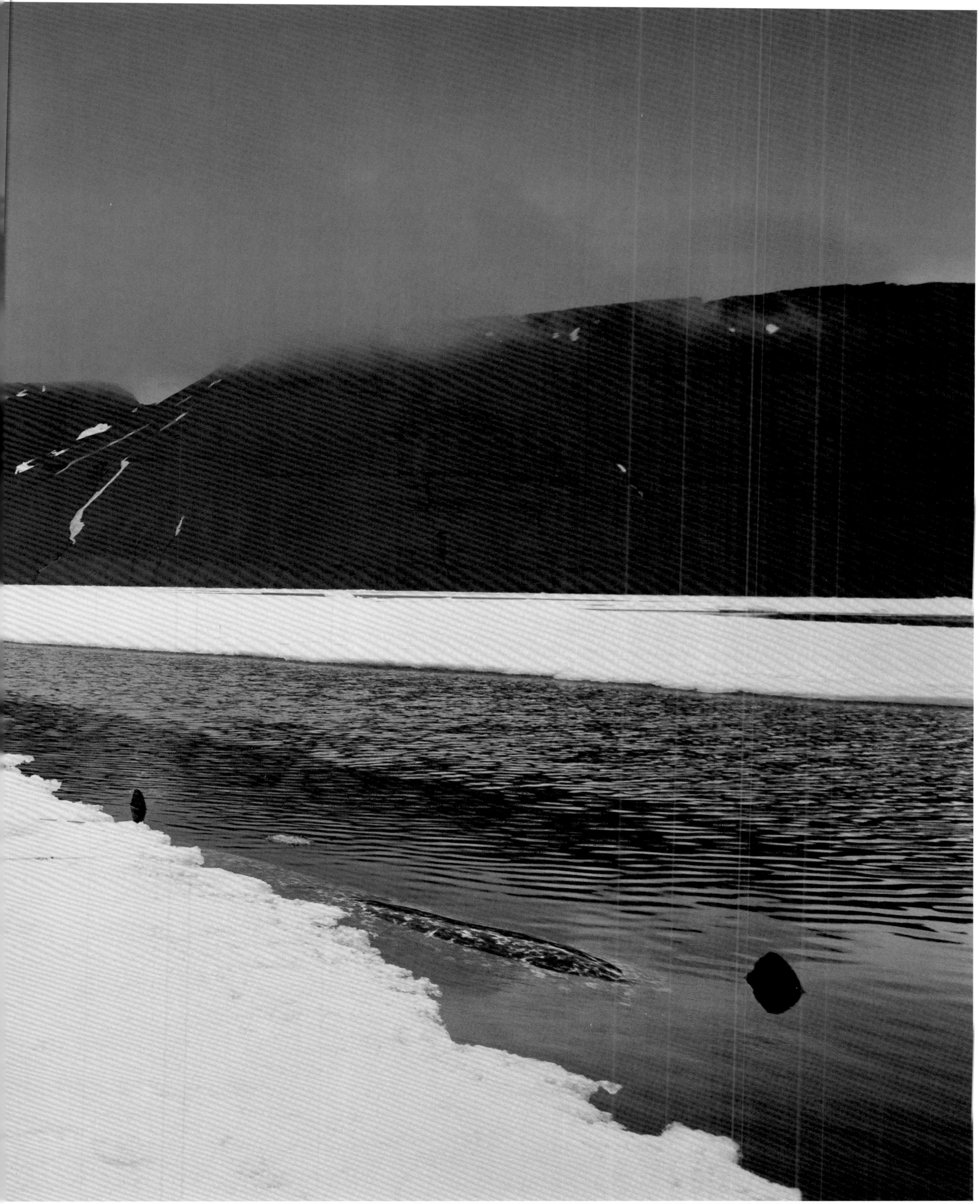

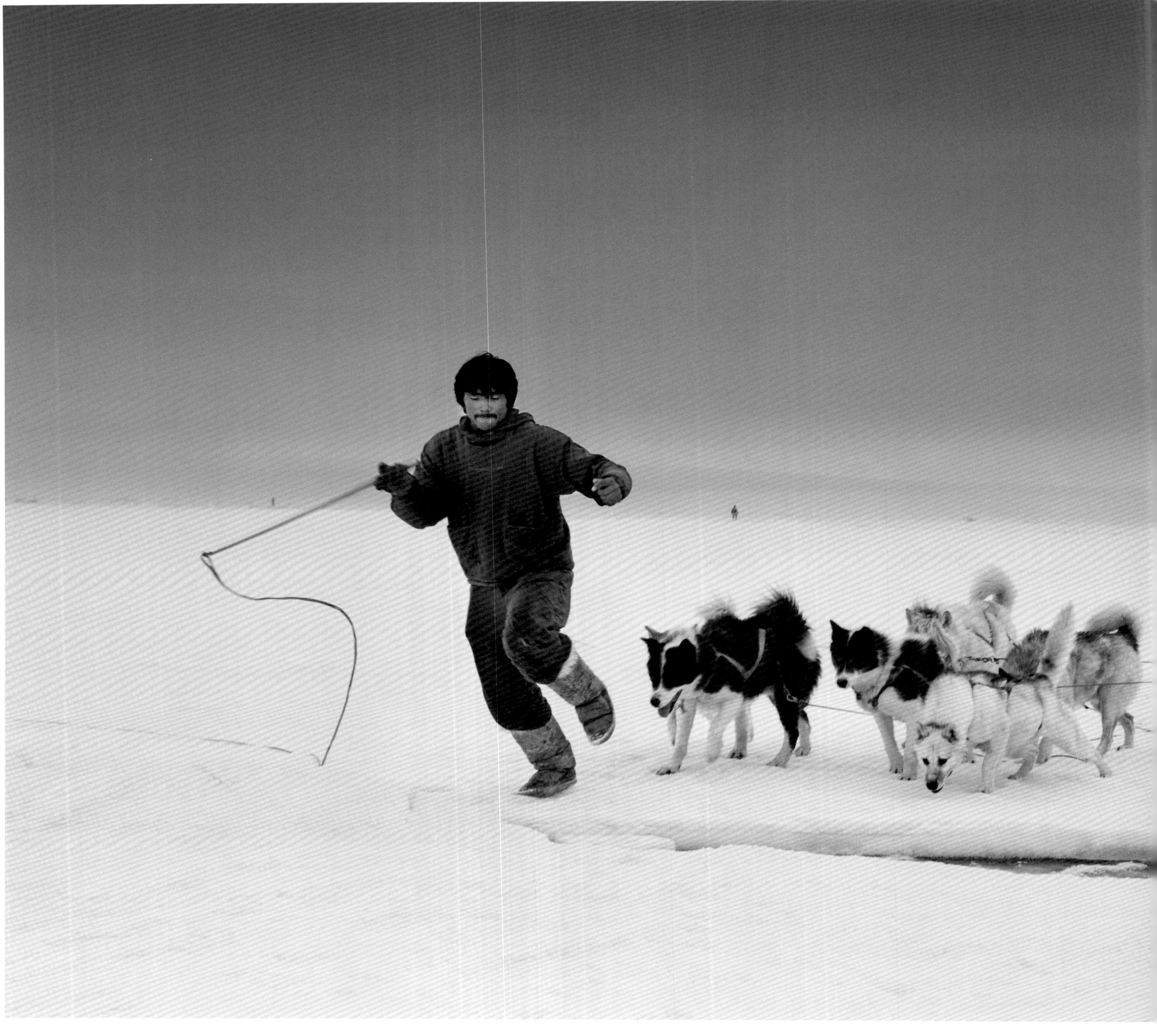

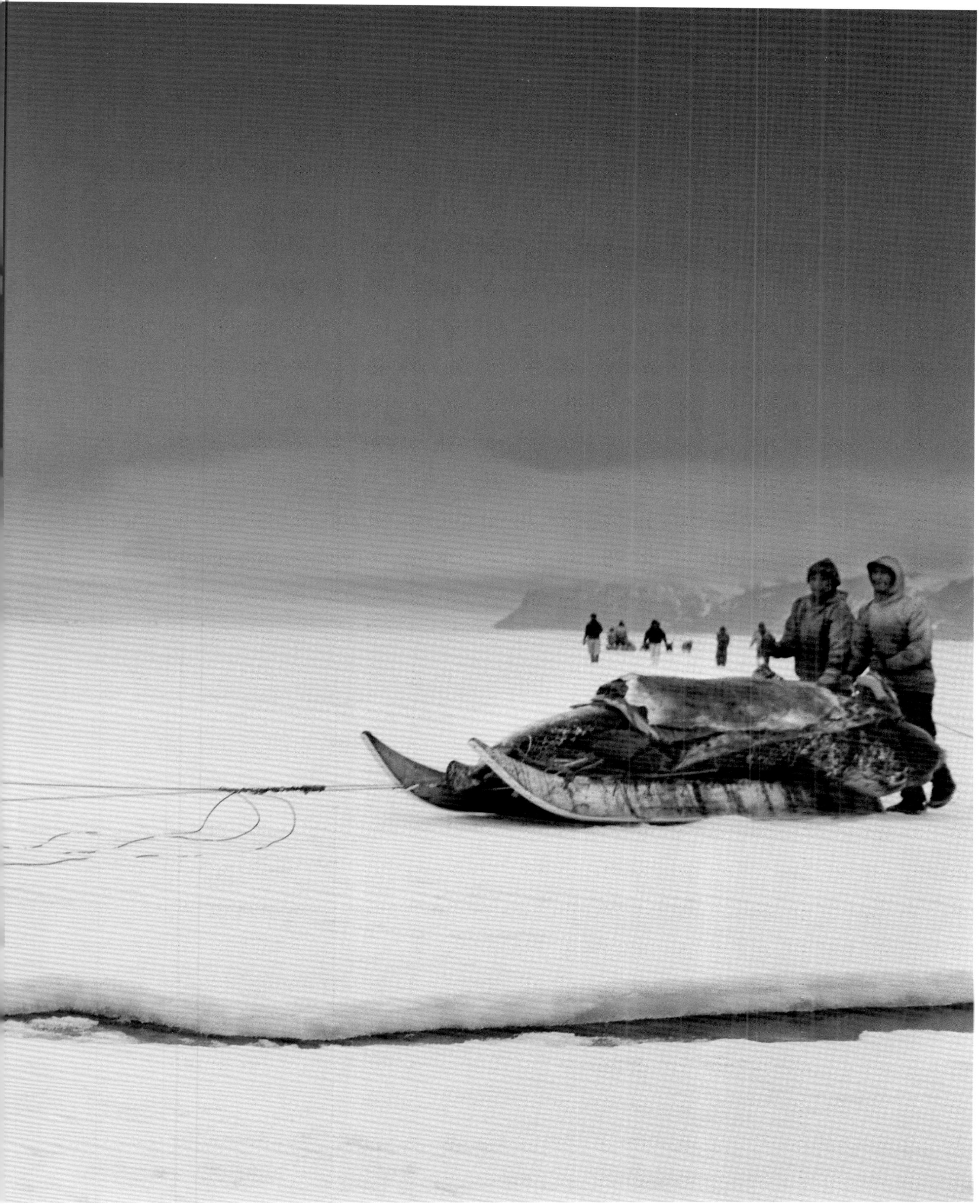

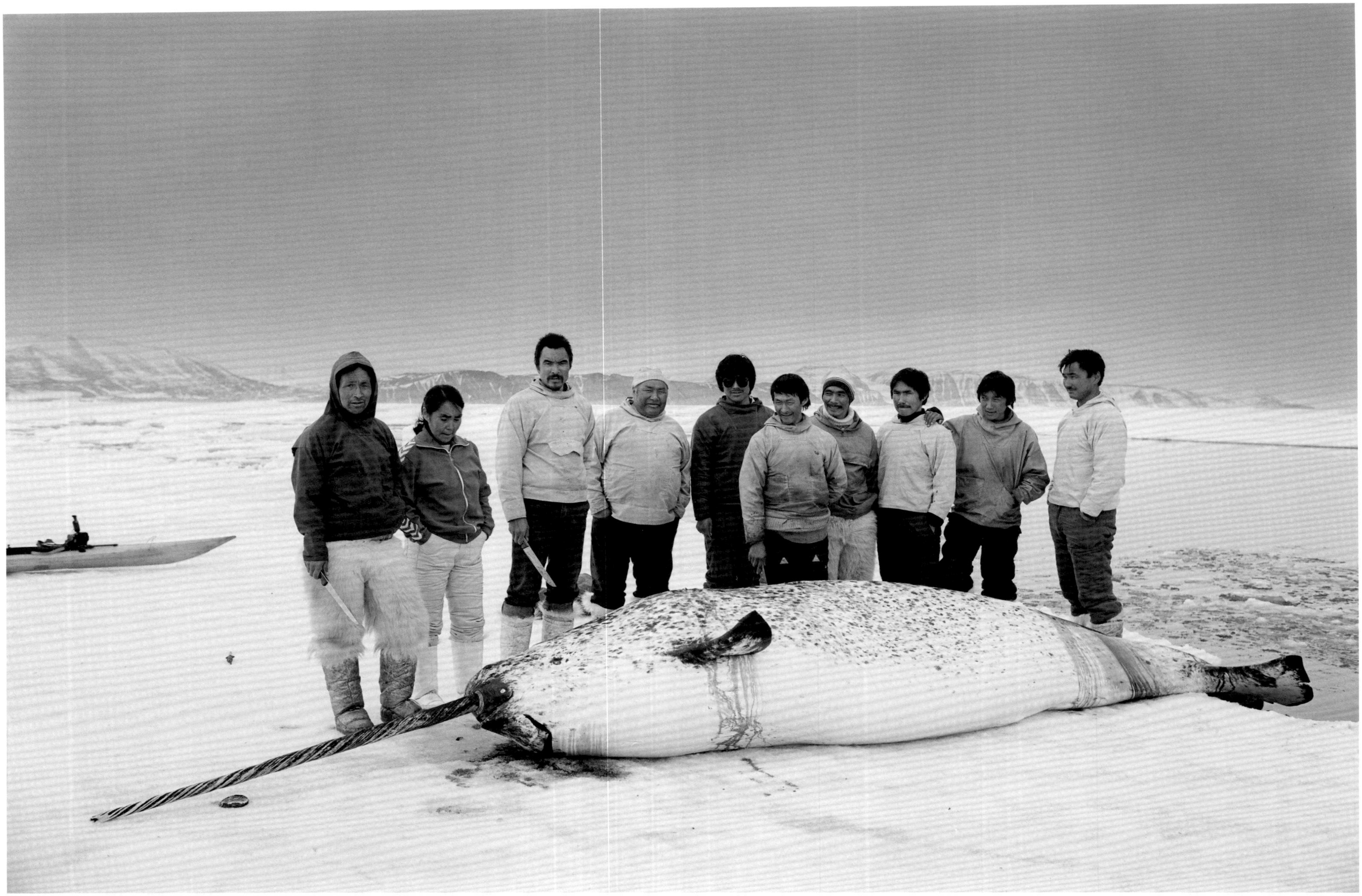

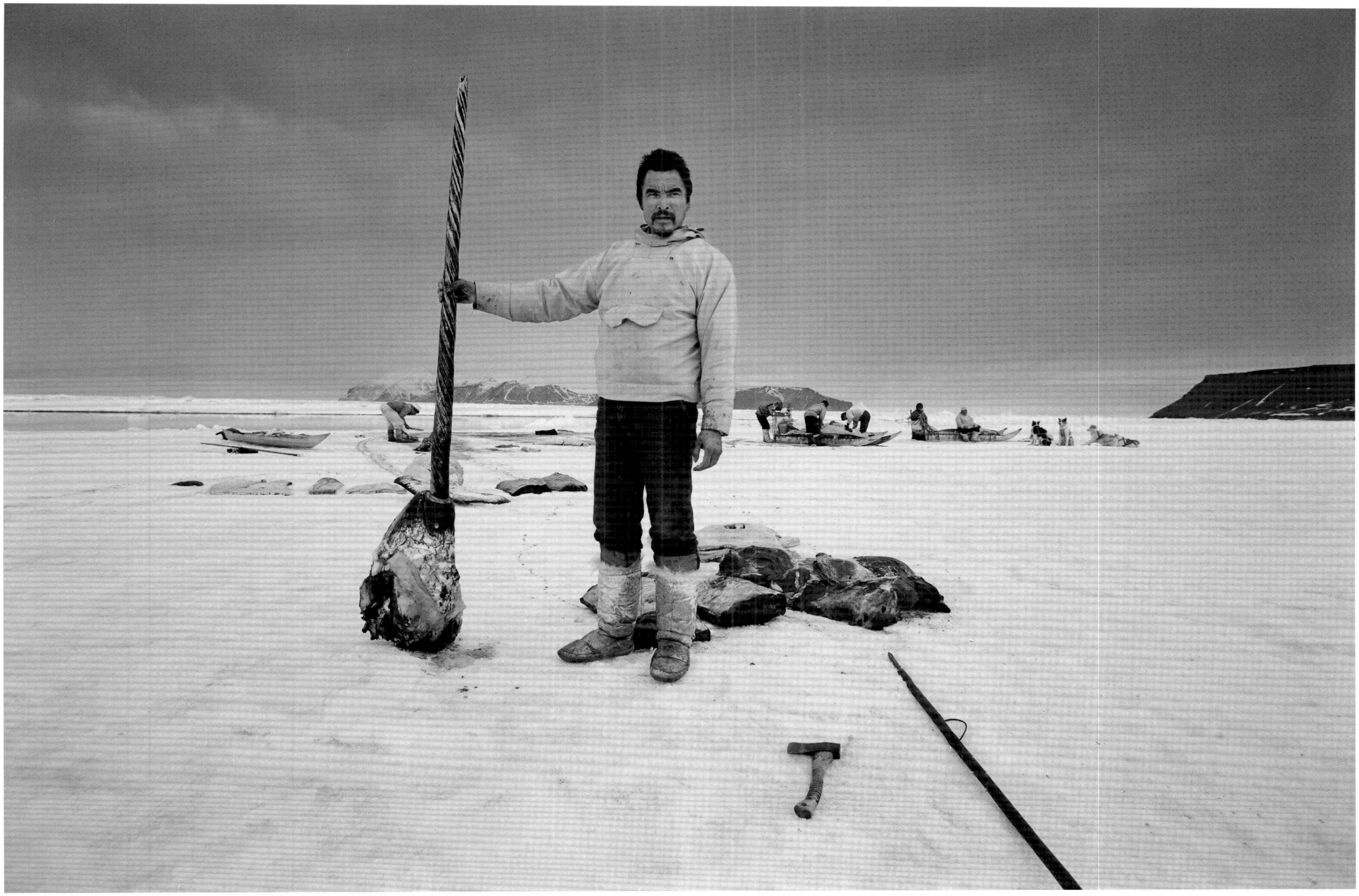

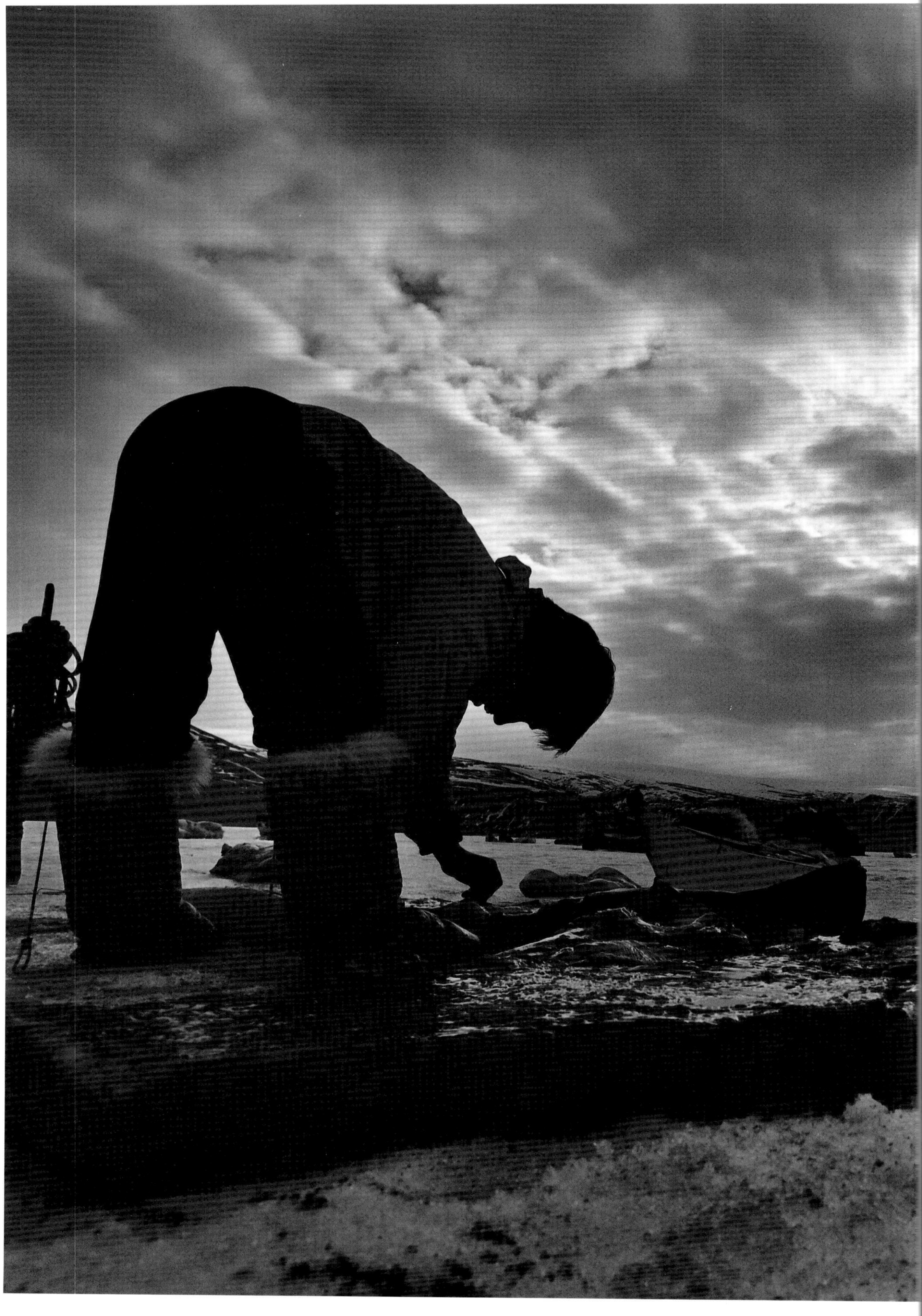

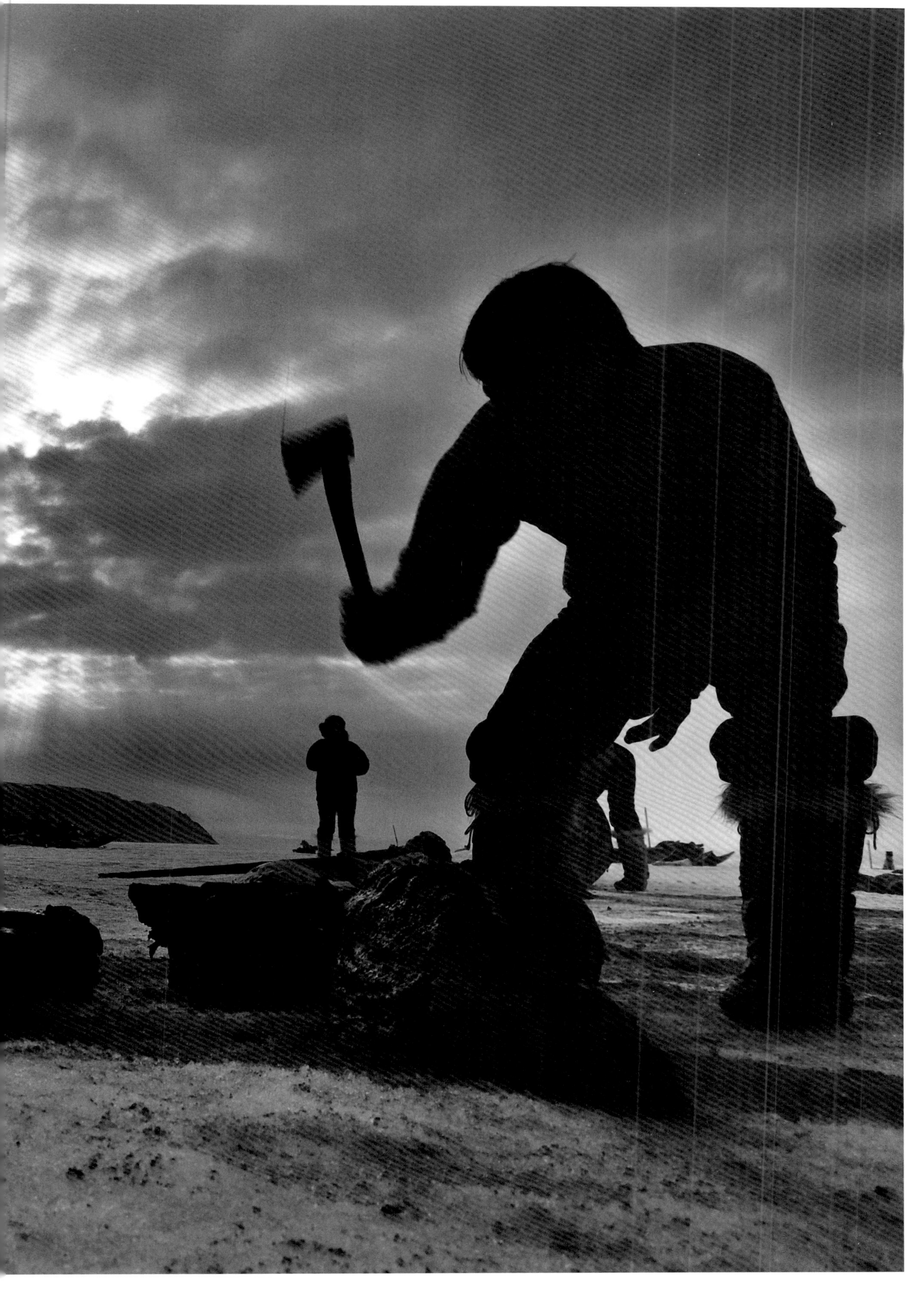

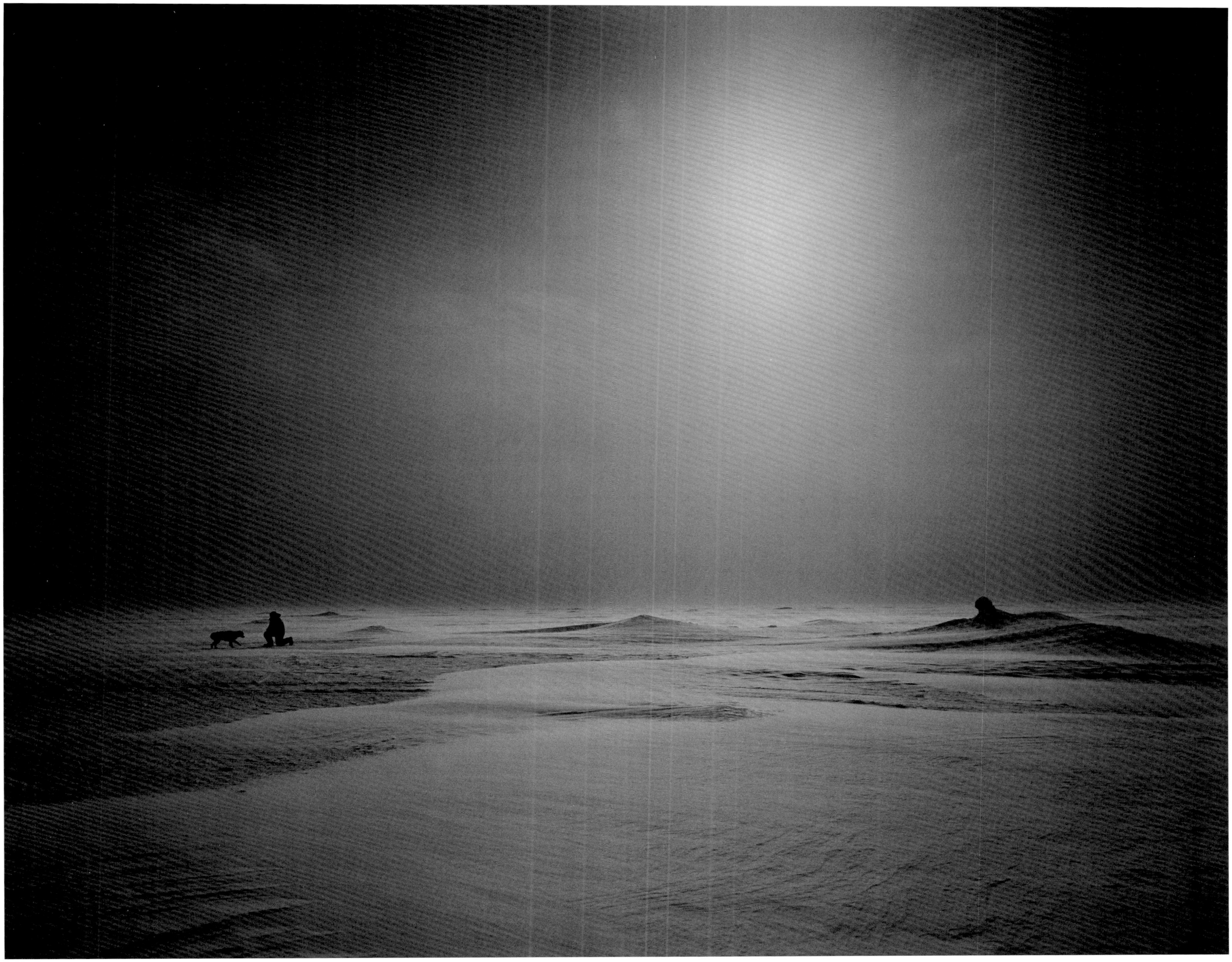

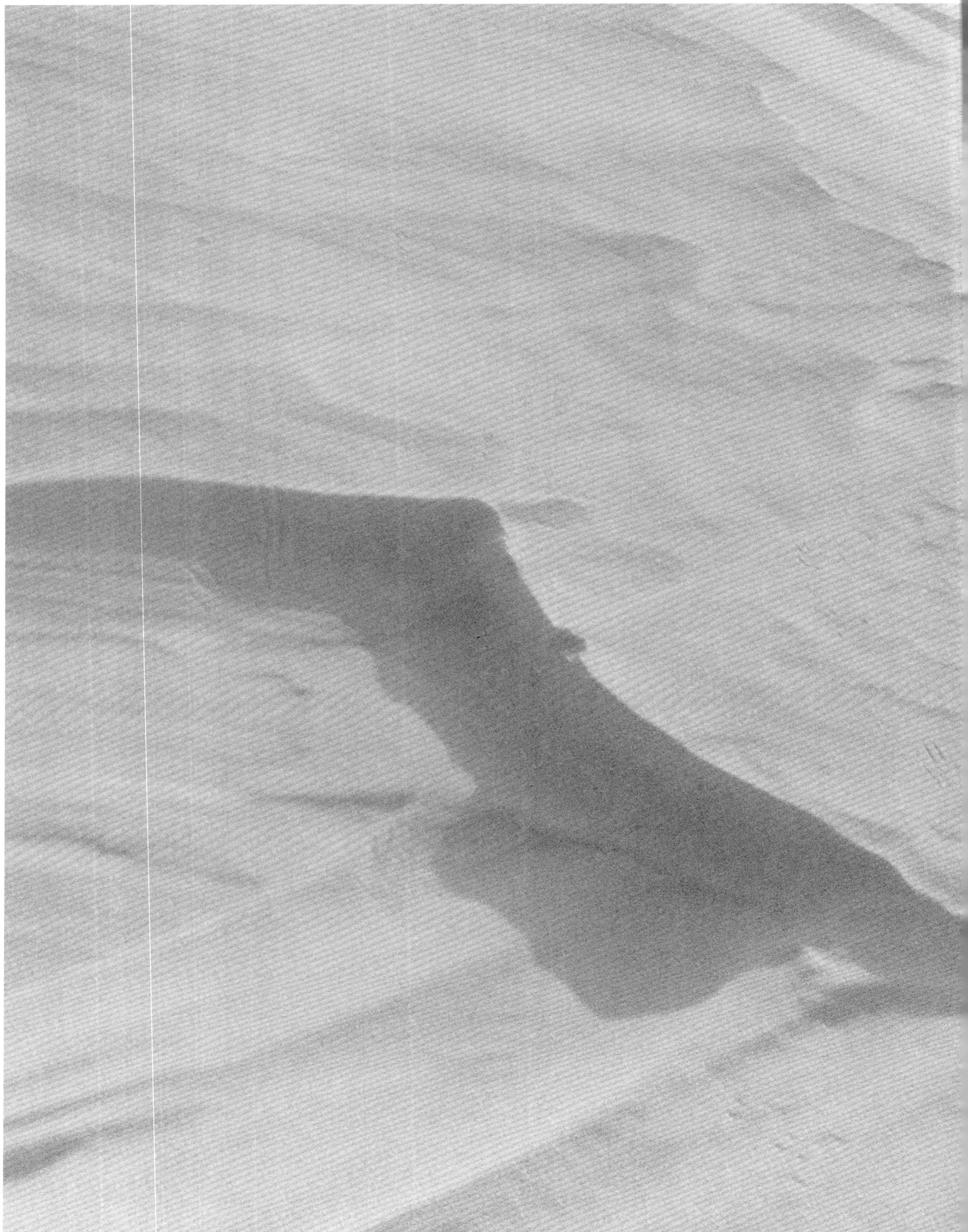

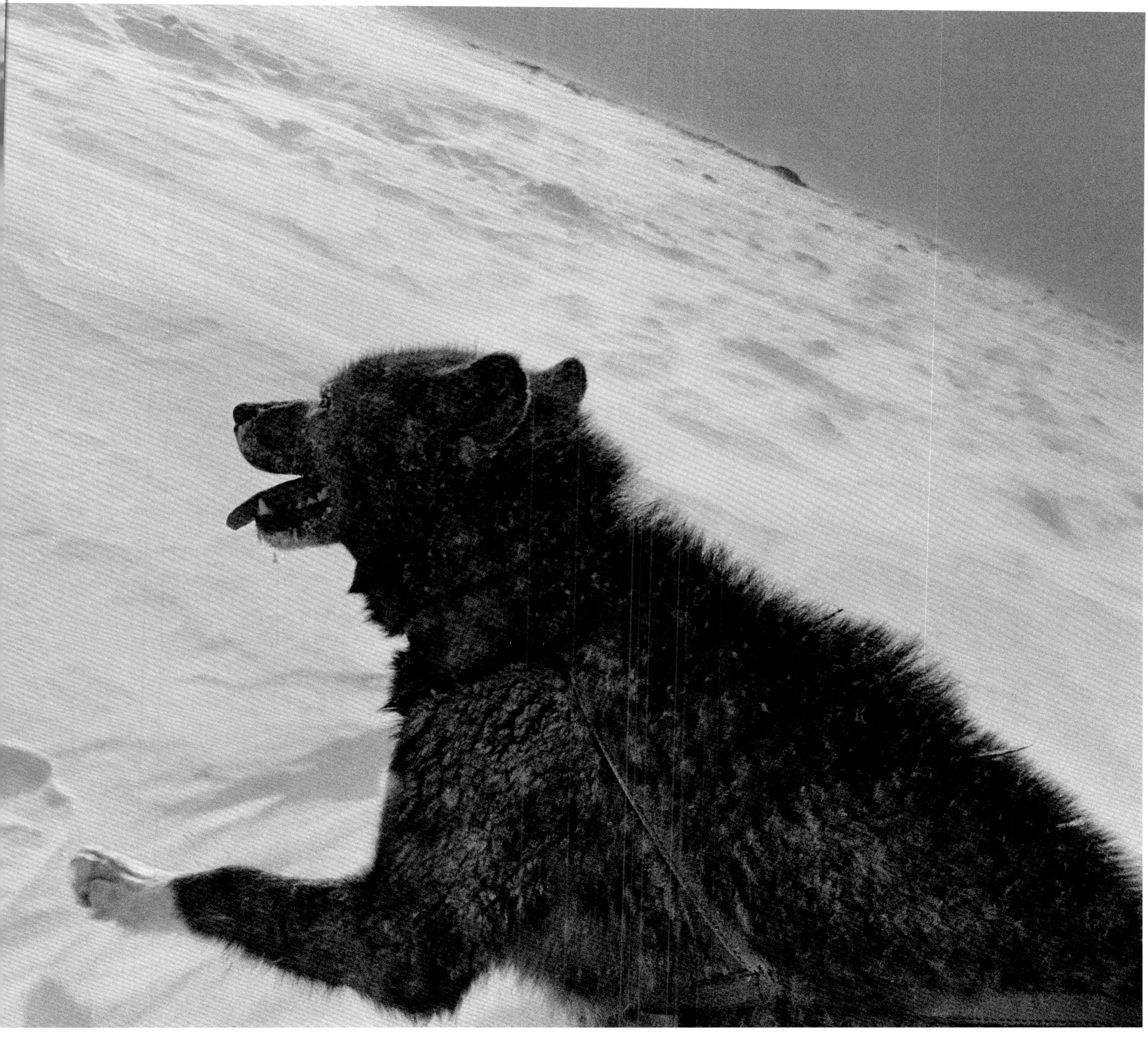

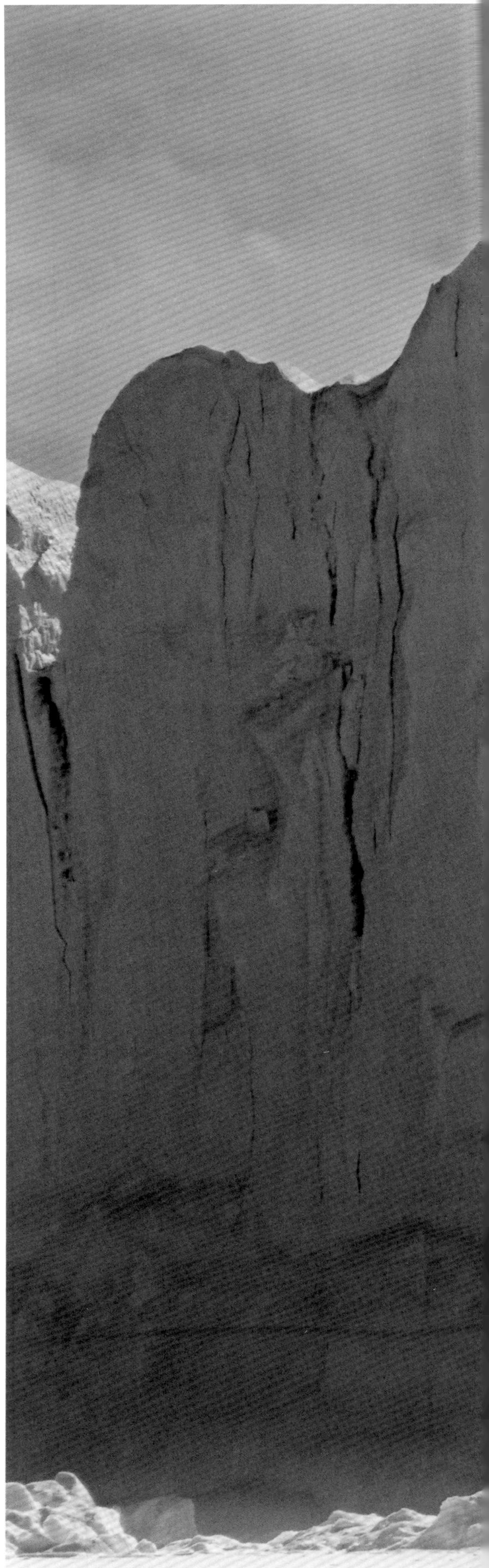

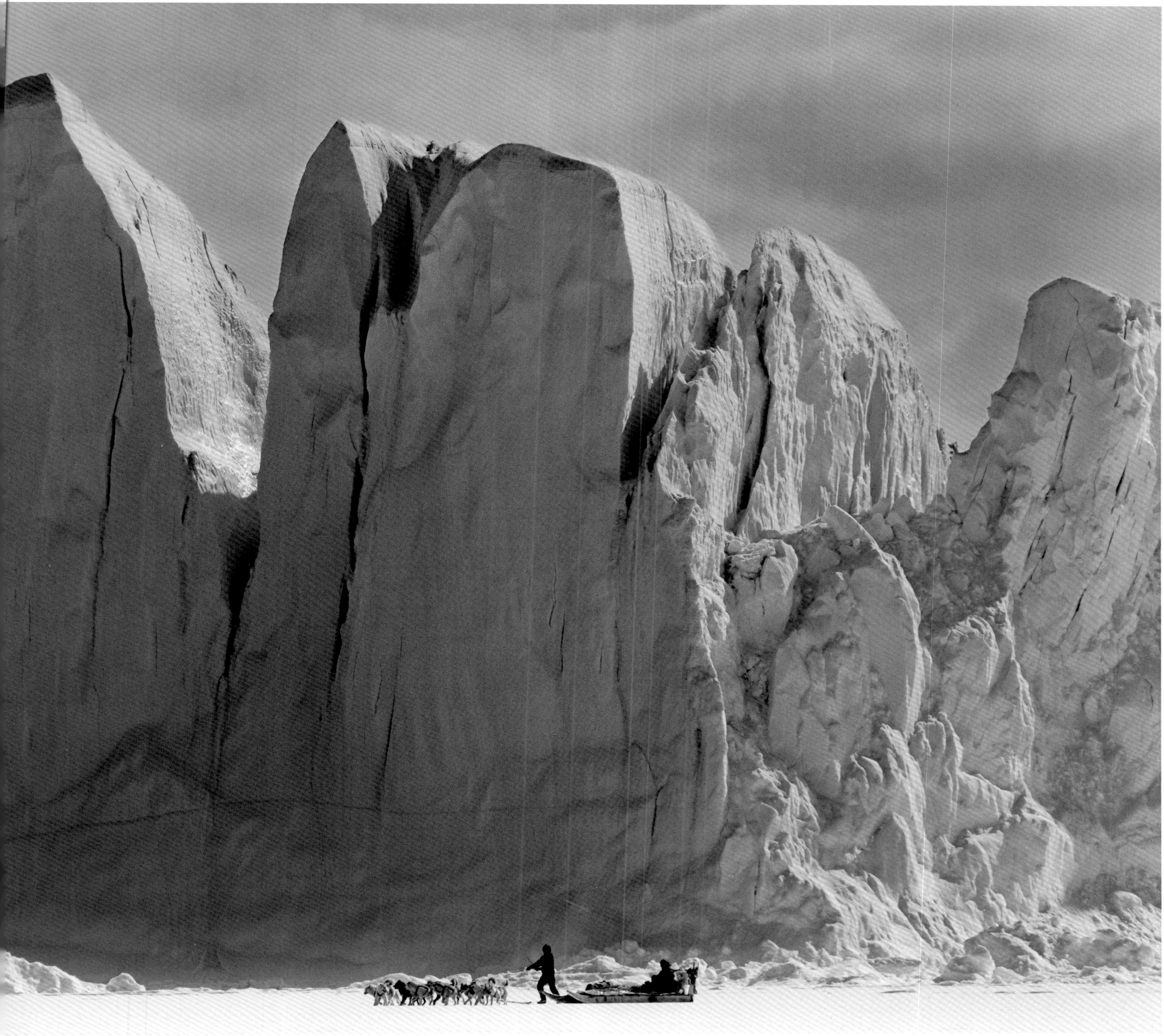

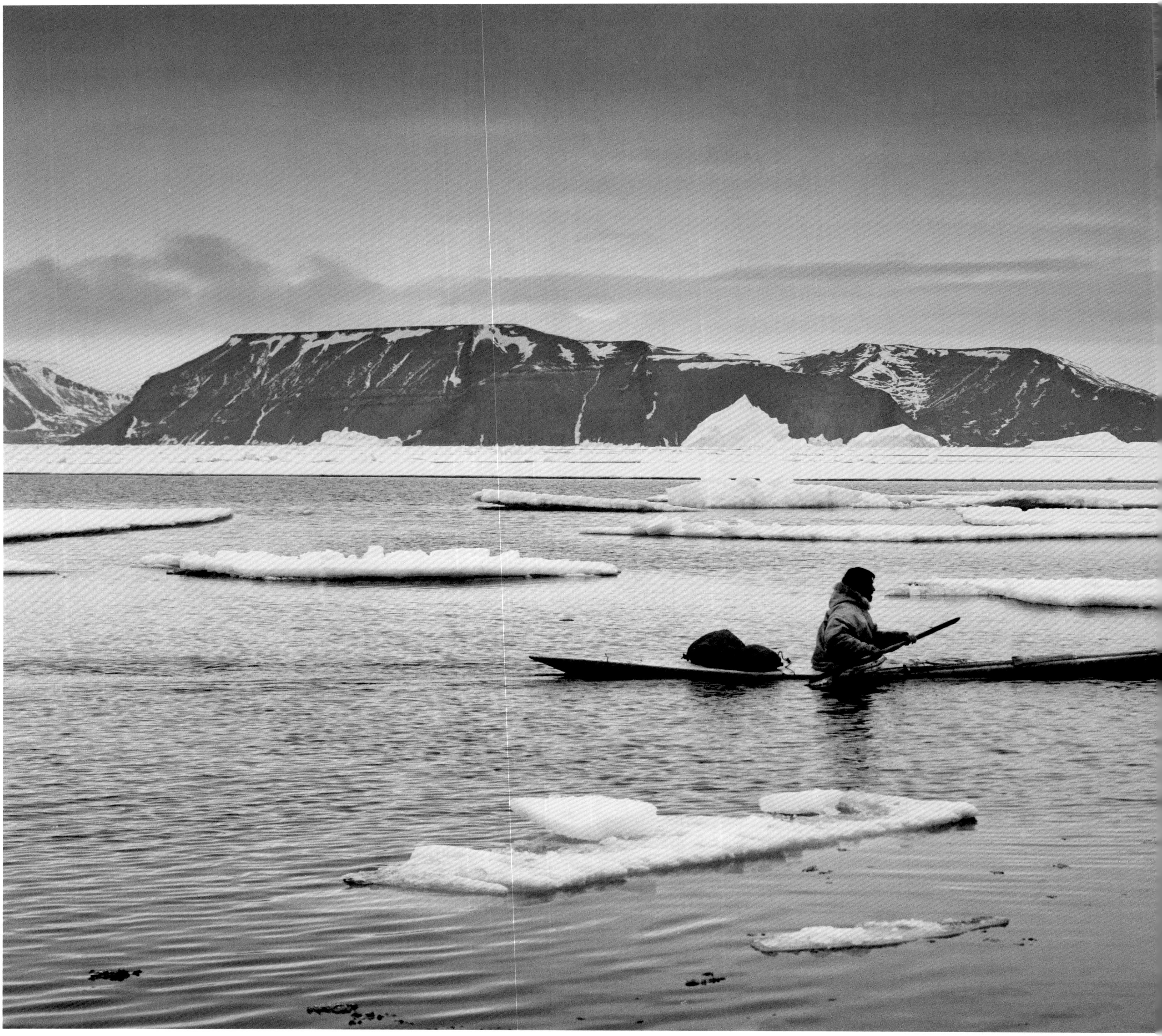

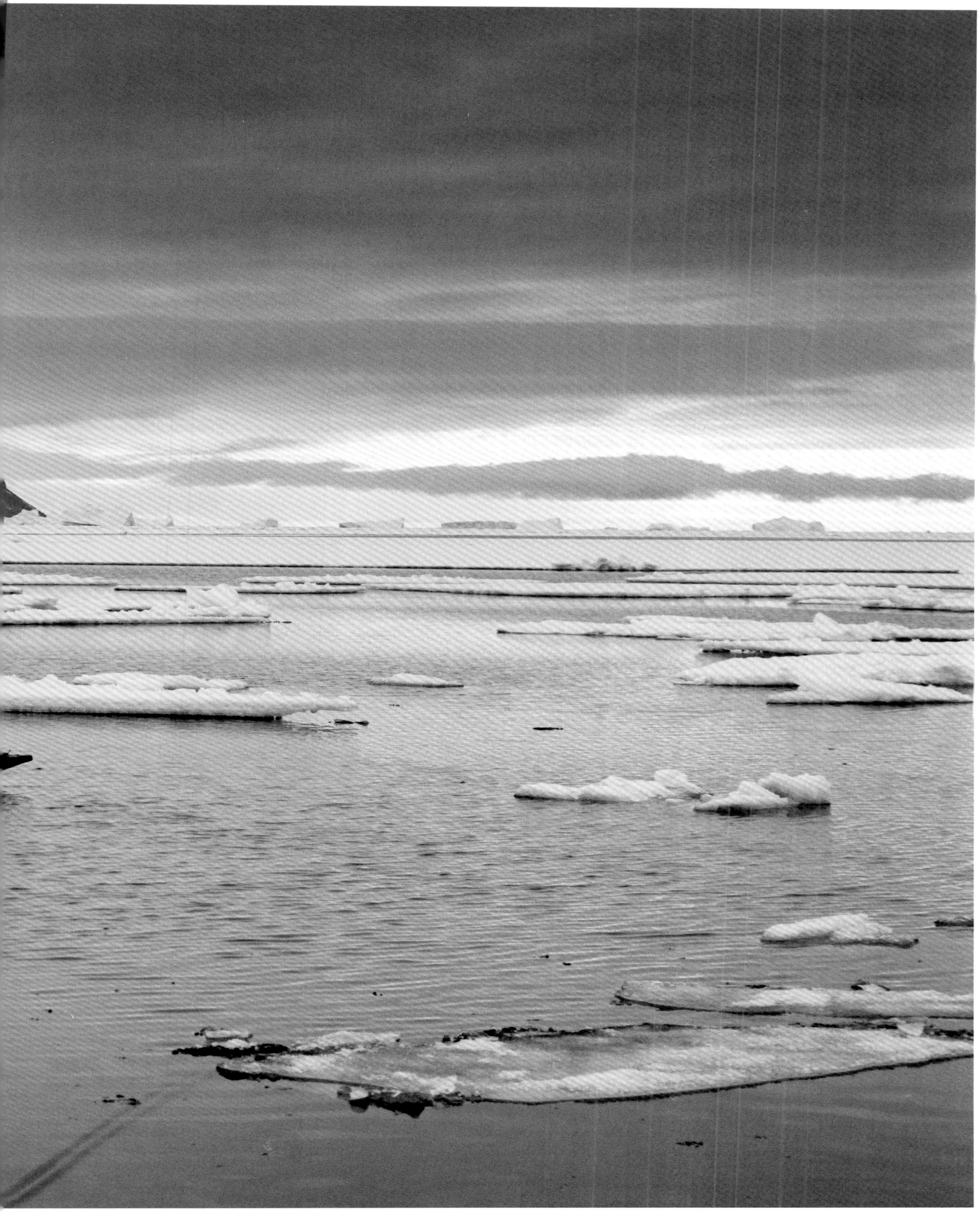

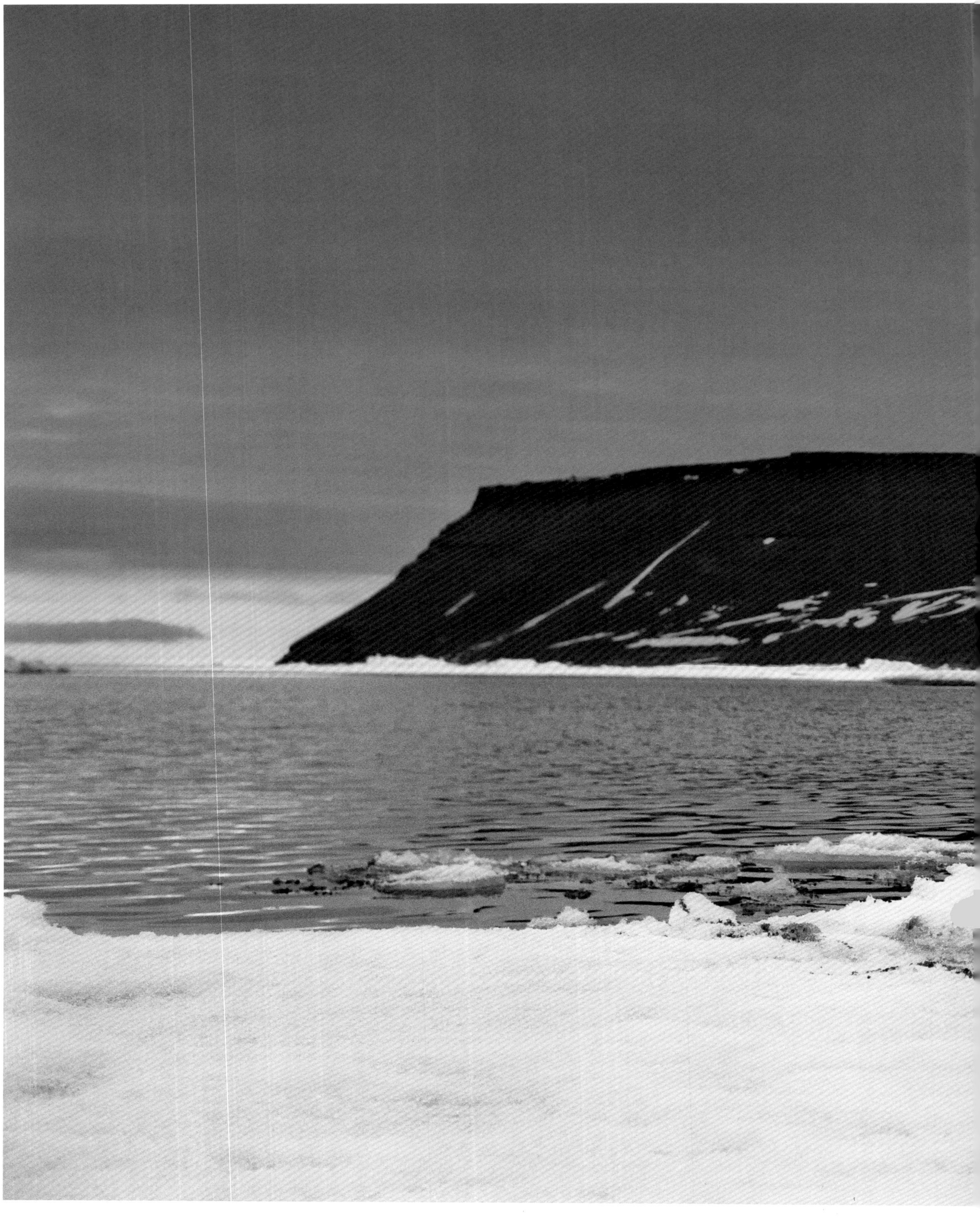

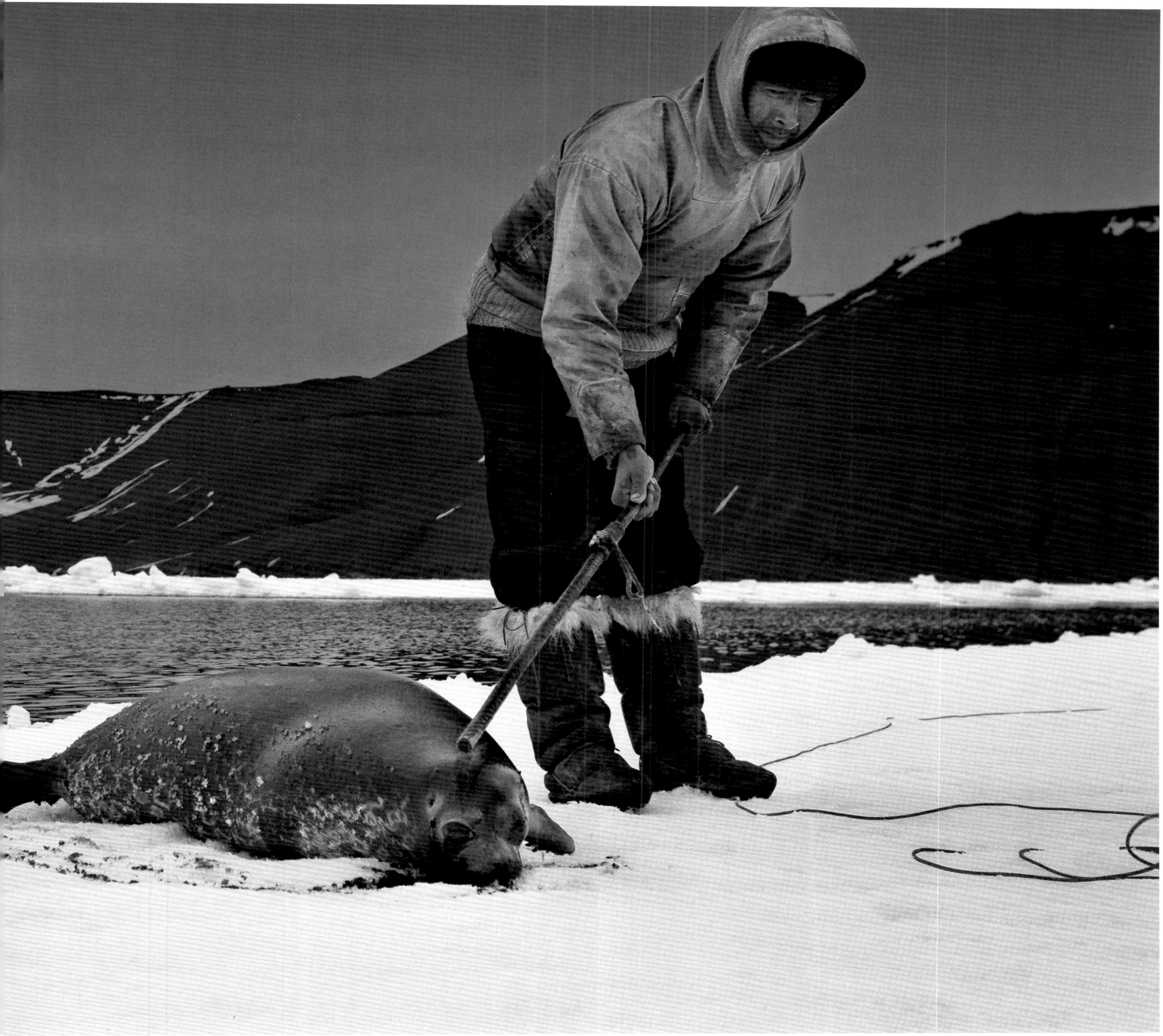

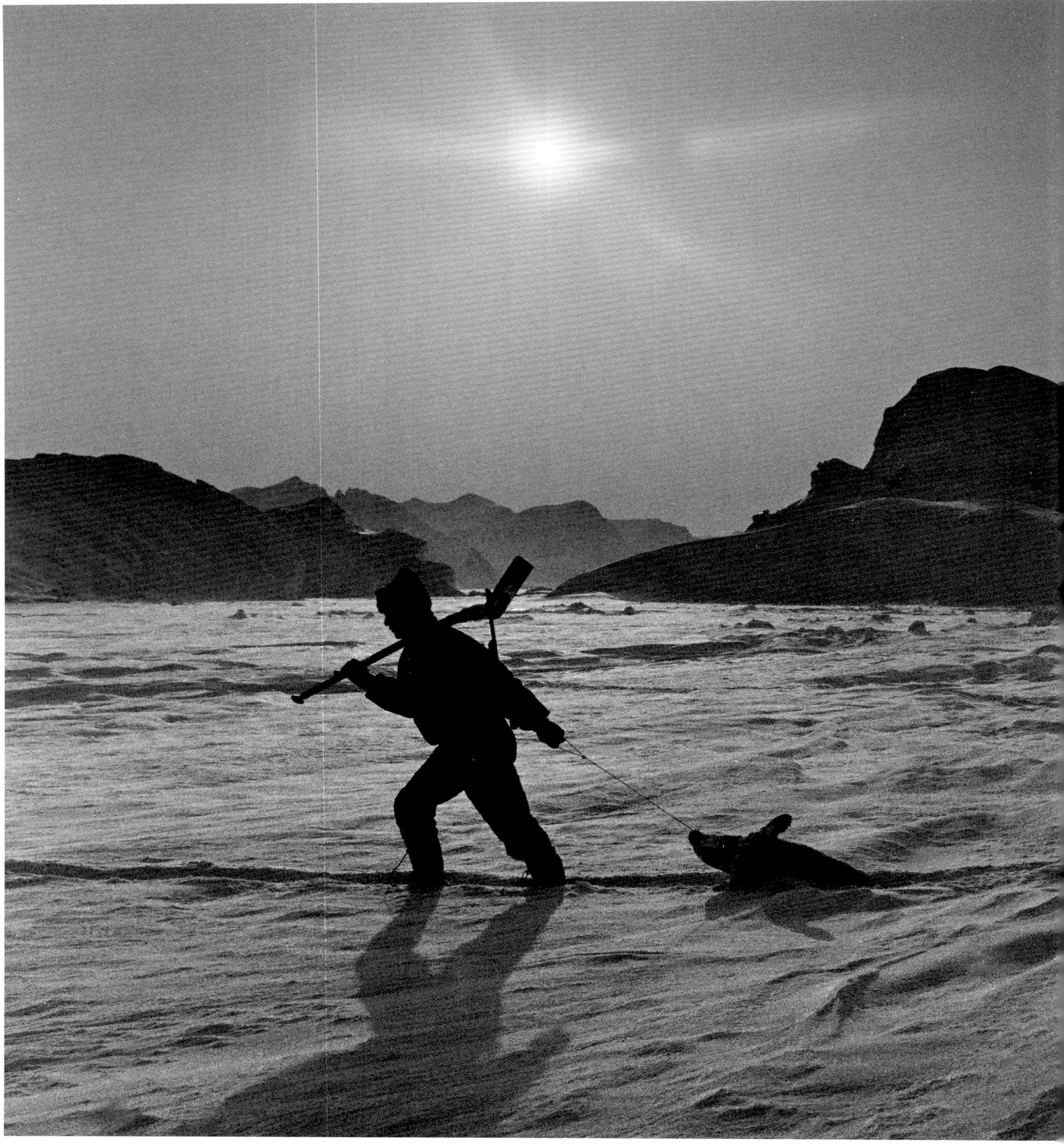

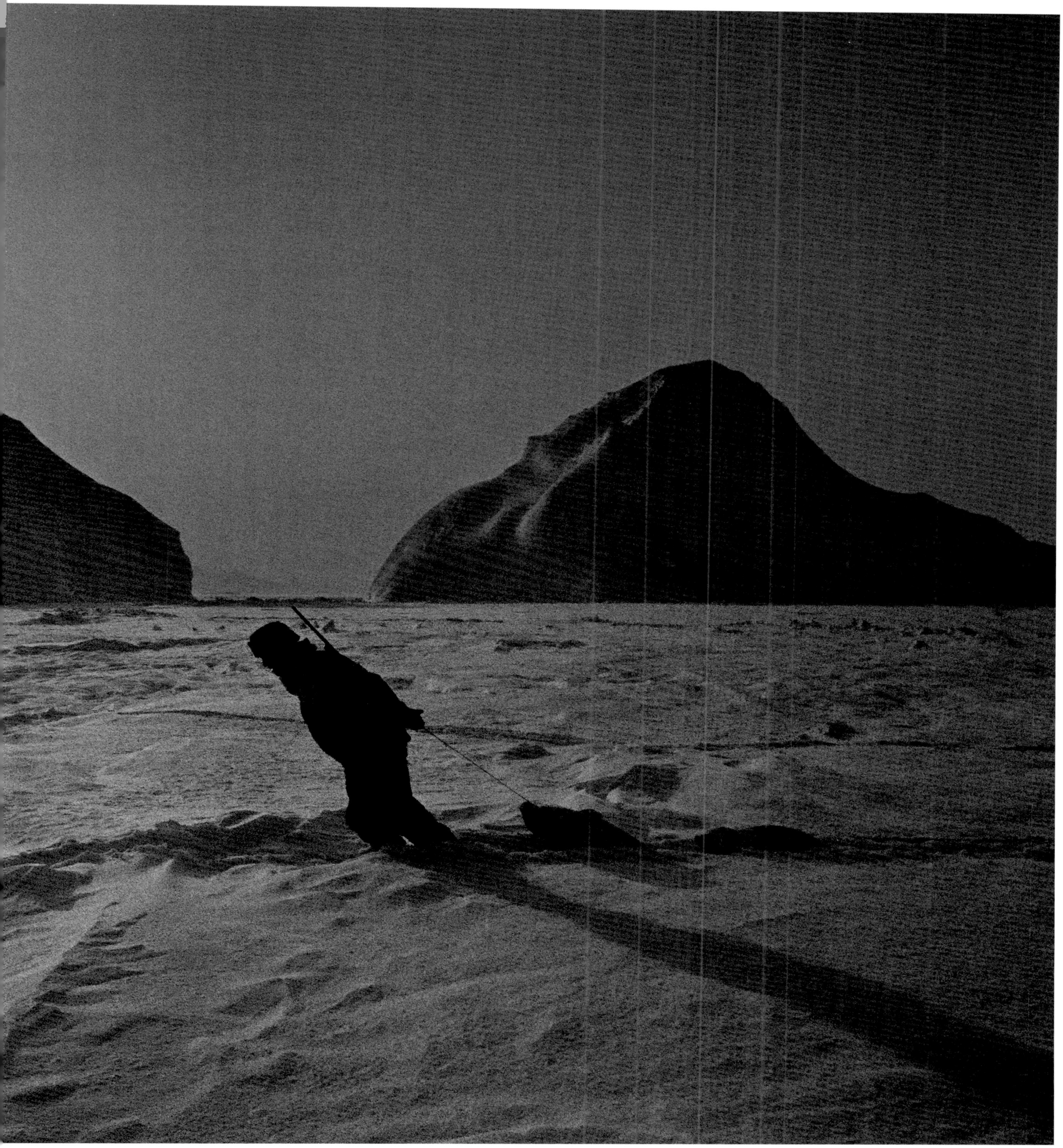

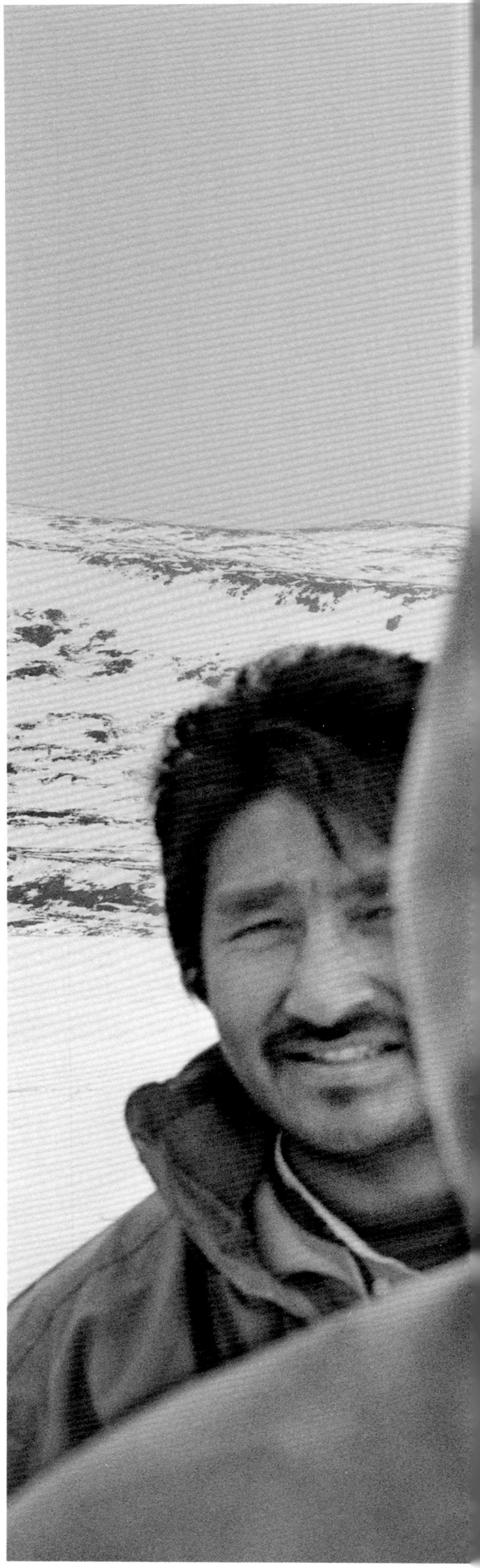

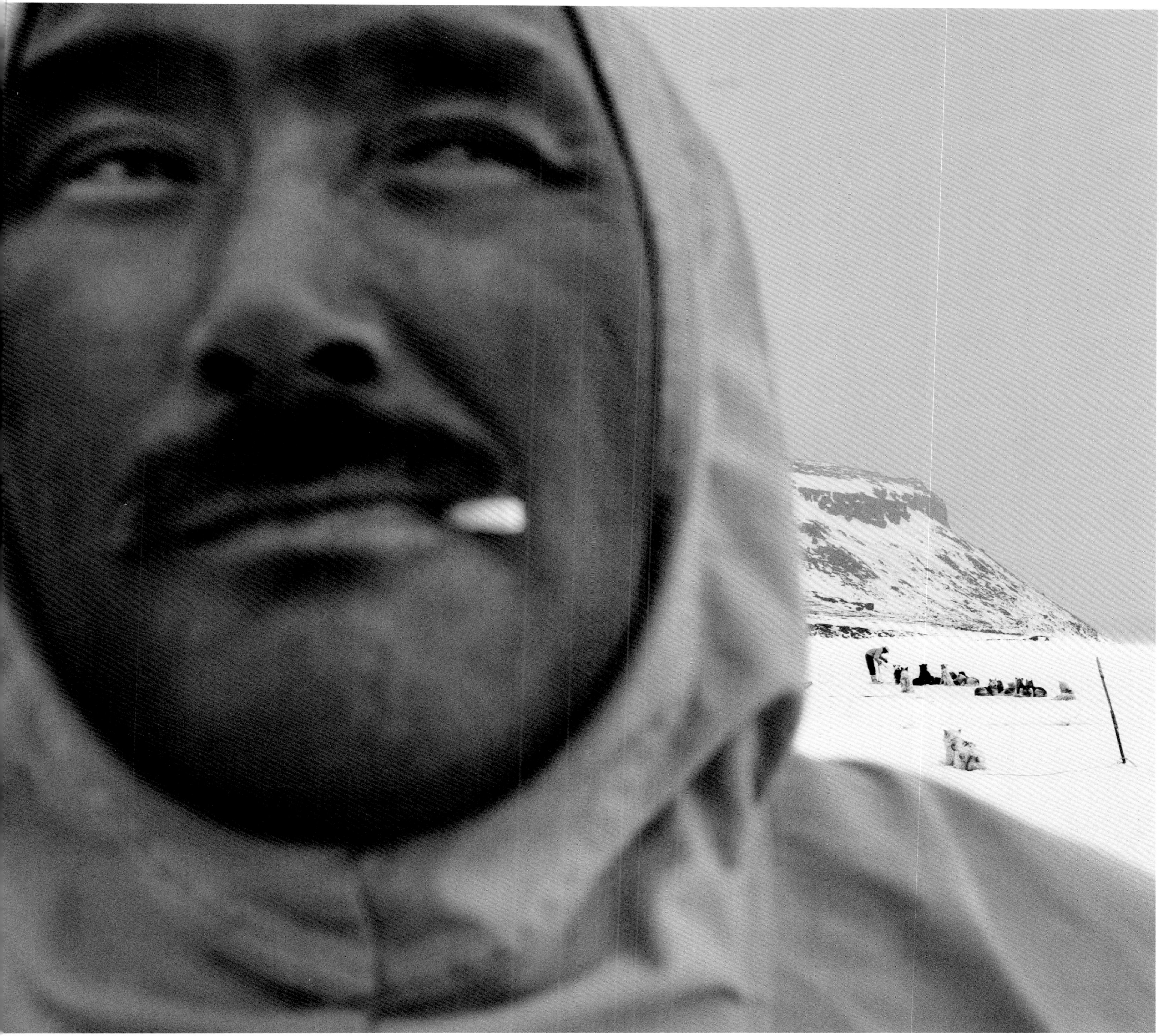

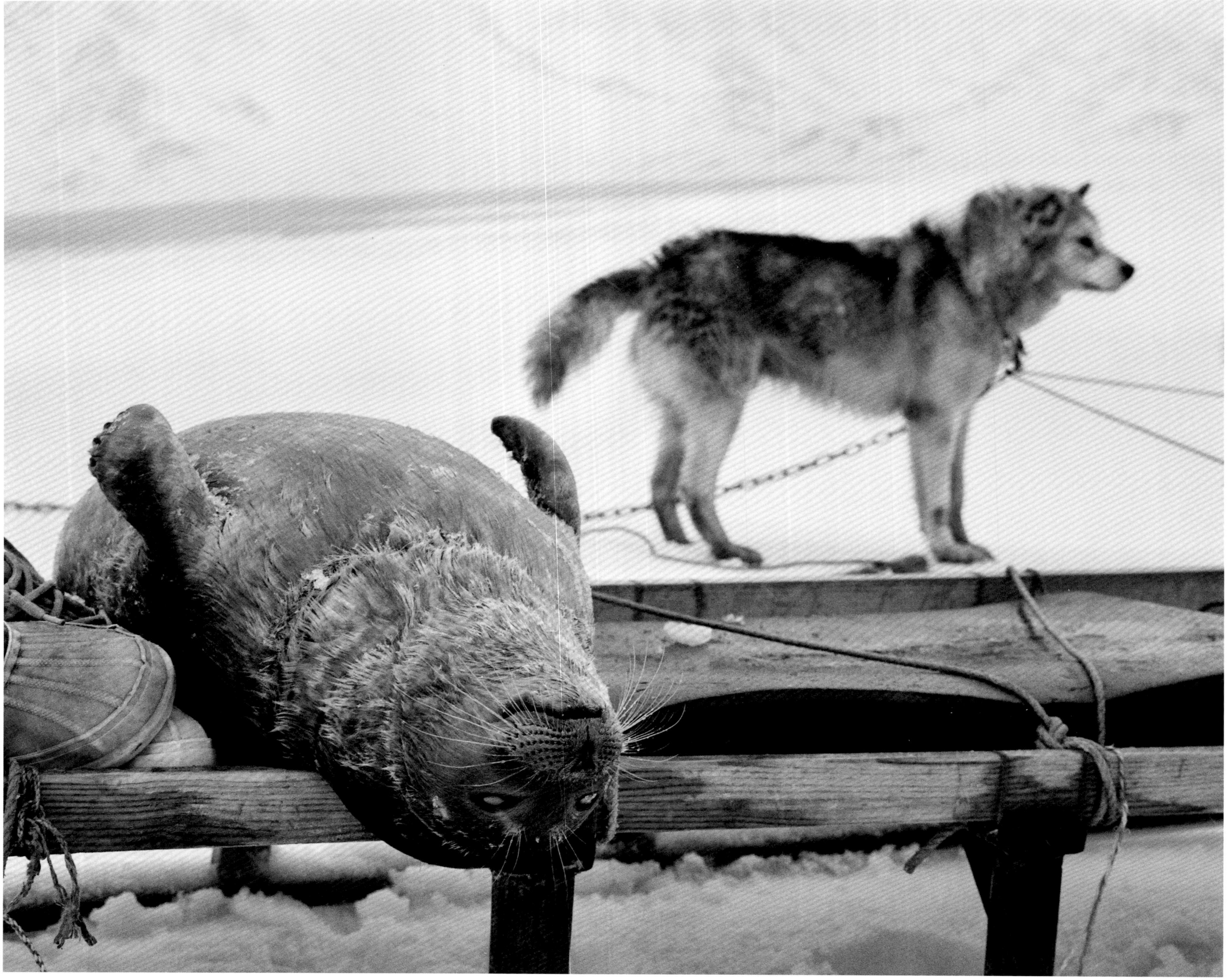

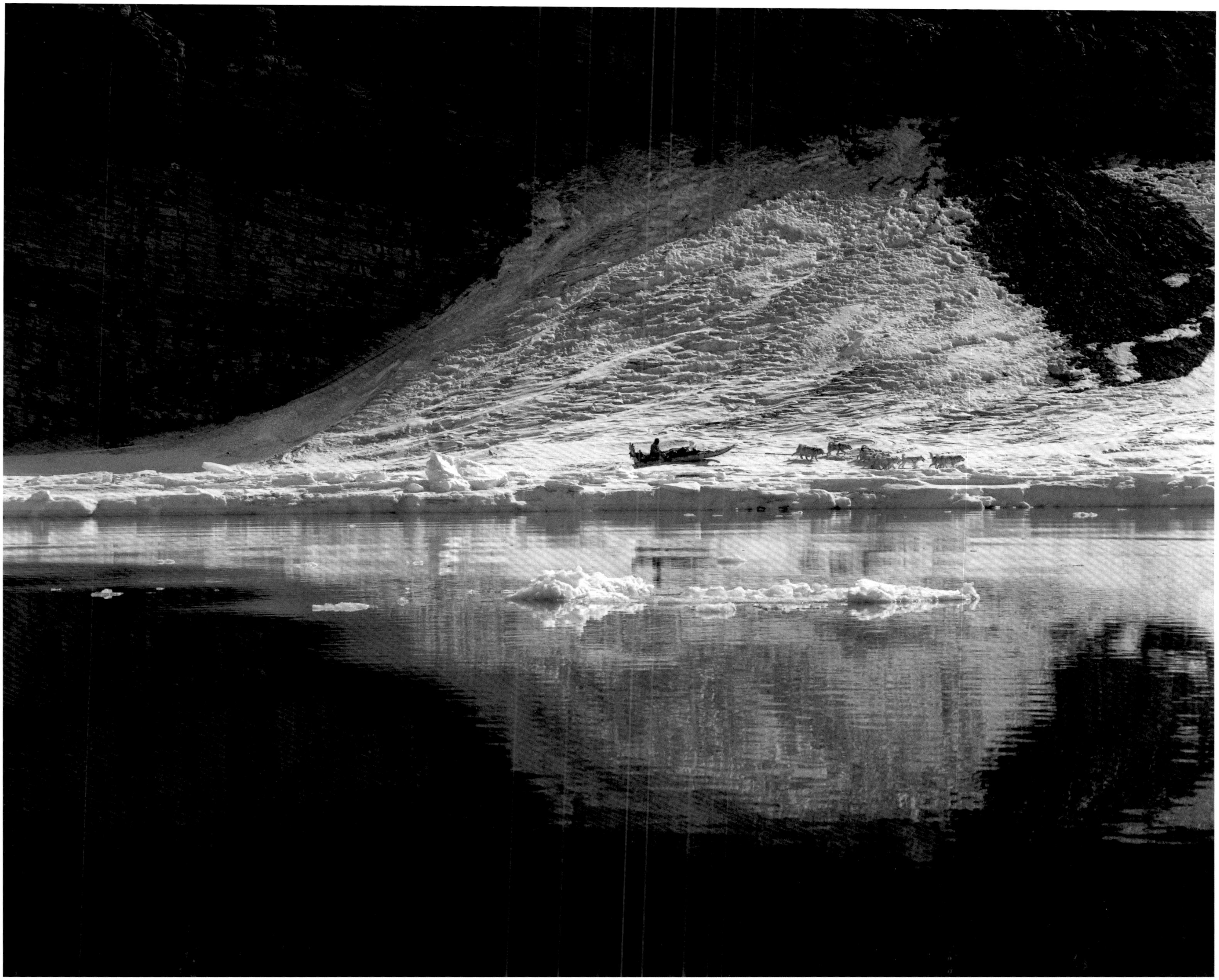

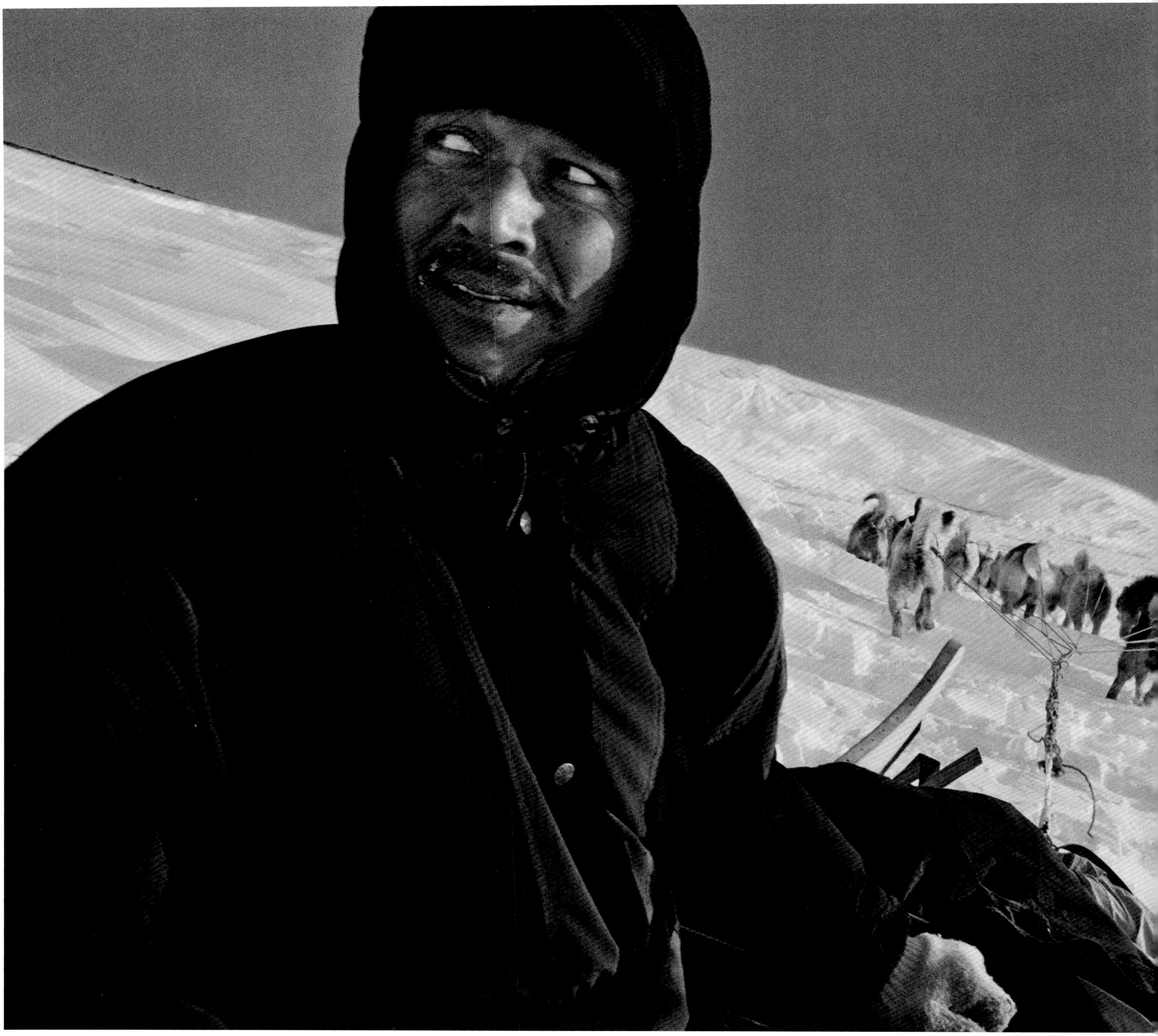

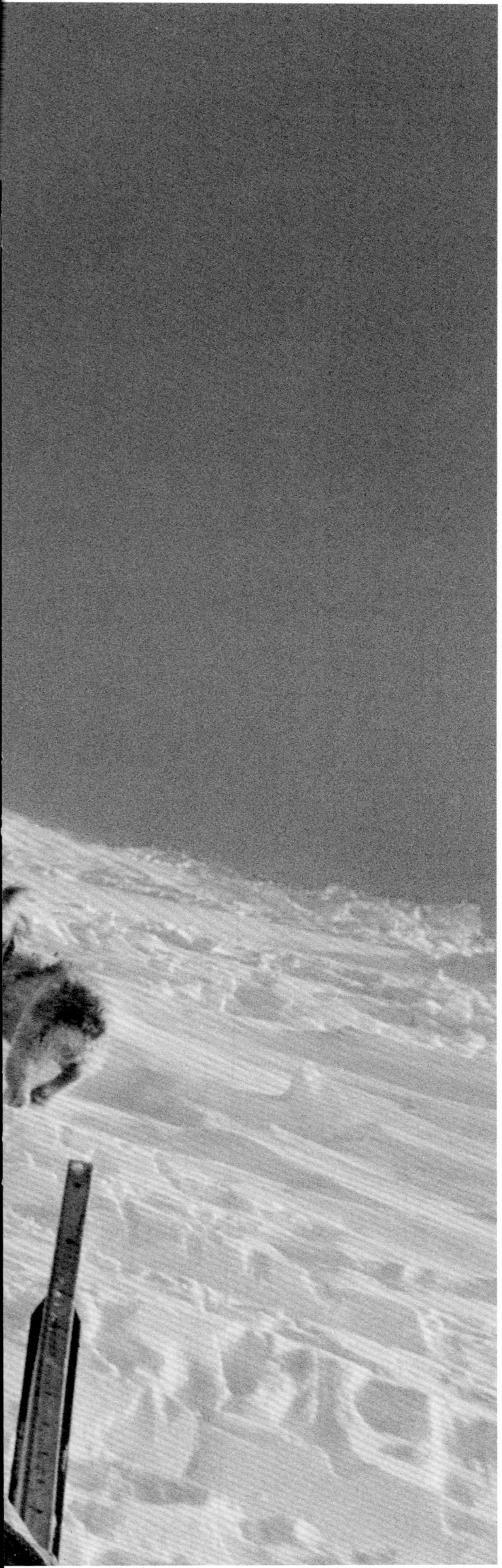

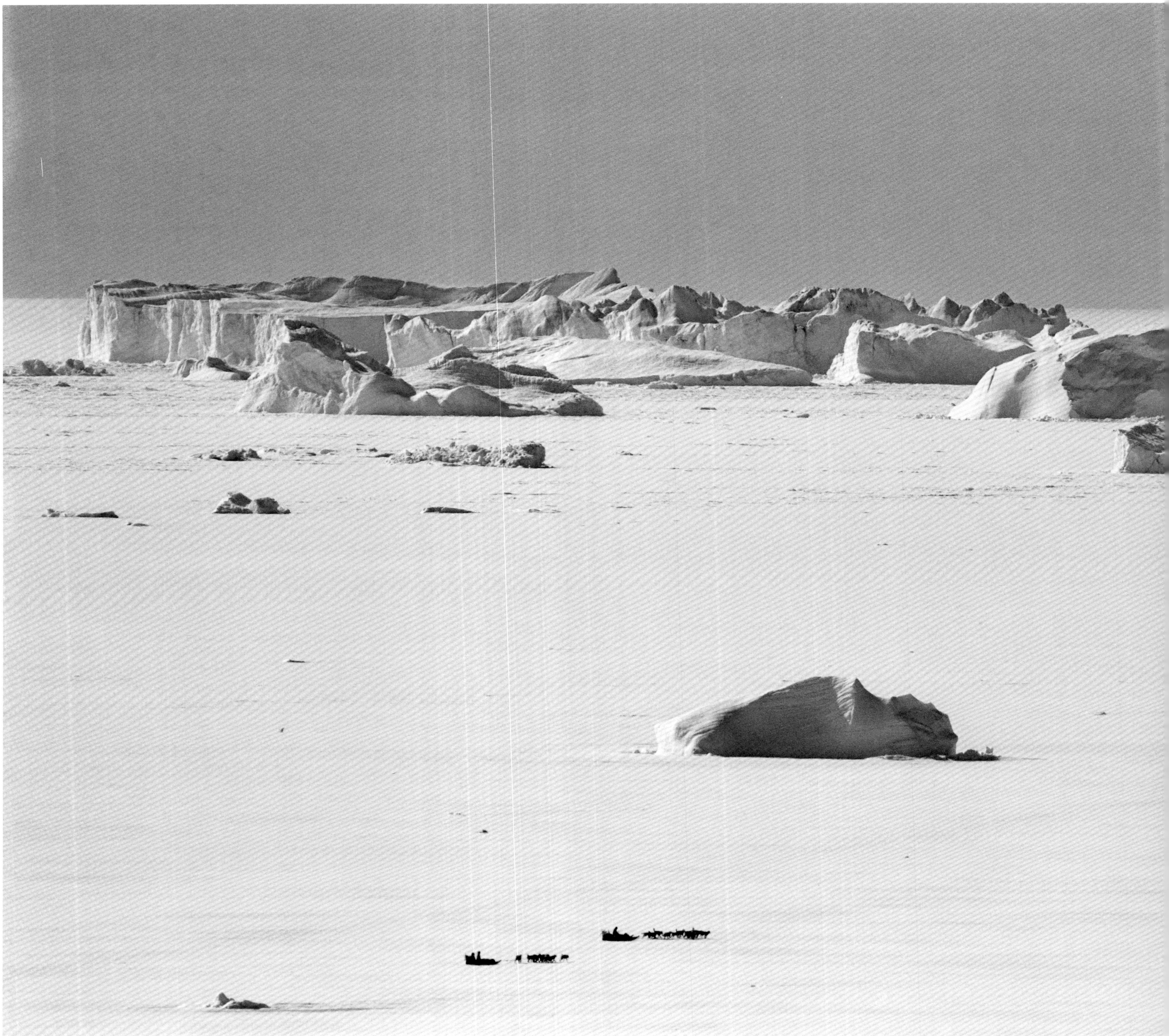

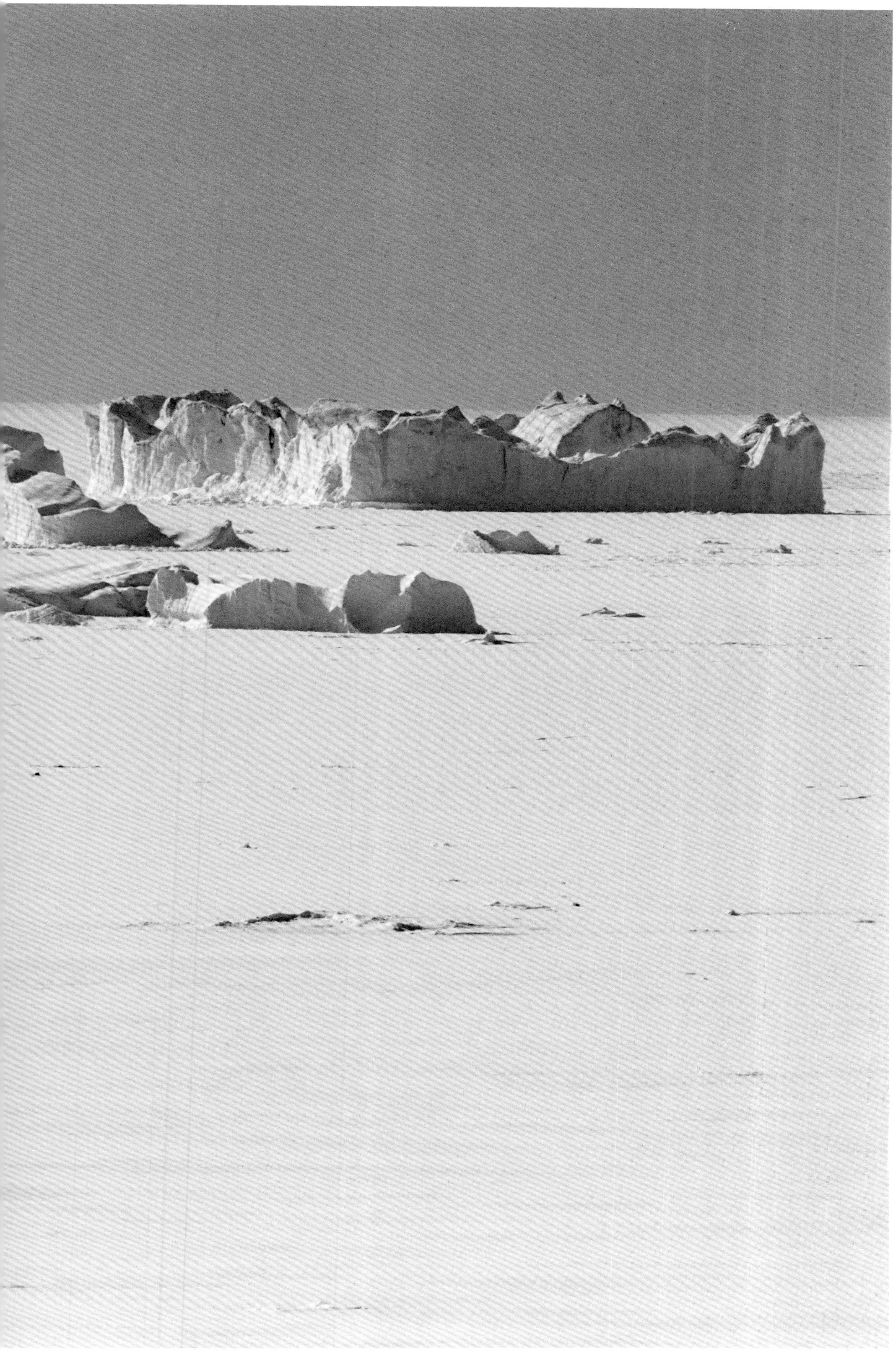

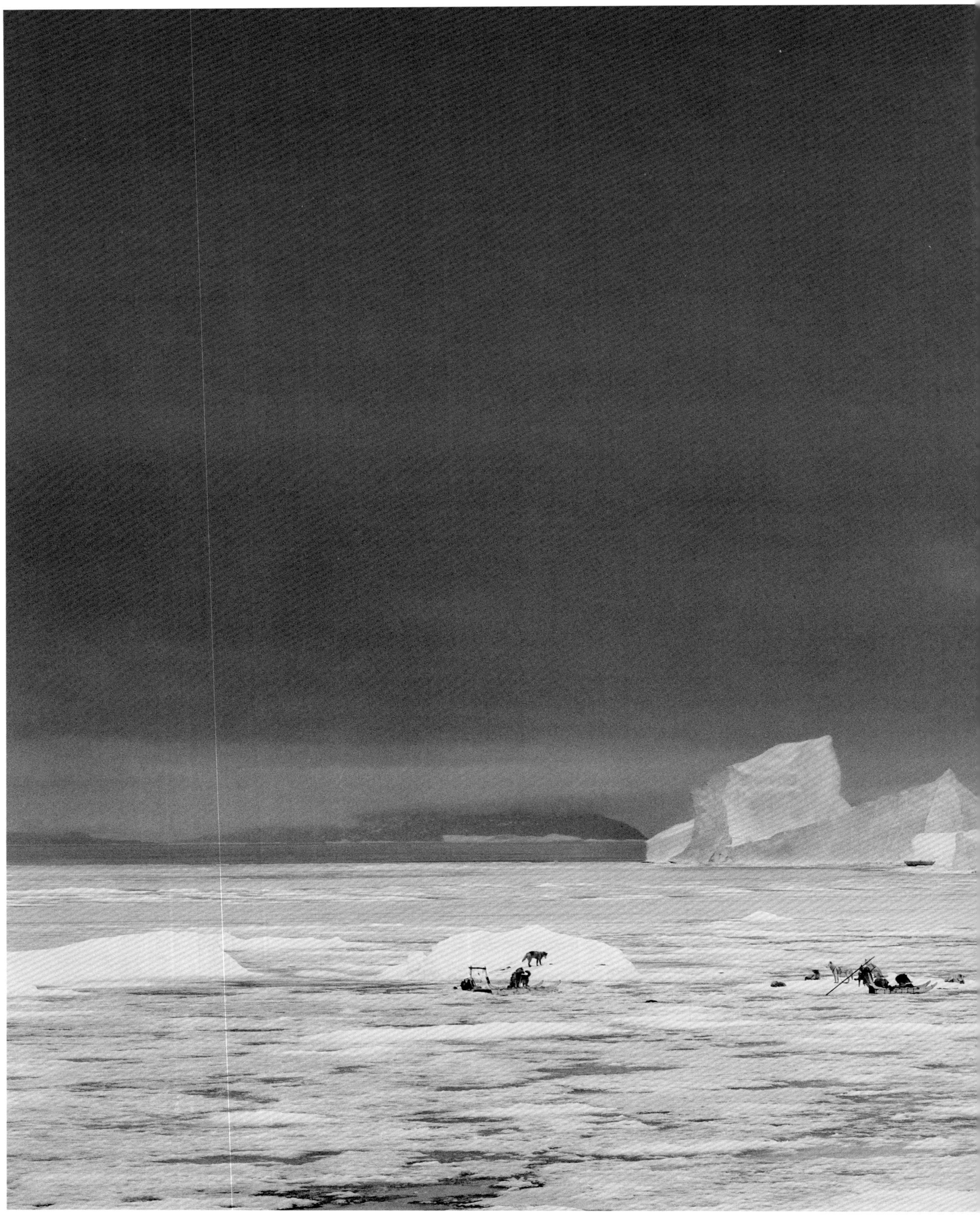

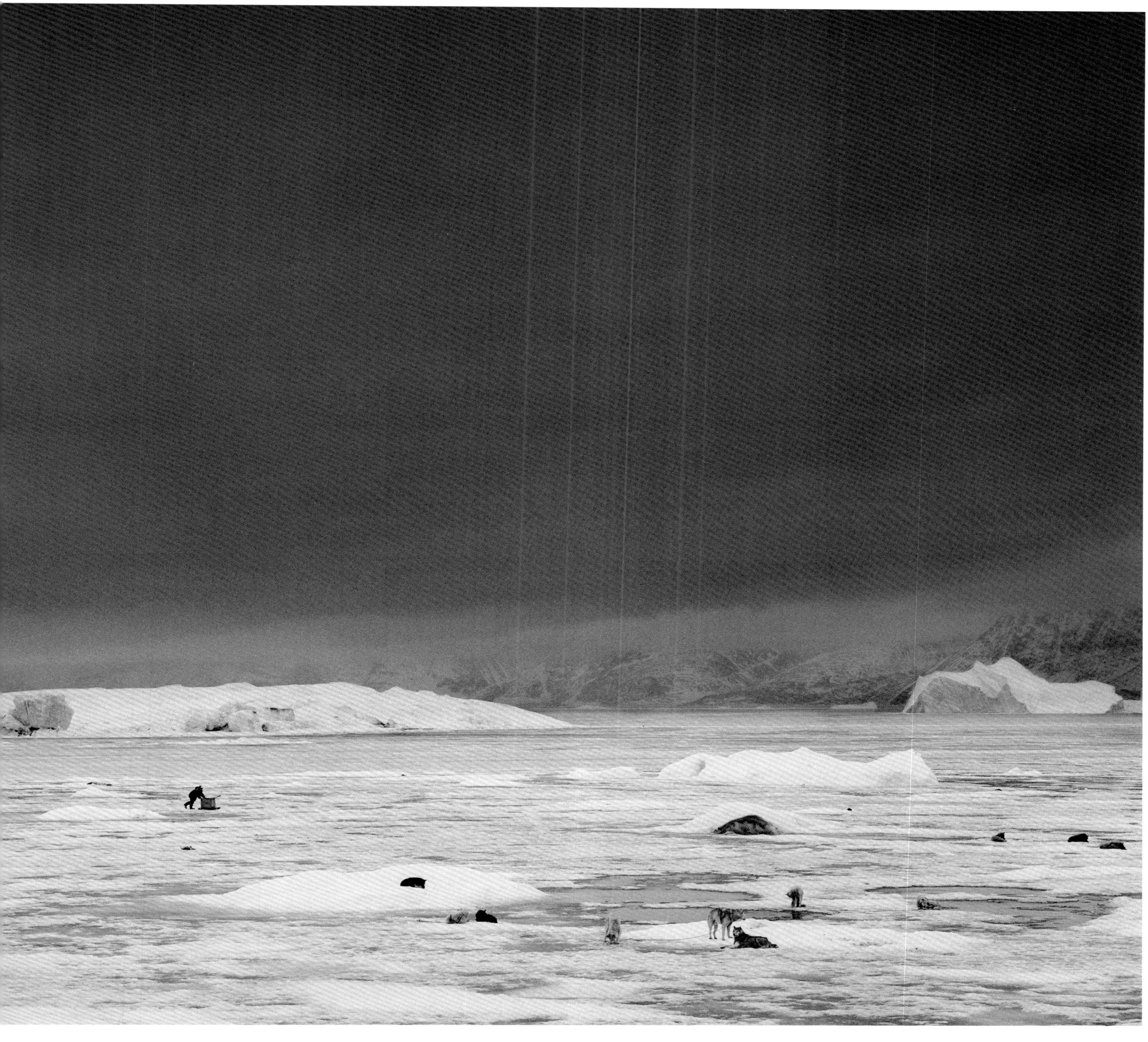

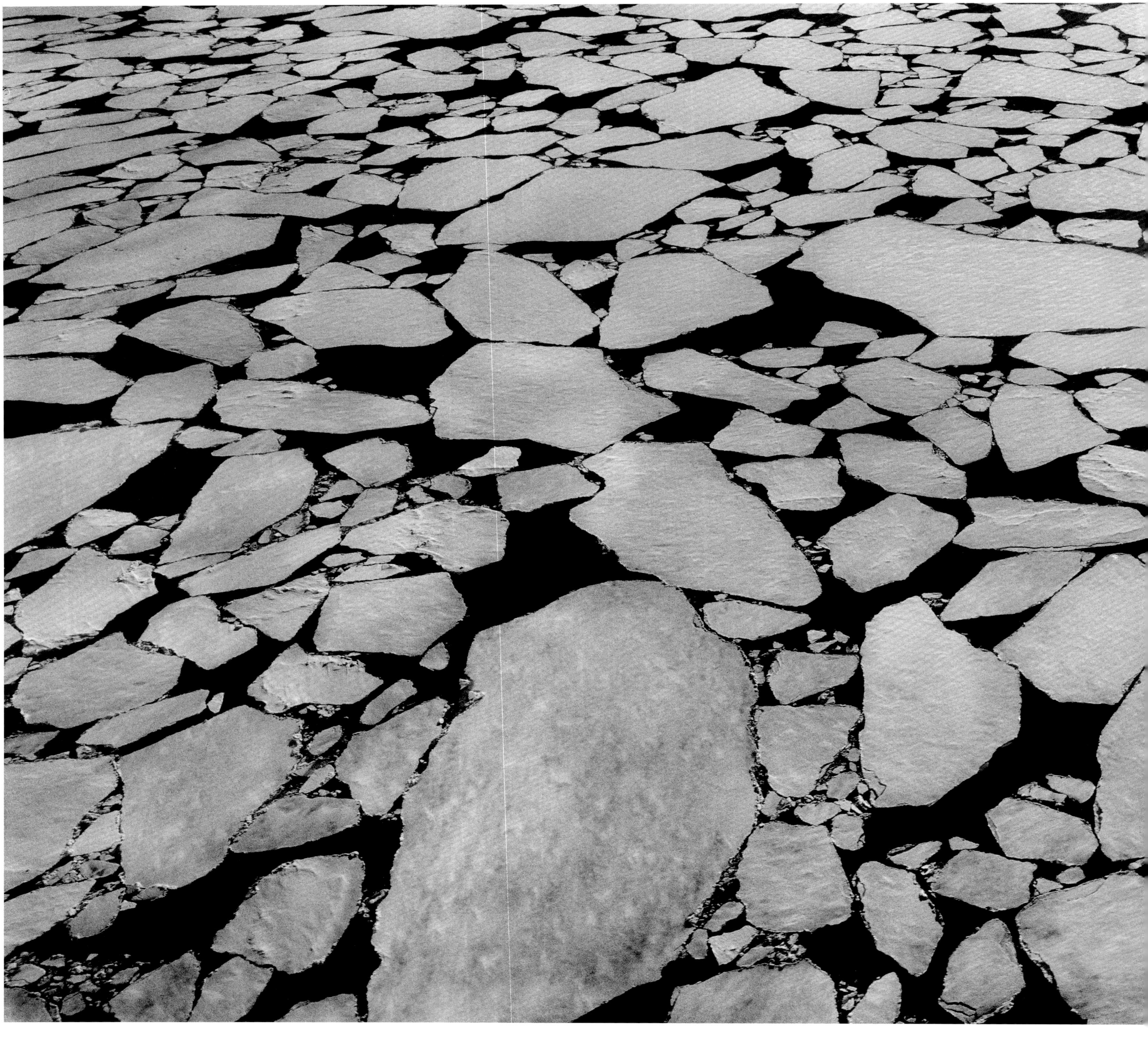

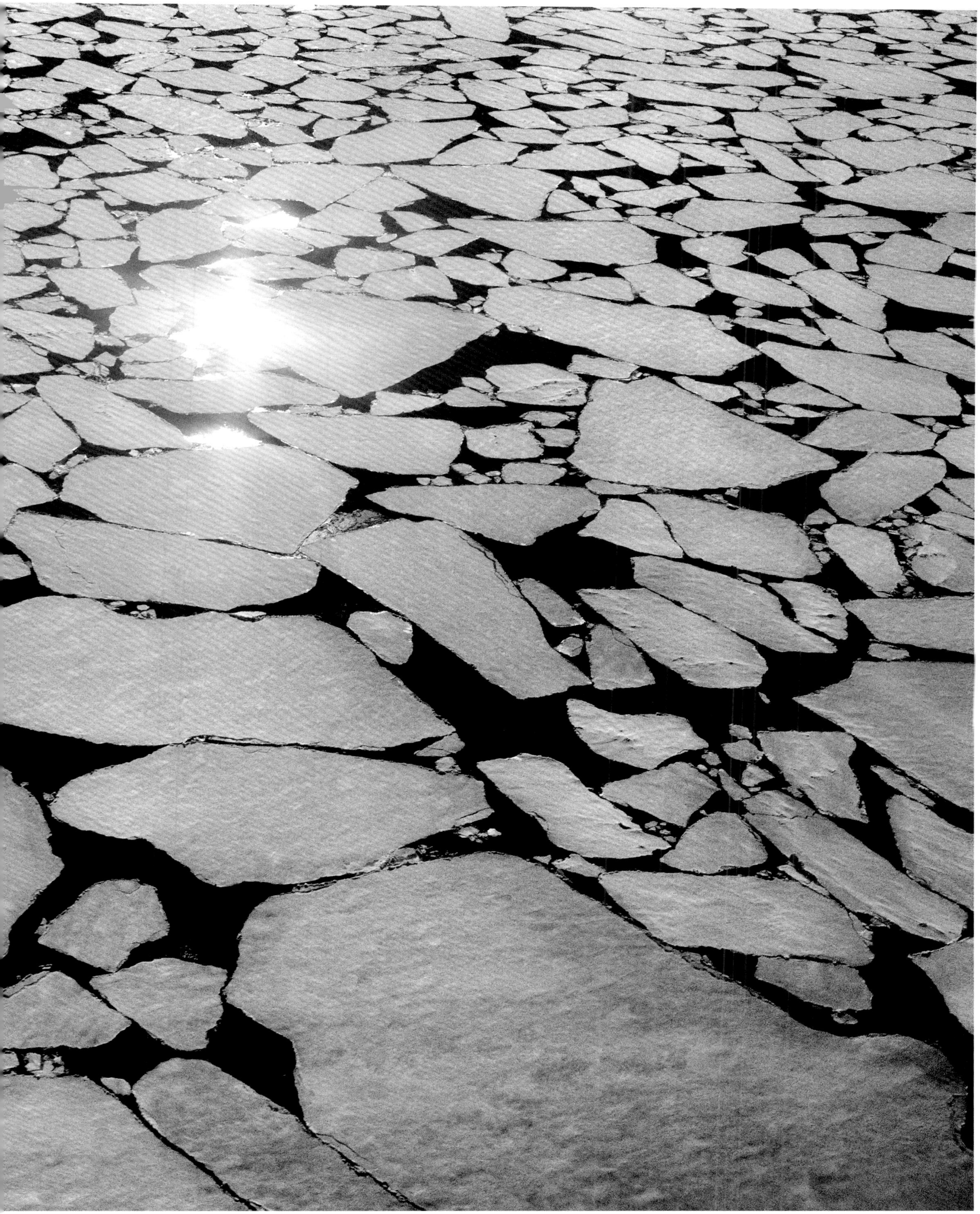

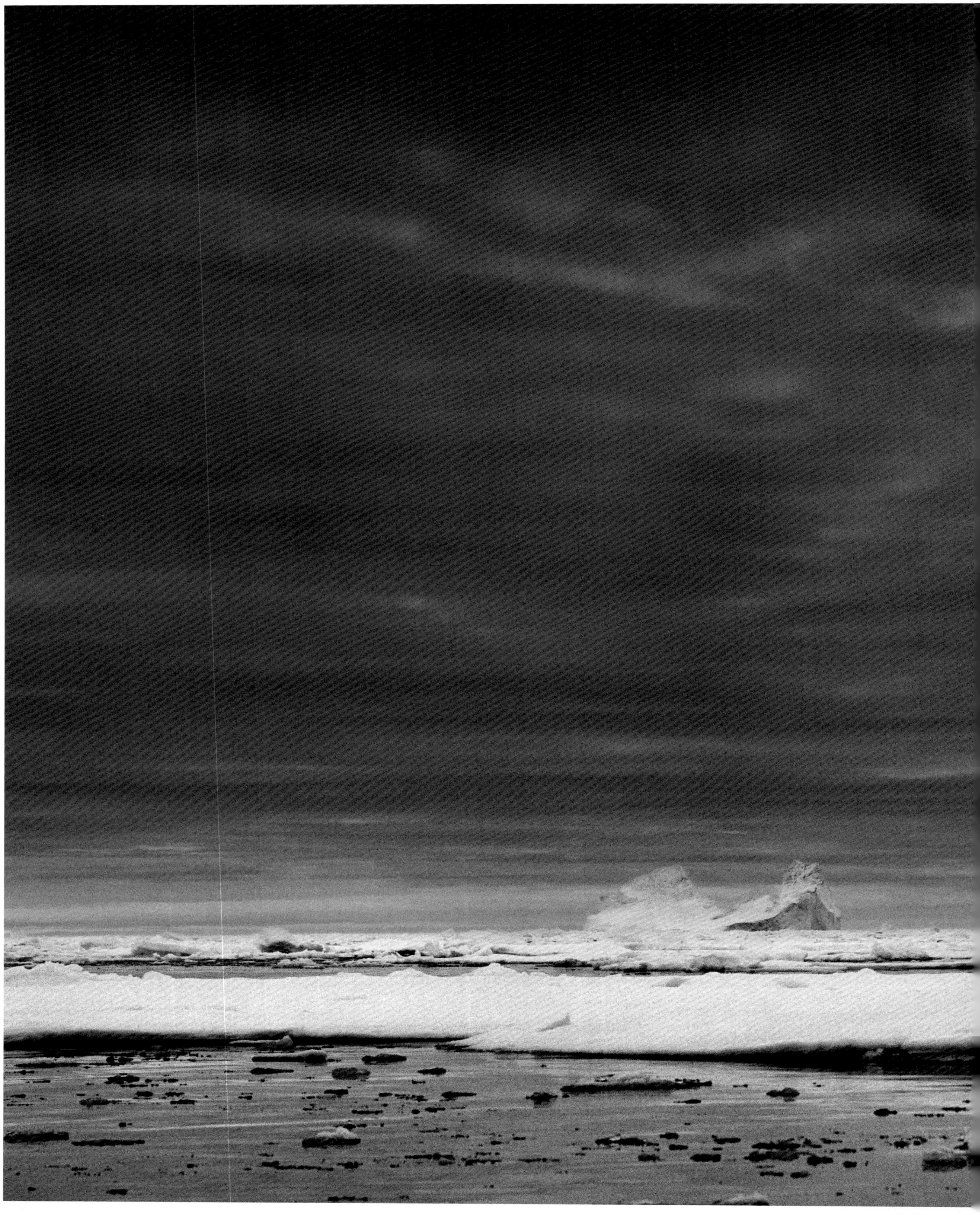

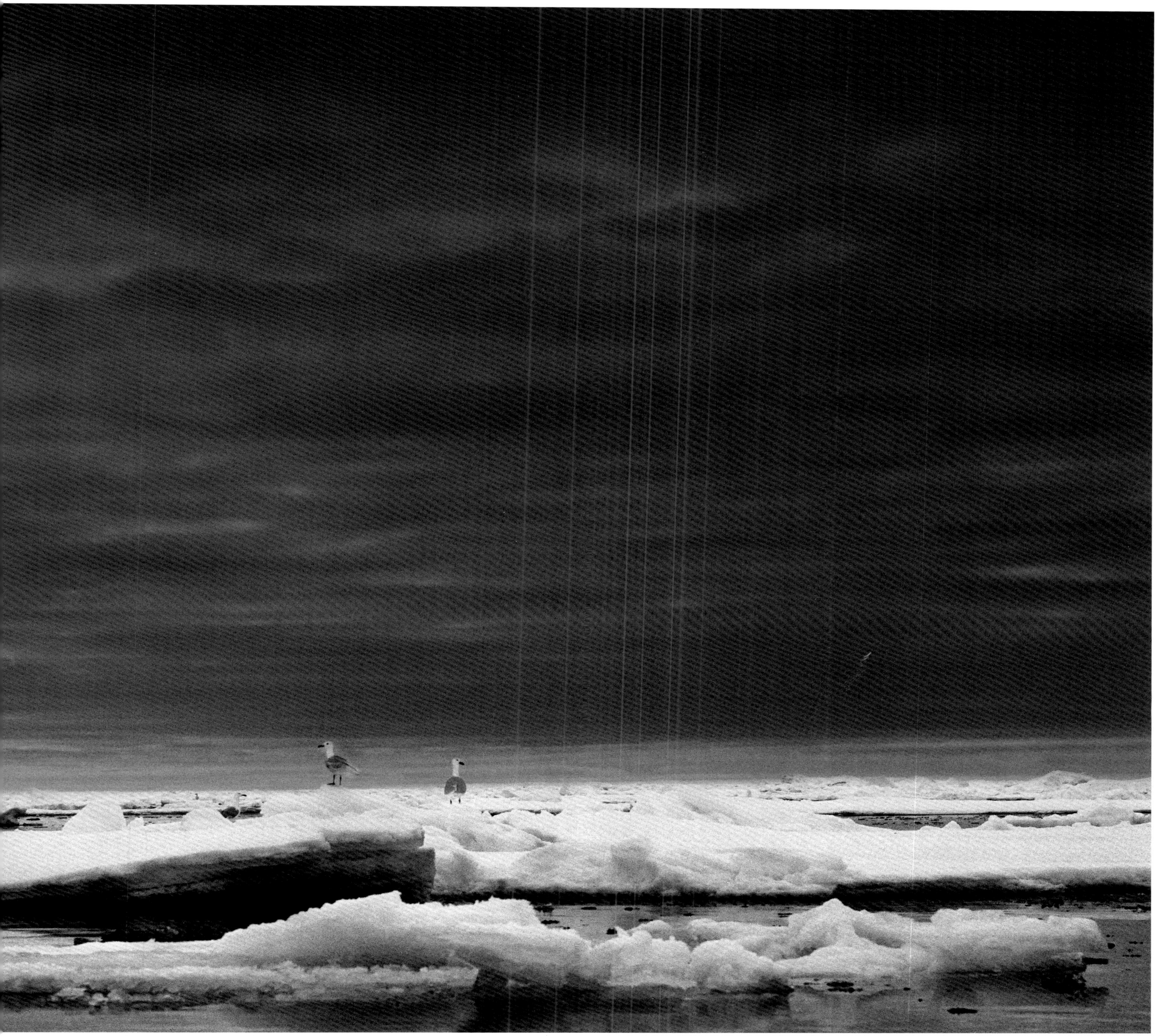

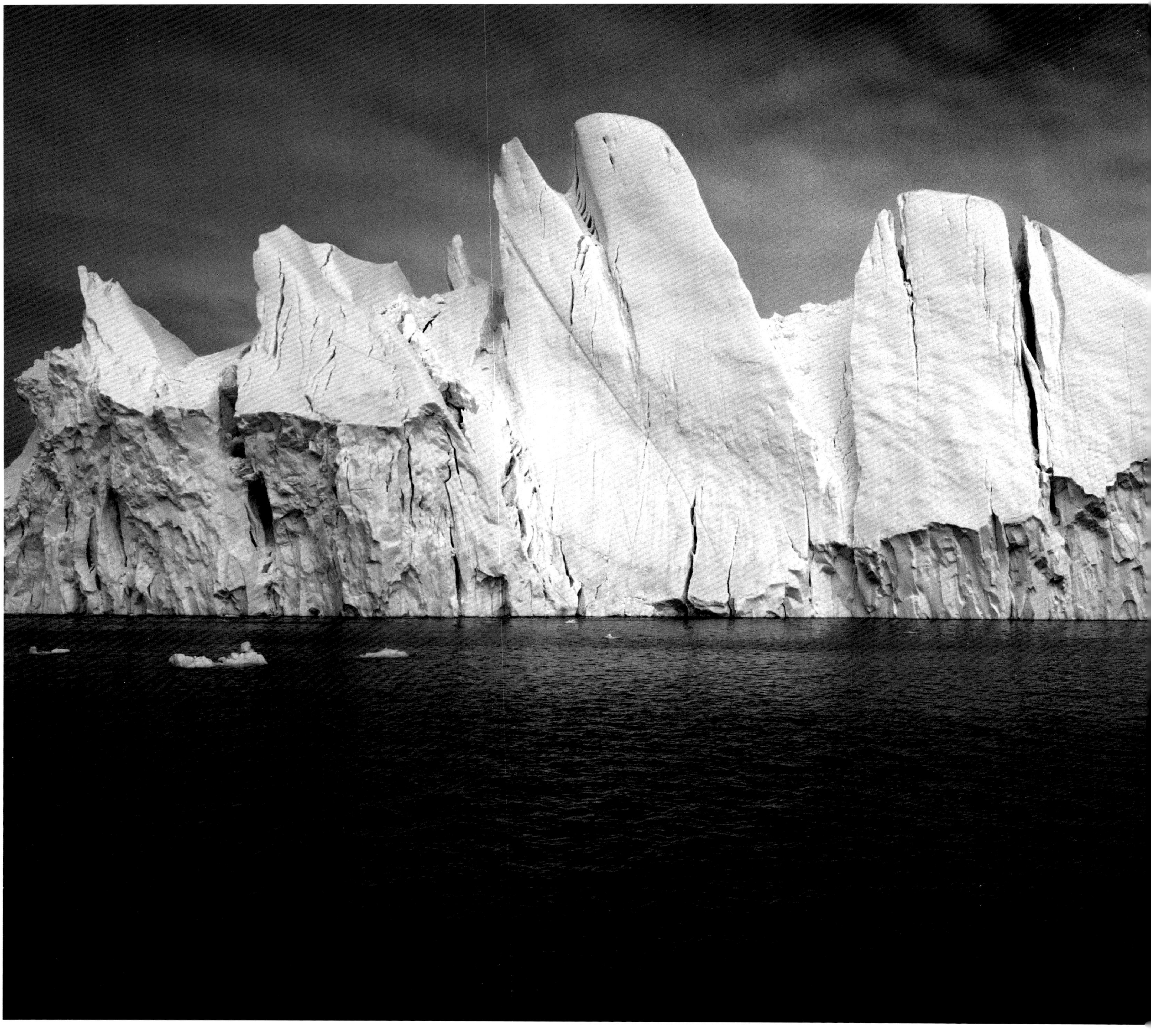

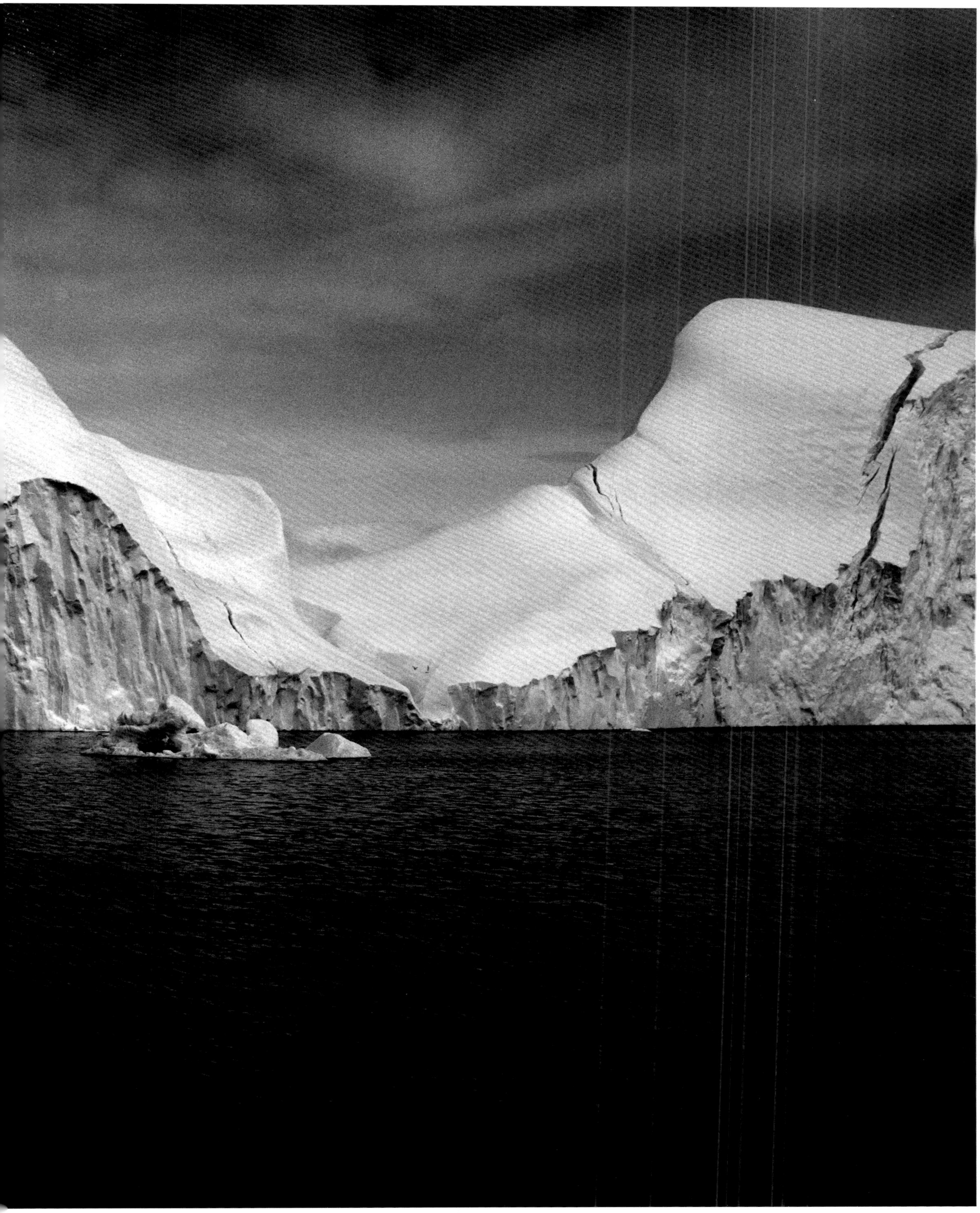

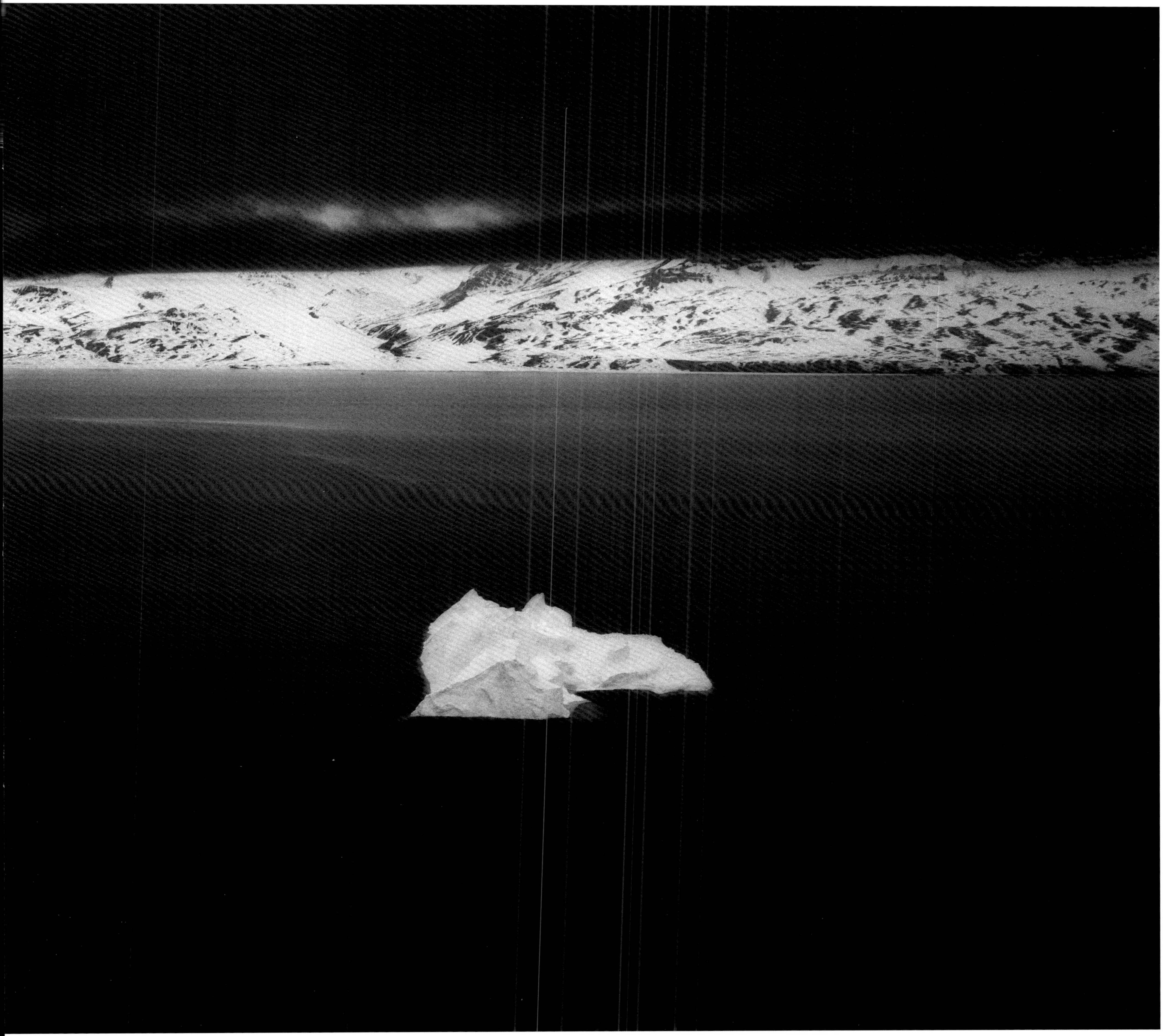

The village

The ice is getting thinner and the hunting season is coming to an end. Ice that was three feet thick, is now only four inches thick. The ocean-icefield that stretched out as far as the eye could see, is now open sea. How will life in these parts be if the ice disappears completely? It is a huge part of life here. The number of hunters decreases every year and it is becoming increasingly hard to survive by hunting. The hunters are worried about the future. They envision the end of a society based on a hunting tradition of many thousands of years.

Spring has arrived, snow melts in the villages and mountains. People get their boats ready and row them out to catch fish and, every now and then, a seal. The dogs sprawl around under the clothes-lines, they are on summer vacation. For a few weeks now there is 24-hour daylight and life is wonderful. The children play and bathe in hot pools in Unatoq or in ponds by the villages.

People travel around, sail to remote places and camp. We venture out from the village to a place that is only a half hour walk away. The village can't be seen from the camping site and it feels like we are in a completely remote place. Thousands of little auks fill the sky and nearly eclipse the sun. People walk up the side of the mountain and catch birds with nets. A few days of good hunting will provide enough food to last them far into the winter.

The days pass, people fish and tell stories of their ancestors at every new place. What will the future hold? No one can answer this. New times are ahead, a different way of life, a different way of working. Times are changing and they might be changing the fastest here in the Arctic, where the effects of climate change are already apparent. Huge, majestic icebergs float around in the fjords, plunging underwater every now and then, some drifting far out to sea and melting. You can see many fantastic images in these icebergs. They have been trapped inside the glaciers for centuries, but now they've been set free and are ready to tell the earth's story.

The sun is shining but the Arctic night is near, with flickering northern lights across the starry sky.

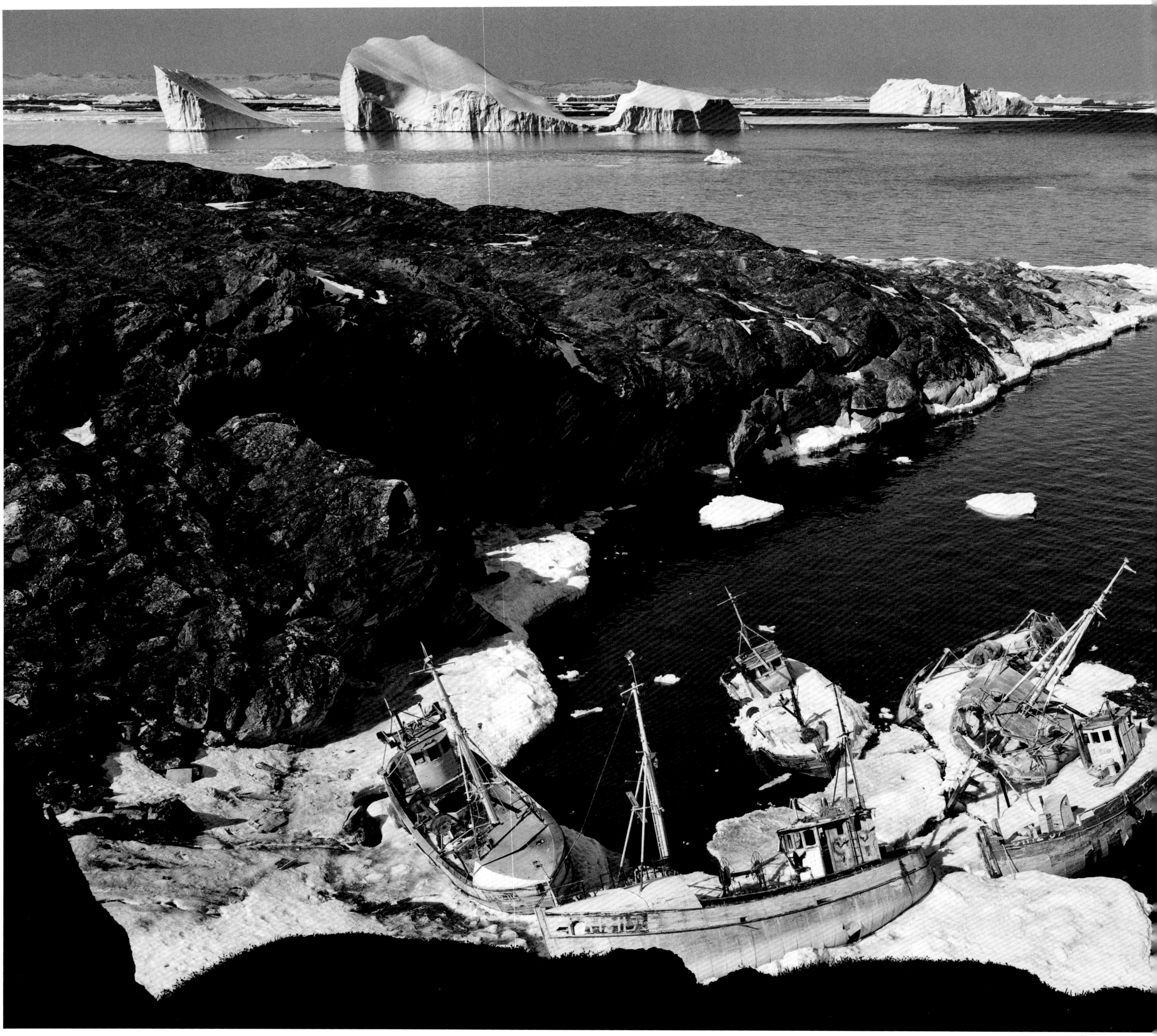

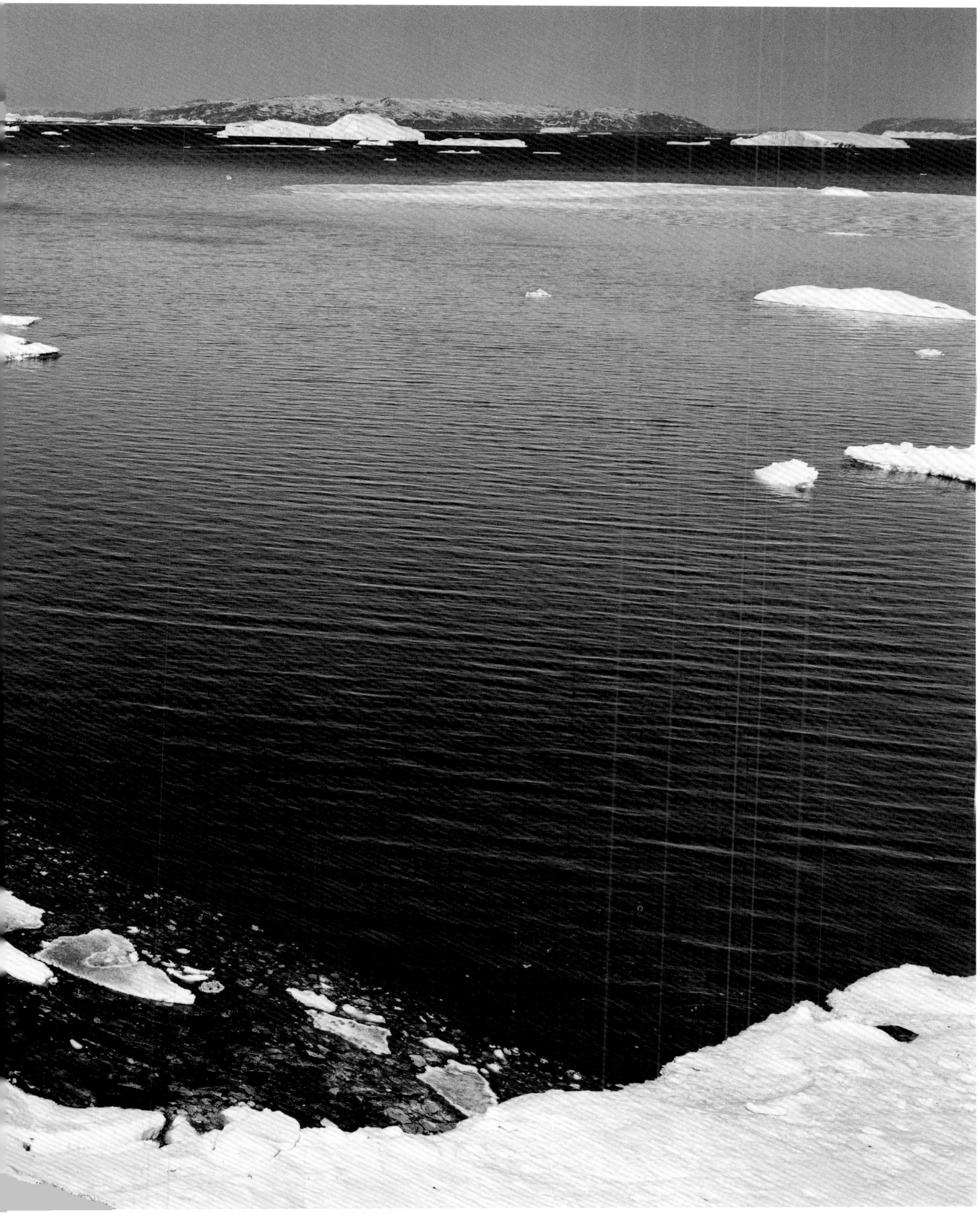

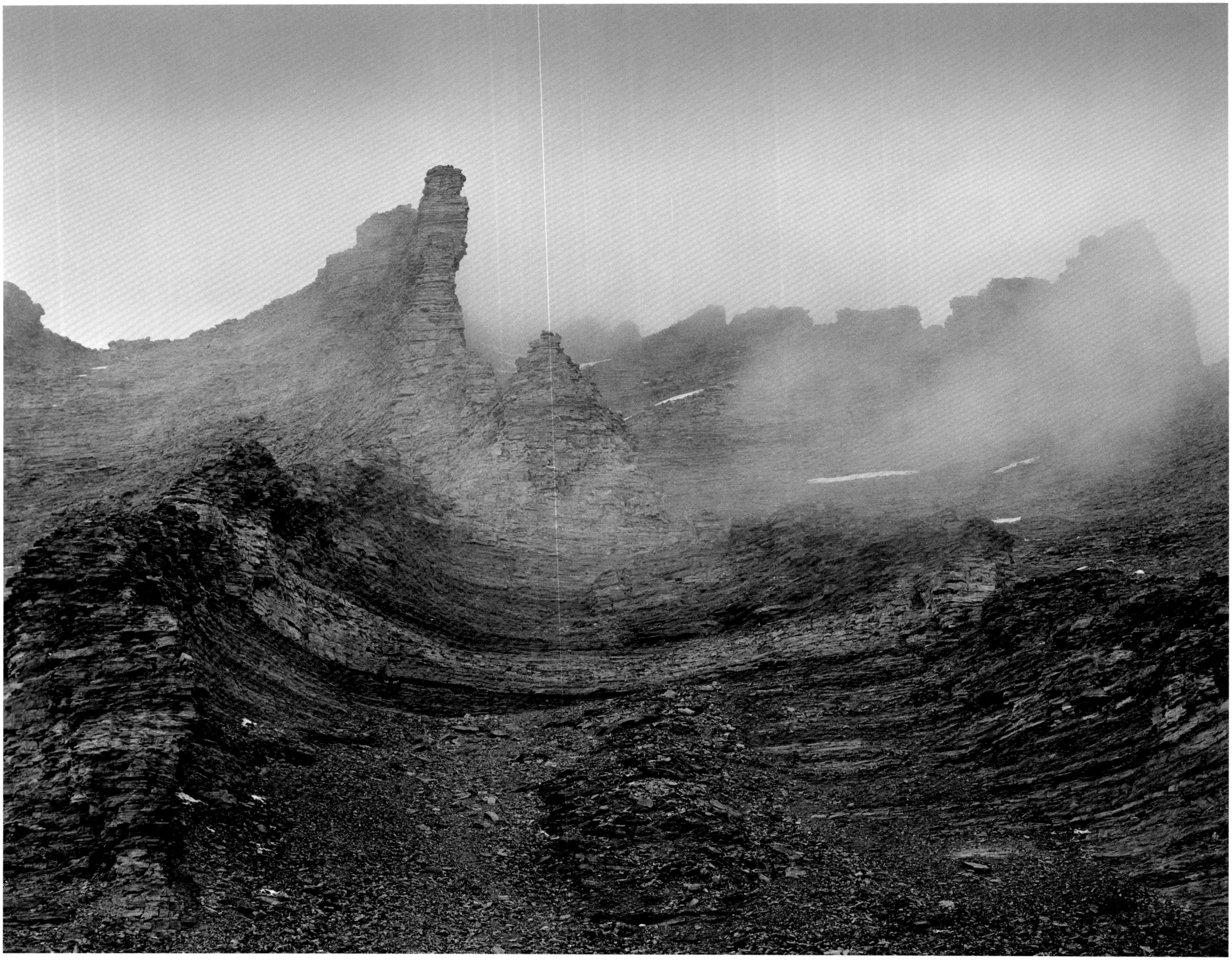

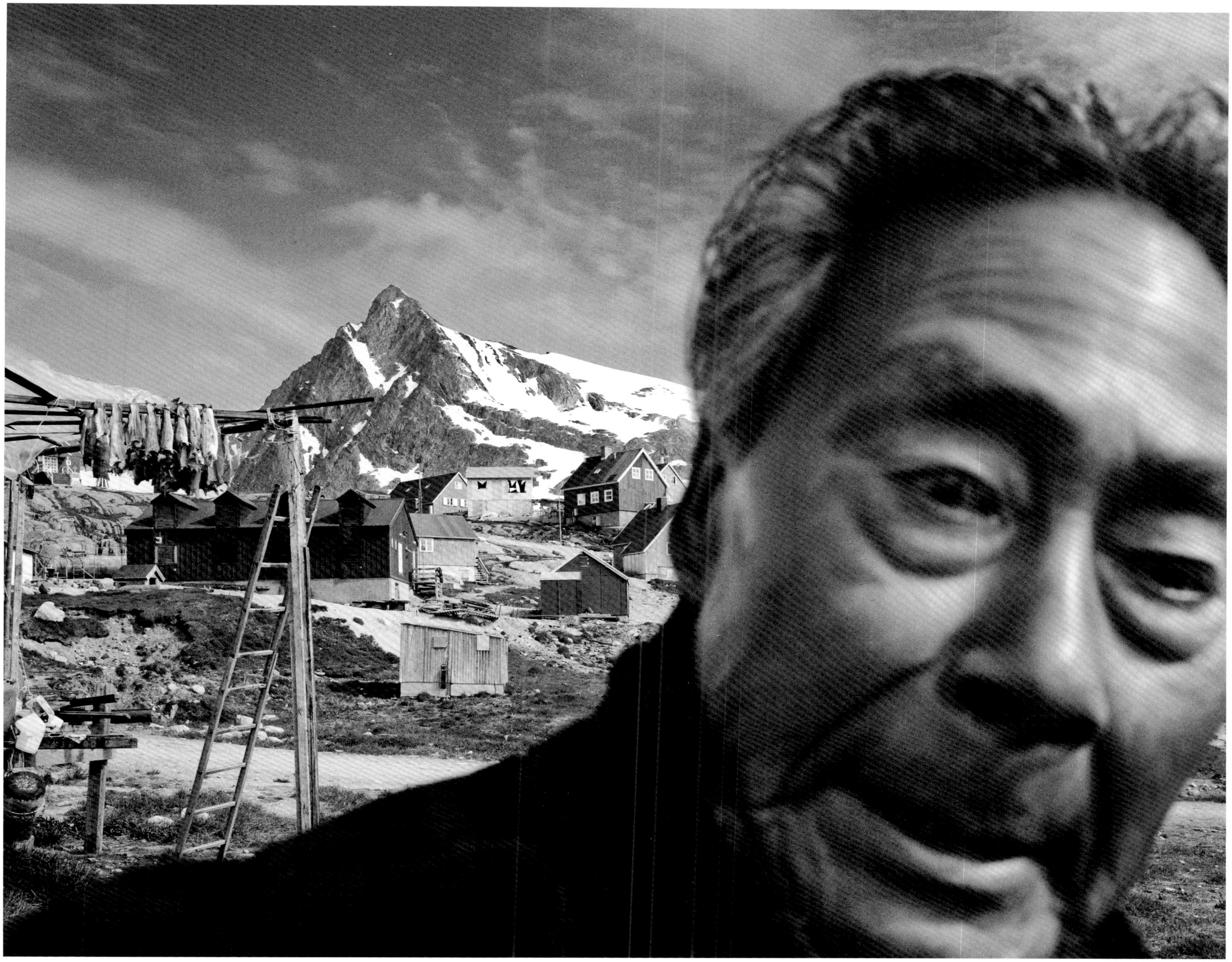

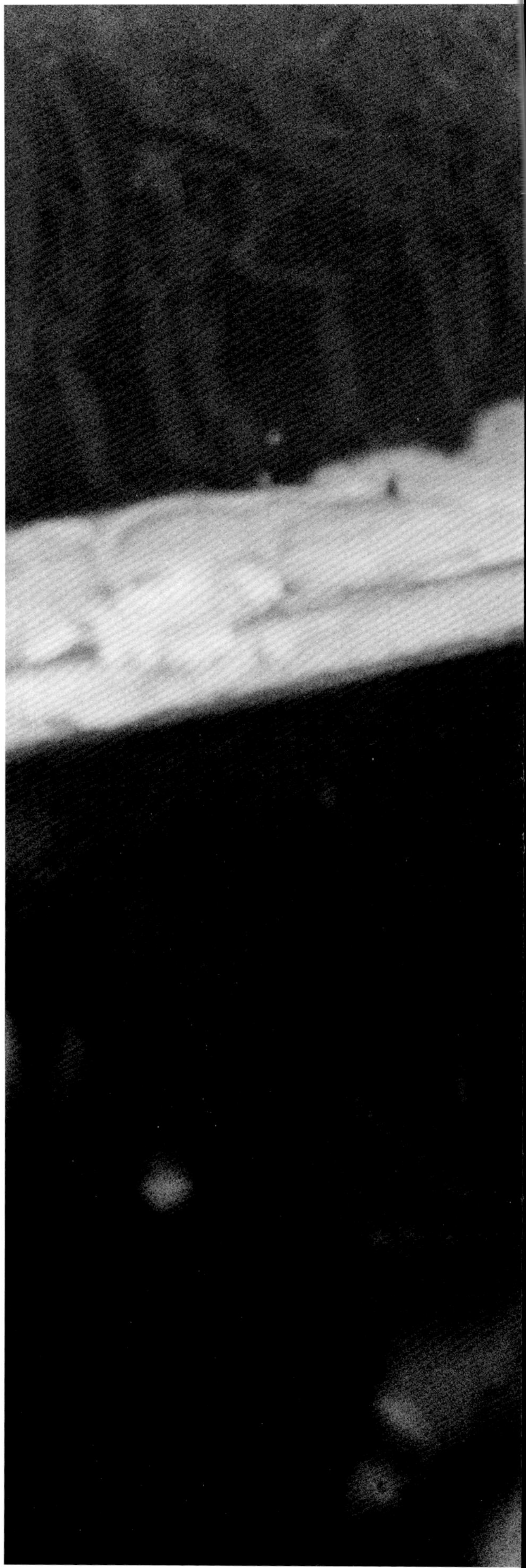

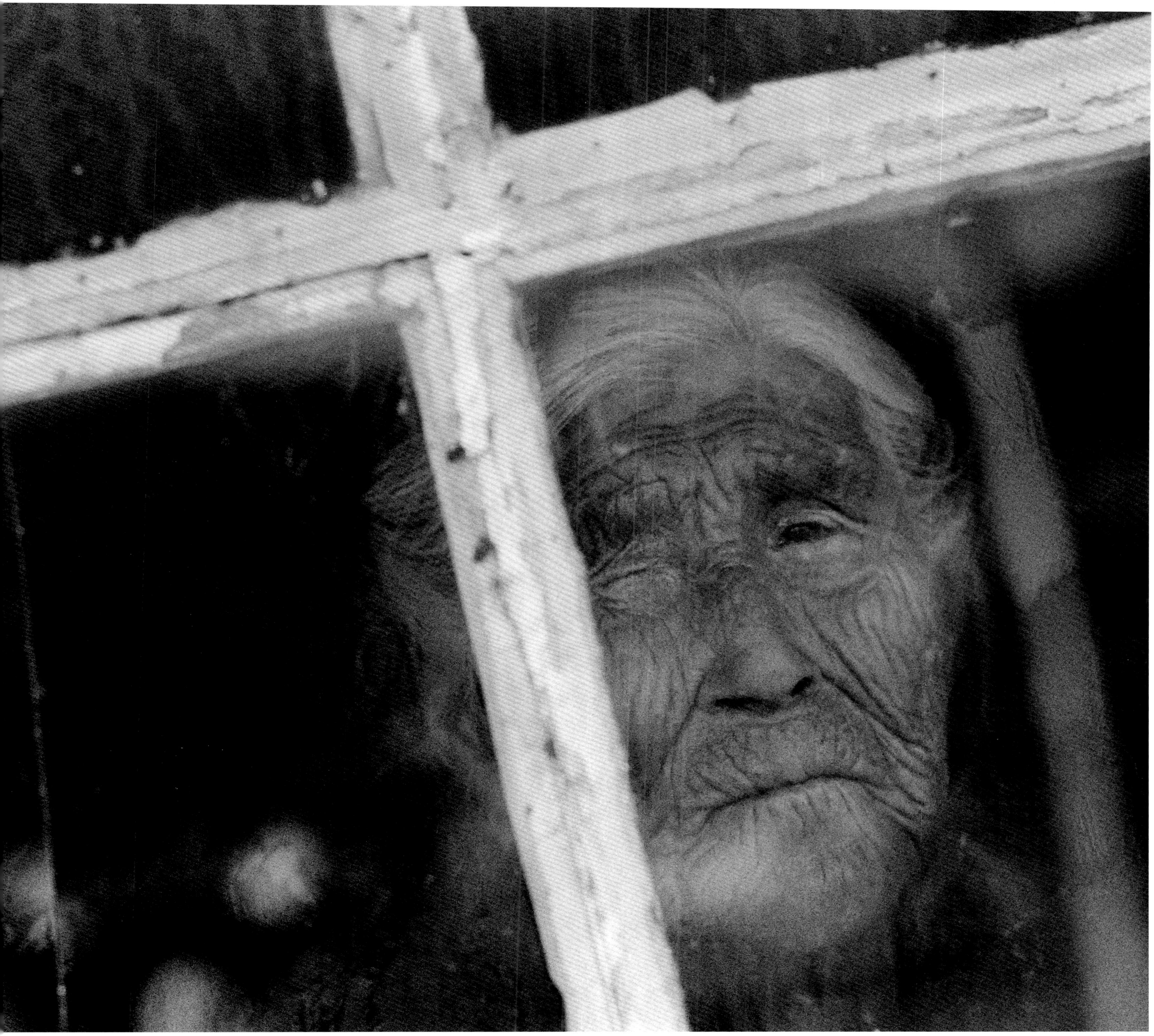

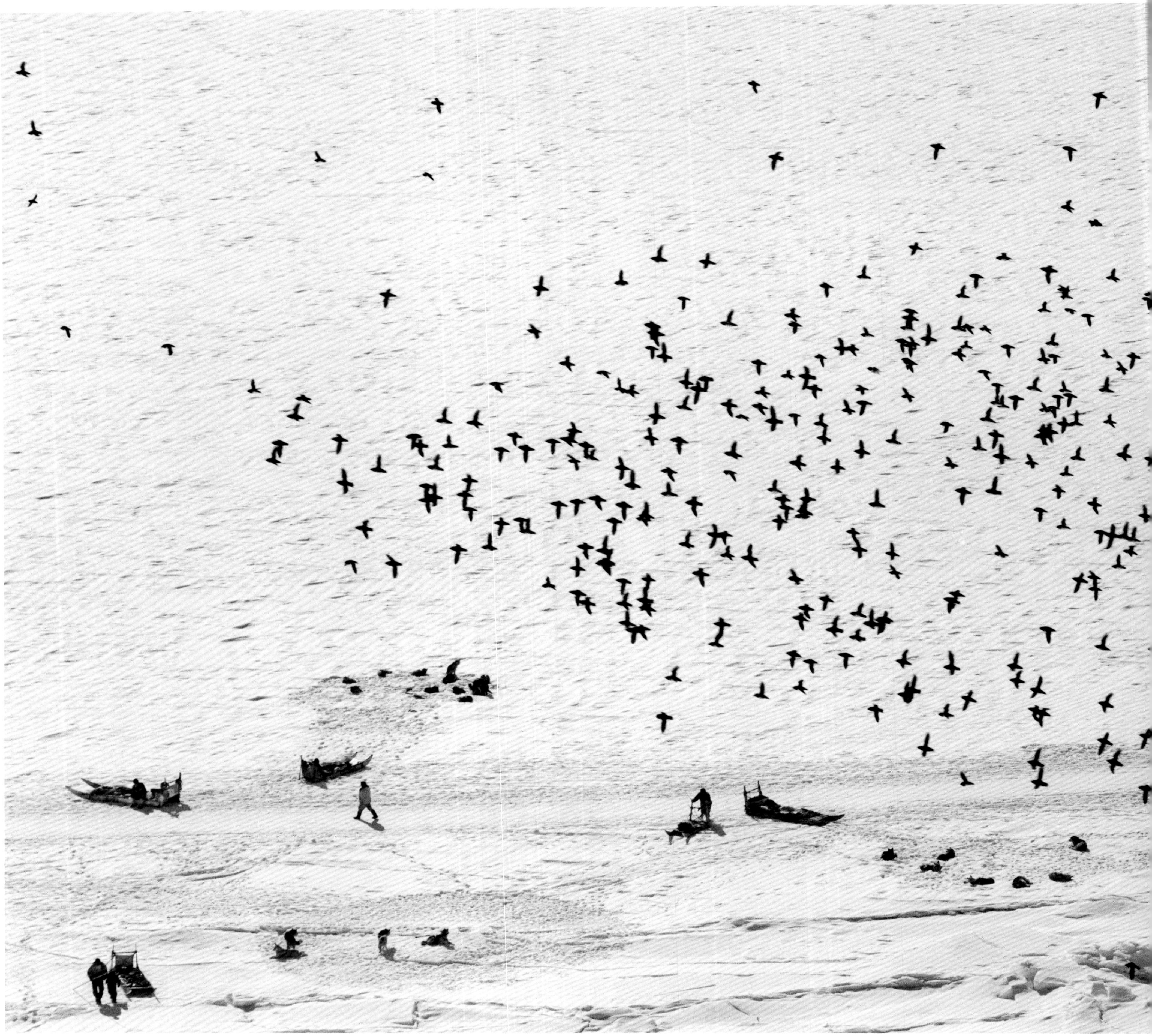

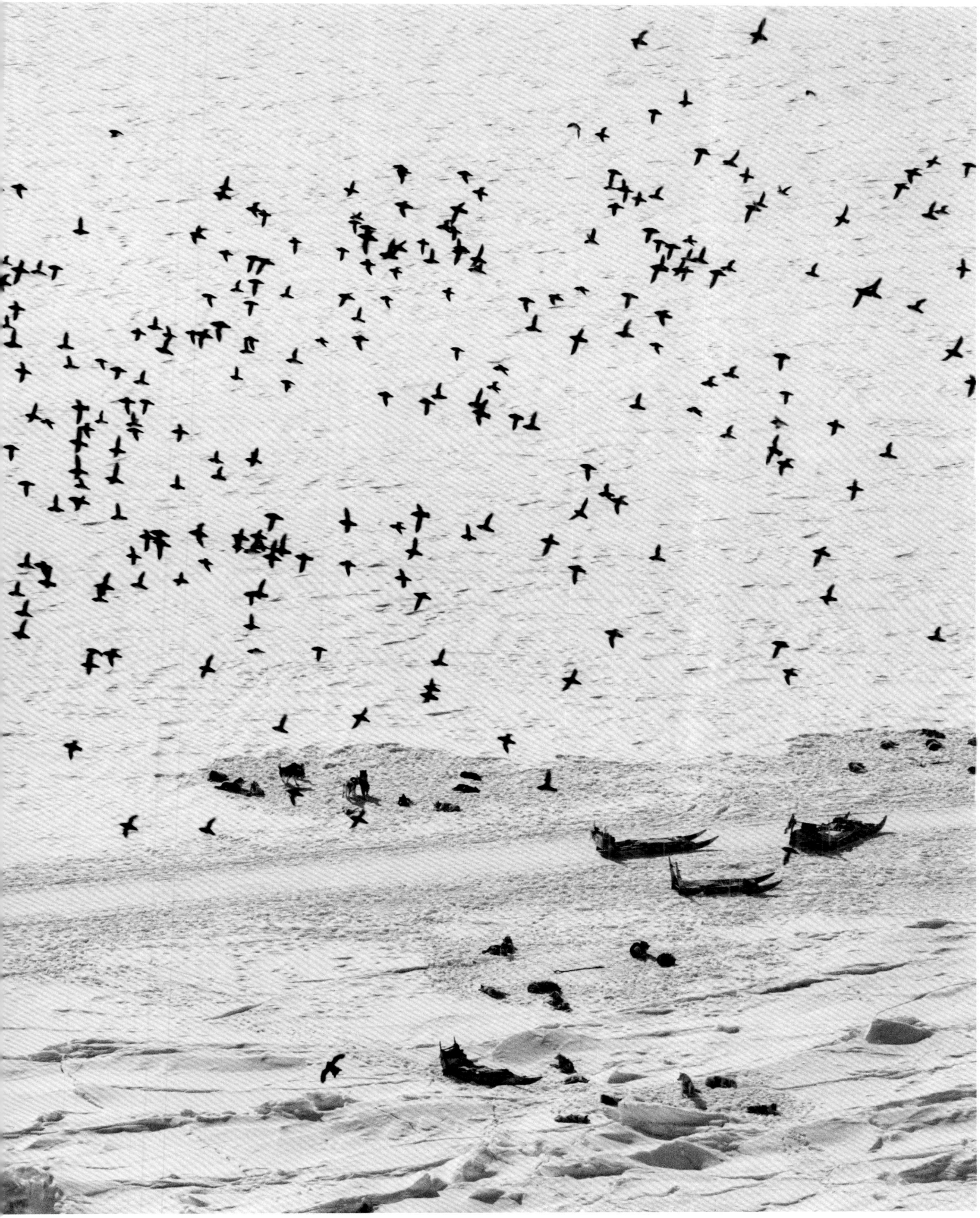

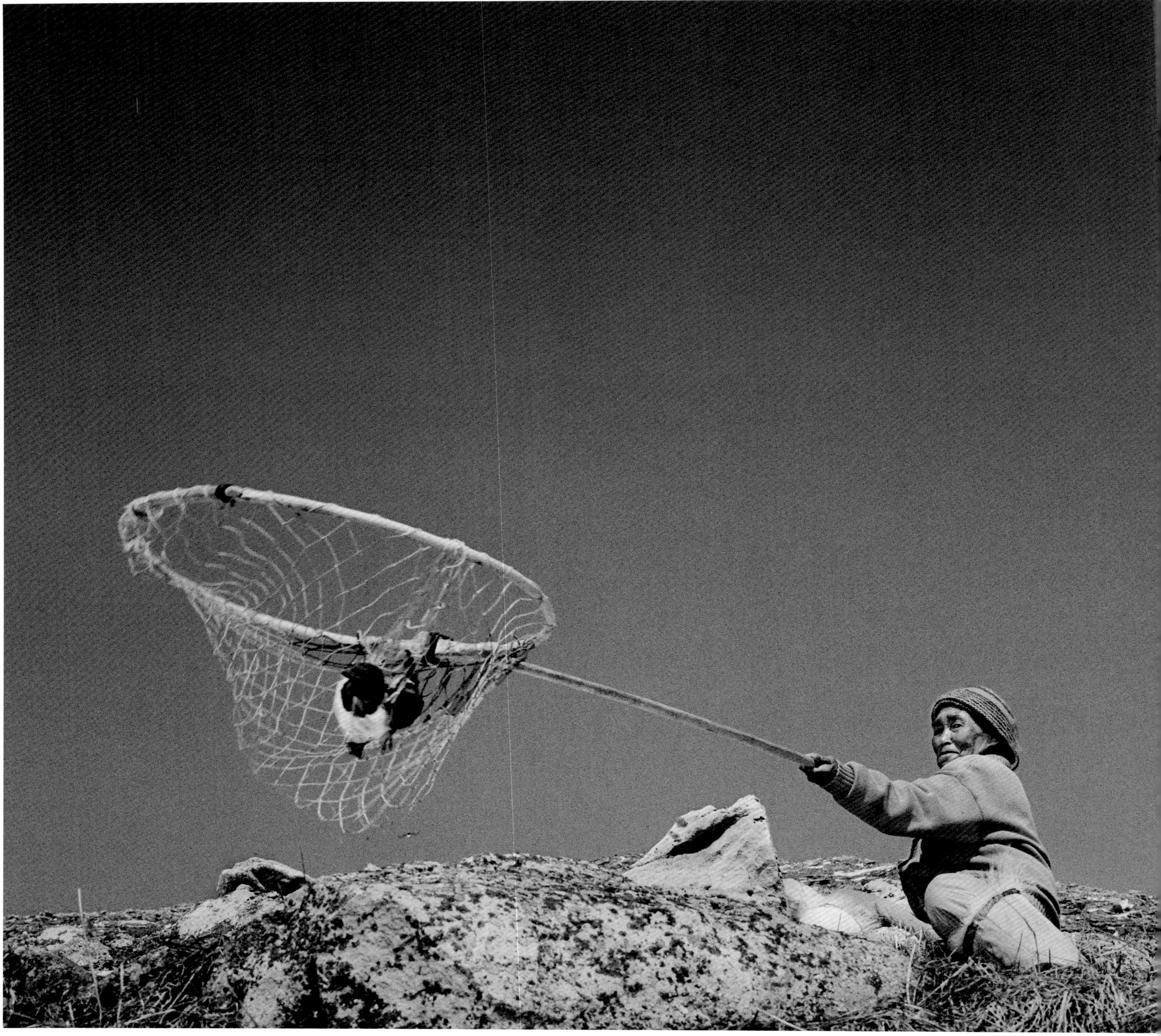

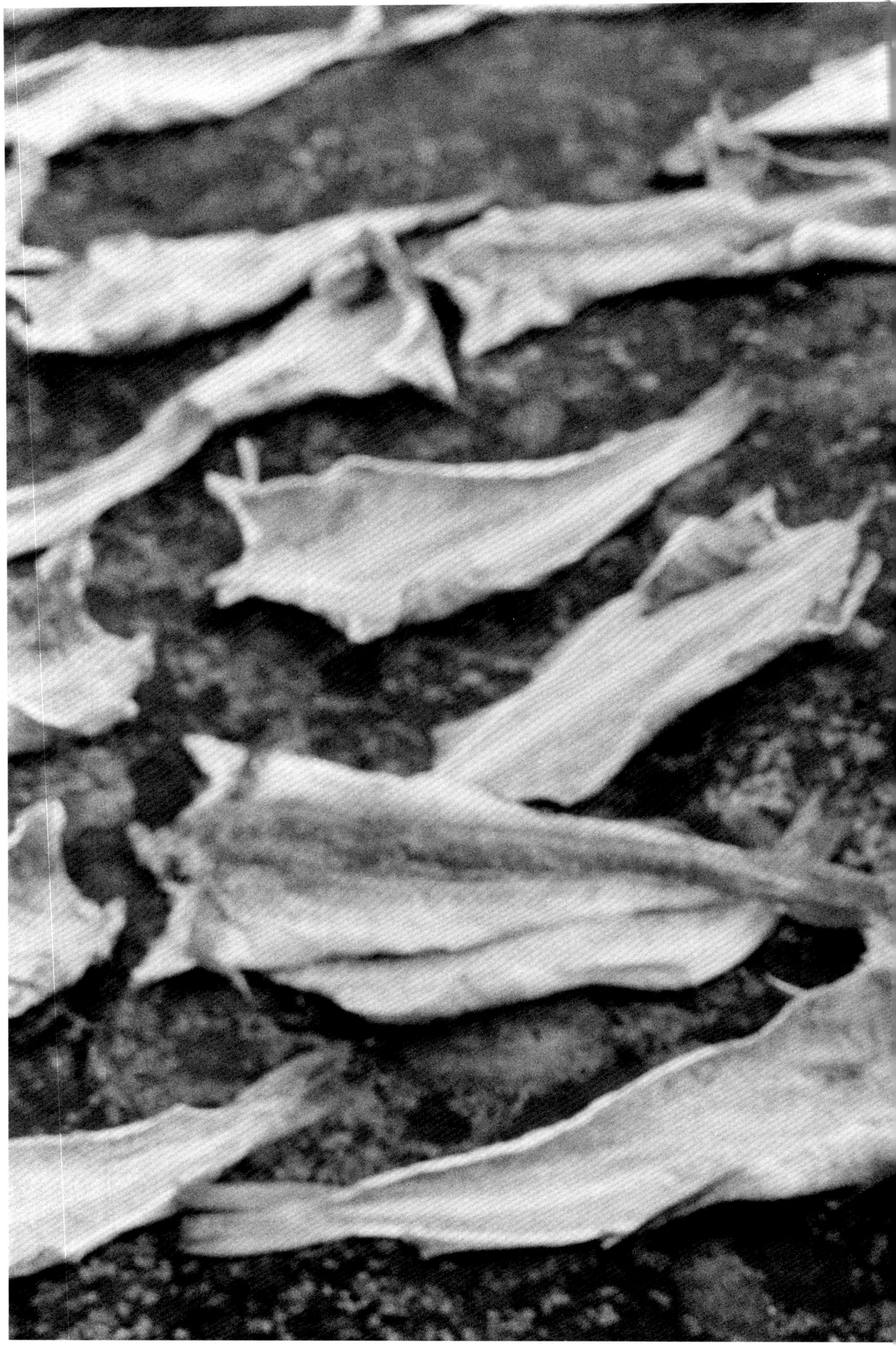

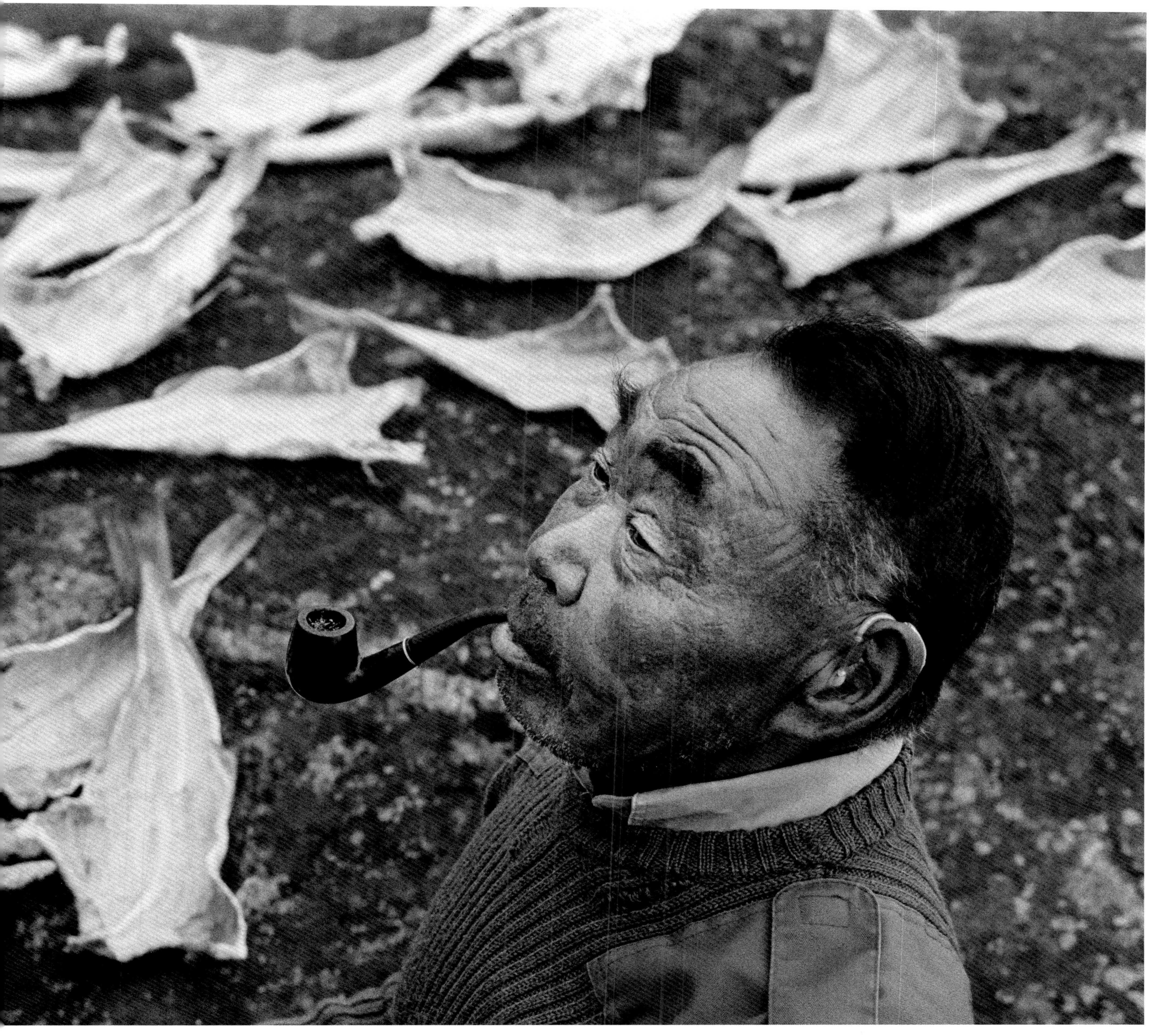

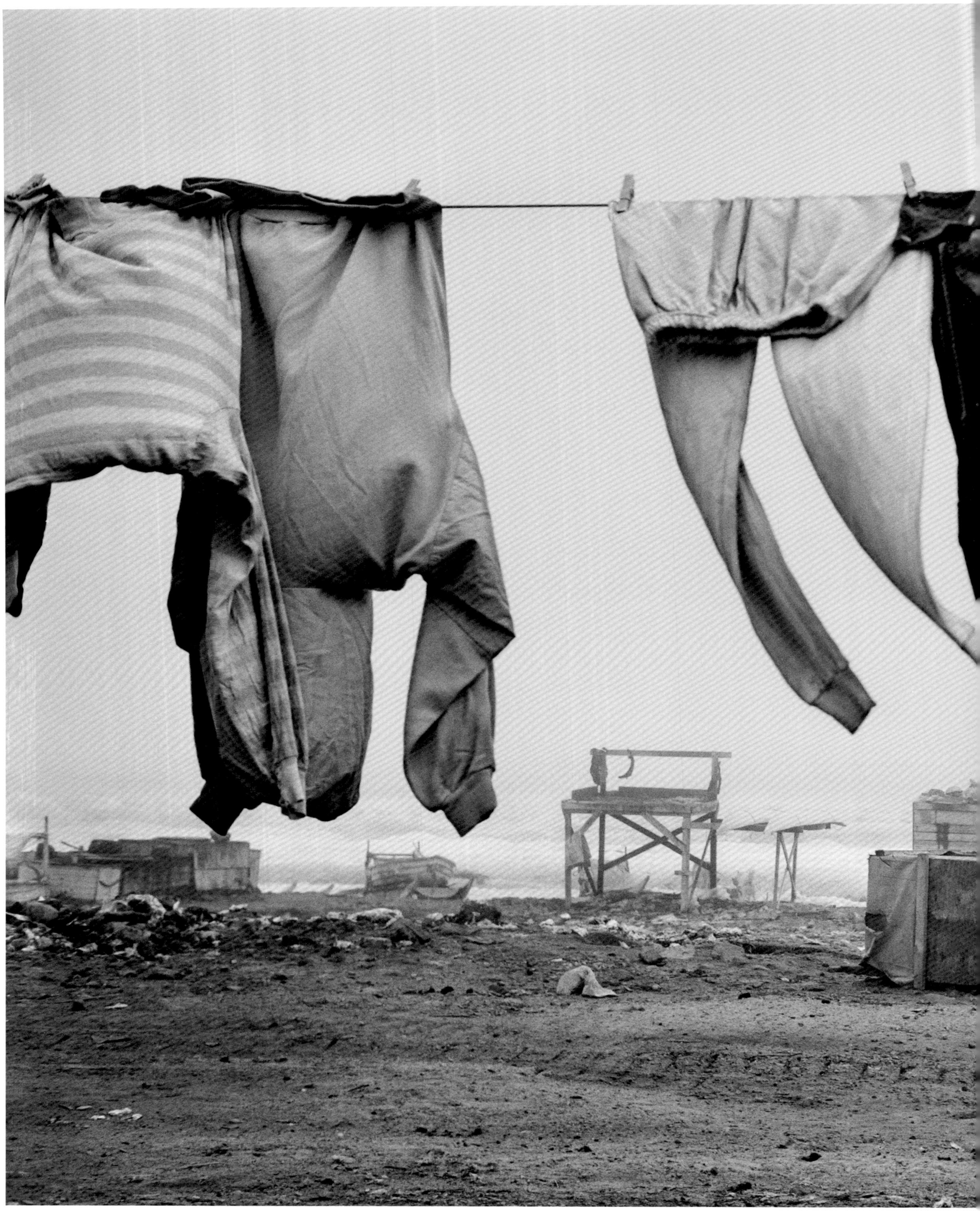

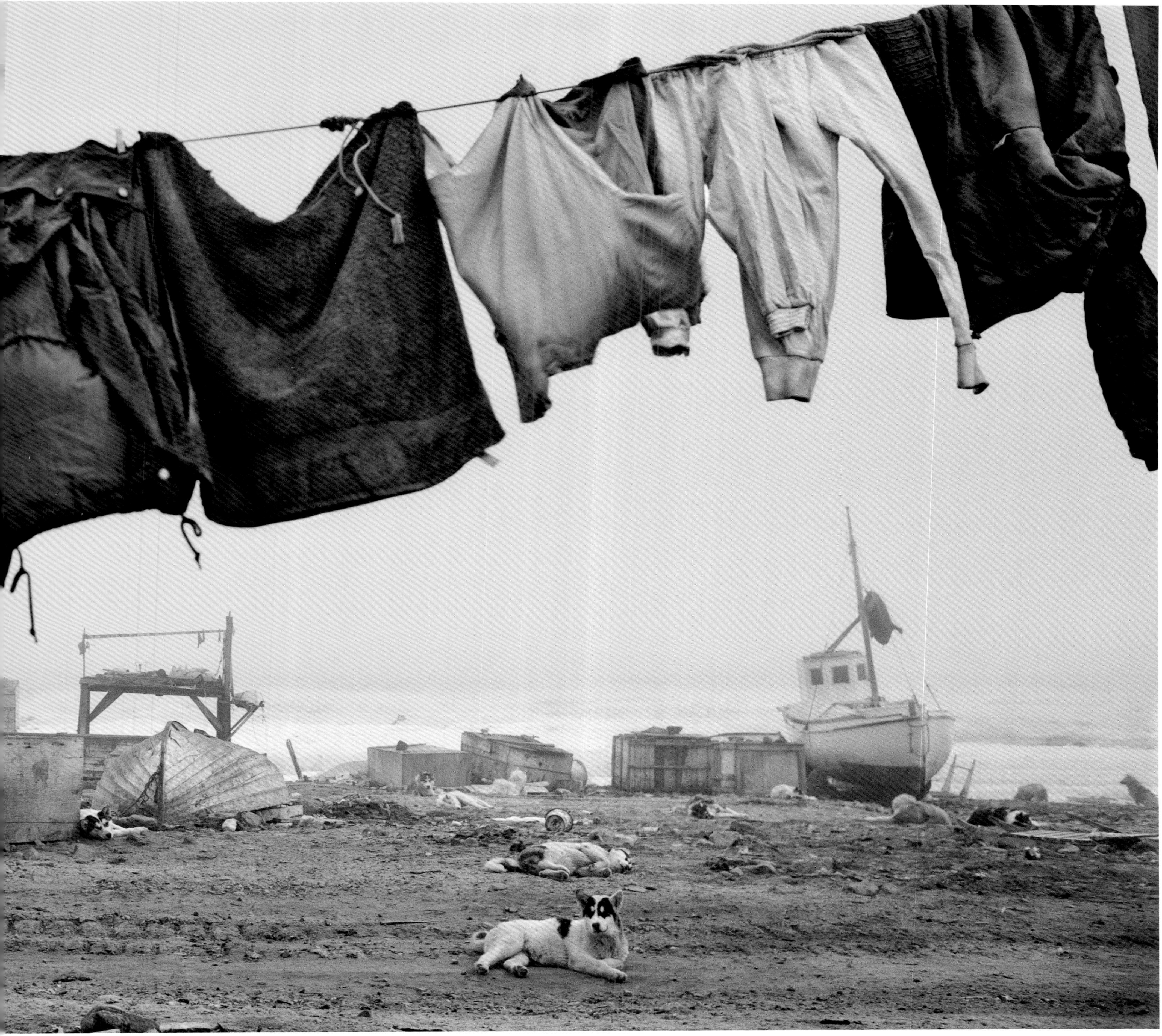

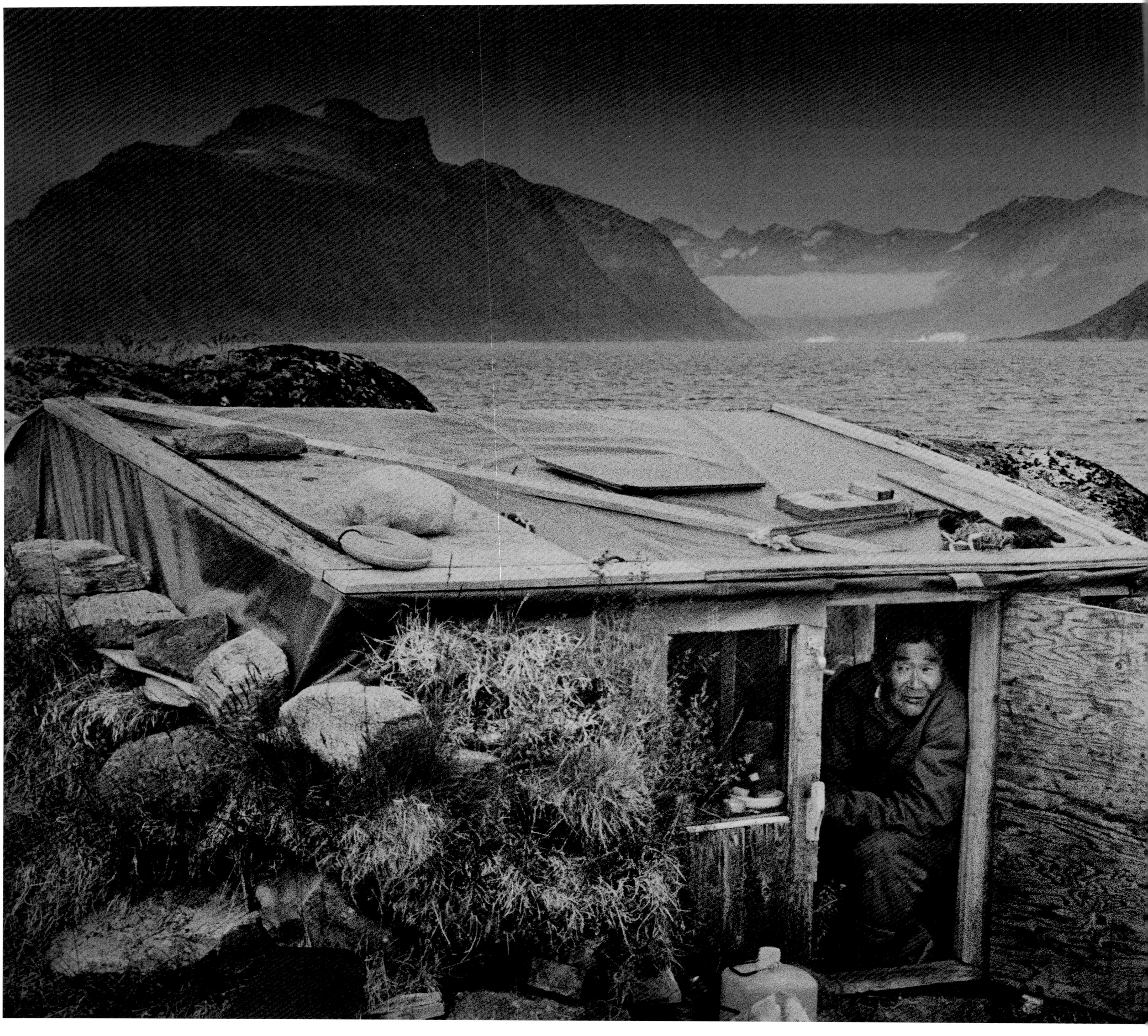

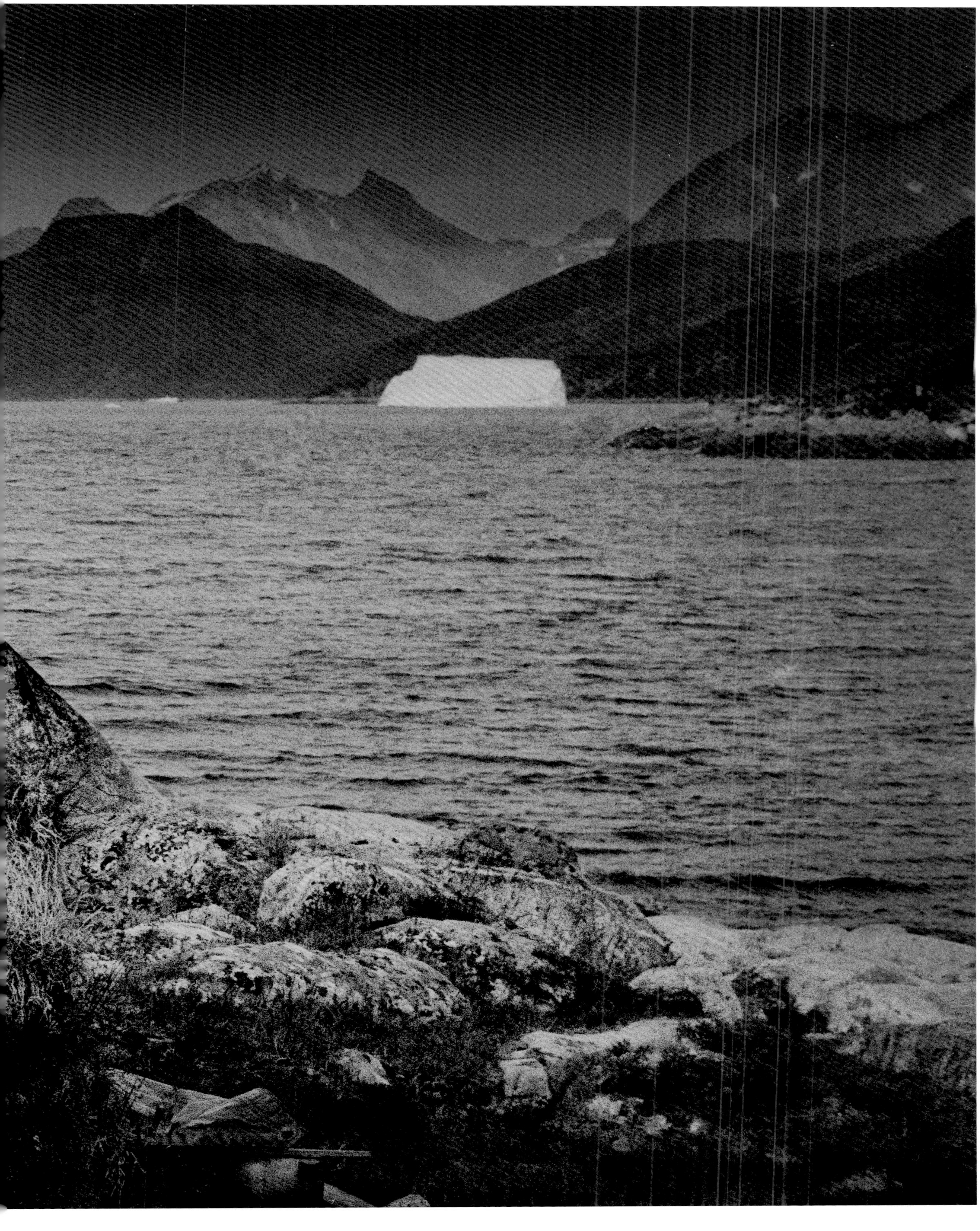

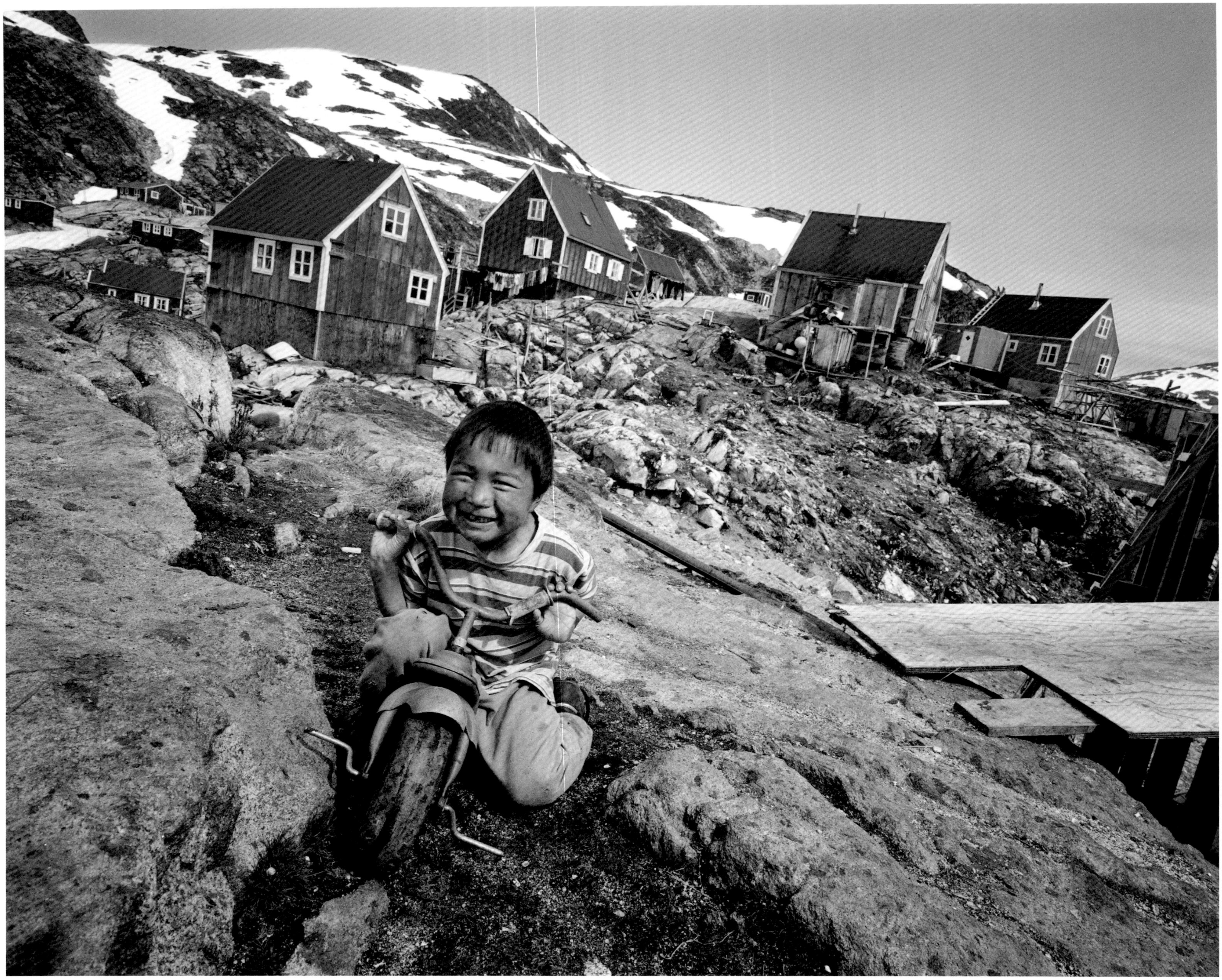

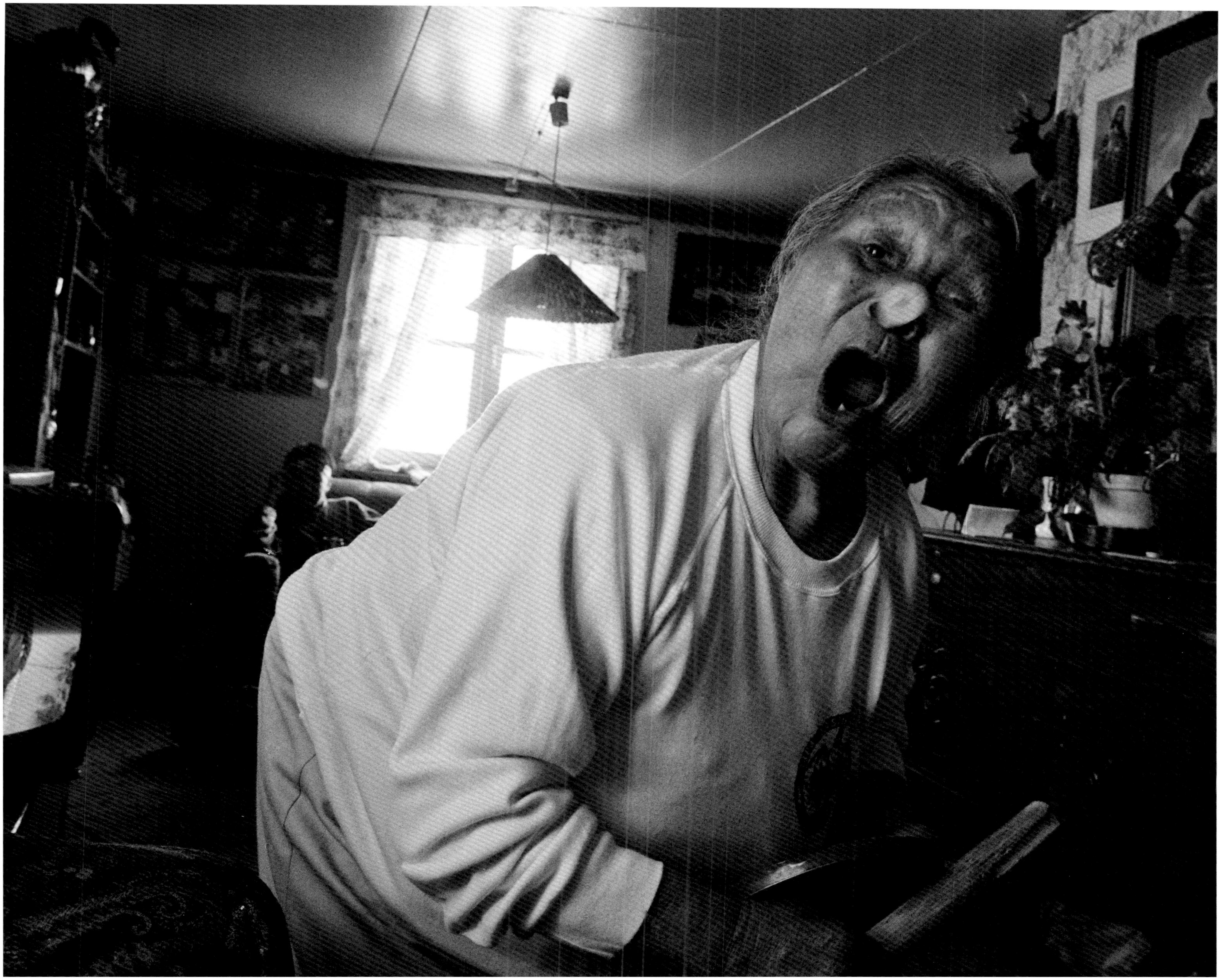

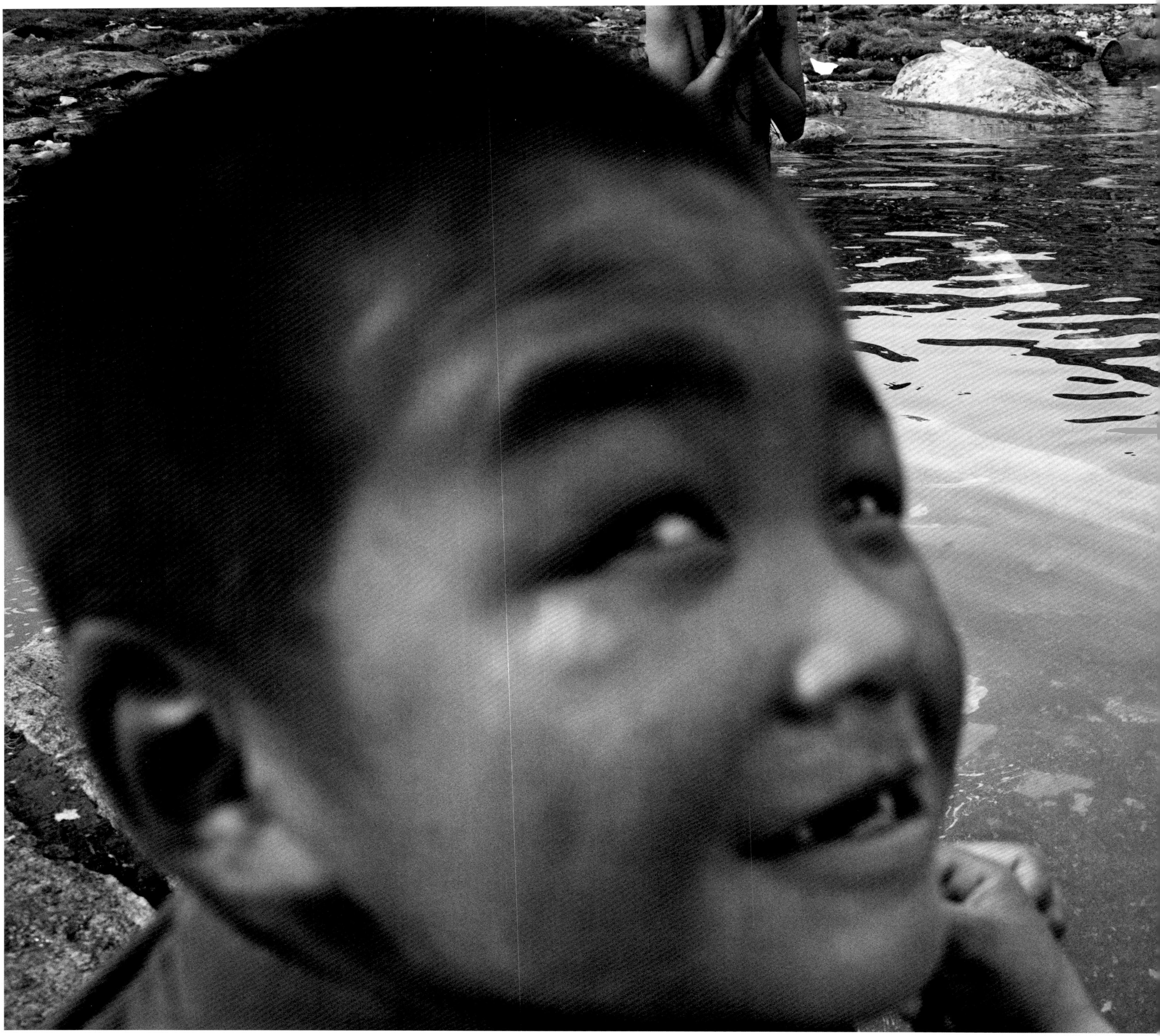

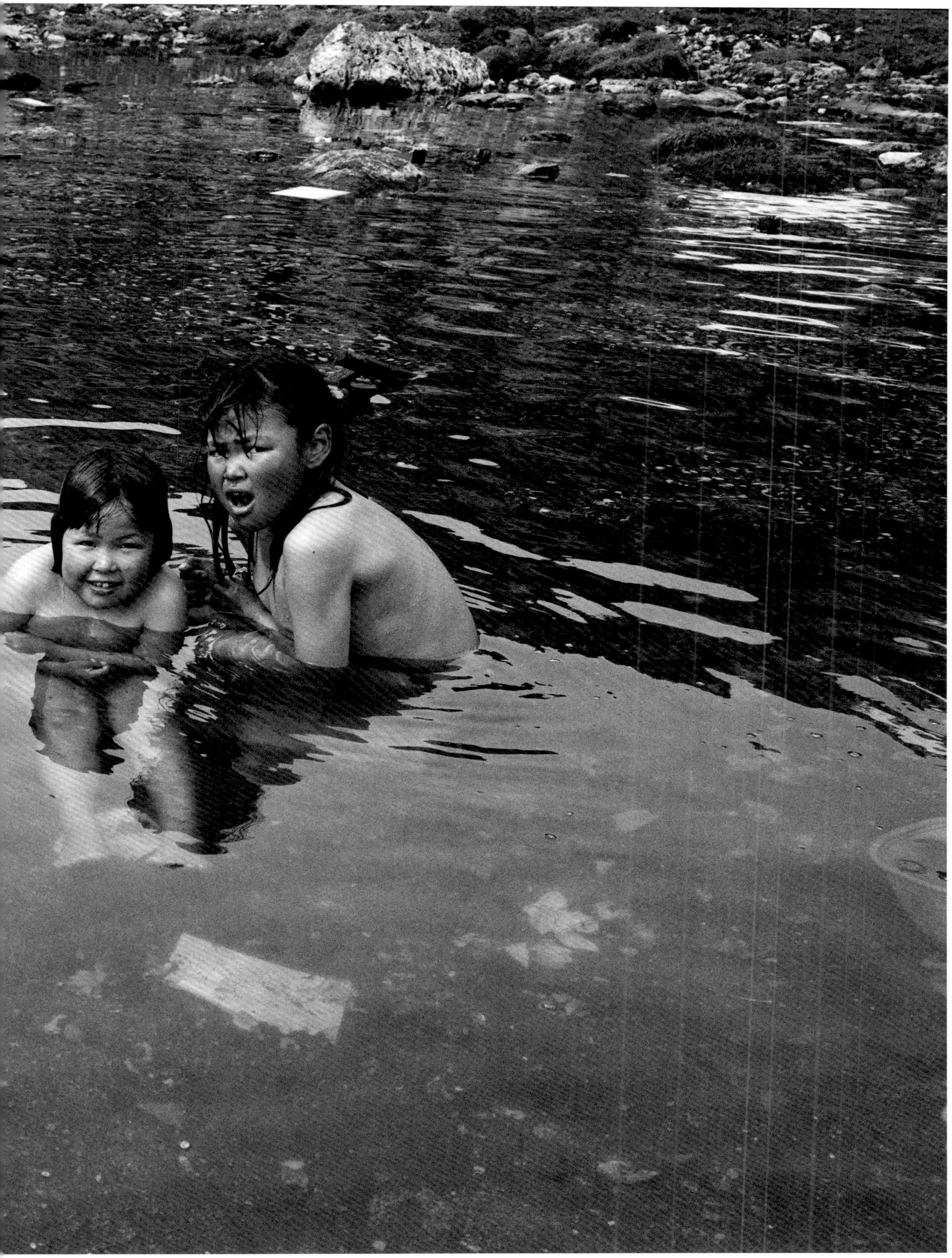

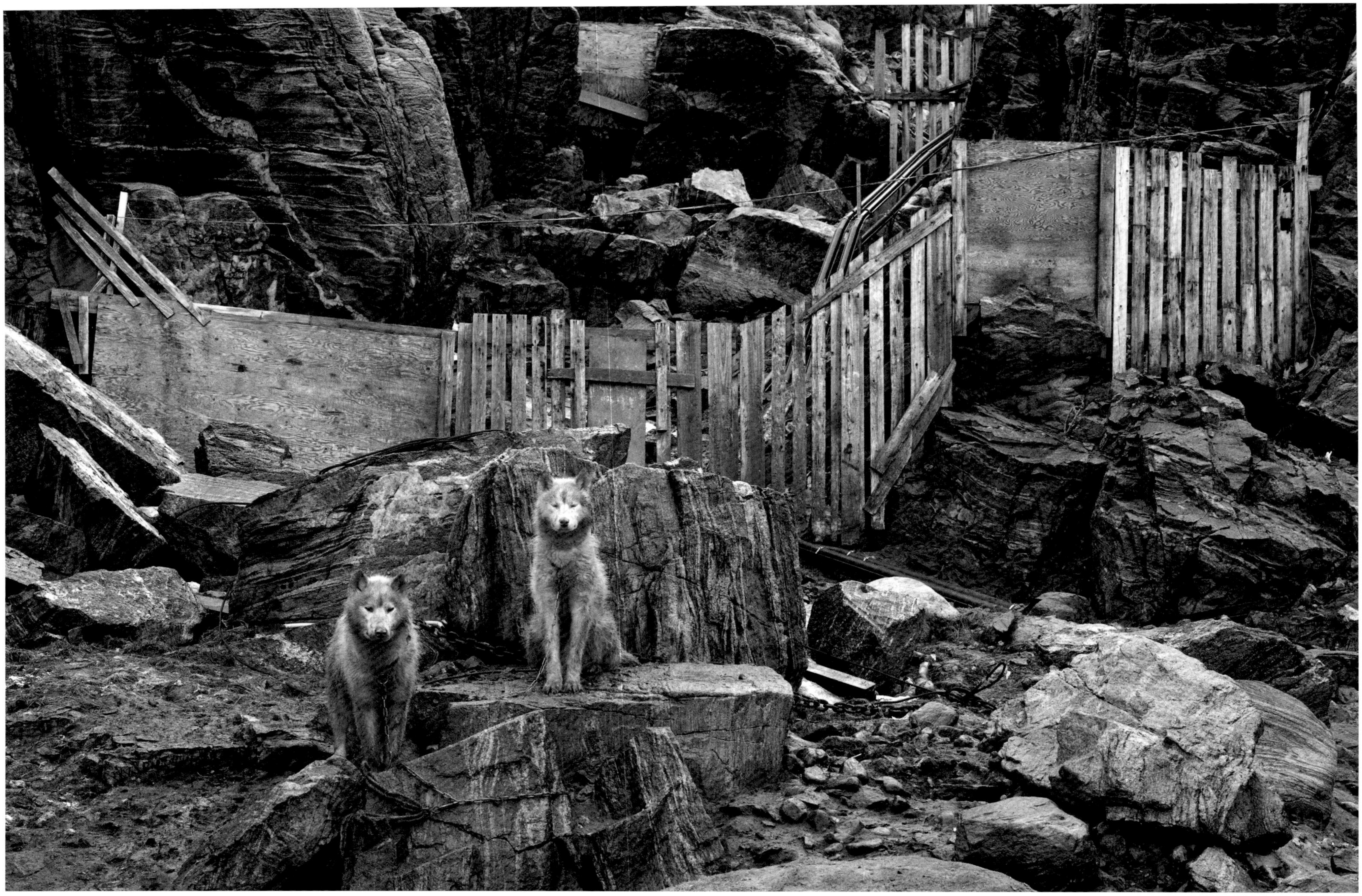

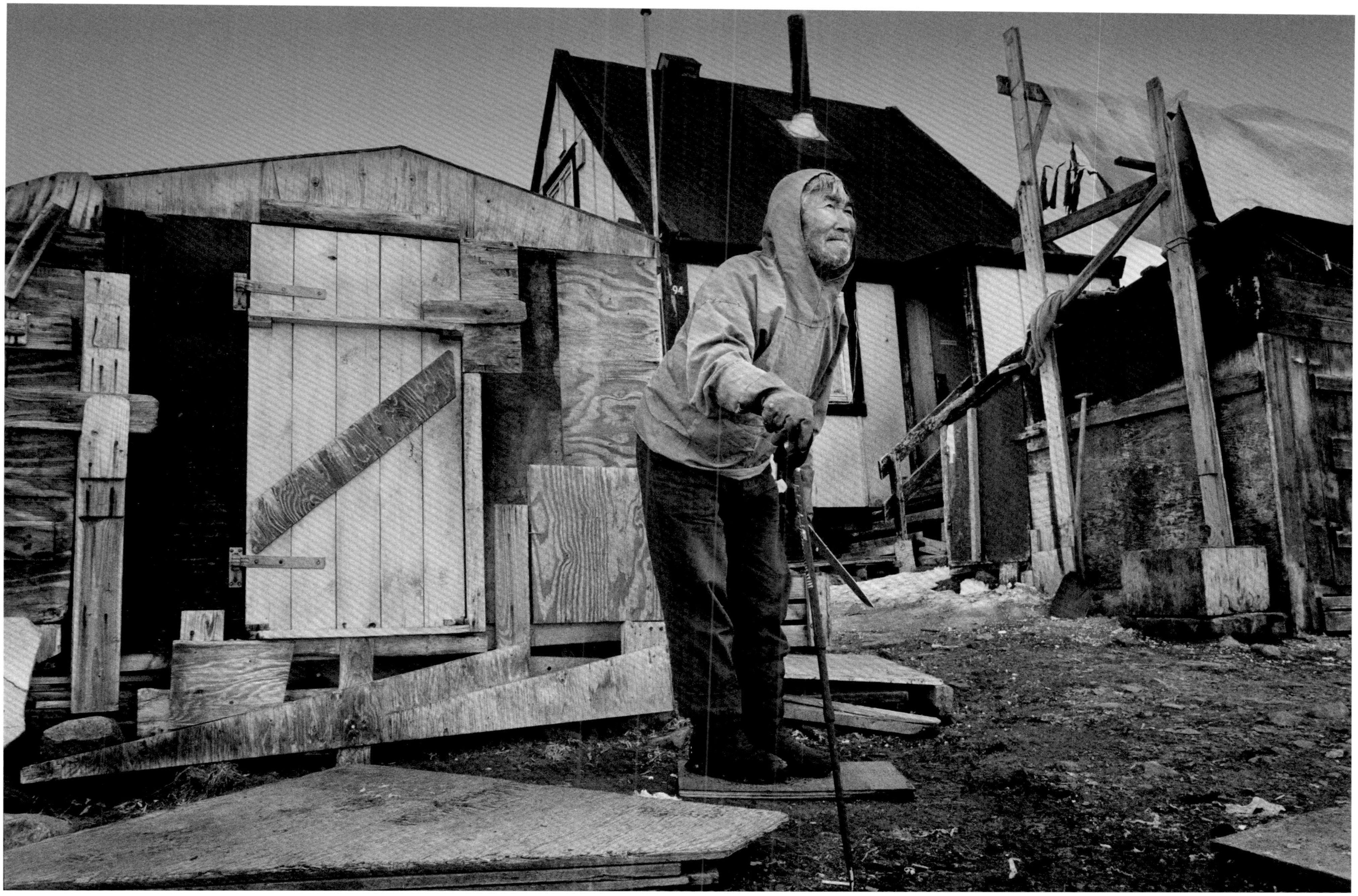

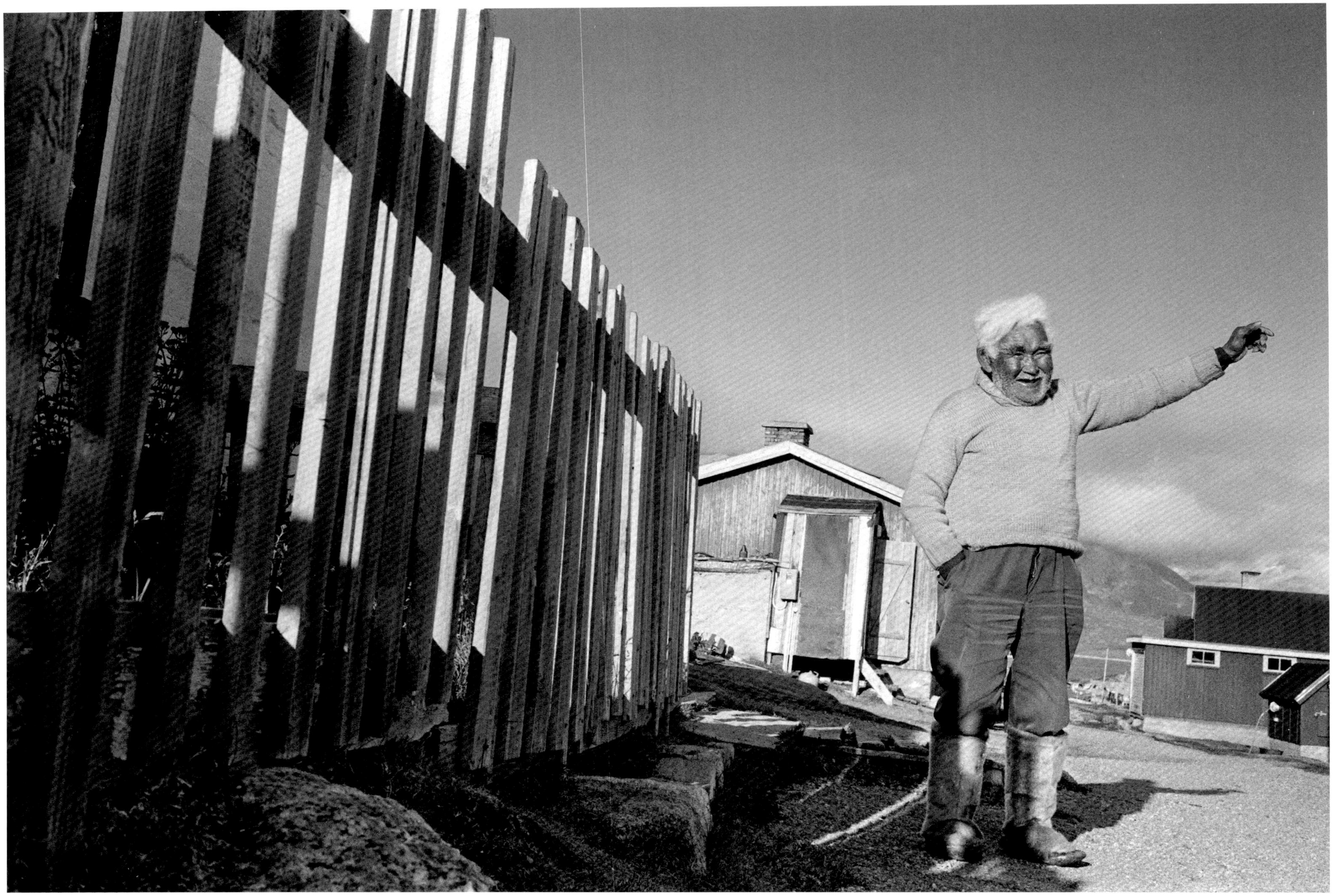

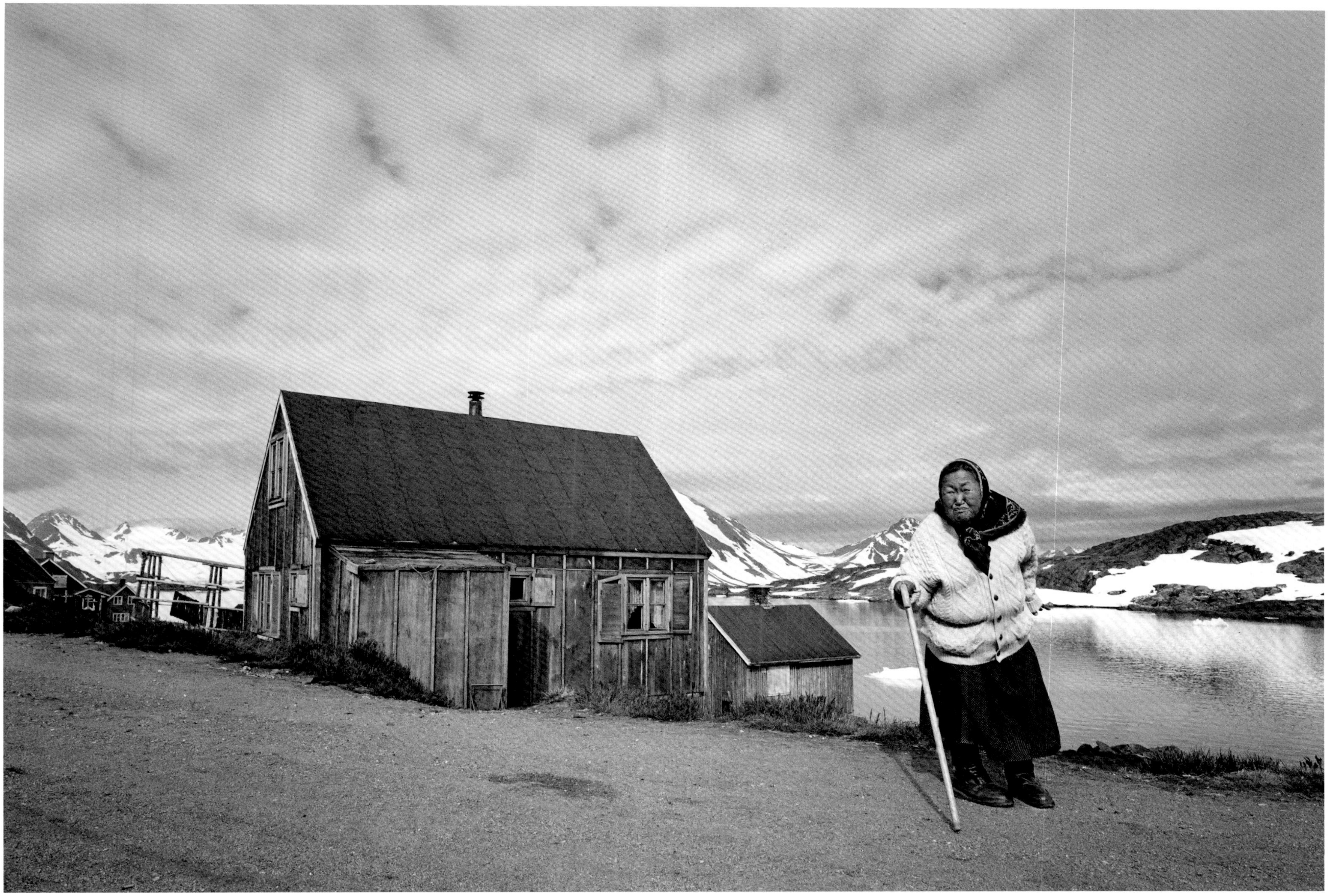

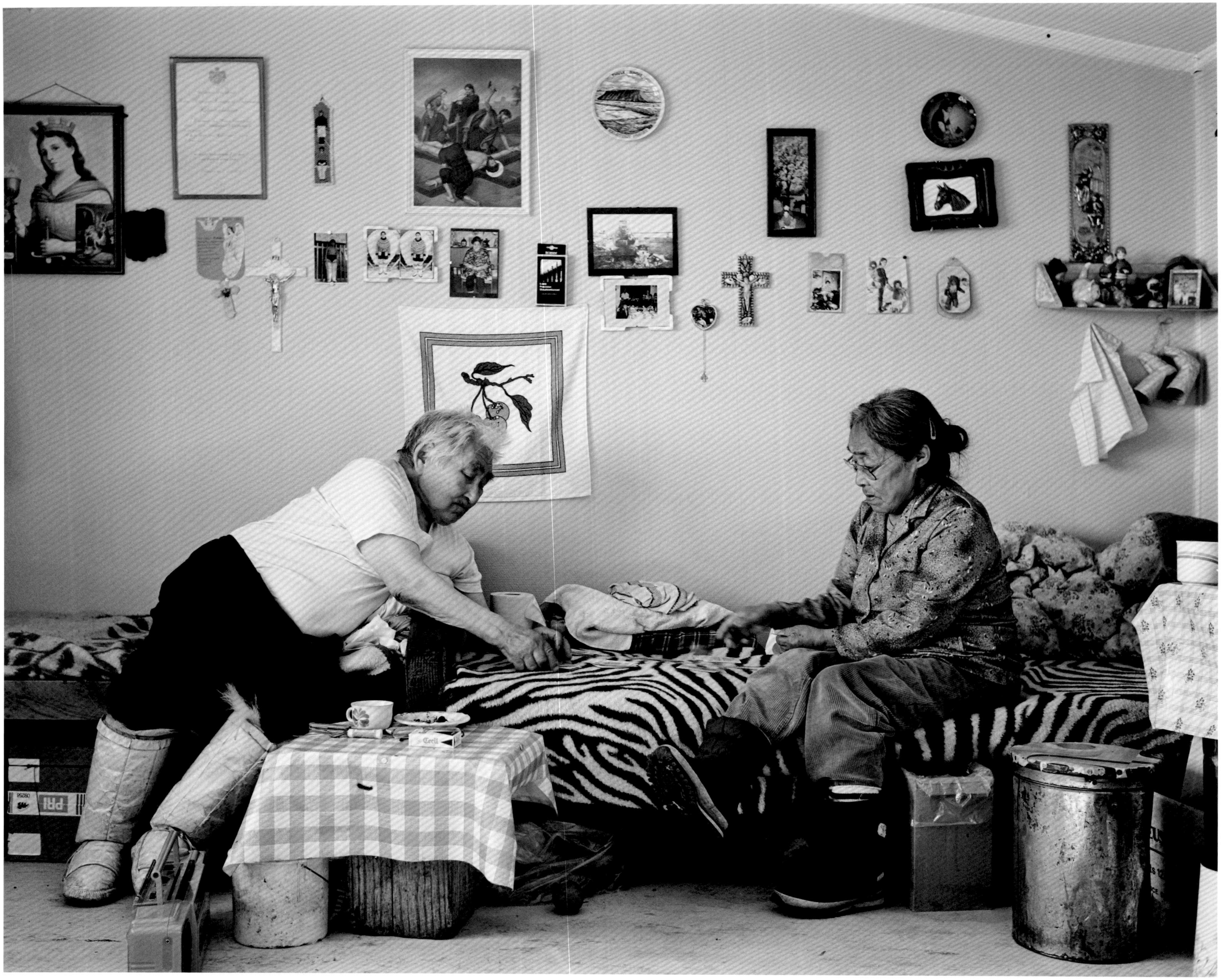

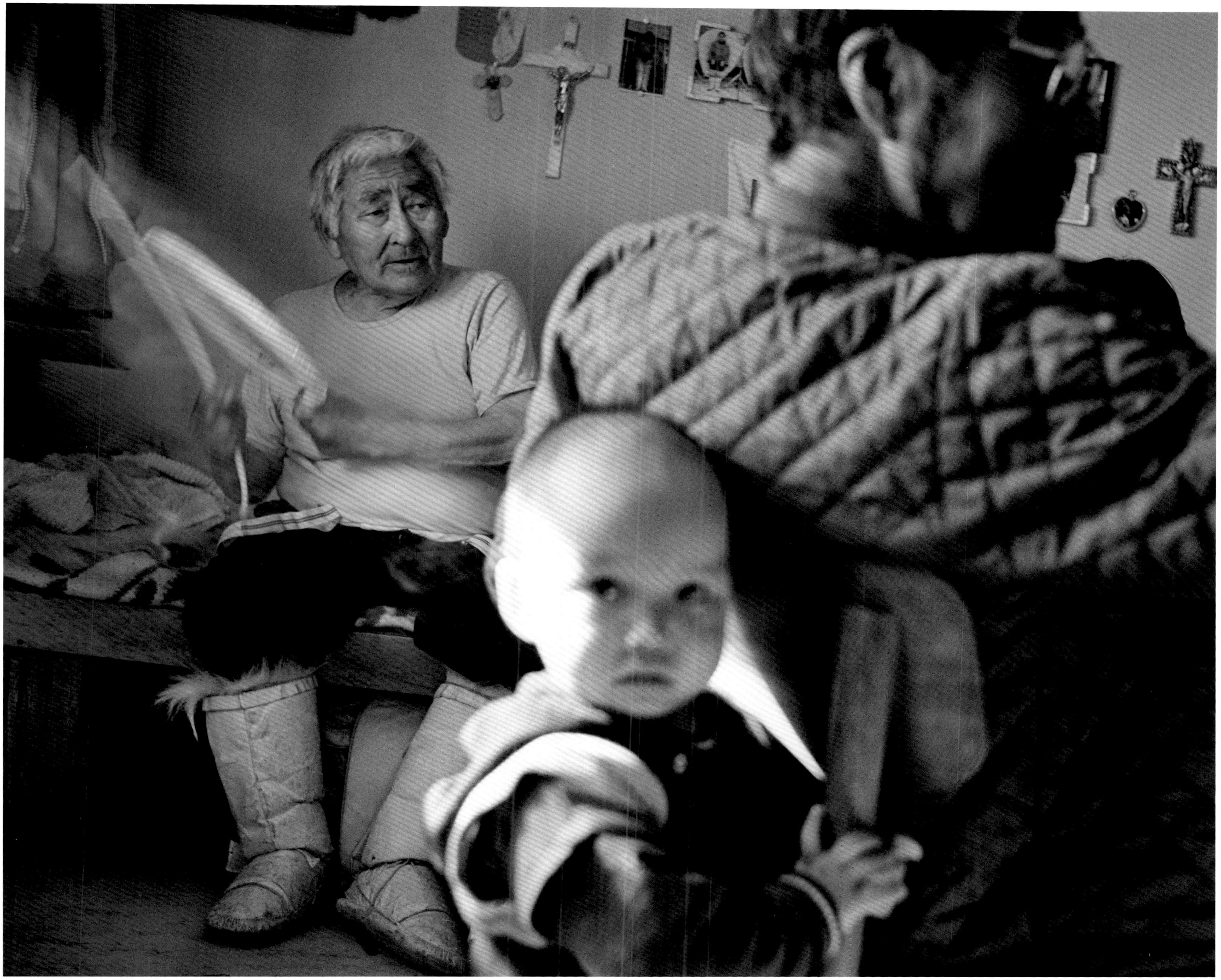

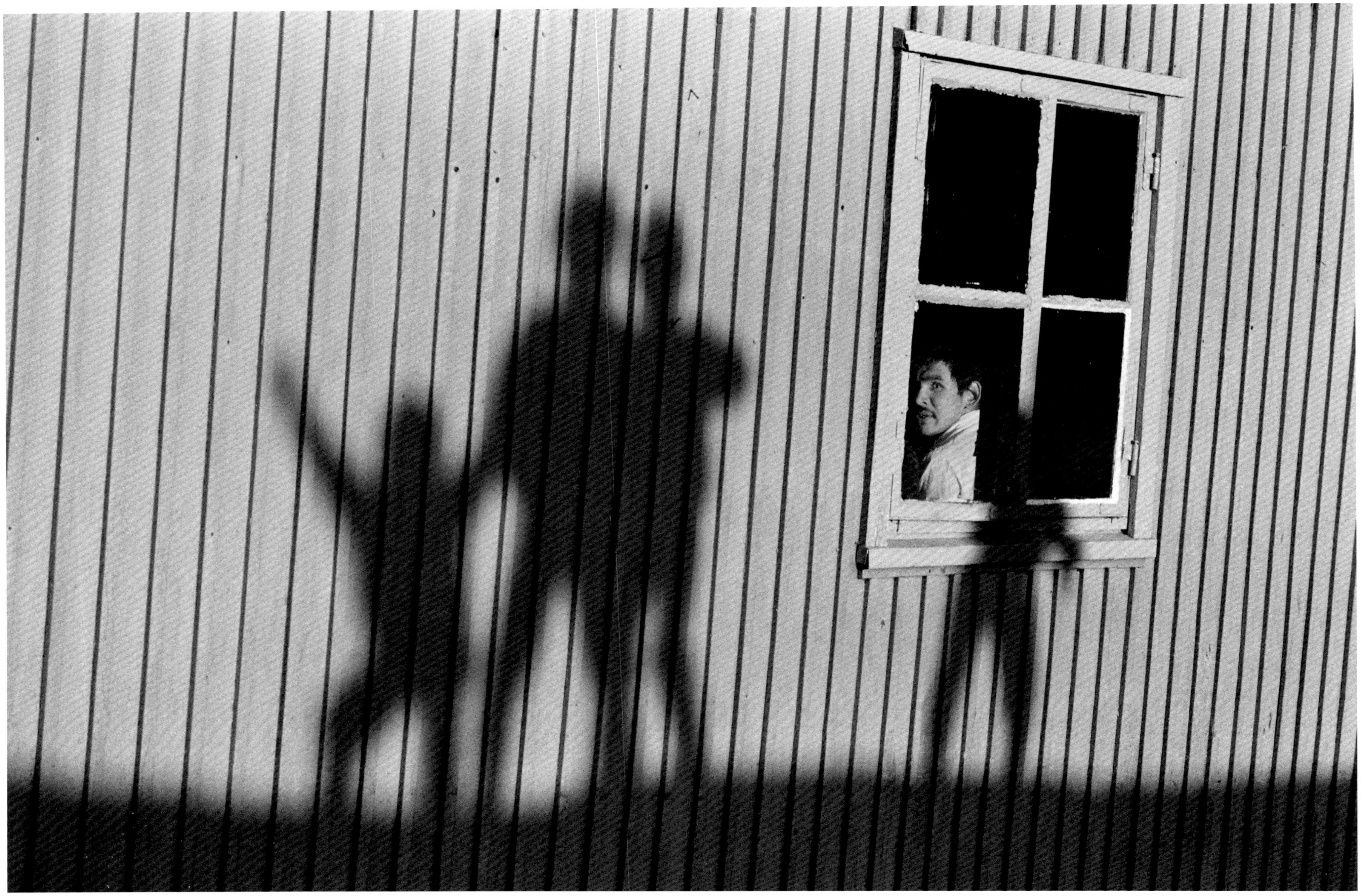

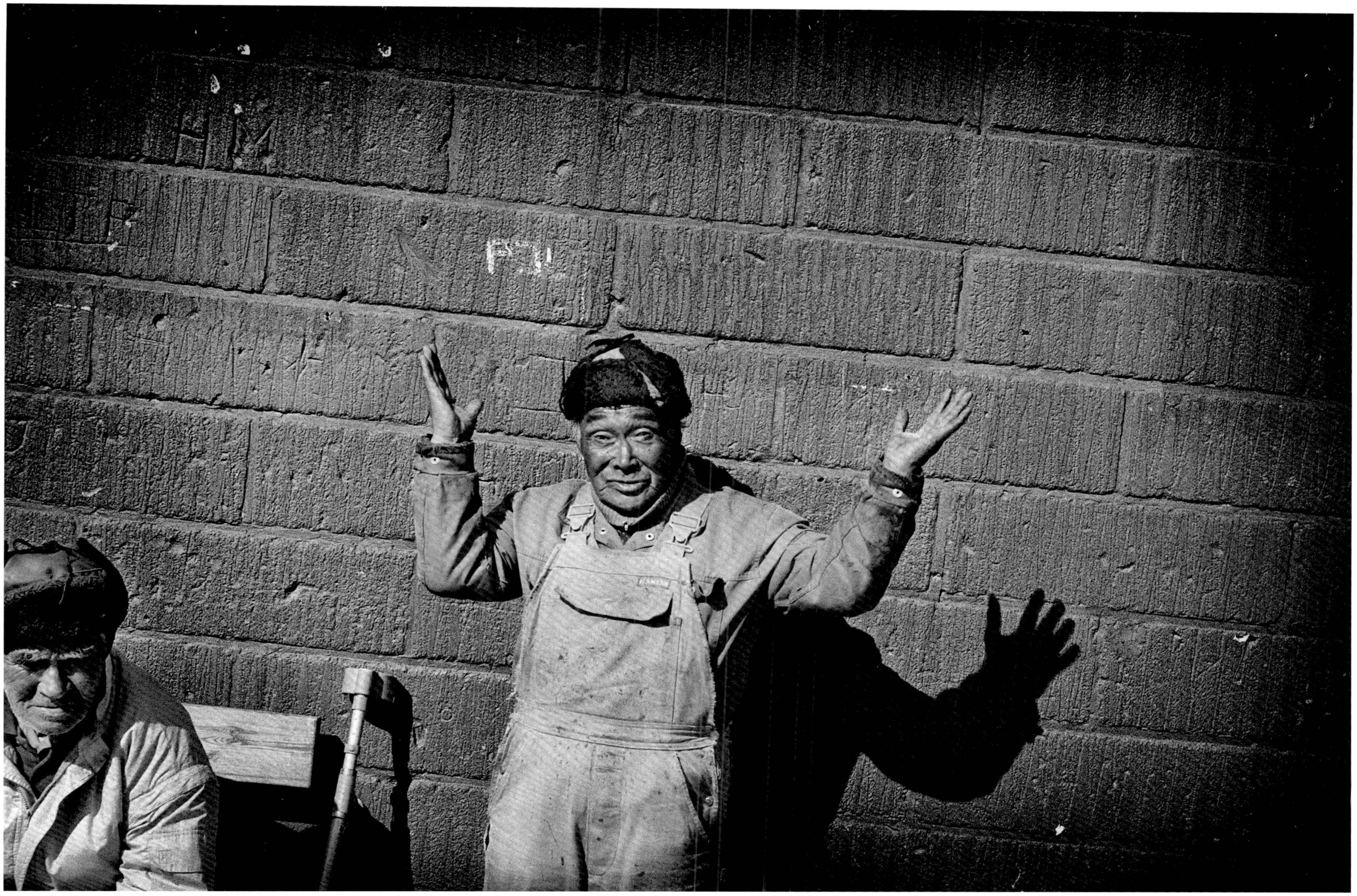

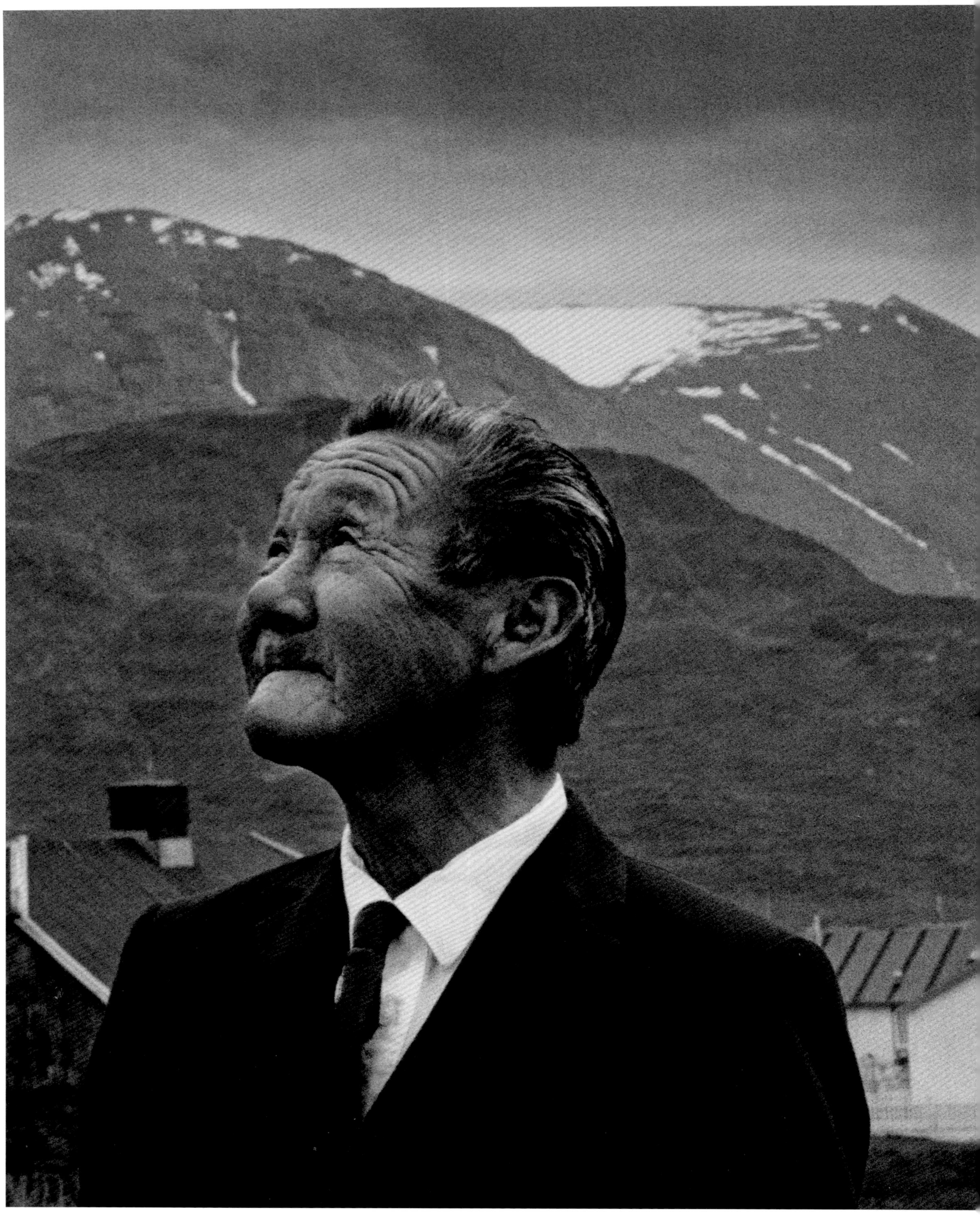

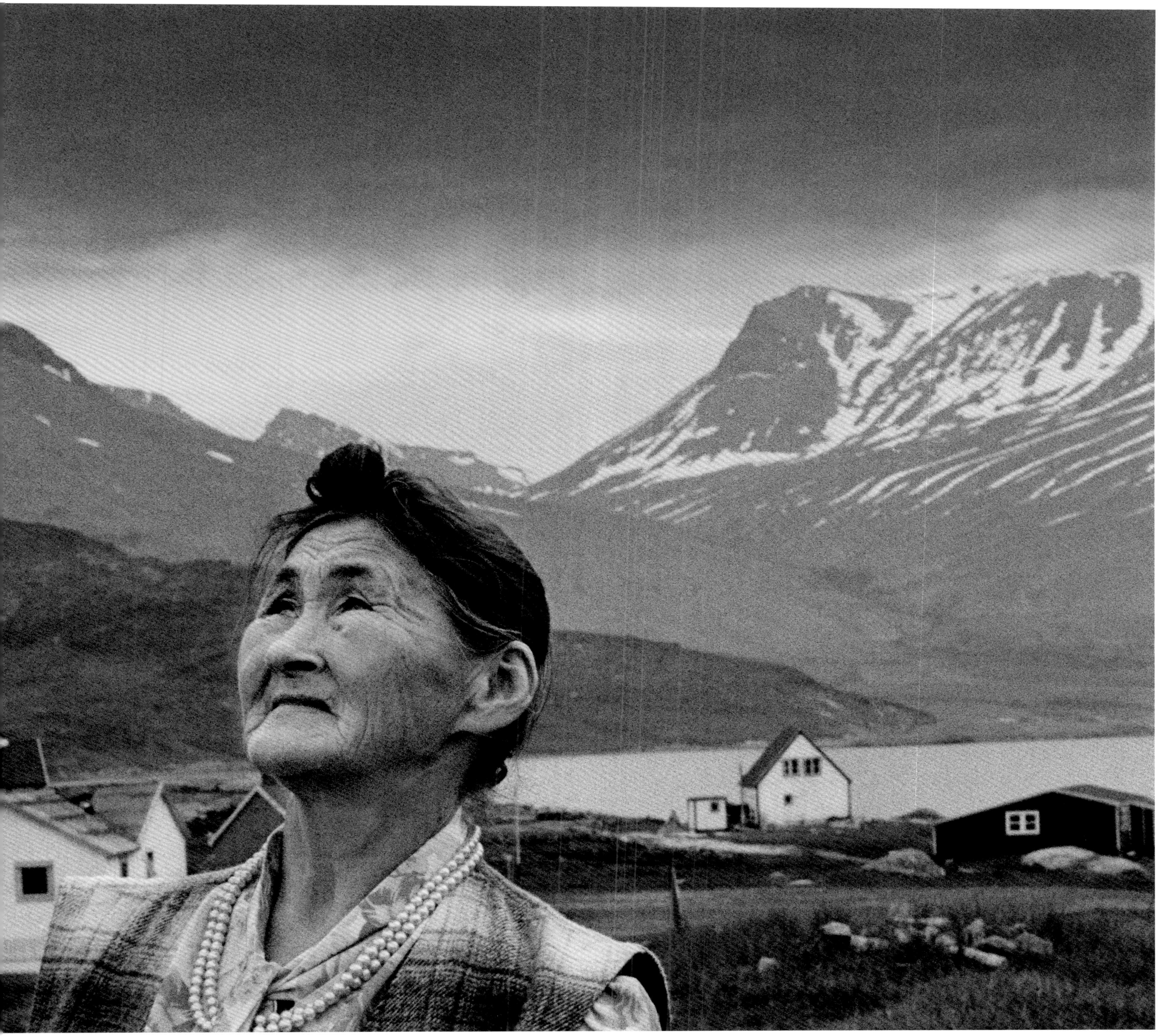

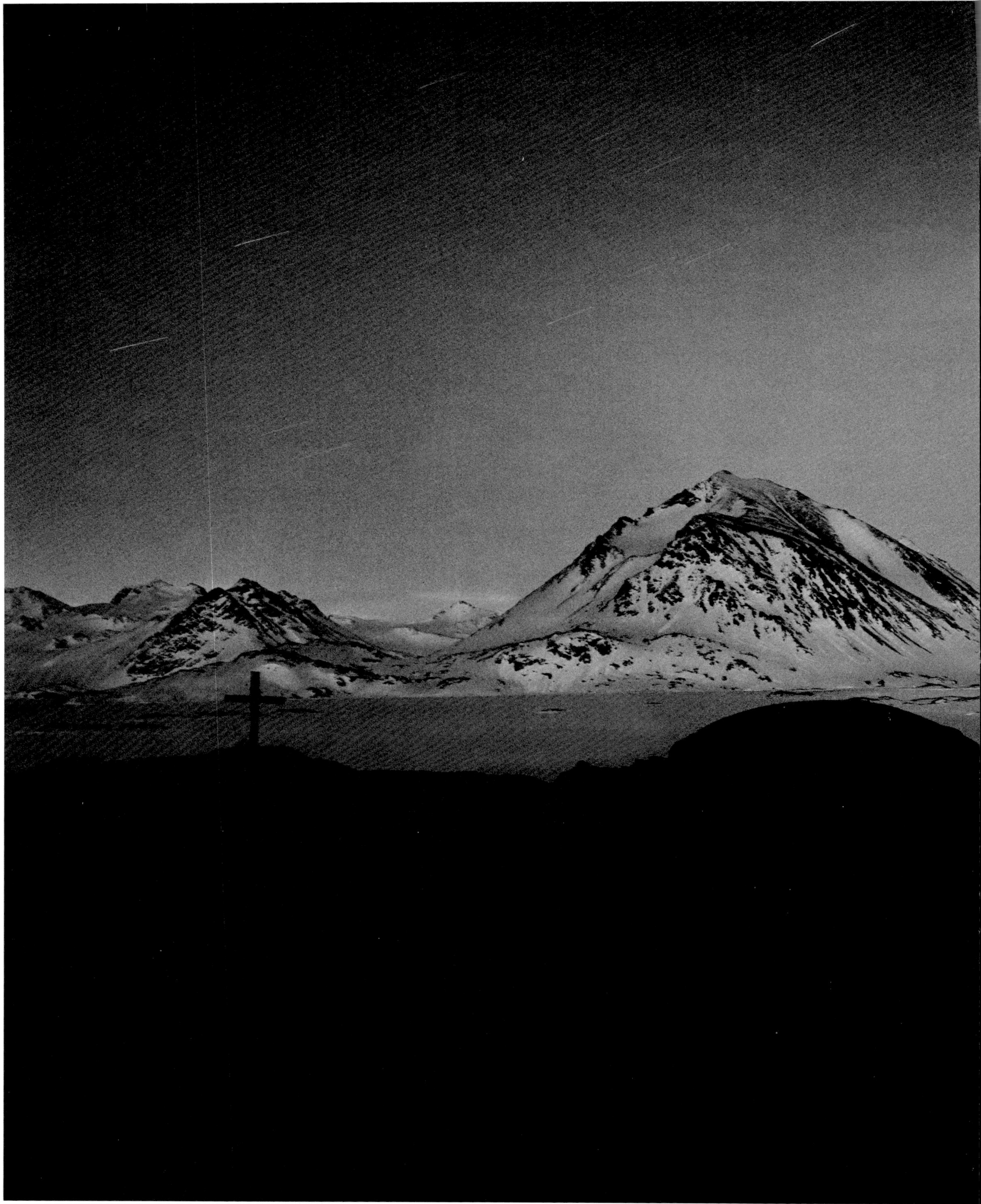

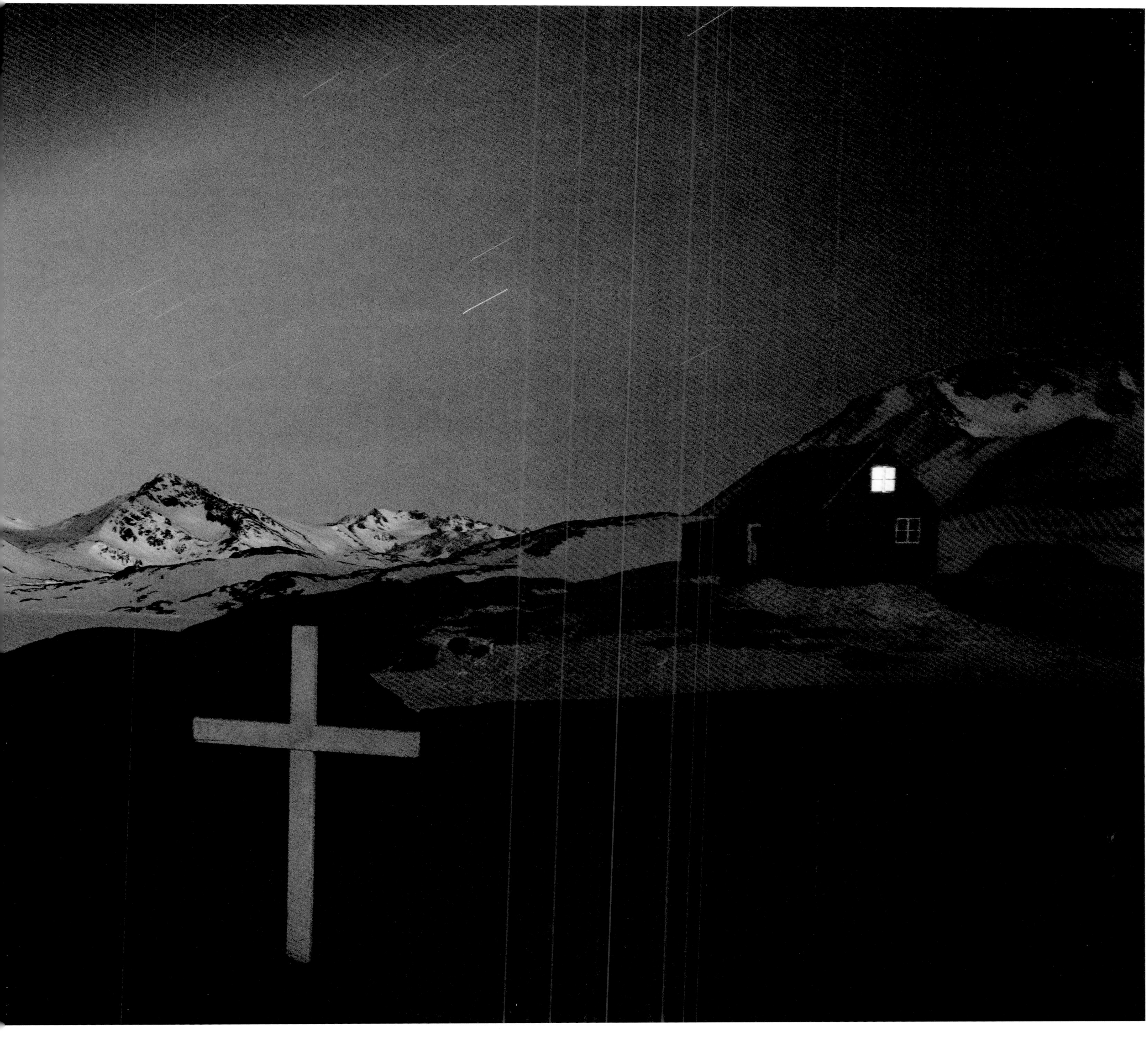

On Kangertittivaq

The largest fjord system and the longest fjord on Earth is found in East Greenland. The Inuit call it Kangertittivaq, but the name Scoresby Sound or Scoresby Fjord is better known. On the northern side of Kangertittivaq, near the mouth of this magnificent waterway, is the settlement Ittoqqortoormiit, a place that I have visited more often than all other settlements and towns in Greenland and where my friend, the hunter Hjelmer Hammeken, lives. His hunting grounds are on and around Kangertittivaq and in this vast space he searches for seals, muskox, whales and polar bears. No other person now living has hunted more polar bears as Hjelmer, somewhere around 300. Since 1990 I have tried over and over again to witness and photograph a successful polar bear hunt after hearing frightening stories about his quests out on the ice in search of this magnificent creature, so immensely important to the Inuit culture and mythology. I myself am not a hunter, can hardly kill a fly, but the Inuit hunters have taught me that there is a big difference between hunting and killing. Their respect for the animals shows an entirely different worldview than most people connect to hunting. Hunting is the foundation of their traditional culture and a man like Hjelmer embodies the wisdom of his culture and the deep understanding of how nature gives and how nature takes what it gives again.

In late winter 2013 I once again ventured out to the ice on Kangertittivaq with Hjelmer and his companions, among them his brother Ababa. Hjelmer had told me two things. First, that this winter polar bears were in abundance for the first time in many years. Secondly, that the ice on Kangertittivaq had behaved strangely in the preceding months. Shortly before I arrived he had narrowly saved his live when a storm on the East Greenland Sea carried waves into the mouth of the fjord and the unusually thin ice started not only to break up, but to move with the waves, throwing him and his dog sled yoke back and forth. He and his hunting companion were in the middle of Kangertittivaq. They had a tiny boat, used for rowing around the ice edge to pick up seals or small whales, attached to their sled. The chances surviving in a storm out on the ocean, around ice floes crushing into each other in the Arctic cold, were alarmingly slim. After fighting their way back for hours, crawling on the ice for the most part, they arrived home in Ittoqqortoormiit. Hjelmer knows that each time he ventures out on the ice, he might not make it back, but that is the way nature works, in his eyes, something he takes from, so sometimes he must give back what he has taken.

Hjelmer was right. We were barely out on the ice when we spotted the footsteps of a polar bear. The hunters found him and he lost his life. Then we thought for a while that we would also lose ours. The storm blew up, it started to snow and we heard the cracks in the ice, those eerie sounds people hear in their nightmares when the ground beneath your feet gives away and you fall into a dark void. An experienced hunter never panics in these circumstances, he remains calm, controlled and firm. The way back was difficult, but we made it. This time we didn't need to give back our living breaths.

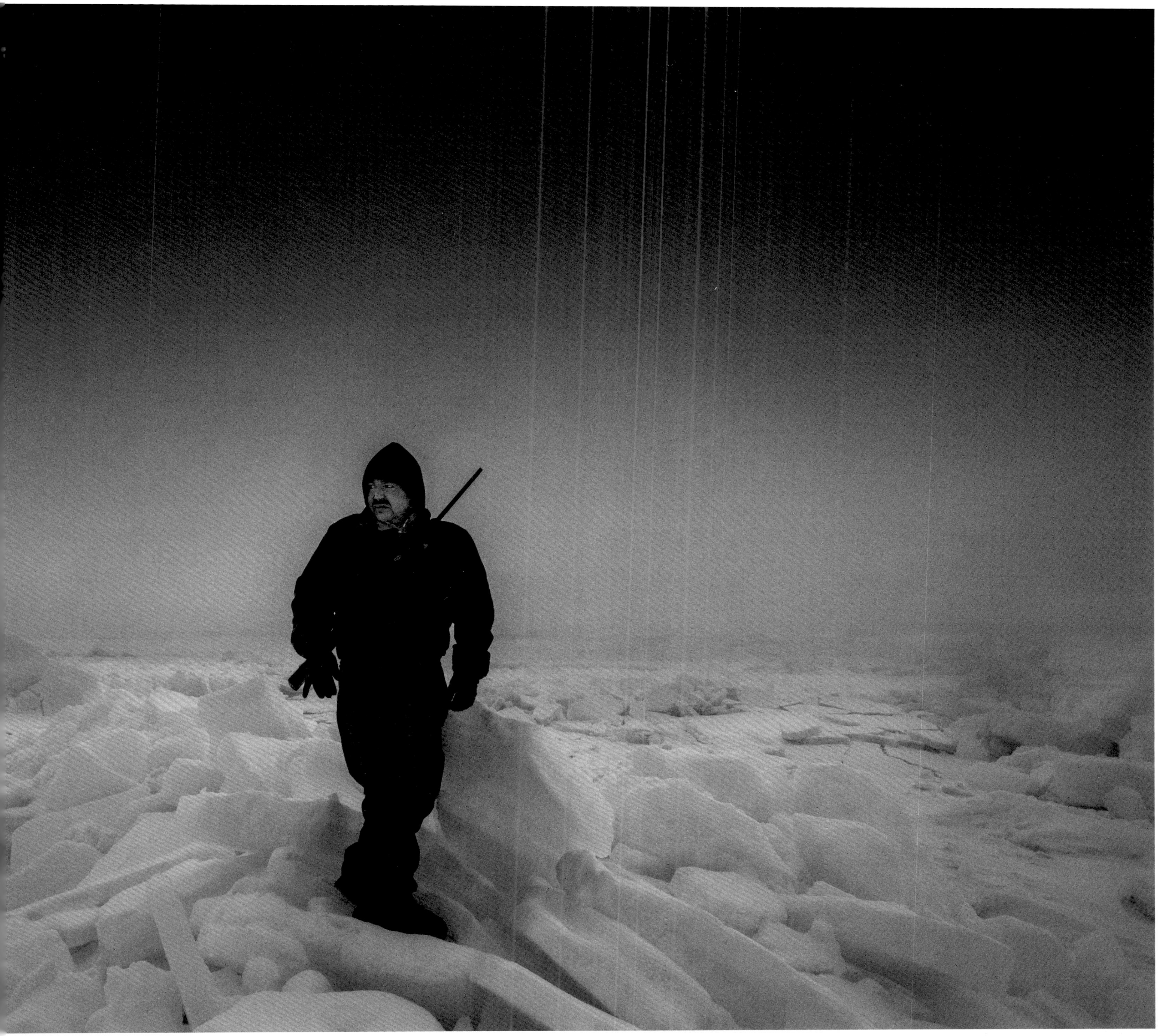

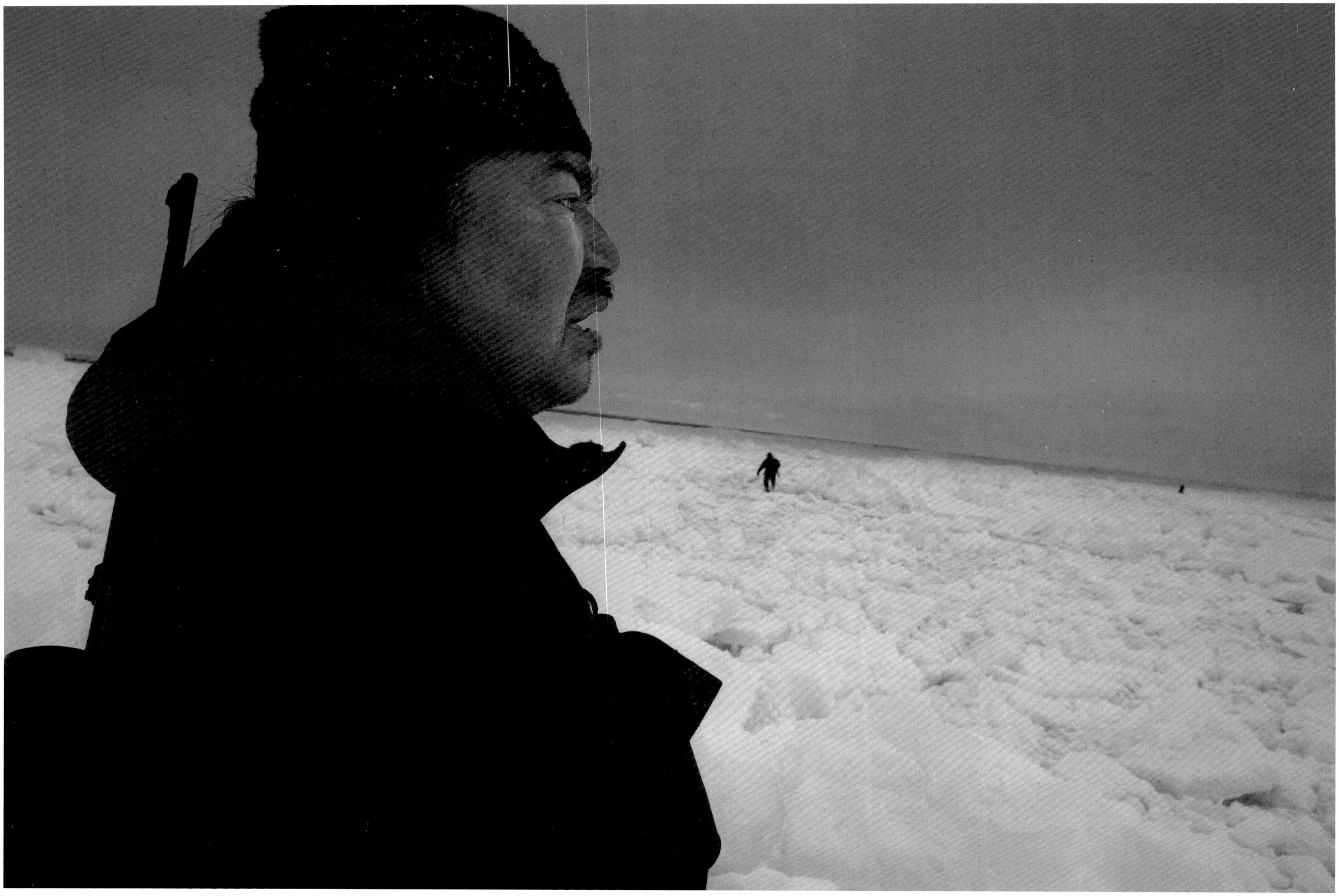

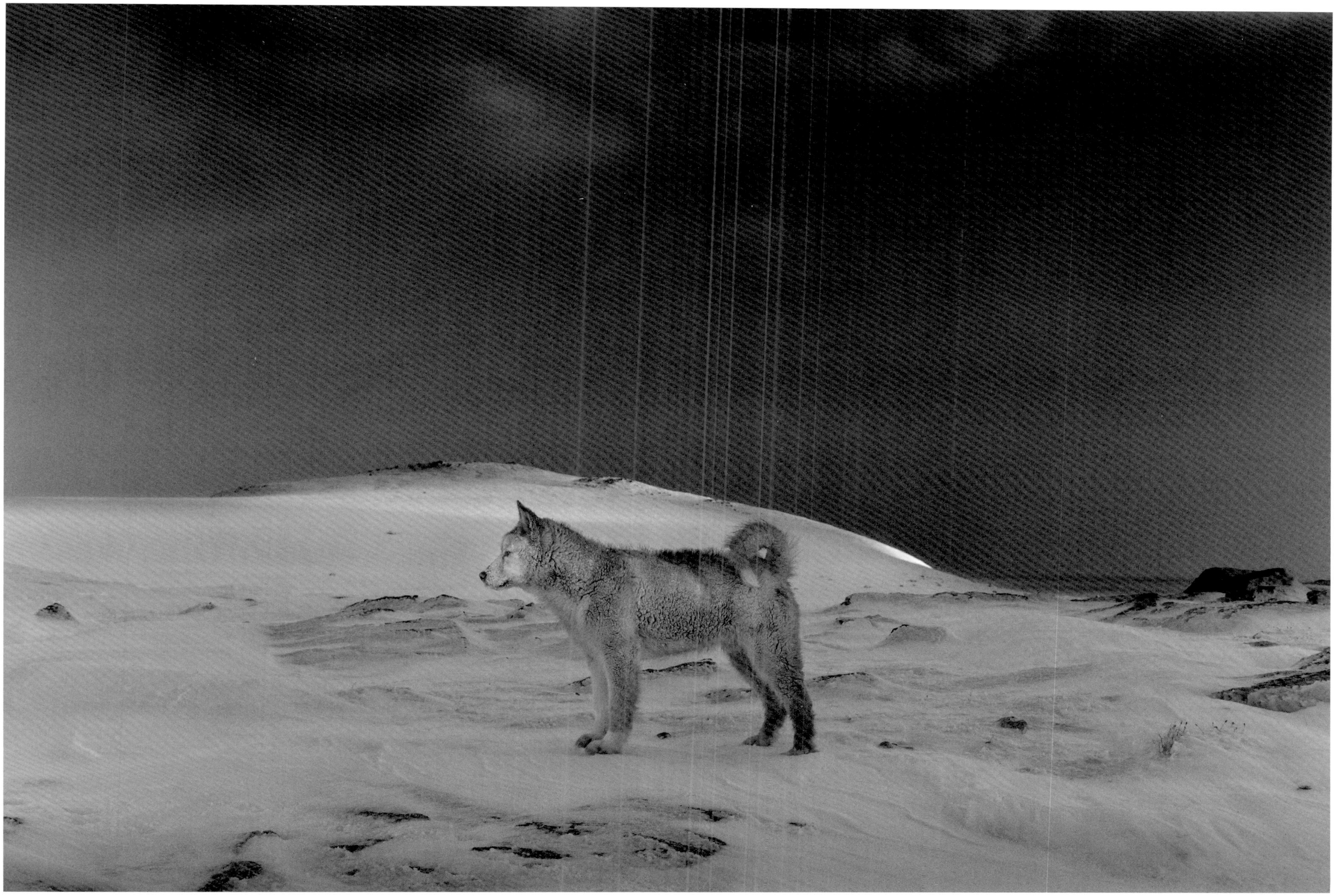

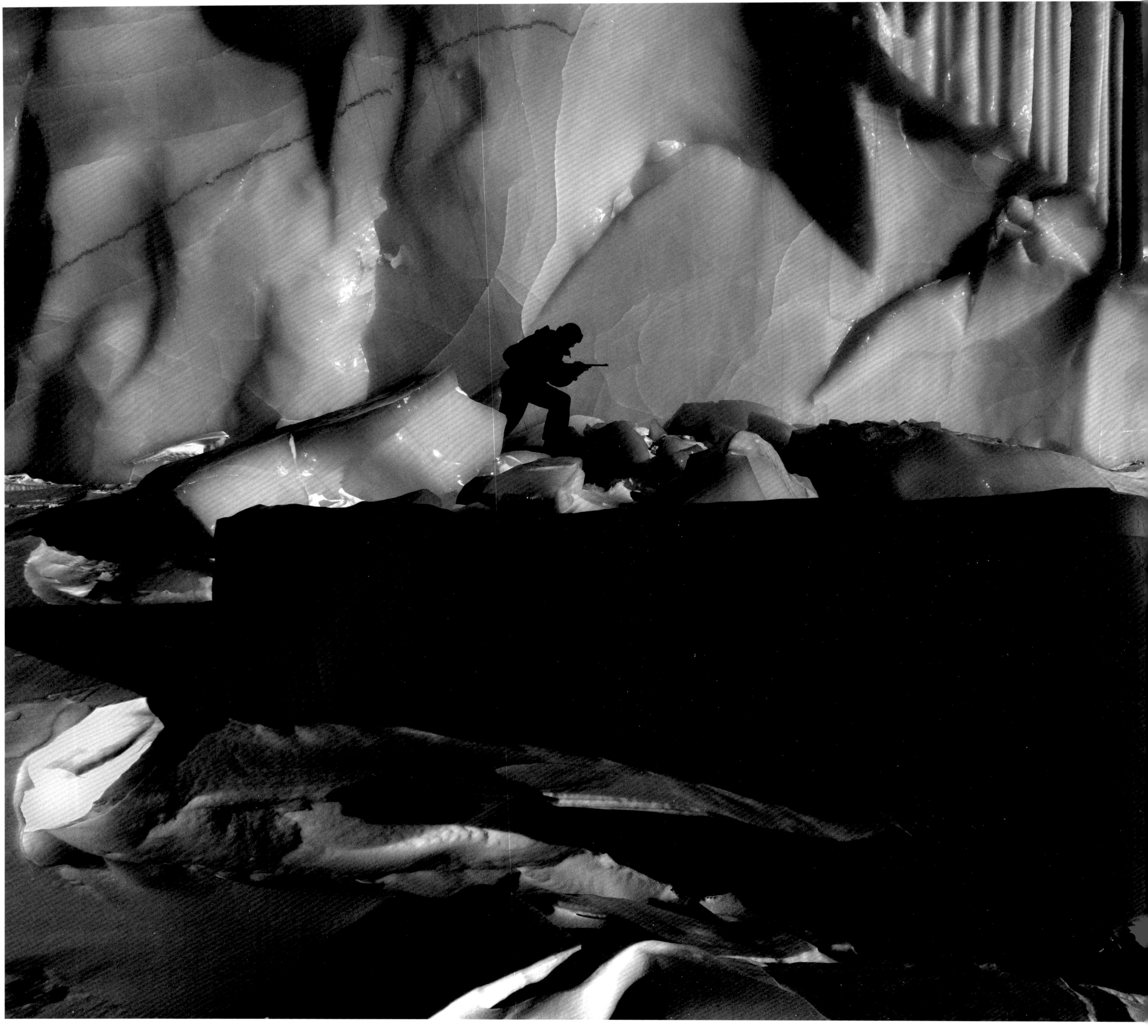

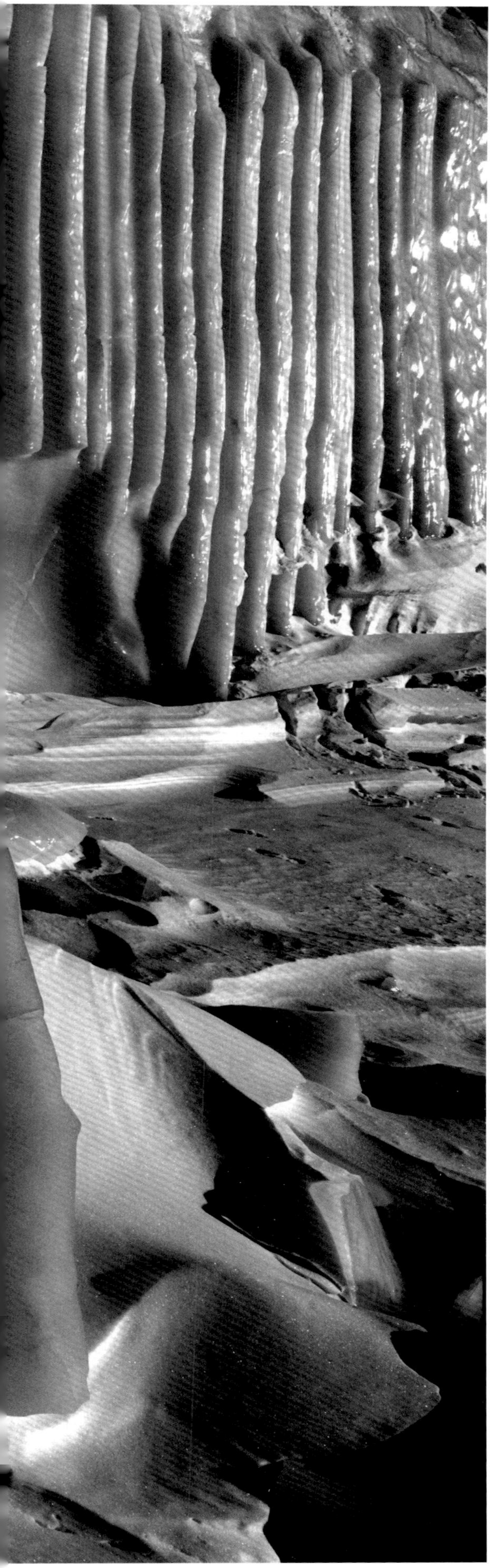

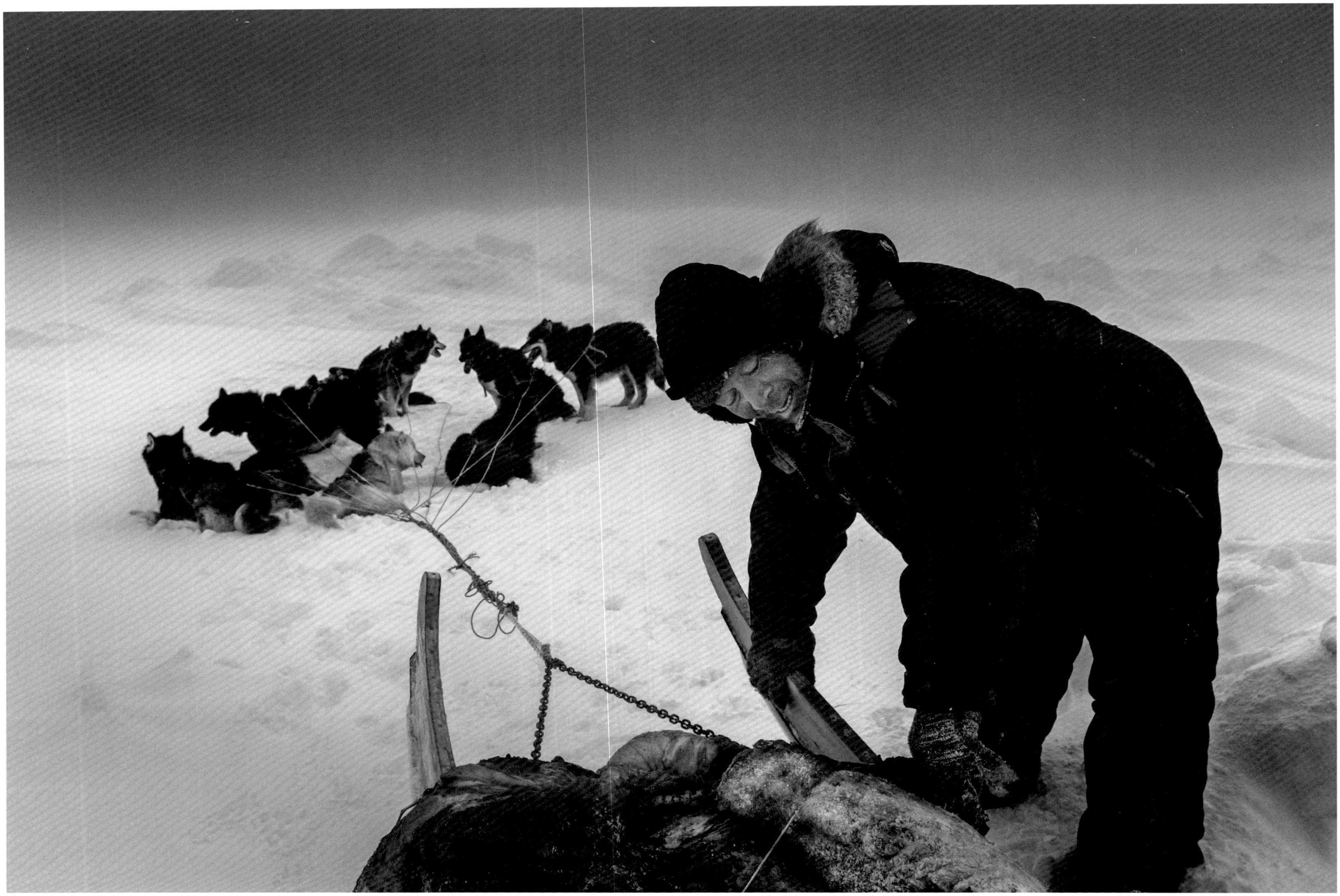

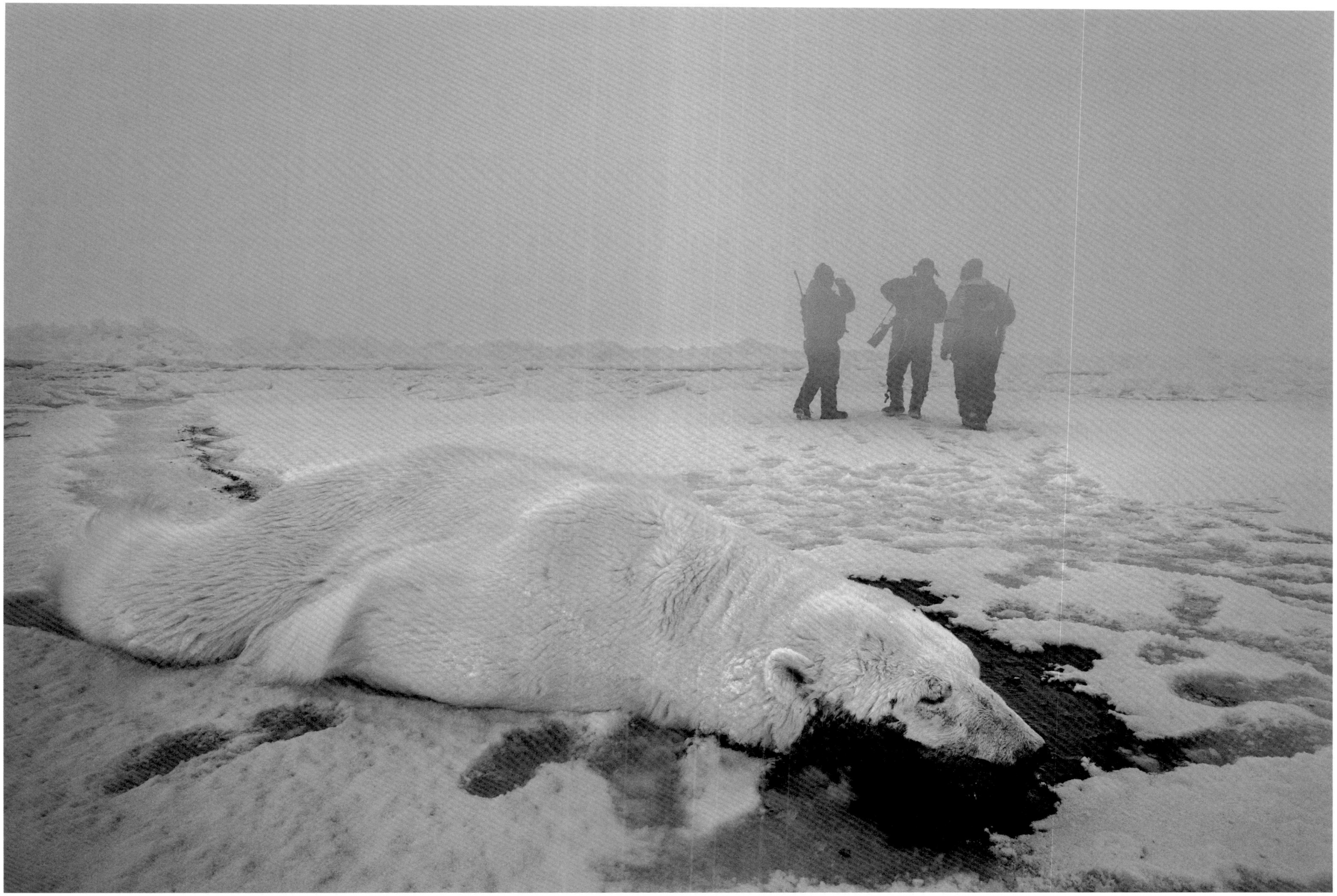

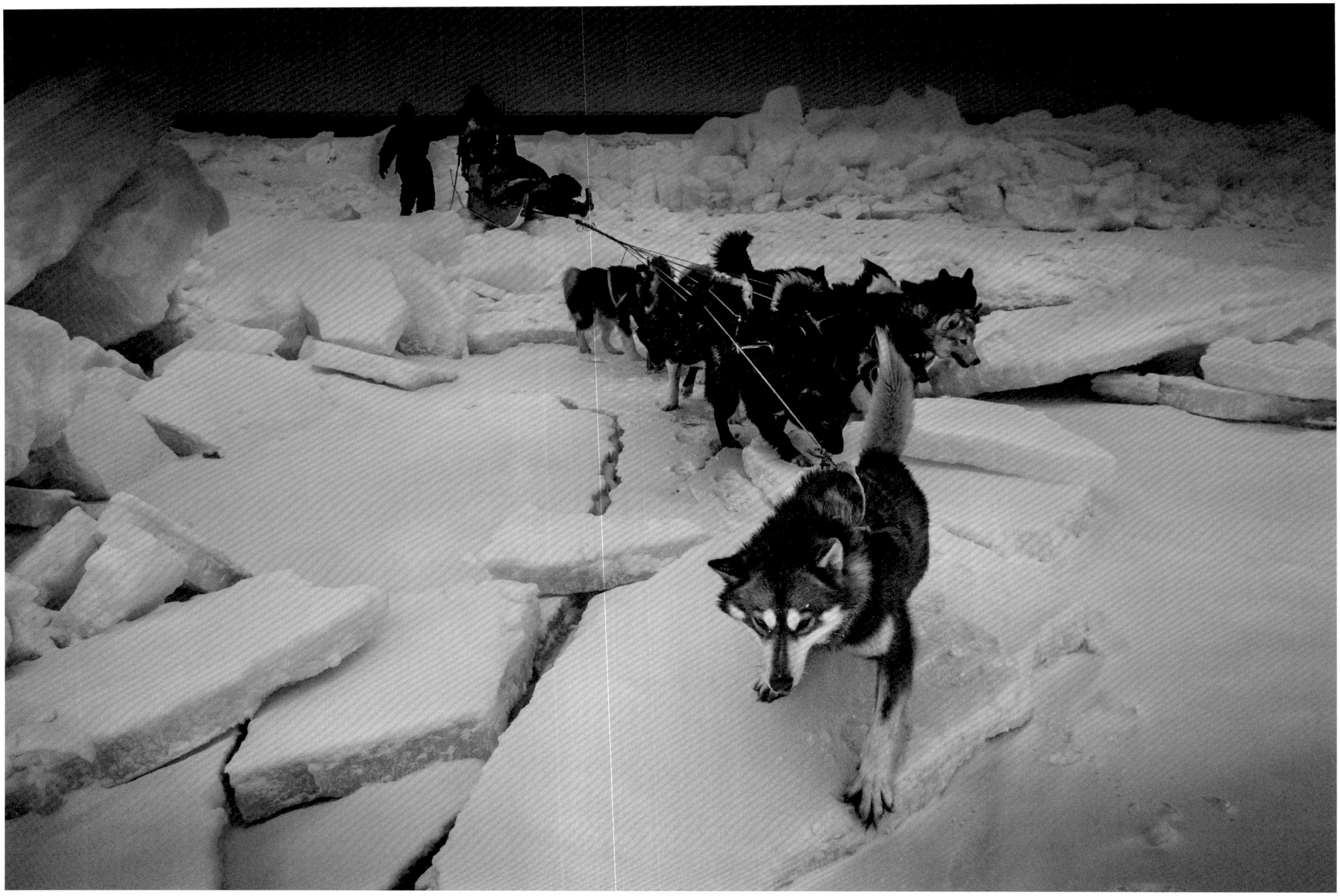

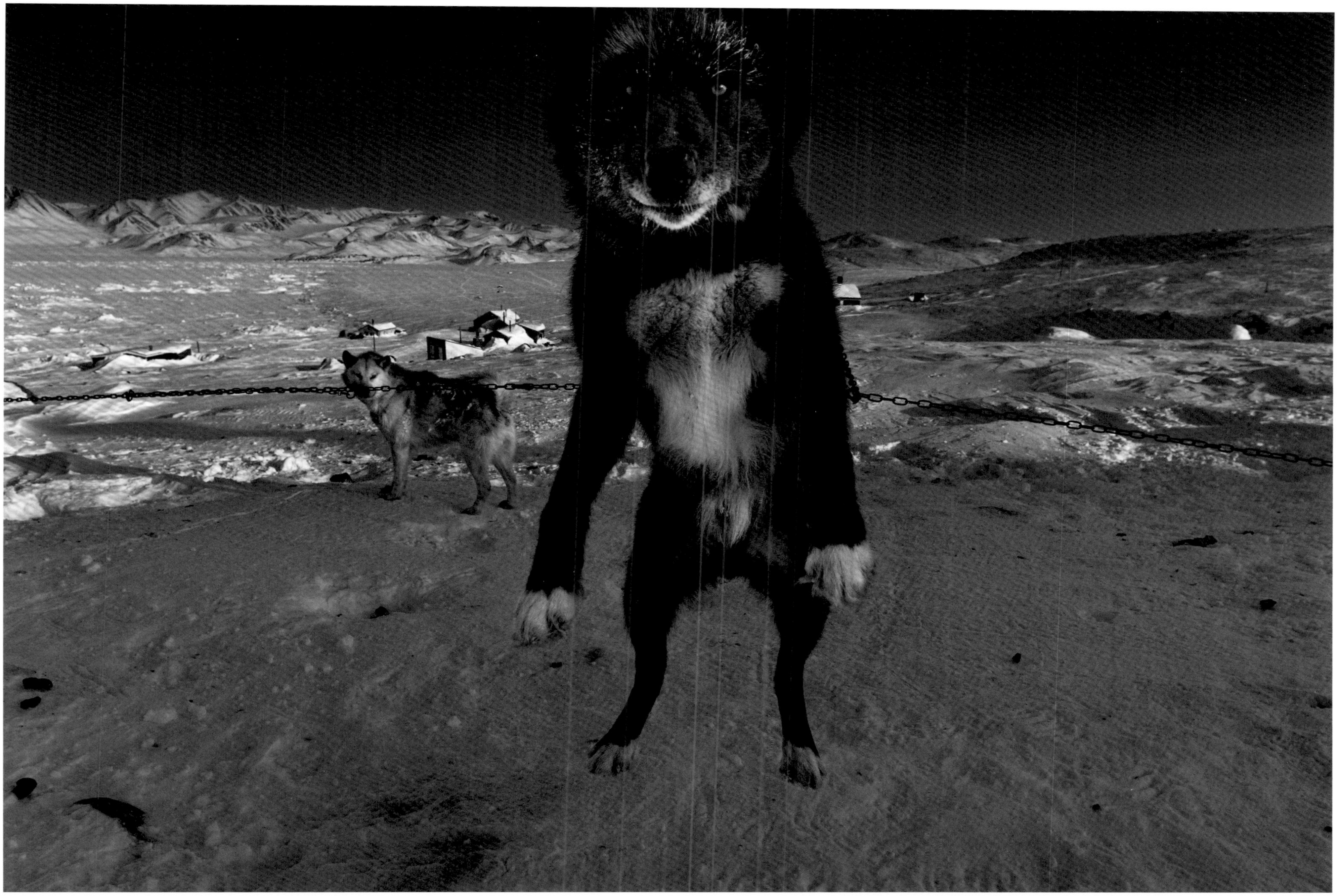

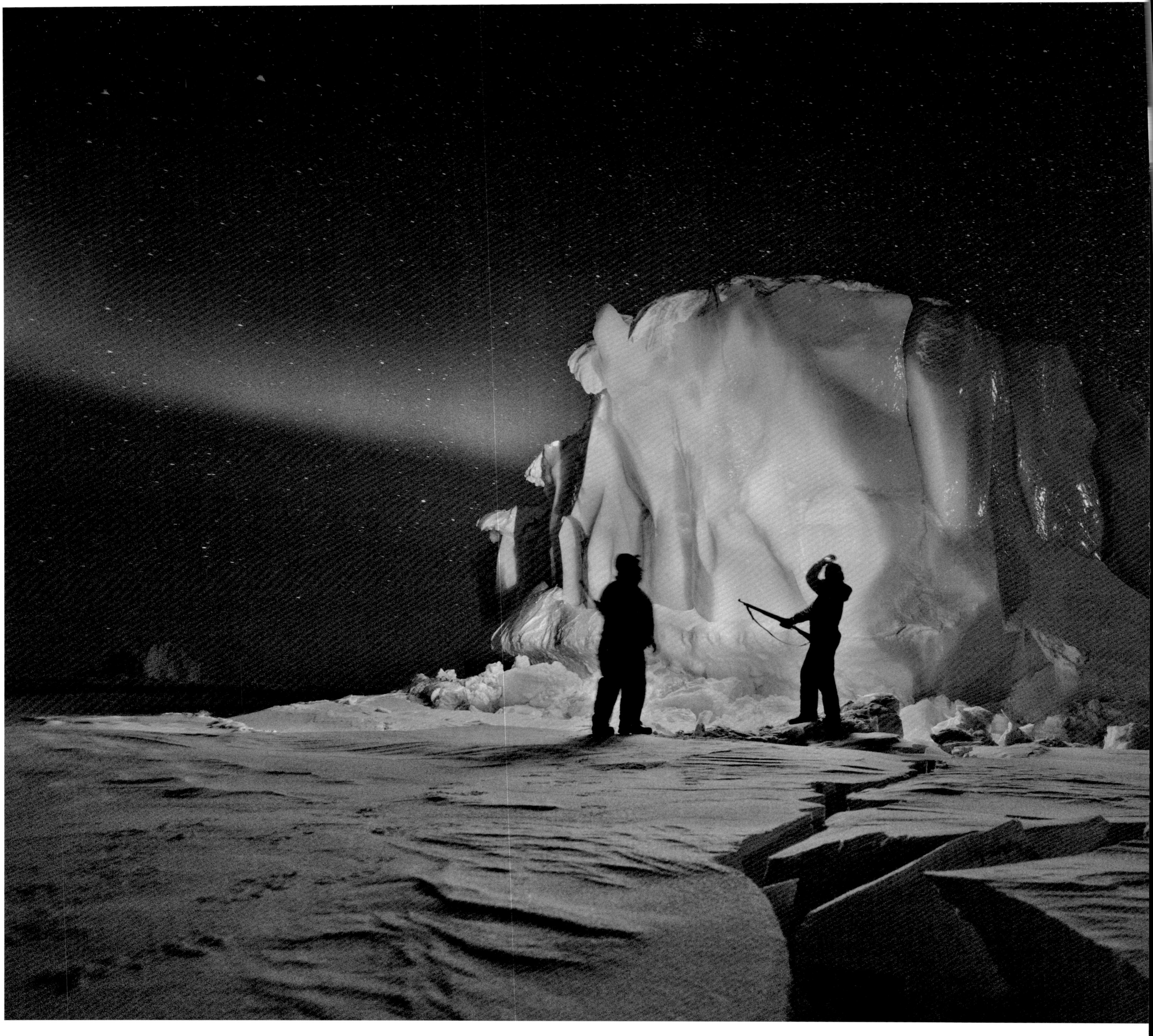

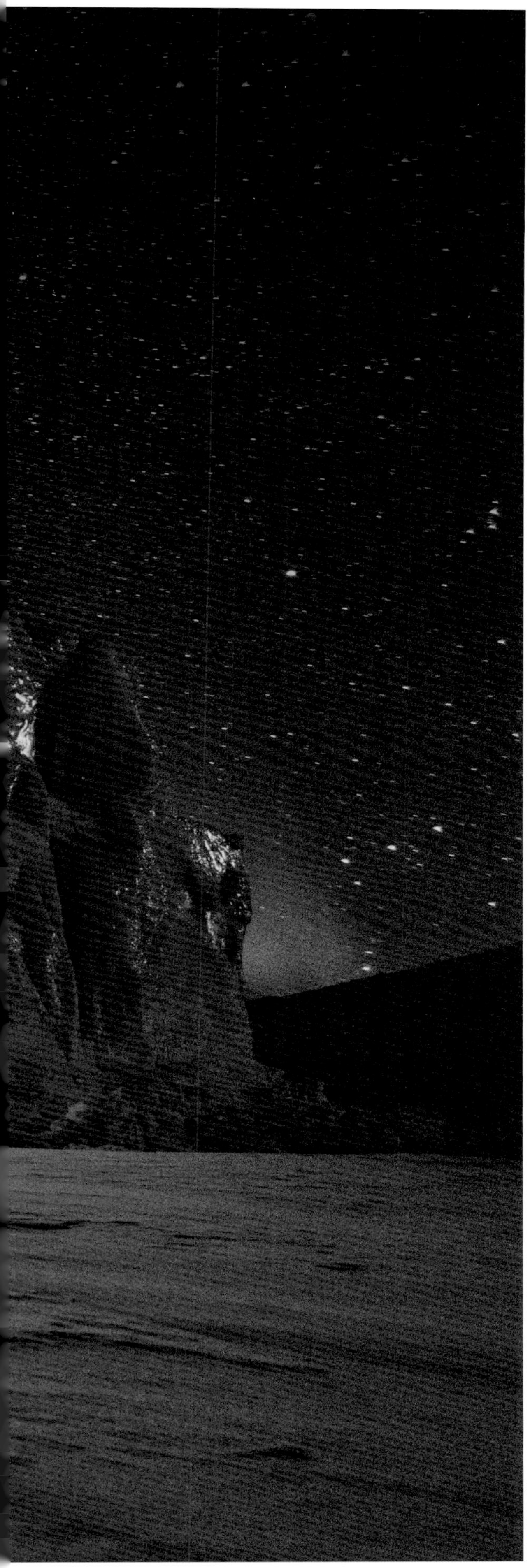

THE ICE THAT ONCE STRETCHED FAR INTO THE HORIZON IS NOW OPEN SEA. THE NUMBER OF HUNTERS DECREASES EVERY YEAR AND IT IS BECOMING INCREASINGLY HARD TO SURVIVE BY HUNTING ALONE. ONE ENVISIONS THE END OF A SOCIETY BASED ON A THOUSAND-YEAR-OLD HUNTING TRADITION.

RAGNAR AXELSSON

CAPTIONS

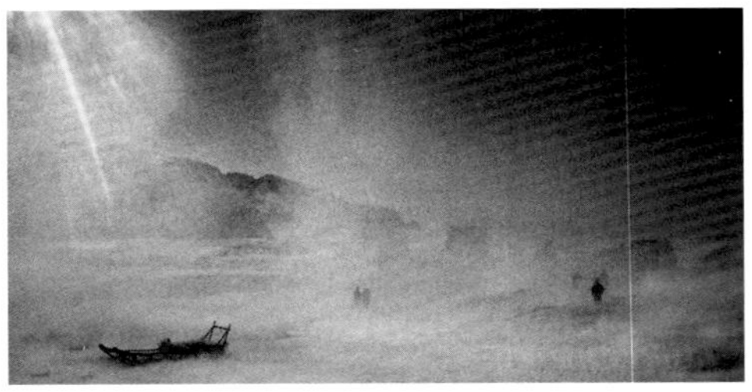

pp. 76-77
The sudden katabatic winds - or piteraq - can be deadly as they descend on the costal towns from Greenland's vast inland glacier. This piteraq killed three experienced mountaineers near the village of Sermiligaaq. East Greenland, 1996.

p. 78
Polar bear hunters in Clyde River, Nunavut, wait for the storm to cease. Canada, 2007.

p. 79
The village Ittoqqortoormiit seen through a frosted window. East Greenland, 1995.

pp. 80-81
A husky in the village Ittoqqortoormiit, East Greenland, 1995.

pp. 82-83
The hunter Bent from the settlement Itterajivit (Kap Hope), East Greenland, prepares for his dog sled ride back home from Ittoqqortoormiit. As many small hunter settlements along the east coast of Greenland Itterajivit is now deserted. East Greenland, 1995.

pp. 84-85
The village Sermiligaaq, East Greenland, 1997.

p. 86
A girl in Sermiligaaq, East Greenland, 1997.

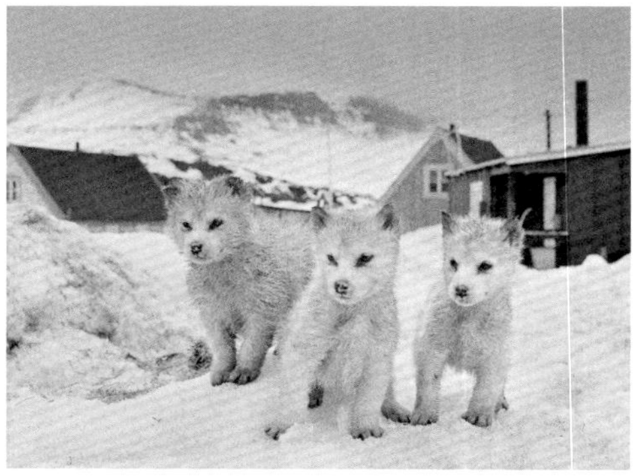

p. 87
Husky puppies on Qeqertarsuaq (Disco Island), 1997. Qeqertarsuaq litterally means "large island" in the Inuit language and is the name of several islands along the west coast of Greenland.

pp. 88-89
The hunter and drum dancer Jakob combs the hair of his grandchildren. Recent research shows that drums were in use among the first inhabitants of Greenland, around 4500 years ago. Drum dancing and singing are one the central elements of traditional Inuit culture. Tiniteqilaaq, East Greenland, 1998.

pp. 90-91
Soccer on the ice. Ittoqqortoormiit, East Greenland, 1995.

p. 93
A woman in Sermiligaaq cuts seal meat with *ulu*, an Inuit knife. East Greenland, 1997.

p. 94
A girl in Tiniteqilaaq on a swing in a rack used for drying seal and polar bear skins. East Greenland, 1997.

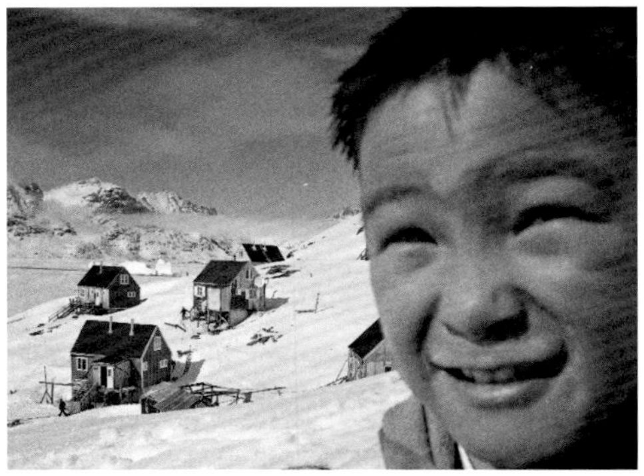

p. 95
A boy in Sermiligaaq, East Greenland, 1997.

pp. 96-97
Sunset in Tiniteqilaaq, East Greenland, 1998.

p. 98
Old woman stands in the door at her house in Siorapaluk in the Qaanaaq area of Greenland, one of the world's northernmost settlements, 1999.

p. 99
Hunter in Sermiligaaq inspects sealskin drying on a rack, East Greenland, 1998.

pp. 100-101
In Siorapaluk, where only around fifty people live. Northwestern Greeland, 1987.

p. 102
In Sermiligaaq, East Greenland, 1997.

p. 103
A hunter in his house in Tiniteqilaaq, East Greenland, 1998.

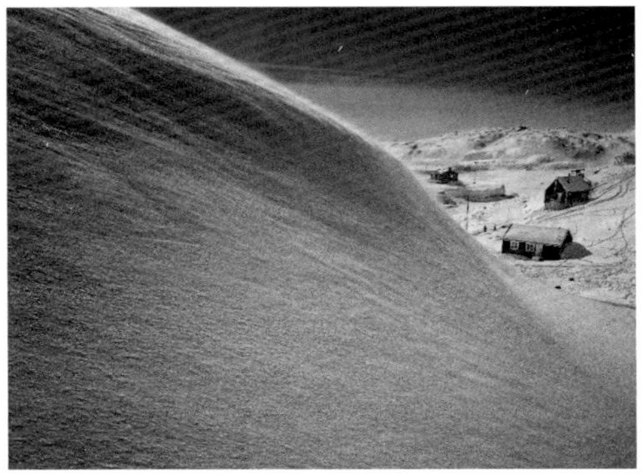

p. 104
Snowstorm descends on Sermiligaaq, East Greenland, 1997.

p. 105
An old and retired hunter in Tiniteqilaaq, East Greenland, 1998.

p. 106
Old man on his way back from the store in Ittoqqortoormiit, East Greenland. 1995.

p. 107
The drum dancer Anda Kuitse fixes his drum at his home in Kulusuk with a help from his son. He is known for his expressive and masculine drum dancing style. Kulusuk, East Greenland, 1997.

p. 109
During a snowstorm, the people of Sermiligaaq, East Greenland, stay indoors but the sled dogs are accustomed to the cold and wind outside. 1997.

p. 110
The hunter and drum dancer Jakob from Tiniteqilaaq. He is considered by his fellow Inuit to be a true shaman or *angakok*, using the drum to gain access to the world of the spirits. East Greenland, 1998.

p. 111
The storm is over and the children flock outside to play. Sermiligaaq, East Greenland, 1997.

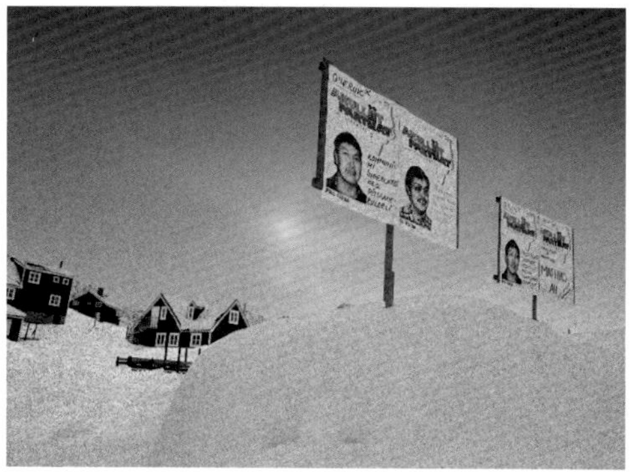

p. 112
Election posters stand out of in the frozen snow in Tasiilaq, East Greenland, 2000.

p. 113
One of the inhabitants of Thule, North Greenland, forced to leave their homes in 1953 and settle in Qaanaaq, when the US army expanded the military base and the airfield in Thule. Qaanaaq, Northwesteren Greenland, 1999.

pp. 114-115
A husky in Qaanaaq has returned home after two weeks out on the ice. Northwestern Greenland, 1987.

p. 116
A husky waits for his food outside an old woman's house in Sermiligaaq, East Greenland, 1997.

p. 117
Skinned seal in a bin. Sermiligaaq, East Greenland, 1997.

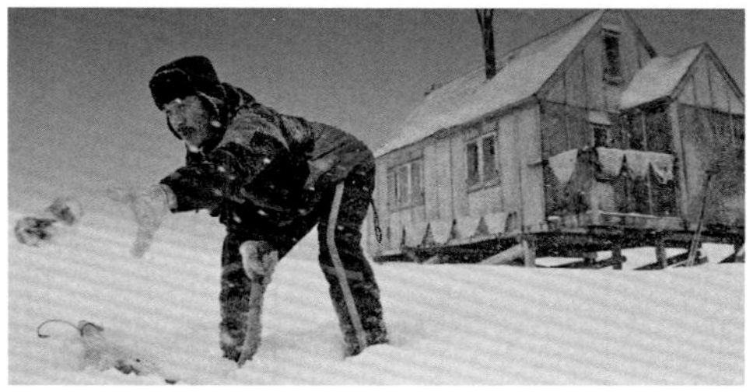

pp. 118-119
The hunter Hjelmer Hammeken feeds his sled dogs in front of his house in the now desterted settlement Uunarteq (Kap Tobin). After the last families moved away from Uunarteq around 2000 some of the houses are used by hunters from Ittoqqortoormiit, the last remaining settlement near the world's longest fjord, Kangertittivaq. East Greenland, 1995.

pp. 120-121
Aurora borealis swirl in the night sky above Tiniteqilaaq. East Greenland, 1998.

p. 122
A heavy storm is about to hit Sermiligaaq, East Greenland, 1997.

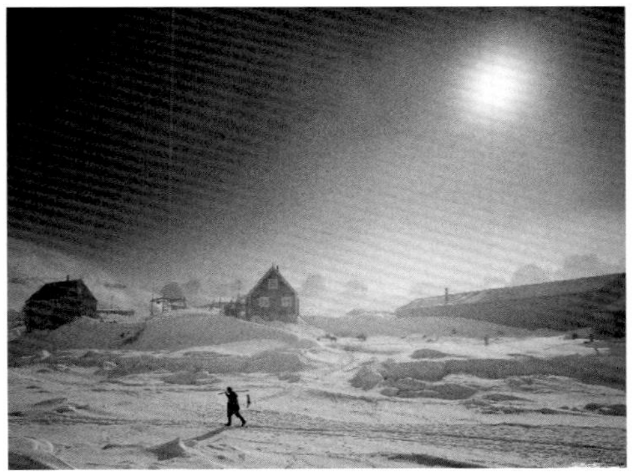

p. 123
A hunter with his fishing net returnes home. Sermiligaaq, East Greenland, 1996.

p. 124
In Sermiligaaq, an old woman lived alone in a small house. East Greenland 1997.

p. 125
Inside her home. Sermiligaaq, East Greenland, 1997.

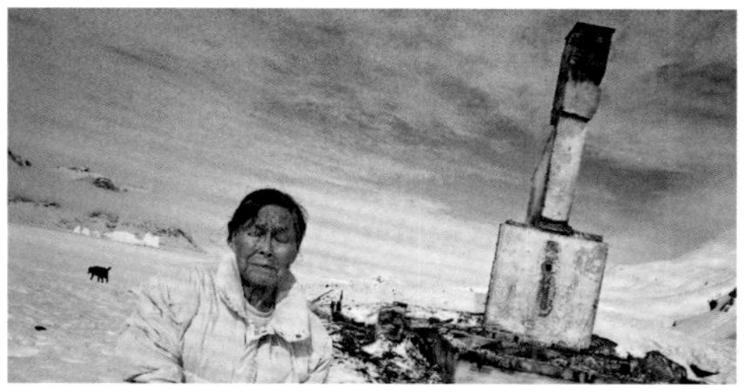

pp. 126-127
The night after the photographs of her house were taken, it burned down. The water tank was empty and no fire brigade is operating in the village so nothing was saved. Sermiligaaq, East Greenland, 1997.

p. 128
Waiting for the skies to clear up, Sermiligaaq, East Greenland. 1997.

p. 129
Feeding the huskies in Sermiligaaq, East Greenland. 1997.

pp. 130-131
Little Bent in Itterajivit (Kap Hope) scolds his puppies for running free around the village. Itterajivit is now deserted like many other small hunter settlements on the east coast of Greenland, 1995.

p. 132
Polar bear pelt, Ittoqqortoormiit, East Greenland, 1996.

p. 133
A hunter's house in the now deserted settlement of Itterajivit (Kap Hope), East Greenland, 1995.

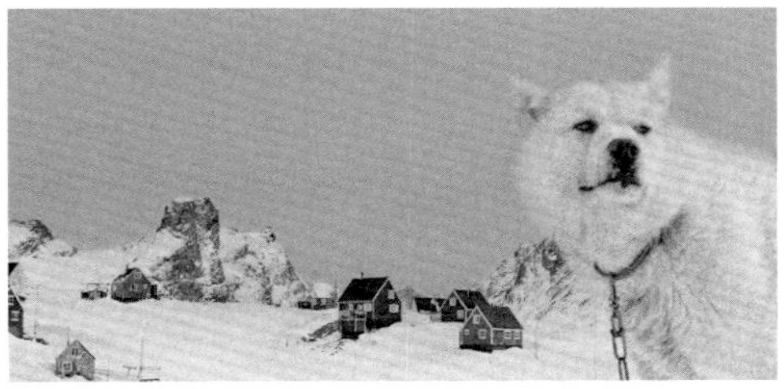

pp. 134-135
Chained sled dog in Sermiligaaq, East Greenland, 1998.

pp. 138-139
A sled doge yoke lined up to go out on the ice hunting in a middle of a blizzard. Ittoqqortoormiit, East Greenland, 1995.

pp. 140-141
Masauna from Qaanaaq, often called the "King of Thule", spurns his dogs with the wip on Inglefield Fjord, Northwestern Greenland, 1987.

pp. 142-143
A husky withers fresh seal meat at the mouth of the Sermilik Fjord, East Greenland, 1999.

pp. 144-145
Blizzard rages on the ice outside Baffin Island. For twenty-six hours, the hunters worked their way back from the ice in a heavy storm. They were glad to see the raven as it was a firm sign that they were getting closer to land. Canada, 2007.

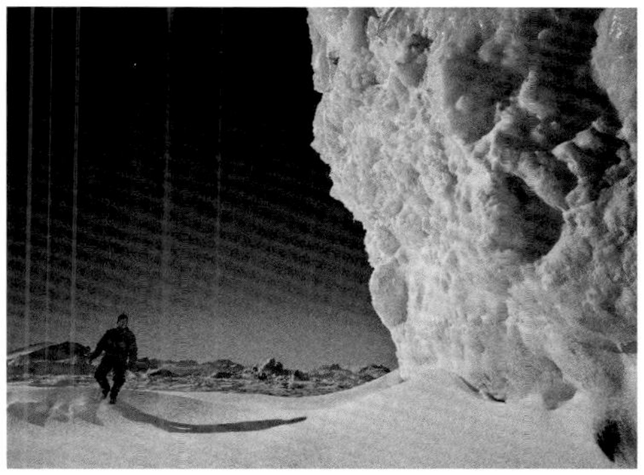

p. 146
Hunter by an ice block on the Sermilik Fjord, East Greenland, 1998.

p. 147
Looking for prey on the ice outside the coast of East Greenland, 1995.

pp. 148-149
The icy wind blows over the ice outside Baffin Island. Canada, 2007.

p. 150
Hunter climbs up an ice block to spot polar bears out on the ice. Baffin Island, Canada, 2007.

p. 151
A husky on the ice near Ittoqqortoormiit, East Greenland, 1995.

pp. 152-153
A polar bear hunter on the ice between Baffin Island and Greenland. Canada, 2007.

pp. 154-155
After following the polar bear tracks for some time, the hunters finally encounter the animal. Canada, 2007.

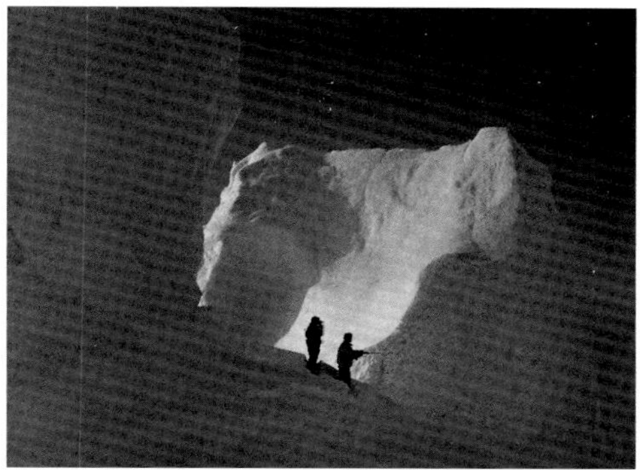

p. 156
Hjelmer Hammeken and his companion Isak watch for signs of polar bears outside Kangertittivaq or Scoresby Sound, the world's largest and longest fjord system. East Greenland, 1995.

p. 157
Hunters face an angry polar bear. The polar bear can attack with astonishing speed and power and should never be underestimated. Baffin Island, Canada, 2007.

pp. 158-159
Hunting polar bears is an integral part of the traditional Inuit culture. The government issues hunting quotas every year. Baffin Island, Canada, 2007.

p. 160
Polar bear shot from a short range. Baffin Island, Canada, 2007.

p. 161
Inuit hunters use all parts of the polar bear, eat the meat and use the skin for clothing. Baffin Island, Canada, 2007.

pp. 162-163
Aurora borealis dancing in the night sky above a hunters camp outside Ittoqqortoormiit, East Greenland, 1995.

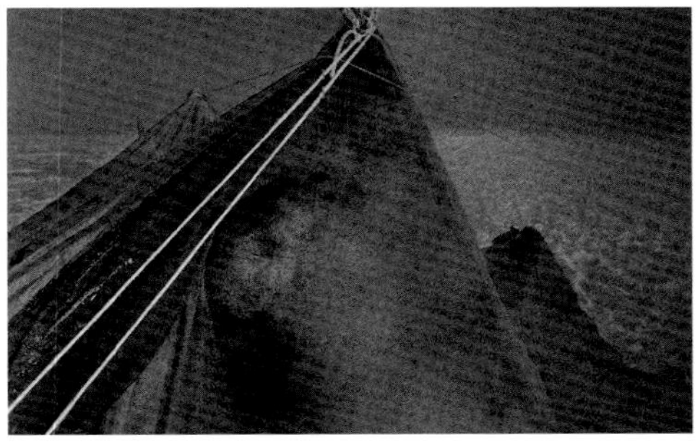

p. 164
Isak from Ittoqqortoormiit wakes up in his tent on the ice on Kangertittivaq. East Greenland, 1995.

p. 165
Hjelmer Hammeken waits for a seal to come up to a breathing hole in the ice on Kangertittivaq or Scoresby Sound. East Greenland, 1995.

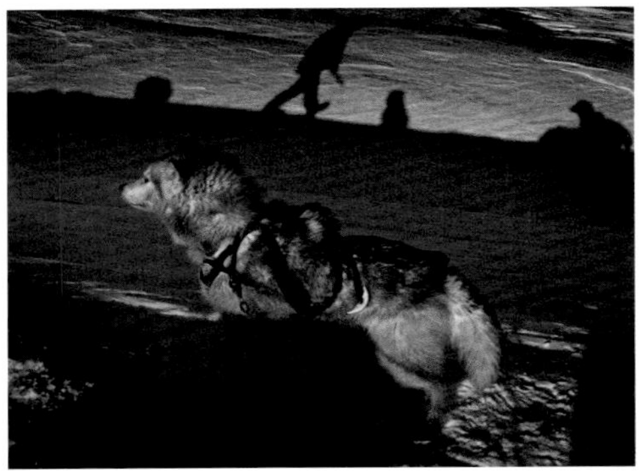

p. 166
A hunter on Baffin Island feeds his huskies. Canada, 2007.

p. 167
Hunter looks for his fishing nets under the ice on Sermilik Fjord, East Greenland, 1997.

pp. 168-169
A hunter near Uunarteq (Kap Tobin) unties a seal from his net. The nets are set under the ice and as the seals come up to breath, they become entangled. East Greenland, 1995.

pp. 170-171
The legendary hunter Masauna from Qaanaaq feeds his dogs on the ice in Inglefield Fjord, Northwestern Greenland, 1987.

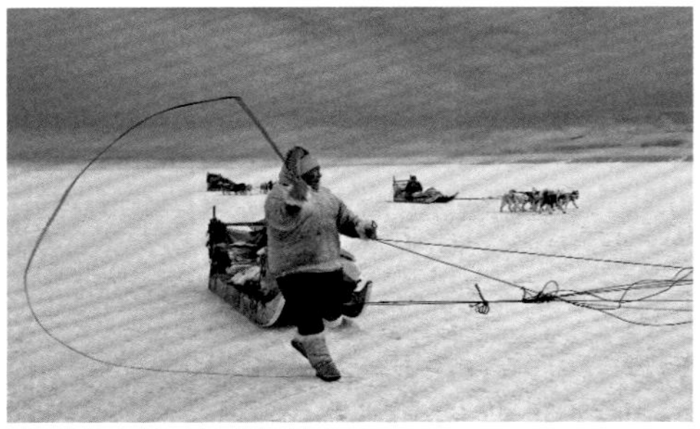

pp. 172-173
Masauna yells at his dogs as the sledges approach a crack in the ice. The dogs fear falling into the sea in the freezing cold more than anything else. Northwestern Greenland, 1999.

p. 175
Masauna yells at his hunting companions after seeing a narwhal swimming nearby. Northwestern Greenland, 1987.

p. 176
Mikide Kristiansen unravels the strings of his yoke out on the ice outside Qaanaaq, Northwestern Greenland, 1999.

p. 177
Mikide Kristiansen, his brother Mamarut and Mamarut's wife on a hunting expedition in Inglefield Fjord, Northwestern Greenland, 1999.

pp. 178-179
The sled dogs of the Inuit fear nothing more than falling through cracks in the ice. Getting wet on the ice in the freezing cold, far away from land, is a certain death if they are not dried and warmed up quickly. Kangertittivaq, East Greenland, 1996.

pp. 180-181
Maren and Knud Qujaukitsoq from Qaanaaq, North Greenland. They spotted a polar bear on an ice floe nearby but the gun was jammed and for a while, it seemed that the animal could only be killed with a harpoon. The polar bear sensed the danger and fled. The hunter cursed his bad luck. Northwestern Greenland, 1987.

p. 182
A hunter from Ittoqqortoormiit on his way out to the edge of the ice to hunt for seals and polar bears. East Greenland, 1996.

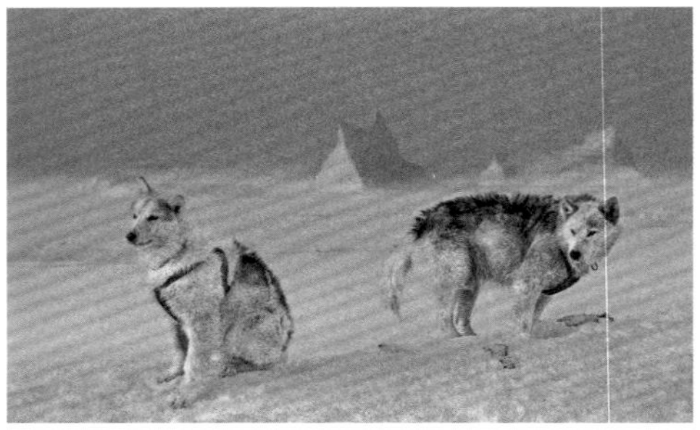

p. 183
Sled dogs rest near Kangigai (Kap Brewster) on Kangertittivaq, East Greenland, 1996.

pp. 184-185
Arctic shark fished through a hole in the ice on Inglefield fjord, Northwestern Greenland, 1988.

pp. 186-187
The hunter Masauna follows a pod of narwhal near Qaanaaq, North Greenland on his kayak. His fellow hunters watch from the ice. The one that harpoons the whale gets his tooth. Northwestern Greenland, 1987.

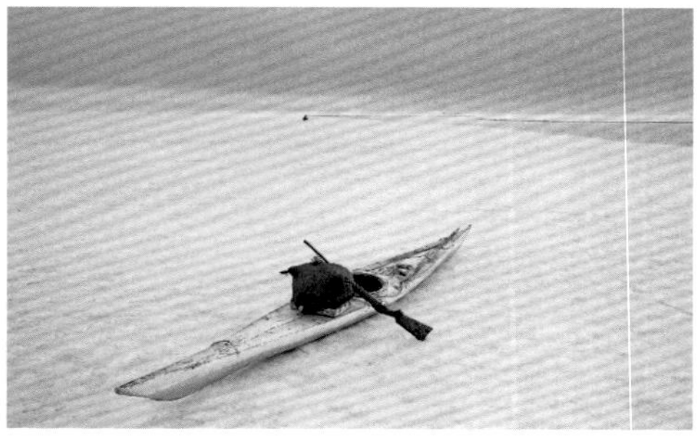

p. 188
The kayak of Ole Neylsen, a hunter from Qaanaaq, his gun and a float, tied to the string of his harpoon. Northwestern Greenland, 1987.

p. 189
Masauna, "The Kind of Thule" rests on his sled at the end of a successful hunting day with one of his fellow hunters. Northwestern Greenland, 1987.

pp. 190-191
The hunter Masauna camping on his dog sled in Inglefield fjord, Northwestern Greenland, 1987.

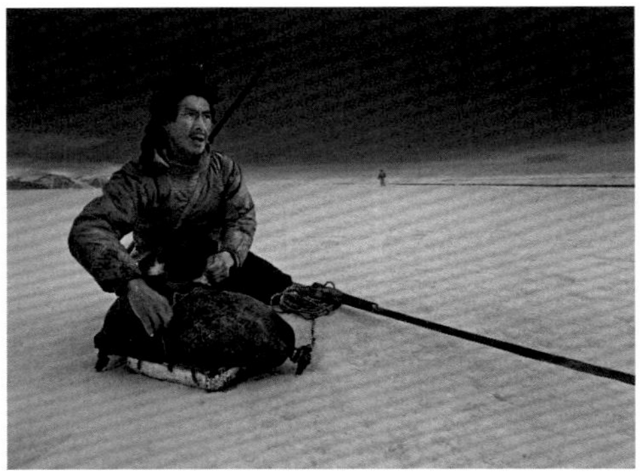

pp. 192-193
Ole Neylsen prepares for harpooning a narwhal in an open crack in the ice nearby. Northwestern Greenland, 1987.

pp. 194-195
Hunters from Qaanaaq jump between ice floes while harpooning a narwhal. The whale tries to escape by swimming under the ice but a float tied to the harpoon shows where he is hiding. Northwestern Greenland, 1987.

pp. 196-197
Narwhal hunters in Inglefield Fjord, Northwestern Greenland, 1987.

pp. 198-199
Hunter Gideon jumps over a crack in the ice on Inglefield fjord, Northwestern Greenland, 1987.

p. 200
The narwhal is not killed with a harpoon but shot with a gun as it finally comes up the breath. It is then tugged up to the ice and the hunters prepare to cut it up and divide the meat according to Inuit customs of sharing food. Northwestern Greenland, 1987.

p. 201
The one that harpoons the whale gets the treasured tooth as a reward. It is Kigutiaq Petersen that managed this time to shoot his harpoon into the whale. Northwestern Greenland, 1987.

pp. 202-203
Mikide Kristiansen and Gidon from Qaanaaq cut narwhal on the ice on Inglefield fjord, Northwestern Greenland, 1987.

p. 205
A hunter and his dog on the ice near Baffin Island. Canada, 2007.

pp. 206-207
A sled dog near Kangigai (Kap Brewster) on the ice on Kangertittivaq, East Greenland, 1995.

pp. 208-209
Hunters pass gigantic icebergs on Inglefield fjord, near Thule. Northwestern Greenland, 1987.

pp. 210-211
Mikide Kristiansen waits in his kayak for a narwhal to come up to blow. Northwestern Greenland, 1987.

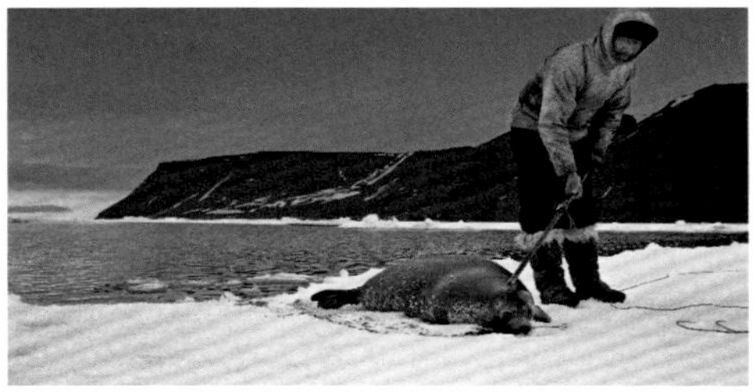

pp. 212-213
Ole Neylsen hunts seals on the ice edge near Qeqertarsuaq (Herbert Island), Northwestern Greenland, 1987.

pp. 214-125
Hjelmer and Isak from Ittoqqortoormiit dragging seals. East Greenland, 1995.

pp. 216-217
Hunters from Qaanaaq. Northwestern Greenland, 1999.

p. 218
Seals are the staple food of dogs and men on their hunting expeditions out on the ice, lasting up to a month. The seals are shy and it is not easy to hunt. A dead seal on a sled near Ittoqqortoormiit, East Greenland. 1995.

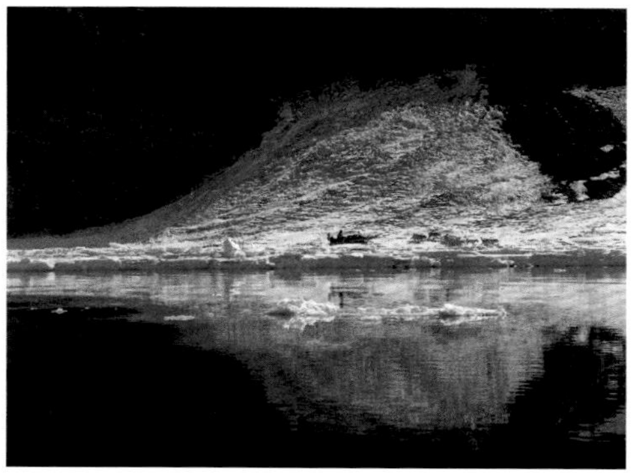

p. 219
Moving over a difficult terrain on Qeqertarsuaq (Herbert Island) near Qaanaaq. Northwestern Greenland, 2001.

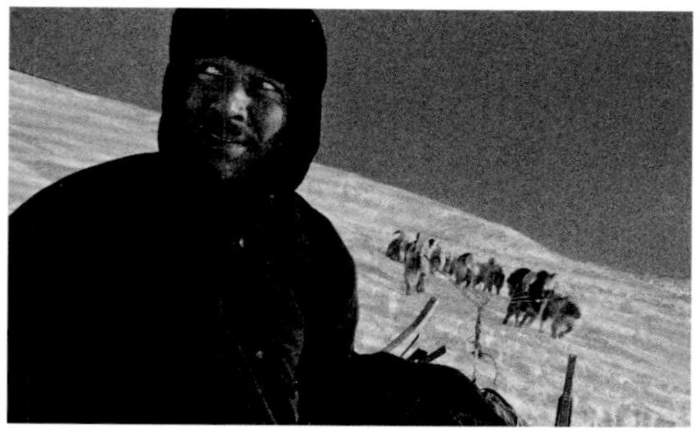

p. 220-221
No other hunter now living has killed more polar bears than Hjelmer Hammeken from Ittoqqortoormiit in East Greenland. He has shot over 200 animals in his lifetime and is still among the few hunters of Greenland that make their living only from traditional hunting of animals, fish and birds, 1995.

pp. 222-223
Hunters move out to the edge of the ice on Inglefield fjord, Northwestern Greenland, 1998.

pp. 224-225
The hunters are near the ice edge where seals, polar bears and whales thrive. The yokes of the huskies are broken up while the hunters await their prey patiently. Near Qaanaaq, Northwestern Greenland, 1999.

pp. 226-227
Ice floes outside the shore of West Greenland, near Disko Island or Qeqertarsuaq. West Greenland, 1998.

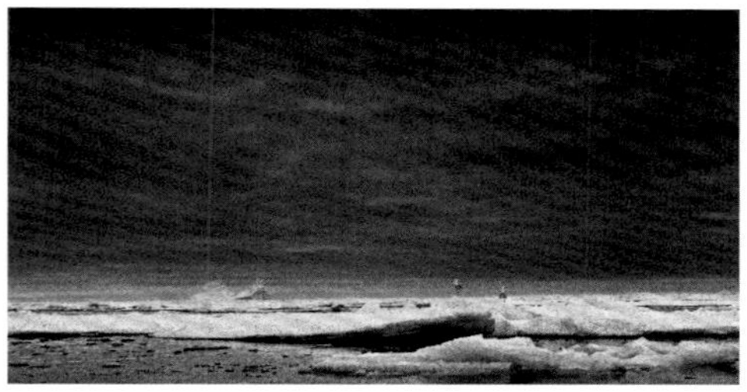

pp. 228-229
Ice drifting away from the shore near Disko Island or Qeqertarsuaq. West Greenland, 1998.

pp. 230-231
Icebergs calved from the Ilulissat Glacier in West Greenland, floating on the fjord. The Ilulissat Glacier is a UNESCO World Heritage Site, known for how fast it slides into the sea, 1996.

pp. 232-233
A lonely iceberg in the ocean outside Uummannaq, West Greenland, 1996.

pp. 236-237
Ship wracks in a cove in Disko Bay, West Greenland, 2001.

p. 238
On the deserted Herbert Island or Qeqertarsuaq outside Inglefield Fjord in Northwestern Greenland, 1999.

p. 239
Old man in the village of Kuummiut, East Greenland, 2003.

pp. 240-241
Old woman looks out through her window in the village of Tasiusaq, South Greenland, 1991.

pp. 242-243
Hunting little auks near Siorapaluk, one of the northernmost settlements on Earth. Northwestern Greenland, 1999.

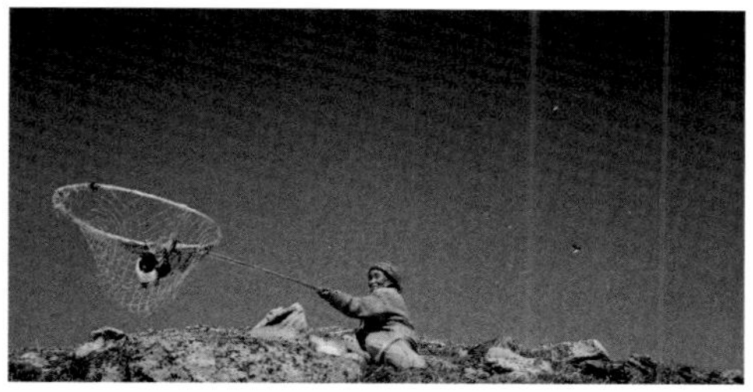

pp. 244-245
Little auks caught in nets in the cliffs around Siorapaluk. The birds are left to ferment in big bags, made of sealskin, covered in stones to protect them from polar bears and arctic foxes. They are considered to be a special delicacy. Northwestern Greenland, 1999.

pp. 246-247
Cod drying on stones in the village of Nanortalik, South Greenland, 1991.

pp. 248-249
Dogs rest during the brief summer in Qaannaaq, Northwestern Greenland, 1987.

pp. 250-251
An old hunter in his cabin in South Greenland, 1991.

p. 252
A boy in Sermiliqaq, East Greenland, 2003.

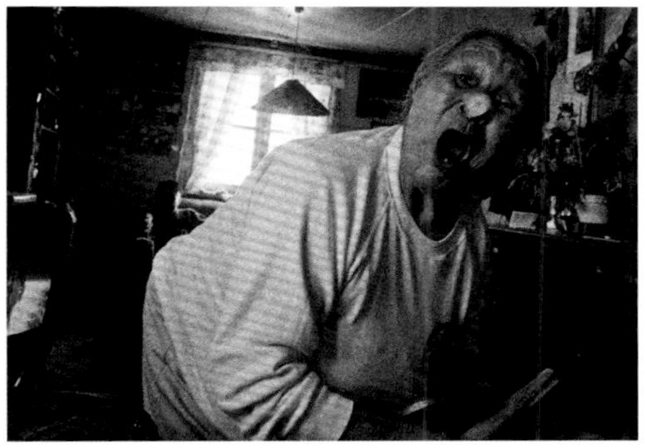

p. 253
An old woman drumdancing, Kulusuk, East Greenland, 1997.

pp. 254-255
Young kids swimming, East Greenland, 2003.

p. 256
Dogs resting in Uummannaq, West Greenland, 1998.

p. 257
Old hunter in front of his house in Qaanaaq, Northwestern Greenland, 1999.

p. 258
An old man in Tasiusaq, South Greenland, 1991.

p. 259
Old woman in Kulusuk, East Greenland, 2003.

p. 260
Old couple in Qaanaaq playing cards. Northwestern Greenland, 1987.

p. 260
Birthday party in Qaanaaq. Northwestern Greenland, 1987.

p. 262
Kids dancing in front of their school in the village of Tasiusaq, South Greenland, 1991.

p. 263
Old men in Ilulissat, West Greenland, 1991.

pp. 264-265
Old couple in the settlement of Igaliku, South Greenland.

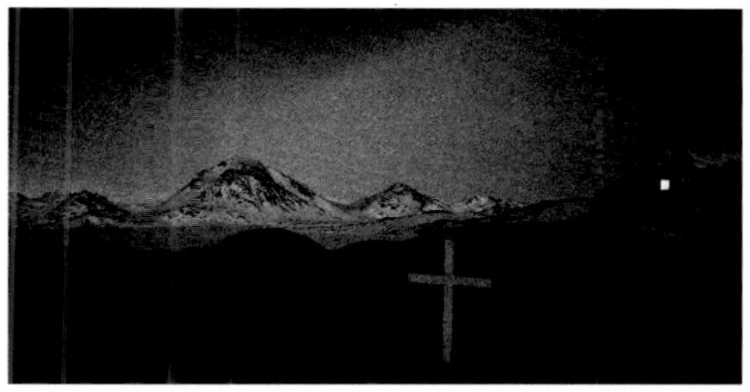

pp. 266-267
A lonely house by the graveyard in Kulusuk, East Greenland, 1998.

p. 269
Ababa Hammeken works his way back from the ice as it suddenly starts to break up. East Greenland, 2013.

p. 270
Ababa Hammeken and his brother Hjelmer. East Greenland, 2013.

p. 271
A sled dog near Ittoqqortoormiit. East Greenland, 2013.

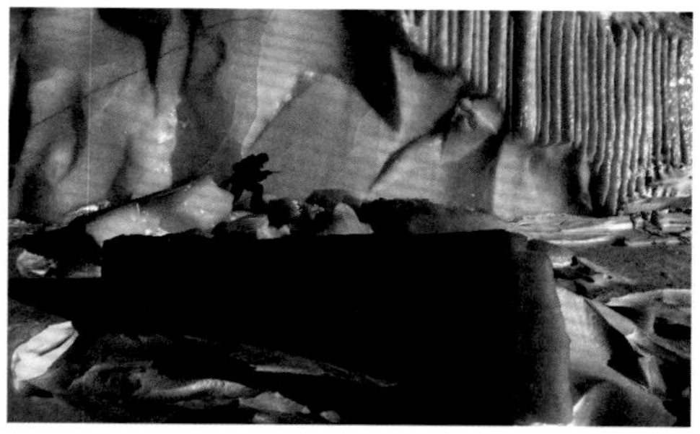

pp. 272-273
Ababa Hammeken nears his prey, a polar bear, East Greenland, 2013.

p. 274
The storm is growing as Hjelmer Hammeken prepears his sled for the ride back to land. East Greenland, 2013.

p. 275
The hunt is over. East Greenland, 2013.

p. 276
As the ice breaks up the dogs move slowly back from the edge by the ocean. East Greenland, 2013.

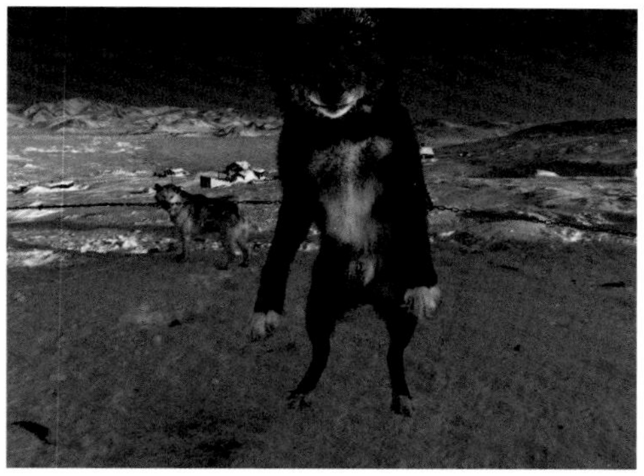

p. 277
Chained dogs in Ittoqqortoormiit, East Greenland, 2013.

pp. 278-279
While northern lights swirl in the sky, the light from a hunter's lamp illuminates an iceberg stuck in the ice sheet on Kangertittivaq. East Greenland, 2013.

RAGNAR AXELSSON

At the end of the road I would like to thank family and friends for bearing with me through the years and everyone who helped while making this book, including my advisors around the world and the staff at Crymogea. Words cannot describe my gratitude.

I also want to thank all of the hunters in Greenland and Nunavut who helped me travel over the vastness of the Arctic ice and allowed me to capture a fraction of their four-thousand-year history on my camera.

The Inuit are extraordinary people. The hunters are reserved and don't brag about their skills, but as soon as you head with them out to the ice their resilience and skills become apparent and you know you can put your life in their hands. It is enough to look them in the eyes.

It has been magnificent to have the opportunity to earn their friendship and trust and learn from them how to read the signs of nature. Their land keeps drawing me back, although their lives have changed faster that I could ever imagine. The ice shelf becomes thinner every year and their way of life is threatened. I hope that the hunting tradition of the Arctic will receive the respect it deserves and people around the world will see how incredibly refined and dignified the culture of the Inuit is.

RAGNAR AXELSSON

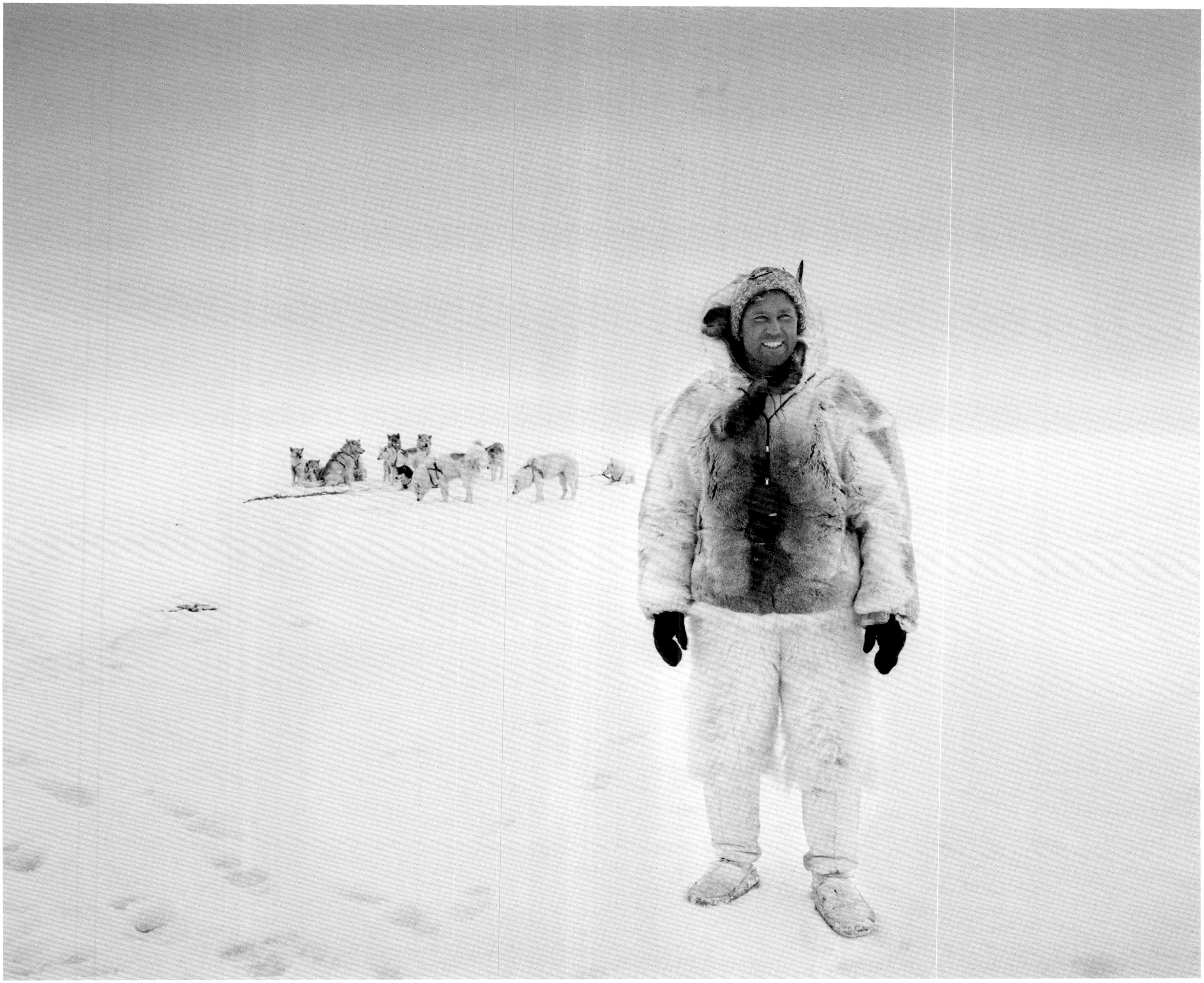

Ragnar Axelsson, Thule, Greenland, 1992.

RAGNAR AXELSSON
LAST DAYS OF THE ARCTIC

The photographs featured in this book were created during travels to Arctic Greenland and Canada from 1987 to 2013.

First English edition published by Polarworld, London, United Kingdom and Crymogea, Reykjavík, Iceland, 2010. Reprinted in 2011.

Second English edition published by Crymogea, Reykjavík, Iceland, 2013.

A CIP catalogue record of this book is available from the British Library.

Direction: Dr Huw Lewis-Jones and Kari Herbert
Editorial assistance: Eliza Reid
English translation of Rax's text: Birna Anna Björnsdóttir
Design: Bergdís Sigurðardóttir
Prepress: borealisworks.com
Printing: EBS, Verona, Italy

ISBN 978-9935-420-30-5

The publishers would like to thank the producers at Saga Film, Reykjavík, and the director, Magnús Viðar Sigurðsson, for the making of the documentary *Last Days of the Arctic*.

Crymogea
crymogea@crymogea.is
www.crymogea.is